COMPLETE PROSE WORKS

OF

John Milton

This publication is made possible
through grants from
the Lucius N. Littauer Foundation
the Andrew W. Mellon Foundation
the National Endowment for the Humanities

Complete Prose Works

OF

John Milton

VOLUME VII
1659–1660

Revised Edition

NEW HAVEN AND LONDON: YALE UNIVERSITY PRESS
MCMLXXX

Library of Congress Catalog Card Number: 52-5371
International Standard Book Number: 0-300-02015-5

Designed by John O. C. McCrillis
and set in Old Style No. 7 type.
Printed in the United States of America by
Vail-Ballou Press, Inc., Binghamton, New York

10   9   8   7   6   5   4   3   2   1

EDITOR OF VOLUME VII

ROBERT W. AYERS

AUTHOR OF HISTORICAL INTRODUCTION

AUSTIN WOOLRYCH

LIBRARY ABBREVIATIONS

BML	Library of the British Museum
BNL	Bibliothèque Nationale
BNV	Biblioteca Nazionale Marciana in Venezia
BOD	Bodleian Library, Oxford
BPL	Boston Public Library
CLL	Columbia University Law Library
CUL	Columbia University Library
EMU	Emory University Library
ENC	New College Library, Edinburgh University
EUL	Edinburgh University Library
FSL	Folger Shakespeare Library
HCL	Harvard College Library
HDSL	Harvard Divinity School Library
HHL	Huntington Library
HLH	Houghton Library of Harvard
IUL	Indiana University Library
JRL	John Rylands Library
LC	Library of Congress
MUL	University of Michigan Library
NEW	Newberry Library, Chicago
NUL	Northwestern University Library
NYPL	New York Public Library
PML	Pierpont Morgan Library, New York
PTSL	Princeton Theological Seminary Library
PUL	Princeton University Library
RUL	Rutgers University Library
SOR	Library of the Sorbonne, University of Paris
UCA	University of California, Clark Library
UCL	University of Chicago Library
UIL	University of Illinois Library
UML	University of Minnesota Library
UPL	University of Pennsylvania Library
UTSL	Union Theological Seminary Library
VAM	Victoria and Albert Museum
WCL	Williams College Library
YUL	Yale University Library

ABBREVIATIONS OF PUBLICATIONS

Bohn	Milton, *Prose Works* (1848–1853)
Columbia	Milton, *Works* (1931–1938)
Complete	
Prose	*Complete Prose Works of John Milton*
CSPD	*Calendar of State Papers, Domestic*
CSP Ven.	*Calendar of State Papers, Venetian Series*
CS	*Camden Society Publications*
DNB	*Dictionary of National Biography*
EETS	*Early English Text Society*
ELH	*Journal of English Literary History*
ELN	*English Language Notes*
ERE	*Encyclopaedia of Religion and Ethics*
HLQ	*Huntington Library Quarterly*
JEGP	*Journal of English and Germanic Philology*
McAlpin	*McAlpin Catalogue*
MLN	*Modern Language Notes*
MLQ	*Modern Language Quarterly*
MP	*Modern Philology*
NED, OED	*New English Dictionary*
N&Q	*Notes and Queries*
PMLA	*Publications of the Modern Language Association*
PQ	*Philological Quarterly*
RES	*Review of English Studies*
SEL	*Studies in English Literature*
SP	*Studies in Philology*
STC	*Short-Title Catalogue*
TLS	*London Times Literary Supplement*
Thomason	*Catalogue of the Thomason Tracts*

Footnote citations designated "E" or "669" refer to British Library press marks for the Thomason Collection. Where available, Thomason's date of acquisition (usually within a few days of publication) is given. For fuller bibliographical detail, see the *Catalogue of the Pamphlets . . . Collected by George Thomason, 1640–1661,* London, 1908. "JOR41x" is the Guildhall Record Office press mark for a volume of unpublished manuscript Journals of the Common Council of the City of London.

PREFACE

The general purpose of the *Complete Prose Works of John Milton* was described in Volume I, p. ix: "to present annotated texts of Milton's prose in the ascertainable order of its composition, bringing to bear in notes, prefaces, and volume introductions the accumulated scholarship of the past century." The present volume effects that purpose with respect to Milton's prose of the tumultuous period, 1659–1660.

All of the writings here presented have been hitherto printed, but only one—the second edition of the *Readie & Easie Way*—has previously received full annotation. The earliest seventeenth-century editions are the bases of all texts, except the *Letter to a Friend* and *Proposalls of Certaine Expedients* (neither of which was published during Milton's lifetime), in which cases our texts are those of the Columbia Manuscript. Furthermore, all documents are here edited, not as belles lettres —which they are not—but as tracts for the times—which they are.

Austin Woolrych, who has written the introduction, has seen it as his prime task to depict the historical background to Milton's last great burst of pamphleteering. This is because the course of politics from Cromwell's death to the Restoration was exceptionally hectic and complex, and because none of Milton's works need to be related more closely to their immediate political context than those here presented. He has therefore chosen to discuss the texts at those points in the historical narrative at which they were written or published, for they were all indeed tracts for the times. His assignment was complicated by the fact that a gap of three and a half years separates *A Defence of Himself,* the last prose work that Milton had previously published, from *A Treatise of Civil Power,* the first in this volume. He faced a consequent gap in the story of national events between Don M. Wolfe's introduction to Volume IV, which ends in 1654, and his own to this volume, which begins logically with Cromwell's death in September, 1658. He has not attempted a comprehensive survey of the intervening years, but he has introduced a few retrospects in order to describe certain new developments in policy and controversy, particularly in the ecclesiastical sphere, which must be understood if these last polemical writings by Milton are to be properly appreciated. Without these retrospects he could not have attempted to explain that crux in Milton's political attitudes which we find in the stark contrast between his eulogy of Cromwell's Protectorate in *A Second Defence* and his revulsion against it in the tracts of 1659–1660.

At a late stage in his work he and Robert W. Ayers, the editor of this volume, mutually benefited from long discussions relating to the social and political complexities of the period, particularly as these bore upon the dating of the last political tracts. These and other personal contacts were made possible by a three months' fellowship of the Folger Shakespeare Library. He thanks the donors of this fellowship for their generosity, the Folger Library Staff for their courteous and expert assistance, and the University of Lancaster for granting him leave of absence.

Except for minor amendments, Mr. Woolrych completed his introduction and Mr. Ayers completed his annotations at the end of 1969; both regret that save in a few exceptional cases they have not been able to take account of work published since then. Both author and editor warmly thank Douglas Bush, Christopher Hill, William L. Sachse, Barbara Taft, David Underdown, the late Don Wolfe, and the late Merritt Y. Hughes, scholars who read all or parts of the historical introduction, or the prefaces or annotations to the various tracts, and offered valuable comments and suggestions. Finally, despite all they have gained by prolonged absorption in one of the greatest of English minds, they share the profound regret of all readers that A. S. P. Woodhouse, the editor originally designated for this volume, whose skill embraced with equal distinction the disciplines of history and English literature, did not live to execute a task so well matched to his unique talents.

R.W.A.   A.H.W.

NOTE TO THE REVISED EDITION

The editor and the editorial board wish to express their gratitude to John T. Shawcross and William B. Hunter, Jr., for their very helpful advice in the preparation of this revised edition. Special appreciation is also due to Leo Miller for his vigilant attention to the text.

September 1979

CONTENTS

INTRODUCTION

By Austin Woolrych

COMPLETE PROSE WORKS

OF

John Milton

INTRODUCTION

PROLOGUE: MILTON IN 1658

Milton was three months short of fifty when Cromwell died in September, 1658, and for several years his life had been running a quiet and even course.[1] It had been lit by one spell of particular happiness, followed by a commensurate grief. On November 12, 1656, he had married Katherine Woodcock, and for more than a year his familiar house in Petty France had been warmed by her gentle presence. He wrote to a young French fellow scholar in March, 1657, of the "serenity of spirit" with which he now bore his blindness: "Why, indeed, should I not endure calmly the loss of my sight, when I may hope that it is not so much lost as retired and withdrawn into myself, so that it sharpens rather than dulls the edge of my mind?"[2] In October of that year Katherine bore him a daughter, but three and a half months later she was dead, and within six weeks more her baby followed her to the grave. Was it out of the keenness of this loss that he wrote that poignant sonnet, "Methought I saw my late espoused Saint"? Some modern scholars have questioned the old assumption, but the latest editor of the sonnets encourages us to go on believing that it was indeed Katherine who in his dream

> Came vested all in white, pure as her mind:
> Her face was vail'd, yet to my fancied sight,
> Love, sweetness, goodness, in her person shin'd
> So clear, as in no face with more delight.
> But O as to embrace me she enclin'd
> I wak'd, she fled, and day brought back my night.[3]

[1] Milton's life is now documented more fully than ever before by William Riley Parker in *Milton: A Biography* (2 vols., Oxford University Press, 1968; hereafter cited as Parker, *Milton*). This magisterial work appeared after the present introduction was complete in draft. Biographical information may be taken as documented by Parker where no further references are given.

[2] Quoted in Parker, *Milton*, p. 502.

[3] *Milton's Sonnets*, ed. E. A. J. Honigmann (London: Macmillan, and New York: St. Martin's Press, 1966), pp. 190–92, where references to the controversy are cited. Parker, in *Milton*, pp. 475–76, 480, 1045, inclines still to the view, which he first advanced, that the sonnet refers to Milton's first wife. For further recent argument of this much-controverted question, see John Huntley, "Milton's 23rd Sonnet," *ELH* XXXIV (1967), 468–81.

Milton probably had fewer visitors now than in the earlier years of his blindness. One of the kindest and most welcome of them, Lady Ranelagh, lived now in Ireland. Her son, his former pupil, was still on his travels abroad, with the poet's old friend Henry Oldenburg accompanying him as tutor. But though the records of Milton's domestic and personal life are sparse in this period, there is no reason to suppose that his other old friends neglected him. At any rate he had his amanuenses, including now a particularly able one called Jeremy Picard. He could work.

A trickle of tasks continued to come to him from the Privy Council in the form of letters of state to compose or translate. He still drew his salary of £200 a year as Secretary for Foreign Tongues, though the routine of the office had been carried since September, 1657, by Andrew Marvell and Nathaniel Sterry, with occasional help from Samuel Hartlib and the young John Dryden.[4] The old Protector's death did not interrupt these mild duties, for Milton wrote fourteen more such letters during the eight months of Richard Cromwell's rule. But he was not in close touch with the men who really handled affairs of state, and he no longer identified his aspirations with theirs as he had done when he wrote *A Second Defence*. In December, 1657, he excused himself from recommending an acquaintance for an official post "because my influential friends are very few (since I stay nearly always at home—and willingly)."[5] Two great projects absorbed his energies in 1658, the last treatise on *Christian Doctrine* and the towering epic of *Paradise Lost*. It was in this year, in all probability, that he embarked on the continuous composition of his poetic masterpiece. How far advanced he was with his *Christian Doctrine* is less certain, but he had probably been working on it for over three years.[6] Whether or not it was substantially complete in draft, its themes still engrossed his mind. It was an astonishing labor for a blind man, dependent on his own memory and the eyes and voices of others for those thousands of proof texts, and dictating out of the dark those reams of involuted argument that he built upon them.

Thus he had largely withdrawn himself from the immediate concerns of the state in order to fulfil his highest missions as a Christian and

---

[4] Parker, *Milton*, pp. 506, 1062.

[5] Below, p. 507.

[6] Parker, in *Milton*, pp. 1052, 1055–57, 1064–65, argues for a conjecture that Milton completed *Christian Doctrine* between May, 1655, and May, 1658, and embarked on *Paradise Lost* in the autumn of the latter year. The most authoritative discussion of the dates of *Christian Doctrine's* composition, however, is by Maurice Kelley in *This Great Argument* (Princeton, 1941), pp. 8–71; and Kelley gives his latest thoughts on the question in his introduction to Volume VI of this edition.

as a poet. This positive motive probably weighed more, in changing the
bent of his activities from 1655 to 1659, than a certain disillusion with
the Protectorate, which we shall examine later. At any rate he some-
how found time for two other ventures in 1658, the first slight, the
second more considerable. In May he published a manuscript which he
owned of *The Cabinet Council,* a compilation of aphorisms mistakenly
attributed to Sir Walter Raleigh,[7] and prefaced it with a brief note to
the reader.[8] Then in the following October he brought out a new and
revised edition of *A Defence of the People of England.* The many
small polishings and amplifications of the text have been fully recorded
in Volume IV;[9] what concerns us here is a new postscript that he
added to the work, and particularly its concluding sentence:

> Now that my toil has won the richest rewards I had hoped for in this
> life, I do delight in them with all thankfulness, but at the same time I
> am earnestly seeking how best I may show not only my own country,
> to which I devoted all I have, but men of every land and, particularly,
> all Christian men, that for their sake I am at this time hoping and
> planning still greater things, if these be possible for me, as with God's
> help they will.[10]

Modern scholars agree that Milton probably referred here not to the
epic poem in English by which he would be known universally but to
the treatise in Latin, the universal tongue of Christendom, in which
he sought to plot from Holy Scripture a new and more perfect chart of
the whole Christian faith. The resolution of his thoughts on church
order in composing *Christian Doctrine* moved him to dictate his next
prose work in English, *A Treatise of Civil Power in Ecclesiastical
Causes.* This favorite theme, vying for his attention with *Paradise
Lost,* so absorbed him that he took no great notice of what was
actually befalling the civil power in England after the passing of the
great Protector. He cannot have foreseen that one more year would
bring such a tragic turn in public events that he would feel compelled
once more to devote all the powers of his pen to saving the Common-
wealth.

[7] On its probable authorship by one "T.B.," see Ernest A. Strathmann in the
Times Literary Supplement, April 13, 1956, p. 228.
[8] J. Milton French, *The Life Records of John Milton* (5 vols., New Bruns-
wick: Rutgers University Press, 1949–58; hereafter cited as French, *Life
Records*), IV, 220–22. For Milton's possible reasons, see Parker, *Milton,*
pp. 516–17; and for the strongly revived interest in Raleigh's writings during
the Great Rebellion, Christopher Hill, *Intellectual Origins of the English
Revolution* (Oxford University Press, 1965), pp. 203–05, 209–11.
[9] *Complete Prose Works of John Milton,* Don M. Wolfe, General Editor
(8 vols., New Haven: Yale University Press, 1953–), IV, 1129–44, hereafter
cited as *Complete Prose.*
[10] *Ibid.,* IV, 537.

CHAPTER I

THE UNDERMINING OF THE PROTECTORATE

1. THE ACCESSION OF RICHARD CROMWELL

September, 1658

AT THREE in the afternoon of September 3, 1658, the news passed through the hushed antechambers of Whitehall Palace that Oliver Cromwell was dead. The day was the anniversary of his great victories at Dunbar and Worcester, and it followed such a night of tempest "as if the Elements had been in Combustion at the flight of a Spirit, which had made so great a Concussion in the Affairs of the World." [1] Cromwell, however, died peacefully; the cares of state passed to the anxious heirs of his power, for none were quite certain what would happen about the succession. Under the new written constitution promulgated in 1657 and known as the Humble Petition and Advice, the Protector was empowered to nominate his successor. This he was believed to have done in a sealed paper addressed to Secretary Thurloe, but he had never parted with it or divulged its contents, and when he sent for it from his death bed it could not be found. According to Thurloe, Cromwell told him on August 30 that he wished Richard, his elder surviving son, to succeed him, and confirmed this choice the night before he died in the further presence of his chaplain Thomas Goodwin, Colonels Whalley and Goffe, and Nathaniel Fiennes, Commissioner of the Great Seal. Recently, this whole story has been denounced as a tissue of fabrications,[2] and it is true that Thurloe's several accounts contain suspicious discrepancies. Nevertheless the probability is that Cromwell did assent to his son's succession, if only

---

[1] Sir Richard Baker, *A Chronicle of the Kings of England* (1670; hereafter cited as Baker, *Chronicle*), p. 653. Baker's original work ended at 1625; the long continuation, which embodies important source material for the period covered by this volume, was written by Milton's nephew, Edward Phillips, and first published in 1665. Much of the material was supplied by Monck's brother-in-law Thomas Clarges.

[2] See E. Malcolm Hause, "The Nomination of Richard Cromwell," *The Historian*, XXVII (1965), 185–209.

with the feeble murmur of a man struggling against coma.[3] Goodwin, Whalley, and Goffe were not the kind of men to perjure themselves in so solemn a matter, and the Privy Council promptly and unanimously accepted the nomination.

Richard, for all his inadequacy, was almost the only conceivable choice. His younger brother Henry, the Lord Deputy of Ireland, had greater capacity, but he reacted to opposition with a degree of suspicion and resentment that would soon have led to trouble with the army officers in England; his letters during the next few months suggest a streak of paranoia. Richard's succession embodied the hereditary principle, which pleased the conservative gentry and lawyers who had been disappointed by Oliver's refusal of the crown, and reassured them that the Protectorate was evolving further towards a limited monarchy in all but name. Furthermore, to have passed over the elder son for the younger might have made other men consider their claims. There was a story later [4] that Oliver, in that lost sealed paper, had named Lieutenant-General Charles Fleetwood, his son-in-law and his deputy in command of the army. But if he had once considered Fleetwood—and it is not unlikely—he had since taken the measure of the man's weakness of judgment and too pliant character. "You are a milksop!" he had cried, when Fleetwood tried to protest his abrupt dissolution of Parliament on February 4, 1658. Major-General John Lambert had once looked a likely contender, but he had pushed his opposition to Cromwell's acceptance of the crown too far, and pressed too hard to know who the successor would be.[5] Stripped fourteen months earlier of all his commissions, and still only thirty-nine, he was the most dangerous of the army's lost leaders.

To nearly everyone's relief, Fleetwood and the rest of the senior army officers promptly recognized Richard's title, and with the ready concurrence of the Lord Mayor and City of London the new Protector was proclaimed with due pomp the next day. With trumpets and

[3] I offer some reasons for rejecting Hause's hypothesis, that Thurloe destroyed a letter by Cromwell nominating Fleetwood and invented his verbal nomination of Richard, in an essay on "Milton and Cromwell," in *Achievements of the Left Hand: Essays on the Prose of John Milton*, ed. Michael Lieb and John T. Shawcross (University of Massachusetts Press, 1974), pp. 185–218. Sir Charles Firth discussed the evidence in *The Last Years of the Protectorate* (2 vols., London, 1909), II, 302–06, and accepted the nomination of Richard as true in substance; so did Godfrey Davies in *The Restoration of Charles II* (San Marino: Huntington Library, 1955; hereafter cited as Davies, *Restoration*), pp. 3–5.

[4] Sources fully cited by Hause, pp. 186–87.

[5] See the document published by David Underdown in *English Historical Review*, LXXXIII (1968), 106. For Cromwell's words to Fleetwood, see *ibid.*, VII (1892), 108.

pageantry, the heralds, the councillors and officers of state, followed by
the Protector's life guard and a long train of persons of quality, pro-
ceeded on horseback from Whitehall to Palace Yard, from Westmin-
ster to the Strand, and from Temple Bar to the City. Each time the
proclamation was read, the shouts and acclamations from the crowds
seemed to testify to a genuine warmth of welcome.[6] Similar ceremonies
throughout the rest of England passed off equally well—except in
royalist Oxford, where Richard was chancellor of the university, and
where the undergraduates pelted the mayor and his attendant troops
with carrot- and turnip-tops.[7] At least a hundred addresses of loyalty
poured in during the next few weeks from counties and boroughs,
churches and ministers, military and naval forces—coin of no great
value, perhaps, but tokens that a large part of the political nation
was willing to accept the new regime.[8]

Only the inveterate enemies of the Protectorate—unyielding roy-
alists, commonwealthsmen, millenarian sectaries, and some malcon-
tents in the army—were disappointed at the deep calm that at first
followed Richard's accession. From the royalists he had little to fear.
The hopes that Charles II's exiled court had placed in a new and more
active leadership in England had been dashed only the previous spring,
when plans for a general rising had fallen into the net of Thurloe's
formidable intelligence system. The activists were still in disarray
after the arrests and executions that had followed—and the activists
were a dwindling minority.[9] One can understand why. A gentleman
had to think not only of his own life and estate but of his family
and descendants when he measured the inexpert recklessness of his
would-be leaders in conspiracy against the powerful efficiency of the
government's security measures. Nor was prudence the only con-
sideration. Richard's own friendly relations with his royalist neigh-
bors in Hampshire, before he came to power, are but one example of
the way in which ties of community were being reknit in many a
county. Civil war was receding into evil memory, and its renewal was

---

[6] *Mercurius Politicus*, September 2–9, 1658, pp. 805–07; F. G. P. Guizot,
History of Richard Cromwell and the Restoration, tr. A. R. Scoble (2 vols.,
London, 1856; hereafter cited as Guizot), I, 232. All references to this work
are to the numerous dispatches of the French ambassador Bordeaux appended
to Guizot's text.

[7] *The Life and Times of Anthony Wood*, ed. Andrew Clark (5 vols., Oxford,
1891) I, 259.

[8] Ninety-four are listed by a hostile pamphleteer in *A True Catalogue*
(September 28, 1659), E999(12); further described in Davies, *Restoration*,
pp. 10–11.

[9] David Underdown, *Royalist Conspiracy in England, 1649–1660* (New
Haven: Yale University Press, 1960), pp. 214–32.

a dreadful prospect. Most royalists whose estates had been seque-
strated had already been astonishingly successful in recovering them,[10]
and they were no longer harried and mulcted by Cromwell's major-
generals, whose rule had come to an end early in 1657. The majority,
so the French ambassador reported,[11] felt that they had no such
quarrel with Richard as with his father, and were glad of an honest
pretext to live on peaceable terms with his government.

The main danger had hitherto been that the royalists would enlist
the co-operation of the many former Parliamentarians, whether Pres-
byterians or uncommitted non-party men, who had been outraged by
the execution of the king and had detested the subsequent triumph of
the army, the Independents and the sectaries. But the debacle of the
past spring had shown how few Presbyterians would yet trust the
cavaliers as allies. They had noted with satisfaction the conservative
trend of Oliver's last years, especially his progressive mitigation of
military dominance in politics and his firm way with sectaries and
commonwealthsmen who tried to rock the ship of state. Richard's ac-
cession mollified them further. Richard Baxter testifies to a change of
heart among those who had looked on Oliver as a traitorous hypocrite
and on Charles II as the rightful claimant to the throne. Government
was an ordinance of God, they told themselves; the person of the
governor was of secondary importance, and if God had meant to re-
store the old royal line He would have moved before now. Richard,
wrote Baxter, "having never had any hand in the War . . . nor ever
seeking for the Government, and now seeming to own the Sober Party,
was like to be used in the healing of the Land." [12] Moderate men every-
where took hope that the new government would stand as a bulwark
against all that they had most disliked in recent years—the power of
the sword, the excesses of the saints, the meddling with private moral-
ity in the name of a "reformation of manners," the whole receding
threat of social revolution.

But in Richard's apparent strength lay also his weakness. Although
he stood well enough with most of the men of substance who formed
the ruling class in town and country, his gentle sway commanded ac-
quiescence rather than any warmth of loyalty. He could not draw upon

[10] Joan Thirsk, "The Sales of Royalist Land during the Interregnum," in
Economic History Review, 2nd series, V (1952), and "The Restoration Land
Settlement," in *Journal of Modern History*, XXVI (1954). See also P. G.
Holiday, "Land Sales and Repurchases in Yorkshire after the Civil War, 1650–
1670," *Northern History*, V (1970), 67–92.

[11] Bordeaux to Mazarin, September 18/28, 1658, in Guizot, I, 234.

[12] *Reliquiae Baxterianae*, ed. Matthew Sylvester (1696), part I, p. 100; *cf.*
Guizot, I, 252–53.

the mystique of monarchy, and his character was not of the build to inspire devotion. His amiable countenance, so unlike his father's in its general softness of feature, hinted at the limitations of intelligence that show through the wooden, laborious phrases of his letters. He was not the feeble clown of royalist legend; he had courage and a good presence, and he could deliver a speech with dignity and effect—if he was told more or less what to say. Even his opponents could not doubt his warm and honest nature, or the decency of his moral life. "I do love the person of the Lord Protector," said Sir Arthur Haslerig, the leader of the republicans who were striving to bring him down; "I never saw nor heard either fraud or guile in him." [13] But at the age of thirty-one his political sense and experience were rudimentary, for he had been brought into the Privy Council only nine months earlier. For about the same brief time he had nominally commanded a regiment of horse, but the army scarcely knew him. The officers reminded each other that he had never drawn sword for the Commonwealth, and referred to him disparagingly as "the young gentleman." [14] The ardors and rigors of Puritan religious experience were totally unknown to him. It is not hard to conjecture what Milton, with his ideal of a commonwealth ruled by an aristocracy of virtue, thought about entrusting the leadership of the state to this easygoing, conventional, unambitious country squire.

Richard was most vulnerable to the heirs of a more radical phase of the English Revolution: officers who had long felt that the "grandees" at Cromwell's court were betraying the army's old ideals, sectaries who still dreamed of a rule of the saints, commonwealthsmen who believed that the Protector's quasi-monarchy had usurped the rights of the sovereign people, and behind them the republican politicians, robbed of power when Cromwell expelled the Rump in 1653. Oliver had always been on his guard against a coalition of these forces, and had held them firmly in check. That strong hand was now removed, and Richard's accession gave a dangerous tilt to a balance that had been subtly changing for some time. The trend had already been manifest in the Humble Petition and Advice, the new parliamentary constitution of 1657. Its creation of a new upper House of Parliament and its stricter limitation of religious toleration were two symptoms of the shift to the right; others were the increase of ceremonial at the Protector's court and Cromwell's creation of knights, baronets, and even

[13] Robert W. Ramsey, *Richard Cromwell, Protector of England* (London, 1935), p. 77.
[14] *Calendar of the Clarendon State Papers* (4 vols., Oxford, 1869–1932; hereafter cited as *Clarendon Calendar*), IV, 100.

peers. Behind these changes lay the rise to power of a party of conservative Cromwellians, opposed to the political ascendancy of the army and hostile to religious extremism. Through Parliament, they had brought the regime of the major-generals to an end, and it was they who had pressed the offer of the crown. In the Privy Council, which Richard took over intact from his father, they were represented by Nathaniel Fiennes and his brother-in-law Sir Charles Wolseley, Edward Montagu, Philip Jones, and Viscount Lisle.[15]

Under Oliver these men had constituted at the most a counterweight to the army officers in the Council, who with the exception of Lambert had learned to live with the changing order of things. The senior officers' ties with their general were old and strong, and he had gratified them by refusing the crown. Richard had no such hold over them, and when the army's discontents rose during the autumn his growing distrust of them strengthened his temperamental affinity with the conservative civilians. He leaned heavily on Secretary Thurloe, who inclined the same way. He was also believed to depend a great deal on the advice of friends of the same stamp outside the Council, especially his brother-in-law Viscount Fauconberg, Lord Broghil, and (slightly later) William Pierrepont, Oliver St. John, and Bulstrode Whitelocke, politicians of the 'forties who had refused to have any part in the proceedings against Charles I.[16] Of these men, Wolseley, Broghil, and Fauconberg had royalist backgrounds, and Fiennes, Montagu, and Pierrepont had been "secluded" from the Long Parliament by Pride's Purge in 1648. This loosely knit group embodied considerably more political competence than the army party did, but Fleetwood, Desborough, and their colleagues were affronted by its influence, and their power for mischief was much greater.

Aligned with the civilian Cromwellians was another former royalist. George Monck commanded the army in Scotland, and he remained as loyal to Richard as he had been to Oliver. He soon sent the new Protector a most interesting letter of advice. He urged him to woo the

[15] Courtesy title of Philip Sidney, later third Earl of Leicester, incorrectly identified in Davies, *Restoration*, p. 30, as John Lisle, the regicide. I believe that it was Philip Sidney, and not his brother Algernon, whom Milton praised in *A Second Defence; cf. Complete Prose*, IV, 677.

[16] Guizot, I, 248; *State Papers Collected by Edward, Earl of Clarendon*, ed. R. Scrope and T. Monkhouse (3 vols., Oxford, 1767–86; hereafter cited as *Clarendon State Papers*), III, 421, 423, 441; *Clarendon Calendar*, IV, 111, 118; Lucy Hutchinson, *Life of Colonel Hutchinson*, ed. Sir Charles Firth (London, 1906), pp. 304–05. Richard seems to have wanted to bring Broghil and Fauconberg and his brother Henry into the Council, and to have been overborne; see Davies, *Restoration*, p. 31.

support of the men of power and interest in the country; to strengthen
the new upper House by admitting the more prudent and loyal of the
old peers and some powerful moderate gentry; to encourage a union
between moderate Presbyterian and Independent divines, and curb the
blasphemies of the sects; to amalgamate some regiments of the army so
as to reduce its burden and get rid of "some insolent spirits"; and in
all this to consult such antimilitarist politicians as Whitelocke, St.
John, Broghil, Pierrepont, and Thurloe.[17] It was excellent counsel, if
only he could have told Richard how to compel the acquiescence of
the ambitious army leaders in England.

2. STIRRINGS OF UNREST

September–November, 1658

It was from the army that Richard met the first hints of trouble.
The officers, however, were not all of one mind towards him, and it is
necessary to distinguish three factions that were taking shape among
them.[1]

The first consisted of a group of the most senior commanders and
came to be known as the Wallingford House party from the name of
Fleetwood's London residence, where it commonly met. Fleetwood had
married Cromwell's daughter Bridget after the death of her first hus-
band, Henry Ireton. In *A Second Defence*, Milton had praised his
"civility, gentleness, and courtesy" as well as his courage in battle and
clemency in victory.[2] All these qualities he possessed, but a term in
Ireland as commander-in-chief, and latterly Lord Deputy, had revealed
his incapacity in politics and his uncritical indulgence towards his fellow
sectaries. "Take heed also of your natural inclination to compliance,"
Cromwell had written to him on his appointment,[3] and Maurice Ashley
has shrewdly commented that "rubbed the right way, he was like putty;
rubbed the wrong way, he grew prickly."[4] He intended no disloyalty

---

[17] *A Collection of the State Papers of John Thurloe*, ed. Thomas Birch (7
vols., London, 1742; hereafter cited as Thurloe), VII, 387–88; discussed in
Davies, *Restoration*, pp. 19–21.

[1] The chief source for the following analysis is *Memoirs of Edmund Ludlow*,
ed. Sir Charles Firth (2 vols., Oxford, 1894), II, 61–62.

[2] *Complete Prose*, IV, 675.

[3] *Writings and Speeches of Oliver Cromwell*, ed. Wilbur C. Abbott (4 vols.,
Cambridge, Mass.: Harvard University Press, 1937–47; hereafter cited as
Abbott), II, 602.

[4] Maurice Ashley, *Cromwell's Generals* (London: Cape, 1954), p. 183.

to his brother-in-law Richard, but he was too open to the promptings of "godly" malcontents and too easily persuaded that any proposition coated in unctuous scriptural phrases had the blessing of the Lord upon it. Next in seniority to Fleetwood, and probably equal in influence because of his firmer will, was Major-General John Desborough, who was also linked to the house of Cromwell through his marriage to Oliver's sister. Desborough was rougher and more rustic in manner than Fleetwood, less given to pious rhapsodies, and several shades less scrupulous in his political dealings. He and Sydenham, another frequenter of Wallingford House, sat with Fleetwood on the Privy Council. All three men had figured in the roll of heroes in *A Second Defence*, but in the coming year Milton's praise was to turn to bitter blame of the whole faction. Its other members included such former major-generals as Berry, Hewson, and Kelsey, and Colonel John Clark. All were united in resentment at Richard's reliance on conservative civilian advisers and in a determination to restore the army to its old political influence and independence.

A second, more diverse group of senior officers stood more steadfastly by Richard and opposed any threat to his authority. Colonel Whalley (another celebrated by Milton in 1654) and Colonel Goffe did so out of simple, honorable loyalty, for they were both intensely devout Independents and they must have felt torn when their co-religionaries turned increasingly against him. Others of this group, including Richard Ingoldsby, Charles Howard (created a viscount by Cromwell), Edward Montagu (general at sea as well as privy councillor, and another whom Milton had lauded), and General Monck, were more secular-minded and stood further to the right. They supported Richard not only out of loyalty to his house and government, but because they actively favored the return to more traditional political and social values that his rule seemed to portend. Thanks to Montagu, Monck, and Henry Cromwell, Richard could count on the fleet and on the armies in Scotland and Ireland.

At the opposite pole to aristocratic traditionalists like Howard and Montagu stood the third group, which included fewer well-known names but was ultimately to emerge as the most potent. It numbered only a few colonels and lieutenant-colonels, such as Ashfield, Robert Lilburne, Mason, Moss, and Farley; its strength lay in the mass of captains and junior officers who mainly composed it. These men had long looked askance at the quasi-regal pomp of Cromwell's court and at the military grandees who lived high on the profits of their offices and commands. Their sympathies lay with old comrades like Overton, Okey, Saunders, Allured, and Packer, who had been drummed out of the army for opposing the Protectorate and upholding commonwealth principles. The yeast of Leveller egalitarianism had not wholly ceased to work upon them, and in religion they were mainly sectarian, if not millenarian. They measured Richard's government not by its prospects of acceptance among men of birth and property but against their own disappointed hopes of the New Jerusalem. They were ripe for the jeremiads of fanatical preachers and the subtle promptings of republican politicians. They would be ready soon, if they were not even now, to own themselves commonwealthsmen.

These groups were still only partially distinct in the autumn of 1658, and the first stirrings in the army were mild enough. On September 21 Fleetwood at the head of over two hundred officers presented an address to Richard in the name of the armies of England, Scotland, and Ireland, declaring their loyalty to him and to the government established by the Humble Petition and Advice. In itself this was reassuring, but there was a presage of future trouble when they reminded Richard how his father had "in his Armies . . . reckoned the choicest Saints his chiefest Worthies," and when they exhorted him to "carry on that good old Cause and Interest of God and his People." [5] We shall meet that ominous phrase "the good old cause" again, and see how it became the rallying cry for all the discontents against the Protectorate. The address went on to ask that the army be kept under the command of honest and godly officers, that vacancies in the Privy Council be "filled up with Men of known Godliness," "that a Work of Reformation, tending to good Life and Manners, may be vigorously carried on by the Hands of good Magistrates," and that the commissions for ejecting unworthy ministers and installing godly ones should be maintained. [6] (Milton would not like that last request.) All this was evidently composed by Fleetwood and a few close colleagues. [7] Were they deliberately courting the more radical junior officers? Whatever their motives, they were asserting the army's right to address the government on the highest affairs of church and state. Perhaps without clearly realizing what they were doing, the men of Wallingford House were throwing the sword into the scales. They would soon find it a two-edged blade.

Early in October a more dangerous petition emanated from the discontented junior officers. It asked that Fleetwood be made commander-in-chief, and that as such he should be empowered to commission all

---

[5] *Parliamentary or Constitutional History of England* (24 vols., London, 1751–66; hereafter cited as *Old Parliamentary History*), XXI, 233–34.

[6] *Ibid.*, p. 235.

[7] Davies, *Restoration*, p. 8.

officers below field rank. It further requested that no officer should be dismissed or cashiered except upon conviction by a court-martial.[8] The implications were alarming. To separate the command of the army from the headship of the state, to deprive the Protector and the Council of power either to prevent the commissioning of unsuitable officers or to dismiss them for persistent political opposition, to subordinate Monck and Henry Cromwell to Fleetwood, to open up the possibility of soldiers choosing whether to obey the protector or the commander-in-chief—what a recipe for anarchy was here! Fleetwood, however, instead of stifling the petition when it was first brought to him, tamely transmitted it to Richard. Well might Henry Cromwell ask him, from Dublin, what he thought he was doing in letting two or three hundred officers meet in his presence and listen to exhortations "to stand up for that good old cause, which had long lain asleep." [9]

Richard wisely refused to part with the ultimate generalship of the forces but assented to what he could of the petition. At another large meeting of officers on October 8, Fleetwood and some senior colleagues belatedly urged their subordinates to give up this dangerous petitioning, but within a week the malcontents were pressing their demands again. Richard decided to address them in person. The speech he made on October 18 was a good one—Thurloe had drafted it—and it quieted them for a while. He told them he had commissioned Fleetwood as lieutenant-general of all the forces, thus making him commander-in-chief under himself, and would always consult him and the other senior commanders when exercising his constitutional authority to grant commissions. No officer would be arbitrarily punished or dismissed.[10]

But the good effect of this speech was fleeting, and the "under officers" soon resumed their agitation, especially at the Friday prayer meetings at St. James' which brought them regularly together. We need not suspect the majority of them of deliberately abusing a religious exercise for political ends, but fiery exhortations to remember the

[8] *Ibid.*, p. 34. The Humble Petition and Advice ruled that the Protector was to dispose of the forces by consent of Parliament when it was sitting and at other times by the advice of the Council. It did, however, provide for the appointment, after Oliver's death, of a commander-in-chief *under* his successors. This did not of course preclude the new Protector from retaining the chief command himself; it simply required the consent of the Council to whatever was arranged. See S. R. Gardiner, *Constitutional Documents of the Puritan Revolution*, 3rd ed. (Oxford, 1906), p. 453.

[9] Thurloe, VII, 454.

[10] Davies, *Restoration*, p. 37, n. 30, gives good reason for assuming that the speech printed in Thurloe, VII, 447–49, was delivered on this occasion.

cause for which they had fought the Lord's battles, to search their hearts for any signs of backsliding, and to resist all who would tempt them back towards Egyptian bondage, could all too easily impart spiritual imperatives to their secular discontents. They also began to voice a new demand that the officers cashiered by Oliver should be reinstated. These of course included not only commonwealthsmen like Okey and Overton but also Lambert, who was credibly reported to have a hand in fomenting the army's unrest.[11] These meetings reached such a pitch that Richard forestalled the one fixed for November 19 and summoned the officers to hear him again instead. Again he talked to them persuasively; he wanted them to know him better, he said, and he warmly assured them of his care for the army, repeating promises he had made a month ago of urgent measures to settle their arrears of pay. He praised their piety and discipline, and appealed earnestly for mutual love, unity, and charity.[12] Most of them seemed genuinely moved, and their agitation died down until well into the new year.

Why had not Fleetwood and his friends at Wallingford House dealt with these motions and mutterings firmly, as Oliver would surely have done? Partly, no doubt, because they felt the undercurrent of resentment against the Protectorate and all its later works lapping around themselves too, and to a considerable extent they shared it. Fleetwood in particular, fuddled with the cloudy language of the saints, was too carried away by emotive invocations of the good old cause to see how far he was undermining his young master. There were far too many officers about London, and a responsible commander-in-chief would have sent many of them back to their regiments. But Fleetwood and Desborough had a strong motive for courting their restless subordinates, for they wanted the army's support in the battles that they themselves were fighting in the Privy Council. The rift between the military councillors and the conservative Cromwellians was widening; they disagreed over the raising of money, the calling of a new Parliament, and the conduct of foreign policy. Early in November there were rumors of a move to purge the Council of all but the Wallingford House men and their allies, and a month later Desborough brought an absurd accusation against Montagu of conspiring with Fauconberg to have Fleetwood and himself seized and sent to the Tower.[13]

---

[11] *Ibid.*, pp. 37–38, esp. n. 35.

[12] *Clarke Papers*, ed. Sir Charles Firth (4 vols., *CS*, 1891–1901) III, 168–70; *Mercurius Politicus*, November 18–25, 1658, p. 24. Davies deals fully with the army's agitation in *Restoration*, ch. 3, and in "The Army and the Downfall of Richard Cromwell," *Huntington Library Bulletin*, VII (1935).

[13] Davies, *Restoration*, pp. 31–33, 38–39, 45–46.

Against the background of such squabbles, Oliver's funeral was at last solemnized on November 23, although his body had been interred much earlier. The Council had planned a costly and magnificent pageant, but the procession started so late, thanks to the foreign ambassadors' quarrels over protocol, and the long train of mourners took so long to wind through the streets, that it was dark before they entered Westminster Abbey. No one had provided a single candle to light the great building, so there were no prayers, no sermon, no oration. A fanfare of trumpets, and everyone went home. Milton probably walked in that shuffling cortège, guided perhaps by the hand of his colleague Marvell; the Council had voted both of them a length of black cloth for the occasion.[14] He probably shared the dislike of many a commonwealthsman for its cost and vanity, and particularly for the regal emblems—crown, sword, sceptre, orb—with which Cromwell's effigy was decked. The glory he had found in Cromwell's triumph when he wrote *A Second Defence* had departed, and as a lover of republican simplicity he would find no fit celebration of it in this empty, ill-ordered pomp.[15]

3. THE PARLIAMENT AND THE REPUBLICAN OFFENSIVE

January–February, 1659

Faced with a heavy burden of debt and the long arrears of the army's pay, the Council decided late in November, 1658, to call a Parliament for January 27. It ran the risk, as Oliver had done in the last two Parliaments, of giving a platform to the Protectorate's republican opponents, who were already laying their plans. "The comonwealth's-men have their daily meetinges," wrote Thurloe to Henry Cromwell on November 30, "disputeinge what kinde of comonwealth they shall have, takeinge it for granted, they may picke and choose; and they hope to prepare a part of the armye to fall in with them, wherein I hope they will be deceived; although I must needs say, I like not the aspect of things, and my feares are greater then my hopes."[1] The scene of these meetings, as the elections drew nearer, was the house of Milton's old hero, Sir Henry Vane.[2]

[14] French, *Life Records,* IV, 235–36.
[15] On the funeral see Davies, *Restoration,* pp. 40–44, and *Old Parliamentary History,* XXI, 238–45.
[1] Thurloe, VII, 541.
[2] Ludlow, *Memoirs,* II, 50. On Milton's admiration for Vane, and Cromwell's breach with Vane in 1653, see *Complete Prose,* IV, 173–76, 215–16.

in the rain till another be built." [6] "If we miss this settlement that we are now under," he said in another day's debate, "we shall never come to it again . . . and the pulling down these will put it into the hands of those that will never be quiet till their bellies be full." [7]

The contest really began on February 1, when Thurloe unwisely introduced a bill whereby Parliament was to recognize Richard as Protector under the Humble Petition and Advice. The republicans, finding the House well disposed towards Richard's Protectorate in principle, professed a bland regard for his person but avidly seized their chance to question the constitutional basis of his authority. They were, as a royalist agent reported, "industrious, popular, plausible, eloquent in the language of the times, cunning in the rules of the House." [8] They made the most of the fact that in its original form the Humble Petition and Advice had named Oliver as king. "This Petition and Advice," said Vane, "was never intended to be the settled government, but only to be a pair of stairs to ascend the throne; a step to King, Lords, and Commons. . . . This Bill huddles up, in wholesale, what you have fought for, and is hasted on, lest you should see it." [9] They particularly attacked the Protector's "negative voice" over the decisions of the Commons and his share of authority over the armed forces. Finding no great support, they spun out time with endless speeches. They filibustered shamelessly; one oration of two or three hours by Haslerig treated the members to a historical survey beginning with the heptarchy. After the House voted at length to recognize Richard as Protector on February 19, they turned their main attack against the Other House. Its high proportion of "swordsmen" and government officials, they claimed, made it a mere extension of the Protector's authority. No extravagance was too wild for them. "If this should pass," said Haslerig, "we shall next vote canvass breeches and wooden shoes for the free people of England." [10] Thanks to their delays, the Commons' formal recognition of the Other House did not pass until March 28, and then only with the proviso that it should not "exclude such ancient Peers as have been faithful to the Parliament." [11] This manifestation of the Parliament's conservative temper must have disquieted Milton if he heard of it, for a House of Lords and a hereditary peerage were anathema to him.

There were other questions upon which the republicans employed

[6] *Ibid.*, IV, 199.
[7] *Ibid.*, IV, 62.
[8] *Clarendon State Papers*, III, 440.
[9] Burton, III, 178.
[10] *Ibid.*, IV, 79.
[11] Davies, *Restoration,* pp. 67–68.

their delaying tactics, such as the right of the Scottish and Irish members to sit and the legality of the excise; but when it came to a division they were generally defeated. Often they fell back on purely procedural wrangles, which they would drag out for hours and even days. If they could not win votes, they could at least frustrate the government's legislative program and hold off the votes of supplies that were so badly needed if the soldiers were to get their pay. They had a vested interest in the army's discontent. Though they could no longer sway the House as they had done in Oliver's time, they had allies to whip up outside it. That was what made time so well worth buying.

4. THE GOOD OLD CAUSE

February–March, 1659

If the republicans had looked for support only among those fellow commonwealthsmen who had always regarded the Protectorate as a usurpation of the people's sovereignty, they would not have been very formidable. The danger lay in their forging links between the commonwealthsmen and two other groups that felt their interests betrayed: the army officers who had already been agitating in the autumn, and the extremer sectaries who looked back with nostalgia to the Nominated Parliament of 1653—the assembly of saints, they often called it—and who regarded the Protectorate as a new guise for the old Babylon. This was a combination that Oliver had feared, and rightly, for it was to bring down his son's Protectorate. William Prynne would then denounce it, quite accurately, as "the confederated *Triumvirate* of *Republicans, Sectaries* and *Souldiers.*" [1] Six years had softened the army's former exasperation with the politicians of the Rump, and since many of the discontented officers were commonwealthsmen at heart and sectarian in religion, it was not hard for subversive propaganda to fuse the three elements.

This was not the first attempt to bring them together. Vane in 1656 had sought to build a common platform for them in his pamphlet *A Healing Question Propounded and Resolved*,[2] and had spent four months in prison rather than retract his opposition. He had sought to rally what he called "the Good Party" against the power-corrupted

---

[1] William Prynne, *The Re-publicans and Others Spurious Good Old Cause . . . Anatomized* (May 13, 1659), E983(6), p. 1.

[2] E879(5), May 12, 1656; reprinted in *Somers Tracts*, ed. Sir Walter Scott (13 vols., London, 1809–15), VI, 303 f.

military leadership which, he maintained, had usurped the rights that
belonged to *all* the true heirs of the cause they had fought for. This
cause he defined as "just natural rights in civil things, and true freedom
in matters of conscience"—terms very similar to Milton's in *The
Readie & Easie Way,* though in fact they were the common coin of
dozens of republican pamphleteers, and Cromwell claimed the same
aims for his own government. But Vane, like Milton and in contrast
with Cromwell, affirmed that liberty of conscience required the civil
magistrate to renounce all authority over matters of faith and wor-
ship. He also appealed to his readers to recover the "primitive sim-
plicity, humility and trust" of the days before the Protectorate, and he
used already that potent phrase, "the good old cause," that was to echo
through tract after tract in 1659.[3]

The good old cause had turned up again in a notorious petition which
the republican leaders promoted among the soldiery and citizenry of
London late in January, 1658, during the brief final session of Oliver's
second Parliament. The petition called on the Commons to restore to
Parliament "the supream Power and Trust, which the People (the Orig-
inal of all just Power) commit unto them," a demand which in its
context implied the exclusion of the Protector and the Other House
from any share in legislation or any powers of veto. It further ap-
pealed to the sectaries by demanding that no tender consciences be
oppressed, and to the army by asking that no officers or soldiers be
turned out of their employments unless convicted by a court-martial.[4]
Cromwell had felt the danger in this petition so acutely that on Febru-
ary 4, 1658, he abruptly dissolved Parliament before it could be pre-
sented.

This same petition was revived soon after Richard's Parliament
met, and its promoters collected somewhere between twenty and forty
thousand signatures to it.[5] The House received the petitioners on
February 15, 1659, the day before Milton registered *Of Civil Power*
for publication. Like Milton's tract, the petition was addressed "To

---

[3] *A Healing Question* is further discussed and the whole literature of the
good old cause surveyed in Austin Woolrych, "The Good Old Cause and the
Fall of the Protectorate," in *Cambridge Historical Journal,* XIII (1957), 133–61,
where much of what follows is more elaborately documented. See also Davies in
Huntington Library Bulletin, VII, 131–67, and in *Restoration,* chs. IV–V.

[4] *To the Parliament. The Petition of Diverse Citizens . . . of London*
(January 25, 1658), 669f20(71); commentary in Firth, *Last Years of the
Protectorate,* II, 30–34, and Davies, *Restoration,* pp. 57–58.

[5] Forty thousand according to Thomas Clarges (Thurloe, VII, 617) and Sir
John Grenville (*Clarendon Calendar,* IV, 148); 15–20,000 according to
Bordeaux (Guizot, I, 302).

the Parliament of the Commonwealth of England," but whereas Milton probably used the word "commonwealth" in the neutral sense of body politic or state, the petitioners were affirming by implication that the Commonwealth as established in 1649 had never ceased to be the legitimate government of England. Three men, all prominent Baptists and wealthy citizens of London, actually presented the petition, and their spokesman Samuel Moyer treated the House to "a great deal of cant language" for nearly an hour. Moyer was to be expected; he had been a leading radical in the Nominated Parliament and a figure of opposition ever since. But his colleagues William Kiffin and Josiah Berners had formerly supported the Protectorate against their more fanatical brethren,[6] and their presence was an ominous sign that Richard's government was alienating the moderate sectaries who had lived at peace with his father. The leading republicans were expecting the petition. One after another, Haslerig, Scot, Vane, Neville, Lambert, and others rose to urge a vote of thanks. But most of the members disliked it, and after rejecting the motion to thank the petitioners by 202 votes to 110 the Commons gave them a cold and noncommittal answer.[7]

Just when this petition was being agitated, there was a move in the army to present a remonstrance on similar lines. Lambert was said to be fomenting it behind the scenes, and one of its demands was that the army should have its own commander-in-chief, distinct from the Protector. Richard, however, went in person to Wallingford House and sharply warned the officers gathered there against countenancing any such address to the Parliament. He would part with the generalship and his life together, he said. Fleetwood and Desborough then agreed to repudiate the proposed remonstrance publicly, though they still permitted a committee of officers "to consider of something, in case itt might bee seasonable to offer any thinge to the Parliament."[8]

[6] See the open letter by Kiffin and others to their fellow-Baptists on January 20, 1654, in *Original Letters and Papers of State . . . Found Among the Political Collections of Mr. John Milton*, ed. John Nickolls (London, 1743), pp. 159–60; also Louise F. Brown, *The Political Activities of the Baptists and Fifth Monarchy Men in England During the Interregnum* (Washington, 1912), pp. 173 f.; Thurloe, V, 755–59; Abbott, III, 509, n. 160; IV, 379. Kiffin and Berners, however, had already turned against the Protectorate in the last year or two; see documents printed in *English Historical Review*, VII (1892), 104, 106–07, and LXXXIII (1968), 105.

[7] Burton, III, 288–96; *Commons Journals*, VII, 604.

[8] *Clarke Papers*, III, 182–83; Guizot, I, 304, 306–08; Thurloe, VII, 612; *Clarendon Calendar*, IV, 148, 150–52, 158; *Clarendon State Papers*, III, 426; Mabbott's newsletter of February 15, 1659, in British Museum, Lansdowne MSS 823, fo. 223.

Firmly though both Parliament and Protector stood against these movements of protest in February, a spate of propaganda was already beginning to pour from the presses that would contribute powerfully and soon to their defeat. Through it all ran the leitmotif of the good old cause, seldom explicitly defined, but always appealing emotionally to memories of a time when the Lord had lent His presence to all who fought His battles, and before their hopes of a new Jerusalem had dimmed amid the inevitable compromises with political realities during the last half-dozen years. So far as these exhortations were inspired by the republican politicians, their object was to identify the cause by implication with the Rump, and if possible to restore that body to power; but the pamphleteers seldom came into the open about this, and most of them appealed more vaguely to the frustrated aspirations of the people of God, often with strong undertones of social radicalism. How far Milton was aware of this campaign in pulpit and press when he published *Of Civil Power* is uncertain, but he would soon endorse emphatically the triumph of the republican old guard. The literature of the good old cause helped to form the intellectual climate in which he composed his last ecclesiastical and political tracts, and to some extent it matches his own disillusion with the Protectorate. He himself would claim in *The Readie & Easie Way* that "What I have spoken, is the language of that which is not call'd amiss *the good Old Cause.*" [9]

The pressure was directed mainly at the army, and its keynote was a call to repentance. *The Cause of God and of These Nations* [10] was typical in portraying the whole Protectorate as a monstrous backsliding, with private interests usurping upon the public, the pomp and vanity of a Court revived, "the old spirit of the *Gentry* brought in play again," Triers keeping the true spirit out of the pulpits, Parliamentary elections corruptly influenced—all indeed running back into the old channels of king, Lords, and Commons, and opposing an "Earthly Lordly Rule" to "the growing light in the people of God." [11] *A Call to the Officers of the Army* [12] exhorted them to awake and repent, to "do our first works, and remember the loves of our Virginity," for the cause that had once shone fresh as a bride was now sullied and faded, "mishapen with a strange dresse, we had almost said, with the attire of an harlot." Satan was exploiting "the divisions of the people of God" to obstruct the work of reformation, "and we must not so

[9] Below, p. 462.
[10] E968(11), March 2, 1659.
[11] *Ibid.,* ch. I, *passim,* and p. 13.
[12] By "S.R. H.W. R.P." (February 26, 1659), E968(8).

much as hope for the happiness of Halcion days, untill they return and embrace each other in love and harmony." *The Good Old Cause Dress'd in It's Primitive Lustre* [13] conveyed the same hint more explicitly: "There was in those virgin daies such a mutuall, strict, and lovely harmony and agreement . . . between the Parliament and the honest unbiass'd people of the Nation." But the political message was usually veiled in a mist of moralizing, thickened with inflammatory scriptural allusions to the travails of an earlier chosen people. Another anonymous scribe, for instance, plainly tilting at the Wallingford House grandees, lamented that some "that once spake the language of Zion, and highly appeared for the Good Old Cause," had become "so besotted and degenerated into a self-seeking slavish, and enslaving Spirit" as to return to Egypt and the bondage of a single person. He denounced the flattering addresses to Richard as emanations of "the Spirit of the Beast and false Prophet in the former and present Monarchs of this and other Nations." [14] Similarly, William Allen, the Fifth Monarchist and former adjutant-general in Ireland, urged the officers to "inquire when could you with joynt satisfaction, say, At such a time the presence of the Lord was with you; and these sore hands of displeasure that have of late years attended you, were not upon you, nor works in your hands as now." [15]

These and other tracts were plain in their denunciation of the Protectorate but coy about what they would erect in its place. Some of them struck a millenarian note, hinting that deliverance from the present apostasy would come not through mere political expedients but by some tremendous divine intervention. God, said one, had recently been testifying with "such interweavings of stupendious Providences . . . and such legible characters of divine ownings, That we are now bigg with just hopes of arriving in the end unto some eminent establishment, even above the magnificence of all those forms, which meerely have the worldly stamp upon them." [16] "How God will do it I know not," wrote another, "but by his own appearing. It is the day of His Power, the day of the Spirit, that is to have its turn next." [17]

Reading these pieces and a dozen other like them, it is often hard to

[13] By R. Fitz-Brian (February 16, 1659), E968(6); quotation from p. 5.

[14] *A Second Narrative of the Late Parliament,* new edition (April 29, 1659), E977(3), pp. 38–40. The quotations are from postscripts written, judging by internal evidence, early in 1659.

[15] William Allen, *A Faithful Memorial of That Remarkable Meeting at Windsor Castle* (1659; written, according to the preface, early in March), p. 7, reprinted in *Somers Tracts,* VI, 489 ff.

[16] Fitz-Brian, *The Good Old Cause Dress'd in It's Primitive Lustre,* preface.

[17] *The Cause of God and of These Nations,* p. 27.

tell the genuine millenarian enthusiast from the republican propagandist who deliberately exploits the rhetoric of the saints. When one finds the good old cause associated with the good old Parliament one naturally suspects the latter, but there is no clear line of demarcation. The sectaries' old resentment against the Rump for its restrictive policy towards religious toleration was half forgotten, and the old conflict of principle between the sovereignty of the people's representatives and a rule of the saints, so acute at the time of the Nominated Parliament, was now kept out of the controversy. The Fifth Monarchist preacher John Rogers, for instance, had rejoiced at the Rump's expulsion in 1653 and campaigned for a Sanhedrin of seventy godly men. But he had evidently cooled during his various imprisonments under the Protectorate, and perhaps Vane had influenced him when they were both confined in Carisbrooke Castle in 1656. At any rate he no longer expected a literal and imminent Second Coming, and he stated the true cause as "submission to the Kingdome of Christ, and *Parliamentary Government* rightly stated, and fixed on a firm foundation." [18] John Canne, another of the same stamp, who in 1653 had said of the Rumpers that "trusting to lying vanities, they forsook their own mercies," and had greeted Cromwell as God's instrument for dissolving them, was soon to give them a qualified welcome when they returned to power and to accept employment as their newswriter.[19]

Whether spontaneous or contrived—and it was something of both—this strain of sectarian fervor in the growing outcry against the Protectorate was highly useful to the republicans. Apart from their emotional force, these flights of Scriptural prophecy and Old Testament parallels were an altogether cheaper currency from their point of view than precise political pledges. How much the sects could really expect from these politicians was very dubious. Vane was their true ally, but Haslerig, courting a different audience, addressed the Commons in April in favor of "a moderate Presbytery," [20] and it would not be long before both Milton and the millenarians would see how far their trust had been misplaced.

Another tactic of the republicans was to take up the cause of Crom-

[18] *The Plain Case of the Common-Weal Neer the Desperate Gulf of the Common Woe* (March 3, 1659), E972(5), p. 31; published anonymously, but acknowledged by Rogers in his *Diapoliteia* (1659), p. 69.

[19] John Canne, *A Voice from the Temple to the Higher Powers* (June 13, 1653), E699(16), epistle dedicatory; *A Seasonable Word to the Parliament-Men* (May 10, 1659), E983(1), *passim*. Canne, however, was outspoken in this last tract about the Rump's former shortcomings, and affirmed that the essence of the good old cause was *"NO KING BUT JESUS"* (p. 5).

[20] Burton, IV, 336.

well's political prisoners, and here they won much more support in the House than on more general issues. They pleased the sectaries by obtaining the release of John Portman, a Fifth Monarchist who had been committed to the Tower for promoting the London citizens' petition [21] on its first appearance in 1658. But the case of which they made most, and which must have warmed Milton's heart, was that of Major-General Robert Overton. In *A Second Defence* Milton had given a very special place to Overton; "You," he hailed him, "who for many years have been linked to me with a more than fraternal harmony, by reason of the likeness of our tastes and the sweetness of your disposition." [22] Yet before that year 1654 was out, Overton had become implicated, how deeply is still not certain, in a stirring of republican protest in the army against the Protectorate, and Cromwell, with a severity quite untypical, had kept him confined without trial ever since. Now the republicans persuaded Parliament to give him a hearing, just when several sectarian pamphleteers—surely not by coincidence —were vindicating him as a martyr to Cromwellian tyranny.[23] He was brought over from Jersey and warned to enter London quietly, but his champions were determined upon a great public demonstration. When he reached Brentford on March 9, fifteen hundred people, in coaches, on horseback, or on foot, waited to greet him, and they turned the last ten miles of his journey into a triumphal procession. Overton rode in the open boot of a coach, crowned with laurel, and four or five hundred riders carrying laurel branches escorted him. As he approached Westminster, the crowd thickened and the cheers rose higher. Vainly the captain in charge of the prisoner tried to steer him towards his appointed lodgings at Lambeth; the crowd forced his coach to drive on towards the Parliament House, where another great concourse was awaiting his arrival. A party of soldiers was sent just in time to get him quietly out of the way, but even without that final scene in Palace Yard it was a triumph that reminded men of the welcome the city had given to Prynne, Bastwick, and Burton when the Long Parliament freed them in 1640.[24] The Commons ordered Overton's release a few days later, despite attempts by Thurloe and other government speakers to justify his imprisonment.

[21] See above, p. 20.

[22] *Complete Prose*, IV, 676.

[23] J[ohn?] R[ogers?], *The Sad Suffering Case of Major-General Rob. Overton* (March 3, 1659), E972(4); *The Cause of God and of These Nations*, ch. 1; *The Plain Case of the Common-Weal*, p. 15.

[24] *Clarke Papers*, III, 184; *Calendar of State Papers, Venetian Series* (hereafter cited as *CSP Ven.*), 1657–59, p. 298; *Clarendon Calendar*, IV, 160. On the earlier triumph of Prynne, Bastwick, and Burton, see *Complete Prose*, I, 44–45.

The rest of March saw something of a lull in the agitation, and at this point the future of the Protectorate still hung in the balance. The majority in Parliament supported it, and Fleetwood, Desborough, and the other senior army commanders had not yet wavered seriously in their allegiance. But the temper of the junior officers was rising again, and the potent appeal of the good old cause was being used to weld soldiers, sectaries, and commonwealthsmen into a single engine of protest. We shall resume the story of Richard's downfall in Chapter IV, but one factor in the situation that we have not yet considered was the Protectorate's ecclesiastical policy. This we must examine before introducing Milton's protest against it in *A Treatise of Civil Power,* which he addressed to Parliament in February.

CHAPTER II

THE BOUNDS OF EITHER SWORD: ECCLESIASTICAL POLICY AND CONTROVERSY, 1654–1659

1. THE CROMWELLIAN SETTLEMENT

FEAR of the state's encroachment on matters of faith and conscience was only one element in the discontent that radicals of all kinds felt towards Richard's Protectorate, but it was the one that Milton most shared. His disillusion with the government that he served was almost certainly not new, and it stemmed mainly from the whole ecclesiastical policy of the Protectorate. Cromwell had been no less sincere a believer in liberty of conscience than Milton, but the two men differed fundamentally over the question whether the state should take responsibility for the provision and maintenance of godly ministers. It was this question that Milton and various sectarian opponents of the Protectorate sought to reopen early in 1659.

Sirluck in Volume II of this edition has traced the process whereby the leading Independent ministers progressed, from 1644 onwards, from requesting a mere "accommodation" under a Presbyterian establishment to allying with the sects for a wide measure of religious toleration.[1] When the Presbyterians lost their political ascendancy through Pride's Purge in December, 1648, their exclusive and intolerant state church was left half built, with most of its classical presbyteries existing only on paper. But it was never formally dismantled, nor was anything positive established in its place until after Cromwell became Protector. The Rump was deeply divided over the settlement of religion; far from being a solidly Independent body, it contained many who would have liked to maintain the Presbyterian church much as it was.[2] With one hand it removed the penalties for not attending parish services, provided that those who objected to them joined in some form of Protestant worship on Sundays; with the other, in the same year of 1650, it passed an act punishing certain atheistic and blasphemous

---

[1] *Complete Prose*, II, introduction, ch. II, esp. pp. 107–20.

[2] William A. Shaw, *A History of the English Church During the Civil Wars and Under the Commonwealth, 1640–1660* (2 vols., London: 1900; hereafter cited as *English Church*), II, 77.

opinions which, though less draconic than the blasphemy ordinance of 1648, clearly asserted the civil magistrate's power to draw the bounds of toleration.

By conceding the right to associate and worship outside the established church the Rump went far to meet the desires of the moderate sects, but it never reached agreement on the constitution of the established church itself. Wolfe has told in Volume IV of the promising scheme that John Owen and a group of fellow-Independents presented to Parliament in February, 1652, with Cromwell's support.[3] It was the embryo of the Protectorate settlement. The state was to regulate the parochial ministry through two sets of commissioners, part lay and part clerical: the one divided into regional circuits, to approve all candidates for livings after they had been attested as sound in the faith by a specified number of local ministers and laymen, the other a single national board whose members were to travel the country and remove clergymen and schoolmasters whom they found unfit. People who dissented from the doctrine or form of service "owned by the state" were to be free to congregate for worship, provided that their meeting-places were certified to the magistrate and that their pastors preached nothing contrary to those principles of the faith which the Scriptures plainly affirm to be necessary to salvation.

The Rump debated these proposals intermittently during the last year of its existence. As Wolfe has described, they roused Roger Williams and others to strong protest, and moved Milton to appeal to Cromwell and Vane in a majestic pair of sonnets.[4] But Cromwell did not see Owen's scheme as "threatning to bind our souls with secular chains," nor did he draw "the bounds of either sword," the spiritual and the civil, as Milton did. As for the Rump, there were probably at least as many members who thought Owen's proposals too permissive as there were who, like Vane, found them too restrictive. On one point, however, the Rump did pronounce. It voted on April 29, 1652, that ministers should continue to be maintained by tithes until a more acceptable provision could be devised. This decision was much resented in the army and among the sects.

The main substance of the proposals was still under debate when Cromwell dissolved the Rump a year later, but they came up again, little changed, in the Nominated Parliament of July–December, 1653.

---

[3] *Complete Prose*, IV, 169–70; see also Shaw, *English Church*, II, 79–85, and Wilbur K. Jordan, *The Development of Religious Toleration in England* (4 vols., Cambridge, Mass., 1932–40; hereafter cited as *Religious Toleration*), III, 138–43.

[4] *Complete Prose*, IV, 170–74.

They were the rock upon which that strange assembly finally ship-wrecked. For six days in early December it debated a report from its committee for tithes which recommended a scheme similar to Owen's for approving and removing parish ministers. It also reaffirmed the clergy's right to their tithes, but when the crucial vote was taken on December 10 it was not on the question of tithes but on the proposed commissioners for ejecting unworthy ministers and installing godly ones. This, the first clause in the report, was rejected by a bare two votes in an exceptionally full House.[5] It was the biggest success so far for the radical party, whose hard core not only opposed tithes but, like Milton, "professed fully against the Magistrate's power in any matters of religion, and particularly in that of placing or sending forth men to preach the Gospel." [6] But it was a pyrrhic victory, because on the next day that the House met, the moderate members, for whom this vote was the last straw, marched out in a body with the Speaker at their head and resigned their authority back into Cromwell's hands.

It was now four years since the Presbyterian ascendancy had been broken, and the common front that the Independents and the sects had formed against Presbyterian intolerance was showing some bad cracks. During 1653 the pamphlet controversy over questions of ecclesiastical settlement had reached its peak. Literally dozens of tracts argued the pros and cons of tithes, but tithes were only one issue among many. For the Independents, there was the difficulty of reconciling the parochial system, within which they might now obtain benefices, with their own Congregational principles, whereby churches were defined not by geographical boundaries but by a free act of covenant. For Independents and sectaries alike there were the old questions of the extent of toleration and of the magistrate's duty to restrain the intolerable, while the Fifth Monarchists raised the comparatively new one of whether God's chosen saints should tolerate any opposition whatever to their designated task of erecting the kingdom of Christ here and now. The problem of a national ecclesiastical order was as open as ever when the Nominated Parliament abdicated its authority on December 12, though two extreme solutions could now be ruled out. There could be no further question of an exclusive, monolithic national church, such as the Westminster Assembly and the majority in the Long Parliament

[5] *Commons Journals*, VII, 361–63. The contested proposal differed from that of 1652 in that the same commissioners were to be responsible for approving fit ministers and ejecting unfit ones, but this involved no difference of principle for Milton.

[6] *An Answer to a Paper Entitled a True Narrative* (January 4, 1654), E725(20), p. 8; *cf. A True State of the Case of the Commonwealth* (February 8, 1654), E728(5), pp. 15–16.

had tried to erect in the later sixteen-forties. Nor was there any further possibility of fusing temporal and ecclesiastical authority in a dictatorial rule of the saints, as the Fifth Monarchist minority in the Nominated Parliament had aimed to do. Cromwell had learnt his lesson from their excesses, and was being denounced by them as "the man of sin, the old dragon, and many other scripture ill names." [7] He broke decisively with the militant Fifth Monarchy men, who would soon be charging him that he "tooke the Crowne off from the heade of Christ, and put it upon his owne." [8]

That left two broad courses of religious policy open when Cromwell became Protector under the Instrument of Government on December 16, 1653. He could conceivably do as Milton and the thoroughgoing sectaries wished [9] and renounce all positive authority by the state over matters of faith, leaving each church to go its own way and maintain its own pastors and preachers by voluntary means. He had, however, always regarded this as an abdication of a Christian commonwealth's essential responsibilities. The alternative lay along the lines that Owen and his friends had proposed to the Rump: to set up agencies that would ensure the provision of godly ministers throughout the parishes, maintained by some form of compulsory contribution, while at the same time imposing as few denominational fetters as possible upon this established clergy, and preserving the right of peaceable dissenting sects to congregate and worship in their own way. This was the policy implicit in the new written constitution, the Instrument of Government. The Christian religion, as contained in the Scriptures, was to "be held forth and recommended as the public profession of these nations," though "to the public profession held forth none shall be compelled by penalties or otherwise." Those who differed from it were to be protected in the exercise of their religion, provided that they professed faith in God by Jesus Christ and did not adhere to popery or prelacy, disturb the peace, or make their beliefs a pretext for practicing licentiousness. There was to be an established clergy, maintained by tithes only until some less objectionable provision could be devised—"as soon as may be," said the Instrument, though none was ever worked out.[10]

The Instrument did not set up the actual institutions for approving and regulating the parochial ministry. This was left to Cromwell and

[7] Thurloe, I, 621.
[8] *Clarke Papers*, II, 244.
[9] We need not distinguish here between the total segregation of authorities advocated by such as Roger Williams and the limited power that Milton would have allowed to the magistrate to punish idolatry and other teachings directly contrary to Scripture. *Cf.* below, pp. 50–51, 256–57.
[10] Gardiner, *Constitutional Documents,* p. 416.

the Council of State, who were given a temporary power to legislate by ordinance until the first Parliament should meet under the new constitution the following September. Two ordinances laid the foundations of Britain's ecclesiastical polity for the next six years. The first, dated March 20, 1654, established a central body of thirty-eight Commissioners for Approbation of Ministers, commonly known as the Triers. They included Presbyterian, Independent, and Baptist ministers, as well as some laymen, and they were centralized at Westminster. All candidates for benefices had to submit their credentials to them, in the form of testimonials from at least three persons of known godliness and integrity, one of them a minister. Five commissioners sufficed to approve a candidate, though it needed nine to reject one. Thus when Milton addressed his famous admonition to Cromwell in *A Second Defence* at the end of May, urging him to renounce all power over the church, he was already too late.[11] The complementary ordinance, providing for the ejection of scandalous or insufficient ministers, was issued on August 28. It entrusted this task to separate bodies of lay commissioners in each county, generally called the Ejectors, who were to act in conjunction with clerical assistants named in the ordinance.[12] No specific confession of faith was imposed on the established clergy, and no ecclesiastical discipline was enforced by the state. The whole spirit and purpose of the settlement was to sink denominational differences in a common effort to evangelize the land. Richard Baxter, a severe critic of the Protectorate in most respects, acknowledged "that though they were many of them [the Triers] somewhat partial . . . yet so great was the benefit above the hurt, which they brought to the Church, that many thousands of Souls blest God for the faithful Ministers whom they let in, and grieved when the Prelatists afterward cast them out again." [13]

Anxious though Cromwell was not to impose on tender consciences, he had to deal on the one hand with a political nation that was on the whole much less tolerant than himself, and on the other with the pathological excesses that inevitably erupted in a period of religious ferment. On the same day that he issued the ordinance establishing the Triers he also published a declaration calling the nation to a day of solemn fasting and humiliation. Foremost among the sins for which he urged the people to abase themselves before God were two grave abuses of the religious liberty that they now enjoyed. One was the mutual intolerance that the various churches displayed towards each other; the other lay

[11] See *Complete Prose*, IV, 263–64.
[12] On both ordinances, see Jordan, *Religious Toleration*, III, 156–60.
[13] *Reliquiae Baxterianae*, part I, p. 72.

in the tendency of men on the brink of religious mania to kick over the traces of morality and authority. Many, said Cromwell's declaration, had "apostatized, running after *Fancies* and *Notions,* listning to filthy *Dreams, worshipping of Angels,* and been carried by their Impulsions, and instead of contending for the Faith . . . contended against *Magistracy,* against *Ministery,* against *Scriptures,* and against *Ordinances."* Such abominations were "justified under the notion of Liberty, it being too commonly said that the Magistrate hath nothing to do either in repressing, or remedying these things." Surely one cause of the Lord's displeasure lay in "the impunity of these things, through the neglect of the Magistracy, throughout the Nation." [14]

It is unlikely that Cromwell wished to punish anything that Milton would not have condemned, but Milton probably saw in this declaration a dangerous assertion of the magistrate's role, just as he undoubtedly disliked the Protectorate's assumption of responsibility for providing the people with able preachers. But this was a duty on which Cromwell remained adamant. In retrospect his gravest charge against the Nominated Parliament was that by its efforts "the axe was laid to the root of the Ministry," [15] and he repeatedly vindicated the work of the Triers. Three months after *A Second Defence* appeared he took satisfaction that the government "hath endeavoured to put a stop to that heady way . . . of every man making himself a Minister and a preacher; it hath endeavoured to settle a way for the approbation of men of piety and ability for the discharge of that work." [16] Two years later he reaffirmed his belief "in giving countenance to Ministers, countenancing a just maintenance to them, whether by tithes or otherwise, for my part I should think I were very treacherous if I should take away tithes, till I see the Legislative power to settle maintenance to them another way." [17]

But if Cromwell's concept of the magistrate's duty extended too far for Milton, it did not stretch far enough for his two Parliaments. Each of them witnessed a *cause célèbre* in the matter of heresy and its penalties. The case of John Biddle the Socinian in 1654–55, and still more that of James Nayler the Quaker, who in 1656 rode into Bristol on an ass in the manner of Christ's entry into Jerusalem, unleashed the pent-up fear and hatred that the average M.P. felt towards the vagaries of sectarian fanatics. The first Protectorate Parliament, when it set

[14] Abbott, III, 226–28; *cf.* p. 436.
[15] *Ibid.,* p. 437; *cf.* IV, 417–18, 489.
[16] *Ibid.,* III, 440.
[17] *Ibid.,* IV, 272.

about rewriting the constitution, claimed the power to pass acts in restraint of atheism, blasphemy, and damnable heresies (which it proposed to enumerate), without allowing the Protector more than a suspensive veto of twenty days.[18] It also sought, with the assistance of a group of divines headed by John Owen, to define more closely the fundamentals of the Christian faith to which the established clergy should assent, as a condition of holding their livings.[19] Its evident desire to narrow the limits of toleration was one of the reasons that prompted Cromwell to dissolve it before any of its measures reached fruition. The second Protectorate Parliament, purged as it was of potential dissidents at the outset, proceeded more gently, but it nevertheless took the opportunity of the Humble Petition and Advice to refine upon the Instrument of Government's religious clauses in a subtly restrictive way. This time Cromwell was prepared to pay the price for a constitution promulgated by Parliament, instead of by a junto of army officers as the Instrument had been. Under the Humble Petition a confession of faith, to be agreed by Protector and Parliament, was to be held forth and recommended to the people, and subscribed by all ministers who received the public maintenance. This was never drawn up in Cromwell's lifetime, but meanwhile toleration outside the established church was, among other restrictions, confined to those who professed a fairly strict trinitarian doctrine and acknowledged both Old and New Testaments to be the revealed will and word of God.[20]

Cromwell, however, took care that these provisions did not in practice lessen the liberty of the sects, most of which lived peaceably and gratefully under his protection. Fifth Monarchists who attempted active subversion were another matter, and so were Quakers who interrupted church services, but his government quite frequently checked the harsh prejudice of country magistrates and certain major-generals against the Friends.[21] Nevertheless, the facts remained that government was now armed with powers that with less good will than Cromwell's could be used to the injury of religious freedom, and that the bulk of the propertied classes would have been glad to see them implemented.

[18] Gardiner, *Constitutional Documents,* p. 443.
[19] Shaw, *English Church,* II, 86–92; Jordan, *Religious Toleration,* III, 162–70.
[20] Gardiner, *Constitutional Documents,* pp. 454–55; Shaw, *English Church,* II, 92–96; Firth, *Last Years of the Protectorate,* I, 145–47.
[21] Abbott, IV, 59, 299, 307, 661, n. 104; Jordan, *Religious Toleration,* III, 176–79.

2. THE DEBATE ON MAGISTRACY AND MINISTRY, 1654–1659

"I have had boxes and rebukes on one hand and on the other," said Cromwell in 1656, "some envying me for Presbytery, others as an in-letter to all the sects and heresies in the nation."[1] He knew how impossible it was for his ecclesiastical policy, indeed for any ecclesiastical policy, to please everybody. We need not dwell further on the extreme opposition of the Fifth Monarchy men, or recount the measures that he was forced to take against some of their leaders. Milton had no sympathy with their wild aspirations to a dictatorship of rough-hewn saints.[2] The sedition preached by such as Vavasor Powell, Christopher Feake, and John Rogers, and still more the crazy insurrection that Thomas Venner the cooper attempted in 1657, made it easy to treat them as a political problem rather than as one of religious principle.

Opposition from the right probably caused him more concern, because of the weight of public opinion behind it and because it was often voiced by men whom he respected. The Presbyterians were its main exponents, committed as they were to the *jus divinum* of their church order and discipline. Generally, however, they were less aggressive and dogmatic than they had been a few years before; adversity was teaching them a more irenical spirit. In London their ministers were still sufficiently numerous and organized to meet in a Provincial Assembly which published during the earliest weeks of the Protectorate a fat manifesto entitled *Jus Divinum Ministerii Evangelici, Or the Divine Right of the Gospel-Ministry.*[3] Here they took their usual stand against a general toleration, unordained preachers, indiscriminate admission to the Lord's Supper, and the heretical, anti-predestinarian opinion that Christ died equally for all men.[4] But they also declared that their differences with their brethren of the Congregational way "shall not hinder Us from any Christian Accord with them in Affection," and that they would welcome any sincere moves towards a *rapprochement* with them.[5] If only they could have displayed a similar latitude in 1644, when a modest accommodation had been all that the Independents had asked of the Westminster Assembly! The next five years saw a number

---

[1] Abbott, IV, 272.

[2] See *The Readie & Easie Way*, 1st ed., below, p. 380.

[3] E728(1), February 7, 1654; it runs to over 360 pages. For a similar vindication *cf.* Robert Walwyn, *A Plea for a Reproached Ministry* (June 11, 1654), E1548(1); and for the continuance of a more intolerant strain of Presbyterianism, John Collings, *Responsaria Bipartita* (April 14, 1655), E832(2).

[4] *Jus Divinum Ministerii Evangelici*, part I, p. 192.

[5] *Ibid.*, "To the Reader" (unpaged, sig. B2, v.).

of attempts by moderate Presbyterians to negotiate an accord with moderate Independents. None of them came to much, one of the main stumbling blocks being the Presbyterians' continuing belief that ecclesiastical censures should be backed by civil sanctions, but the change of attitude since the sixteen-forties was significant.[6]

These same London Presbyterians also sought communion with moderate Episcopalians who did not deny the validity of Presbyterian ordination; indeed they desired a union of all ordained ministers who shared a common Calvinist orthodoxy in doctrine, differ though they might over points of church government. They cited the story from Mary Tudor's reign of Ridley's reconciliation with Hooper in the Tower, and drew the moral *"Adversity united them whom Prosperity divided."* [7] They found some response. Thomas Fuller, former chaplain to the royalist general Sir Ralph Hopton and to Charles I's youngest daughter, and already famous as the author of *The Holy State and the Profane State,* wrote thus in 1654:

> I know the *most Learned and moderate English divines* (though *Episcopal* in their *callings* and *judgements*) have allowed the *Reformed Churches* under the *discipline* for sound and perfect in all essentials necessarie to salvation. If therefore denied my first desire to live under that *Church-Government* I best affected, I will contentedly conform to the *Presbyterian Government,* and endeavour to deport my self quietly and comfortably under the same.[8]

Fuller strongly shared the Presbyterians' detestation of unordained preachers.[9]

Even as Fuller wrote, Baxter was in correspondence with Archbishop Ussher about a possible agreement with moderate Anglicans on the basis of the proposals that Ussher had circulated in 1641 for a fusion of Presbyterian with episcopal church government.[10] In 1656 John Gauden, the principal compiler of *Eikon Basilike,* led a small group of fellow-Anglicans in an initiative to collaborate with moderate Presbyterians in pressing Parliament towards a religious settlement founded upon the same kind of compromise.[11] Although these movements towards inter-

---

[6] For these irenical initiatives under the Protectorate see George R. Abernathy, *The English Presbyterians and the Stuart Restoration* (Philadelphia: American Philosophical Society, 1965), pp. 8–17; and for Cromwell's warm encouragement, Abbott, IV, 271–73.

[7] *Jus Divinum Ministerii Evangelici,* "To the Reader," sigs. B2–3.

[8] Thomas Fuller, *A Tripple Reconciler* (October 23, 1654), E1441(2), pp. 35–36.

[9] *Ibid.,* pp. 57 ff.

[10] See *Complete Prose,* I, 103–04, 117–18.

[11] Abernathy, *English Presbyterians and the Stuart Restoration,* pp. 13–15.

denominational union, whether Presbyterian-low Anglican or Presbyterian-Independent, achieved no striking formal results, they were symptomatic of a widespread desire to break down hitherto rigid barriers.

A more impressive and practical example of co-operation lay in the Voluntary Associations of ministers that sprang up from 1653 onwards in at least fifteen counties.[12] Baxter's Worcestershire Association provided the model for many more, though some others developed independently. In these Associations the ministers of a county commonly met once a month, to determine difficult questions of church discipline, hold disputations, settle matters of common concern, and in some cases to ordain new ministers. The discipline exercised in each member church rested on the voluntary acceptance of the faithful; Cromwell's Protectorate provided no means of coercing the reprobate, unless they fell foul of the law. The Associations arose indeed to supply a need for which the state no longer provided since the abolition of diocesan institutions and the decay of most of the classical presbyteries, and for their part the Associations mostly pursued their activities in singular independence of the civil government. Baxter, for example, reluctantly accepted appointment as one of his county's clerical assistants to the Triers, but he did not act in this capacity more than he could help. The most remarkable feature of the Associations, however, was their sinking of denominational differences. The Worcestershire Association included a very few moderate Independents and moderate episcopalians, but "all the rest were meer Catholicks; Men of no Faction, nor siding with any Party, but owning that which was good in all." [13]

The Voluntary Associations and the more general tentatives towards interdenominational communion were two manifestations of an important development under the Protectorate: the moderate Puritan clergy were closing their ranks towards the center. Whether they were nominally Presbyterians or Independents or episcopal men, or whether they belonged to the large body of "meer Catholicks," they were exploring their mutual interest in maintaining a common, broadly Calvinist orthodoxy, a decent though voluntary ecclesiastical discipline, and a publicly maintained parochial ministry. The main ecclesiastical divide, and the one that most occupied Milton, now ran between these established clergy and those sects that opposed any public maintenance and disliked the state's whole assumption of responsibility for providing and regulating a godly ministry. It had the effect of driving the

[12] Shaw, *English Church*, II, 152–65, 440–56; Geoffrey F. Nuttall, *Richard Baxter* (London: Nelson, 1965), pp. 65–76.
[13] *Reliquiae Baxterianae*, part I, pp. 97, 148.

moderate Independents and the sects further apart, for now that the former found benefices open to them, many of them managed to reconcile their Congregational principles with the parochial system. At least 171 Independents held livings in the established church at the Restoration.[14]

On the side of the sects, there were naturally not a few who opposed Cromwell's commissions as an intolerable intrusion by the state upon matters of faith. Some of them anticipated Milton's arguments in *Of Civil Power*. The millenarian pastor of a gathered church in Lewes, for example, asked

> Can God endure to be prescribed by creatures? Shall Man coin Laws for Rules of acceptable walking with God in Spiritual, Civil, or Ecclesiastical things? It would be and is horrible impudence for any to do it. All the sin and misery in the world, brake in at this door . . . These [Triers] are no competent judges of the doctrine of God in Christ, but must be overthrown.[15]

Another pamphleteer satirized a session of the Triers in a dialogue, introducing them under such names as Dr. Absolute, Dr. Confidence, Mr. Efficax, Mr. Narrowgrace, Mr. Take-o'-Trust, Mr. Knowlittle, Mr. Impertinent, Mr. Dubius, and Dr. Damman.[16]

A particularly interesting opponent of the Triers was John Goodwin, one of London's most powerful preachers and prolific pamphleteers, and ever since 1642 a hammer of the Presbyterians. The similarities and differences between his position and Milton's are instructive. A maverick on the left wing of Independency, Goodwin had gradually travelled from Calvinistic orthodoxy to a conviction that Christ's saving grace was available to all, and from a belief that the civil magistrate should shield the church from the propagation of error and heresy to an advocacy of full toleration.[17] Unlike the wilder sectaries, he did not oppose the Protectorate as such. Twice in its early days he wrote in qualified support of it, and he condemned the Fifth Monarchists roundly. [18] He again professed his entire loyalty to it when on May 23, 1657, he published *Basanistai, or the Triers, [or Tormentors] Tried and*

[14] A. G. Matthews, *Calamy Revised* (Oxford, 1934), p. xlii. The figure is probably an underestimate, and does not include eight listed as "Anabaptists."
[15] Gualter Postlethwaite, *A Voice from Heaven* (April 15, 1655), E1498(3), preface, sig. A4; answered belatedly by Ezekiel Charke in *A Pretended Voice from Heaven, Proved to bee the Voice of Man* (November 17, 1658), E959(5).
[16] *The Examination of Tilenus before the Triers* (December 10, 1657), E1625.
[17] Jordan, *Religious Toleration*, III, 376–412.
[18] John Goodwin, *Synkretismos, or Dissatisfaction Satisfied* (December 22, 1653), E727(7); *Peace Protected, and Discontent Dis-armed* (April 11, 1654), E732(27).

Cast.[19] He warned it, however, against the temptation to encroach on Christ's ordinances and add to the word of God. Christ had manifested his anger against the old monarchy, "and more especially against our late Parliaments, as oft as they presumed to meddle with his golden Scepter, whereby he nurtures and rules the consciences of men."[20] In his opinion the Triers and the Ejectors *were* so meddling. His main gravamen was that they rejected and evicted ministers who did not believe and profess just as they themselves did.[21] With gross exaggeration he inferred that the Triers were narrowing the ministry to a body of timorous conformists, and accused some of them of interpreting their commission in a manner very close to the Spanish Inquisition.[22] He used another argument that Milton would rather conspicuously avoid: that rulers have no right to any authority that is not entrusted to them by the people, and that the Protector had no such mandate for the Triers and Ejectors.[23] Unlike Milton, he was not against an established ministry as such; indeed he held a parish living himself. He even acknowledged, with qualifications, the rights of patrons to present incumbents to livings, though like Milton he really preferred that congregations should be triers of their own ministers, and maintain them too.[24] But he allowed much more to the civil power than Milton would: "If a Ministers tongue prove at any time malignant in the pulpit, there is another Minister of God at hand to restrain him (I mean the Magistrate) who beareth not the sword in vain."[25]

Goodwin's curious position, increasingly at odds both with the Protectorate[26] and with the sects, led him into some inconsistencies, and Marchamont Needham made the most of these in a lengthy counterblast. Goodwin's real complaint, Needham declared, was that the Triers were chary of men who shared his own unorthodox Arminian tenets, and he made the telling point that if parochial congregations were left entirely to choose their own ministers, "the man so chosen in most Parishes would be a man in a Surplice, with the Common-Prayer-Book, devoutly observing all the Ceremonies and Festivals."[27] That was a real possibility, and one wonders whether Milton ever considered it.

[19] E910(12).
[20] *Basanistai,* "To the Reader" (unpaged).
[21] *Ibid.,* pp. 1–5.
[22] *Ibid.,* pp. 11–16, 20.
[23] *Ibid.,* pp. 18–19.
[24] *Ibid.,* pp. 6–7, 23–30.
[25] *Ibid.,* p. 32.
[26] See Abbott, IV, 612.
[27] Marchamont Needham, *The Great Accuser Cast Down, or, a Publick Trial of Mr John Goodwin* (July 30, 1657), E920(1), pp. 43, 56, 65–69, 115.

At the opposite pole of Independency from Goodwin stood Lewis du Moulin, brother of the royalist Peter du Moulin whose *Regii Sanguinis Clamor*, which Milton had so unfortunately attributed to Alexander More, provoked *A Second Defence*. Lewis' career was very different. He was Camden professor of ancient history at Oxford, a wholehearted supporter of the Protectorate, and a voluminous writer on the relations between spiritual and temporal authority. *Of the Right of Churches, and of the Magistrates Power Over Them*, which he published in 1658, was his third massive treatise on these themes.[28] He was an Independent in his belief that particular congregations of Christians constituted the only true visible churches sanctioned by the Scriptures, that pastors and synods should have no coercive jurisdiction in matters of conscience, and that the magistrate therefore should not enforce their determinations. But he implicitly supported Cromwell's commissions when he contended that the magistrate should delegate to a few good men "a particular oversight of the affairs of the church." He was opposed to any formal ecclesiastical jurisdiction distinct from the magistrate's, and indeed to any differentiation of powers and laws between spiritual and temporal. Provided that reasonable rights were assured to nonconformist congregations, he would allow the magistrate or his delegates to establish a public ministry and schools of learning, call synods, restrain blasphemy and heresy, and even appoint "Overseers and Bishops" over ministers and churches. It was an unusually Erastian position for an Independent, but one of Moulin's keenest desires was to reconcile moderate Episcopalians, Erastians, Presbyterians and Independents.[29] As for the power of excommunication, which to Milton was the churches' ultimate sanction and the one to be most jealously preserved from outside influence, Moulin devoted seven chapters to condemning it totally as the very mystery of iniquity.[30]

If John Goodwin represented the left wing of Independency and Moulin the right, the broad center was typified by John Owen, Thomas Goodwin, Philip Nye, and a few other divines who stood very close to Cromwell. We shall shortly see how they stated their position in the Savoy Declaration of 1658, but in the autumn of 1659 Owen further defined his standpoint in *Two Questions Concerning the Power of the*

[28] E2115 (August, 1658). His two previous works were *The Power of the Christian Magistrate in Sacred Things* (March 28, 1650), E1366(4), and *Parænesis ad Ædificatores Imperii in Imperio* (August 2, 1656), E496, a work of 709 pages in Latin. In 1650 he had translated the first chapter of Milton's *Eikonoklastes* into Latin: Parker, *Milton*, p. 434.

[29] The main burden of these arguments is in the epistle dedicatory, the preface, and chs. IV, XV, and XIX.

[30] *Of the Right of Churches*, chs. XXVI–XXXII.

Supreme Magistrate About Religion and the Worship of God.[31] The first question was whether the supreme magistrate in a Christian commonwealth should use his power to promote actively the profession of the true faith and the right worship of God, and to repress such principles and practices as are contrary to them. Owen's answer, in contrast to Milton's in *Of Civil Power,* was a clear affirmative. To renounce this responsibility, he wrote, would entail "The destruction of the Plea of Christs interest in the government of the Nations; especially as stated by them, who in words contend to place him in the head of their Laws and Fundamentall constitutions; where nothing in a Government may be done *for* him, nothing against them who openly oppose him, men can scarce be thought to act under him, and in subordination to him." [32] This was very much in the Cromwellian tradition, which Milton had long rejected; but Milton too had once hoped that it would be through the civil magistrate that God would bring about "the full and perfet reformation of his Church." [33]

Finally it is worth turning from these self-confessed Presbyterians, Independents, and sectaries back to Richard Baxter, that spokesman for "meer Catholicks" and prime representative of an older, more central, less dogmatic Puritan tradition. We have seen the practical expression of his convictions in the Voluntary Associations, but in 1659 he defined his views on magistracy and ministry in *A Holy Commonwealth,*[34] particularly in the chapter entitled "Of the Soveraigns Power over the Pastors of the Church, and of the Differences of their Offices." *"The more Theocratical, or truly Divine any Government is, the better it is,"* he roundly declared, and hence it follows *"that in a true Theocracy, or Divine Commonwealth, the Matter of the Church and Commonwealth should be altogether or almost the same though the form of them and administrations are different."* [35] Baxter carefully distinguishes their spheres of authority and modes of operation, the magistrate ruling by command and coercion, the minister by appeal to the conscience and ultimately by excommunication; but both offices derive *"Immediately and co-ordinately from Christ."* [36] Magistrates, even

---

[31] BOD, Wood 370(9); not in Thomason. It can be dated *ca.* October by a broadsheet reply, *A Serious Letter to Dr. John Owen,* signed "Tho. Truthsbye": BML, 816m24(7). This was evidently written soon after the interruption of the Rump on October 13, 1659, and immediately after the author had acquired Owen's tract.

[32] *Two Questions,* p. 6.

[33] *An Apology against a Pamphlet: Complete Prose,* I, 928.

[34] E1729; registered at Stationers' Hall on June 22, 1659. The arguments here summarized are from ch. x, pp. 285–312, unless otherwise stated.

[35] *A Holy Commonwealth,* pp. 209, 216.

[36] *Ibid.,* p. 285.

princes, are subject to the minister's censure in matters spiritual, but
they are to govern the clergy not as citizens only but as ministers too.
They may punish them for the maladministration of their cures and in
the last resort suspend them. Magistrates are indeed *custodes utriusque
tabulae*, as competent to punish the sins of the first table, including
heresy, as of the second. While they should not normally interfere with
the people's right to call their ministers, or with the ministry's power of
ordination, they should prevent intolerably unfit appointments or un-
worthy ordinations, and guide those concerned to a better choice.
They may assume authority over the clergy's financial maintenance
and over church buildings. Baxter would even have liked a representa-
tive of the magistracy—normally the mayor or a justice of the peace—
to be attached to each congregation in the role of Censor, sitting with
the church officers once a month, hearing the causes brought before
them, compelling offenders to appear, and assenting to sentences of ex-
communication, since these should normally involve civil disfranchise-
ment. Reciprocally, ministers should sit with the judges in their as-
sizes and with the justices of the peace in their sessions, and the
clergy should be represented in both Houses of Parliament.[37] Such an
interpretation of civil and clerical functions was poles apart from Mil-
ton's ideal, though it was close to that of Calvin and other founders of
the reformed churches. At the Restoration, Baxter would be the natu-
ral spokesman for the moderate Puritan clergy; he fairly represented
the mainstream of the English Puritan tradition from which Milton
had so widely diverged.

3. THE SAVOY DECLARATION

October, 1658

When Cromwell's life was drawing to a close, the national confession
of faith, which according to the Humble Petition and Advice was "to
be agreed by your Highness and the Parliament" and subscribed by all
publicly maintained ministers, had still not been composed. The old
Protector lived just long enough, however, to sanction an initiative by
the leading Independent clergy to accomplish what the temporal gov-
ernment had failed to perform.[1]

What they proposed was a conference at the Savoy, at which repre-

---

[37] *Ibid.*, pp. 268–70.
[1] The main authority for what follows is A. G. Matthews (ed.), *The Savoy
Declaration of Faith and Order, 1658* (London: Independent Press, 1959),
which has an excellent introduction.

sentatives from as many Congregational churches as possible should seek agreement on a confession of faith and a statement of church order. Behind this move lay a steady increase during the sixteen-fifties in active communion between Independent congregations. The ritual of "giving the right hand of fellowship" to sister churches had become more formalized, and generally involved mutual assurances of doctrinal orthodoxy.[2] It was thus a natural need for a general assembly and a common declaration, and probably also the example of the New England churches and the articles agreed at Cambridge, Massachusetts, ten years earlier, that inspired the Savoy conference, rather than a desire to push the civil government towards imposing Independent beliefs and practices upon all the established clergy. Baxter was to attack the conference and its promoters, especially Owen and Nye, for frustrating the reunion of all moderate churchmen that he desired by defining too nicely their own concept of church order,[3] but the spirit of the conference was irenical, and sought to minimize the differences between moderate Independents and Presbyterians. The tendency to reconciliation between the two persuasions that we have already noted was growing stronger; it was soon to be encouraged by the *Irenicum* [4] published by one Mr. Hudson in April, 1659, and to bear fruit in a remarkable agreement that the ministers of Lancashire and Cheshire negotiated in the following July.[5] Except in those few areas where classical presbyteries were still active, there was after all very little difference in practice between one parish with a Presbyterian minister who restricted the sacraments to those who submitted to the consistorial discipline and another whose Congregational incumbent tried to preserve the principle that a true church was a congregation of covenanted saints.[6]

The chief promoters of the conference were Thomas Goodwin, John Owen, and Philip Nye. Owen had been involved in every attempt to define the fundamentals of their faith since 1652, but Thomas Goodwin had become something like an unofficial primate of the Congregational churches. It was he who ministered to Oliver on his deathbed; heard the dying man's nomination of his successor; prayed at the solemn session of privy councillors, city fathers, and army officers before which Richard took his oath as Lord Protector; and later presented

[2] On this see, besides Matthews, *Savoy Declaration*, pp. 19 ff., Geoffrey F. Nuttall, *Visible Saints: The Congregational Way, 1640–1660* (Oxford: Blackwell, 1957), ch. II.

[3] *Reliquiae Baxterianae*, part I, p. 104.

[4] E978(1), April 24, 1659.

[5] Shaw, *English Church*, II, 166–71.

[6] Matthews, *Savoy Declaration*, pp. 31–32.

the loyal address to the new head of state from over a hundred Independent congregations. He was now to head the conference's drafting committee and present the results of its labors to the Protector.

The letters of invitation went out in the second half of August. Henry Scobell, Clerk of the Council, played a large part in the preparations, though since he was also an elder of the congregation that met in Westminster Abbey he was not necessarily acting in his official capacity. When the conference opened on September 29, about two hundred elders and messengers, mostly laymen, came together from slightly more than a hundred churches. This was not a very large proportion of all the gathered churches in Britain, and the fact that many were not represented may denote a cleavage between those that identified themselves with the Cromwellian church settlement and those that adhered to voluntaryist principles.[7] Certainly the leading spirits of the conference were closely associated with the ecclesiastical establishment. The drafting committee consisted of Goodwin, Nye, Bridge, Greenhill, Caryl, and Owen, of whom all but Owen had sat in the Westminster Assembly, and all but Bridge served as Triers. Thomas Goodwin stressed their moderate and conservative intentions when he presented the Savoy Declaration to Richard on October 14 and explained its purpose: to clear themselves of the charge "that Independentism (as they call it) is the sink of all Heresies and Schisms," to demonstrate their "harmony with the most Orthodox at home and abroad," and to show how moderately they differed from their Presbyterian brethren.[8] This was entirely in the spirit of the Dissenting Brethren's *Apologeticall Narration* of 1644,[9] and confirmed the partial retreat by "orthodox" Independents towards the center, away from the sectarian alliance, that we have already noted.

The conference completed its work in the amazingly short time of eleven working days. This was because the drafting committee based its declaration of faith on the *Articles of Religion* formulated by the Westminster Assembly, though it made a number of alterations and omissions which were of some significance for the finer points of doctrine. In the articles on church order there were naturally wider differences with the Presbyterians, particularly over the Congregational conception of a church as a voluntary society of saints, the election and ordination of church officers, the powers of censure and excommunication, and the denial here that Christ had appointed any synods "in a way of subordination to one another." But the tone was conciliatory,

[7] *Ibid.*, p. 26.
[8] *Ibid.*, pp. 12–14, quoting *Mercurius Politicus*, October 7–14, 1658.
[9] See *Complete Prose*, II, 72–73.

both in the declaration itself and in the lengthy preface which introduced it to the public, and which has always been attributed to Owen. "The *Spirit of Christ*," wrote Owen, "is in himself too *free*, great and generous a Spirit, to suffer himself to be used by any humane arm, to whip men into belief." He thanked God for a government that *"vouchsafed a forbearance and mutual indulgence unto Saints of all perswasions, that keep unto, and hold fast the necessary foundations of faith and holiness."* [10] Rather disingenuously he attributed this indulgence to the Long Parliament's Accommodation Order of 1644, ignoring the Parliament's subsequent intolerant measures and all that Cromwell had since done to broaden religious liberty. Matthews has seen confirmation here that Owen, who had strongly opposed the offer of the crown in 1657, had already broken with the Protectorate and joined company with the commonwealthsmen.[11] But although we shall find Owen associating with the Wallingford House officers in their defiance of Richard in the spring of 1659, his silence regarding Cromwell's contribution to the liberty of the saints is more probably explained by a desire to appeal to the Presbyterians, who would allow no virtue to the works of the Protectorate but might feel more obliged by a vote passed by the Long Parliament before Pride's Purge. There was no hint of disaffection in his final exhortation to promote the honor and prosperity of the present government, and of "a *Prince* that owns this Establishment, and cordially resolves to secure our churches in the enjoyment of these Liberties." [12]

What did the Savoy Declaration mean to Milton? In the first place it defined the fundamentals of the faith far more restrictively than he believed necessary, and in a sense often contrary to his own *Christian Doctrine*. The chapters for instance concerning the Trinity (ii), predestination (iii), and the state of the soul after death (xxxi) must have been quite unacceptable to him. Further, it countenanced Independent ministers in accepting the public maintenance; chapter xiv defined the obligations of those who held parish livings. To Milton such men were hirelings. But the article that must have interested him most was that which defined the magistrate's power in matters ecclesiastical:

> Although the Magistrate is bound to incourage, promote, and protect the professors and profession of the Gospel, and to manage and order civil

[10] Matthews, *Savoy Declaration*, pp. 53, 56. Since this introduction was written, the theological significance of the Savoy Declaration has been penetratingly analysed by Peter Toon, "The Westminster and Savoy Confessions: a brief comparison," *Journal of the Evangelical Theological Society*, Vol. XV, Pt. III (1972), pp. 153–60.

[11] *Ibid.*, pp. 41–45.

[12] *Ibid.*, pp. 72–73.

administrations in a due subserviency to the interest of Christ in the
world, and to that end to take care that men of corrupt mindes and con-
versations do not licentiously publish and divulge Blasphemy and Errors
in their own nature, subverting the faith, and inevitably destroying the
souls of them that receive them: Yet in such differences about the
Doctrines of the Gospel, or ways of the worship of God, as may befall
men exercising a good conscience, manifesting it in their conversation,
and holding the foundation, not disturbing others in their ways or wor-
ship that differ from them; there is no warrant for the Magistrate under
the Gospel to abridge them of their liberty.[13]

This was the point at which the Savoy Declaration diverged furthest
from the Westminster Confession, and it was far more liberal. Indeed
it was so close to the position that Milton was to take in *Of Civil Power*
that in itself it probably did not offend him.

The main question, however, that the Savoy Declaration probably
raised in his mind was whether it would receive any such sanction from
the state as the Westminster Confession had had. When Parliament
was summoned for January, 1659, he must have anticipated that it
would address itself anew to the long-postponed national confession of
faith, and considered the possibility that the Savoy Declaration, or at
least those parts of it that dealt with faith rather than order, would be
urged as the yardstick of orthodoxy for all the publicly maintained
clergy. Owen was later to state quite firmly that the magistrate ought
not to compel anyone to conform to the public confession of faith or
way of worship,[14] but public confessions of faith were obnoxious to
Milton in principle.

[13] *Ibid.*, pp. 108–09.
[14] Owen, *Two Questions*, p. 7.

CHAPTER III

MILTON'S *TREATISE OF CIVIL POWER*

1. THE ARGUMENT

A T THIS STAGE we can bring together the several circumstances that most probably moved Milton to compose *A Treatise of Civil Power in Ecclesiastical Causes.* When he began it we do not know, but he registered it for publication with the Stationers' Company on February 16, 1659, so it probably occupied him during the early weeks of that year.[1] In the first place Richard's accession had brought with it the possibility of change. Since Richard was credited with a preference for moderate Presbyterians in church as well as state, and relied for advice on men who were inimical to radical or unorthodox religious opinions, the change was unlikely to be for the better from Milton's point of view.[2] Secondly, the Savoy Declaration had defined the position of the most influential Independents in a manner that dissociated them further from the sects and from the voluntarist principles that Milton held; that in itself may have spurred him to reaffirm those principles. Thirdly and most immediately, a new Parliament had been summoned—a Parliament that might, like the last two, seek or set stricter bounds to what both the established clergy and the dissenting sects might profess, but on the other hand might just conceivably be open to conviction by the pen that had laid Salmasius low.

It was the meeting of the Parliament that he himself acknowledged as the occasion for his tract. *"I Have prepar'd, supream Councel, against the much expected time of your sitting, this treatise"*; so run the first words of his introductory address, after the significant dedication "To the Parlament of the Commonwealth of England with the dominions

---

[1] *A Treatise of Civil Power* is not in Thomason, but since it was advertised in *Mercurius Politicus*, February 10–17, it was probably published on or very near the day that it was registered.

[2] *Register of the Consultations of the Ministers of Edinburgh*, ed. W. Stephen (2 vols., Edinburgh, 1921–30), II, 153; *Reliquiae Baxterianae*, part I, p. 101; Guizot, I, 252–53; Prynne, *The Re-publicans and Others Spurious Good Old Cause . . . Anatomized*, p. 3. *Cf.* Monck's advice to Richard to cultivate such moderate divines as Reynolds, Calamy, Cooper, and Manton, in Thurloe, VII, 387–88.

therof." [3] It would be rash to read a denial of the Protector's authority
into the words *"supream Councel,"* or into the form of dedication,
which is identical with that of the subversive petition of the London
citizens presented on February 15.[4] Nevertheless, even allowing for a
rhetorician's natural propensity to magnify the authority of those whom
he addresses, Milton's emphasis implies that he is looking to Parlia-
ment to remedy the errors that the Protectorate has committed. The
impression deepens when he appeals especially to those of its members
whom he himself has often heard debating religious policy *"at a coun-
cel next in autoritie to your own"*—namely the Council of State of the
Commonwealth in the years before Cromwell became Protector. There
he had listened to them *"so well joining religion with civil prudence,
and yet so well distinguishing the different power of either,"* as to
convince any impartial hearer *"that then both commonwealth and re-
ligion will at length, if ever, flourish in Christendom, when either they
who govern discern between civil and religious, or they only who so
discern shall be admitted to govern."* [5] He must refer here to Vane and
others of like mind who had become keen opponents of the Protec-
torate. We cannot know whether he was aware that the republicans had
been concerting their opposition tactics in meetings at Vane's house,
or knew yet of the general attack on Richard's regime in the name of
the good old cause that was just beginning, but the tone of his preface
prepares us for the fuller identification with the Protectorate's republi-
can enemies that he will manifest in *The Likeliest Means* and the last
political tracts. That ominous alternative, *"or they only who so discern
shall be admitted to govern,"* already hints at a readiness to envisage
sweeping changes in government, and even at the drastic solutions that
he would propound in *A Letter to a Friend* eight months later.

His confidence in the republicans would prove to be misplaced. The
campaign to segregate spiritual from temporal authority had flagged
since the fall of the Nominated Parliament, as can be seen from the
steadily diminishing number of pamphlets on the subject (Quaker ones
apart) between 1654 and 1658. The attack on tithes, hireling priests,
and the magistrate's imposition on consciences had been chiefly carried
on by the Quakers in the last few years, and Milton's favorite causes
had grown the more unpopular with men of property through being
associated with these hated and reputedly low-born enthusiasts. Hasle-
rig and his party were ready enough in 1659 to excite sectarian religious
emotions for political ends, but they were not going to prejudice their

[3] Below, p. 239.
[4] See above, pp. 20–21.
[5] *Civil Power*, below, p. 240.

appeal to the country gentry in Richard's Parliament by espousing so widely disliked a policy as Milton advocated. But perhaps he was moved to write by the very need to lift his case above its common association with unschooled extremists and to free it from the taint of anarchism. To state it with a scholar's precision, to enhance it with the eloquence that he uniquely could command, to dignify it further with the authority of his international reputation and his former official commission (as he reminded the Parliament) to defend the Commonwealth's civil liberty—this was a task worthy of his pen. He was probably conscious that he had little new to say. Readers of Sirluck's introduction to Volume II of this edition, or Jordan's *Development of Religious Toleration,* still more those who have browsed deeply in the Thomason Collection, will know how often his main points had been made before; an elaborate discussion of his "sources" would be otiose here. What he aimed at was not originality but the summation of a great argument in a rhetoric at once noble and simple.

After his brief preface, Milton launches his theme with a statement of classic conciseness that will form a symphonic link between this treatise and its future complement in *The Likeliest Means:*

> Two things there be which have bin ever found working much mischief to the church of God, and the advancement of truth; force on the one side restraining, and hire on the other side corrupting the teachers thereof.[6]

The first is his present concern; the second he will treat when God disposes and opportunity invites him. He will argue, he says, solely from Scripture, "and therin from true fundamental principles of the gospel"—no false parallels from the priesthood under the Law, no bandying of dubious patristic or conciliar authorities. His first step is to define broadly those "matters of religion" that he would remove from the magistrate's power. They consist of "such things as belong chiefly to the knowledge and service of God," and either require the light of revelation, being beyond that of nature, or are enjoined or forbidden by divine precept where reason alone gives no rule. No outward force must bear upon the sacred exercise of conscience through which we come to "that full perswasion whereby we are assur'd that our beleef and practise, as far as we are able to apprehend and probably make appeer, is according to the will of God & his Holy Spirit within us." [7] This central thesis he proceeds to support by four cumulative arguments.

The first is that Protestants acknowledge no authority but holy

---

[6] *Ibid.,* p. 241.
[7] *Ibid.,* p. 242.

Scripture as a common ground for their faith. The Scriptures, however, can be understood and interpreted only through the inward illumination that each individual receives from the Holy Spirit, "which no man can know at all times to be in himself, much less to be at any time for certain in any other." [8] Since the light that each receives is to his own conscience alone, no man or body of men can determine questions of faith for the consciences of others. Protestants brand the Pope as antichrist precisely because he assumes such an infallible power, and magistrates who apply compulsion in matters of faith arrogate to themselves a "civil papacie" no less obnoxious.[9] Some will object that this overthrows all church discipline, but Milton retorts that true discipline is to be exercised only over those who submit to it by a voluntary covenant. It extends at the furthest to exclusion from their church, and never to corporal or pecuniary penalties.

Answering the still commoner objection that blasphemy and heresy will flourish unchecked, Milton expounds the sense of these Greek words as they were used in apostolic times. Blasphemy then signified any slander or evil speaking, whether against God or man. Blasphemy against God can claim no sanction in conscience, and Milton praises the way in which "that prudent and well deliberated act *August 9*. 1650" had defined it "as far as it is a crime belonging to civil judicature." [10] In allowing the state this much power to punish opinion—and the punishment was banishment, followed by death if the offender returned—Milton parts company with the total tolerationists such as Roger Williams and John Goodwin. As for heresy, it had originally been "no word of evil note," [11] but had meant only the opting for any opinion, good or bad, rather than another. No man should be censured as a heretic who interprets the Scriptures according to the best light of his conscience, even if he goes against doctrines that the whole church receives; for,

> if by the Protestant doctrine we beleeve the scripture not for the churches saying, but for its own as the word of God, then ought we to beleeve what in our conscience we apprehend the scripture to say, though the visible church with all her doctors gainsay; and being taught to beleeve them only for the scripture, they who so do are not heretics, but the best protestants: . . . concluding, that no man in religion is properly a heretic at this day, but he who maintains traditions or opinions not probable by scripture; who, for aught I know, is the papist only; he the only heretic, who counts all heretics but himself.[12]

[8] *Ibid.*, p. 242.
[9] *Ibid.*, p. 244.
[10] *Ibid.*, p. 246.
[11] *Ibid.*, p. 247.
[12] *Ibid.*, pp. 248–49.

Milton next proceeds to a close exegesis of the classic Scriptural texts
adduced by the opponents of toleration, and concludes that Protestants
who force consciences do worse than papists, since by so doing they
contravene their own professed principles.

Popery Milton brackets with idolatry, and he would have the mag-
istrate tolerate neither. His case for excluding Roman Catholicism is
twofold. In the first place it is "a catholic heresie against the scrip-
ture," which through its demand for implicit faith enthrals the con-
science to man instead of God. But there are reasons of state even
more cogent for repressing it, because of Rome's endeavour "to keep
up her old universal dominion under a new name and meer shaddow of a
catholic religion." [13] As for idolatry, it is so evidently contrary to every
precept of both Old and New Testaments that the civil power is right
to ban "at least the publick and scandalous use therof." [14] In granting
that the magistrate should suppress blasphemy against God, popery,
and idolatry, Milton constantly reminds us that the touchstone of the
permissible is Holy Scripture. Anything that manifestly conflicts with
the Scriptures' teaching or denies the sufficiency of their authority
in matters of faith lies outside the proper bounds of toleration, for
what he is defending is not liberty merely but Christian liberty.[15]

He next advances to his second main argument, which is that even
if the magistrate were able to judge authoritatively in matters of re-
ligion he would still have no right to impose his judgment upon others.
"Christ hath a government of his own, sufficient of it self to all his
ends and purposes in governing his church; but much different from
that of the civil magistrate." [16] Concerned as it is wholly with the in-
ward man, it eschews outward force, the magistrate's natural means
of constraining the outward man, for two compelling reasons. Firstly,
religion consists wholly in faith and charity, or belief and practice.
Faith flows from the understanding charity or practice from the will—
both originally free, but free now "only as they are regenerat and
wrought on by divine grace," [17] and hence not susceptible to coercion.
Force therefore can only frustrate and nullify the fruits of religion;
it can only compel hypocrisy. Secondly, Christ's purpose is to demon-
strate the capacity of His spiritual kingdom to subdue all the powers
of this world by its inward authority alone, so that to attempt to prop
it by enforced conformity is to degrade it to the level of a mere
worldly kingdom. Yet Milton again falls a little short of the position

13 *Ibid.*, p. 254.
14 *Ibid.*, p. 255.
15 See Barker, *Milton and the Puritan Dilemma*, pp. 244–45, 257.
16 *Civil Power*, below, p. 255.
17 *Ibid.*

of the thoroughgoing segregationists when he allows to the civil magis-
trate "the settling of things just, things honest, the defence of things
religious settled by the churches within themselves; and the repressing
of thir contraries determinable by the common light of nature; which
is not to constrain or to repress religion, probable by scripture, but the
violaters and persecuters therof." [18] This left some latitude; magis-
trates might well disagree over what the "contraries" of true religion
were, who were its "violaters," and what was "probable by scripture."

This lengthy and eloquent exposition is followed by refutations of
his opponents' favorite Old Testament authorities for the magistrate's
power in matters ecclesiastical. These in turn lead Milton into elaborat-
ing the distinctions between the status of religion under the Law and
under the Gospel—ground already well trodden by himself and by
countless other controversialists.[19] To those who cite from the New
Testament the rebuke to the church of Thyatira for suffering the false
prophetess Jezebel to seduce it, he replies in a strain that recalls the
Areopagitica, and bears that high comparison:

> I answer, that seducement is to be hinderd by fit and proper means
> ordaind in church-discipline; by instant and powerfull demonstration
> to the contrarie; by opposing truth to error, no equal match; truth the
> strong to error the weak though slie and shifting. Force is no honest con-
> futation; but uneffectual, and for the most part unsuccessfull, oft times
> fatal to them who use it: sound doctrine diligently and duely taught, is
> of herself both sufficient, and of herself (if some secret judgment of God
> hinder not) alwaies prevalent against seducers.[20]

This takes Milton to his third argument, and to what for him is
central territory. The magistrate not only lacks the capacity and the
right to impose in matters of faith; he also does grievous wrong, "by
violating the fundamental privilege of the gospel, the new-birthright
of everie true beleever, Christian libertie." [21] This liberty frees us
not only from the bondage of Judaical ceremonies but from all set
forms, places, and times in the worship of God. Milton rightly stresses
how far Britain has diverged in this from the practice of other Protes-
tant churches, for the intense Sabbatarianism of English Puritans and
Scottish Presbyterians was unique in Europe.[22] Even the Rump's *Act*

[18] *Ibid.,* p. 258.

[19] On Milton's treatment of this theme in this and other works see Barker,
Milton and the Puritan Dilemma; references indexed under "Law and Gospel."

[20] *Civil Power,* below, pp. 261–62.

[21] *Ibid.,* p. 262.

[22] For a full discussion and an attempted explanation see Christopher Hill,
Society and Puritanism in pre-Revolutionary England (London: Secker & War-
burg, 1964), ch. V, esp. pp. 206–13, where he shows how other radical Puritans
besides Milton questioned the strict Sabbatarianism imposed by public authority.

for Relief of Religious and Peaceable People, which in 1650 had re-
pealed the Elizabethan recusancy laws and removed all penalties for
not attending parochial services, still required participation in some
form of worship every Sunday and on appointed days of public thanks-
giving or humiliation.[23] Milton does not dwell on Sabbath-keeping as
such; he argues rather against all human prescription in matters of
worship, but he must have had Sabbatarianism in mind as the chief of
those *"weak and beggarly rudiments"* from which the Gospel had freed
men but which the magistrate still enforced.

His fourth and final demonstration is that the magistrate, in apply-
ing compulsion to religion, is bound to frustrate the very ends that he
purports to promote. Is it for the glory of God? The state can only
diminish it by using means that Christ has renounced. Is it for the
spiritual good of those whom he compels? The aim is self-defeating,
for "whatever we do under the gospel, we ought to be therof perswaded
without scruple; and are justified by the faith we have, not by the
work we do." [24] By making conscientious men do what their own hon-
est convictions reject, the magistrate will only force them to sin. Or
is it, as is so often urged, to prevent the profane and licentious from
giving scandal to the godly, and from neglecting their religious duties
under the pretence of tender consciences? Milton shows how strong a
temptation to encroach on Christian liberty lies in this plea of scandal,
and he distinguishes between scandals taken and scandals given; "to
heal one conscience we must not wound another." [25] As for the outward
performance of religious duties by irreligious men, it is a dishonoring
rather than a worshipping of God. "We read not that Christ ever
exercis'd force but once; and that was to drive prophane ones out of
his temple, not to force them in." [26]

Milton frequently refers to "the church," but he is thinking through-
out of churches in the plural. This is particularly clear in his peroration,
where he states "that the settlement of religion belongs only to each
particular church by perswasive and spiritual means within it self, and
that the defence only of the church belongs to the magistrate." [27] Where
he uses the singular, as in the second half of this sentence, he refers
to the collective visible embodiment of the community of saints in a
given commonwealth, but the only source of ecclesiastical authority

[23] See above, pp. 27–28, and for the act itself Gardiner, *Constitutional Docu-
ments,* pp. 391–94. The requirement to attend Sunday worship was reinforced
in 1657: below, p. 263, n. 69.

[24] *Civil Power,* below, p. 266.

[25] *Ibid.,* p. 267.

[26] *Ibid.,* p. 268.

[27] *Ibid.,* p. 271.

that he recognizes is that of a particular congregation of believers united by a mutual covenant. He ends with an unqualified condemnation of the claim, sustained by Baxter and countless other exponents of the central Protestant and Puritan tradition, that the Christian magistrate is the custodian of both tables of God's law. The Commandments, according to Milton, give the magistrate no mandate but what he has had with regard to civil offences and the outward man "from the beginning, long before *Moses* or the two tables were in being." [28]

Most of his argument in the treatise as a whole is so persuasive, so finely stated, and so consonant with the typical attitudes of modern democratic states towards the religious communities within them, that one needs to exercise one's historical imagination in order to appreciate why it was so widely unacceptable to his contemporaries. To begin with, he gave little indication of how he would have wished actual magistrates, whether ordinary justices of the peace or august privy councillors and members of Parliament, to deal with the typical problems of authority with which religious extremists faced them. Did he, for instance, agree that James Naylor's Messiah-like entry into Bristol amounted to intolerable blasphemy? How did he stand towards the Quakers generally, with their tendency to elevate the inner light above Scripture itself, their frequent interruption of the worship of others, and their implied denial of social subordination when they refused to pay the normal outward respect to magistrates? How would he have treated Fifth Monarchy men whose reading of the Scriptures prompted them to denounce all "carnal" government, or Diggers who found religious sanctions for their denial of the rights of property? Such flashpoints in an age of explosive religious enthusiasm posed genuine dilemmas even for the most liberal of magistrates, and if any of them read *Of Civil Power* they may well have felt some impatience at the olympian heights from which it discoursed.

It may reasonably be answered that most magistrates were not liberal, and that the case for Christian liberty still needed to be stated at the highest level of principle. The commonest grounds for rejecting Milton's contentions were, we can be sure, a belief that heresy and blasphemy imperiled men's souls and a conviction that religious nonconformity generally bore a strong tincture of social subversion. But Milton must have roused the resentment of many men who believed in Christian liberty no less sincerely than he. His distrust of the civil magistrate was so absolute; he assumed so axiomatically that if the state were allowed any initiative in religion it would exercise it re-

[28] *Ibid.*

pressively. This would have been understandable if he had been writing ten years earlier, under the successive experiences of Laudian and Presbyterian intolerance, but it was less plausible after six years of the Protectorate. Ignoring all that Cromwell's regime had done to maintain a liberty of conscience far wider than public opinion in general was prepared to countenance, as well as to improve the quality of the ministry and the tone of religious life throughout the country, Milton refused to admit the Christian magistrate to any true partnership with the churches in promoting the common Puritan ideals of a godly community and a regenerate nation. If he shared at all the zeal of his contemporaries to evangelize "the dark corners of the land," his precepts left no place for such joint enterprises of magistrates and clergy as the Commissions for the Propagation of the Gospel in the North and in Wales.[29]

His experience was largely confined to London, where learned and zealous preachers abounded and every variety of religious worship was at hand. Although he would consider in *The Likeliest Means* how best to instruct the vast numbers of the illiterate and others whom the Gospel had scarcely reached, he was not really much aware of their needs. "All prophane and licentious men," he wrote in *Of Civil Power*, "can be considerd but either so without the church as never yet within it, or departed thence of thir own accord, or excommunicate." [30] Those never yet within the church he dismissed in half a sentence, without considering that their condition might arise from the failure of any church to make contact with them—either because no preaching minister lived within many miles or because traditional social conventions left them outside the pale of communal worship. We do not know how many out of the legions of the poor went to church in seventeenth-century England, but there are indications that many did not.[31] Even in a relatively wealthy and populous county like Worcestershire Baxter found that the main task was one of evangelization, but in remoter regions such as Northumberland [32] there were great tracts where institutional religion had hardly touched the common

[29] See Christopher Hill, "Puritans and the Dark Corners of the Land," *Transactions of the Royal Historical Society*, 5th series, XIII (1963), 77–102.
[30] Below, p. 269.
[31] See Wallace Notestein, *The English People on the Eve of Colonization* (New York: Harper, 1954), pp. 85, 162; Hill, *Society and Puritanism in pre-Revolutionary England*, pp. 472–74, and Hill's article cited in n. 29 above; Peter Laslett, *The World We Have Lost* (London: Methuen, 1965), p. 73.
[32] Roger Howell, Jr., *Newcastle-upon-Tyne and the Puritan Revolution* (Oxford: Clarendon Press, 1967), pp. 63–72.

people before the Puritan Revolution. In face of so much ignorance and superstition, was there not room for the public provision of zealous parish ministers as well as for the spontaneous missionary efforts of the voluntaryist congregations? Milton, in contending that the magistrate ought "in all respects to have more care of the conscientious then of the prophane," [33] may have struck men who knew rural England better as overpreoccupied with consciences as nice and well instructed as his own.

2. COMPARISONS: THOMAS COLLIER AND HENRY STUBBE

The *Treatise of Civil Power* made no perceptible impact on Milton's contemporaries. No other pamphleteer took notice of it in 1659, and the Parliament to which he addressed it soon showed signs of moving in the direction he least desired. Soon after that Parliament was dissolved, however, a Baptist minister named Thomas Collier published *The Decision & Clearing of the Great Point Now in Controversie,*[1] treating exactly the same theme as Milton's and reaching the same conclusions. Collier was a prolific pamphleteer who had preached to the Council of officers at Putney in September, 1647, defended the army after Pride's Purge, vindicated the right of laymen to preach, and answered the orthodox Puritans' objections to the admission of the Jews into England. His presentation of the case against the magistrate's authority over religion is leaden by comparison with Milton's, but it is in places so similar [2] as to raise a momentary suspicion of plagiarism —until one recalls what a large common stock of well-rehearsed argument both men had to draw upon by 1659. Very possibly, Collier did not know of the existence of Milton's treatise; he serves to typify the sectarian tradition in which Milton wrote.

Shortly afterwards, Henry Stubbe dealt with the same questions far more originally in *An Essay in Defence of the Good Old Cause.*[3] Stubbe not only deserves reading in his own right as one of the most gifted of contemporary pamphleteers; he is particularly significant because he was a keen admirer of Milton's earlier prose works and was

[33] *Civil Power,* below, p. 270.

[1] BML, 105a59; not in Thomason, but the dedicatory address (sig. A2) shows that it was published soon after the restoration of the Rump in May, 1659, though written earlier.

[2] *E.g.,* pp. 9–12, 15.

[3] E1841(1); dated September by Thomason, but the introductory "Premonition to the Reader" is dated July 4, 1659.

closely associated with Sir Henry Vane, whose views he probably re-
flected.[4] Vane had helped him through Westminster School and Christ
Church, Oxford, to his present post of Under-Keeper of the Bodleian.
At twenty-seven, Stubbe was the most brilliant classical scholar in
Oxford, and among his acquaintances and correspondents was Thomas
Hobbes. He wrote prolifically during 1659 on all the main themes that
occupied Milton in *Of Civil Power, The Likeliest Means,* and *The
Readie & Easie Way,* and the comparison is in each case rewarding,
for from basically the same premises he often drew somewhat different
conclusions.

Stubbe's *Essay,* however, does not differ from Milton's treatise so
much in its conclusions as in its emphasis and its method of argument.
Whereas Milton rests his case squarely on Scripture, Stubbe's approach
is much more broadly philosophical and historical. He begins with a
lengthy disquisition on the origins of the civil magistrate's authority
and concludes that it is essentially fiduciary and limited: "That our
Magistrate should entermeddle *authoritatively* in such spiritual affairs,
by vertue of any power derived from his *creators,* the *People,* is to me
morally impossible, as well as *unlawful.*"[5] This argument from popular
sovereignty is one that Milton conspicuously avoids. The magistrate,
Stubbe contends, deals by the light of natural reason with such outward
concerns of society as can be judged thereby. He agrees closely with
Milton that there is no "common evidence in the delivery of Spirituall
matters," since "the *Spirit of God* in each Saint is the sole Authentique
Expositor of Scripture unto him that hath it."[6] From here, however,
his argument takes a different turn. He cites the parable of the talents
as testimony that men are variously endowed with spiritual gifts. The
majority, whose stock is only one or two talents, may choose their
magistrates and be eligible for magistracy themselves, but they may
neither exercise nor delegate power over the consciences of the spiritual
elite to whom God has given five talents. Nor may these five-talent
men invoke the civil power in order to dictate the religion of the less
gifted, first because they are always a minority, second because they
should not dare to entrust to men that which should be remitted to the
tribunal of God, and third because it is rash and unjust to try to force
men of one or two talents into a spiritual regimen appropriate to the

---

[4] Parker, *Milton,* p. 507, and *Milton's Contemporary Reputation,* p. 98; An-
thony à Wood, *Athenae Oxonienses* (2nd ed., 2 vols., Oxford, 1721), II, 560,
562; biographical note in Jordan, *Religious Toleration,* IV, 336. Thomason
wrote on his copy of Stubbe's *A Letter to an Officer of the Army* (October 26,
1659), E1001(8), " 'A dangerous fellow'; Sr Henry Vanes Advisor."
[5] Stubbe, *Essay in Defence of the Good Old Cause,* p. 21.
[6] *Ibid.,* pp. 39–40.

improvement of five.[7] Here, as in Vane's thought and Milton's, is a clear conception of an aristocracy of grace, and it is coupled with the most express denial that exceptional spiritual gifts confer either a superior claim to political authority or any coercive power whatsoever over the consciences of others.

Stubbe follows his general thesis with a long and remarkable historical survey of the progress and regress of toleration, and of the changing attitudes to blasphemy and heresy in different ages.[8] He concludes with a plea for toleration that is broader than Milton's. He would extend it to episcopal divines who live peaceably under the government, abjuring royalist politics and the claim to impose their religion on others, and also to papists who renounce the Pope's authority over temporal affairs.[9] In another long tract he pleaded with uncommon charity for the toleration of Quakers.[10] Stubbe and Milton both ran counter to prevailing opinion in their conceptions of Christian liberty, but whereas Milton's manner of argument, focused on a limited range of much-controverted Scriptural texts, was very much of his time, the tone and method of Stubbe's tracts looked forward more to the rational and liberal spirit of the later seventeenth century.

[7] *Ibid.*, pp. 24–31.
[8] *Ibid.*, pp. 42–125.
[9] *Ibid.*, pp. 131–32.
[10] Henry Stubbe, *A Light Shining out of Darknes,* 2nd ed. (November 8, 1659), E770(5), pp. 81–92.

Chapter IV

THE REPUBLICANS TRIUMPHANT

1. THE OVERTHROW OF THE PROTECTORATE

March–April, 1659

THE FIRST HIGH TIDE of pamphlets and petitions hostile to the Protectorate, which coincided with the publication of Milton's *Treatise of Civil Power* in February, ebbed a little during the next few weeks. The lull, however, did not last long. The debates in Parliament were widely discussed in the army, despite attempts to ban the reporting of them, and they steadily inflamed its distrust.[1] The great issue in the Commons during late February and early March was whether to recognize the Other House. Member after member attacked it for the number of officers that it contained, and some hoped frankly that the army would be disbanded or greatly reduced.[2] The same hatred of "swordsmen" appeared when the Commons heard the cases of Overton and other prisoners of the Protectorate. "You have now a military power mixed with your civil," said a republican; "the military act it all now."[3] These were typical republican tactics; but the spontaneous antimilitarism of the unattached country gentry could sway votes too, as when the House debated the disputed elections of Colonel Robert Lilburne and Major Packer. Both were heroes of the army commonwealthsmen, and both were unseated.[4] The army reacted still more sharply when certain M.P.'s sneered at the Rump as "the fag end of the Long Parliament" and disputed the legality of all the Commonwealth's acts since Pride's Purge. The implications were alarming; what indemnity, the officers asked themselves, had they for all they had done in the last ten years, and what security for the estates they had acquired?[5] These endless wrangles, moreover, kept the House from making any financial provision for the soldiers' arrears of pay, so that

[1] Thurloe, VII, 627, 634; Burton, IV, 223.
[2] *E.g.*, Burton, IV, 40, 64.
[3] *Ibid.*, p. 153.
[4] *Ibid.*, pp. 42–46, 148, 249–53.
[5] Davies, *Restoration*, pp. 65–66.

the army came to suspect a deliberate design to increase its unpopularity by driving it upon free quarter.

Before the Commons eventually accepted the Other House as a House of Parliament on March 28, many speeches in favor of the old peerage proclaimed the conservative temper of the country gentry,[6] a few of whom even spoke openly for restoring the monarchy.[7] These members almost certainly had in mind a King Richard rather than a King Charles, if only as second best, and there had indeed been a crop of rumors that this Parliament intended to revive its predecessor's project and crown the Protector.[8] There was little or no foundation for such talk, but it bred a suspicion in the army that "this Gentleman, who they would have made soe much hast to dresse And set on horsebacke, was but to warme the sadle for another whome they better loved and liked." [9]

Two incidents at about this time lowered Richard's stock among the "godly" officers still further. Colonel Ashfield, a favorite of the commonwealthsmen and sectaries, almost came to blows with Commissary-General Whalley in Westminster Hall in an argument over the Other House. Whalley complained to Richard, and Richard ordered Ashfield to apologize or else answer before a court-martial. This brought a deputation to Whitehall from several Baptist churches to plead Ashfield's case, but though Richard refused to retract, he neither had Ashfield court-martialed nor followed Monck's admirable advice to send the man back to his regiment in Scotland. The other episode, significant for the amount of damaging gossip it generated, arose when a subaltern in Colonel Ingoldsby's regiment drew up charges against his major for browbeating honest men and favoring drunkards, liars, and swearers. Richard sent for this pious cornet and exploded at him.

"You article against your Major because he is for me," he said. "You are a company of mutineers . . .[10] and I will hang you and strip you as a man would strip an eele; you talk of preaching and praying men, they are the men that go about to undermine me."

He did indeed strip the cornet of his commission there and then, and clapping his colonel on the shoulder, said "Go thy way, Dick

---

[6] *Ibid.*, pp. 61–62. Prynne seized the moment to defend the peers' rights in *The Antient Land-Mark Skreen or Bank* (March 12, 1659), E972(9).

[7] Burton, III, 125–28, 158, 181, 403; *cf.* pp. 531–34.

[8] *Clarendon Calendar*, IV, 140–43, 176; Historical Manuscripts Commission, *10th Report*, App. VI, p. 194; *XXV Queries* (February 16, 1659), E968(5), pp. 5–7.

[9] *Clarke Papers*, III, 211.

[10] Here the narrator interposes: "meaning the officers who often met to seek the Lord and bewailed their apostacy from the good old cause."

Ingoldsby, thou canst neither preach nor pray, but I will believe thee before I believe twenty of them." [11]

Many an officer genuinely saw the mounting crisis of March and April as a straight fight between the friends and enemies of the people of God. Major Nehemiah Bourne was one of them. The hearts of the Lord's people, he said, were

> greatly awakened and alarumed by the post hast that was made by the majority of the howse to Introdus Kingship, and with it al maner of Tirriny and oppression, both upon the Civill and Spiritual Liberties of the Saints . . . And perceiving plainely that there Cause was desperat as to all human hopes, the honest party in the howse not being able to carry one voate, . . . many of the good people (whose harts and hands the lord had in some measure kept cleane, And Innocent as to the laite general Apostacy) . . . began together to seeke the face of god, And consult what might be there duty at such a time. The lord was pleased to stirre up many of them to apply to the officers of the Armie (who were many of them about the Citty, but there forces scattered about the Countries),[12] And several serius debates were had Amongst them, yet there harts generally down as to any greate exspectations. . . . But in a shorte time the generallity of the officers of the army (who had not soe farre debauched there prinsiples and spirits as to lick up there vomit without Reluctensy) began to gather blood and spirits, and came up to the superior officers, And began to worke upon them alsoe, who by this time were themselves Inclinable to here, and Resolved to mete together, and whet up one anothers spirits, and Revive that good ould Cause for which they had bene ingaiged soe deeply.[13]

That is indeed how it went, with the commonwealthsmen zealously canvassing the army officers and the mass of subordinate officers bringing mounting pressure to bear on the grandees.[14]

In February, Fleetwood, Desborough, and their colleagues at Wallingford House had resisted such pressures and rallied to their young kinsman and master. Towards the end of March, however, they made overtures to his enemies, and thereby they doomed him. They did not really intend to. Fleetwood at any rate was an honest man according to his rather dim lights, and they were all in a trying situation. On the one hand was Richard, alien to them in temperament and values, lean-

---

[11] *A Second Narrative of the Late Parliament* (1659), quoted by Firth in Ludlow, *Memoirs*, II, pp. 62–63. Full sources for both incidents are cited in Davies, *Restoration*, pp. 64–65.

[12] *I.e.*, counties.

[13] *Clarke Papers*, III, 210–11.

[14] "The protector allready relyes upon the great officers of the army, and the republicans on the under officers more than upon the votes of either party. But it is thought the protector will be mistaken in some of those he relyes upon, if the other party appears any whit considerable." Dr. Barwick to Hyde, February 16: Thurloe, VII, 615.

ing upon conservative, civilian counsellors and a Parliament hostile to all that the army stood for. On the other were their own subordinates, grown out of hand through their obsession with the notion of a good old cause betrayed, and encouraged by preachers whose charges of apostasy troubled Fleetwood's heart too. One divine who was no stranger to Milton exerted a special influence upon them. Dr. John Owen had been very close to Cromwell when the Protectorate was set up, but like Milton he had been disquieted by its increasingly traditionalist tendencies, and in 1657 he had actively abetted the officers in their pressure upon Cromwell to refuse the crown. More recently he had preached to Richard's Parliament on a day of prayer and fasting that it held on February 4. He then lamented the tide of wickedness and profanity that he saw engulfing the nation, and inveighed against "old formes and wayes taken up with greedinesse, which are a badge of apostacy from all former ingagement and actings."[15] Shortly afterwards he formed the officers who met at Wallingford House into a gathered church, and by one account this potent little congregation included Lambert.[16]

Late in March, Fleetwood and his confreres took two fatal courses. The first was to seek a secret *entente* with the republicans. They invited Edmund Ludlow to Wallingford House—Ludlow, that stiff-necked commonwealthsman whom Cromwell had had to remove from high authority in Ireland and who was now in close partnership with Haslerig's party in Parliament. They probably sought only a limited collaboration within the framework of the Protectorate, but they did not yet appreciate that the republicans could now negotiate from strength, and they only from weakness. Ludlow warned them that a reconciliation could be based only on their helping to restore the Commonwealth; he suggested that they should prove their good faith by supporting Ashfield against Whalley and by joining heartily with the army commonwealthsmen. Vane and Haslerig approved Ludlow's response, but declined to meet the officers in person; all they offered was a vague assurance "that when they saw it seasonable they would be ready to assist them in all things tending to the publick service."[17]

The grandees' second injury to Richard was to persuade him to sanction a General Council of Officers, including all of whatever rank

[15] John Owen, *The Glory and Interest of Nations professing the Gospel* (1659; not in Thomason). Davies describes this sermon (*Restoration*, pp. 95–96) under the misapprehension that it was preached before the Rump on May 8, 1659, but p. 1 of the original printed edition states the date and occasion plainly.
[16] *Consultations of the Ministers of Edinburgh*, II, 158; Annesley to Henry Cromwell, March 15, 1659, in BML, Lansdowne MSS 823, f.251.
[17] Ludlow, *Memoirs*, II, 63–65.

who were in or about London. They probably did not know what they were unleashing. What they evidently hoped to do was to take the sting out of the army's agitation by putting themselves at the head of it, much as Cromwell had done in the summer of 1647, and to enlist republican support just far enough to force Richard to change his advisers and readmit the army to its former power in national politics. But Fleetwood was no Cromwell. He and his fellow commanders grossly overestimated their influence over their subordinates, and the republican politicians were not to be used for any purposes but their own.

As soon as the General Council of Officers met on April 2 it decided to place the army's grievances before Parliament in a petition. The drafting committee was dominated by Ashfield, Lilburne, Mason, and other commonwealthsmen; not a single Wallingford House man was appointed to it. The officers still loyal to Richard were aghast at its labors, and though they managed to tone it down somewhat in the General Council, the Humble Representation and Petition which Fleetwood and the whole body presented to Richard on the 6th still "smelt of gunpowder and ball." [18] As well as voicing the expected demands concerning pay and indemnity, it complained that "the good old Cause . . . is very frequently and publickly derided and reproached," and that "its implacable Adversaries" were appearing in the highest places. The cavaliers were gathering at home and abroad for a fresh attempt, and were daring to affront the Commonwealth's faithful servants. Let there be, therefore, such a public affirmation of the good old cause that none should dare to speak or act against it. Let freedom of worship also be reasserted, for it had been much violated lately by indictments and imprisonments. The sharpest sting came in a resolution "to stand by and assist your Highness and Parliament, in the plucking the Wicked out of their Places, wheresoever they may be discovered, either amongst ourselves or any other Places of Trust." [19] Who was to pluck out whom?

When Richard passed the Humble Representation to Parliament on April 8, the Commons had it read but shelved it without a debate. They had been spending *their* last few days on a declaration for a fast day throughout the three nations. According to this jeremiad, the decay of trade, the general dearth, and the high mortality of men and

---

[18] [Arthur Annesley], *Englands Confusion* (1659), reprinted in *Somers Tracts*, VI, 518; *Clarke Papers*, III, 187–88.

[19] Text in *Old Parliamentary History*, XXI, 340–45.

cattle were all manifestations of God's wrath at the "many Blasphemies and damnable Heresies" that were rife, and at the remissness of the civil magistrate in not punishing them. The declaration exclaimed in special horror against the "crying up the Light in the Hearts of sinful Men, as the Rule and Guide of all their Actions." [20] It was a plain encouragement to magistrates to be more severe with sectaries in general and Quakers in particular. It may well have clinched Milton's alignment with the Protectorate's opponents, for the republicans opposed it in the House, though in vain. But they made all they could of it; a royalist agent reported that it "has put life into the Commonwealth's men, and they insinuate into the Army, and tell them, 'the Court party intend to force their consciences again, and to set up tyranny.'" [21] Only a few days later the Commons, sitting as the Grand Committee for Religion, ordered that the Westminster Assembly's confession of faith, except for the chapters that dealt with church discipline, should be "held forth as the public profession of the nation." [22] According to one well-informed source,[23] no minister was to receive the public maintenance unless he subscribed it, and unless he further declared his readiness to accept a modified Presbyterian regimen. The Commons were clearly intent on tightening the state's hold over religion. On April 16 their intolerance vented itself on some Quakers who petitioned them for relief from persecution. "They are a fanatic crew," declared one member; "I move to whip them home as vagrants," said another; "wolves under sheep's clothing," a third called them. Only some republicans spoke in their defense.[24]

As if more were needed to drive the senior officers into solidarity with their unruly juniors, the Commons engaged on April 12 in a hue and cry after William Boteler, and proceeded to impeach him for acts he had committed when he was one of Cromwell's major-generals.[25] On the 13th the officers girded up their spirits in a whole day of prayer and fasting at Wallingford House, where Hugh Peters, John Owen, and John Griffith led their devotions. More than five hundred

[20] *Ibid.*, pp. 321–24. For the debate see Burton, IV, 300, 329–33, 335–45.

[21] *Clarendon State Papers*, III, 456.

[22] Burton, IV, 402.

[23] James Sharp, agent in London of the Scottish Resolutioners: *Consultations of the Ministers of Edinburgh*, II, 164, 168. Sharp also heard that the Triers were to be replaced by a much narrower commission, consisting only of eight or nine divines (p. 168).

[24] Burton, IV, 440–46.

[25] Davies, *Restoration*, pp. 72–73. The sources for the ensuing narrative are cited by Davies, unless otherwise stated.

attended the General Council the next day. When Desborough moved that every officer should reaffirm his loyalty by making an "attestation" that the execution of Charles I had been just and lawful, the shouts of approval testified to the widespread suspicion among them that the Protectoral regime had become deeply infiltrated by crypto-royalists.

But what were five hundred officers doing in London anyway? Very many, if not most of them, ought to have been far away with their regiments. Too late, and only after indulging in needlessly provocative and intolerant votes, the Commons recognized the fact. On April 18 they sat far into the afternoon behind locked doors, and finally passed two resolutions that neither they nor Richard proved able to enforce. One was that there should be no further meetings of officers without the consent of the Protector and both Houses of Parliament; the other that no officer should retain his command unless he would engage not to interrupt the free meetings of Parliament.[26] The republicans, who had led the challenge to the swordsmen in the Other House and exploited the antimilitarist temper of the country gentry on many occasions, opposed these votes strenuously, knowing they would be beaten. They were openly courting the army now, confident that the General Council would play into their hands. "There is a 'good old cause,' " said Scot, "if their meetings be, to manage that, I shall not be against them." [27]

Meanwhile, between April 16 and 18, there were tense consultations involving Richard, the privy councillors and some leading officers. Richard still had some loyal friends in the army; Fauconberg, Howard, Goffe, Ingoldsby, and others even offered to seize the Wallingford House leaders so that he could put himself at the head of his troops. Eventually, on the very afternoon that the Commons were debating their two fatal votes, Richard summoned the officers in a body to Whitehall.[28] He ordered that the meetings of the General Council should cease and that they should all return to their regiments. Desborough and Ashfield were openly defiant. Yet when the officers assembled for the next General Council, which had been appointed for the 20th, Fleetwood dismissed them, and went himself to the Other House, which was strongly inclined to contest the Commons'

[26] *Commons Journals,* VII, 641; Lansdowne MSS 823, f.299.

[27] Burton, IV, 454; *cf.* pp. 450, 455, 457.

[28] The most precise accounts, by Mabbott in *Clarke Papers,* III, 191, Anthony Morgan in Lansdowne MSS 823, f.301, and Bordeaux in Guizot, I, 364, all agree that the officers attended Richard early in the afternoon while the Commons were still debating their resolutions. By anticipating these, Richard was taking upon himself the onus for breaking up the General Council.

votes.[29] At some time, probably on the evening of the 20th, Richard saw Fleetwood and Desborough and pledged his good will towards the army; they understood him to promise particularly that he would not countenance any move by Parliament to assert his own generalship in a manner that would override their authority.[30] This was a vital issue, for many officers feared "That the Protector did intend to cast them out of their Places, and put the Army into the hands of the Nobility and Gentry of the Nation, thereby to bring in the King, and destroy that Liberty of the Gospell they had so long contended for."[31] Hence they were agitating again for a commander-in-chief distinct from the head of state.

Richard could still be valuable both to the grandees and to Parliament, and each side was struggling for control of him. April 21 was the day which decided the outcome. Richard consulted with his confidants—principally Broghil, Fiennes, Thurloe, Wolseley, and Whitelocke—as to whether he should dissolve Parliament as the officers were pressing him to do, and most were in favor. But there was still a little hope. The Commons had at last started to consider the soldiers' pay and indemnity, and the lord mayor and aldermen visited Richard on the 21st and promised to stand by him and the Parliament to the last. The city militia, however, declared in support of the army and its Humble Representation, and it was the sword that tilted the scales now. The Commons were well aware of it, and they spent most of the 21st debating the nation's militia. Although they reached no conclusion, they showed such a strong inclination to place all the armed forces under the immediate joint control of the Protector and Parliament that the chief officers judged Richard's pledge to be worthless.

The army would stand no more. Towards midnight, London's citizens stirred in their beds to the sound of hooves and tramping feet. Fleetwood had summoned a general rendezvous of the regiments about the capital to St. James'. Richard called out his life guard; by one account he commanded them to arrest Fleetwood, but they begged to be excused. Then he tried ordering a counter-rendezvous at Whitehall, but all he could muster were two troops of horse and three companies of foot, for the officers who remained loyal could not get

[29] Guizot, I, 366; *Clarke Papers*, III, 192, 212. Despite suggestions in *Clarendon Calendar*, IV, 184, and *CSP Ven.*, 1659–61, p. 11, the best-informed sources agree that there was no further meeting of the General Council before the coup of April 22, though informal conferences continued each evening at Wallingford House.

[30] *Clarke Papers*, III, 192, 212.

[31] Baker, *Chronicle*, p. 659; *cf. Clarke Papers*, III, 212.

their subordinates to obey them. During the night, Desborough faced him with an ultimatum: he must throw himself upon the officers and dissolve Parliament. He put up what resistance he could, but in the end he had to bow to Desborough's threats and sign a commission for the dissolution. Next day, when Black Rod came to the Commons to deliver his summons, they thrice refused to admit him, and he had to content himself with breaking his emblem of office outside their door to signify that the Parliament was at an end.[32]

2. THE RECALL OF THE RUMP

April–May, 1659

Fleetwood, Desborough, and their confederates still had no thought of deposing Richard; they had promised to take care of him, so long as he danced to their tune. "I am suer all indeavours were made by the principal offisers in the Armie to pece and mende up that crakt Goverment," wrote Major Bourne; "the utmost they had in vew . . . was, to Settle the Malitia in safe hands, take away his Negative, And Remove his Sicophants, and Parasits, And fill up the Counsel with good and able men."[1] They did not reckon that a puppet could perform only so long as the would-be puppeteers had control of the strings.

It was the Council of Officers, an assembly of field officers smaller than the all-inclusive General Council of recent weeks, that assumed *de facto* authority after the coup. It promptly acclaimed Fleetwood commander-in-chief, but it weakened the authority of the Wallingford House clique by restoring not only Lambert but thoroughpaced old commonwealthsmen like Overton, Rich, Okey, and Saunders to the command of regiments. Moreover the Council of Officers had no such undisputed power as when Cromwell had expelled the Rump six years before. The junior officers took to holding their own great gatherings at St. James', where they listened to the wilder preachers descanting on the good old cause and grew hot against every relic of the Protectorate. There were also meetings in the city of non-commissioned officers and soldiers who called themselves the Army's Agitators, recalling the heady days of 1647, but it was from the captains and subalterns at St. James' that the really formidable pressure came.[2]

---

[32] *Clarke Papers*, III, 193; Guizot, I, 371–72.
[1] *Clarke Papers*, III, 213–14.
[2] Thurloe, VII, 666; *Clarendon Calendar*, IV, 191–94; *Nicholas Papers* (4 vols., CS, 1886–1920), IV, 122–24.

They were prompted by a veritable spate of republican pamphlets, which now for the first time told the army that the one way to redeem its former "backsliding" was to restore the Rump. It was no small triumph to succeed in identifying the good old cause with the "Good Old Parliament,"[3] considering how vehemently the Council of Officers had denounced the latter six years before for its "bitterness and opposition to the people of God, and His spirit acting in them."[4] But these propagandists were adept at playing upon both the material and moral susceptibilities of the army, and they larded their appeals with the language of the saints. *Some Reasons Humbly Proposed to the Officers*[5] was typical in urging that the present crisis called not only for godliness in the nation's governors but political experience and skill, and that only the Rump could claim the legal authority to make provision for the army's pay and indemnity. But its clinching argument was that the providence of God pointed unmistakably to restoring the Commonwealth's old rulers, since every attempt at settlement had failed since the unity between Parliament and army was broken in 1653. Other tracts probed the army's sense of collective guilt for having departed from the ways of the Lord to serve the self-interest of the house of Cromwell and its creatures, and incited the middle and lower ranks to get rid of all such apostates as remained. "Cleanse therefore and purge your Councils and Commands," urged some petitioners from Southwark, "root out those Canaanites, those Court-Parasites and Apostates . . . if you once touch or give any way to their Politicks, farewel, Good Old Cause."[6] "Court and Camp are universally united in vitiousness," declared *An Invocation to the Officers of the Army;*[7] let the honest officers rise up against "one Person and his prostituted Parasites, who have pawn'd their souls to propagate his Power." *A Seasonable Word*[8] warned them specially of "a Court-designe of a few self-seekers, about a single person, so that now the Militia, and the Negative voice are laid aside, and a round O or Cypher will serve the turn." *A Perambulatory Word to Court, Camp, City and Country*[9] hammered the message home:

[3] So called in a remonstrance signed by nearly 400 men of Goffe's regiment, who had defied their colonel on the night of April 21 when he tried to bring them to Richard's support: *The Humble Remonstrance . . . of Major General Goffs Regiment* (April 26, 1659), E979(6).

[4] Declaration of April 22, 1653, in Gardiner, *Constitutional Documents*, p. 401.

[5] April 28, 1659, E979(8).

[6] *The Petition and Advice of Divers Well-Affected* (April 27, 1659), E980(1).

[7] April 20, 1659, E979(1).

[8] May 5, 1659, E980(17).

[9] May 4, 1659, E980(15), p. 5.

The Grandees we hope will ere long see their errour, & desire no longer to hold that staffe, which they may perceive (if our faithfull inferiour Officers and Souldiers cleave close to what they have declared) they have taken by the wrong end. Our Camp-court creatures going about to bridle the Army, have given them just occasion to take the bit into their own teeth.

The weekly *Faithful Scout* was revived to further the campaign for the Rump, and it often reprinted extracts from republican pamphlets in its editorial pages.

This striking outburst of propaganda, aimed at preventing the Wallingford House party from preserving any shreds of the Protectorate, was dominated by the champions of the Rump, but some other voices were heard too. That indomitable Fifth Monarchy man Christopher Feake thundered that the Rump was still the same accursed thing that it had been six years before, and called upon the hidden remnant of the Lord's people to proclaim "the Name and Interest of the Approaching King of Saints." [10] Another address to Fleetwood celebrated the achievements of Barebone's Parliament, and it was not alone in advocating a new assembly of nominated saints. [11] Some millenarian congregations "confederated" with the assembly of junior officers at St. James' and pressed them to stand out for a government of seventy godly men, on the model of Israel's Sanhedrin; "butt the cry was great against itt, as a thinge the people of England would nott bee bound by, soe att last the Churches were wrought over . . . to restore the Longe Parliament." [12]

At least two pamphlets [13] during this brief interregnum resuscitated parts of the old Leveller program and called for a new, freely elected Parliament, though the particular issue of a democratic franchise no longer seemed to interest anyone. As another variant, James Harrington and his disciples fired an opening shot or two in their campaign for a commonwealth ruled by two elected assemblies, distinct in function. Their main effort, however, was still to come. [14]

[10] Christopher Feake, *A Beam of Light* (May 2, 1659), E980(5), esp. preface and pp. 47–48.

[11] *A True Copie of a Paper* (April 26, 1659), E979(4), erroneously identified in Thomason as a Quaker tract; *A Faithful Remembrance and Advice* (May 4, 1659), E980(16).

[12] *Clarke Papers*, IV, 21.

[13] *The Honest Design: or, the True Commonwealths-man* (May 2, 1659), E980(11); *The Humble Desires of a Free Subject* (May 2, 1659), E980(8). Such echoes of the Leveller movement continued for a short while after the restoration of the Rump; see below, pp. 106–07.

[14] James Harrington, *Pour Enclouer le Canon* (May 2, 1659), E980(6); *The Armies Dutie* (May 2, 1659), E980(12); see also below, pp. 102–04.

Among the mass of junior officers whose collective voice bore the Rump back to power, neither millenarian extravagances nor Harringtonian novelties carried much weight against the simple republican formula of a commonwealth without a single person or House of Lords. Differences that had once been sharp—between Rumper politicians and Levellers, or between advocates of biennial democratic Parliaments and believers in a rule of the saints—had become blurred by the years and by a common revulsion against the Protectorate. Many currents of feeling fed that revulsion: Puritan disgust at the quasi-monarchical trappings of the Cromwellian Court, resentment at the pseudo-aristocratic elevation of the grandees, the slow fading of the vision of a New Jerusalem, the gradual muting of the army's claim to speak for the people of England, the resurgence of traditional gentry influences in politics, and now under Richard an exaggerated fear that crypto-royalists had infiltrated the citadel and that liberty of conscience would shortly be denied. Officers and soldiers were filled with a passionate nostalgia for the high summer of the revolution, when victory had constantly assured them of the Lord's presence and the future lay bright before the people of God. The frequent sexual imagery in the literature of the good old cause, contrasting the "sincere virgin-Spirit" of those earlier days with the political harlotry of the Protectorate,[15] carries clues to its emotional tone. So do the constant references to the fortunes of an earlier chosen people; so does the web of fantasy spun from Revelations and the Old Testament prophets that preachers and pamphleteers wove around the course of recent events. Amid the uncertainty and disillusion of that spring of 1659, the instinct of simple Puritan captains and cornets was to ask when they had strayed from the paths of the Lord. The republicans, smug in the role of wise counsellors and forgiving fathers, gave them the answer and told them what they must do: put the clock back to 1653, before Cromwell usurped the power of the sovereign people.

Under such pressures as these, the men of Wallingford House found themselves powerless. Even in the Council of Officers their efforts to save the Protectorate were overborne, now that Ashfield and Lilburne and their kind were reinforced by the commonwealthsmen whom Cromwell had cashiered and who were now restored to commands. By the beginning of May they had to accept the recall of the Rump as inevitable, and with it the breaking of their pledge to Richard. John Owen, their spiritual mentor, played an equivocal part in reconciling them to this course. As late as May 3 he could still talk of maintain-

[15] *E.g.*, in *A Faithful Remembrance and Advice;* cf. above, pp. 22–23.

ing Richard's title and dignity, and he later denied that he had been instrumental in his deposition.[16] Nevertheless he obtained from Ludlow a list of the surviving Rumpers and took it to Wallingford House.[17] He also officiated at the devotions of the junior officers at St. James', and he preached to the Rump on the day after it returned to power.[18] Baxter exaggerated when he stated that "Dr. *Owen* and his Assistants did the main Work," [19] but Owen's share of the responsibility for Richard's downfall was heavy, even though he probably did not intend it.

When they realized that nothing but the recall of the Rump would satisfy the army, the grandees tried to make what terms they could for Richard and themselves. Two conferences took place at Vane's house, where Haslerig, Ludlow, Salwey, and Vane himself met a small delegation from the Council of Officers, which included Lambert but neither Fleetwood nor Desborough.[20] The officers presented four propositions. To two of them the Rumpers agreed; they were for an act of indemnity to cover the army's past actions and for a reformation of the law and the clergy. But the request "that some provision of power might be made for Mr. Richard Cromwell" met a blank refusal. The Rumpers were prepared to pay his public debts, but not to preserve any part of his authority as Protector. The fourth proposal was the thorniest: "That the government of the nation should be by a representative of the people, and by a select senate." [21] This was to be a contentious issue all through the summer and autumn, and the four Parliament men differed on it among themselves. After four or five hours' debate they declined to pledge their fellow members in advance, but assured the officers that they would secure a sympathetic hearing for any proposals that the army put to the House after it had met.

With these answers the Council of Officers had to be content.[22]

---

[16] *Diary of Sir Archibald Johnston of Wariston* (3 vols., Scottish Historical Society, Edinburgh, 1911–40), III, 107–08; *A Complete Collection of the Sermons of John Owen* (London, 1721), p. xix.

[17] Ludlow, *Memoirs*, II, 74.

[18] Baker, *Chronicle*, p. 660 (misprinted 659); *Commons Journals*, VII, 646. Michael Fixler in *Milton and the Kingdoms of God* (London: Faber, 1964), pp. 201–02, follows Davies in identifying this sermon (see above, p. 61, n. 15).

[19] *Reliquiae Baxterianae*, part I, p. 101. Since this was written, Owen's part has been fully discussed by Peter Toon in *God's Statesman: The Life and Work of John Owen* (Exeter: Paternoster Press, 1971), pp. 111–14.

[20] The main source for what follows is Ludlow, *Memoirs*, II, 74–77.

[21] *Ibid.*, p. 75

[22] In the following October the officers were to claim that the leading Rumpers had accepted their propositions before the Parliament was restored:

When their delegates came again to Vane's house three days later, it was only to declare their assent to the restoration of the Rump and to urge that it should meet as soon as possible. The country had been without a government for a fortnight, and they could provide it with no other. On May 6 the Council of Officers published a declaration which fairly expressed the army's current state of mind. It spoke of the dangers that beset the Commonwealth; of the "Backslidings of many . . . ourselves also contributing thereunto, by wandering divers Ways from righteous and equal Paths"; of the frustration of all their attempts at settlement; and of the daily decline of "the good Spirit which formerly appeared amongst us . . . so as the good old Cause itself became a Reproach." Looking back for the cause of the Lord's withdrawing His presence, and "calling to Mind, that the Long Parliament, consisting of the Members which continued there sitting until the 20th of *April*, 1653, were eminent Asserters of that Cause, and had a special Presence of God with them," the officers judged it their duty to invite those members to resume the exercise of their trust.[23]

Next day a little procession of forty-two Rumpers marched two-by-two into the Parliament House. They had had difficulty in making up a quorum and also in persuading old Speaker Lenthall to take the chair, for he was loath to relinquish the "lordship" that his membership of the Other House had conferred on him. Monday, May 9, should have been their first full working day, but it was disrupted by an interlude of comedy. William Prynne and a group of fellow members who had been "secluded" in Pride's Purge in 1648 managed to enter the House, and they refused to budge. They proposed to debate whether the late king's death had not terminated the Long Parliament's legal existence. The only way to get rid of them was to adjourn the House for dinner.[24]

Nevertheless the Rump soon swelled in numbers, and it assumed at once the full sovereignty that it had exercised during the first four years of the Commonwealth's existence. The question whether that sovereignty was to be shared was sharply raised on May 13, when Lambert presented the Humble Petition and Address of the Officers

---

see *A Declaration of the General Council of the Officers* (October 27, 1659), E1001(12); *Considerations upon the Late Transactions . . . of the Army* (October 20, 1659), 669f21(81); *Clarke Papers*, IV, 73. But Ludlow's statement that he and his colleagues declined to bind the House in advance is supported by Bordeaux (Guizot, I, 383) and Edward Phillips (Baker, *Chronicle*, p. 661).

[23] *Old Parliamentary History*, XXI, 367–68.

[24] William Prynne, *A True and Perfect Narrative* (1659, listed in Thomason under May 7 but published later), E767(1).

of the Army.[25] Its fifteen articles expressed the army's sense of what constituted "the Fundamentals of our Good Old Cause." Most of them were not particularly controversial, for they started by affirming that Britain should be governed as a commonwealth, without a single person, kingship, or House of Lords, and they asked no more for Richard and his heirs than a generous financial provision. But article thirteen pressed the point that had troubled the previous week's discussions. It proposed that the legislative power

> may be in a Representative of the People, consisting of a House successively chosen by the People in such way and manner as this Parliament shall judge meet, and of a select Senate, Co-ordinate in Power, of able and faithful persons, eminent for Godliness, and such as continue adhering to this Cause.

It became clear in subsequent controversy that the advocates of a Senate intended a body with life membership, which would constitute an element of permanence in the state while elected Parliaments came and went. The words "co-ordinate in power" implied that its assent would be necessary to legislation, and its special justification was that it would have the right to restrain the people's representatives if in the future their measures should transgress the "fundamentals," for example by seeking to reintroduce kingship or deny liberty of conscience. At one level it appealed to the senior officers because they hoped that as senators for life they, or at least some of them, would secure a stronger voice in state affairs than they could expect through membership of a Council of State annually elected by Parliament. To some, it would provide handsome compensation for their lost lordships in the Other House. To all, it offered a safeguard against the army being treated by any future Parliament as the Long Parliament had tried to treat it in 1647, the Rump in 1653, and Richard's Parliament in recent weeks.

But on a less self-interested plane the Senate represented an attempt to solve the primary problem which had vexed every regime in the last ten years, and with which Milton was to wrestle in his last political tracts: the problem of how to reconcile the principle that government should rest on the consent and participation of the people's representatives with the fact that the greater part of the political nation would reject if it could the "fundamentals" for which the Commonwealth stood. The Rump's previous efforts in 1653 to control the composition of future Parliaments, the crude expedient of a nominated assembly later that year, and the checks and balances of the two

[25] Text in Baker, *Chronicle*, pp. 662–64, and *Old Parliamentary History*, XXI, 400–05.

Protectoral constitutions can all be seen as reactions to this basic dilemma. In *A Healing Question,* published in 1656, Vane had propounded a solution very similar to the select Senate, though he then called it a standing council. He would shortly return to the idea and elaborate it.[26] The great obstacle to its acceptance lay in the unyielding hostility of Haslerig's party; under no circumstances would they allow any "negative" to diminish the supremacy of the representatives of the sovereign people. A rift would open during the summer between Haslerig's faction and Vane's, over this and other issues, and Haslerig's would command considerably more votes.

Milton's solution would be different again, but since it too would rest on a kind of Senate with membership for life, the army's proposals and the debate that they launched are highly significant as a background to the development of his later political thinking. That debate will be followed in later chapters. For the present, however, he was preoccupied not with models of a commonwealth but with the nature of a true church and the relation of its pastors with the people and the state. We must now see what implications the restoration of the Rump carried in ecclesiastical affairs.

3. THE MATTER OF RELIGION

May–June, 1659

Two articles in the officers' Humble Petition and Address of May 13 were of special concern to Milton, and the Rump accepted both without qualification. One asked that everyone who professed faith in the Trinity and acknowledged the Old and New Testaments to be the revealed word of God should be encouraged and protected in his faith and worship, provided that this liberty did not extend to popery, prelacy, or licentious practices. Milton must have found the trinitarian formula too restrictive, but otherwise this was a welcome reversal of the antitolerationist tendencies that Richard's Parliament had been showing towards the end of its life. He was probably much more suspicious of the next request, "That a Godly, Faithful and Painful Gospel-Preaching Ministry be every where encouraged, countenanced, and maintained."[1] These words were dangerously large; they may have been among the stimuli that set him pondering his next treatise. "Encouraged"? Certainly. "Countenanced"? Yes, so long as the

---

[26] See below, pp. 104–06.
[1] Baker, *Chronicle,* p. 663.

magistrate kept within his proper bounds. But "maintained"? Maintained by whom? If this meant—as it almost certainly did [2]—the continuance of a parochial ministry, ultimately controlled by the state and supported by public contributions, it would be a task worthy of Milton's pen to give the restored Commonwealth better advice.

The Rump made an early gesture towards religious liberty on May 10, when it set up a committee that included Vane, Haslerig, and many other prominent members to consider the cases of people imprisoned for conscience's sake, and how they might be discharged.[3] For the next six weeks, however, it had many more pressing questions to face than the ecclesiastical one, and it did not begin to show its hand on the public maintenance of ministers until mid-June. On June 18 it ordered that a bill be brought in for the ejecting of scandalous ministers and the relieving of oppressed ones.[4] This looks like a revival of a scheme that it had been considering shortly before its expulsion in 1653, whereby commissioners were to tour the six judicial circuits and investigate the beneficed clergy in each county in turn.[5] Two days later it ordered that the Committee for Plundered Ministers be revived, possibly with its powers enlarged.[6] This committee had been extremely active during and after the Civil Wars in removing royalist and Anglican clergymen and installing Puritan ones, and it had acquired considerable funds from impropriated tithes and other sources which it used to augment the stipends of underpaid ministers. After undergoing various changes of function, it had stood in 1653 as a kind of general ecclesiastical commission, directing the disposal of those revenues that the Commonwealth had taken over from the church and retained for ecclesiastical uses.[7] These votes showed that the Rump intended to maintain at least as large a responsibility for the parochial ministry as the Protectorate had done, though by means of different machinery.

Already, however, it had been forced to face the specific issue of tithes, for in June the abolitionists mounted a regular campaign of petitions. The last official pronouncement on this long-vexed question

---

[2] The prevailing opinion among the officers had been in favor of an established ministry, publicly maintained (though not by tithes), since at least the Whitehall debates of December, 1648, and January, 1649, when they modified the second *Agreement of the People* in this respect: see A. S. P. Woodhouse, ed., *Puritanism and Liberty* (London, 1938), pp. 125–70, 361–62.

[3] *Commons Journals*, VII, 648.

[4] *Ibid.*, p. 689.

[5] Shaw, *English Church*, II, 244–46.

[6] *Commons Journals*, VII, 689.

[7] Shaw, *English Church*, II, 194–226.

had been a proclamation by Richard and the Privy Council on November 25, 1658, ordering that the laws requiring the due payment of tithes should be fully enforced.[8] The sectaries took heart when the Commonwealth was restored, and they soon pressed again to get this burden on their consciences and their pockets removed. On June 14 the House admitted a delegation from Somerset, Devon, Dorset, Wiltshire, and Hampshire.[9] The Speaker told them that Parliament was resolved to give encouragement to a godly preaching ministry throughout the nation, and to that end would continue tithes until it could devise a more equitable and acceptable form of maintenance. This it would do with all convenient speed, and the House voted that day to refer the matter to a committee. It divided, however, as to whether this should be a select committee or the whole House sitting as a grand committee. The result was a tie, but the Speaker gave his casting vote for the latter. This was a blow for the abolitionists, since a select committee would have implied that the House desired the supersession of tithes in principle, whereas in a grand committee the question remained wide open.[10]

The Rump sat as a Grand Committee for Religion on June 21, but reaching no conclusion adjourned the debate to the 28th. Before then, however, the House was treated on the 27th to another bulky petition against tithes which claimed to bear fifteen thousand signatures. Its authors praised the great things that the Lord had done in England before Cromwell's usurpation "clouded the Nation with darknesse," but they went on to ask whether it was any part of the Lord's work "To set the Magistrate in Christs throne to try and judge who are fit to be his Ministers, and to send out and restraine whom he thinks fit, and to force a maintenance for them, even from those that for conscience sake cannot hear them, nor own them." [11] They used several arguments that Milton would shortly elaborate, but the House had evidently had enough of mass petitioning, for it proceeded to settle the matter of tithes that very day. The motion was put that "the Payment of Tythes shall continue as they now are, until this Parlia-

[8] Thomason 669f21(15), erroneously catalogued under September 25, 1658, since Thomason himself thus misdated it. The proclamation clearly arose from a petition before the Council on November 25: see *Calendar of State Papers, Domestic* (hereafter cited as *CSPD*), 1658–59, pp. 194–96.

[9] Their petition does not survive, but Thomason has petitions against tithes from Kent (June 4), 669f21(45); Bedfordshire (June 16), 669f21(51); and Hertfordshire (June 21), 669f21(55).

[10] *Commons Journals*, VII, 683; Guizot, I, 412.

[11] *The Copie of a Paper Presented to the Parliament* (June 27, 1659), E988(24), p. 5.

ment shall find out some other more equal and comfortable Maintenance, both for the Ministry, and Satisfaction of the People." The word "until" was challenged and rejected; "unless" was substituted without a division. This small amendment shifted the whole weight of probability against any change during the life of the present Parliament. The vote was published by order as a broadsheet, and read out by the judges on their circuits.[12]

It was a bitter blow to thousands of sectaries, and although we shall find evidence to suggest that Milton was already at work on *The Likeliest Means* before he heard of it, it must have spurred him to his task. Yet it made political sense. The Rump nursed few illusions about the very narrow range of public support that it enjoyed, and it knew that the upholders of an established parochial ministry carried far more political and social weight than the voluntaryists. It would have been rash indeed to alienate the lay patrons of livings and the owners of impropriate tithes—not to mention the great majority of the beneficed clergy, with all the influence that they wielded from the pulpit. Nor should the decision be attributed to mere grounds of expediency, for this was an issue on which the Rump had been genuinely divided throughout its existence.

[12] *Commons Journals*, VII, 694.

CHAPTER V

MILTON AGAINST HIRELINGS

1. THE CURRENT PHASE OF THE TITHES CONTROVERSY

THE English Revolution generated many more exciting controversies than that over tithes, but few so voluminous. To survey here the polemics of nearly twenty years would be both tedious and superfluous; [1] Milton's argument in *The Likeliest Means* ranged over broader territory than tithes. Yet since he felt obliged to descend into this dusty arena, it will be well to take a brief view of the contest as it stood during the few months before he engaged in it.

The case against tithes had always been partly religious and partly economic. The religious argument had taken two main grounds: that tithes were a relic of the Levitical Law that the Gospel had abrogated, and that it was a forcing of conscience to compel men to pay for the maintenance of ministers whose doctrines they rejected. The economic objection lay in the inequality with which tithes were levied upon different sections of the population. They were a burden mainly upon land and the produce of land; the "personal" tithes for which townsmen and traders were liable had long been dwindling into insignificance. Small landholders, from whom the parson commonly collected a tenth of the whole produce of the soil in kind, were much harder hit than rich merchants, who were tithable only on their clear profits and were greatly underassessed even on these. To our modern eyes, the most glaring anomaly would seem to lie in the considerable proportion of the "great" tithes, levied as a rate on land, that had passed from monastic ownership to the crown at the Reformation, and had since become, by purchase or gift, the pure property of lay landown-

---

[1] For a good survey see Margaret James, "The Political Importance of the Tithe Controversy in the English Revolution, 1640–1660," *History*, XXVI (June, 1941), 1–18; for the policies of governments since 1640, Shaw, *English Church*, II, 254–59; and for the prerevolutionary background, Christopher Hill, *Economic Problems of the Church* (Oxford: Clarendon Press, 1956), ch. V. Two great contemporary authorities were frequently appealed to: John Selden, *History of Tithes* (1618), and Sir Henry Spelman, *The Larger Treatise Concerning Tithes* (1647).

ers. But on this aspect there was relatively little emphasis in the controversy of the late sixteen-fifties; it centered mainly on the maintenance of the clergy.

By 1658 the whole issue had rather died down, for there was little more to say on either side that had not been said many times, and both Protectors made it very clear that they would continue tithes, at least until some better maintenance was devised. It revived faintly in the "good old cause" propaganda of early 1659, though usually only incidentally, as part of the larger question whether the state should assume *any* responsibilities over religion.[2] The main attack on tithes developed, as we have seen, after the restoration of the Rump. But before examining its grounds, we should see what kinds of cases the retentionists were currently making, for it was against them that Milton had to contend.

They all agreed that the clergy's right to a settled maintenance was *jure divino,* but they varied in the degree to which they insisted upon tithes as the one form of maintenance that Scripture and the law of the land sanctioned. The strongest defenders of the sacred tenth were the Presbyterians and other right-wing Puritans.[3] They wrested Scriptural texts to prove that tithes were as positively ordained by the New Testament as by the Old. They were also great legalists; they appealed to Ethelwulf's alleged charter of 855, to Athelstan's laws, to Magna Carta, and to a stack of statutes. They argued, as many had done earlier, that the law gave ministers as good a right to their tithes as landlords to their rents, and they often depicted the abolitionists as dangerous subverters of property. Being wholly opposed to toleration, they rejected the plea that laymen should not have to contribute to the maintenance of clergy whose ministrations they could not in conscience accept, since they held that everyone alike was obliged to attend parish worship and submit to parochial discipline. Against the withholding of tithes they could descend to such an argument as this:

> It is a sin that provokes God to curse a man in his outward estate and trading . . . it is usual with God to pay sinners with their own coyn;

[2] *E.g.,* in *XXV Queries,* no. XII; *The Leveller* (February 16, 1659; plausibly attributed to John Wildman by Maurice Ashley in *John Wildman, Plotter and Postmaster* (London: Cape, 1947), pp. 136–37), E968(3), pp. 10–14. A more specific attack on tithes was by Peter Corneliszoon Plockhoy in *The Way to the Peace and Settlement of these Nations* (March 4, 1659), E972(6).

[3] *E.g.,* William Prynne, *Ten Considerable Quæries Concerning Tithes* (June 27, 1659), E767(2); Immanuel Bourne, *A Defence and Justification of Ministers Maintenance by Tythes* (June 30, 1659), E1907(1); *A Caution against Sacriledge* (July 12, 1659), E989(18).

They rob God in *Tithes,* and God robs them of their trade and livelihood;
They grudge the Ministers a maintenance, and God grudgeth them even
bread for their families, so that they usually turn bankrupts, or are so
in debt, that they are ashamed to shew their faces.[4]

Prynne is of special interest among these pamphleteers as the "late
hot Quærist for tithes" whom Milton belabors in *The Likeliest
Means.*[5] Prynne's *Ten Considerable Quæries,* whose publication coin-
cided with Parliament's vote on June 27 to continue tithes, asked
some pertinent questions, such as whether nine-tenths of the present
petitioners against tithes were not "poor mecanical persons, of such
mean inconsiderable fortunes, estates, condition, (without any *Tithable
lands, livings, estates,)* as are no ways interessed nor concerned in the
payment of *Tithes";* and whether there were not a hundred men of
substance who wanted tithes retained for every one tithe payer who
petitioned against them.[6] But he also suggested absurdly that such
petitions were instigated by Jesuits and popish priests, working clan-
destinely through the sectarian congregations to undo true Protestant
ministers. Equally extravagantly, he asked whether the Rump, if it
abolished tithes, would not lay hands on the other nine-tenths of every
man's estate in order to pay the army and sustain its own power.[7]

Presbyterians were not alone in defending tithes. Thomas Boyer,
pastor at Rempstone, took the Congregational position that all true
churches are composed of visible and covenanted saints, but he de-
fended, on grounds of law, the right of ministers to take tithes even
from parishioners who were not church members. He distinguished at
length between conditions in the first-planted churches of apostolic
times and in the Reformed churches of the present age, and he con-
tended that for the latter's ministers Christ had not abrogated tithes
but confirmed them.[8]

A more moderate vindicator of tithes than one would expect from
his opening diatribe against toleration, Anabaptists, and Quakers was
Giles Firmin, who had sailed to New England in 1632, served the first
church in Boston as deacon, and returned home to become vicar of
Shalford in Essex in 1648.[9] He admitted that tithes rested on man's

[4] *The Dreadfull Danger of Sacrilege* (May 8, 1658), 669f21(3).
[5] Below, p. 294. Milton, however, mainly attacked Prynne's earlier and larger
vindication of tithes in *A Gospel Plea* (September 24, 1653), E713(12).
[6] Pp. 1–2.
[7] Pp. 1, 5–6.
[8] Thomas Boyer, *Epidiorthosis* (February, 1659), E1929(2), pp. 20–29. Boyer
was one of the ministers of the Nottinghamshire Association (Shaw, *English
Church,* II, 452).
[9] *DNB.*

law; God's law only enjoined that ministers should be adequately supported. His interpretation of the controverted texts did not conclude, like Milton's, that tithes had been positively abrogated along with the Levitical priesthood. The New Testament might not command tithes, but it did not condemn them. He suggested various devices whereby those whose consciences scrupled their payment might contribute the equivalent by other means, but he held that the state would do wrong if it enacted a general supersession of tithes. They were a revenue set apart by the law for the clergy's maintenance, and no one else could claim them as his own. The prices and rents of tithable land always took account of this burden on it; they would rise if it were abolished, and this would wrong landlords who had sold or leased land at the old rates.[10]

Firmin's views were not far from those expressed later in the year by John Owen, who may be taken as typifying the moderate Independents. He too held that to take away all public maintenance would be a contempt of God's care for His Church, and downright robbery. Tithes *per se* could be justified from the New Testament, but were not prescribed there; yet since they had been paid in Israel *before* the Law was delivered, and since they were customary among nations that lived only by the light of nature, might it not seem a contending with God's providence to abolish them? Nevertheless he went further than Firmin in conceding that an alternative form of maintenance would not necessarily be obnoxious, "but its convenience or inconvenience may be freely debated." [11]

Several pamphleteers offered positive proposals for such an alternative. The radical commonwealthsman who wrote *Englands Safety in the Laws Supremacy* [12] would have had all ministers paid directly out of the public treasury in proportion to the size of their flocks, so that "having no dependance upon the benevolence of the people" they would "be more free to acquaint them with their faults." *The Moderate Man's Proposall to the Parliament about Tithes* [13] advocated a rate on all land equivalent to its tithe dues in an average year, fixed by commissioners appointed by Chancery and collected by the overseers of the poor in each parish. More ambitiously, *A Few Proposals . . . for the Removing of Tythes* [14] proposed that all tithes should be

[10] Giles Firmin, *Tythes Vindicated from Anti-Christianisme and Oppression* (April 6, 1659), E974(4), pp. 15–27.

[11] John Owen, *Two Questions* (1659), pp. 7–8.

[12] June 30, 1659, E988(26), pp. 18–19.

[13] June 29, 1659, E988(23).

[14] August 29, 1659, E993(29).

put up for sale, giving owners of tithable land the option of buying them in. From the proceeds, and from the further sale of all glebe lands, parsonages, and deans' and chapters' estates that did not actually support preaching ministers, the state should purchase land sufficient to yield £80 a year to every rural minister and £100 to those in market towns. But such schemes can have had no appeal for Milton, who utterly opposed a state-maintained ministry on principle.

Turning to the outright abolitionists who shared Milton's voluntaryism, the petitioners who bombarded Parliament during June were apt to couple their requests concerning tithes with others equally radical for Parliamentary reform and the abolition of copyhold tenures.[15] This did not endear them to the Rump; nor did the large part played by Quakers in canvassing signatures to the monster petition which finally provoked its adverse vote on June 27. Three weeks after that, however, John Osborne published a comprehensive statement of the abolitionists' case in *An Indictment against Tythes*.[16] Though unoriginal, it usefully exemplifies the four main lines of argument—economic, historical, legal, and Scriptural—that were common to its kind. Osborne begins with the hardships that tithes impose on husbandmen and farmers; typically, he is concerned mainly with their burden on smaller tenants, whereas the retentionists were generally more sensitive to the rights of landlords. Then, after the usual plunge into the mists of Anglo-Saxon antiquity, he argues that tithes began in England as an idolatrous gift to popish priests for singing masses and later to Anglican clergymen for celebrating the Prayer Book rites; true preachers of the Gospel he regards as a different order of men, not covered by laws made for their superstitious forebears.[17] Nevertheless, he traverses the relevant statutes of Henry VIII and Edward VI, contending that they gave no right to sue for tithes except in ecclesiastical courts that are now abolished. By far his longest section, however—and this too is typical—wrestles with the vexed texts of Scripture, stressing all the apostolic precepts and precedents for a ministry living by voluntary offerings and drawing the sharpest

[15] *E.g., The Humble Representation and Desire of Divers Freeholders* [etc., of Bedfordshire] (June 16, 1659), 669f21(51). For the association of religious with political radicalism, see also *Lilburns Ghost* (June 22, 1659), E988(9), esp. pp. 2–3.

[16] July 18, 1659, E989(28). A John Osborne had been appointed to the living of West Woodhay in Berkshire by the Long Parliament in 1648 and had twice received augmentations; see Shaw, *English Church*, II, 350, 564, 583. *An Indictment* contains no clue as to whether its author was the same John Osborne.

[17] Osborne, *An Indictment*, p. 5.

contrast between the dispensations of the Law and the Gospel. Here, inevitably, he treads much common ground with Milton, though there is nothing to suggest that Milton read him.

Earlier, we found significant points of comparison between Milton's *Of Civil Power* and Henry Stubbe's *Essay in Defence of the Good Old Cause*.[18] Some no less interesting parallels and contrasts can be drawn between *The Likeliest Means* and another work by Stubbe, *A Light Shining out of Darknes*,[19] which in its first and shorter version preceded Milton's treatise by about two months. Stubbe too opposed tithes as they were then enforced, but his main concerns were larger, and very close to Milton's: to deprecate the perversion of a Gospel ministry into a sacerdotal caste, to condemn the whole conception of a church catholic, whether Roman, Anglican, or Presbyterian, and to vindicate the right to preach of any man whom the Spirit called, whether ordained or not.[20] He further anticipated Milton—though of course neither man was original here—by attacking the universities and contesting the assumption that preachers of the Gospel have any need of their formal, outworn, and still papistical learning.[21] He too hankered after primitive simplicity, and praised the example of the apostles who practised an honest handicraft during their ministry, though his rooms in Christ Church and his post in the Bodleian Library made his view of a life of rough toil and itinerant evangelizing as distant as Milton's.[22] Yet he differed from Milton in the power he would allow to the state in disposing of the churches' revenues and providing for their preachers. He argued, from the example of the early Christian churches, that tithes were justifiable so long as they were freely paid by the faithful, without compulsion by the magistrate, and devoted solely to the maintenance of ministers and the relief of the poor. He approved the practice of Geneva and Holland whereby ministers were paid stipends out of the public treasury, and he contended that the English Reformation had given the temporal sovereign plenary power to dispose of the church's wealth.[23] He did not contrast the Law and the Gospel as starkly as Milton did. Since, under the Levitical

[18] Above, pp. 55–57.

[19] First ed. (June 17, 1659), E987(2); 2nd ed., greatly expanded (November 8, 1659), E770(5).

[20] *A Light Shining out of Darknes*, 1st ed., pp. 1–14.

[21] *Ibid.*, pp. 14–22, 26–34; much expanded in 2nd ed., pp. 92–106, 139–50, 156–63.

[22] To do him justice, he was expelled from Oxford later in the year for his attacks on the universities, and subsequently practiced physic at Stratford-on-Avon; see *DNB*.

[23] Second ed., pp. 112–38.

dispensation, tithes had been paid into a common treasury and thence distributed to the priests according to their need, and since the early Christians had brought tithes and offerings to their bishop to share out similarly, he asked

> *Why is there such a clamour against the like management of* Tythes
> *now by the Parlament, since the inequality of the present distribution*
> *is manifest, and the* equity *of such dealing is justified by these examples*
> *from being the suggestion of* Politicians, *nor are there any new emer-*
> *gent difficulties, other then might be objected then?* [24]

It is significant that a writer whose concept of Christian liberty was otherwise as broad as Milton's own was prepared to admit the Christian magistrate into partnership in providing for the ministry of the Gospel.

2. *THE LIKELIEST MEANS TO REMOVE HIRELINGS*

A precious glimpse of Milton's attitude to public affairs in the spring of 1659 comes to us in a letter [1] that he received in reply to one of his own from his friend Moses Wall, a scholar and common-wealthsman known to Hartlib's circle. Wall allegedly wrote on May 26, 1659, and though this date presents some difficulties [2] it is probably close enough not to affect the light that he throws on Milton's dissatisfaction with Richard's Protectorate. Wall is frank with Milton:

> I was uncerten whether yor Relation to the Court, (though I think a
> Cõmonwealth was more friendly to you than a Court) had not clouded
> yor former Light, but yor last Book [3] resolved that Doubt. You com-
> plaine of the Non-progresency of the nation, and of its retrograde Motion
> of late, in Liberty and Spiritual Truths.

[24] Second ed., pp. 118–19. Somewhat inconsistently, Stubbe on p. 126 takes up "the defense of such in our times as would reduce the Ministry to a mainte-nance by voluntary contribution, and abolish Tythes." Was there some conflict here between his own views and those of his patron Vane?

[1] For its text and provenance see below, pp. 510–13, and French, *Life Records*, IV, 267–69.

[2] The letter is thus dated, but it seems scarcely credible that so radical a commonwealthsman as its author could inveigh at some length against the tyrannies of the Protectorate and the army without the slightest reference to the momentous change of government on May 7. He writes as though "the Court" was still in existence; he says "I think a Cõmonwealth *was* more friendly to you than a Court," without mentioning that the Commonwealth had been restored. The letter survives only in an eighteenth-century copy by Josiah Owen; can Owen have misread as May some abbreviation of March?

[3] Obviously *Of Civil Power*, of which Milton may have sent Wall a copy.

But what can poor people do, Wall asks, when those who gained their trust by professing zeal for spiritual and civil liberty lead them back to Egypt and hold them fast in chains? Wall's bitter reflections read as though prompted by similar ones from Milton. His main message, however, is to urge Milton to fulfil the promise he made in *Of Civil Power* and "give us that other member . . . Sc. that Hire doth greatly impede Truth and Liberty."

This Milton was shortly ready to do, though just when he composed *The Likeliest Means* is hard to establish. Thomason assigned it no more precise date than August, and it was advertised among books newly published in the issue of *Mercurius Politicus* for September 1 to 8. This has naturally led scholars to assume a publication date near the end of August, but it has not been previously noticed that parts of James Harrington's *Aphorisms Political*[4] almost certainly refer to Milton's treatise. Aphorism XXI asserts that "To hold that Hirelings, or an endowed Ministry, ought to be removed out of the Church, is inconsistent with a Commonwealth."[5] The verbal echoes of Milton's title are surely too strong to be coincidental. Thomason acquired *Aphorisms Political* on August 31, and although only two pages are devoted to refuting Milton, the time needed to write and print the tract suggests that Harrington had a copy of *The Likeliest Means* not much later than the middle of August.

There is some internal evidence, however, that Milton was already dictating it in June. The preface, for instance, conveys a distinct impression that the restoration of the Rump was still very recent. It speaks of "great expectation . . . whether ye will hearken to the just petition of many thousands best affected both to religion and to this your returne."[6] This sounds as though Parliament had yet to pronounce on the petition with fifteen thousand signatures, which in the event prompted the vote of June 27 to continue tithes. In the same sentence Milton hopes that his treatise will assist "the debate before you," and this too suggests a date soon after June 14, when the Rump referred tithes to a grand committee, but before June 27, after which as far as the Rump was concerned the debate was closed. Again, early in his text, he states that "the maintenance of church-ministers . . . is at present under publick debate."[7] He may of course have been putting the best face he could on the tremendous rebuff of the Rump's

---

[4] August 31, 1659, E995(8). For the sections apparently written against Milton, see Appendix, below, pp. 518–21.

[5] *Aphorisms Political*, p. 3.

[6] *The Likeliest Means*, below, p. 275.

[7] *Ibid.*, p. 278.

vote by assuming that it was a mere interim decision, and he was certainly still at work after it was passed. His snarl against "a late hot Quærist for tithes" was obviously uttered after Prynne had published *Ten Considerable Quæries Concerning Tithes,* which Thomason acquired precisely on June 27. And there is an early passage where he speaks of the practice whereby

> in commonwealths of most fame for government, civil laws were not establishd till they had been first for certain dayes publishd to the view of all men, that who so pleasd might speak freely his opinion therof, and give in his exceptions, ere the law could pass to a full establishment.[8]

Did he insert this after he had heard of the Rump's adverse determination? The evidence is not conclusive, but cumulatively it suggests that he began his work in or shortly after the middle of June, and finished it not later than the first day of August.

He addressed it "To the Parlament of the Commonwealth of England with the dominions therof"—exactly the same dedication as *Of Civil Power* had borne, though this was of course a very different Parliament. The prefatory address opens with an unqualified reaffirmation of allegiance to the Commonwealth's first rulers; Milton reminds them how he had vindicated them in his first *Defence,* but naturally buries in oblivion the strictures he had passed on them in his second one, in 1654. He hails the Rumpers now as England's deliverers from prelatical and regal tyranny, and as "the authors and best patrons of religious and civil libertie, that ever these Ilands brought forth." [9] Then, immediately following, come these astonishing words:

> The care and tuition of whose peace and safety, after a short but scandalous night of interruption, is now again by a new dawning of Gods miraculous providence among us, revolvd upon your shoulders.

Did this "short but scandalous night of interruption" include the whole of the Protectorate? Short, when it had lasted for six years out of little more than ten since the Commonwealth's inception? Could Milton apply such scalding words to the regime that he had eulogized in *A Second Defence*—whose rule moreover he had assisted and whose pay he had drawn throughout its existence? Masson thought not, and took the phrase as referring to the fortnight's interregnum between the dissolution of Richard's Parliament and the return of the Rump.[10]

[8] *Ibid.*
[9] *Ibid.,* p. 274.
[10] Masson, V, 606–07.

But later scholars, including Smart,[11] Wolfe,[12] Lewalski,[13] and Fixler [14] have all accepted it as a description of the whole six years since 1653.

William B. Hunter has recently argued for a third interpretation, which would apply Milton's condemnation only to the eight months of Richard's Protectorate.[15] Hunter postulates that Oliver had definitely designated Fleetwood as his successor, that Fleetwood knew of it, that Milton probably learnt it from Fleetwood, and that he was belatedly denouncing an act of usurpation. This is scarcely a tenable hypothesis. The evidence that Cromwell at one stage nominated Fleetwood is late and dubious, though not inherently implausible. If he did so, it was in a secret paper, and it is hard to believe that Fleetwood knew its contents. He was indeed one of the first to accept the nomination of Richard as valid. Nor does it appear that Milton was intimate with Fleetwood at this time, though he came to know him better after the Restoration.[16]

We are left to decide whether Milton was aspersing the whole span of the Protectorate or merely the army's recent act in breaking an elected Parliament. Don Wolfe presents the fullest and most cogent case for the former view; he cites Milton's salutation of the Rump in this same preface as not authors and assertors only but as "now recoverers of our liberty," and his statement in *A Letter to a Friend* that the army had formerly expelled them "without just autority." [17] Yet though Milton certainly identified himself by now with the republicans against the Protectorate, the present writer long boggled at the word "short" and doubted whether Milton could have brought himself to utter such a harsh indictment of the government that he had served so long and once praised so highly. His doubts, however, were mitigated on reading a pamphlet published in May, 1659, whose lengthy title rejoiced in "this Morning of Freedom, after a Short, but a Sharp Night of Tyranny and Oppression." [18] Its anonymous writer plainly referred here to the whole of the Protectorate and he called

[11] John S. Smart, *The Sonnets of Milton* (Glasgow, 1921), p. 92.

[12] Don M. Wolfe, *Milton in the Puritan Revolution* (New York: Humanities Press, 1963), pp. 289–90.

[13] Barbara Lewalski, "Milton: Political Beliefs and Polemical Methods, 1659–60," *PMLA*, LXXIV (1959), 192–93.

[14] *Milton and the Kingdoms of God*, pp. 189–99.

[15] William B. Hunter, Jr., "Milton and Richard Cromwell," *English Language Notes*, III (1966), 252–59.

[16] These objections to Hunter's interpretation are expanded and documented in my article on "Milton and Cromwell"; *cf.* above, p. 5, n. 3.

[17] Below, p. 324.

[18] *A Publick Plea, Opposed to a Private Proposal* (May 18, 1659), E983(18).

upon the Rump to disgrace Cromwell's memory publicly. Were his words read to Milton, and did they stick in his mind? It seems evident that Milton at least permitted his phrase to be read in the same sense, though one may still wonder with Wolfe "if he purposely left the passage capable of either interpretation." [19]

After this preface, the treatise opens with a symphonic link connecting it with its predecessor *Of Civil Power*, whose statement of the two chief banes of the church it repeats: "force on the one side restraining, and hire on the other side corrupting the teachers therof." [20] The second is Milton's present theme, and he counts it a much greater danger than the first. Hire is not in itself unlawful, in its proper sense of due reward; what makes it dangerous "is either the excess thereof, or the undue manner of giving and taking it." [21] The excess had begun with Constantine, and Milton quotes the legendary voice from heaven that had cried *"This day is poison pourd into the church"* when that emperor had endowed it with his supposed donation.[22] But the evil itself went back to Judas, the first hireling, and Simon Magus, the next, and grew until "hirelings like wolves came in by herds" in the time of the apostles.[23] Yet we have Christ's word that the laborer is worthy of his hire; the question is how to prevent its abuse. Milton proposes to answer under three heads: first, what recompense God has ordained for ministers of the church; next, by whom it should be given; and last, in what manner.

The first section is the longest, for it takes him through all the proof texts that the defenders and assailants of tithes had disputed for many a long year. He had denounced before "the ignoble Hucsterage of pidling *Tithes*," [24] but he had never rehearsed the whole case against them from Scripture, as here he does in the closest detail. The essence of his argument is that God ordained tithes for "the Levitical and ceremonial service of the tabernacle," but that He left the ministry of the Gospel, being totally distinct from the priesthood

[19] Wolfe, *Milton in the Puritan Revolution*, p. 289.

[20] *The Likeliest Means*, below p. 277.

[21] *Ibid.*, p. 279.

[22] *Ibid.* Moses Wall had quoted these words in his letter cited above, and Milton himself had invoked them twice before, in *An Apology* (*Complete Prose*, I, 946–47) and in *A Second Defence* (*ibid.*, IV, 651).

[23] *The Likeliest Means*, below, p. 280. Note the echo of "hireling wolves whose Gospell is their maw," in the sonnet to Cromwell of 1652.

[24] *Of Reformation* (*Complete Prose*, I, 613); see also the diatribe against "a hireling Clergy" in *Animadversions* (*Complete Prose*, I, 717–22), and the more specific references to tithes in *The Tenure* and *A Second Defence* (*Complete Prose*, III, 196, 241; IV, 650–51).

under the Law, to the free charity of the faithful. This is a simplifica-
tion of a long and complex exegesis, but there are places where Milton
breaks from the thickets of pentateuchal technicalities into the clear
light of his own deep conviction. Here is one:

> Yet grant that the people then paid tithes, there will not yet be the like
> reason to enjoin us: they being then under ceremonies, a meer laitie, we
> now under Christ, a royal priesthood.[25]

Christ's calling of all believers to be "coheirs, kings and priests with
him," he claims, "hath freed us by our union with himself, from all
compulsive tributes and taxes in his church." [26] To Milton, a clergy
that retained any of the pretensions of a priestly caste had always
been totally incompatible with a true reformation of religion. More
than seventeen years earlier, in *The Reason of Church-Government*,
he had argued for the participation of laymen in church government
and discipline,

> not now any more to be separated in the Church by vails and partitions
> as laicks and unclean, but admitted to wait upon the tabernacle as the
> rightfull Clergy of Christ, a chosen generation, a royal Priesthood to offer
> up spiritual sacrifice in that meet place to which God and the Congrega-
> tion shall call and assigne them.[27]

But in their jealousy of any lay encroachment on their clerical status
and functions, not only new presbyter but newer Independent had
proved to be but old priest writ large. Hence Milton's contempt in
1659 for those ministers who "for the verbal labor of a seventh dayes
preachment . . . would not take only at the willing hand of liberality
or gratitude, but require and exact as due the tenth, not of spoiles, but
of our whole estates and labors." [28]

"The Levites are ceasd, the gift returns to the giver." [29] The law of
Moses had been finally abrogated with the destruction of the Temple.
The divines of the reformed churches abroad have put ours to shame
by opposing their claim to tithes. The golden rule of the New Testa-
ment is "that they who preach the gospel, should live of the gospel," [30]
and Milton cites further texts to demonstrate that when Christ said
that the laborer was worthy of his hire, He was not enjoining tithes or
any other fixed maintenance, but offering only "a rule of common
equitie which proportions the hire as well to the abilitie of him who

[25] *The Likeliest Means,* below, p. 286.
[26] *Ibid.,* p. 286.
[27] *Complete Prose,* I, 838.
[28] *The Likeliest Means,* below, p. 285.
[29] *Ibid.,* p. 288.
[30] I Corinthians 9:14.

gives as to the labor of him who receives, and recommends him only
as worthy, not invests him with a legal right." [31] Tithes, Milton claims,
are not heard of in Christian history until the Council of Cologne in
356, by which time error had brought back priests, altars, and obla-
tions, and "had miserably Judaiz'd the church." [32] He lashes out at the
apologists, Prynne in particular, who appealed not only to dubious
councils but to the church fathers and canonists of a still darker age.
Likewise he brushes aside the alleged grants of Anglo-Saxon kings, as
being based on equally false authority. He tramples briskly through
the whole structure of legal argument based on statutes, crying shame
on Protestant divines who belie their pretended reformation by per-
suading Christian magistrates and Parliaments to impose a Judaical
ceremonial law. He is even more contemptuous of the claim that
property would be injured if tithes were abolished: "The last and
lowest sort of thir arguments, that men purchas'd not thir tithe with
thir land and such like pettifoggerie, I omitt; as refuted sufficiently
by others." [33] He says he will also omit the clergy's "violent and
irreligious exactions," but he nevertheless devotes some pages to their
extortions upon the poor—pages spattered with such expressions as
"covetousnes and rapine," "spiritual leprosie," "greedy dogs," "the
tricks and impostures of clergie men, contriv'd with all the art and
argument that thir bellies can invent or suggest." [34] Here is as harsh
a strain of anticlericalism as anywhere in his works, and it is directed
now not just against prelates or Presbyterians but against the whole
body of the beneficed clergy. It continues in his attack on the fees that
they exact for christenings, marriages, and burials, which he brands
as simony. Their taking of money for grave-plots and for preaching
funeral sermons is no better. As for marriage, it is "a civil ordinance,
a houshold contract . . . best, indeed, undertaken to religious
ends," [35] but no more requiring a minister's hallowing than any other
solemn undertaking in civil life. He praises the act of the Nominated
Parliament of 1653 which instituted civil marriage, and under which
his own second marriage had been performed by a justice of the
peace.[36]

Milton's next question is who should give ministers their main-
tenance. As usual, apostolic precept and practice provide the only

[31] *The Likeliest Means*, below, p. 290.
[32] *Ibid.*
[33] *Ibid.*, pp. 295–96.
[34] *Ibid.*, pp. 296–97.
[35] *Ibid.*, p. 299.
[36] Parker, *Milton*, p. 480.

authority that he will acknowledge, and from a brief citation of the
texts he concludes that preachers were recompensed only by those who
received their teaching. He denounces the "iniquitie and violence" that
force the maintenance of a parish minister upon men who have neither
chosen him nor received instruction from him. If they prefer to
follow another pastor, "to barr them thir choise, is to violate Christian
liberty." [37] But will this not result in many a poor village being unable
to maintain a minister? He answers that the translated Scriptures
make the "main matters of belief and salvation, plane and easie to
the poorest:"

> certainly it is not necessarie to the attainment of Christian knowledge
> that men should sit all thir life long at the feet of a pulpited divine;
> while he, a lollard indeed over his elbow-cushion, in almost the seaventh
> part of 40. or 50. years teaches them scarce half the principles of reli-
> gion; and his sheep oft-times sit the while to as little purpose of benifit-
> ing as the sheep in thir pues at *Smithfield*.[38]

The needs of poor countryfolk would be sufficiently met, Milton sug-
gests, if ministers would of their own accord follow the example of
Christ and His disciples and go preaching through the villages. If the
clergy will not trust to providence for their subsistence as the disciples
did, let the richer congregations that abound with teachers send some
of them out into the countryside and defray their necessary expenses.
Milton sketches a scheme whereby these intinerant preachers should
stay in a place for a year or two, dividing the inhabitants into several
congregations of moderate size and training the ablest men in each as
teaching elders. Such elders, holding their meetings in church or
chapel, house or barn, armed with the Scriptures in English, "with
plenty of notes," and with "som wholsom bodie of divinitie . . . with-
out schoole terms and metaphysical notions," [39] and occasionally
visited and confirmed by the minister who instructed them, would
(thought Milton) give more edification to their little flocks than a
meanly hired incumbent in many years of preaching. The whole plan
strikingly anticipates the strategy of the Wesleyan movement in the
next century.

Milton would not wholly exclude the civil magistrate from aiding
such an enterprise. He would allow him the custody of revenues that
had originally been bequeathed to superstitious uses, and to these the
churches might apply if they found the support of evangelizing
ministers quite beyond their means. But he also proposes a more in-

[37] *The Likeliest Means,* below, pp. 300–01.
[38] *Ibid.,* p. 302.
[39] *Ibid.,* p. 304.

teresting use for such funds: namely "to erect in greater number all over the land schooles and competent libraries to those schooles, where languages and arts may be taught free together, without the needles, unprofitable and inconvenient removing to another place." [40] These schools are to be very different from the academies that he had projected in *Of Education,* where "our noble and our gentle youth" were to study "that which fits a man to perform justly, skilfully and magnanimously all the offices both private and publike of peace and war." [41] What Milton now outlines are not academies for the sons of the governing class but schools primarily for ministers of religion. Boys who get their schooling free, he suggests, might be bound by a condition that "they should not gadd for preferment out of thir own countrey," but should stay and serve the community which raised them, "without soaring above the meannes wherin they were born." [42] Furthermore, the hours of teaching should be arranged so that they can learn and practice an honest trade at the same time, for Milton would have future ministers equipped, like the apostles, to earn their livings as craftsmen or physicians.

> But our ministers think scorn to use a trade, and count it the reproach of this age, that tradesmen preach the gospel. It were to be wishd they were all tradesmen; they would not then so many of them, for want of another trade, make a trade of thir preaching.[43]

The endowments and possessions of the church may justly be secularized and appropriated to the civil revenue, especially those offered by men of power as a bribe to God for their crimes. Only such funds as were first bestowed in genuine piety may be retained for the purposes above mentioned, and they must not be used by the civil magistrate to "take into his own power the stipendiarie maintenance of church-ministers or compell it by law." [44] Nor ought he "by his examinant committies to circumscribe" each church's free election of its ministers—a clear condemnation of the Triers.[45] The Christian church is not national; it consists of an ever-shifting number and variety of particular congregations, whose proper revenues consist only of their own members' free offerings.

By the time Milton comes to his third question, and considers in

[40] *Ibid.*, p. 305. For a valuable discussion of the educational proposals in *The Likeliest Means,* see Barbara K. Lewalski, "Milton on Learning and the Learned-Ministry Controversy," *HLQ*, XXIV (1961), 267–81.

[41] *Complete Prose,* II, 378–79, 406; *cf.* Sirluck's introduction, esp. pp. 193–94.

[42] *The Likeliest Means,* below, p. 305.

[43] *Ibid.*, p. 306.

[44] *Ibid.*, p. 307.

[45] *Ibid.; cf.* pp. 317–18 for another indictment of the Triers.

what manner God has ordained that ministers should be recompensed, he has largely answered it already. Ministers may take only what is freely given by such as willingly receive them. He commends the primitive church's example whereby offerings were made to the church and not to the pastor, who took only what he needed for bare subsistence and left the rest for distribution to the poor. To a typical country vicar, all this insistence on apostolic poverty must have come hard from one who enjoyed a virtual sinecure, worth far more than most rural livings, without ever having known what it was like to carry the Gospel to a stubborn and ignorant flock. Still harder was the scorn that Milton, who had been privileged to devote long years to scholarship without having to reckon how he would earn his bread, proceeded to pour on those who pleaded the sacrifices that their time at school and university had cost as justification for an assured income when they eventually obtained a benefice. He is at his worst in his comprehensive aspersion of the motives that sent them to the universities and of the use they have made of their opportunities. With more force, he declares that "it is a fond error, though too much beleevd among us, to think that the universitie makes a minister of the gospel;"[46] the one thing really necessary is that inner compulsion to preach that inspired the apostles. Rather than listen to theological disputations that "perplex and leaven pure doctrin with scholastical trash,"[47] the aspiring preacher may acquire what learning he needs in any private house, and his essential library need cost him not £600, as some claim, but £60. He goes further:

> To speak freely, it were much better, there were not one divine in the universitie; no schoole-divinitie known, the idle sophistrie of monks, the canker of religion; and that they who intended to be ministers, were traind up in the church only, by the scripture and in the original languages therof at schoole.[48]

Milton has nothing here to propose for the reform of the universities; he simply turns his back on them. The educational schemes that he propounds in *Of Education, The Likeliest Means,* and *The Readie & Easie Way,* different though they are one from another, have this in common: they all propose some kind of schooling, whether for the ministry or the governing class, that would save the young from having to leave their native counties for the unnourishing air of Oxford or Cambridge.[49]

[46] *Ibid.,* p. 315.
[47] *Ibid.,* p. 317.
[48] *Ibid.*
[49] For Milton's strictures on the universities in *Of Education* see *Complete Prose,* II, 370–76, where n. 34 refers to similar passages in his other works.

The final pages of peroration, amid rhetoric heightened still further against the "hireling crew," return to the innermost conviction that inspires Milton's animosity. *All* the faithful are now a holy and a royal priesthood. "The Gospel makes no difference from the magistrate himself to the meanest artificer, if God evidently favor him with spiritual gifts." [50] Christendom might soon be happy "if Christians would but know thir own dignitie, thir libertie, thir adoption, and let it not be wonderd if I say, thir spiritual priesthood, whereby they have all equally access to any ministerial function whenever calld by thir own abilities and the church." [51] Milton's fundamental objection is not so much to tithes or any other "hire" as to what they create and endorse: a clergy as a caste apart from other Christians, "a peculiar tribe of levites, a partie, a distinct order in the commonwealth." [52]

What distinguishes *The Likeliest Means* from the common run of anti-tithe tracts is that whereas they generally stressed the burden on the consciences and pockets of the payers, Milton cared much more about the corrupting effect on the recipients, and on the whole quality of Christian life. He called for a total return to the simplicity and inspiration of apostolic times, not greatly reckoning the profound contrast in social and political circumstances between the churches of the first century and those of the seventeenth. Relatively undeveloped though the historical sense still was in his time, there were contemporaries as diverse as Stubbe, Harrington, Baxter, and Boyer—not to mention the Anglicans in the tradition of Hooker—who realized that St. Paul's directions to the earliest churches were not all equally applicable in a settled and deeply hierarchical society whose ecclesiastical organization had been the growth of a thousand years. Milton's uncompromising biblicism, by contrast, was essentially anti-historical, and it ministered to his painful lack of charity towards hundreds if not thousands of honest clergymen who ruled their lives by their duties rather than their rewards. He was insensitive to certain aspects of the very Protestant tradition that he claimed to interpret: the positive value, for instance, that it attached to clerical marriage, the example that it expected ministers to give of a decent and godly family life, and the obligations of hospitality and personal charity that it laid upon them. Those who pleaded such reasons for a settled maintenance had a case.

See also the appendix on "Milton and the Universities" in James H. Hanford, *A Milton Handbook* (New York: Crofts, 1946), pp. 355-64.

[50] *The Likeliest Means*, below, p. 319.

[51] *Ibid.*, p. 320.

[52] *Ibid.*, p. 319.

To suggest objections to Milton's argument does not of course imply any commitment to his opponents' case for an established church and ministry. But if one takes as given, in the historical context, the common Puritan ideal of making England a regenerate nation, and asks how far Milton's means conduced to that end, one is bound to consider, as earlier when discussing *Of Civil Power*,[53] whether they would adequately have met the challenge of "the dark corners of the land." Most Puritans certainly believed that a publicly endowed ministry should have an essential, though not necessarily an exclusive, role in the enterprise. Granted that John Wesley and his disciples achieved wonders in the next century by methods not unlike those proposed in *The Likeliest Means*, Wesley would have been the last to claim that these could or should satisfy the entire religious needs of the country. It may be too that Milton, in his contempt for pensioners of the state, underrated the dangers of making all ministers the pensioners of their particular congregations. How long would they have remained untempted to mitigate the rigor of the Gospel's demands? It was mainly after the Restoration that Puritanism, driven out of the established church, came to terms with Mammon. Again, how many formal Christians would have lapsed if they could have worshipped only as members of congregations of covenanted saints? Would Milton have counted them well lost? And finally, did he reckon how many village communities, loving old ways and associating the new with sequestrators, assessment commissioners, and the like, might, if left to choose their pastor, pick one who would use the Prayer Book services and keep the feasts and holidays of the old church?

One thing at any rate is certain: Milton's tract made not the slightest impact upon the Parliament's policy. Its indiscriminate rancor against the clergy, its cavalier attitude to the sensitive questions of property that tithes raised, and its hostility to the universities, which many members were proud to have attended, were ill calculated to endear it to the House. Nor was it mentioned by name in the voluminous pamphlet literature of the next few months until *The Censure of the Rota* struck it a glancing blow in March, 1660.[54] Nevertheless, as has already been suggested, it is tolerably certain that Harrington was deliberately replying to it in certain of his *Aphorisms Political*. His arguments are too interesting to dismiss in a mere summary, and are therefore reproduced in an appendix.[55] Especially significant is his contention that the religious instinct is so much a part of man's

[53] See above, pp. 53–55.
[54] See below, p. 199.
[55] Below, pp. 518–21.

nature that a government that makes no provision for it defaults on its obligations. The majority of mankind expect a "publick leading" in religion, and a national religion requires an endowed clergy. To deny the majority the religious provision that they expect is to deprive them of liberty of conscience, and will drive them inevitably to deny religious liberty to the minority. Harrington's arguments were remarkable in 1659 for their philosophical detachment; they were as applicable to a Moslem state as to a Christian one. Three centuries later we can relish the paradox of this cool rationalist contending for an established church against so committed a Puritan as Milton.

CHAPTER VI

RIFTS IN THE RESTORED COMMONWEALTH

June–October, 1659

URING those weeks of early summer in which he worked on his tract against hirelings, Milton evidently had no inkling that the very survival of the republic was at stake. His preface to *The Likeliest Means* breathed optimism; indeed he let slip a faintly disparaging remark about those who bombarded the Parliament with new models of a commonwealth. Constitutional settlement could and should wait, he implied, until religion was rightly ordered.[1] As far as he could see, power was back in the hands of the men who had sustained the Commonwealth against all its enemies during the first four critical years of its existence. Its arms had never ceased to bring victory; why should he fear for it now? His own involvement in affairs of state had been tenuous for some time, and now it dwindled to a close. He wrote two State Letters for the new Council of State on May 15, and with the doubtful exception of another on June 30 they were his last.[2] Now that the "short but scandalous night of interruption" was over and authority restored to "the authors and best patrons of religious and civil libertie, that ever these Ilands brought forth,"[3] he could retire to more congenial tasks than politics.

But the situation was more precarious than he realized. English society remained strongly hierarchical, and government still depended greatly on the men of property who were the natural rulers of the counties and the major towns. Each change of regime from the first Civil War to the Protectorate had brought a narrowing of support from the men of broad acres who thought they had a prescriptive right to participate in the rule of their county communities. Oliver's last years had witnessed a slight reversal of this trend, especially after he dropped the major-generals. The country gentry were learning to bury old quarrels and reknit still older ties of neighborhood. A royalist past was no longer quite the bar it had been to a share in political

[1] *The Likeliest Means,* below, p. 275.
[2] French, *Life Records,* IV, 264–65, 272.
[3] *The Likeliest Means,* below, p. 274.

life; Lord Broghil, Viscount Fauconberg, and Sir Charles Wolseley, for example, were harbingers of a new generation that was coming to terms with the new order and quietly smoothing out its contrasts with the old. When death removed the arch-regicide in 1658, this tendency accelerated, for the squirearchy could recognize Richard Cromwell as one of themselves.

To the broad mass of the gentry the return of the Rump was most unwelcome. Richard's Parliament, which represented them better than any other legislature since 1648, had been brought to a violent end by the hated swordsmen. If the Good Old Cause in whose name the act was done meant anything, it meant the rejection of the whole conservative trend of the last few years. Worse still, the Rump soon proceeded to purge the county lists of justices of the peace, commissioners for the militia, commissioners for the monthly assessment, and other local bodies, weeding out many Cromwellian moderates, installing or reinstating more radical commonwealthsmen, and generally lowering the social level of the county administrators a stage further. The Rump had been little mourned when Cromwell had sent it packing in 1653, and it was no more popular when it came back six years later. Harrington testified in July 1659 "that there is a general dis-affection, nay hatred, thorowout the Counties, unto the Government; and that more now, then in the time of the late Usurper."[4] The French ambassador and the Venetian resident bore him out.[5] There were miserably few addresses of congratulation to the Rump compared with the great sheaf that had greeted Richard's accession, and those few were said to have been mostly concocted at Westminster.[6] Ominously, the city of London could not be stirred to produce one, despite the efforts of the lord mayor.[7]

The Rump had to reckon with opposition from both the left and right. During May and June quite a crop of pamphlets by sectaries or commonwealthsmen warned it that it was on trial and must clear itself of the old suspicion of perpetuating its power for selfish ends. At

[4] James Harrington, *A Discourse, Shewing that the Spirit of Parliaments,* . . . (July 28, 1659), E993(9), p. 5.

[5] Guizot, I, 386, 431, 437; *CSP Ven.,* 1659–61, pp. 37–38, 47–48, 50–52.

[6] *Nicholas Papers,* IV, 152.

[7] *Clarendon Calendar,* IV, 206. The London addresses referred to in Guizot, I, 151 n. 1 were from groups of private citizens, not from the city government: see *Commons Journals,* VII, 647, 649–50. When the city corporation did eventually address the Rump on June 2 (*ibid.,* p. 671), it was not so much to pledge allegiance as to press for a guarantee of the city's liberties and for relief from over-taxation: see Reginald R. Sharpe, *London and the Kingdom* (3 vols., London, 1894–95), II, 353.

the other end of the political spectrum the royalist activists were
planning another rising and making greater efforts than ever before
to enlist the Presbyterian gentry on their side. The royalists would
fail, and the radicals would rally to the Commonwealth's support—for
a time. But if the Commonwealth were to have any future it would
have to reassure the uncommitted country gentry, and the men of
substance in the town corporations, that it had their interests at heart
—and that could not be done without promising them reasonably
representative Parliaments at reasonably regular intervals. The Rump's
task was harder because the army had borne it back to power. The
gentry hated the swordsmen, but the Rump could not afford any
grand antimilitary gestures. To quarrel with the army, before the
constitution was settled and measures taken to woo the political
nation, would be suicide. Yet that is just what the Rump proceeded
to do.

1. THE RUMP AND THE ARMY

May–June, 1659

The Rump was not long back in the Parliament House before it
began to show who was master in the new state. It had avoided mak-
ing any positive pledges to the army leaders before its restoration, but
it was soon faced with their version of "the Fundamentals of our Good
Old Cause" in the Humble Petition and Address that Lambert pre-
sented on their behalf on May 13.[1] It responded by acceding to the
non-controversial requests in this document and shelving most of the
contentious ones. These last included a very large financial provision
for Richard, his mother, and his heirs, in recognition of Oliver's ser-
vices to the nation; confirmation of the army's acceptance of Fleet-
wood as commander-in-chief; and the vesting of legislative authority
jointly in a Parliament and a select Senate, co-ordinate in power
with the people's representatives.

Richard was the most easily disposed of, for he soon signed a decla-
ration that he would live peaceably under the new government as a
private citizen. Instead of the £20,000 a year that the officers asked
for him, the Rump voted him a mere £2,000 down and then forgot
about him. He was soon in acute trouble with his creditors. The
Senate was a harder matter to shrug off, but the Rump avoided any
positive pronouncement on it, and the grievance festered among the

[1] See above, pp. 71–72.

Wallingford House party until the crisis of the autumn brought it into the open again. As for Fleetwood, the House could hardly challenge the army's demand directly, but it confirmed his command only for the duration of the current session, and then proceeded to whittle down his authority as far as it dared. It entrusted the selection and promotion of officers not to the commander-in-chief but to a Committee of Nominations, in which Fleetwood was partnered by the politicians Haslerig, Vane, and Ludlow as well as the soldiers Lambert, Desborough, and Berry. Even this Committee's recommendations were subject to the approval of Parliament in every case. To rub it in further, the House ordered on June 6 that every single officer who could attend must come and receive a new commission from the hands of the Speaker.[2] Vane, Ludlow, and Salwey opposed this tactless flaunting of the army's new subordination, but Haslerig, Algernon Sidney, and Henry Neville drove it through. The Council of Officers was deeply resentful; "Col. Desborough openly said, that he accounted the commission he had already to be as good as any the Parliament could give, and that he would not take another."[3] But next day Haslerig persuaded Colonel Hacker to lead all his officers to the House for their commissions, and after that the grandees and the rest had to follow. In the ensuing weeks the Rump subjected every regimental list to close scrutiny, and the large purge of the Cromwellian party that it carried out goes far to explain the army's subsequent unrest.

Meanwhile the grandees were being made very conscious of their diminished role in national politics. They were swamped on the new Council of State, which consisted of twenty-one M.P.'s and ten non-members, all elected by and responsible to the House itself. Fleetwood, Sydenham, Lambert, Desborough, and Berry gained places on it, but the preponderance of Rumper politicians was overwhelming. Legislature and executive were virtually one—an old grievance that the Protectorate had taken pride in rectifying.[4]

Further friction arose over an Act of Indemnity, which the army had requested on May 13 in order to protect all who had served the Protectorate from legal proceedings against anything they had done in the course of duty during the past six years. It was not perhaps so much the act itself that caused disquiet as the length of time—over seven weeks—that it took to pass, and the hostile proposals that were

---

[2] *Commons Journals*, VII, 649–51, 672–73; *Acts and Ordinances of the Interregnum, 1642–1660*, ed. C. H. Firth and R. S. Rait (3 vols., London, 1911), II, 1283–84.

[3] Ludlow, *Memoirs*, II, 90.

[4] See *A True State of the Case of the Commonwealth* (February 8, 1654), E728(5), pp. 8–11, 51–52.

made in the course of debate. One was that all who had accepted public office under the Protectorate should be made to refund their salaries. Nevertheless, although such wild amendments were defeated, the act itself seemed to some insufficient. Lambert complained angrily to Ludlow and Haslerig that "it left them still at mercy." "You are only at the mercy of the Parliament," Haslerig replied, "who are your good friends." "I know not why they should not be at our mercy as well as we at theirs," Lambert retorted.[5]

The remodelling of the militia gave yet more ground for suspicion. It was only politic for the Rump to remove its known enemies from the militia commissioners in the counties and cities, but to require that Parliament itself should approve each local militia officer by name and that the Speaker should sign every single commission was a foolish over-assertion of central authority. To the county communities, with memories of the major-generals still raw, such purges carried the whiff of a one-party state. The army for its part suspected a design to raise a rival force, perhaps in preparation for a general disbandment of the regular regiments. Its discontent bred rumors during July that it was about to dissolve the Parliament again—some said to restore the Protectorate.[6] Such fears reached the highest places. Sir Archibald Johnston of Wariston, a Scottish laird in whom vanity and ambition jostled with a cringing kind of Presbyterian piety, had been glad to accept nomination to the Council of State and flattered at being invited to preside over it. But on July 6 he confided this to his diary:

> I was troubled to find such jealous and hott words between Fleetwood and S[ir] H. Vayne, and I perceive jealousyes rooting both in the members of the House and Airmye, which may readily break out agayn unto flammes if God prevent not.

Five days later he confessed

> Their is a strange contempt and haytred throw the nation of this present Parliament, and their counsels and ways hes been very infortunated and deserted-lyk.[7]

Yet the shadow of the common enemy kept the army and the Rump from quarreling openly. Both knew in July that the plans for a new rising on the king's behalf were approaching the point of action. The

---

[5] Ludlow, *Memoirs*, II, 100; Davies, *Restoration*, pp. 112–14.

[6] Guizot, I, 432, 434–35, 437; *Clarendon State Papers*, III, 508–09, 518–19; *Clarendon Calendar*, IV, 262–64, 286; *Nicholas Papers*, IV, 167–69; *CSP Ven.*, 1659–61, pp. 44–46. *Cf. Truth Seeks No Corners* (July 14, 1659), E989(21).

[7] Wariston, *Diary*, III, 123–24.

Commonwealth would have to set its own house in order if it was to survive.

2. THE SEARCH FOR A SETTLEMENT

Naturally the Rump did not let the summer of 1659 go by without debating how the constitution should be set on a more permanent footing. As a pledge that it did not mean to perpetuate its own authority it voted on June 6 that it would not continue sitting beyond May 7, 1660,[1] and it spent many days in Grand Committee discussing schemes for a future settlement. Many a pamphleteer contributed to the great debate. The dilemma for all republicans, however, was to reconcile their principle that lawful authority must derive from the people's consent with the fact that a genuine appeal to the political nation would probably send most of them packing and reveal how slender a hold the very idea of a commonwealth had on the people's affections. That was the central problem with which Milton was to wrestle in his last political tracts, and though these lay yet some way in the future, the summer's dialogue in Parliament and press forms an essential background to the development of his own ideas.

In the House itself,[2] many republicans were content with the simple old solution of a sovereign single-chamber legislature, elected under suitable qualifications at stated intervals and for a stated duration, and committing executive authority to a Council of State on roughly the present model. The Council would govern in the intervals between Parliaments and render an account to the new House before laying down its authority. Haslerig, however, evidently sensed how insecure the good old cause would be if it were wholly entrusted to a new Parliament every few years. He was toying with the idea, doubtless influenced by Harrington, of a Parliament continuously in being but with one-third of both the House and the Council of State retiring each year. As a further safeguard the annual elections to the vacant seats in Parliament should be indirect, with each parish sending one in ten of its primary voters to a county electoral assembly.[3] The army officers' solution, backed probably by Vane and his supporters, was of course a perpetual select Senate co-ordinate in power with the people's representatives. But this was anathema to most of the Rumpers, both

[1] *Commons Journals*, VII, 673.

[2] Much of what follows is based on Ludlow, *Memoirs*, II, 98–99. No diary of the Rump's debates in 1659 is known to survive.

[3] This seems to be the sense of Johnston of Wariston's slightly confused account of a conversation with Haslerig recorded in his *Diary*, III, 125.

in principle as an encroachment on the sacred rights of the sovereign people and in probable practice as a device for prepetuating the political influence of the chief army officers. A variant of the Senate scheme which commended itself to Ludlow was a proposal "that there might be joined to the popular assembly, a select number of men in the nature of the Lacedemonian Ephori, who should have a negative in things, wherein the essentials of the government should be concerned, such as the exclusion of a single person, touching liberty of conscience, alteration of the constitution, and other things of the last importance to the state." [4] Ludlow was to return to this notion in his proposal for Conservators of Liberty in the following December.[5]

Another much canvassed model of a commonwealth was that which James Harrington had put before the world three years earlier in his *Oceana*. Henry Neville and a few others urged it in the House, and a regular campaign of Harringtonian pamphlets pressed it on the public at large. Harrington's basic idea was that the form of government is determined by the balance of property in a state, and that since early Tudor times the distribution of landed wealth in England had become so wide as to support no government but a commonwealth. All that was needed to construct a perpetually healthy state was the erection of the right "superstructures" or political institutions upon these economic foundations. These must begin with an agrarian law, to prevent the concentration of landed property in too few hands. But the constitution of the sovereign legislature was crucially important, for Harrington held that government by a single assembly is inevitably an oligarchy, and a prey to faction. "A *Common-wealth* consisting of a party," he contended, "will be in perpetuall labour of her own destruction." [6] So he advocated a legislature consisting of two elected assemblies: a Senate of three hundred, empowered only to debate and propose laws, and a popular assembly of about a thousand whose sole function was to ballot in silence for or against the Senate's proposals. Both the Senate and the popular assembly were to be subject to a system of rotation, one third of their number retiring each year without the possibility of immediate re-election. Harrington distrusted professional politicians, and still more professional soldiers; he would have the whole adult male population organized and trained as a militia, with the exception of servants, whom he considered unfitted by their dependence either for military service or for the exercise of political rights. He was no egalitarian. His

[4] Ludlow, *Memoirs*, II, 99.
[5] See below, pp. 148–49.
[6] *Oceana* (1656), ed. S. B. Liljegren (Lund and Heidelberg, 1924), p. 55.

Senate, his magistrates and three-sevenths of his popular assembly were to be drawn from men worth more than £100 a year, and the mode of election that he proposed was elaborately indirect. "There is something first in the making of a *Common-wealth,*" he wrote, "then in the governing of her, and last of all in the leading of her Armies; which . . . seems to be peculiar unto the Genius of a Gentleman." [7]

Earlier in 1659 he had published a shorter, simpler exposition [8] of his ideal commonwealth in which he pruned the epigrammatic exuberance, the exotic nomenclatures, and the fantastic elaboration of detail and ceremonial that had perhaps hindered *Oceana* from being taken as seriously as he intended. But with the fall of the Protectorate he thought he saw a real chance to get his ideas implemented, and from then on he wrote with a directness, a concision, and a note of passion that were new. Against all forms of oligarchy, whether in a single-chamber Parliament, a select Senate, or a rule of the Saints, he waged war. He himself published five pamphlets between May and August, and his supporters brought the number up to a dozen.[9] The campaign in press and Parliament was furthered by a debating club in Bow Street that foreshadowed the more famous Rota Club of later months.[10] Harrington was, as it were, moving out of his study into the

[7] *Ibid.,* pp. 34–35.

[8] In *The Art of Lawgiving,* which is not in the Thomason collection but is dated "Feb. 20. 1659" on the final page. I do not know why Charles Blitzer in *An Immortal Commonwealth* (Yale University Press, 1960), p. 52, suggests a publication date as late as June, 1659; on internal evidence March seems likelier. Harrington had already defended his proposals in *Oceana* at length in *The Prerogative of Popular Government* (1657).

[9] Harrington's own tracts were: *Pour Enclouer le Canon* (May 2, 1659), E980(6); *A Discourse upon This Saying* (May 16, 1659), E983(12); *A Discourse, Shewing that the Spirit of Parliaments is not to be Trusted for a Settlement* (July 28, 1659), E993(9); *Politicaster,* E2112(2), dated August 1659 by Thomason, but March 20, 1656, at the end of the Epistle to the Reader, where the year is an obvious misprint; *Aphorisms Political* (August 31, 1659), E995(8). Directly associated with Harrington (and printed by Toland with his works) were: *A Proposition in Order to the Proposing of a Commonwealth or Democracie* (June 14, 1659), 669f21(49); *A Petition of Divers Well-affected Persons* (July 6, 1659), E989(11) said to have been promoted if not written by Wildman (see Maurice Ashley, *John Wildman,* pp. 141–42). Also part of the Harringtonian campaign were: *The Armies Dutie* (May 2, 1659), E980(12), signed by six pairs of initials, including Neville's and Wildman's and probably those of Henry Marten and John Jones; *A Common-Wealth or Nothing* (June 14, 1659), E986(17); *A Commonwealth, and Commonwealths-men, asserted and vindicated* (June 28, 1659), E988(19); *A Model of a Democraticall Government* (August 31, 1659), E995(9).

[10] For the Bow Street club see Ashley, *John Wildman,* p. 142; for the Rota Club see below, pp. 129–30. Since this introduction was written, John G. A. Pocock's introduction to his edition of *The Political Works of James Harrington*

marketplace and contending with the demagogues and the preachers on their own ground. The baroque flourishes of *Oceana*'s prose were gone, but though his new rhetoric was in a different vein from Milton's it could rise to a pitch of eloquence and passion not unworthy of the comparison:

> We hope ye are Saints: but if you be men, look with all your might, with all your prudence, above all, with fervent imploration of GOD's gracious Assistance (who is visibly crowning you) unto the well-ordering of your Commonwealth. In the manner consists the main matter. Detest the base itch of the narrow Oligarchy. If your Commonwealth be rightly instituted, seven years will not pass, ere your clusters of Parties, Civil and Religious, vanish, not through any force, as when cold weather kills flies; but by the rising of greater Light, as when the Sun puts out Candles. These in the reason of the thing are demonstrable, but suit better with the spirit of the present times, by way of Prophesie. *England* shall raise her Head to ancient Glory, the Heavens shall be of the old Metal, the Earth no longer Lead, nor shall the sounding Air eternally renounce the Trumpet of Fame.[11]

Alas for Harrington's optimism! Rumpers and army officers alike were afflicted with "the base itch of the narrow Oligarchy," and few shared his sublime confidence that "good orders" would of themselves make good men. Yet there is no denying his intellectual influence. No serious writer on politics in the later 'fifties dared ignore his propositions, which were far more discussed than those of Hobbes. Men as diverse as Vane and Baxter, Stubbe and Prynne, Matthew Wren the royalist and John Rogers the Fifth Monarchist, all joined issue with him; and Milton, as we shall see, was to be very much aware of him in *The Readie & Easie Way*.

Closer to Milton in thought than Harrington, and (unlike either of them) deeply involved in the Commonwealth's daily political affairs, was Sir Henry Vane. Yet such was the fascination of *Oceana*'s model of government that when Vane set down his own thoughts on a settlement he did so in the form of a letter to Harrington. He published this short tract anonymously, probably in May, and he called it *A Needful Corrective or Ballance in Popular Government*.[12] He agreed with Harrington in seeking a government of laws and not of men, and granted that it should derive from "the right of consent and free gift by the common vote of the whole Body."[13] He was drawn to the

---

(Cambridge, 1977) has become the standard work on all Harrington's writings and activities.

[11] *A Discourse upon This Saying*, pp. 13–14.

[12] BOD C.13.6 (16) Linc.; undated, and not in Thomason. I have set forth the evidence as to date and authorship in *Cambridge Historical Journal*, XIII, 154.

[13] *A Needful Corrective*, pp. 3–4.

notion of a Senate proposing laws and a broadly representative assembly assenting to them, but he could not believe that if both bodies were chosen without considering the commitment of electors and elected to the essentials of a Christian commonwealth they would worthily fulfil the main ends of government. For Vane, very much as for Milton in the political tracts still to come, the central problem remained

> to shew how the depraved, corrupted, and self-interested will of man, in the great Body, which we call the People, being once left to its own free motion, shall be prevailed with to espouse their true publick interest, and closely adhere to it, under the many tryals and discouragements they must be sure to meet with, before they obtain what they pursue.[14]

The will of man itself needed a balance, "the ballancing and ruling motion of Gods Spirit to keep him stedfast." [15] In the fullness of time, so Vane trusted, that spirit would be poured out upon all flesh, and then "the publick sentence and judgement of such a restored People and holy Nation, in their Assemblies of Judicature, may not so much be the judgement of Man, as of the Lord himself, their King and Law-giver." [16] But this ultimate dispensation was "very remote, as to the redress of the evil now in question," [17] and meanwhile ordinary human prudence must be employed to secure the choice of men fit for their trust.

Vane therefore proposed that full political rights should be restricted for a season to

> either such as are free born, in respect of their holy and righteous principles, flowing from the birth of the Spirit of God in them, (restoring man in measure and degree, as at the first by Creation, unto the right of Rule and Dominion) or else who, by their tryed good affection and faithfulness to common right and publick freedome, have deserved to be trusted with the keeping or bearing their own Armes in the publick defence.[18]

Only these select citizens were to elect the Ruling Senate or Body of Elders, whose authority was evidently to be permanent. Here we see a compromise very like Milton's own between the ideal of an aristocracy of grace and the practical necessity of keeping the ultimate power of the Commonwealth in the hands of men with an interest in its preservation. Vane's Senate was to wield supreme executive au-

[14] *Ibid.*, p. 6.
[15] *Ibid.*
[16] *Ibid.*, p. 11.
[17] *Ibid.*, p. 7.
[18] *Ibid.*, p. 8.

thority and to have the power of framing and proposing laws. Its legislative rights were however to be qualified "by the help of a second order of men, ordained and constituted by the Peoples suffrage; who, in the capacity of their Deputies and Representative Body, are from time to time to make up one general Assembly with the Senate, . . . and there to give the consent of the People to all Acts and Decrees that are Legislative and binding to the Common-wealth." [19] This Ruling Senate was a direct development of the "standing council" that Vane had proposed in *A Healing Question* in 1656. The difference between his scheme and Milton's in *The Readie & Easie Way* was that Vane thought popular assent could best be given in a single national assembly, whereas Milton preferred a multiplicity of county assemblies; but it was not a difference of principle. Did Vane, one wonders, send Milton a copy of his new tract?

Vane was now parting company with Haslerig and the majority of the Rumpers, who disliked any form of Senate. Shortly after the middle of June, addressing the Grand Committee on the constitution, he declared that the people must not be trusted with authority over the state lest they abuse it to their own ruin. Charge over them should be entrusted to a small body of choice and godly spirits—"but a few, a very few." [20] Vane was losing ground in the House. By the latter part of July he was reckoned to command no more than sixteen or seventeen votes.[21]

Outside Parliament, some of the smaller fry of pamphleteers kept up the radical notes that had been sounded during the agitation of the spring months. Some still tried to hoist anew the colors of the Leveller movement, others sought to revive Fifth Monarchist enthusiasms. "We are your Principals, and you our Agents," one H.N. reminded the Rump, and he called on all true noble spirits to meet weekly at Lilburne's tomb.[22] *Lilburns Ghost* exhorted the people to arise and show both army and Parliament that *their* will was the source of all just power.[23] Samuel Duncon called for a settlement based on a new Agreement of the People, subscribed by all true citizens.[24] Demands

[19] *Ibid.*, p. 5.

[20] *Clarendon State Papers*, III, 505–06. *Cf.* Guizot, I, 426–27; *Nicholas Papers*, IV, 161; Wariston, *Diary*, III, 120–21.

[21] Thurloe, VII, 704; *Nicholas Papers*, IV, 165; *Clarendon State Papers*, III, 511, 529; *Clarendon Calendar*, IV, 250.

[22] H.N., *An Observation and Comparison between the Idolatrous Israelites, and Judges of England* (May 25, 1659), E983(29), pp. 5–6, 9.

[23] *Lilburns Ghost*, p. 5.

[24] Samuel Duncon, *Several Proposals Offered to . . . the Keepers of the Liberties* (July 6, 1659), E989(9), p. 3.

for unqualified manhood suffrage were scarcely heard now, but the anonymous *Speculum Libertatis Angliae Re Restitutae* would have disfranchised only the dissolute and those openly disaffected to the Commonwealth, and hinted at a mulcting of the rich to abolish beggary.[25]

From the Fifth Monarchist front Christopher Feake proclaimed "the Name and Interest of the Approaching King of Saints" and called the "faithful remnant" to stand ready to unite in shaking the foundations of the kingdom of the Beast, destroying the Great Whore, and other apocalyptic exertions.[26] John Canne told the Rumpers that the essence of the Good Old Cause was *"NO KING BUT JESUS"* and that a righteous God had let them be broken in 1653 in order to purge out their dross and tin.[27] Peter Chamberlen revived the project, frustrated six years before, of a new Parliament elected solely by the gathered churches.[28] Another scribe denounced the restoration of the Rump as "a further fruit of backsliding" and "another invention to withstand the true heir the Lord Jesus." [29]

But these sorts of voices, useful though they may have been in swelling the bedlam chorus against the Protectorate earlier in the year, went quite unheeded by the Rump now it was back in the saddle. The Leveller movement had lost its coherence years ago; the Fifth Monarchists were blowing on dying embers. If these rallying cries from the past had any effect, it was probably to increase the nostalgia of moderate, conservative men for a government with the will and power to silence them once and for all.

3. THE AUGUST RISINGS AND THEIR AFTERMATH

August–September, 1659

The long-planned risings on the king's behalf were launched on August 1. Here we need not delve into the depressing story of their failure:[1] the divided leadership, the treachery of a few, the careless-

---

[25] E989(19), (July 13, 1659), pp. 6–7.

[26] Christopher Feake, *A Beam of Light,* preface and pp. 58–59.

[27] John Canne, *A Seasonable Word to the Parliament-Men,* p. 5.

[28] [Peter Chamberlen], *The Declaration and Proclamation of the Army of God,* 2nd ed. (June 9, 1659), E985(26), p. 5.

[29] *The Fifth Monarchy, or Kingdom of Christ, in Opposition to the Beast's, Asserted* (August 23, 1659), E993(31), pp. 48–50.

[1] The best accounts are in Underdown, *Royalist Conspiracy in England,* pp. 234–85; Davies, *Restoration,* ch. VIII; J. R. Jones, "Booth's Rising in 1659,"

ness of many, the lukewarmness of most of the cavalier squirearchy, the still prevalent distrust between royalists and Presbyterians, and the final rash decision to go ahead after too many indications that the enterprise was doomed in advance. The design was for risings to begin simultaneously in many widely separated parts of England, but good intelligence by the government nipped nearly all these plans in the bud. When August 1 dawned after a dismally wet and stormy night, most of the appointed places of rendezvous either slept quiet under the grey clouds or witnessed an undignified *sauve qui peut*. There was only one exception, in a region not greatly reckoned on by the leaders of conspiracy in the south. From Cheshire, south Lancashire, and the adjacent parts of north Wales, Sir George Booth and his friends got about four thousand men under arms and led them in revolt for nearly three hectic weeks. But unsupported as they were their plight was desperate, and when Lambert caught up with them near Northwich on August 19 they melted in flight at the first clash.

The interest of the episode lies in what it can tell us about the state of political opinion in the country just before Milton turned his mind again to the Commonwealth's great problems, and also in the kind of appeals to the nation's discontents that the leaders of the insurrection thought worth exploiting. One is struck first by the contrast between the feeble response to the August risings and the surge of enthusiasm for the monarchy only six months later. The rebels did not even dare at first to declare their real purpose. Most of their leaders were Presbyterians who had once fought for Parliament, and the Presbyterian ministers of Lancashire called their flocks to arms in fiery sermons—not in support of the king but against the Quakers and Anabaptists.[2] This was not the only region in which the bogy of a Quaker or Fifth Monarchist rising was made a pretext for gathering arms—proof of how unwise the Rump would have been to bow to sectarian pressures or endorse Milton's attack on the established clergy.

Three manifestoes were printed in support of the rising, and none mentioned the king. The one most likely to be Booth's own accused the Rump of relying on social upstarts to govern the county communities. Through crippling taxes, and still more through the new militia, this government was "subjecting us under the meanest and fanatick spirits of the Nation, under pretence of protection." Its

---

Bulletin of the John Rylands Library, XXXIX (1956–57), 416–43; R. N. Dore, "The Cheshire Rising of 1659," *Transactions of the Lancashire and Cheshire Antiquarian Society*, LXIX (1959), 43–69.

[2] Underdown, *Royalist Conspiracy in England*, pp. 256–57; Dore, pp. 62–63.

power rested on the same army that had violated Parliament in 1648 and 1653. "And what will be the issue of all this? A mean and schismaticall party must depresse the Nobility, and understanding Commons."[3] What then did the insurgents demand? Either a new Parliament freely elected or the restoration of the old one with both Houses composed as they were in 1648, before Pride's Purge. This call for "a full and free Parliament" would become the rallying cry of all monarchists in the coming winter, but it needed the growing anarchy of the intervening months to bring it massive popular support.

In clean contrast with this appeal to the conservative nobility and gentry, another broadsheet,[4] issued in the name of the Cheshire insurgents but probably concocted in London, professed friendship towards the "Gathered Seperate Churches" and condemned all coercive power in matters of religion. It called for the annual election of all officers and magistrates, drastic reform of the law, abolition of the excise, and restitution of the enclosed commons to the poor—a program as inconsistent with the rising's real objectives as can be imagined. The gathered churches of London were not deceived. They promptly offered to raise three volunteer regiments to defend the Commonwealth, and the government gratefully accepted.[5] These attempts by the organizers of conspiracy to be all things to all men merely alienated many Presbyterians by their "lying and deceit," and especially by their promises of toleration,[6] while eminent royalists "decried ye undertaking as totally presbiterian"[7] and sneered at this "Bellum Presbiterale".[8] Yet in the coming months cavaliers and Presbyterians would learn from the disaster to co-operate more fruitfully, whereas the army and the Rump would drift ever further apart.

Their divisions reopened as soon as Lambert's too easy victory freed them from immediate danger. Fleetwood moved the House on August 23 that Lambert should be promoted once more to major-general. It would not have been a very costly acknowledgment of his services, but Haslerig opposed it strenuously and successfully. Instead, Lambert

[3] *A Letter from Sir George Booth to a Friend of His*, dated Chester, August 2, 1659: 669f21(66). For another and even less specific declaration, allegedly sent down from London for distribution by the insurgents, see Baker, *Chronicle*, p. 671.

[4] *An Express from the Knights and Gentlemen Now Engaged with Sir George Booth* (August 9, 1659), 669f21(68).

[5] *CSPD*, 1659–60, pp. 94, 111, 115; Whitelocke, *Memorials*, p. 683; *Clarke Papers*, IV, 42.

[6] Davies, *Restoration*, p. 137; Underdown, *Royalist Conspiracy in England*, p. 275.

[7] *The Letter-Book of John Viscount Mordaunt, 1658–1660*, ed. Mary Coate (*CS*, 1945; hereafter cited as *Mordaunt Letter-Book*), p. 31.

[8] Underdown, *Royalist Conspiracy in England*, p. 275.

was voted £1000 to buy a jewel—a sum which he promptly distributed among his troops in the recent campaign.[9]

Tensions rose again on September 3, when Haslerig's party split the House over a new Engagement, whereby all officers of the militia, and originally all members of Parliament too, were to abjure anew the pretended title of the house of Stuart and swear fidelity to "this Commonwealth" without a king, single person, or House of Lords. This roused several objections. One was that so solemn a pledge to "this Commonwealth" before its form was even settled suggested a sinister design to perpetuate the power of a party—Haslerig's party. Another was the conscientious scruple that many sectaries felt against public oaths and covenants in general, as a tempting of God. A third arose from a plausible belief that what really moved Haslerig and his friends was a suspicion that Lambert was aiming at some such position as Protector. Vane, whose ties with Lambert were close, took sharp issue with Haslerig, and the House was violently divided. Johnston of Wariston tells us that "the greatest heats that could be in words was between Sir [Arthur] Hazelrig and S[ir] H. Vayne, and that Mr. Nevil and uthers was jeering at their division, and taking advantage of it, and saying that honest men will com to their awen when theeves reckon." [10] In the upshot the proposal to make M.P.'s take the Engagement was referred to a committee and eventually allowed to drop.

The Rump's relations with the City of London were second in importance only to its good understanding with the army, but they too were deteriorating. The city authorities had resented the extent to which the Rump had overridden their authority when it completely reorganized London's militia in July.[11] The lord mayor was Sir John Ireton, a brother of Cromwell's famous son-in-law Henry Ireton, and he and most of the aldermen supported the Rump. Thanks to them

[9] *Commons Journals*, VII, 766, 769; Guizot, I, 464; Ludlow, *Memoirs*, II, 114–15; Clarendon, *History of the Rebellion* (ed. W. Dunn Macray), VI, 143; Davies, *Restoration*, p. 146.

[10] Wariston, *Diary*, III, 135; and on the whole affair, *Commons Journals*, VII, 773–74; *CSPD*, 1659–60, pp. 187–88, 207, 234; *Clarke Papers*, IV, 49–50; *A Collection of Original Letters . . . Found among the Duke of Ormonde's Papers*, ed. Thomas Carte (2 vols., London, 1739; hereafter cited as *Ormonde Papers*), II, 203, 216; *CSP Ven.*, 1659–61, pp. 68–69; Guizot, I, 474, 478.

[11] George V. Chivers, *The City of London and the State, 1658 to 1664* (unpublished Ph.D. thesis, University of Manchester, 1961), pp. 133–36. I am much indebted to Dr. Chivers for placing his thesis at my disposal. Further evidence of the city's discontent is in Guizot, I, 437; *Nicholas Papers*, IV, 172; *CSP Ven.*, 1659–61, pp. 47–48; *Clarendon State Papers*, III, 531; *CSPD*, 1659–60, pp. 57–58.

and to a large movement of regular forces into the city, London stayed quiet during Booth's rising. But many citizens sympathized with Booth's proclaimed intentions, and there was a strong move among the Common Councilmen to petition the Rump for a free Parliament. The lord mayor had to resist heavy pressure to call a Court of Common Council in August; he even had to have troops posted at the Guildhall to prevent it from assembling without his consent.[12] So dependent did the Rump feel on Ireton's loyalty that it voted on September 2 to override the city's right of annual election and continue him in office for a further year. The city fathers were highly incensed, and their strong protests induced the Rump on September 28 to rescind its former vote and allow the election to proceed.[13] But the city was henceforth on its guard. During the coming months it would increasingly justify Lord Mordaunt's description of it as the "master wheel by whose motions the successive rotations of all the lesser must follow." [14]

Amid these distractions the Rump took up again the intractable question of the constitution. On September 8 it set up a committee of twenty-nine, instructing them to sit daily and present a draft of a settlement by October 10 at the latest. With Haslerig and Scot ranged against Vane and Salwey, Fleetwood against the conservative lawyers Whitelocke and St. John, and Neville sniping from the Harringtonian sidelines, these twenty-nine were no likelier to reach agreement than the Grand Committees of the earlier summer. One scrap of news from Wariston's diary on September 24 would have depressed Milton: the committee rejected a "fundamental of Toleration" by sixteen votes to six.[15] It is unlikely that it intended to deny liberty of conscience outright; the proposal was probably one from Vane's party to exclude religion from the authority of the civil magistrate. On September 17 the Parliament received a Fifth Monarchist petition telling it that the prevailing party in it had deserved their expulsion in 1653, and calling for perpetual rule by an oligarchy of saints dedicated to establishing the kingdom of Christ.[16] It was signed by Milton's old friend Robert Overton, as well as by Vavasor Powell and other well-known millenarian preachers. The French ambassador heard that it was instigated by Vane. This is unlikely, but Bordeaux may well have been right that

[12] *Clarendon Calendar*, IV, 322, 328; Guizot, I, 450, 453, 458; *CSP Ven.*, 1659–61, pp. 52–53, 57–58; *Cf. The Londoners Last Warning* (August 15, 1659), E993(24), pp. 5–6.

[13] Chivers, *City of London*, pp. 139–40; *Commons Journals*, VII, 773, 785, 787–88; *CSP Ven.*, 1659–61, pp. 70–72, 74–75; *Ormonde Papers*, II, 203.

[14] *Clarendon State Papers*, III, 659.

[15] Wariston, *Diary*, III, 138.

[16] *An Essay towards Settlement*, 669f21(73).

Vane was joined by the army officers in advocating a council of forty with supreme authority in the state and a veto over the resolutions of Parliament.[17] The pressure for a select Senate was still on, and the settlement of the government as far away as ever. The words that the Fifth Monarchist John Rogers had lately addressed to the Council of State might equally well have been spoken to the present committee: "I see you like Men in the Dark, up at MIDNIGHT, in a confused State; ready to knock your *Heads* at every Post, and to break your *Legs* at every Block!"[18]

4. THE SECOND EXPULSION OF THE RUMP

September–October, 1659

Tense though relations were between army and Parliament by mid-September, there was no public breach yet to warn a comparative recluse like Milton that the very foundations of the Commonwealth were about to be shaken. The train of events that woke him to its peril and led to the explosion on October 13 began on September 22 when Parliament received a petition from the brigade that Lambert had commanded against Booth's little band of insurgents.

The Derby Petition,[1] as it was called from its place of origin, was a provocative document, but not so subversive as to justify the violent reaction to it by Haslerig and his party. It asked that the officers' Humble Petition and Address of May 12 should not be laid asleep but be given fresh life, as the best prescription yet offered for securing both civil and spiritual liberties. The principal unfulfilled request in that petition was of course the one for a select Senate. The Derby Petition further asked that Fleetwood's commission as commander-in-chief should be made permanent and that general rank should also be conferred upon Lambert as second-in-command, Desborough as chief officer of the cavalry, and Monck as commander of the infantry. The remaining articles reflected a suspicion that the Rump was not proceeding rigorously enough against the participators in the August risings, and called for sharper action against both the individuals and the corporations concerned.

Although the petition was addressed to the Parliament, its authors sent it in the first place to Fleetwood, to be communicated to the Gen-

---

[17] Guizot, I, 474–75.
[18] Rogers, *Diapoliteia*, preface, sig. B2.
[1] It is printed in Baker, *Chronicle*, p. 677.

eral Council of Officers. Less wisely, they also sent it to Monck in Scotland and to the commanders in Ireland, asking them to invite their officers to subscribe it. Fleetwood, worried and indecisive as usual, showed it to Haslerig and suggested a meeting with Vane and Salwey to discuss what should be done. If Haslerig had had any sense he would have persuaded Fleetwood to suppress it, as he was inclined to do, on his own authority. Instead he took it at once to the House, dramatically moved that the doors be locked, and denounced it in an exaggerated and inflammatory speech.[2] For two days the Rump was in a great heat over it. Lambert's enemies immediately assumed him to be responsible, and Haslerig led a clamor to commit him to the Tower for high treason. This was as unjust as it was impolitic. Lambert was under suspicion because he had delayed returning to London until September 20, but it seems clear that he had left his brigade before the petition was drafted. He himself strenuously denied that he had any part in it, and a colonel who helped to draw it up wrote positively that Lambert "was not informed of their desires drawn up and subscribed."[3] Vane and Fleetwood believed him innocent, and said so. Lambert even asked Fleetwood to move Parliament on his behalf that he should be allowed to resign his commission in order to relieve the army of suspicion, but Fleetwood would not have it.[4]

The motion to commit Lambert was dropped, but the Rump voted "that to have any more General Officers in the Army than are already settled by the Parliament, is needless, chargeable, and dangerous to the Commonwealth."[5] It further ordered Fleetwood to admonish his officers for their irregular conduct and to stop it from going any further.

"Dangerous to the Commonwealth": how those gratuitous words were to rankle in the army! The officers about London were meeting daily now, as they had done when trouble was brewing in April. They were not prepared to accept Parliament's rebuke of their comrades. They set up a committee to draft an address that would clear their reputation by publicly affirming their loyalty to the Commonwealth, but instead of the healing assurances that Fleetwood hoped for a rather different kind of document emerged. Fleetwood could no longer

[2] *The Armys Plea for Their Present Practice* (October 24, 1659), E1000(24), pp. 15–17; Ludlow, *Memoirs*, II, 134–35; Baker, *Chronicle*, p. 676; Guizot, I, 482.
[3] Historical Manuscripts Commission, *Leyborne-Popham MSS*, pp. 122–23. *Cf.* Guizot, I, 479, 482–83; Ludlow, *Memoirs*, II, 135, 143, 154–55; *A Declaration of the General Council of the Officers*, p. 8; *Clarke Papers*, IV, 58, n. 1.
[4] Wariston, *Diary*, III, 138; Guizot, I, 479.
[5] *Commons Journals*, VII, 785; 'needless' is supplied from Baker, *Chronicle*, p. 678, where *Commons Journals* have 'dangerous,' which in view of its immediate repetition appears to be a clerical error.

control the Council of Officers, while Lambert sat silent, as if uncon-
cerned, and let the hotter spirits make the running.[6] The republican
zeal with which the mass of junior officers had acclaimed the Rump
five months before was evaporating. The army felt itself even less
valued than in Richard's time; much of it was living at free quarter for
lack of pay, and to the powerful sectarian element the Rump's religious
policy looked little different from the Protectorate's.

Belatedly, in the early days of October, the Rump sought means of
meeting the soldiers' long arrears of pay and discussed measures to
relieve their widows and orphans. It also debated how to fill the va-
cant seats in the House.[7] But would a mere recruitment of the Rump
satisfy its critics now any better than in 1653? Vane told Johnston of
Wariston "he thought that to be by a syde wynd a settling the gouver-
ment as Sir Arthur [Haslerig] would haive it. He thought they should
not taike so much offence at what the airmy did, but settle the gouver-
ment with their consent." Haslerig was even more bitter towards
Vane. He "sayd on Saterday in the Counsel-chamber that S[ir] H.V.
would ruyne the nation, and he desyred never to come in the place
wheir he was, and the uther chalenged." Having now a regiment of his
own, Haslerig carried the quarrel into the Council of Officers, where
"their was high and hotte debaytes between S[ir] A. H. asserting the
absolut power of Parliament and the officers asserting their being im-
ployed against arbitrary gouverment in whatsoever, and my Lord
Fleetwoods urging them to sleepe upon the whol busines." [8] Haslerig
bore a heavy responsibility for the collision course on which army and
Parliament now seemed set—"a man of a disobliging carriage," Lud-
low says of him at this time, "sower and morose of temper, liable to be
transported with passion, and to whom liberality seemed to be a
vice." [9]

On October 5 Desborough presented to the House the promised
address, styled *The Humble Representation and Petition of the Of-
ficers of the Army.*[10] There was really nothing humble about it. True,
it closed with a curt assurance of fidelity to the Parliament and Com-
monwealth, but it was essentially a vindication and not a repudiation
of the Derby petitioners. It blamed the present tension on those who
had misrepresented them and the army in general. It vehemently
denied any intention to interrupt the Parliament's sitting, or "to set

[6] Ludlow, *Memoirs,* II, 135; *Ormonde Papers,* II, 225; *CSP Ven.,* 1659–61,
p. 74.
[7] *Commons Journals,* VII, 789–91; Baker, *Chronicle,* pp. 678–79.
[8] Wariston, *Diary,* III, 139.
[9] Ludlow, *Memoirs,* II, 133.
[10] Printed in Baker, *Chronicle,* pp. 679–81.

up a *Single Person,* or another *General."* It urged the Rump to get on with the job of settling the foundations of government, and reminded it again of the officers' address of May 13. Then came a series of fresh requests: that all who in future wrongfully aspersed the army should be tried and punished; that soldiers should enjoy the same right as other citizens to petition the Parliament; and that Parliament would hasten to provide for their pay, their maimed comrades, and their widows and orphans. But the demand that stuck most was one revived from the agitation a year earlier: that except in cases of disbandment, no officer or soldier should be dismissed unless he was convicted by a court-martial. As Monck wrote to Fleetwood, "it might encourage the more inferiour Officers and Souldiers to affront the Superiour, and the General himself, and would in time make the Army a kind of separate Corporation from the Parliament." [11]

Monck was right; there was danger in this address. Yet a wiser and less frightened assembly than the Rump would not have provoked it, and if it were provoked, would have made the most of its conciliatory gestures towards "a Cordial and Affectionate Union of the Parliament and Army, and an uninterrupted good understanding of each other." For a few days, that seemed to be its policy. It debated the first five articles of the Humble Representation and Petition one by one and framed reasonable answers to them. But then on October 11 it abruptly dropped this business in order to rush an emergency bill through all its stages in a single day. The resultant act, which was immediately published, declared that all legislation since April, 1653, was null and void unless specifically confirmed by the Rump, and made it high treason as from October 11 to collect any taxes, excise, or customs without the consent of Parliament. Clearly the House was in fear of an immediate dissolution by the army, and its object was to make lawful government impossible if this should happen.

The reason for this panic measure probably lay in a letter that Colonel Okey showed to Haslerig on the morning of the 11th. It was signed by Lambert and eight other senior officers, and it invited Okey and the officers of his regiment to subscribe the Humble Representation and Petition. Though Haslerig cannot have known it yet, similar letters had been sent to other regimental and garrison commanders in England and to the armies in Scotland and Ireland. It was of course indefensible to canvass all the forces for signatures to an essentially political petition *after* it had been presented to Parliament. It was an exercise in blatant military pressure. But it was folly on Haslerig's part to jump to the conclusion, without even sending for the nine

[11] *Ibid.,* p. 678.

officers concerned, that they intended an immediate violence upon the Parliament. Haslerig did not divulge the letter to the House on the 11th, though he probably hinted enough to put it in fear of imminent dissolution.

Early on the morning of the 12th, Haslerig, Scot, and Walton received a secret message from Monck that if Parliament were resolute in asserting its authority against the army, he would if necessary march the forces in Scotland to its defence.[12] As soon as the House met, these three caused the doors to be locked and had the letter to Okey read. After a long debate the Rump voted to deprive the nine signatories of their commissions. It was a rash decision to cashier such senior and popular commanders without even a hearing, especially as they included not only some former Cromwellian major-generals (Lambert, Desborough, Berry, and Kelsey) but hitherto staunch commonwealthsmen like Ashfield, Packer, and Creed. Equally rashly, the House revoked Fleetwood's commission as commander-in-chief and vested the command of all the forces in seven commissioners. They were Fleetwood, Ludlow, Monck, Haslerig, Walton, Morley, and Overton, which meant in effect that Haslerig and his fellow Rumpers could assume direct and overriding control of all the forces in England —if they would obey.

But would they? The votes of October 12 were a challenge to a trial of strength, and the next twenty-four hours provided the answer. That evening Haslerig, Walton and Morley, acting under their new commission, ordered Morley's own regiment and Moss's to occupy Westminster Hall and the other environs of the Palace of Westminster. Some leading Rumpers camped in the House for the night. Lambert called out the regiments that supported him—the majority, as it turned out—and posted them so as completely to surround the Parliament's defenders. For much of the night and all next day the opposed forces faced each other with muskets loaded and match burning.[13] Action threatened at several of the approaches to the Parliament-house, for Morley ordered his men to fire if Lambert's moved in any closer, and there were some similar challenges from the blockaders. But when Lambert rode up and confronted Major Evelyn, the commander of the Parliament's life guard, Evelyn tamely dismounted and his troops changed sides. The soldiers did not really want

[12] Baker, *Chronicle*, p. 682; *Ormonde Papers*, II, 246. Other sources for the crisis of October 11–13 are fully cited in Davies, *Restoration*, pp. 150–52, and are referred to here only for incidents and quotations not found in Davies' narrative.

[13] *The Diurnal of Thomas Rugg 1659–1661*, ed. William L. Sachse (*CS*, 1961), p. 8.

to fight. There was a good deal of speechmaking on both sides, and the risk of bloodshed dwindled as more and more of the defenders went over to Lambert.

Next day, the 13th, Lambert's men turned back the members who tried to enter the House. They stopped the Speaker's coach almost at the gate of Palace Yard. "I am your General," he said, and told them that he expected their obedience. They answered that "they knew no such thing; that if he had marched before them over *Warrington-bridge*, they should have known him." [14] Lambert told him "hee was a foolish, impertinent fellow, and bid him get home." [15] The members who had spent the night in the House sent to the city for the help of its militia, "but they answered they would not meddle with the dispute, but endeavour to preserve the peace of the City." [16] The citizens indeed, even those of Westminster, took the day's excitements very calmly, "for in all the hurly burly the streets were full, every one going about their business as if not at all concerned." [17] They would not for long be so tolerant of their masters' squabbles.

Eventually, in the evening, the Council of State issued orders that all the troops should return to their quarters, and most of them gladly obeyed. But the army was left in possession of the field; Fleetwood posted two or three companies in and around Westminster Hall. The Rump was out of doors again, and nobody knew what was to happen next.

[14] *Ormonde Papers*, II, 266: the story is retailed by Hyde. Warrington is an error for Winnington, where the brief action against Booth's rebels had been fought. See also Davies, *Restoration*, p. 152.

[15] *Clarendon Calendar*, IV, 411.

[16] *Clarendon State Papers*, III, 581; Wariston, *Diary*, III, 144; *Mordaunt Letter-Book*, p. 60; *A Declaration of the Proceedings of the Parliament & Army* (October 17, 1659), E1000(14), p. 5.

[17] *Clarendon State Papers*, III, 581.

CHAPTER VII

MILTON AND OTHERS IN QUEST OF A SETTLEMENT

1. A WEEK OF CONFUSION

October 14–20, 1659

U NTIL that fatal breach on October 13, Milton had on his own
confession left questions of politics "to the wisedome & care
of those who had the government . . . not finding that either
God or the publick required more of me then my prayers for them
that govern." [1] Shocked now into awareness that the Commonwealth
lay naked to her enemies, he felt impelled to turn his own mind
to the question of how she could be constitutionally clothed and
protected. The result was *A Letter to a Friend, Concerning the Rup-
tures of the Commonwealth,* and for once he appended a precise date:
October 20, 1659. Before examining it, however, we should see how
events were shaping in the anarchic week between the army's *coup*
and Milton's setting down of his thoughts.

The Council of State met again on the 14th, still uncertain whether
the army's occupation of the Palace of Westminster signified a dissolu-
tion or merely a suspension of the Parliament's session. Even the
military members seemed not to know; indeed their total unprepared-
ness argues strongly against the Rumpers' assumption that the army
had been planning a political take-over. The leading officers, together
with Vane's group, would probably have been content—even relieved
—for the Rump to return on condition that it annulled the votes of
October 11 and 12 and took the army's demands into speedy con-
sideration. But Haslerig's party, fortified by Monck's promise of sup-
port, was in no mood for concessions. Wariston "found at Counsel
som asserting the Parliaments absolut authority, som that it was
limited not to be prejudicial to the cause." [2] All that the Council de-
cided that day was to demand the withdrawal of the forces from the
Parliament's doors. This the army ignored. The Council of Officers
was taking its own decisions; it agreed to recognize Fleetwood as still

[1] *Letter to a Friend,* below, p. 324.
[2] Wariston, *Diary,* III, 145.

commander-in-chief and to take orders from no one else. It also suspended those officers who continued to obey the Parliament.[3]

Next day the Council of State resumed its deliberations. Towards the end of a fruitless morning, Vane produced a draft plan whereby the army would undertake to let Parliament sit again on December 1 and to obey the Council's orders until then; meanwhile the Council would consider the army's proposals for a settlement and present them to the House on its resumption.[4] This found little favor. Colonel Sydenham made a speech justifying the army's actions as necessitated by a particular call of divine providence. An emaciated figure rose and interrupted him. It was John Bradshaw, the former president of the court that had tried Charles I and the subject of a great eulogy by Milton in *A Second Defence*.[5] He was now a mortally sick man. He said "that being now going to his God, he had not patience to sit there to hear his great name so openly blasphemed." He walked out of the Council, never to sit there again, and by the end of of the month he was dead.[6]

Most of his colleagues also withdrew, though a rump of the Council sat on until October 25. One of its last acts was to order payment of the salaries due to eighty-six of its servants, including Milton.[7] Real power passed however to the Council of Officers, though they had little enough idea of how to wield it. To consider how the government should be carried on they appointed five of their number—Fleetwood, Lambert, Desborough, Sydenham, and Berry—to confer with five of the Council of State who could still be persuaded to sit down with them: Vane and his shadow Salwey, Bulstrode Whitelocke, Sir James Harrington, cousin of the author of *Oceana*, and Johnston of Wariston, torn as ever between vanity and fear.[8] How much grip Fleetwood had on the situation as commander-in-chief can be gauged from a letter that he wrote to Monck on the 18th. After much cant about the necessity of providence and the preciousness of their cause, all he could really report was that "the Lord is pleased to give the army very

[3] *Ibid.; A True Narrative of the Proceedings in Parliament* (December 2, 1659), E1010(24), hereafter cited as *True Narrative*, p. 21; *Clarke Papers*, IV, 62–63.

[4] Wariston, *Diary*, III, 145–46.

[5] *Complete Prose*, IV, 637–39.

[6] Ludlow, *Memoirs*, II, 140–41. He left Milton £10 in his will: see French, *Life Records*, IV, 287, where, however, Bradshaw's death is misdated November 22. That was when he was buried in Westminster Abbey; he died on October 31. French corrects the misdating, *Life Records*, V, 455.

[7] French, *Life Records*, IV, 280–81.

[8] *True Narrative*, p. 21; Wariston, *Diary*, III, 146; Whitelocke, *Memorials*, p. 686.

greate union, though as to what is intended and resolved upon there is noe conclusion yett taken [that] I know." [9]

2. A LETTER TO A FRIEND

Milton's *Letter to a Friend* would have filled a typical eight-page pamphlet if set in fairly large type, but so far as is known it was not printed in his lifetime. It was quite a common literary device among contemporary pamphleteers to cast a tract addressed to the public in the form of a letter to a friend, and Milton's piece may be an example of this *genre*. He may have thought of circulating it in manuscript, as was commonly done, in order to get the reactions of friends and critics to the ideas that he was to develop more fully in *The Readie & Easie Way*. Yet, although the style and tone of the letter often suggest a public rather than a purely private communication, the friend in the title probably existed. There is an air of verity about Milton's opening references to "the sad and serious Discourse" that he had had with him last night, and to his friend's request, after imparting all he knew of the state of political affairs, that Milton should set down his own thoughts upon them. At the close, Milton commits those thoughts to his friend with the words:

> With this you may doe what you please: put out, put in, communicate, or suppresse; you offend not mee who only have obeyed your opinion, that in doing what I have done, I might happen to offer something which might be of some use in this great time of need.[1]

It sounds as though Milton were furnishing a man nearer the center of affairs with matter for a speech or writing of his own, but he may well have kept a copy with the idea of circulating it more widely or of working up its proposals at greater length.

It is fruitless to speculate as to who the friend was. Masson and Barker have suggested Vane,[2] but this is implausible because of the general accord between writer and recipient that the letter assumes. Vane at this stage would not have endorsed Milton's harsh and one-sided condemnation of the army leaders—particularly not the obvious allusion to Lambert in his exhortation to the army "to finde out that Achan among them whose close ambition in all likelyhood abuses their honest natures against their meaning to these disorders." [3]

---

[9] *Clarke Papers,* IV, 64.
[1] *Letter to a Friend,* below, p. 332.
[2] Masson, V, 618; Barker, *Milton and the Puritan Dilemma,* pp. 260, 393.
[3] *Letter to a Friend,* below, pp. 328–29.

Vane was still in close touch with Lambert,[4] and had as we have seen tried constantly to moderate the animus of Haslerig's party against the officers. Is it possible that the dying Bradshaw sent for Milton, in the hope of enlisting his pen against the army's usurpation? This is a mere guess, and the question of the friend's identity must remain open.[5]

Even more explicitly than in *The Likeliest Means,* Milton now dissociates himself from the Protectorate and pins his colors to the restored Commonwealth. He was overjoyed last May, he says, when the army was brought "to confesse in publick their backsliding from the good old cause, & to shew the fruits of their repentance in the righteousnesse of their restoring the old famous parlament, which they had without just autority dissolved." [6] This is a sharp reversal of the attitude that he had taken towards that dissolution in *A Second Defence.*[7] But he hastens to qualify his vindication of the Rump: "I call it the famous parlament, though not the blamelesse, since none well affected but will confesse, they have deserved much more of these nations, then they have undeserved." [8] This perhaps hinted how hard he had found it to swallow the vote of June 27 concerning tithes.[9] There follows a lengthy passage in which he condemns in the strongest terms the army's second interruption of the Rump.

The main interest of *A Letter to a Friend* lies, however, in its second half, which contains the embryo of *The Readie & Easie Way.* The first remedy for the current anarchy, Milton says, must be "a senate or generall Councell of State," empowered to preserve the public peace, conduct foreign relations, and raise revenue. It must be bound to two fundamental principles: "Liberty of conscience to all professing Scripture the rule of their faith & worship, And the Abjuracion of a single person." [10] It should consist either of the Rump, or, if the Rump is held to be justly dissolved for failing to establish full liberty of conscience and to abolish the enforced maintenance of ministers, a Council of State chosen by the army and including as many Rumpers as hold fast to the two fundamentals. Milton would evidently prefer a simple restoration of the Rump, though it is interesting to note the only two grounds on which he could consider its authority forfeit.

[4] Wariston, *Diary,* III, 146; Ludlow, *Memoirs,* II, 143.

[5] Other names that have been suggested include Meadows, Frost, and Whitelocke: French, *Life Records,* IV, 276.

[6] *Letter to a Friend,* below, p. 324.

[7] *Complete Prose,* IV, 671, 682–83.

[8] *Letter to a Friend,* below, pp. 324–25.

[9] See above, pp. 75–76.

[10] *Letter to a Friend,* below, p. 330.

His most extraordinary proposal was that the Senate, whichever form it took, should enter into a solemn league with the army, whereby senators and army officers should swear to maintain each other in their places *for life,* unless any should be found false to the two fundamentals or guilty of criminal conduct in the judgment of both parties. Anything less acceptable to the political nation could scarcely be imagined. Yet immediately after this proposal of life tenure, Milton says

> And whether the civill government be an annuall democracy or a perpetuall Aristocracy, is too nice a consideracion for the extremities wherein wee are & the hazard of our safety from a common enemie.[11]

This strange indecision on a matter that every politician would have regarded as fundamental would be eliminated in Milton's later versions of his scheme, as his mind set more firmly on a perpetual Senate.

He was well aware that such a government would be open to the charge of oligarchy. To counter this he suggested that "the well ordered committies of their faithfullest adherents in every county may give this government the resemblance & effects of a perfect democracie." [12] Here is an adumbration of the larger plan for county assemblies that he would develop in *The Readie & Easie Way,* but it is unhappily phrased, and Milton was wise not to publish it in this over-compressed form. Too many unpopular regimes had already based themselves on the narrow support of "their faithfullest adherents in every county," and committeeman had become a dirty word.

As a contribution to solving the constitutional impasse at which both Rump and army had arrived in October, 1659, *A Letter to a Friend* is negligible. It claims our attention as an indicator of Milton's progressive disillusion with genuinely popular government and as a stage in the formulation of his final scheme for establishing an incorruptible republic. It stands alone among the pamphlets of that autumn in advocating the perpetuation of the Rump, for the simple reason that every other political writer realized that that was precisely what had to be avoided if the Commonwealth was to gain the acceptance of the nation. But in principle it is not out of line with other proposals for a Senate that had been canvassed in recent months, including the army's; indeed within a few weeks we shall find Major-General Desborough making the very suggestion that the Senate should be constituted forthwith from the membership of the Rump.[13]

[11] *Ibid.,* p. 331.
[12] *Ibid.*
[13] See below, p. 153. Barbara Lewalski, in "Milton: Political Beliefs and Polemical Methods, 1659-60," *PMLA,* LXXIV (1959), 194, states that Milton

The differences are that Milton envisaged a larger body than did most other advocates of a Senate, and that whereas they generally looked to a national representative assembly to share the legislative function with it, he was already hinting that popular assent could be better conveyed through select local assemblies.

3. MORE SALVES FOR A SICK COMMONWEALTH

October, 1659

Milton's was of course not the only pen that tried to point a way out of the anarchy created by the open breach between army and Parliament. In this section we shall examine first what the principals had to say for themselves; then a few of the more interesting proposals for a settlement advanced by writers who were not immediately engaged in the quarrel; and finally the whimsical forum for verbal debate established by Harrington and his friends in the Rota Club.

On the Rump's behalf, *The Parliaments Plea*[1] had little to offer beyond such threadbare commonplaces as that the people, being the original of all just authority, have the right to be governed by their deputies and trustees in Parliament. The gist of its argument can be conveyed in two quotations: "The Sword of *England* is to be subject to the Civil Authority of *England,* to be *servus servorum Populi Angliae"*; and "This Parliament is the only remaining Branch, of the Peoples Authority, to whom of right belongeth the settlement of our Government."[2] It held forth the hope, if the Rump were restored, of the summoning of a new and lawful Parliament, and proposed "a firm Foundation of Settlement by way of *An Agreement of the People,* to be subscribed by the Parliament, Army, and People."[3] Had the writer forgotten the contempt with which the Rump had treated the last Agreement of the People that had been presented to it more than

---

"ignored completely the army's Select Senate plans (and all other contrivances for a "godly" council to checkmate the legislature)." I find a rather closer relationship between those plans and Milton's own.

[1] *The Parliaments Plea* (October 25, 1659), E1001(7). It claimed to be "printed and published by special permission and command of the Members of Parliament." Most of it is an expansion of certain "National Proposals" that had been printed together with a declaration by the northern nobility and gentry in support of the Rump and General Monck in *The Rendezvous of General Monck upon the Confines of England* (October 20, 1659), E1005(11).

[2] *The Parliaments Plea,* pp. 6, 7.

[3] *Ibid.,* pp. 21–22.

ten years before? What the new Agreement should contain and how the new Parliament should be constituted were questions that he left conveniently vague. Another and lengthier vindication of the Rump entitled *The Grand Concernments of England Ensured*[4] had equally little to offer for the future, beyond conventional assurances of a constant succession of free Parliaments. It was not surprising that these republican apologists revealed their political bankruptcy. The Rump had had five months in which to frame a constitutional settlement, and it had framed none.

On the army's side, two pamphlets of a very different temper claimed to be "published by special command." *The Armys Plea for Their Present Practice* was for the most part a sermon on the text *salus populi suprema lex,* as cliché-laden as the republican attacks that it attempted to answer. It argued predictably that governors have no authority but what the people commit to them, that their commands and laws cease to be binding when they frustrate the true ends of government or jeopardize the people's safety, that the army were not mercenaries but had been called into being to defend the same ends of civil and religious liberty as the Parliament itself—and so on. These generalities prefaced a highly colored narrative of the recent crisis, culminating in the charge that the Rump designed "either totally to destroy, or quite change and alter the very spirit and temper of this Army, and to form another for their own ends and purposes"—purposes which included the perpetuation of its own power and the persecution of consciences.[5]

The second pamphlet, entitled *The Armies Vindication of This Last Change,*[6] offered a far more full-blooded justification of military power and harked back to the millenarian enthusiasm that had fired a large section of the army in the earlier 'fifties. It dated the army's right to act for the people back to the first Civil War. When the Parliament was forced to raise the good people of the land into a military body "of much greater force and strength than that which was Civill: The power and greatness of the Parliament did hereby necessarily descend into the Army." The Parliament "became a lesser and more inferiour

---

[4] E1001(6), (October 25, 1659); much of this long tract was written before October 13, but pp. 55–70 were added later and strongly condemn the army's violation of the Parliament. Another vindication of the Rump, equally unoriginal, was by "E.D.," *A True Relation of the State of the Case between the . . . Parliament and the Officers of the Army* (October 11, 1659), E1000 (12).

[5] *The Armys Plea for Their Present Practice*, pp. 18, 20, 25.

[6] London, 1659; not in Thomason or BML. The copy here cited is in the Brotherton Collection in the University of Leeds.

power, by pouring out and devolving their greatness and strength into another Society of men, more formidable than themselves."[7] After the abolition of kingship and the House of Lords no legal form of civil government was left, for the Commons alone had no mandate or authority to constitute a commonwealth. Sovereignty fell back into the hands of the people, whence it sprang, and in that situation "the good people embodied in an Army, together with those that adheared to them, must of undoubted right, be receptable of all Power and Soveraignty."[8] The Commons, such as were left, continued to sit only on the army's sufferance, and when they ceased to be of use to the nation "they were by the Army *gently* laid aside."[9] The people's approbation of this act finally cancelled the trust that they had originally reposed in the Parliament.

This stark equation of might with right was bolstered by various arguments for the proposition that "the Army is the principall body of the People, in whom the Soveraignty doth at present reside."[10] It embodies "the ordinary and common bulk of the people, which are the greatnesse and strength of the Nation;"[11] "the Army are the people in an active body"—not a sluggish mass but a great company of choice spirits geared for action, "carrying the interest of the people of God" and supported by the prayers of "the honest party of the Nation."[12] The army had admittedly been guilty of backsliding in "dancing after the pipe of a single person,"[13] but when it had restored the Rump in May it had acted not from wisdom and judgment, and certainly not in deference to any legal right of the Rump to authority, but because this had seemed the readiest expedient at the time. Now it could be seen as a second apostasy, because the Rump, despite many worthy members, had been so signally disowned by God prior to April, 1653. "Why doe we speak so high for a Parliament, is it not a worldly Constitution, a Body fitted for a King, the Interest of the Nation, not of the people of God; and every whit as Babylonish as Kingship itself?"[14] Specifically condemning the Rump for seeking "to espouse a National Interest, intending to have thrown the Government upon the spirit of the Nation,"[15] this anonymous writer turned his

[7] *The Armies Vindication*, pp. 2–3.
[8] *Ibid.*, pp. 3–4.
[9] *Ibid.*, p. 4.
[10] *Ibid.*, pp. 4 ff.
[11] *Ibid.*, pp. 4–5.
[12] *Ibid.*, pp. 5–6.
[13] *Ibid.*, p. 11.
[14] *Ibid.*
[15] *Ibid.*, p. 9.

back on Cromwell's long endeavors to reconcile the interest of the
nation with the interest of the people of God. His tone becomes more
and more apocalyptic towards the close:

> It is a time of breaking, and pulling down all worldly Constitutions:
> God is staining the *pride of all glory,* and *treading down strength.* . . .
> Our condition at present is not a *fixed Station,* but a posture of *direct
> motion;* we are upon our March from *Egypt* to *Canaan,* from a Land of
> bondage and darkness, to a Land of Liberty and Rest: Now the Army is
> a Body of Activity of life and motion, and so fit for such a Work; being
> full of Spirit and vigor, inlarged in love and kindness, separated from the
> old Forms and Customes of the world.[16]

And what is its great goal? No less than "the Kingdom of Christ,
which is at the very Birth, and no man knows how to give it a deliver-
ance." [17]

How much response such chimerical aspirations still roused within
the army it is impossible to say. They certainly did not characterize
the leadership, to judge by the Committee of Safety's feeble gropings
in the coming weeks. But the very existence of this vein of anarchic
enthusiasm served to intensify the nation's exasperation with the
army, and to render still more hopeless Milton's plea for a perpetual
league between army and Parliament.

Of the many pamphleteers who offered advice on a settlement from
a relatively disengaged position the most interesting is Henry Stubbe,
who wrote most of *A Letter to an Officer of the Army Concerning a
Select Senate* just before the *coup* on October 13 and published it
shortly after.[18] Stubbe again affords a significant comparison with
Milton, partly because he was wrestling with the same political prob-
lems from a not dissimilar standpoint, and partly because of his close
association with Vane.[19] Like Milton, Stubbe regarded liberty of
conscience as the very essence of the cause, and looked upon the Pres-
byterians both political and ecclesiastical as no less enemies than the
royalists. Stubbe too had been driven to narrow drastically the extent
to which he would dare entrust government to the people's freely
elected representatives. But whereas Milton basically took the part of
the Rump against the army, Stubbe (in a preface added after October

[16] *Ibid.,* p. 20.
[17] *Ibid.,* p. 21.
[18] E1001(8); text dated at the end "Ch[rist] Ch[urch] Oct. 13. 1659," though
the preface was written subsequently; acquired by Thomason on October 26.
[19] See above, p. 56. *The Grand Concernments of England Ensured* sneered
(p. 65) that Stubbe "hath written a Book on purpose to prove Sir *Henry Vane*
no *Jesuite.*"

13) condemned the Parliament for denying a full toleration, threatening "the illustrious Lord Lambert" with the Tower, and generally doing the work of the common enemy. To Stubbe the lesson of Booth's rising was that it had been a Presbyterian design, and the Rump was not free from the Presbyterian taint. The main issue as he saw it lay between the would-be forcers of conscience and the defenders of toleration rather than between the friends and enemies of the house of Stuart.[20] He warned the moderate Independents, who had produced the Savoy Declaration and sought a *rapprochement* with the Presbyterians on the basis of a broadly common theology, that they did not know their danger. With the Presbyterians, he acutely remarked, it is far more dangerous to oppose their clergy than their doctrine.[21]

Stubbe advanced a series of fundamentals on which the Commonwealth should be based. These, though more extensive than Milton's, included Milton's essential points: no single person, and no power in the people's trustees to meddle with matters of religion. To safeguard these fundamentals he believed there must be some permanent body, distinct from the elected legislature, with powers comparable to those of the tribunes of Rome or the Justicia of Aragon.[22] In proposing how it should be constituted, he elaborated and refined upon the suggestions made by his patron Vane in *A Needful Corrective or Ballance.* All who adhered to the army and Parliament at the time of Booth's rising should be given special status as "Liberators of their country" and embodied as a kind of permanent militia. Their names should be recorded in county registers and their fame preserved by courts of honor; except in the gravest national emergency they alone should be permitted to bear arms, and for a time at least they alone should be eligible for places of trust in the state. At their musters they should choose a suitable number of deputies, who should in turn elect by ballot "the *Select Senate,* or Conservators of the liberties of England."[23] These senators should serve for life, subject to the scrutiny of a body of "inquisitors into the deportment of the Senate," elected for the purpose every two years. Both the Senate and its inquisitors must be composed exclusively of Independents and sectaries; Presbyterians must be excluded as rigorously as papists and prelatists.[24] The Senate should have sole control over the militia, the universities, and the ministry, so far as the latter was subject to the authority of

20 *A Letter to an Officer,* pp. 9–11.
21 *Ibid.,* pp. 14 ff.
22 *Ibid.,* pp. 3–6, 19–36.
23 *Ibid.,* pp. 59–61.
24 *Ibid.,* p. 61.

the state, but it should not normally interpose in the executive or legislative functions of government. Legislative power should be vested in biennial Parliaments, each sitting for three months, and elected through a two-stage system by all duly qualified electors—not merely by the Liberators. Each Parliament should choose a Council of State to manage the nation's affairs until the next one met. But even this degree of separation of powers was qualified: the senators should sit in Parliament as of right, and between Parliaments three of them should also sit on the Council of State as non-voting members.[25] Furthermore, Stubbe concluded by offering a simpler alternative scheme, closer to Vane's own: namely that the Senate should be invested with the whole executive power, and have a right of veto over Parliament's legislative proposals if they contravened the fundamentals.[26]

Readers of Milton's *Letter to a Friend* and *The Readie & Easie Way* will note the similarities and differences in Stubbe's approach. Both men grappled with the problem of guaranteeing certain principles and rights that most of the nation would reject if they could, but Stubbe thought out a more sophisticated system of checks and balances which was several degrees less impracticable than Milton's in that it recognized the sheer impossibility of denying the political nation its treasured right to elect Parliaments.

No other commonwealthsman during this interregnum published anything approaching Stubbe's treatise in intelligence or constructiveness, and the rest of the pamphlet literature can be very briefly surveyed. There were, for example, sketches of a settlement more quaint than practical from a Quaker, who was probably either Edward Billing or Edward Burrough,[27] and from John Eliot, the millenarian and apostle of the American Indians.[28] More significantly, at the other end of the political spectrum the advocates of monarchy were beginning to come more boldly into the open. The tireless William Prynne [29] called on the traditional members of the political nation to defy the present usurpers and reassert their rights. Let the ancient nobility, he urged, or at least all those who adhered to the Long Parliament, reassemble at Westminster and exercise the powers conferred on them by the Triennial Act of 1641 to issue writs for a new Parliament. To ensure their execution he called on the freeholders in each county to

[25] *Ibid.*, pp. 61–63.
[26] *Ibid.*, pp. 75–76.
[27] "E.B.," *A Mite of Affection* (October 25, 1659), E1001(5).
[28] John Eliot, *The Christian Commonwealth* (October 26, 1659), E1001(10).
[29] William Prynne, *A Short, Legal, Medicinal, Usefull, Safe, Easie Prescription* (dated October 31, 1659, by Prynne, and November 4 by Thomason), E772(1).

meet in strength at the next county court and elect their own sheriffs, in order both to conduct the elections and to take over control of the militia. The natural leaders of every county and city should declare unanimously that they would pay no taxes and obey no officials but those appointed by a free Parliament elected by themselves. Prynne's standpoint was Presbyterian, and it was moderate in comparison with the extreme royalist sentiments expressed by the diarist John Evelyn in *An Apology for the Royal Party*.[30] Evelyn declared that the Presbyterians who had managed Booth's rising deserved the ruin it had brought upon them, because of the part they had played in the Civil War. His unmeasured diatribe against the blasphemy, the atheism, the hypocrisy and oppression that rebellion against the king had entailed upon England gave a foretaste of the huge reaction to come and lent substance to Milton's blackest fears.

Some time during October the campaign to propagate Harrington's doctrines entered a new phase with the establishment of the Rota Club.[31] It was not a pressure group in the sense of aiming at direct influence on current politics, for its avowed purpose was to debate the theoretical problems of government and political philosophy. The leading spirits were Harrington himself and his close companion and coadjutor Henry Neville, though the chair was sometimes taken by Milton's young friend Cyriack Skinner. The club attracted a lively and varied group of virtuosos. They included John Wildman, now very much a Harringtonian, and another former Leveller who had participated in the famous Putney Debates, Maximilian Petty; Sir Charles Wolseley, once prominent in Cromwell's Council of State; Dr. William Petty, the pioneer of "political arithmetic"; the barrister Sir John Hoskins, like Petty an early member of the Royal Society and later its president; Richard Sackville, Earl of Dorset; Samuel Pepys and John Aubrey; and a number of others who were to make considerable reputations after the Restoration. They met at Miles' coffee house in New Palace Yard, close to where river passengers

[30] E763(11), (November 4, 1659). Other royalist tracts, serious and satirical, can be sufficiently identified in Thomason, II, 259–64.

[31] Of the many accounts of the Rota Club, the more informative include H. F. Russell Smith, *Harrington and His Oceana* (Cambridge, 1914), pp. 101 ff.; Blitzer, *Immortal Commonwealth*, pp. 56–61; Ashley, *John Wildman*, pp. 145–47; Masson, V, 484–86, 508–09; Parker, *Milton*, pp. 537–38. Aubrey dates the inception of the club from the beginning of the Michaelmas (law) term, which in the seventeenth century fell on October 9: see the passage from John Stow's *Survey of London* printed in Geoffrey R. Elton, *The Tudor Constitution* (Cambridge University Press, 1960), p. 154.

landed for Westminster Hall and the Parliament house. Aubrey's famous description of their proceedings will bear quoting once more:

> [There] was made purposely a large ovall-table, with a passage in the middle for Miles to deliver his Coffee. About it sate his [Harrington's] Disciples, and the Virtuosi. The Discourses in this Kind were the most ingeniose, and smart, that ever I heard, or expect to heare, and bandied with great eagernesse: the Arguments in the Parliament howse were but flatt to it. Here we had (very formally) a *Balloting-box,* and balloted how things should be caried, by way of *tentamens.* The room was every evening full as it could be cramm'd.[32]

Another jotting of Aubrey's seems to convey the Rota's opinion on current proposals for a perpetual Senate, and reads almost as if it were a comment on Milton's suggestion that the Rump itself should assume the role:

> Pride of Senators-for-Life is insufferable; and they were able to grind any one they owed ill will to to powder; they were hated by the armie and the countrey they represented, and their name and memorie stinkes —'twas worse then Tyranny.[33]

The Rota provided sophisticated entertainment and attracted a certain amount of satirical attention in the prints, but one has a feeling that some of the seriousness had gone out of Harrington's purpose since the summer. To generate discussion of his ideas among intelligent men-about-town was doubtless good long-term policy, but the accounts we have of the Rota's proceedings breathe a slightly dilettante air compared with the passion and urgency with which Harrington had pressed his ideal commonwealth between May and August. He published only one more brief tract [34] during the autumn, and in the club's heyday from October to January he probably felt that for the time being at least the chance for a successful settlement on the lines he advocated had passed. It is ironical that one of the Rota's claims to fame is that the cleverest contemporary satire on Milton masqueraded as a record of the club's transactions.[35]

[32] *Aubrey's Brief Lives,* ed. Oliver Lawson Dick (London: 1949), p. 125.
[33] *Ibid.*
[34] James Harrington, *Valerius and Publicola* (dated October 22, 1659, by Harrington, and November 7 by Thomason), E1005(13).
[35] See below, pp. 199–200.

CHAPTER VIII

THE DRIFT INTO ANARCHY

1. THE COMMITTEE OF SAFETY

October–November, 1659

AT THE BEGINNING of the last chapter we left the army officers fumbling for some viable alternative government after they had so precipitately interrupted the Parliament's sitting on October 13. The first reports ran that they would set up the select Senate for which they had long contended, and then reinstate the Rump with this curb upon it.[1] But the leading Rumpers would accept no such terms, so the officers had to shoulder the burden of state as best they could. After a whole fortnight had gone by, they announced that government was entrusted for the time being to a Committee of Safety. Their intention, they declared, was to secure the people's liberties as men and Christians, reform the law, provide for a godly preaching ministry by means less vexatious than tithes, and settle the constitution without a single person, kingship, or House of Lords.[2] How threadbare these formulas had become!

The Committee of Safety numbered twenty-three. There were rumors abroad that these were to be but the nucleus of a Senate of seventy [3]—a number which, being that of the Jewish Sanhedrin, suggests that the old millenarian agitation for a rule of the saints was afoot again. But in fact the officers had great difficulty in assembling as many names as they did, and the list was far from impressive. While it was being decided, some sectarian officers objected to the inclusion of old Cromwellians like Henry Lawrence, Walter Strickland, and Bulstrode Whitelocke and tried in vain to recall from oblivion such old Fifth Monarchist leaders as Major-General Harrison and John Carew. This roused counter objections against Vane and Salwey,

---

[1] Guizot, II, 267; *Clarendon Calendar*, IV, 415–17.

[2] *A Declaration of the General Council of the Officers;* also printed in *True Narrative*, pp. 42–53.

[3] Guizot, II, 272, 277; *Clarendon Calendar*, IV, 425–26; *CSP Ven.*, 1659–61, pp. 83–84.

but they were overruled.[4] Even so, nomination did not necessarily imply consent to serve. Ludlow for instance had great misgivings; he and Vane and Salwey were subjected to earnest persuasion by Lambert, Fleetwood, Desborough, and Sydenham, but the three Rumpers "desired to be excused, till such time as the common cause might be secured to the satisfaction of good men."[5] On the other hand, when Whitelocke showed equal hesitation about serving, Desborough and other leading officers pressed him urgently to do so on the plea that *"Vane, Salwey, and others, had a design to overthrow Magistracy, Ministry, and the Law."*[6] No wonder the Committee's meetings tended to be both thin and stormy. Wariston remarked of the first day's session that "Thir divisions are lyk to plunge us al in blood," and by November 3 no more than nine or ten of the twenty-three had yet sat down together.[7] Nevertheless Vane, Salwey, and Ludlow, despite their doubts, kept up a qualified collaboration with the Committee, and labored at the same time to bring their fellow Rumpers to a better understanding of the army's viewpoint. This brought them only the increasing distrust of both sides.

Barbara Lewalski has remarked[8] that the Committee of Safety exactly conformed to Milton's compromise plan in *A Letter to a Friend* for a single-chamber legislature composed of army officers and members of the Rump, and that this "argues Milton's intimate knowledge of the army's intentions." This can hardly be maintained. For one thing the Committee was much smaller than the Senate envisaged by Milton[9] and contained only half-a-dozen Rumpers, even on paper. More important, it was never conceived as a legislature at all, or as more than a merely provisional government.

Yet the outlines of something closer to Milton's Senate began to emerge after November 1, when the Committee appointed a subcommittee "to prepare a form of government."[10] Vane, Salwey, and Ludlow were of its number, as well as the inevitable Wallingford House men; so were Whitelocke and Wariston. We have only glimpses of its deliberations. Vane had a draft constitution ready prepared, which shocked Wariston as much as it would have pleased Milton by ex-

[4] Wariston, *Diary*, III, 147–48.
[5] Ludlow, *Memoirs*, II, 144.
[6] Whitelocke, *Memorials*, p. 687.
[7] Wariston, *Diary*, III, 150; *Clarke Papers*, IV, 92–93. The Committee's membership is analysed in Davies, *Restoration*, pp. 157–58.
[8] In *PMLA*, LXXIV, 194.
[9] "That it be not an Oligarchy or the faction of a few, may be easily prevented by the numbers of their owne chusing." (*Letter to a Friend*, below, p. 331).
[10] *True Narrative*, pp. 62–63; Whitelocke, *Memorials*, p. 687.

cluding religion from the civil magistrate's authority and upholding an unlimited toleration. Wariston labored against this with his earnest Scottish persistence and his thick Scottish tongue; he pleaded instead for a regimen based on a covenant with God and a confession of faith —surely the last gasp of Presbyterian theocracy in English politics. Others sought a basis in the version of the Agreement of the People which the Council of Officers had presented to the Rump more than ten long years before.[11] But rumors trickled through of continuing projects for a supreme Senate. One spoke of each county electing six candidates, of whom the Council of Officers was to choose three; the resultant assembly would govern under the title of either Parliament or Senate, with a Council of State drawn from its membership.[12] Others suggested that a Council or Senate of fifty or seventy—probably the Committee of Safety enlarged—should nominate four hundred candidates as a kind of "party list" from which the people should elect a supreme legislature of two hundred.[13]

Throughout the discussion of these fanciful schemes, however, some members of the Council of Officers continued to believe that the only way forward to a settlement lay through the Rump. If only, they thought, a quorum of forty members could be persuaded to co-operate with them a compromise could be worked out.[14] But the Rumpers saw less and less reason to compromise as Monck prepared to implement his promise of armed support. All these deliberations in London began to look insubstantial as the General in Scotland cast his lengthening shadow over them from the north.

2. GENERAL MONCK TAKES A STAND

October–November, 1659

Although he was to pull off one of the most striking political confidence tricks in history, George Monck was basically a professional soldier and a plain man. In his lifetime both his apologists and his enemies read endless subtleties into his words and actions, and credited him with a foresight and cunning in planning the Restoration that were really beyond his scope. Tough and shrewd though he was, his

[11] Wariston, *Diary*, III, 150–52.
[12] *CSP Ven.*, 1659–61, pp. 88–90.
[13] Guizot, II, 286; *cf. Clarendon Calendar*, IV, 428; *Ormonde Papers*, II, 248. How far these various reports refer to a single scheme is uncertain, but they contain some common elements.
[14] Guizot, II, 286; *Clarke Papers*, IV, 125.

sheer intellectual capacity was limited. He could be a stout liar when
the need arose and he held his cards close to his chest, but he decided
how to play his hand from one day to the next. When he declared for
the Rump in October, 1659, it is most unlikely that he felt any posi-
tive commitment to the king's cause or looked more than a few moves
ahead. The deviousness and deception into which the events of the
next few months forced him were foreign to his nature. He had
boasted quite sincerely to the Speaker on June 18 of "haveing had my
education in a Comonwealth [the Dutch Republic] where souldiours
received and observed comands, but gave none. Obedience is my greate
principle, and I have alwaise, and ever shall, reverence the Parlia-
ment's resolutions in civill things as infallible and sacred." [1] He was
singularly free from ideological prepossessions in either politics or
religion. If he had a political preference it was for a regime broad-
based on sober, moderate, propertied support; he hated fanatics,
whether in church or state.

He had fought loyally for Charles I until he was captured in 1644,
but after the king in turn became a prisoner Monck made no bones
about accepting a commission from the Parliament to fight the Irish
rebels, against whom he had first engaged. Later he fully justified
the great trust that Cromwell placed in him as General in Scotland,
and he remained equally loyal to Richard for as long as the Protector-
ate survived. When the Rump supplanted Richard Monck was far
from pleased, but it was the *de facto* government and he obeyed it. He
made no move during Booth's rising,[2] and took no notice when his
brother brought him at that time a flattering letter signed "Your
affectionate Friend, Charles R." [3] The Rump nettled him by tamper-
ing with his regiments in Scotland, removing and installing officers
without consulting him, and he evidently went as far as to offer his
resignation.[4] But it is significant that this was his reaction rather than
to intrigue with the royalists as other Cromwellians such as Admiral
Montagu did.

Why then did he take so firm a stand for the Rump in October? The
simplest explanation, and his own, is that he thought that the army
leaders in England had a bad case and that their actions would plunge
the country into anarchy. His parson brother, who had delivered the

[1] *Clarke Papers*, IV, 22.
[2] Later statements by his apologists that he was about to march to Booth's
support when he heard of his defeat, *e.g.* in Baker, *Chronicle*, pp. 674–75, should
be treated with scepticism.
[3] Printed in Baker, *Chronicle*, p. 673.
[4] *Ibid.*, pp. 675–76; *Clarke Papers*, IV, 90, 152; Guizot, I, 475, 486; *Clarendon
Calendar*, IV, 393.

king's letter, told a royalist correspondent that George inclined more
to the Rump than to the army but would have preferred a free
Parliament to either.[5] That was not yet in his power to promote,
though on October 13 he did respectfully remind the House through
the Speaker "to hasten the Settlement of the Government of these
Nations in a Commonwealth Way, in Successive Parliaments, so to
be Regulated in Elections as You shall think fit."[6] Meanwhile his
only choice lay between supporting the Rump and acquiescing in the
military usurpation in England. Since he had no intention of involving
himself in common ruin with the Wallingford House grandees, he put
all his weight behind the only civil government that could claim a
shred of legal authority.

But first he had his own forces to reckon with, for they contained
many officers, chiefly sectaries, whose sympathies lay with Fleetwood
and their brethren in England. These he swiftly and drastically
purged; then he spent great pains in cementing the loyalty of the rest.
He toured and addressed the key regiments in person. He summoned a
great council of all his officers, even the most junior, and patiently
debated the issues with them, stilling their qualms about his evident
threat to set one army against another. He sent a stream of letters
into England, and his aides published pamphlets and broadsides, all
designed to sow doubts among the soldiery and to divide them from
their self-seeking commanders. For consumption by his own troops
and the Scots, circular letters and printed tracts were reinforced in
December by a carefully slanted newspaper called *Mercurius Britan-
icus*.[7] His care was necessary, for his own forces as well as his po-
tential supporters in England already needed convincing that he was
not playing Charles Stuart's game.

Meanwhile he backed up his threat to march into England by mov-
ing troops rapidly towards the border. The Council of Officers in Lon-
don was forced to send all the forces that it could spare to the north,
and on November 3 Lambert departed to take command of them.
Neither side, however, really wanted to fight. The English grandees
realized that a civil war would finally ruin them, while Monck for his
part was outnumbered at least three-to-two by the twelve thousand
or so men that Lambert was gathering in northern England. It was
Fleetwood who made the first pacific gesture. He wrote to Monck on
October 25, hinting that the interruption of the Rump's sittings was

[5] John Barwick to the king, October 13, 1659, in *Mordaunt Letter-Book*, p. 59.
[6] *True Narrative*, pp. 22–23. His public declaration for the Rump, dated
October 20, is in *ibid.*, pp. 24–25.
[7] Davies, *Restoration*, pp. 162–64, 167–71.

not necessarily permanent and urging him to send commissioners to treat. He even offered to meet Monck personally, as far north as York. Monck replied on November 3, proposing a negotiation between three commissioners from each army. Fleetwood promptly accepted.[8] The commissioners met in London on the 12th, and by the 15th the terms of a treaty were agreed.

Unfortunately Monck's commissioners went far beyond their brief. They were instructed to insist that the Rump should be readmitted, and that "noe forme of Governement bee established over these Nations butt by Parliament, unlesse they shall refuse to sitt."[9] One of them, however, betrayed these secret instructions to the Wallingford House party. He was Colonel Wilkes, said to be a member of Christopher Feake's Fifth Monarchist congregation—why Monck chose such a man is a mystery.[10] At any rate the draft treaty provided that the future form of government should be determined not by the Rump but by a special general council of the army and navy, consisting of two officers from each regiment throughout the Commonwealth, the governors of garrisons, and ten officers of the fleet. It was to meet at Whitehall on December 6. The treaty further laid down

> That a Parliament, or a Supreme Delegated Authority of this Commonwealth, be with all possible speed Constituted and Summoned in such manner and form, as shall be by the afforesaid General-Council agreed unto.[11]

The qualifications of the members were however to be decided by a special committee of nineteen, representing the Committee of Safety and the armies in England, Ireland, and Scotland. Vane and others persuaded Monck's commissioners that the terms they signed did not preclude the restoration of the Rump, but the plain sense of the articles was surely that a new Parliament was to be convened.

Monck certainly could not accept the treaty. If the negotiation did not succeed in restoring the Rump its only value to him was as a delaying tactic; so much is clear from a letter he wrote to the lord mayor and Common Council of London while it was actually in progress. He knew that many of the city fathers greatly disliked the army's usurpation. He had already appealed for the support of London's militia, and the militia commissioners had wrangled long and hard before deciding by a majority of one to return a hostile answer. He had more friends,

[8] The exchange of letters is in *Clarke Papers*, IV, 70–74, 85–87.
[9] *Ibid.*, p. 98.
[10] *Ibid.*, pp. 299–300; Historical Manuscripts Commission, *Leyborne-Popham MSS*, pp. 130–31.
[11] The treaty is printed in Baker, *Chronicle*, pp. 693–94.

however, among the aldermen and common councilmen, and his letter of November 12 virtually incited them to resist the Committee of Safety by force:

> If this good Cause shall miscarry in my Hands, through want of your timely Assistance, it will be too late for you to endeavour to support it with your own Strength; and if it prosper, it will be dishonourable for a City so famous, and so much concerned, that its Liberties should be asserted, without its own Help.[12]

This letter naturally appalled the Committee of Safety when it arrived a week after the treaty was signed, and its two bearers were clapped into prison. Monck's embarrassed commissioners gave their opinion that it was a forgery.

The issues as they appeared to both sides while the outcome of the treaty hung in the balance are vividly conveyed in an exchange of letters between the Independent divine John Owen and Monck. Owen had countenanced the Wallingford House party in breaking Richard's Parliament and restoring the Rump; now perhaps he regretted it. At any rate he was prepared to jettison the Rump for the sake of a settlement. This is part of his eloquent plea to Monck on November 19:

> Their are, my Lord, two evills that wee have cause to feare: the one is the prevailing of the Comon Enemy over ous; the other the prevailencie of fanaticall selfe seeking persons amongst ous. By your union both of these, through the mercy of God, wilbee prevented. By a continuance in your breaches, . . . either the Comon Enemy will devoure ous all, which is the most likely, or another sort of men will have opportunity to lay hould on that power which will not easily be wrested from them.

As for the Rump,

> Most of the persons of that number are my old freinds and acquantance. I may say freely that I ventered somwhat for their sitting. . . . Yet this I shall say, that it were better that both they, and I, and hundreds of better men then my selfe were in the ends of the earth, then that this [cause] should be ruined by the armies contest about them.[13]

But Monck would not accept Owen's contention that a free commonwealth could be settled without the Rump's authority. Owen, he replied, had only confirmed "the greate cause of my owne feares—I meane the fanaticall and selfe seeking party, which doe threaten much danger to these three Nations." Fleetwood was too credulous and charitable towards these firebrands, and Owen should press him to care for the safety of sober and judicious Christians, which could be

---

[12] *Old Parliamentary History*, XXII, 47–48; Chivers, *City of London*, pp. 142–50; *Clarke Papers*, IV, 91–94.
[13] *Clarke Papers*, IV, 122–23.

done only by bringing the army back into obedience to the civil authority.

> I am ingaged in conscience and honnour to see my Country freed . . .
> from that intollerable slavery of a sword Goverment, and I know England cannot, nay, will not indure it; and if this army heere had concurred with them in England, wee had bin all exposed to the fury of the three Nations, which they would some time or other have executed. . . .
> As to the Cavaliers' interest, I think I may modestly averre it hath not a greater enimy in the three Nations then my selfe, soe that I shall not trouble my selfe to confute those slanders that fanaticall spiritts would asperse mee withall. I doe assure yow in the presence of God that I shall oppose it to the last dropp of my bloud.[14]

How much hypocrisy there was in this when Monck wrote it on November 29 is difficult to say. A fortnight earlier he had summoned a special convention of representatives of the Scottish shires and burghs to agree on measures for maintaining order in the land if he should march into England. It elected as president the royalist Earl of Glencairn.[15] That may not have meant much by itself. Monck, however, was already in touch then with Lord Fairfax, who had sent him the interesting message that he and other Yorkshire gentlemen were prepared to rise in his support against the army in England, but that they disliked his pledges to restore only the Rump, without the members secluded in 1648, and to countenance no government but a commonwealth. Monck sent a message in reply that his published declarations did not reveal his whole mind, but were governed by the need to reassure his army that he was not working for the king's restoration.[16] He welcomed Fairfax's offers warmly and encouraged the Yorkshire gentry to go ahead with their plans for a rising in Lambert's rear.

Fairfax and his friends certainly wanted to see monarchy restored, but that is no proof that Monck was yet committed to the same cause. He was upon a risky venture; he could not be too nice about his choice of associates or what he said to them. It is probable that he still intended to give the Rump one more chance to effect a republican settlement. If it delayed too long, or if it sought to base the Commonwealth on narrow sectional interests, above all if it sought to perpetuate its own power, he would look elsewhere for a solution. He was nothing if not empirical.

[14] *Ibid.*, p. 153.
[15] *Ibid.*, pp. 78–79, 113–16, 120–21, 140.
[16] Baker, *Chronicle*, p. 690; Austin Woolrych, "Yorkshire and the Restoration," *Yorkshire Archaeological Journal*, XXXIX (1958), pp. 487–88.

3. *PROPOSALLS OF CERTAINE EXPEDIENTS*

It was probably in November, 1659, that Milton dictated another brief paper, propounding a solution to the Commonwealth's latest problems. He may not have found it easy to decide just where he stood between the quarrelling factions. On the one hand the Rump had rejected his most cherished policies with regard to religion. On the other, the army's cause was popularly associated with that of the "anabaptists" who stood as he did for unlimited toleration and against a state church. Without their support, it was said, the grandees could never have defied the Parliament. Monck, the Rump's champion, was reviled because he had "put out all the godly"; and indeed most of the officers whom he dismissed were sectaries.[1] When he first threatened to march, the congregated churches about London sent Joseph Caryl and Matthew Barker, two of their most eminent ministers, in company with Colonels Whalley and Goffe to remonstrate with him.[2] Milton's old friend Robert Overton, now Governor of Hull, remonstrated too, and urged Monck to "drive not so furiously against the dispensation of God, though it be clouded with the weaknesse and failings of the instruments."[3] Overton saw the breaking of the Parliament as an act of providence, for "though there be many pious, prudent and publick Patriots and spirits amongst them; yet they were so intermixed with the late Court Creatures and Kingling Champions . . . that neither Christ, his Peoples, nor the Nations ends were likely to be answered: And I feare some were so misled by principles of a persecuting tendancy . . . that endeavours were not closely wanting to bring all to bow to their Baal."[4]

Yet the religious alignment was not clear-cut. Some of the most prominent sectarian officers, including Rich, Okey, Allured, Saunders, Streater, and Lawson, adhered to the Rump and denounced its violators. So did Praise-God Barebone and his congregation; so did that

---

[1] *Clarke Papers,* IV, 91–92, 101–02; *A True Relation of the State of the Case,* pp. 5, 13–14; *Twelve Seasonable Quæries* (November 1, 1659), E1005(5), p. 2; *The Northern Queries from the Lord Gen. Monck His Quarters* (November 7, 1659, misdated October 7 in Thomason Catalogue), E1005(15), pp. 4, 6–7.
[2] *Clarke Papers,* IV, 81–82.
[3] *The Humble and Healing Advice of Colonel Robert Overton* (1659), BML 100.f.75, p. 5.
[4] *Ibid.,* p. 3.

powerful preacher of the Fifth Monarchy, Christopher Feake.[5] The army was indeed divided, with the sectarian element growing more and more distrustful of Lambert and his motives.[6] It was scarcely plausible any longer to portray the quarrel in terms of principle rather than power. The wisest and truest friends of the Commonwealth were those who, like Vane and Owen in their different ways, avoided violent partisanship and strove only to heal the breaches.

This was what Milton now sought to do in his *Proposalls of Certaine Expedients for the Preventing of a Civill War now Feard, & the Settling of a Firme Government*. This short piece, which remained unpublished until 1938, refers to "the present committee of safety"[7] and so was certainly composed between October 27 and December 24. Two or three indications suggest a date in November. The reference to "this civill war now at point to ensue"[8] was most probably dictated after Lambert departed on November 3 to command the forces sent against Monck but before the temporary *détente* which followed the abortive treaty of November 15. Admittedly the danger of war revived in December, but by that time the debates afoot on the calling of a new Parliament had introduced such an important new factor into the situation that Milton would surely have referred to them. Furthermore, the restoration of the Rump by agreement with the army, which he advocated, was still a plausible possibility during much of November but had almost ceased to be so by December.

We do not know for whom he framed these proposals. The Columbia editors, who first printed them, considered the possibility that they were actually published as a pamphlet,[9] but it is surely inconceivable that Milton sent them to the press in the rough form in which they survive. They begin thus: "First to lay before them in power the scorne we are to forreigne nacions by these our continuall changes." This opening, like all that follows, conveys a strong impression that Milton was dictating mere "heads," to be worked up more fully by himself or another. Perhaps they were intended, as *A Letter to a Friend* may have been, to prompt some acquaintance who stood nearer to "them in power" than he did. Perhaps they represent the outline sketch of a pamphlet of his own, which he was discouraged from

---

[5] L. F. Brown, *Baptists and Fifth Monarchy Men*, p. 191; *Mordaunt Letter-Book*, p. 118; *The Humble Representation of some Officers* (November 1, 1659), E1005(8).

[6] Guizot, II, 275–76.

[7] *Proposalls of Certaine Expedients,* below, p. 336.

[8] *Ibid.*

[9] *Notes and Queries,* CLXXIII (1937), 66.

completing by the rapid changes in the political situation during December. Whatever their purpose, they are interesting as a further stage in the formulation of the ideas that would be fully developed in *The Readie & Easie Way.*

The *Proposalls* differ from *A Letter to a Friend* in their comparative neutrality of tone. There is no more belaboring of the army leaders; Milton accepts the Committee of Safety as a fact and urges it both to go on providing vigilantly for the public safety and to hasten the settling of a durable government. But "the only probable way" of doing this is by treating with the Rump to sit again, since "no government is like to continue unlesse founded upon the publick autority & consent of the people which is the parlament." [10] There must however be conditions: an act of oblivion for past acts of hostility, full liberty of conscience for all who base their faith and worship only on the Scriptures, and an abjuration of government by a single person or a House of Lords. Furthermore the members, once restored, should "sitt indissolubly"; they and all who are elected in the future should hold their seats for life, unless they deserve expulsion for misconduct. This time Milton allows no alternative to life membership. He would change the name of this sovereign body to "Grand or Supreme Counsell," since Parliament "is a Norman or French word, a monument of our Ancient Servitude, commonly held to consist necessarily of 3. Estates, King, Lords, & commons." [11] Vacancies should be filled either by the Grand Council nominating candidates for the well-affected people to choose between, or by such people electing the candidates and the Grand Council making the final choice—evidence of Milton's distrust of unregulated popular elections, which was to become even more explicit in the second edition of *The Readie & Easie Way.* He reveals his misgivings as to whether all the Rumpers are worthy for so great and permanent a trust by tentatively suggesting that if any are judged to be manifestly insufficient they should be excluded and others worthier chosen in their place; "but this is not urged, lest it be misinterpreted" [12]—words which confirm that this paper was not meant for publication as it stood.

Like *A Letter to a Friend,* but unlike *The Readie & Easie Way,* the *Proposalls* would have the restored Rump confirm all the chief officers in their commands for life, though an oath of obedience to it should be required of all ranks of the army. Further articles propose a

[10] *Proposalls,* below, p. 336.
[11] *Ibid.,* p. 337.
[12] *Ibid.,* p. 338.

Council of State, similar in constitution and function to that appointed by the Rump, and (inevitably) the relegation of all authority over matters ecclesiastical and the maintenance of ministers to the particular congregations. Rather strikingly, Milton does not repeat here his hint that the Grand Council's supreme authority should be mitigated by an element of democratic consent at the county level, though he does again recommend that justice should normally be rendered without appeal by judges chosen by each county and city. He closes with an adumbration of *The Readie & Easie Way*'s plan for schools of arts and sciences in every major town, and a rare incursion into economic matters in a plea for "the just division of wast Commons."

4. THE COLLAPSE OF ORDER

November–December, 1659

"If my Lord Generall Monck can but keepe himselfe and army about Barwick for a month or two his business wilbee done."[1] That was the message that a keen-sighted London news-writer sent to Monck on November 5, and a week later his intelligence was still more encouraging:

> Things heere in the South are in a perplexed condition; the lawe is tottering, the Citty is wavering, the Clergy declineing, the people murmering, and nothing but the face of confusion appeares; the divisions are so greate, military and civill, certainely some greate judgement attends this place and the whole land.[2]

Thus informed, Monck had no hesitation in refusing to ratify as it stood the treaty that his commissioners had signed on November 15. He proposed a renewal of negotiation at York or Newcastle with two additional commissioners on each side, and to spin out time still further he demanded that Lambert should send a safe-conduct for his own two nominees.[3] Lambert protested: "The course yow propounde," he wrote, "is soe long and delatory as will give the Common Enimy all the advantage they can expect." More than a hundred of Lambert's officers signed an emotional remonstrance to Monck, asking "will nothing satifie yow but the hazard of the lives and well beeing of your freinds and brethren in England?" But they pleaded in vain;

[1] *Clarke Papers*, IV, 102.
[2] *Ibid.*, p. 112.
[3] *Ibid.*, pp. 129–31.

Monck's proposals were accepted, subject to the new treaty propounding nothing directly contrary to that of the 15th, and to the special representative Council of Officers meeting as formerly agreed on December 6.[4]

As the Committee of Safety ran further into trouble, a nucleus of the old Council of State began to meet again privately, dominated by such men as Haslerig, Scot, Morley, Walton, Neville, and Ashley Cooper. They contrived a meeting with Monck's three commissioners, and on November 19 they wrote to the general warmly encouraging his resistance. On the 24th they sealed a commission to him as commander-in-chief of all the armies in England and Scotland, and entrusted it to his brother-in-law Thomas Clarges. It empowered him to march into any part of England or Scotland and "to feight with, kill, and destroy, or by any waies put to death all such who are in hostility against the Parliament, or doe oppose or hinder . . . the sitting of the same."[5]

Meanwhile, as November advanced, the Committee of Safety rode uneasily upon a growing swell of popular hostility, especially in London. Fleetwood, Whitelocke, Desborough and others visited the city twice, first to put their case to the Court of Aldermen on November 4 and then to address the Common Council on the 8th. But although they got vague assurances that the city fathers would help to keep the peace of the capital, their reception was guarded and equivocal; and on the second occasion they rode home amid shouts from the populace for a free Parliament.[6] The aldermen, drawn from the wealthiest citizens and including some who had invested heavily in confiscated lands, were chary of taking sides and risking a renewal of civil war; but the much more numerous common councilmen were less easily restrained from challenging the Committee's authority and asserting the city's liberties. Fear of such men led the Committee to lay aside the militia commissioners whom the Rump had appointed for the city, and on November 11 to appoint new ones whom it could better trust. It also ordered that all London's militia officers should receive their indi-

[4] *Ibid.*, pp. 144–45, 148. Monck's two additional commissioners were instructed to insist on the recall of the Rump, though they were given some further secret instructions, permitting them to consent to a new Parliament if the Rump should prove altogether recalcitrant: see Historical Manuscripts Commission, *Leyborne-Popham MSS*, pp. 128–30.

[5] *Clarke Papers*, IV, 138; Baker, *Chronicle*, p. 695; K. H. D. Haley, *The First Earl of Shaftesbury* (Oxford: Clarendon Press, 1968), pp. 117–18.

[6] *True Narrative*, pp. 67–68; Whitelocke, *Memorials*, p. 688; *Mercurius Politicus*, November 3–10, 1659, pp. 851, 859; *Old Parliamentary History*, XXII, 10–17; *Clarendon State Papers*, III, 601–02.

vidual commissions from Fleetwood.[7] This caused an angry scene
in the Common Council. One member asserted that the city alone had
the right to dispose of its militia, and urged it to secure itself by a
general call to arms.[8] But more cautious counsels prevailed, to the
chagrin of many bolder spirits in the provinces. A lady in the north
was heard to say that "The Citizens would lye on their Backs, till
They were Gelt, before They would stirre to restore the Nation to the
Liberty of a Parliament." [9]

Amid all this tension London's already depressed trade was grinding
to a standstill. As a further sign that the rule of law was collapsing,
the few judges who had consented to dispense justice at Westminster
since the interruption of the Rump closed their courts on November
20 in mid-term because their commissions from the Parliament had
expired.[10] The lord mayor and Common Council ordered a day of
fasting and prayer on December 2, on the ground that it had "pleased
God to shew us so much of the Fruit of our own Hearts and Evil ways,
as to let us see the very Foundations of Government Razed." [11]

The common citizenry soon turned to more militant protests. They
were stirred up to refuse to pay any taxes that were not lawfully voted
and to clamor for "a full and free Parliament." This movement,
which was evidently organized, soon spread to a series of associations
in the provinces.[12] Money could be levied only with the help of troops,
and the soldiers so employed ran a real danger of being lynched.
Their morale was wilting visibly—"Indeed, the soldyers generally say
they will not fight, but will make a ring for their officers to fight in." [13]
The younger citizens took the lead in the mounting agitation, and
none were busier than those distant forbears of modern student pro-
testers, the city apprentices. They circulated petitions for a free
Parliament and canvassed all and sundry for signatures. On Decem-
ber 1 the Committee of Safety framed a proclamation forbidding this

[7] *True Narrative*, pp. 70–77; Whitelocke, *Memorials*, p. 689; *Mercurius
Politicus*, November 10–17, 1659, pp. 866–67. The new commission issued by
the Committee of Safety is in Guildhall Record Office, box 5.

[8] *Clarendon Calendar*, IV, 443.

[9] *A Narrative of the Northern Affairs* (dated York, November 16, 1659),
E1010(19), p. 5. The militia commissioners of Westminster were more boldly
defiant: see *Clarke Papers*, IV, 112–13.

[10] Guizot, II, 267, 294; *Clarendon Calendar*, IV, 428; *Clarke Papers*, IV, 300.

[11] Order of Common Council, November 23, 1659, 669f22(11*).

[12] Guizot, II, 293; *CSP Ven.*, 1659–61, p. 97; *Clarendon State Papers*, III,
624; *Clarendon Calendar*, IV, 458; *Mordaunt Letter-Book*, p. 118; *The Re-
monstrance of . . . the late Eastern, Southern and Western Associations*
(November 16, 1659), 669f22(11).

[13] *Clarke Papers*, IV, 300.

practice and ordered the lord mayor to publish it. The lord mayor first pleaded indisposition, then asked time to consult the Common Council on the 5th; but the Court of Aldermen met specially on the 3rd and directed each of its members to go round his ward with his constable and charge every master of a family to prevent his sons and servants from disturbing the peace.[14]

Early on the morning of December 5, without waiting upon the Common Council's deliberations, the Committee of Safety despatched the Parliament's serjeant-at-arms with the backing of a squadron of cavalry to read the new proclamation at the Royal Exchange. Poor Serjeant Dendy did not get far. The apprentices harried the trumpeters and moved in threateningly upon the troopers, while more of them manned the nearby roofs and pelted the soldiers with tiles and great lumps of ice from the gutters. The horsemen retired in disorder to the nearest garrison at St. Paul's, the apprentices pursuing, and the city streets rapidly filled with angry demonstrators. All the shops were now shut, and the rioters closed the gates at Temple Bar. The Committee then sent in a stronger force under Colonel Hewson, who had once been a shoemaker. He broke down the Temple Bar gates, but as he advanced towards the storm center at the Exchange with his troopers' swords drawn and their pistols cocked, shouts of "a cobbler! a cobbler!" greeted him all along the way. The apprentices so goaded his men, first with jeers and then with stones, that eventually they opened fire, killing at least two and wounding more. Meanwhile the Common Council had met and admitted a deputation of apprentices with a petition bearing thousands of signatures and calling for either a new free Parliament or the readmission of the Long Parliament as it had sat in 1648 before Pride's Purge. The Common Council appointed a committee to consider it, but it also reinforced the orders to all householders to keep their sons and apprentices from raising tumults. The day's disturbances ended only late in the evening, when a deputation from the Common Council persuaded Fleetwood to withdraw his troops, and Desborough obtained a reciprocal order from the lord mayor commanding all citizens to return to their homes.[15]

The toll in killed and wounded was lighter than it might have been,

[14] Guildhall Record Office, *Repertories* (Court of Aldermen), vol. 67, f. 21v.; Davies, *Restoration*, p. 181; Chivers, *City of London*, pp. 151–52; Guizot, II, 299.

[15] *Clarke Papers*, IV, 164–70; Guizot, II, 299–301; *CSP Ven.*, 1659–61, pp. 101–02; *The Letters and Second Diary of Samuel Pepys*, ed. R. G. Howarth (London, 1932), pp. 14–15; *Mercurius Politicus*, December 1–8, 1659, p. 939; Guildhall Record Office, *Journals* (Common Council), JOR 41x, f. 212. The apprentices' petition is in Thomason, 669f22(14).

but set against the economic misery and seething resentment of the time its emotional impact was not unlike that of the Peterloo massacre 160 years later. It even stiffened the cautious city fathers. When the Court of Aldermen was summoned to Whitehall the next day it flatly refused to attend, though it sent three of its numbers to find out what the Committee of Safety wanted. Three days later the Common Council appointed a committee of safety of its own, to take measures for the peace of the city and to confer with Fleetwood as necessary "concerning the exercise of the power of the Militia of this City by the citizens thereof as also concerning [the government] of this Nation in a Parliamentary way."[16] So far from recognizing the Committee of Safety's authority, the city was claiming now to treat with it on equal terms—or rather to treat merely with Fleetwood as the *de facto* commander of the regular forces about London. The Common Council requested that the troops be kept in their quarters unless the lord mayor or sheriffs saw cause to call them out, and that the stocks of grenades and fire-bombs that had been brought into the city since the riots should be removed.[17] As for the victims killed in those riots, a coroner's court found a verdict of wilful murder, and Hewson was indicted.[18]

Worse news was coming in from the country. On the very day of London's uproar the Committee of Safety heard that Haslerig, Walton, and Morley had donned buff-coats and swords once more and had ridden into Portsmouth, where the governor, the town magistrates, and the citizens warmly welcomed them. From now on the partisans of the Rump had a military base in southern England, and their example was infectious. The same small nucleus of the old Council of State that had organized the securing of Portsmouth commissioned Ashley Cooper to attempt an insurrection in London itself. Cooper, Scot, Okey, and others laid a neat little plot to surprise the Tower in the early hours of December 12. The Lieutenant of the Tower, Colonel Fitch, was in league with them, but Fleetwood heard of their plans just in time and Desborough hastily took over London's ancient fortress.[19] Colonel Fagg was caught gathering forces in Sussex to march

[16] Guildhall, *Journals*, JOR 41x, f. 212v.; words in square brackets supplied to fill an apparently inadvertent omission in the MS.

[17] Guidhall, *Repertories*, vol. 67, ff. 22–23; Chivers, *City of London*, pp. 154–55; Guizot, II, 302–05; *Clarke Papers*, IV, 186–87; *Nicholas Papers*, IV, 190.

[18] *Clarendon State Papers*, III, 626; Guizot, II, 305; *Letters . . . of Samuel Pepys*, p. 17.

[19] *Mercurius Politicus*, December 8–15, 1659, pp. 954–55; *Clarke Papers*, IV, 186–88; Guizot, II, 305–06; Haley, *Shaftesbury*, pp. 119–20. Ludlow's

to the support of Portsmouth. There was also an attempt to raise Colchester, and further west there were broils in Bristol and Taunton, though whether these were for the Rump or for a free Parliament is not clear.[20] At any rate they were against the Committee of Safety, whose authority by mid-December was tottering.

5. THE GENERAL COUNCIL OF OFFICERS

December, 1659

The Committee of Safety's last hope lay in the representative General Council of Officers that met on December 6 under the shadow of the news from Portsmouth and the deep unrest in London. The council was itself only a shadow of what it was meant to be, for no delegates came from either Scotland or Ireland, or even from Lambert's forces in the north. After six days' sitting it mustered only thirty-seven members.[1] Yet although its debates were abortive and can be pieced together only imperfectly from the sketchy evidence that survives,[2] they claim the attention of anyone who seriously studies the ideas in Milton's last political writings. Here were men, many of whom Milton knew, struggling with the same dilemmas: how to establish a durable government on the basis of "fundamentals" that the political nation was increasingly inclined to reject, and how to reconcile civil liberty with what must essentially be minority rule.

When it first met, the General Council was presented with a "model or form of civil government"—presumably the work of the Committee's sub-committee on the constitution, though its content is unknown. Against this Ludlow and Colonel Rich strenuously and repeatedly urged the recall of the Rump, but the majority present inclined neither to the Rump nor to the draft constitution before them, and fell on December 7 to debating a Parliament and a Senate in the most general terms.[3] The grandees took alarm at meeting so much opposition and sent several officers back to their regiments on the pretext of

---

statement (*Memoirs*, II, 169) that the lord mayor informed on this plot is countered by Colonel Whitley in *Nicholas Papers*, IV, 191.

[20] *Mercurius Politicus*, December 15–22, 1659, pp. 963, 965; *Clarke Papers*, IV, 188; *Clarendon Calendar*, IV, 481, 487; Guizot, II, 303.

[1] *Clarendon Calendar*, IV, 481.

[2] What follows is mainly based on the memoirs of Ludlow and Whitelocke, the diary kept of Wariston, the cautious reports in the official newspaper *Mercurius Politicus*, and an occasional gleaning by the French ambassador.

[3] Ludlow, *Memoirs*, II, 163; Wariston, *Diary*, III, 155.

the growing public danger. They also made a last attempt at a settle-
ment behind the scenes by inviting Vane and Salwey to meet them at
Wallingford House. Vane had ceased to attend the Committee of
Safety since his views found no acceptance there,[4] but he and Salwey
consented to the conference provided that Ludlow accompanied them.
The three republicans taxed the officers with intending to restore
Richard Cromwell—a course which had apparently been proposed in
the Committee of Safety by the City Alderman Robert Tichborne.[5]
When this was denied, Salwey pressed them to say whether their
desperate position might not drive them into a deal with Charles
Stuart. "Thus they stood upon their guard on both parts," says
Ludlow, "not adventuring to trust one another; that mutual confi-
dence by which they had done so much being intirely lost." [6] When
Ludlow again pressed them to recall the Rump, Fleetwood admitted
that they had pledged themselves to Lambert not to do this without
his consent.

Meanwhile the General Council had agreed with little opposition
that a new Parliament should be called. Ludlow believed that the
grandees had already come to an agreement on this with the leading
Independent divines, promising at the same time that tithes should be
continued until some other equally ample revenue was provided for
the clergy and that toleration should not extend as far as the Quakers
and other sects which they held to be subversive of civil society.[7] On
December 9 the General Council voted that the Parliament should
consist of two assemblies, as had apparently been proposed in the
draft constitution that it had at first wanted to reject. One assembly
was evidently to be of the nature of a Senate, for the main debate
next day was whether the Senate should be nominated there and then
or left to the election of the people.[8] Ludlow made another impas-
sioned plea for restoring the Rump, but found himself almost alone.
He was convinced that the officers wanted only such a Parliament as
would be a cloak for their own power, and that if it were not content
to be their creature they would dissolve it like its predecessors. To
avert this he changed his tactics. He moved and carried that the
General Council should define the inviolable fundamentals of their

[4] Guizot, II, 293, 304; *Clarendon State Papers,* III, 620; *Clarendon Calen-
dar,* IV, 457.

[5] Ludlow, *Memoirs,* II, 164, 173. The French ambassador heard that this
course was considered by the General Council: see Guizot, II, 306.

[6] Ludlow, *Memoirs,* II, 164.

[7] *Ibid.,* 169. It was at about this time that John Owen published his *Two
Questions,* considered above (pp. 39–40): see Wariston, *Diary,* III, 156.

[8] Wariston, *Diary,* III, 156.

cause, and set up twenty-one Conservators of Liberty with the final power to determine any disagreement that might arise over them between army and Parliament. Several obvious fundamentals were easily agreed, and the General Council proceeded to elect the Conservators by ballot on the basis of a list submitted by Ludlow. The first seven or eight names were accepted, and they included Vane and Salwey as well as Wallingford House men. But thereafter the officers went on to reject Haslerig, Walton, Morley, Wallop, Neville, and Monck, and to elect in their stead such stalwarts of the Committee of Safety as Tichborne, Wariston, Strickland, and Pickering. Ludlow was disgusted, but he was naïve to expect anything else.[9]

By December 13 the General Council had approved "Seven Principles and unalterable Fundamentalls." [10] Four were old familiars that Milton too had stipulated: no kingship, no single person as chief magistrate, no House of Lords, and no imposition on God-fearing consciences. Another laid down that the army was not to be disbanded nor to have its command altered except by consent of the Conservators. The sixth required that the legislative and executive powers should be in separate hands, though it did not say whose. The last was the most cryptic: "That both the Assemblies of the Parliament shall be elected by the people of this Commonwealth, duly qualified." That is all that was announced—not a word as to how the two were to be differentiated in function or membership. But since it is extremely unlikely that the General Council had been suddenly converted to Harrington's model of a commonwealth, the probable explanation is that one assembly was to be a House of Commons and the other an elected Senate of the kind proposed by Vane in *A Needful Corrective or Ballance* or by Stubbe in *A Letter to an Officer*.[11] Yet the Senate had always been conceived in the army as a guardian of the fundamentals; how then was its function to be squared with that of the Conservators?

The General Council referred all such unanswered questions to the Committee of Safety, which drafted a proclamation on December 14 announcing that writs would be issued for the election of a new Parliament to meet on January 24. But the Senate and its manner of election bristled with unsolved problems, and the Committee spent that afternoon debating them with a committee of officers whom it

[9] Ludlow, *Memoirs*, II, 172–74.

[10] *Mercurius Politicus*, December 8–15, 1659, pp. 955–56.

[11] See above, pp. 104–06, 126–28. The French ambassador reported "that the Parliament shall be composed of two Houses, one of which shall hold the place of a Senate co-ordinate in power with the other." Guizot, II, 308.

had asked to attend for the purpose.[12] That day the General Council considered the apportionment of seats in the Commons among the counties and boroughs, and on the next it debated the qualifications of the members and the manner of electing them. This led to an angry brush with Whitelocke, the only Commissioner of the Great Seal who was still acting. Whitelocke told them that some of the things they proposed were contrary to law, and that he could not seal the writs as they demanded without breaking his oath of office. Some officers retorted that they would then seal the writs themselves. One colonel even declared that it was not fit in a time like this for the Great Seal to be entrusted to a lawyer who had not gone through the dangers of war with them.[13]

After this the General Council of Officers rapidly disintegrated. Some were called away by the growing threats to the Committee of Safety, others talked of marching to York to join Lambert, and all were beginning to realize the hopelessness of their efforts as politicians. "Everyone of the officers," wrote Wariston on December 17, "told to us their confusion and unfittnesse to manage such a busines as gouverment." [14]

6. THE FALL OF THE COMMITTEE OF SAFETY

December, 1659

Threats to the Committee's survival were appearing now from all quarters. The most serious came from the fleet in the Downs. Encouraged by the same small group of Rumper Councillors of State who had secured Portsmouth, Vice-Admiral Lawson and his captains wrote to the lord mayor and city government on December 13, declaring that they were ready to use force in order to restore the Rump and desiring the city to assist them. They set sail for London, entering the Thames on the 16th and bringing with them Scot, Okey, and others who had escaped to the fleet after the failure of their plot to seize the Tower. The Committee of Safety sent four of its members, including Vane and Salwey, to try to avert an open breach between army and fleet and to seek some kind of agreement. Lawson had difficulty in per-

---

[12] Wariston, *Diary*, III, 157–58; *Mercurius Politicus*, December 8–15, 1659, p. 956.

[13] Whitelocke, *Memorials*, p. 691; *Mercurius Politicus*, December 15–22, 1659, p. 962.

[14] Wariston, *Diary*, III, 159.

suading Scot and Okey to sit down with these renegades, as they now regarded them, but he dropped anchor off Gravesend and presided for four or five days over a conference between them. He would not, however, be persuaded to join in imposing terms on the Rump before readmitting it.[1]

More bad news came in while these talks were in progress. In Ireland a party of the army seized Dublin Castle on December 13, arrested the governor and commissioners who still took their orders from Fleetwood, and published next day a declaration for the Rump.[2] On the 20th a force that the Committee had sent to reduce Portsmouth went over to the defenders and declared with them for the Parliament. The packets from the north were equally bleak. Monck had advanced his quarters, first to Berwick and then to Coldstream on the Tweed, and was using every pretext for delaying the resumption of negotiations. On the 16th he proposed Alnwick as the venue for the new treaty, but he requested Lambert first to withdraw all his forces from Northumberland, Cumberland, and Westmorland as a pledge of good faith.[3] Three days later, however, he completely changed his tune. He had heard now of Haslerig's, Morley's, and Walton's success in Portsmouth, and on the ground that these three had been appointed fellow commissioners with him for the command of the army by the Rump's act of October 12 he informed Lambert that he could conclude no treaty without their concurrence.[4] It was tantamount to breaking off the negotiation.

Very much depended now on whether the Committee of Safety could keep London quiet. The first effect of the General Council's decision to call a new Parliament was to take some of the steam out of the city fathers' new-found militancy. After Fleetwood and other officers had reported their plans to the corporation's own committee of safety on the evening of December 13, the Common Council at its meeting next day appeared satisfied and renewed its orders to all householders to keep their sons and servants and apprentices from assembling in the streets.[5] These younger citizens, "ripe and almost mad for action,"[6] were furious. They got up fresh petitions and

[1] Davies, *Restoration*, pp. 183–84; Ludlow, *Memoirs*, II, 180–81.

[2] Ludlow, *Memoirs*, II, 184–85.

[3] *Clarke Papers*, IV, 195–96; Historical Manuscripts Commission, *Leyborne-Popham MSS*, pp. 133–34; *Mercurius Politicus*, December 15–22, 1659, p. 970.

[4] Baker, *Chronicle*, p. 698; *Clarke Papers*, IV, 208–10.

[5] *Mercurius Politicus*, December 8–15, 1659, p. 956; Guildhall, *Journals*, JOR 41x, f. 213; *At a Common Council . . . on Wednesday, 14 December*, 669f22(23); *Clarendon State Papers*, III, 630; Guizot, II, 307.

[6] *Nicholas Papers*, IV, 192.

remonstrances, aimed particularly against the redcoats' continuing presence in the city and the Common Council's failure to assert the sole right of its own militia to defend the capital.[7] They railed at the lord mayor as he drove by, and some of them stoned his coach.[8] Fleetwood was forced to keep large guards at the gates and other key points; "yᵉ army men are almost watched off theire legs," it was said.[9] They were also constantly affronted and assaulted. Officers dared no longer wear their swords off duty; soldiers who wandered into back streets were in danger of being beaten and even killed, and shots were fired at sentries in the dark.[10]

All this vigilance was needed not only against apprentice riots but against the royalists. The king's agents had been planning an insurrection in London for the early hours of December 18. The lord mayor gave Fleetwood warning of it, and Desborough had little trouble in stamping it out.[11] But the continuing agitation for a free Parliament indicated that a great part of the citizenry wanted the king back by more peaceful means, and the Common Council could not remain deaf to it. When it met on the 20th it had a declaration drafted to vindicate the lord mayor and his committee of safety from the popular charge that they had betrayed the city's interests to the army. So far from consenting to the army's seven "fundamentals" as a basis for calling a new Parliament, the declaration said, the Common Council had never had a sight of them until they were "printed in a late scandalous Pamphlet styled *The Publick Intelligencer*"—one of the two official newspapers! The Common Council reaffirmed their support for the true reformed Protestant religion, a settled magistracy and the ancient fundamental laws, "And for these ends will endeavour, all they lawfully may, the speedy convening of a Free Parliament to sit and Act without Interruption or Molestation, by any persons whatsoever."[12]

This was not so uncompromising a manifesto as the hotter spirits would have wished, but it indicated that the city was now taking a

[7] *The Engagement and Remonstrance of the City of London*, "Subscribed by 23,500 hands" (December 12, 1659), 669f22(18); *To . . . Our Worthy and Grave Senators* (December 13, 1659), 669f22(19); *The Final Protest, and Sense of the Citie* (December 19, 1659), 669f22(26).

[8] *Clarendon Calendar*, IV, 486–87; *Clarendon State Papers*, III, 630; *Mordaunt Letter-Book*, p. 141; Guizot, II, 308–09.

[9] *Nicholas Papers*, IV, 192.

[10] *Ibid.*; *Clarke Papers*, IV, 166; *CSP Ven.* 1659–61, p. 103.

[11] Guizot, II, 312; *Clarke Papers*, IV, 210–11; *Mercurius Politicus*, December 15–22, 1659, pp. 970–71.

[12] Printed as a broadsheet, 669f22(28), and in *Mercurius Politicus*, pp. 967–68; *cf.* Chivers, *City of London*, pp. 157–59.

line independent alike of Monck, the Rump, and the Committee of Safety. This line was greatly strengthened when the annual elections to the Common Council were held next day. The citizens voted "as if God had directed them for the Kings good"; [13] 83 of the 240 Common Councilmen lost their seats to newcomers, and the result was a large incursion of Presbyterians favorable to monarchy and an exodus of commonwealthsmen and sectaries. The new Common Council promptly resolved to put the city "forthwith into a posture of defence" and set about reorganizing the militia under its own exclusive authority.[14]

But in defying Wallingford House the city found itself pushing at an open door, for the Committee of Safety was collapsing. Haslerig was preparing to march on London with fifteen hundred horse, and news was coming in daily from the provinces of troops and regiments declaring for the Rump. On December 21 two regiments on guard near Whitehall did the same, in defiance of their colonels, and on the previous evening sixty infantrymen who were marching to St. James "laid downe their arms till they bee satisfied for what and whome they engage." [15]

At about this time Ludlow broke in upon a meeting of the chief officers and warned them of the ruin they were bringing upon themselves and the people of England. Desborough took him aside and suggested that they should select sixty of the best and ablest of the old Parliament and constitute them as the select Senate, with a veto over the representative body about to be elected.[16] Sixty was about the whole active strength of the Rump in its latter days. No Milton scholar has remarked how close this came to Milton's own proposals, though he of course envisaged not a House of Commons but a plurality of county assemblies as a balance to the Senate's autocracy. Ludlow rightly pointed out that such a Senate would be as objectionable as the Cromwellian "Other House" if, as was inevitable, it were to contest the decisions of the nation's representatives with no other support than that of the army.[17]

By December 20 Fleetwood was having agonizing doubts about calling a new Parliament at all, but after long debates the attenuated

[13] *Mordaunt Letter-Book*, p. 146; the elections are thoroughly analysed in Chivers, *City of London*, pp. 99–110, 114–15.

[14] Chivers, *City of London*, pp. 159–61.

[15] *Clarke Papers*, IV, 211, 216; Guizot, II, 317; Wariston, *Diary*, III, 160.

[16] Ludlow, *Memoirs*, II, 182–83.

[17] *Cf. A Negative Voyce* (November 20, 1659), E1010(10), p. 3, which said that the proposed Senate "is as like the other House, as an *Ape* is like a *Monkey*."

Council of Officers requested the Committee of Safety to send out the writs. Next day, however, some leading members of the Committee were talking of shutting themselves up in the Tower, and an envoy was despatched to Lambert to recall him and his forces to London. Writs for parliamentary elections were sent to the city on the 21st, only to be countermanded on the 22nd.[18] All was confusion; "the sojours everywheir was lyk to mutiny for want of sylver, and saying they would not feight against the Long Parliment." Owen, Desborough, and Sydenham indeed were now urging that there was nothing left but to treat with the Rump.[19] Whitelocke, according to his own account, proposed a more drastic expedient. Confirmed after a visit from some very prominent Presbyterians in his own opinion that Monck was already set on restoring the king, he privately urged Fleetwood to get in first and make what terms he could for himself, his friends, and his cause. He suggested two possible courses: either Fleetwood should muster such forces as would obey him, occupy the Tower and join with the city in declaring for a free Parliament, or he should send direct to the king—Whitelocke offered himself as an envoy—and offer to further his restoration on whatever terms Charles would agree to. Whitelocke believed he had persuaded Fleetwood to this second course, but as he left the room Vane, Desborough, and Berry went in. A quarter of an hour later Fleetwood came out, deeply agitated. "I cannot do it! I cannot do it!", he cried. The others had reminded him of his pledge to Lambert to take no such step without his consent.[20]

As the Committee's authority crumbled, the small nucleus of the old Council of State acted once more. Rejoined now by their friends who had sailed in with Lawson's fleet, they sought out the Speaker at his home on December 23. By his authority they issued orders to all the forces in London to rendezvous next day in Lincoln's Inn Fields under the faithful Colonels Okey and Allured. The Speaker sent to Fleetwood for the keys of the Parliament House. As he surrendered them, Fleetwood confessed "that the Lord had blasted them and spitt in their faces, and witnessed against their perfidiousnesse." [21] He who eight months earlier had called out the regiments about London to a demonstration of strength that left his brother-in-law Richard naked to the army's demands now learned in his turn what it was to be de-

[18] Wariston, *Diary*, III, 159–60; *Clarke Papers*, IV, 215–16.
[19] Wariston, *Diary*, III, 160.
[20] Whitelocke, *Memorials*, p. 692.
[21] *Clarke Papers*, IV, 220; Historical Manuscripts Commission, *Leyborne-Popham MSS*, p. 136.

serted by them. On the 24th they all paraded obediently in Lincoln's Inn Fields and marched to Speaker Lenthall's house in Chancery Lane, where they greeted him with joyous acclamations and volleys of shot. Lenthall and a small delegation then called upon the Lord Mayor and obtained that flexible gentleman's acquiescence in the resumption of authority by the Rump. Next they took formal possession of the Tower.

The day that would soon be recognized again as Christmas was evidently spent in rounding up the surviving Rumpers. Lenthall and his colleagues just managed to collect a quorum. They had announced their intention to sit again on December 27, but they apparently got wind of a design by the secluded members of 1648 to take their seats too. So the Speaker assembled his little flock at Whitehall on the evening of the 26th and led them by back ways to the Parliament-house, where they held a token sitting at 7 o'clock.[22] In such a hole-and-corner way began the last act of the tragi-comedy of the year 1659.

[22] In addition to the sources cited in Davies, *Restoration,* p. 189, I have drawn on Guizot, II, 318–19 and *A Brief Narrative* (December 30, 1659), E1011(4), pp. 2–5, 7.

CHAPTER IX

THE WANING OF THE GOOD OLD CAUSE

MILTON beheld the death throes of the Committee of Safety with a tragic sense of all that was being betrayed by the squabbling children of the Commonwealth. In mid-December he received a letter from Henry Oldenburg asking whether he was planning to compose a history of England's commotions. He replied on the 20th that England's troubles were worthier of silence than of celebration:

> nor is the need with us for someone who can prepare a history of our commotions, but for someone who can happily settle the commotions themselves; for I fear with you lest amidst these our civil discords, or rather madnesses, we may seem all too exposed to liberty's and religion's enemies, now newly conjoined; but they will not have inflicted a severer wound on religion than we ourselves have long been doing by our crimes.*

Why Milton did not contribute his own prescription for "settling the commotions" sooner—why in other words he did not compose *The Readie & Easie Way* in December or January rather than February —is difficult to guess. He surely cannot have imagined that the return of the Rump in itself provided a solution. But whatever the reason, the events described in this chapter constitute the immediate background to his last major prose work, and he must have scanned them anxiously for their omens.

1. THE RUMP AND THE CITY

December, 1659–January, 1660

Only forty-two members were present when the Rump assembled for serious business on the morning of December 27. Twenty-two of the secluded members, with the indomitable Prynne prominent among them, attempted to take their seats too, but Colonels Okey and Allured

* French, *Life Records*, IV, 287–88. The translation, where it departs from French's, is my own.

turned them back.[1] The first work was to reassert parliamentary authority over the broken forces in England, especially Lambert's, and if possible to pay them. But then arose the more controversial question of an act of indemnity for members of the army who submitted to Parliament's authority. How far should it extend? Some members wanted to proceed against Lambert as a traitor, and when Vane spoke in his defense their tempers rose.[2] On the 29th Haslerig, Morley, and Walton rode into London from Portsmouth amid cheers from the citizens. They came straight to the House in their riding habits, though Haslerig refused to enter it until Vane left.[3] Haslerig was in exuberant spirits, "so elevated, that for some time after he could scarce discern his friends from his enemies."[4] He arrived just in time for the election of a new Council of State, and he topped the poll. It was a very different Council from that of the past summer, for the Rump made a clean sweep of all who had had any dealings with the Committee of Safety. Out went Vane, Salwey, Ludlow, Whitelocke, and Algernon Sidney,[5] as well as Fleetwood, Lambert, Desborough, and Berry; in came a phalanx of Haslerig's henchmen, together with a few republican officers and city aldermen. But the triumph of the republican old guard was premature, for the sands would shortly be quaking under their feet too.

The reactions of the city should have warned them.[6] Their own dramatic return to power stole the limelight from some scarcely less significant developments in the Common Council, which met nine times between December 20 and January 4—more often than it had been wont to do in a whole year in prerevolutionary times. The change of government at Westminster made at first no difference to the new Common Council's resolve to put the city in "a posture of defence" and to reorganize its six regiments of militia. The list of officers whom

---

[1] *A Brief Narrative*, pp. 2–5, 7. Attendance rose to a peak of 62 on December 30, when the House was counted, but declined again thereafter.

[2] Guizot, II, 323. On January 3 Lambert was included in the indemnity after a division, but on the 13th the House instructed the Council of State to secure him and other officers: *Commons Journals*, VII, 802, 812.

[3] Whitelocke, *Memorials*, p. 693; Wariston, *Diary*, III, 164. According to Wariston there was a move to impeach Vane, but the House eventually contented itself with expelling him.

[4] Ludlow, *Memoirs*, II, 204.

[5] Sidney had not acted with the Committee of Safety; he was in Copenhagen on a mission to the kings of Sweden and Denmark.

[6] The next two paragraphs are based mainly on the Common Council's *Journals* in Guildhall JOR 41x, ff. 214–18, and in Thomason 669f22(45); *Mercurius Politicus*, December 29–January 5, 1659–60; Guizot, II, 323, 325; *Clarendon State Papers*, III, 639.

it approved for these regiments on December 24 must have gladdened
royalist hearts. It busied itself about the gates and posterns and
portcullises, and ordered the setting up of posts and chains to bar
the streets if need be. On the 27th it instructed its own new com-
mittee of safety to inform the Rump of its measures and to assert its
right to dispose of London's militia as it thought fit. Even more
boldly, it ordered the drafting of a petition for a free Parliament. This
was approved the very next day; it called for the readmission of the
secluded members and the filling of the other vacant seats by free
elections. But it was never presented. When the city's committee of
safety duly met Haslerig, Morley, and Walton, the latter evidently
used enough diplomacy to secure a respite, for the Common Council
voted on the 29th to suspend the petition. The Rump followed up this
temporary gain on the 31st by sending the Speaker and a powerful
delegation to meet the Court of Aldermen.

As usual, the cautious aldermen proved much more conciliatory
when they met on their own than did the larger body of the Common
Council, and Haslerig was content with the assurances of obedience
that he carried back to the House.[7] But this did not stop the Common
Council from voting on January 4 to complete the raising of its six
regiments or from naming commissioners to confer further with the
Rump's delegates about the readmission of the secluded members or
the calling of a free Parliament. The same courses were also urged
in a letter to Monck that the city's swordbearer was already carrying
northward. Many a county and city would soon follow London in
serving notice that the fate of England did not rest exclusively with
the Rump, or even with its enigmatic General.

2. MONCK'S MARCH INTO ENGLAND

January, 1660

For the Rump, the whole future hung on whether Monck's pledges
of obedience could be taken at face value. Now they were back in
power, Haslerig and his colleagues probably hoped he would remain
quietly in Scotland. The Speaker wrote to him on December 27
to convey the House's hearty thanks, but said not a word of marching
into England.[1] His letter crossed one from Monck written on the 29th,
which explained that he had long been ready to put the Parliament's

---

[7] *Commons Journals*, VII, 801.
[1] *Clarke Papers*, IV, 222–23.

righteous cause to God's determination, but that friends in England
had advised him that if he could stand posted on the border without
engaging Lambert in battle until January 1, "the Work would be done
without Blood." He thanked the members of the Council for the great
honor of his commission as commander-in-chief, and promised such
absolute obedience to the Parliament's commands "that I shall be
more ready to return that Commission than to receive it." "I have
made ready to march," he concluded, "but am unwilling to hazard
your Justice and Authority upon a Fight, when it may be done with
more Security. I shall attend your farther Commands." [2]

Yet three days later, *without* any further commands, Monck
launched his army across the Tweed into England, even though he
now knew for certain that the Rump was sitting again.[3] He had, it is
true, an excellent pretext. Lord Fairfax kept his promise and began
to raise the Yorkshire gentry on December 30. Many of Lambert's
forces came over to them, and the various scattered parties were
skillfully directed to a single rendezvous. On New Year's Day, as
Monck's advance began, Fairfax mustered about eighteen hundred
men on Marston Moor—what memories that field must have held
for him! Thence he marched them to York, and by the evening the
city was his.

Monck naturally felt obliged to engage Lambert's army frontally,
lest it turn and stamp out Fairfax's insurrection piecemeal. Yet
there was no fight in Lambert's men—what was there to fight for
now that Wallingford House had capitulated to the Rump? The only
consideration that roused a few of his officers to resist was a well-
grounded suspicion that most of these Yorkshire gentry were for the
king, but Fairfax was circumspect in concealing his intentions and
preventing his royalist neighbors from joining openly in his enter-
prise. Most of Lambert's forces that did not either join Fairfax or
desert proved ready enough to obey the Parliament's orders and
disperse to scattered quarters. By the time Monck followed his
forward units into England on January 2, Lambert had only a few
officers and about fifty troopers still with him, and these he soon
left in order to make his way as inconspicuously as possible to
London.[4]

With the total collapse of resistance in England and with Scotland

[2] *Old Parliamentary History*, XXII, 40–41.
[3] He so informed Sir Hardress Waller on January 1, countermanding his
former request for cavalry from Ireland because they were no longer needed:
Clarke Papers, IV, 237.
[4] Woolrych, *Yorkshire Archaeological Journal*, XXXIX, 491–98.

virtually undefended, Monck might have been expected to withdraw beyond the border and await further orders from the Parliament. Instead he advanced steadily southward, arriving in York on January 11. Quite obviously he had no intention of watching the Rump's efforts to settle the Commonwealth's future as a distant spectator; he meant to be on the scene himself. On January 7 the Parliament did request him to come to London with such forces as he thought fit, to confer about the ordering of the Commonwealth's armies,[5] but there is an air of face-saving about this letter, and Monck had already advanced nearly 150 miles into England before he can have received it. Everyone in England from Rumpers to royalists was speculating about his intentions. "He is a black Monck," wrote Lord Mordaunt to the king, "and I cannot see through him." [6]

He continued however to profess his unqualified adherence to the Rump. To the city's letter in favor of readmitting the secluded members he replied on January 6 that he and his army were resolved "to stand by and maintain this present Parliament, as it sat on *October* 11," and that he hoped the city would concur [7]—"a cunning piece, and that which they did not much trust to," noted Pepys,[8] but it sufficed to check the Common Council's challenge to the Rump until after he had arrived in London. How far he meant what he said, we could judge better if we knew what passed between him and Fairfax when they conferred privately in York. The stand that he took in public was virtually dictated by the need to allay suspicions among his own regiments and the other forces still afoot in England; paradoxically, he could only preserve his freedom of action by pledging and demanding implicit obedience to a government which he trusted little, and which only half trusted him.

Yet throughout his march to London he was greeted as a hero by thousands of people who cordially detested the Rump. This was the time when declarations for a free Parliament poured in from every quarter of England.[9] Some were addressed to Monck, some to the Speaker, and some that refused all recognition of the Rump to the

[5] *Clarke Papers*, IV, 240–41; *Commons Journals*, VII, 804.

[6] *Clarendon State Papers*, III, 651. "All the world is at a loss to think what Monck will do," wrote Pepys on January 18, "the City saying that he will be for them, and the Parliament saying he will be for them." *The Diary of Samuel Pepys*, ed. Henry B. Wheatley (8 vols., London, 1904; hereafter cited as Pepys), I, 22.

[7] *Old Parliamentary History*, XXII, 51.

[8] Pepys, I, 16.

[9] See Thomason, *CSPD*, 1659–60, and *Mercurius Politicus*, from January 12 onwards.

lord mayor and Common Council of London. Some demanded a new Parliament based on free elections, others the readmission of the secluded members; many offered either course as equally acceptable. Either would indeed have led to the same desired end, and although care was usually taken to prevent overt royalists from signing these addresses, no one was deceived about their promoters' intentions. Some were launched with riotous demonstrations, and not a few undertook to refuse all taxes until the county concerned was properly represented in a free Parliament. Some were apparently spontaneous; some were certainly promoted by royalist agents in collaboration with Presbyterians like Prynne, Annesley, and the Earl of Manchester.[10] Getting them up was not without risk. Some gentlemen were sent to the Tower for it, and Haslerig even proposed that those who signed them should have their estates sequestered.[11] These declarations, together with the agitation in London, brought home to Milton the swelling public demand for a return to monarchy that he bitterly acknowledged in *The Readie & Easie Way*.

One of the first of them came from Monck's native county of Devon. On January 23 he wrote a reply to it which was read in Parliament three days later and promptly published. Naturally it received enormous attention. The Civil Wars, wrote Monck, had given birth to many new interests in both church and state: Presbyterians, Independents, sectaries of all colors in the one, and purchasers of crown lands, church lands, and delinquents' estates in the other. No government could be good or lasting that did not provide for their security. That being so,

> Then that Government under which we formerly were both in State and Church, *viz.* Monarchy, cannot possibly be admitted for the future in these Nations, because it's support is taken away, and because it's exclusive of all the former Interests both Civil and Spiritual, all of them being incompatible with Monarchical Uniformity in Church and State thus expired.[12]

As for the secluded members, whose recall the Devon gentry demanded, many (Monck continued) were monarchists, and wanted to annul all laws passed since 1648. This the army would never endure; the result

[10] *Clarendon State Papers*, III, 660, 663; *Clarendon Calendar*, IV, 527, 531, 534; *Mercurius Politicus*, February 2–9, 1660, p. 1073.

[11] *Clarendon State Papers*, III, 661; *CSPD*, 1659–60, p. 330; *Mercurius Politicus*, January 26–February 2, 1660, pp. 1068, 1073; *cf. CSP Ven.*, 1659–61, p. 114.

[12] *A Letter of General Monck's* (dated Leicester, January 23, 1660), E1013(20), p. 5; reprinted in *Old Parliamentary History*, XXII, 68–70, where it is misdated January 21.

would be a new and bloody civil war. He therefore urged his fellow countrymen to submit to the determinations of the present Parliament, for that way lay the best hope of settling a Commonwealth that would comprehend all interests both spiritual and civil.

When Monck wrote this letter he had just been joined by two Rumpers, Thomas Scot and Luke Robinson, who henceforth accompanied him in the role of latter-day political commissars. He was not however the man to write under dictation. How far was his tongue in his cheek? He was already in close touch with Sir Charles Coote and other crypto-royalists in Ireland who would shortly help him by taking over control of the military forces there, and who were to declare for the secluded members five days before he himself let them in.[13] He was not necessarily committed yet to this course, but he must surely have been contemplating it as a possibility in case the Rump should prove refractory.

3. THE RUMP IN DISARRAY

January–February, 1660

During January the Rump did show some limited awareness that this was its last chance to provide for the future. It voted on the 3rd to hold elections to the seats of members who had died, and then on the 5th to fill also those of the secluded members, whose expulsion was finally confirmed.[1] A bill to define the qualifications of electors and elected was read a second time on the 11th and referred to a large committee, which was further instructed "to consider, In what manner this Parliament may be made, so as to be a Foundation for future Parliaments, and the Settlement of the Nation." [2] Did this decision to fill up the House imply a tacit abandonment of the past summer's promise to terminate the present Parliament's life not later than May, 1660? Nothing was clear, although a declaration published on the 23rd denied the charge that the present members intended to perpetuate themselves in authority. Otherwise this declaration offered

[13] Ludlow, *Memoirs*, II, 209, 228–31; in p. 228 n. 2 Firth marshals the evidence that Monck instigated this declaration, which he must have done well in advance owing to the slowness of communications. On Monck's complicity cf. Davies, *Restoration*, pp. 250–51, 267.

[1] *Commons Journals*, VII, 803. The latter vote, which was expunged from the *Journals* after the secluded members' return, is printed in *Mercurius Politicus*, January 5–12, 1660, p. 1009.

[2] *Commons Journals*, VII, 807.

little but platitudes, though it did promise to provide for a learned and pious ministry and to continue its maintenance by tithes, since this was "already established by Law, and is in itself the most certain, convenient, and comfortable Way of Maintenance that, in the Judgment of the Parliament, can be settled." [3] This was an even more positive rejection of Milton's plea in *The Likeliest Means* than the Rump had voted the previous June, and it is a measure of his desperation that he was prepared in the original version of *The Readie & Easie Way* to perpetuate the authority of a body so opposed to his deepest convictions in matters ecclesiastical. Nothing more specific was decided until February 4—was it coincidence that Monck had arrived in London the day before?—when the House resolved to bring up its strength to four hundred, with the seats apportioned "as they were agreed on in the Year 1653." [4] This at least tells us the size of the perpetual Grand Council that Milton envisaged when he dictated *The Readie & Easie Way*.

The slow progress of these deliberations is largely explained by new divisions that were rending the House. After the expulsion or withdrawal of Vane, Salwey, Whitelocke, Fleetwood, Sydenham, and all who had acted with the Committee of Safety, it might be imagined that Haslerig now commanded a monolithic party. Nothing was further from the truth. The rift began to open on January 2, when a clause was added to the oath to be taken by Councillors of State whereby they must comprehensively renounce the pretended title of Charles Stuart and swear to oppose the setting up of any single person or House of Lords. The House further voted that Haslerig—surely the main instigator—should bring in a bill requiring all M.P.'s to take the same engagement. [5] This proposal, though carried, caused such bitter language that the Speaker threatened to leave the chair. [6] Despite long debates the bill never passed, but the obligation on the Council of State remained. Only twelve of the thirty-one councillors were prepared to take the oath. [7]

The fact was that many members suspected that Monck might bring in the king and did not want to prejudice their chances of working their passage with him. Some would have to turn their coats, but faced with the hopeless intransigence of Haslerig's party it was not unnatural to prefer a bloodless restoration, perhaps on terms that would

[3] *Old Parliamentary History*, XXII, 61.
[4] *Commons Journals*, VII, 834.
[5] *Commons Journals*, VII, 801.
[6] Guizot, II, 329.
[7] Davies, *Restoration*, p. 263. A thirteenth councillor eventually swore.

save something of the old cause, to a republican *Götterdämmerung*.
These *politiques* were a mixed body. Chief Justice St. John and Sir
Thomas Widdrington, Commissioner of the Great Seal, had never been
antimonarchical in principle, but others such as John Weaver and
Robert Reynolds, the new attorney-general, certainly had. The group
also included Colonels Morley, Fagg, White, and Thomas. An in-
creasingly prominent role was played by Sir Anthony Ashley Cooper,
who came into the Rump for the first time on January 7 upon the
redetermination of a disputed election in 1640.[8] All these were on the
Council of State. Probably only a very few, such as Colonel Feilder,
Richard Ingoldsby, and Francis Lascelles, had undergone any positive
conversion to the king's cause, but they would not be dictated to by
Haslerig and Scot, and if Monck were to let in the secluded members
they would not oppose him. Speaker Lenthall also entered into close
correspondence with Monck, and when he pleaded ill health to gain
ten days' leave of absence from January 13 his indisposition was sus-
pected to be of a diplomatic nature.[9]

These men were all hostile to the more extreme sectarian and radical
wing of the Rump's remaining supporters, and Monck encouraged
them. He wrote on January 21 to congratulate St. John on his "noble
resolution to endeavoure the just settlement of these Nations in a
Commonwealth way, with care and provision to avoide those two
rocks of the Malignant and fanaticall interests."[10] "Fanatical" was
Monck's favorite term of reproach during these weeks, and in the
sweeping way that he used it it would doubtless have embraced
Milton.

A crucial contest between Monck's supporters and Haslerig's took
place in Parliament on January 30. Monck's whole success hung on it.
He had now reached St. Albans, only twenty miles from London. He
had about 5,800 men with him, and they were outnumbered by the
regiments already stationed in and around the capital. The discipline
of those regiments was uncertain, owing to their long arrears of pay
and the frequent changes among their officers, but their colonels in-
cluded men like Haslerig, Rich, Okey, and Streater who would stand
by the Rump if Monck should fall out with it. The only two regiments
that Monck felt he could trust were Morley's and Fagg's. He therefore

[8] Haley, *Shaftesbury*, pp. 123–26. Evidence for the other names in this
paragraph is drawn from Baker, *Chronicle*, p. 700; Ludlow, *Memoirs*, II, 205–
06, 209–11, 217; Guizot, II, 329, 331; *Clarendon State Papers*, III, 650–51;
Clarendon Calendar, IV, 519–20, 524; *Clarke Papers*, IV, 249–51.
[9] *Commons Journals*, VII, 811; Guizot, II, 332; *Clarendon Calendar*, IV, 520;
Historical Manuscripts Commission, *Leyborne-Popham MSS*, pp. 206 ff.
[10] *Clarke Papers*, IV, 249.

wrote to the Speaker on the 28th, proposing that all the regiments except these two should be ordered out of the London area to make way for his own. He further proposed to quarter them so as not only to scatter them widely over southern and eastern England but to divide each one of them, company from company and troop from troop. He was in fact requesting the Rump to neutralize the military resources of which it still disposed and to entrust him with the crucial military dominance of the capital. The debate in the House was long and violent. Haslerig, speaking for the Council of State, proposed a compromise: only four regiments should march out, and only four of Monck's seven should march in. After four hours' debate this was rejected; the House voted Monck's requests to the letter. It was a measure of the ground that Haslerig had lost in the past month.[11]

As if to justify Monck's request for their removal, the infantry in London and Westminster staged a serious mutiny when they got their marching orders. It began in a regiment that was being paraded in St. James' fields on the morning of February 1, prior to going on guard. An officer struck a soldier for insolence; the soldier laid him flat with the butt of his musket. Soon all the men were shouting that they would not march without their money. They threatened to hang their officers and strip them naked, and they drove them from the field. This particular regiment was quieted with promises of pay, but the contagion spread to others. Somerset House was the storm center on the 2nd. There too the soldiers refused to stir without their pay; they tore up their colors and hauled guns to the main gate. Pepys was drawn to the Strand by the sound of gunfire—did Milton hear it too? By afternoon, as more and more companies marched in to join them, over two thousand men were in full mutiny. Some were shouting for a free Parliament, some for Lambert and their old officers, and many declared they would serve anyone who gave them their pay. Enough money was somehow found to quiet the majority of them, but a hard core retreated into Somerset House, where many got drunk. To such a rabble had Cromwell's once splendid redcoats declined. With the active help of royalist agents the trouble spread to the city. Crowds of apprentices gathered that night at the Royal Exchange with swords and halberds, and they were already marching to join the mutineers when two determined troops of horse arrived and broke them up.

All this gave the Council of State such a scare that it sent Thomas Scot posting in the dark to Monck's headquarters to urge him to

[11] Baker, *Chronicle*, pp. 701–03 (where Clarges' claim to the credit for Monck's letter should be treated with scepticism); Guizot, II, 338; *Commons Journals*, VII, 826.

march in immediately. Monck was roused from his bed after midnight, but he soon went back again. He would make his entry on the morrow, as planned; in the meantime, he probably thought, it would not hurt the Rump to learn how much it depended on him. London, however, was much calmer by the morning. The mutinous regiments marched out quietly after their officers had striven with them all night and promised them pay at their next quarters—all save the one at Somerset House, which held out till later in the day for ten shillings a head on the spot.[12]

4. MONCK AND THE CITY

February, 1660

The sun shone as Monck entered the city at noon on February 3 at the head of his life guard, followed first by some hundred men of quality in coaches and on horseback and then by his cavalry. He was finely mounted, and though his own dress was sober, trumpeters, footmen, and grooms attended him in red livery decked with silver lace. As he rode through Holborn and Chancery Lane to Temple Bar, he met little sign of popular welcome but many cries for a free Parliament. The Speaker arrived by coach to greet him before Somerset House, whose gates were still barred by the mutineers. Monck dismounted, and the two men embraced with lavish assurances of mutual respect. Thence to Whitehall, where most of the Rumpers came in to attend upon him.[1]

The next two days were full of compliments on both sides, but beneath them ran a strong undercurrent of suspicion. Invited to take his place on the Council of State, Monck to the consternation of Haslerig's party declined to take the councillors' oath that had already caused such dissension.[2] For his part he cannot have failed to remark that Parliament regularly referred to him now as Commissioner-General Monck, as if he were no more than one of the seven appointed to command the army by the act of October 12, despite its having at his own

[12] This account of the mutinies is based on Historical Manuscripts Commission, *Leyborne-Popham MSS*, pp. 144, 214; Pepys, I, 37–40; *Diurnal of Thomas Rugg*, pp. 34–35; *Mercurius Politicus*, pp. 1073–74; *Clarendon State Papers*, III, 668; Guizot, II, 342; *CSPD*, 1659–60, pp. 344, 357; *CSP Ven.*, 1659–61, p. 115; Ludlow, *Memoirs*, II, 214.

[1] *Diurnal of Thomas Rugg*, p. 35; Historical Manuscripts Commission, *Leyborne-Popham MSS*, p. 144.

[2] See above, p. 163.

direct request confirmed the former Council of State's commission to him as commander-in-chief.[3] During his march, "Haslerigge could not endure to hear him called General by anyone in the House, but would presently startle at it and ask whom they meant and angrily say that he was no more General than himself was." [4]

The republicans' suspicion was by no means allayed when Monck attended the House in state on February 6 to receive its formal thanks. After the Speaker's high-flown oration, his speech in reply sounded all the blunter by contrast. He told the members of the correct and chilling responses he had made to the many addresses presented to him on his way for a free Parliament or the readmission of the secluded members. But then he advised them "That the less *Oaths* and *Engagements* are imposed . . . your Settlement will be the sooner attained to." This settlement, he urged, should be such as would satisfy "all the sober Gentry . . . knowing it to be the Common Concern to amplifie, and not to lessen our Interest,[5] and to be careful that neither the Cavaleer, nor Phanatick Party have yet a Share in your Civil or Military Power." He closed with brief advice about Ireland ("as well there as here, it is the sober Interest must establish your Dominion") and Scotland, where "nothing was to them more dreadful, than a fear to be over-run with Phanatick Notions." Scot and others of Haslerig's party were much offended that Monck should so presume to tell them their business. Did commonwealthsmen like themselves come under his censure as "fanatics," they asked themselves, and did his "sober interest" extend to include the cavaliers? [6]

Two days later came a challenge from the city that determined them to put him to the test. On February 8 the Common Council held its stormiest meeting yet. Monck's discouraging letter of January 6 had checked its pressure for a free Parliament until now, but it would contain its discontents no longer. It debated whether the city should pay any taxes voted by the Rump, and the majority seemed in favor of refusing. They talked gallantly of shedding the last drop of their blood in defense of the city's and the whole nation's liberties and they pressed the lord mayor hard. Yet despite confident reports [7] of a

[3] *Commons Journals*, VII, 823 and *passim; Clarke Papers*, IV, 256.

[4] Historical Manuscripts Commission, *Leyborne-Popham MSS*, p. 210.

[5] So in Baker, *Chronicle*, p. 705, the version quoted throughout this paragraph; but that in *Old Parliamentary History*, XXII, 89, follows *Mercurius Politicus* and reads "to expatiate, and not to narrow our Interests."

[6] Baker, *Chronicle*, p. 706.

[7] *Clarendon State Papers*, III, 674; *Clarendon Calendar*, IV, 555; Pepys, I, 46; *CSP Ven.*, 1659–61, p. 116; BML, Stowe MSS 185, f. 143.

vote to allow no taxes to be collected that were not imposed by a full
and free Parliament, nothing of the kind is recorded in the Common
Council's *Journals,* and somehow the lord mayor must have staved
it off.[8] Nevertheless the Common Council gave thanks to the pre-
senters of two petitions for a tax strike, and promised to consider
them "so far as concerns this Court." [9]

The Council of State concluded, probably rightly, that London was
on the verge of repudiating the Parliament's authority. If that were
allowed to happen, county after county would follow suit. It therefore
called Monck to an urgent conference and issued orders for an im-
mediate military occupation of the city. Monck and his army were
to remove the posts and chains from the streets, take down the gates,
wedge the portcullises open, and arrest eleven ringleaders of the Com-
mon Council. Subsequently there was much argument whether the
Rump's leaders deliberately imposed an odious task on Monck in
order to deflate his popularity, or whether Monck himself urged this
punishment of the capital, foreseeing a heaven-sent chance to turn
against the Rump with his army's full support. His closest associates
contradict each other, but both versions, and especially the latter, are
probably too subtle. The situation was stark and simple, as the
Council of State saw it: the city's defiance must be met if the gov-
ernment were not to fall, and the only forces within many miles
were Monck's. Perhaps these Rumpers over-reacted, but that was
typical; they had done so in October. Monck probably disliked his
mission quite genuinely, but he could not decline it without raising
still more dangerous suspicions, which his own officers might well
share.

At daybreak on the 9th, only five or six hours after leaving the
Council of State, Monck was marching into the city.[10] His officers
protested against their orders but obeyed them. Great silent crowds
of citizens watched London's humiliation.[11] Meanwhile the Rump con-
firmed the Council of State's instructions, adding to them that the
city's gates and portcullises should be totally destroyed. Then it lis-

[8] Guizot, II, 345; *cf.* Chivers, *City of London,* pp. 166–67. Perhaps the Lord
Mayor invoked the aldermanic veto; at any rate the Rump voted next day to
thank him for his "discreet Carriage": *Commons Journals,* VII, 838.
[9] Guildhall, *Journals,* JOR 41x, f. 219v. The Londoners' petition is in Thom-
ason 669f23(34); the other was from Warwickshire.
[10] Haley, *Shaftesbury,* pp. 127–28; Baker, *Chronicle,* p. 706. All but two of
Monck's regiments had so far been quartered either west of the city proper
or on the south bank: *ibid.,* p. 702.
[11] Guizot, II, 346.

tened to an address presented on behalf of London's sectarian brethren by Praise-God Barebone, the godly leatherseller and Baptist lay preacher who had lent his name to the Nominated Parliament of 1653. This address alleged that the royalists had been insinuating their subtlest friends into many places of trust, both civil and military, "under the Notion of a moderate Party," and were now boldly advancing the king's interest with their demands for a free Parliament or the secluded members. It prayed that no one should be admitted to Parliament, office, command, or pulpit without solemnly abjuring the house of Stuart and the promotion of any single person, Senate, or House of Lords, and also renouncing "all coercive Power in Matter of Religion." [12] Milton would have heartily endorsed most of this petition and may have been cheered when the House thanked its authors for their constant good affections. But to Monck it was the very voice of the "fanatic party," and he took the Rump's kindly reception of it as prime evidence of its unfitness to govern.

When the House met again in the afternoon and heard that Monck was about his business, Haslerig was jubilant. "All is our own," he cried, "he will be honest." [13] But then came a letter from the General that quickly dashed his spirits. Monck asked for a respite of his orders, now that he had removed the posts and chains and arrested nine Common Councilmen. Further action against the gates and portcullises would only exasperate the city, whereas he believed that the Common Council would come to heel over the taxes when it met next morning. In a postscript he begged the Parliament to hasten its decisions on the qualifications of members so that the promised elections could proceed.[14] Haslerig's party took deep offense. They carried the House in a curt order to Monck to destroy the gates and portcullises forthwith and in a vote declaring the present Common Council dissolved. This was sheer folly, for Monck had just given them their very last chance. He had been moved by the appeals of the Lord Mayor and other leading citizens and by their readiness to come to reasonable terms—moved too by the passionate hatred that his officers felt for their task. Some of the most loyal of them begged to resign their commissions. It is more than possible that he had been prepared until now to uphold the Rump if it took reasonable steps towards a broad-based settlement, but he had reached a turning point. Now he started preparing, very cautiously, to take the reins.

[12] Text in *Old Parliamentary History*, XXII, 95–97.
[13] Ludlow, *Memoirs*, II, 219.
[14] Text in *Old Parliamentary History*, XXII, 92–93.

Next day he made a show of complying with his orders, even to the point of burning some of the city gates.[15] But he conferred long and earnestly with his senior officers, his chaplains, his brother-in-law Clarges, and other confidants, letting them feel that they and not he were making the running. He was helped by the stupidity and bad faith of the Rumpers. That morning they gave a first reading to a bill which, like that of October 12, put the command of the army into commission. So much for his brief authority as commander-in-chief; they evidently thought he had served his turn. He thought otherwise. He returned to Whitehall that afternoon with some of his forces, only to be treated by Haslerig and Scot with intense suspicion because he had withdrawn them from the city without orders. Did he hear that the Council of State had just agreed to recommend Colonel Allured to Parliament as a good man to be made Major-General of London? At any rate he conferred again closely with his friends that evening, and summoned fourteen of his most trusted senior officers to meet him at six the next morning.[16]

At that cold dark hour on February 11 he put before them the heads of a momentous letter that he proposed to send to the Rump. To these they readily agreed. The letter was drafted, they signed it after him, and two colonels were despatched with it to the Parliament-house. He next sent words to the Guildhall that he and his whole army would quarter that night in the city, and thither he returned from Whitehall to await the results of his bombshell.

This famous letter was nothing less than an ultimatum.[17] It protested that the use of force against the city was grievous to him and his army, and tended to fresh confusion rather than the establishment of peace and liberty. He and his officers and "sober" people in general had further grounds for their fears: that men who stood impeached of treason still sat in the House; [18] that Lambert and Vane remained at large in London, contrary to Parliament's orders but apparently with its connivance; that men involved in the Committee of Safety's rebel regime were boldly justifying themselves, and were not all

[15] Guizot, II, 347.

[16] Davies, *Restoration,* pp. 279–81; Baker, *Chronicle,* p. 707; *Commons Journals,* VII, 840; *CSPD,* 1659–60, p. 354.

[17] Text in *Old Parliamentary History,* XXII, 98–103.

[18] Ludlow and four other former commissioners for the government of Ireland had had factious articles of impeachment brought against them by the Council of Officers in Dublin, headed by Sir Charles Coote, and Monck had supported the charges. Ludlow and Miles Corbett had hurriedly returned from Ireland and taken their seats on January 30. See Ludlow, *Memoirs,* II, 209–12, 464–72.

purged from the army; above all that Parliament had countenanced that venomous petition from Barebone which proposed the forcing of a new oath upon the nation, the exclusion of "the most conscientious and sober Sort of Men" from civil and military employment, and (by implication) the robbing of godly ministers of their just maintenance. The fiercest sting came in the tail. Monck gave the Rump until the next Friday—just six days—to issue the writs for the promised elections. Furthermore, he made it clear that even when it had filled its vacant seats its stay must not be long:

> And we must not forget to remember you, that the Time hastens wherein you have declared your intended Dissolution; which the People and ourselves desire you would be punctual in. Hereby the Suspicion of your Perpetuation will be taken away, and the People will have Assurance that they shall have a Succession of Parliaments of their own Election.

How long Monck had contemplated this step we shall never know, but he timed it perfectly. He had gone on obeying the Rump until his own officers and men were itching to defy it, and his studied reluctance and hesitation before he finally rounded upon it disarmed their suspicions that he was playing a deeper game. Perhaps he was not; quite an assortment of people—Ashley Cooper, Clarges and his chaplains among them—were subsequently to claim the credit for persuading him to take a stand against his would-be masters. But it is far likelier that the decision and the timing were essentially his own, and that in seeming to follow rather than to lead he was displaying—or rather concealing—something of the wisdom of the serpent. Did he also pass a hint to his friends in the House to hold their hands until he showed his own? It is noticeable that they never forced a division over the Council's orders for the punishment of the city, or the rejection of Monck's plea to mitigate that punishment, or the vote dissolving the Common Council. Yet we see them in action again immediately after his letter arrived on the 11th. The plain soldier who had boasted that he obeyed commands but gave none was ripening fast as a politician.

5. THE ROASTING OF THE RUMP

February 11–21, 1660

Monck's challenge exploded upon the political scene just as Milton was laboring at *The Readie & Easie Way*. But the way to establish a free commonwealth had for long been far from ready or easy, and on February 11 it suddenly became far harder. The effect of Monck's letter on Parliament that morning can be imagined. Haslerig stalked out of the House in high anger. At the door Edward Billing, the Quaker pamphleteer, took him by the arm and cried "Thou man, will thy beast carry thee no longer? Thou must fall!" Pepys, loitering in Westminster Hall for news, saw men's faces change from gloom to joy within half an hour.[1]

But when the House reassembled in the afternoon the republicans persuaded it to fight. Although it sent Monck a conciliatory reply, it went straight ahead with its bill to entrust the command of the army to commissioners. There were to be five. It could not do less than name Monck first, but then almost as inevitably it appointed Haslerig, Walton, and Morley. Morley however was Monck's man now, so the fifth name was vital. Monck's friends proposed Ashley Cooper, but he gained only fifteen votes against thirty for the staunch republican Colonel Allured. They then moved that Monck should always be one of the quorum of three, but this too was defeated.

Parliament however found itself defying a national hero. That same afternoon Monck went to the Guildhall and explained what he had done to a thronged meeting of Aldermen and Common Councilmen. As he came out, Pepys heard the people greet him with such a shout as he had never heard in all his life. "God bless your Excellence!" they roared, and "God bless them!" they cried to his soldiers whenever they passed. That night the city rang with bells from all the churches and blazed with bonfires in every street. The young found cheap sport in smashing Barebone's windows, but the general mood was of rejoicing and release. Pepys stood on Strand Bridge and from that one spot counted thirty-one fires,

> and all along burning, and roasting, and drinking for rumps. There being rumps tied upon sticks and carried up and down. The butchers at the May Pole in the Strand rang a peal with their knives when they were going to sacrifice their rump. . . . Indeed it was past imagination, both the greatness and the suddenness of it.[2]

Boys stopped passers-by to beg pennies for "the roasting of the Rump," and men dared to drink the king's health on their knees in the street.[3] At least Milton's blind eyes were spared that great glow in the London sky, lit by the funeral pyre of the good old cause.

There followed ten days of outward calm and intense conjecture,

---

[1] Pepys, I, 49.
[2] Pepys, I, 49, 51.
[3] Historical Manuscripts Commission, *Leyborne-Popham MSS*, pp. 219–20.

during which Milton probably completed all but the final touches to his treatise. Monck stayed in the city and moved into the house of Alderman William Wale, whose royalist sympathies were well known. Twice, on February 12 and 13, the Council of State requested him to come to Whitehall and take his seat, but the councillor's oath still stuck with him and he respectfully declined. The danger from "phanatique and disaffected persons," he said, required his presence in the city.[4] Even when the Rump substituted for the oath a simple engagement against a king, single person, or House of Lords, he would not budge.[5] The House went further to meet him, with renewed orders to Vane to leave London, a proclamation commanding Lambert to surrender, and a threat of disciplinary action against all M.P.s who had acted with the Committee of Safety. It spent most of the week settling the qualifications of electors and candidates and on Saturday the 18th it finally passed an act regulating the elections to its vacant seats.

Monck made a show of being satisfied. He assured Haslerig "in the presence of God" that the desire of his soul was for a commonwealth to be settled without a king or single person or House of Lords, and he told an anxious Ludlow that if Parliament proceeded to readmit the secluded members he would interrupt it.[6] On the 17th he received a declaration, signed a week earlier by Lord Fairfax and many of the leading Yorkshire gentry, threatening to withhold all taxes until the county was fully represented in a free Parliament. This caused more of a stir than most such addresses, since Fairfax and Monck had lately been in such close touch.[7] Yet Monck's reply virtually told Fairfax and Yorkshire to be content with the steps that the Rump was taking to fill up the House.[8] At the same time, however, the secluded members were gathering in London for secret conferences, and on the 14th Monck brought several of them face to face with a select group of Rumpers at his headquarters. He made no secret of it; indeed he invited Haslerig and others to another such meeting a few days later. Haslerig came, but stormed out in a rage. The others however were mostly Monck's supporters, and there was some progress towards an

[4] *CSPD*, 1659–60, pp. 358–60; *Clarke Papers*, IV, 261–63.

[5] *Commons Journals*, VII, 843–45. When Monck did propose on February 15 to remove his forces from the city, the Court of Aldermen begged him to keep them there: Sharpe, *London and the Kingdom*, II, 370.

[6] *Clarendon State Papers*, III, 678–79; Ludlow, *Memoirs*, II, 224–27.

[7] Woolrych, *Yorkshire Archaeological Journal*, XXXIX, 500–03; Davies, *Restoration*, pp. 286–87.

[8] Historical Manuscripts Commission, *Leyborne-Popham MSS*, pp. 154–55. It was written on the 18th.

entente.[9] Then came news that the officers in Dublin under Monck's close confederate Sir Charles Coote had declared for the secluded members on the 16th.

Yet the indications are that Monck kept an open mind about re-admitting the men of 1648 until a very late stage. Possibly he really did believe that a commonwealth would provide the best government for Britain, if it could be securely settled. Possibly he was waiting to see how the Rump would determine the qualifications of electors and members, and decided when they were published that they were more restrictive than the nation would stand for. Very probably he meant to find out what the secluded members intended, and made up his mind to do business with them only when he was satisfied as to how far they would do his bidding.[10] Certainly he had to conceal his own intentions until the last moment; that in itself suffices to explain his dusty answer to Fairfax. By February 20, and probably not much earlier, he had reached an understanding with the most influential secluded members and determined what he would do. On that date the Rump ordered the Speaker to sign a warrant for the Commissioners of the Great Seal to issue writs for the promised elections. Lenthall, however, stubbornly refused to do so, on the ground that every secluded member whose seat was thereby filled might sue him at law. It is difficult to explain this timorous man's obstinate stand except by a conjecture that Monck had quietly instructed him to secure a crucial day's delay.[11]

Whatever secret cabals prepared the ground, seventy-three of the secluded members—far more than enough to outvote the still active Rumpers—met Monck at Whitehall early on the morning of February 21. They were asked to signify their assent to a declaration [12] that his secretary read to them. In it he said he would not impose anything as to the way of future settlement, but he nevertheless treated them to a

[9] Davies, *Restoration,* pp. 287–88.

[10] He told them on February 21 that he had "at length received fuller Satisfaction from [them] than formerly." *Old Parliamentary History,* XXII, 140.

[11] For another version, based on an account written by Ashley Cooper towards the end of his life, see Haley, *Shaftesbury,* pp. 130–32. But the story that Monck only consented to readmit the secluded members in the early hours of February 21 under the combined persuasions of Cooper, Clarges, Mrs. Monck, and Colonels Clobery and Knight does not explain why Lenthall was so obstructive on the 20th or how more than seventy secluded members were so readily assembled between 3 and 8 a.m. on the 21st. If the meeting took place as Cooper described it, perhaps it was one more comedy played by Monck to sustain his famous reputation for "honesty."

[12] *Old Parliamentary History,* XXII, 140–43.

little sermon on the theme that monarchy could only be re-established upon the ruin of the people. It would lose them the liberty of their representatives in Parliament; it would bring back prelacy, whereas religion would best be settled in a "moderate, not rigid, Presbyterian Government, with a sufficient Liberty for Consciences truly tender." As for the city, only a commonwealth government could make it "the Metropolis and Bank of Trade for all Christendom." Finally, and this was his main purpose, he commended four tasks to them: to settle the command of the armies (which they promptly did by making him commander-in-chief); to provide for the pay of all the forces; to appoint a new Council of State and instruct it to issue writs for a new Parliament to meet on April 20; and to enact at last the legal dissolution of the Long Parliament. Thus charged, the secluded members were straightway escorted by Monck's Adjutant-General to the House, where their arrival took the Rumpers by complete surprise.

Monck cannot have really doubted what the consequences would be of restoring these men, who had been secluded precisely for their efforts to preserve Charles I's kingship; after all, he himself had predicted those consequences to the Devon gentry. But he had to act out his part before the armed forces. He therefore sent out a specious declaration to every regiment and garrison, assuring them that there was no intention of returning to the old bondage, but that the sole objects of his action were the better securing of their civil and religious liberties and the calling of successive Parliaments "upon a Commonwealth accompt." [13] The forces kept quiet, whatever they thought, but the citizens of London read the signs aright. They made holiday on the night of the 21st as exuberantly as they had done on the 11th. Pepys sat with Henry Purcell (the composer's father) and Matthew Locke in a Thames-side coffee house and watched the spectacle.

> Here out of the window it was a most pleasant sight to see the City from one end to the other with a glory about it, so high was the light of the bonfires, and so thick round the City, and the bells rang everywhere.[14]

If any doubts remained, the first votes of the transformed Parliament should have dispelled them. It released Sir George Booth; it restored to the city all its liberties. Above all its new Council of State was dominated by a galaxy of political Presbyterians whose desire to restore monarchy was no secret, while the few Rumpers who gained places were all allies of Monck and ready to swim with the tide. Six of

[13] Baker, *Chronicle,* pp. 710–11.
[14] Pepys, I, 61.

these councillors were to receive peerages when the king came home. The instincts of countless revellers in London and many a market town were proved sound: February 11 had marked the downfall of the republican diehards, and February 21 ensured that however the government was settled, King Charles II would be at the head of it.

CHAPTER X

THE READIE & EASIE WAY

1. THE FIRST EDITION

O F ALL Milton's prose works, *The Readie & Easie Way* needs to be read in closest relation to the political circumstances in which it was composed. Between the first and second editions events moved so fast, and prompted Milton to make such large amendments to his text, that one should try to read the original version with a mind uncolored by his later alterations and additions. Even while he was at work on the first edition the situation changed radically.

We can safely assume that he composed it during the first three weeks of February, 1660. As he confesses in his opening sentence,[1] he was overtaken by Monck's readmission of the secluded members on February 21, after he had written his treatise but before it went to press. In the second edition he spoke of the haste with which the first was composed. Furthermore, he was plainly aware of the Rump's plans for filling up its numbers, which though voted in principle early in January were only given definite shape on February 4. He therefore began dictating when a Parliament dominated by diehard republicans was proposing to fill its vacant seats with men subject to stringent qualifications and the strict scrutiny of the sitting members. Monck, even after his *volte face* on the 11th, continued to pledge himself to a Commonwealth without a king, single person, or House of Lords. The dikes, it seemed, might still be made to hold against the surging tide of the "misguided and abus'd multitude's" clamor for a return to monarchy. Yet when *The Readie & Easie Way* appeared on the bookstalls, probably a day or two before Thomason acquired it on March 3 but possibly before the end of February,[2] the Restoration had become an overwhelming probability. Milton must have known that by publishing such a scathing attack on monarchy, and particularly that terrible parallel in the closing peroration between Charles II and Coniah King of Judah, he might be endangering his life—and not

[1] *The Readie & Easie Way*, below, p. 353.
[2] For evidence of the date see French, *Life Records*, IV, 300–01, Parker, *Milton*, p. 1072, and below, p. 345, n. 26.

his life only but the great epics on which his immortality as a poet would chiefly rest. In a real sense, and this applies even more to the second edition than to the first, Milton was setting *The Readie & Easie Way* in the scales against *Paradise Lost*. He was not deterred.

One wonders again why he left it so late. The Commonwealth's cause sadly lacked able defenders during January and early February, when the presses poured forth addresses for a free Parliament and scurrilous satires against the Rump, the sectaries, Lambert, Haslerig, Vane, Salwey, Wariston, and others. Milton's old opponent Prynne was pamphleteering with gusto, and royalists of the old school were growing bold again in print. The honor and the execration for defending the good old cause at almost the last ditch fell to Barebone and his fellow petitioners; it was Barebone's windows that the city youths smashed on February 11, and again on the 21st.[3]

Yet late or not, Milton chose to publish his treatise in spite of the fact that its central proposal to erect the self-enlarged Rump into a perpetual Grand Council was clearly no longer feasible. In an introductory paragraph added at the last moment he expressed a strained hope "that it may perhaps (the Parlament now sitting more full and frequent) be now much more useful then before: yet submitting what hath reference to the state of things as they then stood, to present constitutions." [4] Did this convey, as Lewalski thinks, "a clear suggestion to the newly restored Long Parliament to perpetuate itself"? [5] It is doubtful. Milton was surely aware that Monck had adjured the secluded members "to a legal Dissolution of this Parliament, to make Way for Succession of Parliaments," [6] and that the House promptly voted on February 22 to hold general elections in the near future. The key words in this prefatory paragraph are surely, as Wolfe has pointed out, "and so the same end be persu'd, not insisting on this or that means to obtain it." [7] They should guard us against taking *The Readie & Easie Way* as a fully wrought political testament, let alone a model of an ideal commonwealth. The means are not its main matter; the essential message lies in its prophetic warnings of the bondage that monarchy will entail and its reassertion of the ideals and virtues for which a Christian commonwealth should stand.

[3] Pepys, I, 53, 62.
[4] *The Readie & Easie Way,* below, p. 355. All quotations in this chapter are from the first edition unless otherwise stated.
[5] *PMLA,* LXXIV, 195.
[6] *Old Parliamentary History,* XXII, 143. This declaration of Monck's was promptly published.
[7] Wolfe, *Milton in the Puritan Revolution,* p. 296; *The Readie & Easie Way,* below, p. 355.

Into the first of these themes Milton plunges after a brief celebration of the triumphs of the Commonwealth in its earlier years. What a scorn we shall be to all our neighbors, he argues, if after God has "wonderfully now the third time brought together our old Patriots, the first Assertours of our religious and civil rights," we abandon the chance of settling a free commonwealth "for ever" in order "to fall back, or rather to creep back so poorly as it seems the multitude would, to thir once abjur'd and detested thraldom of kingship." [8] The example of the Dutch Republic and its much longer and harder struggle for liberty should particularly shame us. This is the first of a series of references to the United Provinces, and Milton had several reasons for keeping them in his and the reader's mind. They were Protestant —*the* other great Protestant power; they had survived not only without a king but for the last ten years without even a stadtholder; their prosperity countered the argument that only monarchy could restore England's languishing trade; and their federal constitution afforded parallels with his own proposals for decentralizing government. Perhaps he also recalled that Monck had learnt his trade as a soldier in their service and admired their institutions.

The pages that enlarged on the evils that must attend a return to monarchy are among his most eloquent. Monck, too, in his letter to the Devon gentry and his declaration to the secluded members, had argued that monarchy was no longer a fit government for England. But whereas Monck had dwelt on the various "interests" that would suffer, especially the purchasers of confiscated land and the city with its ambition to be the *entrepôt* of Europe, Milton's standpoint is overwhelmingly moral and religious. He dwells on the thousands who bought England's liberty with their lives, he wrests Scripture to prove "the brand of *Gentilism* upon kingship",[9] he scourges the luxury, the debauchery, the gross extravagance, and the base servility that a royal court imposes on a nation, and especially on its nobility and gentry. What he hates most is the degrading servitude to one man— one who may be a cipher at best and "a mischief, a pest, a scourge of the nation" [10] at worst. With "the base necessitie of court-flatteries and prostrations," with "the perpetual bowings and cringings of an abject people," he contrasts the integrity of a free commonwealth "wherin they who are greatest, are perpetual servants and drudges to the publick at thir own cost and charges, neglect thir own affairs; yet are not elevated above thir brethren, live soberly in thir families,

---

[8] *Ibid.*, pp. 356–57.
[9] *Ibid.*, p. 359.
[10] *Ibid.*, p. 361.

walk the streets as other men, may be spoken to freely, familiarly, friendly, without adoration." [11] "The happiness of a nation must needs be firmest and certainest in a full and free Councel of their own electing, where no single person, but reason only swayes." [12]

Yet it is just on the score of the people's right to elect their governors, and remove those who offend them, that Milton's own proposals are most vulnerable. For what has he to offer as the embodiment of these heroic republican virtues? Only the Rump and its yet unnamed and unknown recruits. To the "rabble's" complaint that the Rumpers are but the tiny remnant of a Parliament, he retorts that "rather they should be therefor honourd, as the remainder of those faithfull worthies, who at first freed us from tyrannie, and have continu'd ever since through all changes constant to thir trust." [13] (Constant even in that vote less than a month before to perpetuate tithes?) In any case they have voted to fill up their number, and if the people will but elect able men, "according to the just and necessarie qualifications decreed in Parlament, . . . the work is don." [14] Let the resultant body assume the sovereign powers of commanding the forces by sea and land, raising and managing the public revenue, making laws, and treating of peace or war with foreign nations. Let it commit urgent or secret matters to a strictly subordinate Council of State. And (here came the shock, for Milton's previous proposals to this effect were yet unpublished) let it "sit perpetual." [15]

> The ship of the Commonwealth is alwaies undersail; they sit at the stern; and if they stear well, what need is ther to change them; it being rather dangerous? [16]

Milton dismisses in a few facile sentences the "conceit" of successive Parliaments elected at regular intervals, to which the Rump, the former army leaders, and Monck had all pledged themselves, and which dozens of petitions had urged. Transitory Parliaments would only breed commotions, novelties, and uncertainties, and nurture undesirable political ambitions. If such ambitions *must* be countenanced, he would reluctantly concede that every two or three years "a hun-

[11] *Ibid.*, p. 360.
[12] *Ibid.*, pp. 361–62.
[13] *Ibid.*, p. 366.
[14] *Ibid.*, p. 368. These qualifications were only finally "decreed" in the act passed on February 18, but they had been referred to a committee on January 3.
[15] *Ibid.*, p. 369.
[16] *Ibid.*

dred or some such number may go out by lot or suffrage of the rest" and be replaced by fresh elections; "but in my opinion better nothing mov'd, unless by death or just accusation." [17] Elections in Milton's Commonwealth were to be rare and purely local occasions, upon the death of a senile senator or the removal of a corrupt one.

Milton would abolish the name of Parliament, "as originally signifying but the *parlie* of our Commons with thir *Norman* king when he pleasd to call them," and call his supreme assembly "a Grand or General Councel." [18] It was indeed less like an English Parliament than the kind of permanent Senate that Vane and Stubbe and others had advocated, though its authority was more nearly absolute. Desborough, as we have seen, had actually suggested in December that sixty of the Rump should be constituted as the Senate. Milton himself refers to the Grand Council's members as senators, and seeks precedents for them in the Jewish Sanhedrin, the Athenian Areopagus, the thirty Ancients of Sparta, the Roman Senate, and in more recent times the full Senate of the Venetian Republic. This, a perpetual assembly of aging oligarchs, was surely the extreme solution to the problem of safeguarding the Commonwealth against change. Well might Milton's readers ask, *quis custodiet ipsos custodes?*

Later in the tract he offers his own palliative to the autocracy of the Grand Council, but meanwhile he is adamant that it should not share its sovereignty with any kind of chief magistracy vested in a single person. He warns against "the fond conceit of something like a duke of *Venice,* put lately into many mens heads, by som one or other suttly driving on under that prettie notion his own ambitious ends to a crown," and urges "that our liberty shall not be hamperd or hoverd over by any ingag'ment to such a potent family as the house of *Nassaw*." [19] This is cryptic. If the two warnings are meant to be separate, which is uncertain, that concerning a duke of Venice may arise from a surprising crop of rumors, current in the latter part of February and the early days of March, of a move to restore Richard

---

[17] *Ibid.*, pp. 369–70. Milton's "partial rotation" was far more restricted than Harrington's much discussed scheme whereby the retirement of a third of the membership was to be annual and automatic. Milton not only proposed longer intervals and smaller numbers, but would have had retirement determined by lot (*i.e.* by divine providence) or by the votes of the Grand Council itself. The second edition proposed something closer to Harrington's scheme, though again grudgingly; see below, pp. 434–35.

[18] *Ibid.*, p. 369. For the objection to the word Parliament, *cf. Proposalls of Certaine Expedients,* below, p. 337.

[19] *Ibid.*, p. 375.

Cromwell as Protector.[20] Thurloe, St. John, Montagu, Colonel Birch, and others were said to be making a party for him. How this story gained currency is a mystery; perhaps it took strength from Thurloe's reappointment as Secretary of State and from the presence of a number of former Cromwellians among the secluded members and on the new Council of State. In any case, who could be aiming at a crown? Here Milton was more probably hinting at Monck, who might also covet such a role as the head of the house of Nassau (or Orange) had played in the United Provinces. A pamphlet published early in February purported to trace Monck's descent from Edward III and other medieval kings,[21] and the French ambassador reported on February 12 that the general was believed to aspire to "a post similar to that held by the Prince of Orange." [22]

Mention of a single person brings Milton back to the ills that a restored monarchy would inevitably bring in its train: a Parliament dependent on the king's pleasure and hamstrung by a court faction, a Council packed with the king's creatures, a spirit of vengeance against which no conditions or terms could protect the former Parliamentarians. This section, trenchant as it is in the first edition, was to be greatly expanded in the second.

Finally, Milton expounds the essential liberties which he looks to a free commonwealth to secure, they being inevitably compromised under monarchy. Beginning with the conventional assertion that "The whole freedom of man consists either in spiritual or civil libertie," [23] he treats each in turn. The spiritual part, which lies for each man in serving God and saving his soul by the light he receives from the Scriptures and the Holy Spirit, "hath bin heertofore prov'd at large in other treatises," [24] alluding to his tracts of the previous year. Nevertheless he cannot resist a further disquisition, most of which will disappear in the second edition, on the harms that ensue when civil states meddle with ecclesiastical matters. Remove this power, he urges, and there will be less faction in parliamentary elections, no

---

[20] *Clarendon State Papers*, III, 689–90, 693–94; *Clarendon Calendar*, IV, 572, 581, 583, 584, 586, 592, 595; *Ormonde Papers*, II, 310; *CSPD*, 1659–60, pp. 385–86; Guizot, II, 370; *CSP Ven.*, 1659–60, p. 126; Pepys, I, 74, 77. Most of these reports date from shortly after *The Readie & Easie Way* must have gone to press, but rumors may well have been circulating before Milton put the finishing touches to it.

[21] *The Pedigree and Descent of General George Monck* (February 3, 1660), E1015(9).

[22] Guizot, II, 351; cf. *Clarendon Calendar*, IV, 543, 583.

[23] *The Readie & Easie Way*, below, p. 379.

[24] *Ibid.*, p. 380.

hypocritical pretexts for army leaders to violate Parliaments, and "no more pretending to a fifth monarchie of the saints." [25] Again he cites the United Provinces, contrasting their present concord and prosperity under religious toleration with the strife and danger of civil war when they persecuted the Arminians. Even Queen Elizabeth, so moderate and so well loved, persecuted the Presbyterian reformers out of fear that they would diminish her regal authority.

> What libertie of conscience can we then expect from others far worse principld from the cradle, traind up and governd by Popish and *Spanish* counsels, and on such depending hitherto for subsistence? For they hear the Gospel speaking much of libertie, a word which monarchie and her bishops both fear and hate; but a free Commonwealth both favours and promotes.[26]

Turning to civil liberty, Milton introduces his most interesting and original constitutional proposals, though he had adumbrated them in *A Letter to a Friend*.[27] Whereas Vane and Stubbe and the General Council of Officers of last December had all sought a balance to a permanent Senate in some sort of periodic co-ordination with a single, nationally elected representative assembly, Milton would vest the function of popular consent and participation in a multiplicity of local bodies. Civil rights would be best secured

> if every county in the land were made a little commonwealth, and thir chief town a city . . . where the nobilitie and chief gentry may build, houses or palaces, befitting their qualitie, may bear part in the government, make their own judicial lawes, and execute them by their own elected judicatures, without appeal, in all things of civil government between man and man.[28]

County courts with elected magistrates had figured largely in the Leveller program and had often been advocated since, but to give legislative powers to such local bodies was a novel idea. Milton sees them as training grounds for future members of the Grand Council. He seems still to be thinking of the natural leaders of society when he goes on to propose that the local communities should have in their county cities "schools and academies at thir own choice, wherin their children may be bred up in thir own sight to all learning and noble education, not in grammar only, but in all liberal arts and exer-

[25] *Ibid.*, p. 380.
[26] *Ibid.*, p. 383. This bold passage was retained and explained in the second edition.
[27] Below, pp. 329–32.
[28] *The Readie & Easie Way*, below, p. 383.

cises." [29] Tantalizingly brief though this is, there seems a clear difference in conception between these academies and the schools that he had advocated in *The Likeliest Means,* where boys were to be brought up "to a competence of learning and to an honest trade" in hours that would not hinder them from working for their living.[30] The context suggests that he now has in mind an education for public service intended primarily for the gentry. Probably he hopes to wean them from their practice of using the ancient universities, which he so disparaged in *The Likeliest Means,* as finishing schools. Some commentators [31] have treated the proposals in *The Likeliest Means* and *The Readie & Easie Way* as essentially similar and have contrasted them strongly with Milton's earlier treatise *Of Education,* but Barker perceives their differences and observes in *The Readie & Easie Way* a partial return to the humanistic confidence of that tract of 1644.[32]

How strong an injection of democracy did these county assemblies give to Milton's otherwise oligarchic commonwealth? Their constitution is left in the first edition extremely vague. Only from the letter that he wrote soon afterwards to Monck do we learn that they are to be chosen by some process of election, "by such at least of the People as are rightly qualifi'd." [33] But he refers to them there as "standing Councils," and conveys an impression that they are to be neither large nor frequently subject to the suffrages of the people. The whole picture in *The Readie & Easie Way* of the nobility and greater gentry running local affairs from their palazzos in the county towns suggests a kind of English equivalent to the hereditary regent class in the cities of the Dutch Republic. The impression is strengthened in his letter to Monck when he considers how best to secure assent to national legislation. The "Judicial Lawes" that the local councils may make are evidently by-laws, binding only on the counties that enact them. When the Grand Council frames general laws of more than routine import, it is to submit them to the "Assent of the standing Council in each City, *or such other general Assembly as may be call'd on such occasion.*" [34] In other words, the standing councils may need to be enlarged in

---

[29] *Ibid.,* p. 384.

[30] *The Likeliest Means,* below, pp. 305–06.

[31] Wolfe in *Milton in the Puritan Revolution,* pp. 356–58, and in *Complete Prose,* IV, 142; Sirluck in *Complete Prose,* II, 142.

[32] Barker, *Milton and the Puritan Dilemma,* pp. 276, 281; *cf.* Lewalski, *HLQ,* XXIV, 279–80.

[33] *The Present Means, and Brief Delineation of a Free Commonwealth,* below, p. 393.

[34] *Ibid.,* p. 394; my italics. Compare the similar proposals in the second edition of *The Readie & Easie Way,* below, p. 459.

order to convey popular assent convincingly—but only when major national legislation is proposed, and Milton frankly hopes that such occasions will be rare.[35]

What Milton proposes is almost a federal constitution, with as much decentralization of justice and administration as is practicable. He sees his local councils "communicating the natural heat of government and culture more distributively to all extreme parts, which now lie numm and neglected." [36] He would not, however, go as far as the Dutch Republic, where in theory the decisions of the States-General required the concurrence of each constituent province. He makes the distinction thus:

> We shall also far exceed the United Provinces, by having not as they (to the retarding and distracting oft times of thir counsels on urgentest occasions) many Sovranties united in one Commonwealth, but many Commonwealths under one united and entrusted Sovrantie.[37]

He is probably aware that the United Provinces had become less rather than more democratic under the republican regime of John de Witt, and it probably troubles him little. He is not concerned with universal participation in political activity; indeed the second edition will make brutally clear how little he trusts it. "The people" in his usage means those who are fit to participate. His care is for virtues, not satisfactions: "a Commonwealth aims most to make the people flourishing, vertuous, noble and high spirited," whereas monarchs may seek to make them wealthy in order to fleece them, "but otherwise softest, basest, vitiousest, servilest, easiest to be kept under; and not only in fleece, but in minde also sheepishest." [38] Striving against the materialism that is submerging the old Puritan aspirations, he vents his scorn on those who would "prostitute religion and libertie to the vain and groundless apprehension, that nothing but kingship can restore trade." If "we must forgoe & set to sale religion, libertie, honor, safetie, all concernments Divine or human to keep up trading, . . . our condition is not sound but rotten, both in religion and all civil prudence; and will bring us soon, the way we are marching, to those calamities which attend alwaies and unavoidably on luxurie." [39] These pages attain a splendor of utterance rarely equalled in

[35] In the second edition (*loc cit.*) he cites as an advantage of his scheme "fewer laws to expect or fear from the supreme autoritie."

[36] From a passage added in the second edition, below, p. 460.

[37] *Ibid.*, p. 461. I again quote the second edition, which makes Milton's point more clearly.

[38] *Ibid.*, p. 460.

[39] *Ibid.*, pp. 461–62.

Milton's later prose, and surpassed only in the moving peroration that closes the whole treatise. Yet how must they have struck contemporary readers who had lived through two years of deepening economic depression and knew that the quarrels of the bankrupt claimants to the good old cause had brought trade to its lowest ebb? The "general defection of the misguided and abus'd multitude"—Milton's closing words—represented not mere fickle sentiment but a reasonable desire to restore the rule of law and enable the nation to get on with its business.

It would be otiose to dwell at length on the impracticability of Milton's proposals as a whole, even if they had appeared before the readmission of the secluded members relegated them almost to the sphere of fantasy. One must however contest claims like Barbara Lewalski's that Milton's was "an eminently practical attempt to rescue the Puritan cause",[40] or William Riley Parker's that "if the Rump had retained its fleeting popularity, if Monk had chosen to support the Rump, Milton's scheme might also have been acceptable—and it might have worked." [41] The Rump's fleeting popularity rested solely on the fact that it had supplanted the still more unpopular Committee of Safety, and was totally conditional on its readiness to make way for a regular succession of free Parliaments, which Milton's scheme expressly denied. No one who has read the whole gamut of contemporary comment in correspondence, pamphlets, diaries, memoirs, and the reports of foreign residents could imagine that England would have stood for any kind of perpetual Grand Council—least of all one based on the Rump. The longevity of the Long Parliament was itself a reproach, and its own members knew it. Nor would Milton's "little commonwealths" in the counties have provided an acceptable substitute for the chance to compete for seats in the national legislature through reasonably frequent general elections. They offered too small an arena to the broadest and most politically sensitive governing class in Europe. They would either have had to be as unrepresentative as the Grand Council itself, or they would soon have been engaged in just such a strike against it as many a county had been threatening in January and February.

The most attractive of Milton's proposals are those for establishing centers of culture and liberal education throughout provincial England. If the reform of the law could have been undertaken in happier circumstances there would probably have been wide support too for the decentralization of justice. But to have given larger *political*

40 *PMLA,* LXXIV, 195.
41 Parker, *Milton,* p. 543.

autonomy to the counties would probably have been retrograde. They were too numerous and too small to form the basis of a genuinely federal solution to the problem of government. The county communities were already strong, and one of the great difficulties of governing seventeenth-century England effectively lay in what Alan Everitt has called "that latent intransigence of the provincial world which, in the last resort, was one of the principal factors in the failure of both Charles I and Cromwell." [42] The challenges of the next half-century were to confirm the need for a dynamic rather than a static concept of the function of government, and Milton's concept was so essentially static as to seem to reflect more his reading of classical authors than his limited experience of actual government in the service of the Council of State. Harrington had shown more awareness when he distinguished between a *"Common-wealth for encrease,"* such as Britain, and a *"Common-wealth* for *preservation,"* such as Venice.[43]

The assumption that the standing councils in the counties would function harmoniously under the general direction of a Grand Council whose members were irremovable except (presumably) by itself is only one of the difficulties in the way of taking Milton's scheme seriously as a model of government. The central one is surely the gulf that it leaves between ends and means—between its noble celebration of the virtues of responsible self-government and the pitiably meagre participation that it actually allows to the people in the shaping of their political destiny. The powers committed to the Grand Council are so very large, and its accountability to public opinion so very small. Seventeenth-century Europe was strewn with examples of what happened when a single authority gained absolute control over the armed forces and the raising of revenue. It was usually a prince, but a perpetual oligarchy was potentially no less oppressive an embodiment of Leviathan. The Grand Council must have struck contemporary readers as a crude engine for fastening a type of government and a set of values upon a people that desired, more strongly each month, to reject both.

But in evaluating *The Readie & Easie Way* we must constantly remember what kind of document it is, for it has sometimes been subjected to a weight of exegesis that it cannot reasonably bear. It is not in any sense a utopia, and we should not do Milton the injustice of regarding it as his model of an ideal commonwealth. It is naïve to take at face value the note of desperate optimism with which he attempted

---

[42] Alan M. Everitt, *The Local Community and the Great Rebellion* (Historical Association pamphlet G.70, London, 1969), p. 27.

[43] *Oceana* (ed. Liljegren), pp. 11, 32.

to erect his defenses against the tide of monarchy, or his claims that
they might last forever. In an age when self-confessed political em-
pirics were rare, every constitution-builder felt constrained to do the
same. Milton's generation had been nurtured on the idea of an ancient
constitution, unchanged in essentials since the mists of antiquity.[44]
Monarchists were making the most of the plea that they sought only
to return to this perfect embodiment of the nation's accumulated po-
litical wisdom, and anyone who advanced an alternative felt obliged
to claim for it nothing less than perfection and immortality.

We must also recall that Milton returned to the task of defending
the republican cause only when it had already become almost desper-
ate, and after his personal contacts with England's actual governors
had long grown few and rare.[45] Until the crisis of October 1659 he had
resigned himself "to the wisedome & care of those who had the gov-
ernment," [46] for he had other and greater tasks in hand. Even in the
six months spanned by his last political writings his proposals vary
considerably. In *A Letter to a Friend* he is somewhat tentative about
erecting the Rump into a perpetual Senate, and adds that "whether
the civill government be an annuall democracy or a perpetuall Aris-
tocracy, is too nice a consideracion for the extremities wherein wee
are." [47] In the *Proposalls* of a few weeks later his opinion had
hardened in favor of the Rump, though his reservations as to its fit-
ness are manifest in both these short works. In the original version of
The Readie & Easie Way his Grand Council is a body of some four
hundred, of whom the active Rumpers would constitute only a small
nucleus. In the second edition it is the unknown new Parliament in
process of being elected.

The constant ingredient is indeed a sovereign Senate or Council
with life membership. But how far did his extreme distrust of popular
elections and successive Parliaments spring from the enormous swing
of popular sentiment in favor of monarchy that began to gather real
momentum precisely in the autumn of 1659? How confident can we be
that if he had given his full mind to the framing of a commonwealth
even six months earlier, when the republican revival was still full of
hope, he would not have reached a solution closer to that of his old
hero Vane? These are questions that we shall be wise to leave open.

[44] On this see J. G. A. Pocock, *The Ancient Constitution and the Feudal
Law* (Cambridge University Press, 1957).
[45] French, *Life Records*, IV, 189–90.
[46] *A Letter to a Friend,* below, p. 324.
[47] *Ibid.,* p. 331.

2. MILTON WRITES TO MONCK

March, 1660

It must have been a bitter blow to Milton that Monck's readmission of the secluded members on February 21 rendered the central proposals in *The Readie & Easie Way* inoperable, even before they went to the printer. But he would not give in to it; there were two things he could yet do. One was to work on a new edition, adapting his model of a commonwealth as best he could to the radically changed situation. But that in turn would be too late unless some preventive measures were taken at once. The most immediate need was a plan to secure that the forthcoming elections should return a body of men fit to assume the role of permanent General Council for which he had hitherto cast the Rump.

This was the evident purpose of the brief piece which Toland first published in 1698 from a manuscript of Milton's, now lost, entitled *The Present Means, and Brief Delineation of a Free Commonwealth, Easy to be Put in Practice, and Without Delay*. It may have been Toland who added "In a Letter to General Monck,"[1] a description for which he had the clearest internal evidence. But was it simply a private letter, or did Milton plan also to follow a common pamphleteering convention by publishing it as a tract? There is no means of knowing, but the elaborate title rather suggests the latter.[2] No such contemporary publication survives, nor does any evidence that Monck received such a letter. What seems certain is that Milton cannot have intended it to go either to Monck or to the press in the rough form[3] in which it has come down to us.

There are several indications that what survives is only a draft. There are no words of address or compliment to Monck. The text begins very abruptly, in a manner that seems to presuppose at least a prefatory sentence or two. *The Readie & Easie Way* is referred to as "that book," as if it had been previously named, though it nowhere is. The letter is undated, and attempts to date it from internal evidence have differed quite widely. Some commentators have suggested the end of March or even early April,[4] but so late a date cannot be ac-

[1] Parker, *Milton*, p. 1073.
[2] Assuming that the title is Milton's own; it has an authentic ring.
[3] See below, p. 389.
[4] Wolfe, *Milton in the Puritan Revolution*, pp. 294, 461; Lewalski, *PMLA.* LXXIV, 195.

cepted. Nor can the assumption that Milton could only have been certain of a new Parliament after the old one had dissolved itself on March 16.[5] The House resolved as early as February 22 that a new Parliament should meet on April 25, and voted on March 1 to dissolve on the 15th [6]—a date that it failed to keep by one day. Both votes were immediately and widely publicized.

The key to the date lies in the purpose of the letter. It was not a mere digest of *The Readie & Easie Way* for Monck's easy reading, but an urgent plan of action to secure favorable elections. Milton had enough experience to reckon that elections to a Parliament called for April 25 would begin before the end of March; they did in fact begin on March 24.[7] The time-scale of the action he proposed would, as we shall shortly see, make his plan inoperable if he offered it any later than the first few days of March. He may of course have abandoned it in draft form on realizing that time did not permit him to put it before Monck or the public early enough for it to work, but the evidence is nevertheless strongly in favor of Masson's assumption that Milton dictated *The Present Means* immediately after *The Readie & Easie Way* was first published.[8]

Milton shows at the outset his desperate concern that the elections should be so managed as to return members favorable to a commonwealth without a single person or House of Lords. Without powerful pressures to this end, "who foresees not, that our Liberties will be utterly lost in this next Parlament?" [9] He therefore urges Monck to summon immediately the chief gentlemen of every county and lay before them the danger, the confusion, and the royalist vengeance that they must expect if kingship is restored. He should then charge them to return home and forthwith conduct elections to a "standing Council" in every city and major town. Although on this occasion he talks of "a competent Territory adjoin'd" rather than actual counties as the areas to be administered by these local councils, their role is to be much the same as in *The Readie & Easie Way*.

Under the conditions of travel in an English March three centuries ago, it would probably have taken two weeks to send to the leading gentry of the remoter English counties and assemble them in London and at least another week for them to return home and bring their local "standing Councils" into being—longer, indeed, if the process

[5] This is part of Barbara Lewalski's argument (*loc. cit.*) for dating the letter at about the end of March.

[6] *Commons Journals,* VII, 848, 855, 857.

[7] See below, pp. 205–06.

[8] Masson, V, 655–56.

[9] *The Present Means,* below, p. 393.

were to be remotely democratic. Yet it is only after this has been done that the Parliamentary elections are to proceed—a sequence impossible if Milton proposed it much after the beginning of March. Here is what he says of these elections:

> Next, That in every such Capital Place, they will choose them the usual number of ablest Knights and Burgesses, engag'd for a Commonwealth, or (as it will from henceforth be better called) the Grand or General Council of the Nation.[10]

Whom does he mean by "they," who are to have the vital trust of electing the Grand Council? In the context it could refer either to the leading gentry whom Monck is invited to convoke or to the standing councils whose functions have been the subject of the long previous sentence. It is perhaps conceivable that the word "they" has no such specific reference, but Milton can hardly mean the normal electorate—the men, that is, who were actually to elect the Convention Parliament—since he recommends that the elections should be held not in the traditional constituencies but only in those "Capital Places" where the standing councils are to have their seats. The likeliest construction is that he would have the standing councils to be the sole electors of the Grand Council. How else indeed could he hope to counter the enormous swing of popular opinion towards royalism? What he envisages is thus a two-stage electoral process, with the standing councils first chosen "by such at least of the People as are rightly qualifi'd," [11] and then themselves acting as electoral colleges for the perpetual Grand Council. This accords in principle with the more elaborate system of indirect election that he would shortly advocate in the second edition of *The Readie & Easie Way*.

For the rest this short piece consists of a summary of *The Readie & Easie Way*'s proposals, though with two significant departures. One is a playing down of the Grand Council's autocracy and an enhancement of the role of the local assemblies.

> Though this grand Council be perpetual . . . yet they will then, thus limited, have so little matter in thir Hands, or Power to endanger our Liberty; and the People so much in thirs, . . . that we shall have little cause to fear the perpetuity of our general Senat.[12]

Here for instance he allows his local councils the right to approve decisions of peace or war, a surely impracticable proposition that is not found in either edition of *The Readie & Easie Way*.

The other recommendation, for obvious reasons unique in this letter,

[10] *Ibid.*, pp. 393–94.
[11] *Ibid.*, p. 393.
[12] *Ibid.*, p. 394.

is that if the gentry summoned by Monck should reject his proposi-
tions he should use his veteran army to implement them, even in the
teeth of opposition. This anticipates the famous passage that Milton
would add to *The Readie & Easie Way*, justifying the right to force
men to be free.[13] The whole letter is of great interest in showing how
little he can have hoped, when he came to revise that treatise, that the
elections then in progress would really secure a Parliament disposed
to perpetuate the Commonwealth.

3. "A LITTLE SHROVING-TIME"

February 22–April 25, 1660

From here on we need not follow the course of politics in such de-
tail as in earlier chapters. It was now set inexorably towards the Res-
toration, and Milton soon knew it in his heart. Writing of the new
Parliament during that fateful electiontide, he expressed the poignant
hope that "if thir absolute determination be to enthrall us, before so
long a Lent of Servitude, they may permitt us a little Shroving-time
first, wherin to speak freely, and take our leaves of Libertie."[1]
After Monck let in the secluded members on February 21, they took
just over three weeks to carry out his injunctions and bring the Long
Parliament to an end. The House spent many days on the ticklish
business of settling the militia. It swept away all those prominent
republicans whom the Rump had installed; the new militia commis-
sioners, like the new Council of State, consisted of men who though
Parliamentarians in the first Civil War had never sought the abolition
of monarchy. Among them was Sir George Booth, the leader of the
previous August's rising in Cheshire.
Here lay danger, for there were still many officers and soldiers scat-
tered about the country who might attempt a last stand for the good
old cause, and some of them were gathering unobtrusively in London.
The early days of March were heavy with reports of plots.[2] Suspicion
ran high even among Monck's regiments, and the Militia Bill evi-
dently brought it to a head. A group of officers met on March 6 to
draft an engagement for a Commonwealth and against any single per-
son, which they would have had Monck present to the Parliament in
the name of himself and his whole army. Monck deferred his answer

---

[13] *Cf.* below, p. 455.
[1] *The Readie & Easie Way*, 2nd ed., below, pp. 408–09.
[2] *Nicholas Papers*, IV, 197–99; *Diurnal of Thomas Rugg*, p. 49.

until next day, when a General Council of Officers was to meet. It was a large and uneasy gathering. Colonel Okey set the tone with a long speech about the inundation of evils that threatened their civil and religious liberties and the care they must take to prevent their enemies from bringing back Charles Stuart. The army, he urged, should press Parliament to engage for a commonwealth without a king or House of Lords; if it refused, let them "take such a Remedy as God should put into their hearts to save the Nation from destruction." [3] Had Monck just read a similar suggestion in Milton's letter to him? At any rate he would have none of it. Such violence, he said, would make the Parliament dissolve itself in haste and leave the country in confusion. If that happened, "they must not expect"—as some of them evidently did—"he would take upon him the Government, which he had rather lose his life than accept." "Nothing was more injurious to Discipline," he went on, "than their meeting in Military Councills to interpose in Civil things." [4] To mitigate suspicion he arranged a conference next day between ten officers and ten M.P.'s. It was inconclusive, but immediately afterwards he ordered all officers back to their commands.

Nevertheless there was a fresh stir in the army when Parliament on March 13 annulled the famous Engagement of 1650, whereby every citizen had been required to declare his faithfulness to the Commonwealth "as it is now Established, without a King or House of Lords." [5] Monck felt impelled to write to Parliament, probably with his tongue in his cheek, and ask it to suspend the execution of the new Militia Act lest the commissioners named in it should try to bring in Charles Stuart. The House sent Morice, Annesley, and Holles to give him satisfaction, and the agitation simmered down.[6]

Meanwhile the wind was already blowing cold upon the last champions of the Commonwealth. Lambert was summoned before the Council and asked for a surety of £20,000. He declined, and was committed to the Tower. Colonel Rich too was examined and committed. Overton was dismissed from his colonelcy and his governorship of Hull, and haled before the Council shortly after. John Owen was removed from the deanship of Christ Church. Even Haslerig, though he clung to his seat till the last, was under investigation by the Council. Scot dared to tell the House that he wished to have it inscribed on his

---

[3] Baker, *Chronicle*, p. 716; *Nicholas Papers*, IV, 200–03; Davies, *Restoration*, pp. 298–99.
[4] Baker, *Chronicle*, p. 716.
[5] *Complete Prose*, IV, 5.
[6] Davies, *Restoration*, p. 300.

tomb that he had "had a hand and heart in the execution of Charles Stuart late King of England."[7] He narrowly escaped summary punishment.

Yet all was not yet running the king's way, for in its last days the Long Parliament took a surprisingly strong stand on religion. It reaffirmed the Presbyterian Westminster Confession as the public profession of faith of the Church of England, and ordered that the Solemn League and Covenant be reprinted and read in every church in the country. It even tried to complete the division of the counties into classical presbyteries, so abortively begun in 1648. It confirmed the right of beneficed clergy to their tithes and passed a new Act for the Approbation and Admittance of Ministers, naming a strongly Presbyterian group of clergy to judge their fitness.[8] Futile as all this was, it can only have deepened Milton's depression to see England's religious future narrowed once more to a contest between new presbyter and old priest. He must have groaned too at a vote affirming the right of the House of Lords to constitute a part of future Parliaments. The twenty-year-old House of Commons was taking much upon itself, and it was persuaded not without difficulty to enact at last its own demise on March 16.

"And now they begin to talk loud of the King," wrote Pepys in his diary that evening, recording the general joy in Westminster Hall at the dissolution.[9] For a brief while, however, there was much speculation about another possibility: might not Monck himself make a bid for the headship of the state? True, he had repudiated such a proposal to his officers, but that only suggested the more that it had been seriously advanced, and his denials were somewhat debased in currency by now. There were many to whom George Protector would be less obnoxious than Charles Rex; Milton was soon to declare himself among them.[10] Although none of the evidence is above suspicion, it seems that Scot and Haslerig and some others approached Monck with just such a suggestion a day or two before the dissolution.[11] He

---

[7] Ludlow, *Memoirs*, II, 250.

[8] Davies, *Restoration*, pp. 297–98.

[9] Pepys, I, 86.

[10] *Brief Notes upon a Late Sermon*, below, p. 482.

[11] Baker, *Chronicle*, pp. 715–16; *Clarendon State Papers*, III, 706–07; *Clarendon Calendar*, IV, 611, 616; Historical Manuscripts Commission, *Leyborne-Popham MSS*, pp. 225–26; Guizot, II, 372, 375–76, 388. Clarges' story in Baker, *Chronicle*, p. 717 that Bordeaux offered France's support for such a venture deserves little credit; *cf.* Bordeaux's full reports on his contacts with Monck in Guizot, II, 384–94, and his subsequent explicit denials cited in Haley, *Shaftesbury*, p. 132.

had far more sense than to entertain it. Although he still carefully
kept up his pretense of expecting a Commonwealth settlement, he
waited only until the Parliament was gone before at last allowing his
kinsman Sir John Grenville to deliver a letter to him from the king.
Grenville had been carrying it for nearly eight months, but he got his
reward. Monck told him that he had never been in a position to do the
king service until the present, but that he was now ready to sacrifice
life and fortune in his cause. He put nothing in writing, however,
and until Grenville reached Brussels more than ten days later even
Charles II did not know how Honest George stood. The public and
particularly the army had to be kept in the dark for considerably
longer, so that in April Milton could still profess to vindicate him as
true to his public promises against the preacher Dr. Griffith's assump-
tion that he was about the king's business.[12] Nevertheless, from the
time of that secret interview with Grenville on March 16 or 17 Monck
was at last fully committed.

The real question, however, from mid-March to late April was not
whether Charles II would return, but whether his restoration would be
bound by conditions. At first it was natural to assume that it would,
for the Presbyterians who dominated the Council of State could be
expected to exact some safeguards for the causes that they had sup-
ported in the 'forties. They appeared to be strengthened by the Long
Parliament's last votes concerning religion, and by a declaration, im-
posed on all the new militia commissioners, that the war waged
against Charles I's forces in the 'forties was a just and lawful war.[13]
There was much talk and not a few cabals about resuscitating the
terms that Parliament had been negotiating with Charles I on the Isle
of Wight before Pride's Purge had cut the treaty short. These schemes
need not concern us closely, firstly because they were abortive and
secondly because they can have held little interest for Milton. He was
of course aware of them, and in the second edition of *The Readie &
Easie Way* he powerfully warned "the new royaliz'd presbyterians"
of their folly in pinning any trust upon a conditional Restoration.[14]
With their aim to re-establish an exclusively Presbyterian Church of
England he had no sympathy at all, and their constitutional safe-
guards must have struck him as hollow.

Three principal factors militated against their efforts to set any con-
ditions at all. One was the sheer surge of national feeling in favor of
monarchy, which would brook no half-way house. The elections to the

[12] *Brief Notes upon a Late Sermon,* below, pp. 470–71.
[13] *Commons Journals,* VII, 871.
[14] *The Readie & Easie Way,* below, pp. 451–54.

Convention Parliament would soon reflect this very powerfully. Another lay in the growth to manhood of a whole generation that had no personal memories of Charles I's personal monarchy, and cared only to be rid of swordsmen, Puritan repression, over-taxation, and the exclusion from political life of half the political nation. Thirdly, even if Parliament retained the power to appoint to a few leading offices of state, it could hardly recall the king without restoring also his right to dispose of a mass of lucrative or honorific places in the royal household, the central administration, and local government—places for which the nobility and gentry would soon be competing again as keenly as in the century before the Civil War. Was it worth risking proscription for being stiff-necked? There might be no room on the bandwagon for men who tried too hard to stop the clock at 1648.

Nevertheless, while Milton pondered and dictated the second edition of *The Readie & Easie Way*, there were many uncertainties and even alarms about England's future government before the temper of the new Convention set all doubts at rest. The army was still to be feared. On March 17 the Council of State issued two proclamations, the one banishing all disbanded officers from London, the other ordering all papists and all who had fought for Charles I to their homes in the country, at the same time enjoining a strict watch at the ports for suspicious persons entering or leaving the country. A week later, having intelligence that republican emissaries were being sent out to the scattered regiments, it set a price on the heads of anyone who was found trying to subvert the soldiery.[15] Monck sent this out to all commanding officers with a letter containing specious assurances of the army's continuing zeal to defend the nations' religious and civil liberties against the known enemies thereof.[16] There was cause for concern about the surviving commonwealthsmen in the army. Ludlow was in the thick of a conspiracy to rally them to a series of rendezvous up and down the country and to raise money to pay them. He and his friends naturally tried to enlist Haslerig, who still nominally commanded two regiments and four garrisons. But they found him slumped with his head in his hands, quite broken in spirit: "We are undone, We are undone," he told them. At about this time he threw himself on Monck's mercy, and Monck good-humouredly promised to save his life and estate for twopence if he would go home and lie quiet at his country house. The twopence were duly sent, and Ludlow too gave up hope and retired to the country.[17]

[15] Thomason 669f34 (24), (25), (40).
[16] *Clarke Papers*, IV, 266–67.
[17] Ludlow, *Memoirs*, II, 242–44, 251–53; *Clarke Papers*, IV, 268, 302–03.

Early in April Monck judged the time ripe to bring the army finally to heel. He required all officers whatsoever to subscribe an engagement, binding them and their men to obey their superiors' orders without dispute, to hold no meetings for the promotion of political declarations, and to submit to whatever the forthcoming Parliament should settle in both church and state. Then on the evening of April 10, a few hours after most of the officers about London had been summoned to sign this document, Lambert escaped from the Tower. Here was the great test, for Lambert was bent not on flight but on a call to arms. For two days he lay hidden in London; then he lit out for the midlands, fixing his rendezvous at Edgehill. There were signs of a response from York and Hull, but these movements were quickly repressed. Only a few small bodies of horse rode in to join him. What use were four troops, even with such brave and desperate men as Okey, Axtel, Cobbet, and Creed to help him lead them? Monck entrusted the job of rounding them up to Colonel Richard Ingoldsby— the Dick Ingoldsby who could "neither preach nor pray" [18]—doubtless to help him redeem his regicide past. After an almost bloodless skirmish, Lambert was duly brought back to London. He was made to stand under the gallows at Tyburn before he was recommitted to the Tower, to resume an imprisonment that was to last for the remaining twenty-three years of his life.

It was the last fling of the good old cause before the Restoration. Milton was now one of very few who dared still to resist the tide with their pens, and we shall see next what obloquy and threats he incurred for his pains.

4. MILTON UNDER FIRE

During March and April of 1660 the utterances of press and pulpit underwent a striking change. When Milton completed his first version of *The Readie & Easie Way*, anyone who directly and publicly advocated the king's cause still risked serious penalties, but by the time he published the second there was far more hazard in defending the Commonwealth. The royalist clergy were among the boldest harbingers of the new order. February 28 was appointed a day of thanksgiving for the readmission of the secluded members, and one of the preachers at St. Paul's was Dr. John Gauden,[1] who eleven years earlier had dared

---

[18] See above, pp. 59–60. Ingoldsby was knighted in 1661 and sat in every Parliament from 1660 to 1685.

[1] John Gauden, *Kakourgoi, sive Medicastri* (February 28, 1660), E1019(4).

to denounce the trial of Charles I. Milton had assailed him in *The Tenure of Kings and Magistrates,* not knowing of course that his adversary was the compiler of *Eikon Basilike.*[2] Gauden's sermon was discreet, but next Sunday the Book of Common Prayer was read openly in several London churches, and from the pulpit of St. Clement's Mr. Masterton told a congregation containing many M.P.'s that "hauing contributed soe much to ye ruine of ye father, they had nothing now to thinke of but restoring ye son."[3] Masterton was suspended from preaching for this, yet a fortnight later Pepys heard "a very gallant sermon" on the text "Pray for the life of the King and the King's son."[4]

Even in April, however, there were still limits to the license that royalist parsons could allow themselves, as we shall see shortly in the case of Dr. Griffith.[5] The nameless writers of pamphlets and broadsheets risked less, and they observed fewer restraints. Scurrilous Rump ballads poured forth, to be hawked in the streets and bawled in the taverns. A spate of crude satires found in Milton only one of many targets, while more serious monarchical propaganda and personal eulogies of Charles II swelled from a trickle to a broad river in the course of March. Soon the danger lay on the other side. Livewell Chapman, the bookseller who had published so many republican and sectarian tracts, including *The Likeliest Means* and *The Readie & Easie Way,* went into hiding, and on March 28 the Council of State issued a proclamation for his arrest.[6]

Milton fell specially foul of the satirists because so few others dared now to speak out against monarchy, and because he alone, by those famous initials "J.M.," acknowledged his authorship. One other bold spirit was Marchamont Needham, who cleverly and damagingly impersonated the vengeful attitude of a fire-eating cavalier in *Newes from Brussels.*[7] Even Needham, however, published his piece anonymously, though he was promptly identified as its author and removed from his editorship of the official newspaper *Mercurius Politicus.* Milton's name was coupled with Needham's in at least four hostile tracts, one of which envisaged them standing side by side under the gallows at Tyburn.[8] Both were named, groundlessly, as probable au-

---

[2] *Complete Prose,* III, 105, 191, 195.

[3] *Nicholas Papers,* IV, 198.

[4] Pepys, I, 87.

[5] Below, pp. 201–02.

[6] Thomason 669f24(47).

[7] Dated March 10, 1660, E1017(38); summarized in Davies, *Restoration,* pp. 315–16. On Needham see *Complete Prose,* IV, 49–58.

[8] Parker, *Milton's Contemporary Reputation,* pp. 99–102; the Tyburn reference is from *The Character of the Rump,* quoted by Parker on p. 99.

thors of another antimonarchical pamphlet entitled *Plain English.*[9]
It must have galled Milton that after his two ecclesiastical treatises of
1659 had sunk into a pool of utter silence, *The Readie & Easie Way*
provoked such a chorus of croaks.

Few of these royalist attacks hold any intrinsic interest beyond
the mention of Milton's name. French and Parker have documented
them thoroughly, and Masson quotes and discusses them at length.[10]
First in the pack came Sir Roger L'Estrange, who had at least risked
his life in royalist conspiracy and had pamphleteered in 1659 when
the hazards were still real. In *Be Merry and Wise,* published about
ten day after *The Readie & Easie Way,* he taunts Milton that
Monck has wrecked his model of a commonwealth, just as he had fin-
ished it, by letting in the secluded members. L'Estrange dismisses
Milton's proposal to erect the Rump into a perpetual Grand Council
in a couple of sentences of gentle irony.[11] By contrast, the anonymous
writer of *The Character of the Rump* aims mere crude abuse at the
Rump's "Goos-quill Champion." [12] Three of the thirty facetious que-
ries in William Collinne's *The Spirit of the Phanatiques Dissected*
concern Milton, but the only one of any interest suggests that Milton's
proposed commonwealth constitution is "borrowed in copy from the
States of Holland." [13]

There is more wit and substance in *The Censure of the Rota upon
Mr. Miltons Book, Entituled, The Ready and Easie Way,* which came
out at the end of March.[14] This purports to be a record by Harrington
of an evening's proceedings in the Rota Club, but the aim of the un-
known royalist author is to satirize Harrington and belabor Milton at
the same time. His heavier guns are, however, trained on Milton:

> For you have done your feeble endeavour to Rob the Church, of the
> little which the Rapine of the most sacrilegious Persons hath left, in
> your learned work against Tithes; You have slandered the Dead, worse
> then envy it selfe, and thrown your dirty out-rage, on the memory of a
> Murther'd Prince, as if the Hangman were but your Usher.[15]

[9] *Ibid.,* p. 100.
[10] Parker, *loc cit.;* French, *Life Records,* IV, 304–09, 311–15; Masson, V,
657–63, 689–94. See also Wolfe, *Milton in the Puritan Revolution,* pp. 236–40.
[11] *Be Merry and Wise* (March 13, 1660), E765(6), p. 86; quoted in French,
Life Records, IV, 304.
[12] *The Character of the Rump* (March 17, 1660), E1017(20), pp. 2–3;
quoted in French, *Life Records,* IV, 305.
[13] Thomason E1017(39) (March 24, 1660), pp. 7–8; also quoted by French,
p. 307.
[14] E1019(5*); dated March 26 on title page, acquired by Thomason on
March 30; reprinted in facsimile in Parker, *Milton's Contemporary Reputa-
tion,* pp. 229–44.
[15] *The Censure of the Rota,* pp. 8–9.

He charges Milton among other things with sanctifying mere success, with wresting the Scriptures, and with a large abuse of historical evidence.[16] Milton's "stiffe formall Eloquence," he complains, takes for granted everything that will serve its turn, right or wrong.[17] There is a grain of truth in his reproaches "That you fight alwayes with the flat of your hand like a Retorician, and never Contract the Logical fist," and "That you trade altogether in universals the Region of Deceits and falacie." [18] This writer has read Milton closely, and probes his weaknesses with some precision, as here:

> For though you bragge much of the Peoples Manageing their own affaires, you allow them no more share of that in your *Utopia* (as you have ordered it) then only to set up their throates and Baul (instead of every three yeares, which they might have done before) once in an Age, or oftener, as an old Member drops away, and a new one is to succeed, not for his merit or knowledge in State affaires, but because he is able to bring the greatest and most deep mouth'd Pack of the Rabble into the field.[19]

This last taunt may have prompted Milton's advocacy of indirect elections in the second edition of *The Readie & Easie Way,* though his actual current experience of elections probably provided sufficient incentive.

Far longer and duller was *The Dignity of Kingship Asserted: in Answer to Mr. Milton's Ready and Easie Way,*[20] which ran to 248 insufferably prolix pages. Its author, "G.S.", has been convincingly identified by Parker as George Starkey, an American-born graduate of Harvard who had lived in England for ten years or more, purveying quack medicines.[21] Starkey treats Milton with marked respect as "the most able and acute Scholar living"; [22] he finds his "Language *to be* smooth and tempting, *the* Expressions pathetical, *and apt to move the* Affections." [23] These and other praises, however, have the rather obvious object of enhancing the service that Starkey is rendering to the royal cause by refuting so formidable and insidious an adversary. His whole performance looks like a bid for patronage, coupled perhaps with an expiation of his indiscretion in having formerly dedicated one

[16] *Ibid.*, especially pp. 9–10.
[17] *Ibid.*, p. 9.
[18] *Ibid.*, p. 13.
[19] *Ibid.*, p. 14.
[20] Reprinted in facsimile (Columbia University Press for the Facsimile Text Society, 1942) with an introduction by William R. Parker, who argues plausibly for a publication date shortly before April 25, 1660.
[21] *The Dignity of Kingship,* ed. W. R. Parker, pp. x–xxi.
[22] *Ibid.*, p. 5.
[23] *Ibid.*, Epistle Dedicatory, sig. a 2.

of his treatises on "chemical philosophy" to the regicide Robert Tichborne.[24] He is clearly not much interested in Milton's specific proposals, of which his discussion is brief and trite. He wants a peg on which to hang some invective against the Commonwealth and much flattery of Charles II, Monck, and the forthcoming Parliament, and he finds in *The Readie & Easie Way* the only one that will bear the weight. His standpoint is that of a political Presbyterian. His favorite contemporary authorities are Prynne's works and Walker's *History of Independency;* [25] he is ambivalent as to whether the Civil War was initially justified; [26] he hopes that monarchy may be restored without *"Episcopal Lordly* power" and that moderate Anglicans will fuse with moderate Presbyterians in a common front against papists and sectaries.[27] He is of course rabidly opposed to Milton's concept of liberty of conscience, though he crudely mistakes what Milton had proposed in *The Likeliest Means.*[28] Like William Collinne, he believes that Milton has borrowed his model of a commonwealth from the Dutch, whom he hates.[29] Their revolt against Spain's authority, to Milton a paradigm of heroic virtue, Starkey denounces as heinous rebellion against a legitimate monarch. With one eye doubtless on the two states' recent treatment of Charles II, he contrasts the boorishness, the treachery, the disrespect for authority, and the greed for money of the United Provinces with the courtesy, the honor, and the charity of the Spanish Netherlands—"a most clear argument of the degenerate effect of *Popular Government.*" [30] Yet before we dismiss this somewhat foolish and leaden pamphleteer, let us acknowledge that he treated Milton, who could no longer hurt him, with a decency greater than the poet had always shown towards his own adversaries.

5. MILTON AGAINST DR. GRIFFITH

Milton did not return the fire of his assailants, but he did take public issue with one particularly indiscreet royalist clergyman. Dr. Matthew Griffith was brave, bigoted, and foolish. He had been chaplain to Charles I, and since his master's death he had ministered to clandestine royalist congregations according to the Book of Common

[24] *Ibid.,* p. xx.
[25] *Ibid.,* pp. 18, 45, 54, 95, 96.
[26] Compare pp. 29 and 215 with p. 62.
[27] *Ibid.,* pp. 142–44.
[28] *Ibid.,* p. 141.
[29] *Ibid.,* pp. 103–09, 113–19.
[30] *Ibid.,* p. 114.

Prayer. He had been several times imprisoned. Scenting the whiff of victory in the spring air of 1660, he preached an inflammatory sermon in the Mercers' Chapel on March 25, taking as his text "My son, fear God and the King, and meddle not with them that be seditious or desirous of change." "Seditious" was apparently a sheer interpolation of his own.[1]

Two features in particular made his performance more objectionable than many another royalist sermon that went unpunished during March and April. One was his vengeful tone against Presbyterians, Independents, and sectaries alike. His portrayal of Charles II as an avenging Samson and his prophecy of sudden destruction to all who had been guilty of sedition against the Lord's anointed embarrassed the exiled Court and frustrated the current efforts of many responsible royalists to proclaim that they desired only the burial of old quarrels and the healing of the nation's breaches.[2] Griffith's second indiscretion was worse. He not only published his sermon, together with a political tract entitled *The Samaritan Revived,* but he prefaced them with a fulsome dedication to Monck, calling on him to win "that immarcescible crown of glory due to you" by restoring the king. "It is a greater honour to make a king than to be one," he told him.[3] Monck was very angry, for he could not afford to be compromised in his ticklish task of keeping a suspicious army quiet. Nor could the Council of State pass this open challenge by, and it promptly committed Griffith to Newgate.

Milton clutched at this straw of hope that England's present masters might yet resist monarchy. His purpose was not only to confute Griffith's politics and divinity but to try to hold Monck to his pledges to maintain the Commonwealth. Hastily he dictated his *Brief Notes upon a Late Sermon,* which were published in mid-April or slightly earlier, over his initials.[4] No one would rate this piece high in the Miltonic canon, and we need not dwell on the pages that retort the charge of sedition on Griffith's head and refute his appeals to Scripture. More surprising is Milton's rebuttal of the doctor's claim that kingship is rooted in the fundamental laws of England. He counters

[1] The Authorized Version reads merely "meddle not with them that are given to change": Proverbs 24:21. On Griffith, see *DNB* and Masson, V, 667–69.

[2] Royalist declarations to this effect were published in a number of counties. For an example see Baker, *Chronicle,* pp. 722–23.

[3] Most of the dedicatory epistle is printed in Masson, V, 668–69.

[4] Not in Thomason, but clearly after Griffith's commitment on April 5 and before L'Estrange's reply in *No Blinde Guides,* dated April 20 by L'Estrange himself.

that no law can be *fundamental*, but that which is grounded on the light of nature or right reason, commonly call'd *moral law:* which no form of Government was ever counted; but arbitrarie, and at all times in the choice of every free people, or thir representers. This choice of Government is so essential to thir freedom, that longer then they have it, they are not free.[5]

This is a reversion to an earlier and simpler kind of appeal to natural law than could easily be sustained in 1660, and it is difficult to square with Milton's vindications from 1651 onwards of the well-affected minority's right to impose their own government on the unworthy majority. How far it can consist at all with the extreme restriction of choice proposed in *The Readie & Easie Way* will be considered later,[6] but it is probable that Milton, in the heat and haste of controversy, was justifying a choice already made in 1649 rather than asserting a similar right in 1660. If this be inconsistency, let us remember the desperate circumstances in which he was writing.

He goes on to contend, in terms that would convince only the dwindling ranks of his fellow commonwealthsmen, that kingship has been abolished by a law of Parliament—a law no less valid for being enacted by so truncated a Parliament as the Rump. And whatever doubts may be cast upon the Rump's legislation, the Civil War was a just war, and therefore (the most dubious step in his argument) the victors' right by conquest to dispose of the government was equally just. That right still stands; but at this point Milton makes a startling concession. If we *must* regress from a free commonwealth into monarchy,

we may then, conscious of our own unworthiness to be governd better, sadly betake us to our befitting thraldom: yet chusing out of our own number one who hath best aided the people, and best merited against tyrannie, the space of a raign or two we may chance to live happily anough, or tolerably.[7]

Better, in fact, King George than King Charles, for Milton can only refer to Monck. But he makes clear how poor an alternative to a commonwealth this will be, and he has already expressed the strained hope that the general will yet confound his slanderers by fulfilling his public promises.[8]

His short tract drew an immediate reply. *No Blinde Guides*,[9] dated

[5] *Brief Notes upon a Late Sermon,* below, p. 479.
[6] See below, pp. 209–10, 217–18.
[7] *Ibid.,* p. 482.
[8] *Ibid.,* pp. 470–71.
[9] Acquired by Thomason on April 25, and reproduced in facsimile in Parker, *Milton's Contemporary Reputation,* pp. 245–60.

April 20, 1660, was Roger L'Estrange's second tilt at Milton, though he acknowledged his authorship only after the Restoration. He takes Milton to task not only for his latest piece but for his doctrine of divorce, his first *Defence, Eikonoklastes*, and *The Readie & Easie Way*. His style is brisk, his tone sharp but not scurrilous, and he challenges Milton's appeals to law and Scripture with sufficient force to raise a casual reader's doubts about them. He scores his best points where Milton's own argument is most vulnerable: on the nature of fundamental laws, on the validity of the Rump's enactments, and on the claim that victory in a war of limited objectives conferred an unlimited right of conquest. At its conventional level, *No Blinde Guides* is a lively and effective exercise in polemics, though the work that it attacks is among Milton's weakest.

Fortunately Milton had yet time to "take his leave of freedom" in an altogether nobler utterance: a version of *The Readie & Easie Way* so revised and enlarged as to constitute almost a new work.

6. THE SECOND EDITION OF *THE READIE & EASIE WAY*

April, 1660

It is not easy to establish exactly when Milton composed this new edition. It must have been after the dissolution on March 16, for he refers to "this last Parliament" and to the writs issued for a new one,[1] and well before mid-April, since he hoped to influence public opinion "in the midst of our Elections."[2] He may have begun the work of revision very soon after the first edition went forth. One new passage expresses a hope that the people will elect their representatives "according to the just and necessarie qualifications (which for aught I hear, remain yet in force unrepeald, as they were formerly decreed in Parlament)."[3] This closely resembles the reference to qualifications in *The Present Means*. But the act for a new Parliament passed on March 16 threw overboard many of the stringent qualifications imposed by the Rump on February 18, and debarred from membership only papists, abettors of the Irish Rebellion, and men who had actually fought (or whose fathers had fought) against the Long Parliament in the Civil Wars. Even these categories were not disqualified from voting. Since Milton is unlikely to have been unaware of so significant

---

[1] *The Readie & Easie Way*, below, p. 407.
[2] *Ibid.*, p. 408.
[3] *Ibid.*, pp. 431–32.

and well publicized a change of policy, this passage may have survived inadvertently from an earlier stage of rescension.

Masson, arguing for a date of composition between April 9 and 24, pointed to indications that Milton had read *The Censure of the Rota,* which Thomason acquired on March 30.[4] These are not convincing, for the expanded references to Harrington and rotation in the second edition were more probably prompted by Harrington's own *The Wayes and Meanes whereby an equal & lasting Commonwealth may be suddenly introduced,* which Thomason dated February 8,[5] and which may have come a little late to Milton's notice. But Masson found another clue in the motto which Milton now placed on his title page, perhaps as a final touch:

et nos
Consilium dedimus Syllae, demus populo nunc [6]

By Sulla, the military dictator, he can only have referred to Monck; so far we can agree with Masson. But is this evidence that the second edition of *The Readie & Easie Way* postdated *Brief Notes upon a Late Sermon,* published probably in mid-April? I find no reason to think so, and I share Ayers' opinion to the contrary.[7] Milton's hopes of Monck's integrity in *Brief Notes* are obviously not to be taken at face value, and his melancholy suggestion there that the general would make a less intolerable king than Charles Stuart does not betoken a high degree of confidence. All that we can reasonably infer from this motto is that Monck had ignored the "consilium" that Milton had sent him in *The Present Means* concerning the management of the Parliamentary elections, and this must have been obvious well before the end of March.

Milton gives us the closest indication to the date of composition where he hopes that his tract "may now be of much more use and concernment to be freely publishd, in the midst of our Elections to a free Parlament, or their sitting to consider freely of the Government."[8] He was probably aware very soon that writs for elections were issued almost immediately after March 16,[9] and he knew that the new Parliament was to meet on April 25. He could easily estimate that most elections would be held early in April, if not before the end of March; in fact the first were held not later than March 24 and the last about

[4] Masson, V, 682–84, 689 n. 1.
[5] E1015(14); notice the similarity between Harrington's and Milton's titles.
[6] "And we gave counsel to Sulla; now we give it to the people."
[7] See below, pp. 398–400.
[8] *The Readie & Easie Way,* below, p. 408.
[9] *The Form of Writs* was published as a broadsheet on March 17, 669f24(21).

April 20, though most returns were in by mid-April.[10] He hoped to publish in the midst of these elections, and the literal midst lay around April 6. It is therefore likely that he finished his work on the second edition by the end of March, or by the first few days of April at the latest.

By the end of March Livewell Chapman, who had brought out the first edition, was as we have seen a fugitive from the Council of State, so Milton presumably had to bear the cost and risk of the venture himself. Did that clause beginning "or their sitting" indicate a fear that the delays and hazards of fugitive printing might delay publication until the Convention had actually assembled? It is possible, but "or" may bear here its more archaic sense of "ere" or "before." At any rate it is perfectly evident that at the time of composition Milton hoped to have his new edition out while the elections were still in full progress, and this points inescapably to an earlier date than has been accepted by Masson and most subsequent scholars. Whether his unknown printer worked fast enough to satisfy him is completely unknown. The extreme rarity of the second edition, of which only three copies are known to survive,[11] suggests that it had a very limited circulation before the Convention's manifest royalism made it dangerous to handle, and it may indeed have been delayed in the press.

The course of the elections [12] could hardly have been more discouraging to Milton. This was the first time in nearly twenty years that the whole traditional electorate had been allowed to vote, without subjection to political tests. Never before had so many candidates contested so many seats, or fought so widely on great political issues. Many a tract and broadsheet urged the electors to reject all regicides, Rumpers, army men, sectaries, purchasers of confiscated land, and enemies of kingly rule in general. At the county hustings, where the franchise was generally broadest, the contest was not so much between supporters and opponents of monarchy as between royalists who wanted an unconditional Restoration and Presbyterians who might try to set terms to it. In Middlesex, for example, the royalist voters set up a cry of "Noe Rumpers, no Presbiterians that will put bad conditions on the King." [13] Sir George Booth and Sir Thomas Myddelton, leaders

---

[10] *Mercurius Politicus*, March 22–29, 1660, p. 1195; Whitelocke, *Memorials*, pp. 700–01; *Clarendon Calendar*, IV, 614 and *passim;* Historical Manuscripts Commission, *Report V*, p. 199, and *Laing MSS*, I, 310–11; *Old Parliamentary History*, XXII, 208. Other elections investigated all fell between the above terminal dates.

[11] Parker, *Milton*, pp. 556, 1074.

[12] Davies gives a full acount of the elections in *Restoration*, pp. 320–34, and an even fuller one in *Huntington Library Quarterly*, XV (1952), 211–35.

[13] Davies, *Restoration*, p. 322.

of the previous August's risings, were both elected by their counties, and in general success went to the men who were strongest for the king. The results in the boroughs naturally showed greater variety, but many of them reflected the same animus against republicans, swordsmen, and sectaries. Only sixteen of the Rumpers who had sat since last May were re-elected, and three of them were subsequently expelled by the House.

Milton cannot have been deaf to the voice of the political nation. Against such a background, one can but marvel at the courage and conviction with which, guided only by the voice of his amanuensis, he went through every word of his former text, polishing its roughnesses, modifying points that its attackers had shown to be vulnerable, and above all enlarging those great set pieces that condemned monarchy and extolled a commonwealth government. He had of course to revise his central prescription for securing a free commonwealth, now that the swift current of events had swept the Rump into limbo. He could not retract the expressions of forced optimism in the first edition without admitting the defeat of his cause; he had to help keep open that outside chance that the nation's representatives might yet opt against monarchy. He must have been aware of the hiatus between the heroic aspirations and virtues that he attributed to republican government and the pathetically implausible means that were all he could now propose for achieving them. But more strongly than in the first edition, one senses that the means were not his sole or even his main concern now. What chiefly impelled him was surely a desire to distill more perfectly for posterity the essential nobility of the ends for which the best minds of the Commonwealth had striven, to vindicate the right of the nation's better part to prevail over the more numerous, and to prophesy even more forcefully the servitude and degeneracy that a relapse into monarchy would entail. It is worth remarking how many of the new passages heighten the *moral* contrast between republican and kingly rule.

Not that the new version is indifferent to immediate issues: far from it. The first large addition, several pages long, begins by justifying the Rump in considering itself no longer bound by the Solemn League and Covenant when it proceeded against Charles I.[14] This is obviously prompted by the Long Parliament's recent attempt, since the first edition had appeared, to reimpose the Covenant. But this passage soon leads Milton into deeper philosophical waters, when he comes to vindicate the minority of the Parliament in its actions against the majority. They were, he says, "not bound by any statute of preceding Parlaments, but by the law of nature only, which is the

---

[14] *The Readie & Easie Way*, below, pp. 409 ff.

only law of laws truly and properly to all mankinde fundamental; the beginning and the end of all Government; to which no Parlament or people that will throughly reforme, but may and must have recourse." [15] This begs many questions, and skates over all the vicissitudes that natural-law theory had undergone at the hands of Hobbes and others since the early Parliamentarian apologists had first appealed to the concept.[16] It is probably to be read as a simple invocation of *salus populi suprema lex*, for Milton's point is the obligation of the members who were "under free conscience" to act for the people against those who were "under force." [17] But he faces difficulties beyond that of justifying the parliamentary minority in dictating to the majority. Only the force applied by the army had enabled the minority to act at all, and while he has to approve the immediate effect of that force in bringing the king to trial and the Commonwealth into existence, he cannot any longer defend the motives or the subsequent actions of the men who wielded it. Nor can he, especially amid the execration of 1660, rest his defence on the purity of intention of all who had sided with the Independents or sat in the Rump in its earlier days.[18]

Whence then did the acts of the minority receive their sanction? Milton answers thus:

> The best affected also and best principl'd of the people, stood not numbring or computing on which side were most voices in Parlament, but on which side appeerd to them most reason, most safetie, when the house divided upon main matters.[19]

Moreover "neither did they measure votes and counsels by the intentions of them that voted," for they were aware "that a greater number might be corrupt within the walls of a Parlament as well as of a citie; wherof in matters of neerest concernment all men will be judges." [20] They preferred sound policies advanced by ill-motivated men to unsound ones promoted with the best intentions. They judged "that most voices ought not alwaies to prevail where main matters are in question . . . there being in number little vertue, but by weight

[15] *Ibid.*, pp. 412–13.

[16] The earlier development of natural-law theory is discussed in *Complete Prose*, II, 12–52, 130–36; III, 65–80.

[17] *The Readie & Easie Way*, below, pp. 413–14.

[18] *Cf.* another added passage slightly later, exhorting his fellow countrymen not to "betray a just and noble cause for the mixture of bad men who have ill manag'd and abus'd it": below, p. 422.

[19] *Ibid.*, p. 414.

[20] *Ibid.*, pp. 414–15.

and measure wisdom working all things." [21] These may seem dangerous doctrines in a treatise whose central proposal is a perpetual Grand Council whose decisions in many great matters of state are to be as unquestionable by the people as its members are to be irremovable, except presumably by itself. Even the right of assent to national legislation that Milton accords to the county assemblies is to be subject to majority rule, all counties being bound by the decision of the greater number. Milton, however, is concerned here to denounce the terms that the majority in the Long Parliament had been bent on concluding with Charles I in the later months of 1648—terms that were often referred to in March and April, 1660, as a possible basis for the restoration of Charles II. One can see why he seeks to credit their former rejection to "the best affected and best principl'd of the people" rather than to the army officers who actually carried out Pride's Purge.

The reader will not miss the newly inserted reference—yet another! —to Milton's victory over Salmasius,[22] or the eloquent expansions of his sections on the shame of reverting to the thraldom of kingship [23] and on the debasement to which Court service will subject the nobility and gentry.[24] Then, after many pages that undergo only occasional amendments and enlargements, radical alterations begin again in the central section that proposes the actual means whereby a commonwealth may be established, and treats in particular of the Grand Council. All references to the Rump as its nucleus are suppressed, for obvious reasons. How then is the Grand Council to be constituted? Only by casting the forthcoming Convention in the role, for the elections are already in progress, and no other assembly lies now within the bounds of possibility. Milton takes what comfort he can from the fact that the writs have been issued, not in the name of the king (an assumption of royal authority that the Long Parliament had expressly rejected) [25] but of the Keepers of the Liberties, the old Commonwealth style.

Cautioned perhaps by his critics, he is more circumspect this time in defining the Grand Council's authority. "In this Grand Councel," he writes, "must the sovrantie, not transferrd, but delegated only, and as it were deposited, reside." [26] This sounds like the delegation of a limited trust rather than a Hobbesian total surrender of natural rights; but though the Grand Council's powers in the spheres of

[21] *Ibid.*, pp. 415–16.
[22] *Ibid.*, pp. 420–21.
[23] *Ibid.*, p. 422.
[24] *Ibid.*, pp. 425–26.
[25] Masson, V, 554.
[26] *The Readie & Easie Way*, below, p. 432.

revenue and legislation are now qualified, they remain in other re-
spects large. He would still have its authority to be perpetual, and he
expands his arguments against successive Parliaments. Nevertheless
he gives more consideration to the alternative of rotation, and in place
of the preposterously limited device in the first edition he offers the
Harringtonian scheme whereby a third of the members would retire
annually—though "if the space be longer, so much perhaps the bet-
ter." [27] "But," he adds, "I could wish that this wheel or partial wheel
in State, if it be possible, might be avoided; as having too much affin-
itie with the wheel of fortune." [28]

The next lengthy addition follows the section in which he supports
his plan for a commonwealth from the examples of other republics,
past and present. He answers the objection that in states such as
Athens and Sparta and Rome, which had some form of perpetual
Senate, this was balanced by a more popular assembly that could hold
it to account. Yes, he replies, but "these remedies either little availd
the people, or brought them to such a licentious and unbridl'd democ-
ratie, as in fine ruind themselves with thir own excessive power." [29]
This talk of a balance serves to introduce a compact but devastating
criticism of Harrington's favorite scheme for dividing the legislature
between an elected Senate, to propose laws, and a larger popular as-
sembly, to ballot on them. Balloting in turn provides a link with an-
other topic which he had not paused to discuss in the first edition,
namely how elections should be held when death or retirement cause a
vacancy in the Grand Council. He sketches an elaborately indirect
method in three or four stages, "not committing all to the noise and
shouting of a rude multitude." [30] This and the following sentences pro-
vide a *locus classicus* for Milton's rejection of anything approaching
direct democracy and for his ideal of an aristocracy of virtue. Finally,
before reverting to his former text, he suggests how much more con-
veniently and effectively his own proposed county assemblies will
perform the function of popular assent than the unwieldy national
assembly of *Oceana*.

Two sizable cuts in the original text soon follow, both passages
being rendered inapposite by their references to the former Parliament.
Then Milton returns to his criticism of Harrington, affirming that his
own proposals can be effected "without the introducement of new or

[27] *Ibid.*, p. 434.

[28] *Ibid.*, p. 435.

[29] *Ibid.*, p. 438.

[30] *Ibid.*, p. 442. Wolfe, in *Milton in the Puritan Revolution*, p. 301, eluci-
dates this scheme of election with a diagram.

obsolete forms, or terms, or exotic models; idea's that would effect
nothing, but with a number of new injunctions to manacle the native
liberty of mankinde; turning all vertue into prescription, servitude, and
necessitie, to the great impairing and frustrating of Christian lib-
ertie." [31] That he is tilting particularly at Harrington is indicated by
his specific criticism, a few lines later, of the latter's agrarian law,
which he claims will be needless under his own scheme.

The additions to the next section, which treats of the particular evils
to be expected if monarchy is restored, are considerable in length and
splendid in utterance. Except for the magnificent closing peroration
that is shortly to follow, no passage in Milton's later prose sustains the
grand style more eloquently than the chain of rhetorical questions
that begins "Can the folly be paralleld, to adore and be the slaves of
a single person for doing that which it is ten thousand to one whether
he can or will do, and we without him might do more easily, more
effectually, more laudably our selves?" [32] If it is difficult here to keep
our judgment unclouded by the risk that Milton is running by parad-
ing his contempt for the particular single person whose return is now
all but inevitable, it is so no less when he proclaims, even more boldly
than before, the shame that will fall upon the English people if they
surrender now the fruit of their blood and treasure.[33] But for sheer
defiance, and for invective raised to the level of art, what can surpass
his warning to "the new royaliz'd presbyterians"?

> Let them but now read the diabolical forerunning libells, the faces,
> the gestures that now appeer foremost and briskest in all public places;
> as the harbingers of those that are in expectation to raign over us; let
> them but hear the insolencies, the menaces, the insultings of our newly
> animated common enemies crept lately out of thir holes, thir hell, I
> might say, by the language of thir infernal pamphlets, the spue of
> every drunkard, every ribald; . . . Let our zealous backsliders fore-
> think now with themselves, how thir necks yok'd with these tigers of
> Bacchus, these new fanatics of not the preaching but the sweating-tub,
> inspir'd with nothing holier then the Venereal pox, can draw one way
> under monarchie to the establishing of church discipline with these new-
> disgorg'd atheismes.[34]

Still in the full flood of moral revulsion against the whole royalist
crew, Milton challenges the argument, now heard everywhere, that
since the great majority of the nation wants kingship restored, the

---

[31] *The Readie & Easie Way*, below, p. 445. Milton nowhere names Harring-
ton, but the references would be unmistakable to Harrington's readers.
[32] *Ibid.*, p. 448.
[33] *Ibid.*, pp. 449–50.
[34] *Ibid.*, pp. 452–53.

rest must yield. The greater part, he retorts, have forfeited the right to choose their government, both in reason and through trial by battle. And even if the majority of those who are *not* disfranchised by earlier royalism are now in favor of monarchy,

> Suppose they be; yet of freedom they partake all alike, one main end of government: which if the greater part value not, but will degeneratly forgoe, is it just or reasonable, that most voices against the main end of government should enslave the less number that would be free? More just it is doubtless, if it com to force, that a less number compell a greater number to retain, which can be no wrong to them, thir libertie, then that a greater number for the pleasure of thir baseness, compell a less most injuriously to be thir fellow slaves. They who seek nothing but thir own just libertie, have alwaies right to winn it and to keep it, when ever they have power, be the voices never so numerous that oppose it.[35]

It is a terrible argument. Milton would never have willed the horrors that have since been committed in its name,[36] but we in our time have shuddered at its distant echoes in Hungary, in Czechoslovakia, and in lands that Milton had never heard of.

The next pages, which define spiritual liberty, suffer his largest single excision. He deletes the whole passage that had asserted once more his favorite contention against allowing the civil state any power over matters ecclesiastical. Why? According to Barker, "because the practical political situation in 1660 seemed to demonstrate conclusively that the state must be so constituted as to provide for the defence of true spiritual religion, and that in consequence (while true religion must remain free, and church and state therefore separate) the strict segregation of the spiritual and natural was not only undesirable but impossible." [37] But whatever Milton may have wished, he can have had no hope whatever "that the magistrates shall be only such as already recognize the religion which is true." [38] The current elections were determining who England's new masters were to be, and he must already have guessed that the Convention would regard the segregation of temporal and spiritual authority as a worse evil than a

[35] *Ibid.*, p. 455.

[36] Compare Robespierre, addressing the National Convention on February 5, 1794: "Is our government then like despotism? Yes, as the sword that flashes in the hand of the hero of liberty is like that with which the satellites of tyranny are armed . . . The government of the Revolution is the despotism of liberty against tyranny." Quoted in G. H. Sabine, *History of Political Theory* (1937), p. 498.

[37] *Milton and the Puritan Dilemma*, p. 279.

[38] *Ibid.*, p. 280.

return to episcopacy. He probably did not waver in his old convictions; he simply recognized that he would only prejudice his almost desperate plea for a commonwealth if he reaffirmed a demand which every government since the Civil War had rejected. Consequently he changed his emphasis and added a new passage, warning the Presbyterians how hopeless was their attempt to reimpose the Covenant and how certain it was that monarchy would bring back with it an inveterately hostile episcopacy. "But let our governors beware in time," he admonished, "least thir hard measure to libertie of conscience be found the rock wheron they shipwrack themselves," for by abandoning those they call sectaries they will reject "thir own chief strength and interest in the freedom of all Protestant religion." [39] This was sound prophecy.

In the ensuing section on civil liberty, the role of the county assemblies is expanded and elaborated on lines that have already been discussed.[40] Aware now how ill received his proposal for a perpetual Senate has been, he seeks to show that a sufficient decentralization of justice and administration will remove its powers for harm.

The superb peroration stands much as it did in the first edition until the closing sentences. In these the specific reference to Coniah is excised, for the terrible words spoken to that king in Jeremiah 22 : 24–30 were the plainest treason when applied to Charles II. But it may not have been prudence that prompted this slight change; Milton probably wanted to shift the emphasis from Coniah's seed to earth's "perverse inhabitants," the better to introduce the parenthetical prayer that he so poignantly inserts at this point: "Nay though what I have spoke, should happ'n (which Thou suffer not, who didst create mankinde free; nor Thou next, who didst redeem us from being servants of men!) to be the last words of our expiring libertie." [41] Men who knew their Bibles well, and there were many then, would recall which prophet cried the words "O earth, earth, earth," and in what context. Milton was certainly not heeding the consequences when he inserted another sentence which talked of the people "now chusing them a captain back for *Egypt*." In comparing the two editions one feels him to be striving only to enhance the pathos and eloquence of these last words that he addresses "to som perhaps, whom God may raise of these stones, to become children of reviving libertie." [42] That word "reviving," added in the second edition, hints at a

[39] *The Readie & Easie Way,* below, p. 458.
[40] See above, pp. 183–85.
[41] *The Readie & Easie Way,* below, p. 463.
[42] *Ibid.*

hope that a new generation will heed his message, even if his contemporaries are deaf to it.

7. *THE READIE & EASIE WAY* AND ITS CRITICS

We have already argued that Milton's last political treatise is not to be taken as a model of the ideal commonwealth.[1] Only its general celebration of republican liberty and virtue in contrast with monarchical tyranny and servitude stands for certain above the limitations of time and place; the actual machinery that it propounds is geared to the rapidly contracting political possibilities of certain months— even weeks—in 1660. That is the reason for the pathetic rift between ends and means that runs like a geological fault through the whole work. We wrong Milton if we seek too far in his last political tracts what Barker calls "the influence of the Platonic search for that ideal city whose pattern is laid up in heaven," [2] and Wolfe is surely right that they present "indisputable evidence that Milton's proposed commonwealth was not his ideal commonwealth." [3]

We should be equally wary of accepting Zera Fink's contention that Milton "proposed . . . to set up, like Harrington, nothing less than a perpetually healthy state which would work perfectly and last unchanged even to the very end of the world." [4] There are strong expressions in *The Readie & Easie Way* that seem to support such a case, but Milton, like most of his contemporaries, wrote under at least two powerful pressures to conform to this convention: the persistent classical tradition that the best form of state is not only just but immutable, and the still stronger common law tradition, synthesized on a monumental scale and with enormous authority by Coke, that England's pre-revolutionary constitution had come down, unchanged in essence, from the dawn of history. At a time when chronic instability had sickened men of constitutional experiment, and when the strongest card in the royalist pamphleteers' pack was their appeal to return to a regimen that perfectly embodied the nation's immemorial political wisdom, it would have been suicidal for Milton to claim less than permanence for his own scheme. Yet he let fall more than one hint that the achievement of the perfect commonwealth would not be the work of a day. Of the Grand Council, for instance, he wrote that it

[1] See above, pp. 187–88.
[2] *Milton and the Puritan Dilemma*, p. 288.
[3] *Milton in the Puritan Revolution*, p. 297.
[4] *The Classical Republicans*, p. 120.

would be better "in this wavering condition of our affairs, to deferr the changing or circumscribing of our Senat, more then may be done with ease, till the Commonwealth be throughly setl'd in peace and safetie, and they themselves give us the occasion"; [5] and of his local assemblies, "for it may be referrd to time, so we be still going on by degrees to perfection." [6]

It will be seen how strongly the present writer agrees with the recent remarks on *The Readie & Easie Way*'s commentators by Parker, in his magisterial biography of the poet:

> A good deal of this criticism and analysis has unfortunately been vitiated by a quite unwarranted assumption: that the tract presents its author's final, considered theory of an ideal Commonwealth. . . . The truth of the matter is that Milton was dealing, not with ultimate ideals, but with desperate expedients. He modified his proposal each time he uttered it, from October of 1659 to April of 1660; and if a seventh such document had been produced in May or June, it would probably have offered a still different solution.[7]

Some of his exegetes have contorted themselves in their efforts to save his consistency at all costs, as though it were a failing in him to modify his political convictions under the experience of nineteen years of revolutionary change. Fink, for instance, drives too far the thesis that the keynote of Milton's politics lies in the concept of the mixed state—mixed, that is, in Aristotle's and Polybius' sense of combining monarchical (or magisterial), aristocratic, and democratic elements in an ideal balance.[8] But belief in the mixed state had been a commonplace in English political thought for over a century,[9] and in 1660 the moderate royalists were making far more play with it than any republicans. In Milton's work, surely, the principle is progressively eroded. Monarchical and magisterial are not closely equivalent terms, and in *The Readie & Easie Way* even the magisterial element is reduced to a Council of State that is little more than an executive committee of the Grand Council.

More than any of his previous political tracts, *The Readie & Easie Way* leans towards aristocracy. Its condemnation of monarchy is ab-

[5] *The Readie & Easie Way*, below, pp. 441–42. Lewalski, in *PMLA*, LXXIV, 199, has boldly suggested that Milton "thought of this body merely as another temporary expedient, and that he himself might well have been the first to demand its liberalization once the threat of a Stuart restoration was removed."

[6] *The Readie & Easie Way*, below, p. 444.

[7] Parker, *Milton*, p. 557.

[8] Fink, *The Classical Republicans*, chapter IV, esp. p. 120.

[9] See for instance the excerpt from John Aylmer, *An Harborowe for Faithful and True Subjects* (1559), printed in Elton, *The Tudor Constitution*, p. 16.

solute, and although Milton claims something of a democratic role
for his county assemblies, the picture that he essentially conveys is
one of a central oligarchy balanced by a multiplicity of local aris-
tocracies.[10] But what kind of an aristocracy is he advocating? Not the
traditional aristocracy of birth, for he more than once commends the
abolition of distinctions between lords and commoners.[11] On the other
hand the role that he allocates to the nobility and chief gentry in the
counties, and his concern lest these orders be corrupted by Court ser-
vice, show him to be no opponent of social hierarchy as such. The in-
teresting question, however, is that raised chiefly by Barker: whether
his ideal lay in an aristocracy of virtue or in one of grace. Was he
content that his senators should be imbued with the civic loyalties of
good commonwealthsmen and endowed with sound political judgment?
Or did he intend ideally that they should be visible saints, "men
whose natures have been regenerated by the Spirit"?[12]

   The case for the latter rests on very tenuous textual support from
The Readie & Easie Way itself, and on a great deal of inference from
certain passages in *Christian Doctrine*. In that work, Milton goes far
towards the view that original sin has so polluted the springs of man's
will and understanding that only those illuminated by the Spirit
through the experience of regeneration can form right judgments and
exercise true liberty, even in temporal affairs. But it is unsound on this
basis to identify the law of nature, as invoked in *The Readie & Easie
Way*, with the law of the Spirit, or to infer that the minority who are
credited there with retaining their freedom include only the regener-
ate. As Lewalski has cogently argued,[13] Milton's Arminian theology
blurs the sharp predestinarian lines between regenerate and unregener-
ate, and allows mere natural man to attain a degree of wisdom and
virtue sufficient for the purposes of the secular state. Although Milton
stops short of the total segregation of temporal and spiritual that
Roger Williams and the Levellers had advocated, a reading of *The
Readie & Easie Way* as a whole conveys the overwhelming impression
that the capacity of civil magistrates is to be judged in terms of hu-
man prudence and of their faithfulness to the main ends of a common-
wealth—which of course include liberty of conscience. He justifies
those who had valued the cause itself above the men who had man-
aged it: "Safer they therefor judgd what they thought the better coun-

[10] *Cf. above*, pp. 183–85.

[11] *The Readie & Easie Way*, below, pp. 445, 461.

[12] Barker, *Milton and the Puritan Dilemma*, p. 285; for the main develop-
ment of Barker's argument see pp. 278–90, 308–26.

[13] In *PMLA*, LXXIV, 199–202. Michael Fixler supports Lewalski's arguments
in *Milton and the Kingdoms of God*, pp. 204–10.

sels, though carried on by some perhaps to bad ends, then the wors, by others, though endevord with best intentions." [14] Nowhere does he stipulate godliness as an essential qualification for magistracy, either in the Senate or the local councils. Nor are the "free" who have the right to impose on the degenerate majority identified with the saints; it is enough that they hold fast to the principles of a commonwealth.[15] In all this, Milton's tract speaks in a quite different tone from even the more moderate advocates of a rule of the saints. There is no perceptible "fusion of the principles of 'the mere commonwealths man' with those of 'the rigid Fifth Monarchy Man,' " [16] and no ground for believing that Milton's excision from the second edition of a specific condemnation of Fifth Monarchists [17] marks a change of attitude towards them between February and April, 1660. Milton's commonwealth depends certainly upon an aristocracy of virtue, but civic virtue stands sufficiently in its own right to distinguish his elite from an aristocracy purely of grace.

One more crux demands discussion. How far can Milton's revised proposals be squared with his assertion, in that answer to Dr. Griffith that he dictated in this same month of April, of the fundamental right of every free people to choose its form of government? [18] Lewalski has labored bravely to save his consistency by arguing that on his definition the free meant only those who had attained such inner freedom as would merit political liberty and maintain it. She points also to the second edition's greater emphasis on the local assemblies as safeguards against the Grand Council's autocracy, and sees at worst a pardonable disingenuousness in his using the popular-sovereignty argument in a sense different from that in which it was commonly understood.[19] This is difficult to sustain. It is surely wiser to face the

[14] *The Readie & Easie Way,* below, p. 415.

[15] *Cf. A Second Defence:* "just as to be free is precisely the same as to be pious, wise, just, and temperate, careful of one's property, aloof from another's, and thus finally to be magnanimous and brave, so to be the opposite to these qualities is the same as to be a slave" (*Complete Prose,* IV, 684).

[16] Barker, *Milton and the Puritan Dilemma,* p. 286.

[17] *The Readie & Easie Way,* below, p. 380.

[18] *Brief Notes,* below, p. 479; *cf.* above, p. 210.

[19] *PMLA,* LXXIV, 199. Lewalski was of the opinion that Milton "frequently hinted that the army might overthrow this 'perpetual' legislature if it should act against freedom of religion or commonwealth government." He only gave such a hint once, in his letter to Monck (below, p. 395), and he limited it to the eventuality of the leading gentry of the counties refusing to manage the forthcoming elections in the manner he proposed. It was never a suggestion that the army might eject the Grand Council, once it was established.

fact that *The Readie & Easie Way* does *not* allow the people—even the "free" people in Milton's sense—any considerable power to choose or to alter the form of their government, and that its assertion of the right of the minority to impose "their own just liberty" upon the majority by force is not only incongruous with popular sovereignty but capable of infinite abuse. One senses how dearly Milton must have wished that the people *were* fit to erect a government of their free choice, and how deeply he felt the tragic gap between his aspirations for his fellow countrymen and the political realities as he saw them. On that notorious passage about forcing men to be free, Barker's comment is just and compassionate:

> The frustration of a great idealism is a painful spectacle; and it would be a bold man who should sit in judgment on this pitiful declaration of failure in which strength and weakness, determination and despair, hope and fear, are so inextricably combined.[20]

[20] *Milton and the Puritan Dilemma*, p. 272.

EPILOGUE: THE RESTORATION

WHEN the Convention Parliament assembled on April 25, 1660, it lost little time in demonstrating just how desperate Milton's proposal was that it should erect itself into a bulwark against monarchy. The overwhelming majority of members shared the now quite uninhibited desire of the country as a whole to bring back the king. The greater number were Presbyterian in the sense that their antecedents in the Civil War had been Parliamentarian, but it was soon clear that many ex-royalists and sons of royalists-in-arms had been returned, despite the prohibition enacted by the expiring Long Parliament. The French ambassador reported a proposal to exclude a hundred or six score as being thus disqualified,[1] but no action followed; indeed the weapon of expulsion was soon turned against the tiny handful of regicides and republicans who had secured election. Equally depressing to Milton was the presence from the start of a few determined peers. At first they were all former Parliamentarians, but they were shortly joined by the "young lords" who had not sat before, and slightly later by the royalist peers, so that the House of Lords was quickly re-established as an essential component of Parliament.

As for the king, the only question now was whether or not his restoration would be conditional. The exiled Court cleverly forestalled any move to make it so. On May 1 Sir John Grenville, Charles II's emissary to Monck, appeared before the Lords with letters from the king to the Speakers of both Houses and a declaration that Charles had signed at Breda four weeks earlier. The Declaration of Breda was a skillful piece, drafted by Edward Hyde, now Lord Chancellor, and allegedly owing much to Monck's advice.[2] In it the king made promises regarding four matters on which the former Parliamentarians were likeliest to press for conditions: a free and general pardon for all but such as Parliament should except, liberty to tender consciences in matters of religion, determination by Parliament of titles to confiscated and otherwise disputable estates, and payment of the army's arrears. On all these thorny issues, however, Charles bound himself no further than to assent to such acts as Parliament should pass con-

[1] Guizot, II, 412.
[2] Baker, *Chronicle*, p. 718. The Declaration of Breda is printed in many collections, including Gardiner, *Constitutional Documents*, pp. 465–67.

cerning them, so that he would have the credit for clemency and con-
ciliation, and Parliament the odium for the inevitable failure to satisfy
all parties.

Both Houses warmly welcomed the king's letters and declaration.
That very day they voted "That, according to the ancient and funda-
mental Laws of this Kingdom, the Government is, and ought to be, by
King, Lords, and Commons." [3] As that memorable May Day drew to a
close, London celebrated with another night of bonfires, bell ringing,
and loyal toasts drunk deep.

Milton knew now that there was nothing more to hope. He had
banked about £2000 that he had saved from his salary in the Excise
Office, both for security and for the steady interest that excise bonds
had hitherto offered. Now, too late, he tried to redeem them. Did he
suddenly realize at this late stage that he might lose them, as Parker
suggests? [4] He was never a very good manager of his financial affairs,
but it is at least possible that he was all along aware of the risk but
scorned to act as though he despaired of the Commonwealth's future
until there was no future left. At any rate he transferred at least one
and probably all of these bonds to Cyriack Skinner, but neither Skinner
nor any other of his friends could salvage them.

On May 8 Charles was proclaimed king with all the old pageantry,
and the populace celebrated its joy in another round of revels. That
May was a mad month for the "tigers of Bacchus," and to Milton's
ears it must have sounded as though the forces of hell were let loose.
Two days later came the last spasm of the movement for a conditional
Restoration, with a motion in the Commons for a committee to con-
sider which of the terms accepted by Charles I in the abortive negotia-
tion on the Isle of Wight in 1648 should be presented to his son.
Monck himself opposed it, and moved instead that commissioners be
sent over at once to bring the king home. The shout that acclaimed
him put the House's wishes beyond all doubt.

We need not follow further the train of events that brought Charles
II to Dover on May 25, or describe the triumph of his entry into
London four days later. This is not the place for a general account of
the Restoration settlement. We must concentrate on what closely con-
cerned Milton: his personal fate first, and then the cruel attrition of
that dearest of rights to him, liberty of conscience.

Personal danger he must have expected, and he felt it close enough
to go into hiding—just when we do not know, nor what friend found

---

[3] Davies, *Restoration,* p. 342. What follows concerning the events of the Res-
storation is fully documented in chapter XVII of Davies' work.

[4] Parker, *Milton,* p. 562.

refuge for him in a narrow alley off West Smithfield called Bartholomew Close.[5] A bill for a general pardon, indemnity, and oblivion was introduced in the Commons on May 9, but it was obvious from the start that some would be excluded from its benefits, starting with the regicides. Orders for their arrest and for the seizure of their estates went out on May 14. The Commons decided that seven of them, and five others who had been implicated in the proceedings against Charles I without actually signing his death warrant, should suffer the death of traitors. On June 8 they voted that in addition to the remaining regicides a further twenty men should be excepted from the act, though for penalties short of death. The next ten days, during which the House selected its sacrificial victims, must have been among the worst of Milton's life. Slowly and suspensefully the names came out: Speaker Lenthall first, then such other old associates on the Council of State as Vane, St. John, Haslerig, Sydenham, Desborough, Lambert, and Fleetwood, together with some others who must have struck Milton as more obscure than himself. The pamphleteers were still baying after him,[6] though he was only one of many republicans who came in for their mockery and abuse.

On June 16, before the Commons had completed their list, they ordered the immediate arrest of Milton and John Goodwin, and requested the king to issue a proclamation calling in *A Defence* and *Eikonoklastes*, together with Goodwin's *Obstructors of Justice*, to be burnt by the common hangman. In the next few days they nominated the last seven of the twenty non-regicides to whom pardon was to be denied. The nineteenth was Goodwin, denounced by Prynne "because of his book"; it was getting horribly close. The last name was keenly debated. One Mr. Powell actually proposed Milton,[7] but he apparently found no seconder. The choice finally fell on Colonel Ralph Cobbet, who had promoted the Derby Petition the previous year and joined Lambert's desperate rising in April, 1660.[8] Now and later, Milton was

[5] The ensuing paragraphs are based on Parker, *Milton*, pp. 567 ff., 1079 ff., and Godfrey Davies, "Milton in 1660," in *Huntington Library Quarterly*, XVIII (1955), 351–63.
[6] See Parker, *Milton's Contemporary Reputation*, pp. 101–04, and *Milton*, pp. 568–69.
[7] The bald entry in Bowman's MS diary, quoted by Davies in *HLQ*, XVIII, 356, reads "Mr. Powell (Berks) against Milton." This is ambiguous: did Powell accuse Milton (as Davies reads it) or defend him (as Parker assumes in *Milton*, p. 1085)? I incline to Davies' interpretation, but what matters of course is that Milton's name was certainly proposed by someone.
[8] Parker (*Milton*, pp. 572, 1085) names instead Miles Corbet, on the authority of "Davies's quotation from the *Old Parliamentary History*." This is inexplicable. The *Old Parliamentary History*, XXII, correctly names "Colonel

well served by his friends, not only in Parliament but on the Privy Council, and none was stauncher than the member for Hull—his old colleague Andrew Marvell. There is also a late though not improbable story that the royalist poet and dramatist Sir William Davenant, for whom Milton had interceded when he was in danger of being tried for his life in 1650, now in turn used his influence to protect Milton. On the Council itself, Milton's advocates may have included Sir Thomas Clarges and Sir William Morrice—both intimates of Monck—Arthur Annesley, and perhaps Monck too. And who knows what Lady Ranelagh may have done for him through her brothers the Earl of Cork and Lord Broghil? [9]

But his danger was by no means past. From about mid-July to August 10 the Lords went over the whole Bill of Indemnity and tried to add both to the number and the penalties of those excepted from it. Save in a very few cases, including Vane's,[10] their amendments were rejected, and the bill received the royal assent on August 29. But there was still that order of June 16 for Milton's arrest, and the royal proclamation—strangely delayed until August 13—calling in *A Defence* and *Eikonoklastes*. This proclamation stated that Milton and Goodwin "are both fled, or so obscure themselves, that no endeavors used for their apprehension can take effect, whereby they might be brought to Legal Tryal, and deservedly receive condigne punishment for their Treasons and Offences." [11] Early in September a few copies of Milton's two treatises were actually burnt by the common hangman at the Old Bailey.

The blind poet probably thought that this was as far as his enemies would pursue him, for soon after this he came out of hiding and rented a house near Red Lion Fields in Holborn. But no sooner was his *Defence* against Salmasius consigned to the flames than that old adversary came back at him from the grave with a long-delayed reply. *Ad Johannem Miltonum Responsio*,[12] registered in London on September 19, 1660, had been left less than half finished when Salmasius

---

Ralph Cobbet," as does Davies (*HLQ*, XVIII, 355–57), but Davies cites not the *Old Parliamentary History* but its source, Bowman's MS diary. Moreover, the twenty men under consideration were not regicides; whereas not only was Miles Corbet a regicide, he was executed as such in 1662.

[9] On Milton's friends in this crisis, see Parker, *Milton*, pp. 571–72.

[10] Vane and Lambert were made liable to capital punishment, but the king granted a petition from both Houses that their lives should be spared. In spite of this, Vane was shamefully executed in 1662.

[11] Full text in French, *Life Records*, IV, 328–30.

[12] Bibliographical particulars in Parker, *Milton*, p. 1086; extracts in Masson, VI, 204–11, and French, *Life Records*, IV, 344–48.

died in 1653, but it ran nevertheless to over three hundred splenetic pages of very small print. What gall it added to Milton's darkest hour of defeat we can only imagine—and he could not reply. Posterity at any rate can be grateful that he was not distracted from *Paradise Lost* by another laborious and sterile exercise in polemics. For him, however, it must have been bitter that his freedom was too precarious to risk, even if he could find a printer for another reply to Salmasius.

He soon discovered just how precarious his freedom was. Probably in November, the Commons' sergeant-at-arms suddenly executed the order of June 16 and took him into custody. His imprisonment did not last long, for he was persuaded, perhaps reluctantly, to sue out his pardon under the Act of Indemnity and Oblivion. The Commons considered his case on December 15 and ordered his release, on payment of his fees. The sergeant-at-arms, however, charged him the exorbitant sum of £150, and on the 17th Andrew Marvell brought the matter up in the House. Colonel Edward King and Colonel Robert Shapcot seconded the motion for an investigation, whereupon Sir Heneage Finch, the new solicitor-general and future Earl of Nottingham, remarked that Milton deserved hanging. How the matter ended is unknown, but Milton certainly received an official pardon in December and was not molested again.[13]

But there was plenty to distress him during that autumn besides his personal troubles. The hanging, drawing, and quartering of ten regicides and others in mid-October must have harrowed him. Even though none of them had been close associates of his, he had known Thomas Scot, Major-General Harrison, John Carew, and Colonel John Jones on the Commonwealth's Council of State, and Hugh Peters was no stranger to him. In a more general way he must have felt that the gloomy prophecies of *The Readie & Easie Way* were fulfilling themselves. The royal Court was rapidly resuming its old social ascendancy and more than its old political influence. Ambition good and bad was drawn irresistibly towards this great honeypot, with its luxury and fashion, its sweet sinecures and ceremonial offices, its capricious favors and its fascinating intrigues. Its corrupting effect on the manners and morals of the governing class was only just beginning, but already its tone encouraged a massive and vituperative reaction everywhere against the religious and political ideals which Milton had given up his calling as a poet to defend. If the spirit of vengeance was less unbridled than he had forecast, that was partly because Charles II and Hyde had the honor and good sense to check it and partly because the decencies of neighborhood among the gentry that had mitigated the

[13] Parker, *Milton,* pp. 575–76.

lot of the royalists in the past decade did not wholly succumb to the fevers of the year of Restoration. Furthermore, the new government was by no means a wholly cavalier body; room had to be found in it for many former Parliamentarians who had helped to bring the king home.

But if Milton had exaggerated the political evils that the Restoration would entail, he scarcely did so with regard to liberty of conscience.[14] At first it seemed as though his fears would be belied, for Charles II's Declaration of Breda promised "a liberty to tender consciences, and that no man shall be disquieted or called in question for differences of opinion in matter of religion, which do not disturb the peace of the kingdom." [15] Hyde, who drafted these words and was to be the main architect of the Restoration settlement on the political side, certainly intended to restore the historic Church of England, but he probably overestimated the power of moderate Puritans to exact concessions. He could not foresee how rapidly the intellectual climate would turn against them in the next year or so.

When Milton had published his ecclesiastical tracts in 1659, Anglicanism was officially proscribed, and he could see the main line of cleavage as running between the "orthodox" Puritan groups—whether moderate Presbyterians or Independents or non-denominational men like Richard Baxter—who upheld an established parochial ministry supported by the state, and the separatists who contended as he did for a purely voluntaryist system. He spoke for a small minority even then, but the very fact of the Restoration shifted the lines of controversy much further to the right. It was now the separatists who were in the wilderness, and moderate Independents like John Owen and Thomas Goodwin saw their chances of toleration dwindling fast. The Long Parliament's bid in March, 1660, to restore a Presbyterian establishment proved to be a chimera. As the lines redrew themselves after the king's return, the main confrontation lay between on the one hand moderate Puritans like Baxter (commonly though inaccurately labeled Presbyterians) who were willing to come to compromise terms with an Elizabethan-type episcopacy, together with equally moderate Anglicans such as John Gauden and Thomas Fuller whose consciences had permitted them to hold livings during the Inter-

[14] The chief modern authorities for the ensuing summary of the Restoration religious settlement are Anne Whiteman, "The Restoration of the Church of England," in *From Uniformity to Unity,* ed. Geoffrey F. Nuttall and Owen Chadwick (London: S.P.C.K., 1962), pp. 19–88; Robert S. Bosher, *The Making of the Restoration Settlement* (Westminster: Dacre Press, 1951); Abernathy, *English Presbyterians and the Stuart Restoration,* pp. 60–91.

[15] Gardiner, *Constitutional Documents,* p. 466.

regnum; and on the other hand the uncompromising heirs of the Caroline Church of England who had suffered deprivation and whom for want of a better term historians call the Laudians. The former side felt an essential community with the orthodox reformed churches abroad, the latter with the Church Catholic universal, not excluding the Church of Rome. The Laudians or "New Prelatists" held the doctrine, still regarded by most as a dangerous novelty in Laud's own time, that the office of bishop was ordained *jure divino*. To them, nonepiscopal churches were no true churches, and ministers who lacked episcopal ordination were no true priests.

It is their triumph that we have to explain, since in 1642 they had commanded very little lay support, even among royalists. But their staunchness in the royal cause and their consequent sufferings had changed all that. As tutors and chaplains in royalists households and as ministers to Anglican conventicles when the Prayer Book services were officially forbidden, they had gained a firm hold over a whole new generation of cavalier squires, while others who embraced exile won a like moral ascendancy at Charles II's Court. When the Court came home again the old bishops were a spent force. Only nine were still alive (the youngest was sixty-eight), and as a group they had been miserably pusillanimous in defending their faith and order. The real leaders of the Church of England now were not these old men but Hyde's fellow exiles Gilbert Sheldon and George Morley, who were not going to concede to any Puritans a jot more than they had to.

Yet if the Convention Parliament had been allowed to settle religion in its own way, the new Anglican leaders might have had to concede much. The Presbyterians were strong enough in the Convention to carry some measures that made Hyde and the Laudians anxious to defer a definitive settlement until they had had time to marshal their own forces. To discourage the two parties from taking up entrenched positions, Charles was persuaded to summon a conference of the leaders of both at Worcester House, Hyde's London residence, to advise him on the terms of a royal declaration. By this he would cut the knot of their differences, if only for the time being. The conference was heated, but the so-called Worcester House Declaration was published on October 25, 1660. It went surprisingly far to meet the desires of Baxter, Calamy, Reynolds, and the other moderate Puritan negotiators. It grafted certain elements of Presbyterianism upon the old Episcopalian stock, somewhat in the manner of Archbishop Ussher's proposals of 1641, and if its provisions had been made permanent they might have gone far to revivify the ideal of a genuinely comprehensive national church. But their details need not concern the student of Milton closely, for Milton would have found little comfort in a solution that still offered the layman no choice but to worship in his parish church. "Comprehension" was all that these right-wing Puritans were interested in; the alternative policy of a limited toleration for peaceable Christian sects outside the establishment was discussed, only to be flatly opposed by Baxter himself, on the ground that it might be extended to Roman Catholics.

In any case the whole purport of the Worcester House Declaration was uncertain, and still remains so. What is a mere interim indulgence or the blueprint for a permanent settlement? Was it a sincere attempt at accommodation or a tactical feint to delude the Presbyterians while the Laudians entrenched themselves in the establishment? These questions are still disputed, and the Anglican negotiators may not all have been of one mind. Perhaps the most genuinely tolerant person present at Worcester House was Charles himself.

The next move was a surprise. The Presbyterians in the Convention put the declaration to a rude test by bringing in a bill in November to give it the force and permanence of law. The Anglican members, however, mustered all their strength, and with the strong backing of the government they defeated the bill. Some Independent members are also said to have opposed it, out of a natural resentment that the Presbyterians were trying to secure the sole benefit of the royal indulgence for themselves. There the matter rested when the Convention was dissolved in December, 1660.

Already that promise of "a liberty to tender consciences" was beginning to look delusive, though through no wish of its royal author. Already some 695 ministers had been ejected from their livings, only 290 of them on the reasonable ground that they had supplanted a still-living Anglican incumbent.[16] Angry royalist justices of the peace and patrons of livings were taking the law into their own hands. More ominously, all but two of the many vacant bishoprics were filled between October 28, 1660, and January 6, 1661, and the complexion of the new episcopate was strongly Laudian. Baxter, Calamy, and other moderate Puritans had been offered sees, but all but Reynolds had refused. This was high-principled but unwise. One promise in the Worcester House Declaration had been that a synod or conference of Puritan and Anglican divines would be convened to consider a revision of the Book of Common Prayer, but when it assembled at the Savoy on April 5, 1661, the Anglican opponents of compromise already commanded the key positions in the church and dominated its convocations. The Savoy Conference failed miserably. Baxter's ill-judged

[16] A.G. Matthews, *Calamy Revised*, p. xiii.

handling of the reformers' case, the non-attendance or non-cooperation
of his colleagues, the growing dissensions among the Presbyterians
generally, all played into the Anglicans' hands.

But the crucial factor in the situation was the new Parliament that
met on May 8, 1661. Not for nothing is it known to history as the
Cavalier Parliament. One of its first acts restored the bishops to the
House of Lords. Before June was out the Commons went ahead with a
Bill of Uniformity, even though the Savoy Conference was still sitting
and nothing further had yet been done to determine what kind of
prayer book the bill was to enforce. Well before the Conference broke
up on July 24, the cause of comprehension was doomed as surely as
that of toleration. Whether the breasts of the faithful Commons
swelled more with love of the old liturgy or with hatred of their old
enemies, the course was irrevocably set towards the eventual passage
of the Act of Uniformity on May 29, 1662. The new Book of Common
Prayer, as approved by the revived convocations, contained numerous
minor alterations but differed little in substance from the old, either
in doctrine or in the disputed ceremonies. The act itself was harsher
than Hyde, now Earl of Clarendon, or even Sheldon and Morley would
have wished. As for the king, the weakening of the royal supremacy
was driven home when he tried and failed to assert a dispensing power
in order to exempt loyal Puritan ministers from the act's more strin-
gent provisions.

Stringent they certainly were. Every beneficed clergymen had pub-
licly to declare his "unfeigned assent and consent" to everything in
the Book of Common Prayer, and no other form of worship was per-
mitted. Nor was conformity the only test imposed on all who con-
ducted services or who taught in schools or universities; they had
further to declare that the Solemn League and Covenant was an illegal
oath and that armed resistance to the king was unlawful in any cir-
cumstances. All ministers who had not been ordained by a bishop—
and that of course meant all who had entered the ministry since 1642
—must seek episcopal ordination forthwith or renounce the exercise
of their orders. All these requirements had to be met by St. Bartholo-
mew's Day (August 24, 1662) on pain of immediate deprivation. The
number who then lost their livings for not complying was 936, but
when to these are added their brethren who had already been deprived
since the king's return the total of the ejected comes to about 1,760.[17]
Despite the penalties of the act against any form of nonconformist
worship, many of the deprived clergy held the most stalwart of their
flocks together and continued to minister to them. Their lot was made

[17] *Ibid.*, pp. xii–xiii.

still harder by the Five Mile Act of 1665, and that of their congrega-
tions by the Conventicle Acts of 1664 and 1670. These measures were
irregularly enforced, but persecution, though intermittent, was a fact
that dissenters had to live with until the Toleration Act of 1689
brought them lasting relief.[18] Milton, not being a member of any
particular sect or congregation, was personally unaffected, but he
would show how keenly he still felt for the cause of religious liberty
in his last tract, *Of True Religion,* which he published in 1673.

Another liberty for which he had striven, that of the press, went
down before the Licensing Act, which became law on the same day as
the Act of Uniformity. Among its casualties would be his *Christian
Doctrine,* and for the rest of his life the printing and publication of
books and pamphlets were more closely controlled than he had ever
known them. He would be long in his grave before it would be safe
to reprint *Areopagitica.* Fortunately there was no hindrance to the
publication of his epic masterpieces, and we can close this story of the
defeat of the pamphleteer with the comfort that the triumph of the
poet was still to come.

[18] See Gerald R. Cragg, *Puritanism in the Period of the Great Persecution,
1660–1688* (Cambridge University Press, 1957).

A TREATISE OF CIVIL POWER

February 16, 1659

AND

CONSIDERATIONS TOUCHING THE LIKELIEST MEANS

August, 1659

PREFACE AND NOTES BY WILLIAM B. HUNTER, JR.

To recognize that Milton conceived *Civil Power* and *Hirelings* as companion tracts is both interesting and instructive. Each is addressed to a "Parlament"—though not the same one—and each begins with a Prcfacc in which Milton reviews his earlier service to the country with special emphasis upon his attack on Salmasius in the Latin *First Defense,* which he continued, perhaps until his death, to regard as his greatest public achievement. The argument of each begins with a reference to the other, claiming correctly that they are complementary in their support of civil liberty, a theme which Milton viewed as running through all of his prose works since *Of Reformation* had attacked religious restraints in 1641 and one which would be the major subject of his publications in prose until the *History of Britain* appeared in 1670.

After a short introductory paragraph each tract moves to a summary of its subject in a second short paragraph which concludes with a precise statement of the thesis and an outline of the argument of the rest of the treatise. In *Civil Power* Milton will present arguments—four as it turns out—to prove that "for beleef or practise in religion according to this conscientious perswasion no man ought to be punishd or molested by any outward force on earth whatsoever."[1] The four supporting statements each receive a long paragraph which in turn argues (1) that interior illumination by the divine Spirit (or conscience) is superior to all external traditions, (2) that civil authority has no absolute right to judge religious matters, (3) that if this authority does so judge, it achieves evil rather than good by restricting religious

[1] Below, p. 242.

liberty, and (4) that in doing so it can accomplish no good ends. A final paragraph sums up the argument. Thus, after the Preface to Parliament, the tract consists of an introductory paragraph, a paragraph stating the thesis, four longer paragraphs offering four different proofs of that thesis, and a paragraph of summation.[2]

In *Hirelings,* on the other hand, Milton will hold that despite the difficulty of removing those who serve the church for the financial return it may bring, we must still exercise "our utmost diligence, how it may be least dangerous." The argument that follows will consider the "likeliest means" to effectuate this outcome: "first, what recompence God hath ordaind should be given to ministers of the church . . . ; next by whom; and lastly, in what manner."[3] There are, then, a paragraph of introduction, a paragraph stating the thesis and dividing it into three sub-theses, and a very long paragraph elaborating each sub-thesis. There is no summation; the effects of reading the last page are quite different from those of reading *Civil Power,* which in its conclusion acknowledges its own limitations and intimates further discussion in another publication—probably the *Christian Doctrine,* which Kelley has convincingly argued was being written at this time.[4] *Hirelings,* in contrast, offers no summary but refers to some contemporary problems in Scotland and, with a brief restatement of its subject, simply stops with the request that readers recognize Milton's sincerity in bearing such "witnes not out of season to the church and to my countrey."[5] There is no suggestion of a further analysis of tithing in a larger context, although the *Christian Doctrine* argues the same views.[6] Clearly then, Milton conceives in quite different ways the arguments which support his related theses: as four mutually supportive propositions in the one case, and as a partition of the subject into three related but separate problems in the other.

[2] Comparison with the structure of *Areopagitica* as a classical oration is instructive. See E. Sirluck's Introduction, *Complete Prose,* II, 170 ff.

[3] Below, pp. 280–81.

[4] *Complete Prose,* VI, 23 ff. The equivalent material appears on pp. 525–31.

[5] Below, p. 321.

[6] *Complete Prose,* VI, 595–600. The reference to Scottish problems (which had most recently occurred in 1653), the failure to mention the treatment of tithes in the *Christian Doctrine,* the failure to allude in any way to the slaughter of the Waldensians in 1655 (in this treatise which cites them more often than any other of Milton's), and the response primarily to books printed in 1646 and 1653 (by Spelman and Prynne; see below, notes 9 and 10 to *Hirelings,* pp. 278, 279) all suggest that the tract may have been planned and in part composed in 1653, to be put aside when the issue became moot with the dissolution of the Nominated Parliament in December (see Introduction above, p. 29). On the other hand, mention of the "hot quaerist for tithes" (below, p. 294) suggests Prynne's *Ten Considerable Quæries,* which was dated by Thomason on June 27, 1659, only a few weeks before *Hirelings* itself appeared.

Just as the disposition of the argument is fundamentally different in the two tracts, the evidence upon which each is based is different. *Civil Power* develops almost entirely from interpretation of various biblical passages. Time and again Milton cites particular verses which have been quoted by his unnamed opponents to justify their Erastian position that the civil magistrate—the state—had authority from the Bible to intervene in religious matters. Because Milton never identifies an opponent or cites any book (except, of course, the Bible), one has some difficulty today in placing *Civil Power* in its contemporary context. Clearly, his antagonists were supporters of Cromwell's state church, some of whose leading clergy had composed the Savoy Declaration of 1658.[7] One may, however, inquire about what tradition Milton was responding to as he answers arguments based upon specific biblical verses which he reinterprets to his own advantage. It seems clear that in doing so he is recognizing some particular public authority.

Although the Savoy Declaration must have been in his mind (it was certainly a major motivation in the composition of *Civil Power*), its body does not contain any biblical proofs; indeed, its Preface observes "That there are not Scriptures annexed." [8] But one may recognize that the Declaration was directly based upon the *Westminster Confession of Faith*, which it accommodated to the demands of certain powerful Independents, and that the *Confession* was buttressed at every turn by biblical proof texts. It is these texts which Milton examines in his treatise.

Despite later embarrassment to some of its Presbyterian supporters in this respect, the *Confession*, which had been reported out from the Westminster Assembly of Divines to Parliament early in 1647, was a strongly Erastian document. Its Chapter 20 ("Of Christian Liberty, and Liberty of Conscience") asserted that "because the power which God hath ordained, and the liberty which Christ hath purchased, are not intended by God to destroy, but mutually to uphold and preserve one another; they who, upon pretense of Christian liberty, shall oppose any lawful power, or the lawful exercise of it, whether it be civil or ecclesiastical, resist the ordinance of God." Accordingly, "they may lawfully be called to account, and proceeded against by the censures of the Church, *and by the power of the Civil Magistrate.*" [9] Again,

---

[7] See Introduction above, pp. 41–45.

[8] Philip Schaff, *The Creeds of Christendom* (3 vols., New York, 1919; hereafter cited as Schaff), III, 715. For the use of proof texts to establish a historical context, see William B. Hunter, Jr., "The Theological Context of Milton's *Christian Doctrine*," in *Achievements of the Left Hand*, pp. 269–87.

[9] Schaff, III, 645. Italics added. The paragraph is deleted in the Savoy Declaration (*ibid.*, III, 720).

in Chapter 23 ("Of the Civil Magistrate"), "he hath authority, and it is his duty to take order, that unity and peace be preserved in the Church, that the truth of God be kept pure and entire, that all blasphemies and heresies be suppressed. . . . For the better effecting whereof he hath power to call synods, to be present at them, and to provide that whatsoever is transacted in them be according to the mind of God." [10] Clearly, in both of these sections the Assembly had delegated to civil authority the regulation of religious matters—such confidence in 1647 indicating the control which they exercised at the time in the English government. Finally, Chapter 31 ("Of Synods and Councils") gives the magistrate power to "call a synod of ministers and other fit persons to consult and advise with about matters of religion." [11] These are the three chapters which most concerned the members of the Savoy Conference, and they provide the proof texts to which Milton is responding. Although *Civil Power* should not be conceived as merely a response to the *Confession* alone, the tract does address contemporary Erastians who shared its views of this subject and who argued from the same biblical passages. [12]

Although *Civil Power* is thus argued almost entirely from the interpretation of biblical texts, *Hirelings* employs them to only a limited extent. The real issue of the later tract is *not* the removal of hirelings from the church but the rescinding of the public tax (or forced tithe) by which the state supported a church—Anglican, Presbyterian, or whatever. Milton's thesis is that hirelings will disappear when they are no longer paid; only those with a genuine spiritual calling will remain to minister to the people. Tithers had argued perforce from the Bible, and especially from the Mosaic law which required the contribution of part of one's income or property in support of the priesthood. The tithers thus tried to show how Old Testament laws like this were continued in the New. Milton accordingly has to spend a good deal of time emphasizing the difference between the Law and the Gospel, in effect denying the authority of the former over a Christian. The tithers had met that argument by asserting that the book of Genesis depicted a pre-Mosaic society, its laws presumably authorita-

[10] Schaff, III, 653. The final sentence is omitted and the rest rephrased in the Savoy Declaration (*ibid.*, III, 720).

[11] Schaff, III, 669. Not in the Savoy Declaration.

[12] Although, of course, they were a negligible force in 1659, there is no reason to think that Anglicans would disclaim such Erastian conclusions; see, for instance, the eighth book of Richard Hooker's *Laws of Ecclesiastical Polity*. But Milton's antagonists here were the vast number of conservatives of various denominations who were represented in Parliament and who would have subscribed to the statements of the *Confession* quoted above.

tive for all people instead of only the Jews, who were subject to the laws of Moses. In Genesis the tithers found the example of Melchizedek, to whom Abram offered a tenth of his recent conquests; furthermore, they could assert that the author of the New Testament book of Hebrews had argued that Melchizedek represented an Old Testament type of Christ. Hence, the tithers concluded, Christians were obligated to tithe to his representatives, the priests. Milton's answer denies at length the applicability of this example.[13]

In addition to their biblical authorities, tithers also pleaded their case from English constitutional law under the leadership of one of the greatest English antiquarians, Sir Henry Spelman. Tracing the practice of tithing ultimately to classical pagan times, they made much of the tithing laws of pre-Conquest Britain. In response, Milton drew upon the extensive knowledge of English history that he had developed to write his then-unpublished *History of Britain*. And he found support from an even greater scholar than Spelman, John Selden, whose *History of Tithes* had exhibited the same orientation and had drawn the same conclusions in 1618 that Milton was to display in 1659.

Just as *Civil Power* is addressed to all Erastians, Reformed or Anglican, so *Hirelings* is addressed to all tithers. Here, however, the *Westminster Confession* and the Savoy Declaration are silent, providing no official position towards which Milton might orient his argument. Instead, he responds primarily to a major representative of each faith: the Presbyterian William Prynne and the Anglican Henry Spelman. A single response would serve, for Anglican and Presbyterian were at one on this issue and did not hesitate to use each other's arguments, as they were in agreement on the authority of the civil magistrate in religious matters. Milton's strategy is to deny their interpretations of the pertinent biblical passages and to undermine the authority of their constitutional history.

Given the assumption of the separation of church and state held as dogma in much of modern society, an act of the imagination is required to appreciate the fundamental nature of the causes which Milton was supporting—vainly as it turned out then. Like most of his other arguments for liberty, these ideas had to await their time. That he was arguing real issues and that he was right by modern standards can be shown by the actions in 1787 of the Presbyterian Synod meeting in the United States as the new national Constitution with its firm cleavage between church and state was being established. The offensive statements quoted above from Chapters 20, 23, and 31 of the *Confession* were restated or withdrawn, and they appear in no subsequent Ameri-

[13] Below, pp. 284 ff.

can edition. The English waited until 1846, when a General Assembly disclaimed Erastian principles (though the offending statements remain, inconsistently, in the English *Confession*). Milton could have judged himself as Norman Thomas did: "I am not the champion of lost causes, but the champion of causes not yet won." [14]

Both *Civil Power* and *Hirelings* deserve to be better known for their stylistic achievements. The former especially contains statements every bit as worthy of quotation as the more famous counterparts in *Areopagitica:* "he [is] the only heretic, who counts all heretics but himself," or, let us proceed "by opposing truth to error, no unequal match; truth the strong to error the weak though slie and shifting," or, "To heal one conscience we must not wound another," or, the busy civil magistrate "hath anough and more then anough to do, left yet undon; for which the land groans and justice goes to wrack the while." [15] *Hirelings* has nothing quite so good: it is more an argument from reason; *Civil Power* is also an affective argument from rhetoric.

An unusual but successful rhetorical device is employed in dramatic dialogues between two disputants which unexpectedly appear in each of the two texts. In *Civil Power* an Erastian quotes a series of biblical texts which he supposes will support his case. His opponent answers him in abrupt sentences. A change to modern paragraphing immediately reveals the dramatic conflict:

> *But why dost thou judge thy brother?*
> How presum'st thou to be his lord, to be whose only Lord, at least in these things, Christ both dy'd and rose and livd again?
> *We shall all stand before the judgment seat of Christ.*
> Why then dost thou not only judge, but persecute in these things for which we are to be accountable to the tribunal of Christ only, our Lord and lawgiver?
> *Ye are bought with a price; be not made the servants of men.*
> Some trivial price belike, and for some frivolous pretences paid in their opinion, if bought and by him redeemd who is God from what was once the service of God, we shall be enthrald again and forc'd by men to what now is but the service of men. . . .
> *Ye are complete in him, which is the head of all principalitie and power.*
> Not completed therfore or made the more religious by those ordinances of civil power, from which Christ thir head hath dischargd us.[16]

The same technique appears again in *Hirelings*. There a member of the tithe-supported Establishment enumerates the clerical duties for which he should be reimbursed and is answered by an opponent:

[14] As recorded on a commemorative plaque in the Princeton University Library.
[15] Below, pp. 249, 261, 267, 258.
[16] Below, p. 264. A similar dialogue appears on p. 250.

At burials thir attendance they alleage on the corps.
All the guests do as much unhir'd.
Thir praiers at the grave . . .
Superstitiously requir'd: yet if requir'd, thir last performance to the
deceasd of thir own flock.
The funeral sermon . . .
At thir choise: or if not, an occasion offerd them to preach out of
season, which is one part of thir office.
Somthing must be spoken in praise . . .
If due, thir duty; if undue, thir corruption. . . .[17]

Consideration of these companion tracts may conclude with some
observations about Milton's quotations from the Bible, which are the
primary proofs for almost all of the earlier treatise and for much of
the later one. As was usual when he wrote in English, at least in these
later years, he relied upon the Authorized Version of these texts. He was
evidently satisfied with its general accuracy, for he does not appeal to
another textual authority in either tract, and he assumes its acceptance
by his opponents. Usually his quotations are in exact agreement with
this translation, but check against the original discloses a surprising
number of minor discrepancies, enough to suggest that he was quoting
from memory, possibly with the original language or the Junius-
Tremellius Latin translation in mind. Reference to the Geneva version
shows that it is not the source of the alterations, which are always made
to synonymous expressions with occasional slight change in the mean-
ing. In a few cases Milton's biblical citation is simply wrong.[18] On at
least one occasion he translates directly from the Greek in order to
emphasize another meaning of the Greek word than was expressed in
the Authorized Version.[19] But most of the variations are those which
Milton seems to have made unconsciously,[20] sometimes leading to a
near paraphrase.[21]

[17] Below, pp. 298–99. Italics added.
[18] In *Civil Power*, p. 245 below, Matthew 13:26 should be 13:29; on p.
263 Galatians 5:14 should be 5:1. In *Hirelings*, p. 296 below, Isaiah 46:10
should be 56:11; on p. 302 I Timothy 3:7 should be II Timothy. A full study
appears in Harris F. Fletcher's monograph, *The Use of the Bible in Milton's
Prose*, in *University of Illinois Studies in Language and Literature*, 14, No. 3
(1929), with conclusions which differ from those drawn here.
[19] "certain of the heresie [Junius-Tremellius "haeresi," Authorized Version
"sect"] . . . after the exactest heresie [sect]," below, p. 247.
[20] "*The earth* is the Lord's" becomes "The *whole earth*," below, p. 288;
"weak and beggarly *elements*" becomes *rudiments*, p. 262; "They *rejected* the
counsel of God" becomes *frustrated*, p. 259; *heart* ("cor," Junius-Tremellius)
in I John 3:20 becomes *conscience*, p. 243; "be not *ye* the servants of men"
becomes *made*, p. 264; and so on for many minor variants.
[21] Romans 14:4 in the Authorized Verson is "Who art thou that judgest
another man's servant? to his own master he standeth or falleth. Yea, he shall
be holden up: for God is able to make him stand." Milton instead writes, "who

Contemplation of such differences from the Authorized Version evokes a vivid and moving impression of the blind polemicist in his early fifties, possessed of such prodigious learning and memory that he could recall much of the Bible almost perfectly, citing not only text but chapter and verse as he dictated to one or another of his amanuenses. One error strikingly suggests, however, the difficulty under which Milton worked. Where the Authorized Version reads, "there is no man which shall do a miracle in my name, that can *lightly* speak evil of me," his text reads *likely,*[22] a transformation which is surely the consequence of auditory confusion by an amanuensis. Such is the silent testimony to the difficulties of a blind man arguing his cause.

TEXTUAL NOTE: *A TREATISE OF CIVIL POWER IN
ECCLESIASTICAL CAUSES*

A Treatise of Civil Power was advertised on February 14, 1659,[1] and registered on February 16.[2] The text presented here is that of the Princeton University Library copy, which has been compared with the Harvard University Library and the Henry E. Huntington Library copies. All three show defective running head, p. 60, *"A Treati of seCivil power,"* B3 is signed B2, and all have the typographical errors noted in the text below. Page 13 exists in two states: "powr" and *"Feed,"* which are corrected in the New York Public Library copy to "power" and *"feed."* This second state is followed here. Parker, II, 1067, n. 77, prints a finding list of other copies. Collation: 12mo; A-D[12]; 48 leaves; pp. [1–12] 83 [1]. Contents: [A], title page (verso blank); A2-[A6v], "To the Parlament"; ·[A7]-[D12], the work; [D12v], blank.

TEXTUAL NOTE: *CONSIDERATIONS TOUCHING THE
LIKELIEST MEANS TO REMOVE HIRELINGS
OUT OF THE CHURCH*

Hirelings was advertised on September 8, 1659;[3] Thomason had dated his copy [E.2110.(2)] "Aug." without the day.[4] The text pre-

art thou that judgest the servant of another? to his own Lord he standeth or falleth; but he shall stand; for God is able to make him stand" (below, p. 244). Similarly Milton's list of the various damnations differs from the authorized text in Galatians (below, p. 250).

[22] Below, p. 246.

[1] *The Publick Intelligencer*, No. 163, February 7–14, 1659, p. 221. For other early notices, see French, *Life Records*, IV, 253–54. The Thomason collection does not have a copy.

[2] *Stationers' Registers, 1640–1708*, ed. G. E. Briscoe Eyre, II, 214.

[3] *Mercurius Politicus*, No. 585, September 1–8, 1659, p. 713. For another early notice, see French, *Life Records*, IV, 275.

[4] See Thomason, *Catalogue*, II, 255.

sented here is that of the Harvard Library copy, which has been compared with the Newberry Library and the Henry E. Huntington
Library copies. All three misnumber p. 85 as 58, and they all have the
typographical errors noted in the text below. Page 36 has a textual
correction: the uncorrected Huntington copy reads ". . . *Abraham,*
and all the faithful with themselves included in him, cannot both give
and take tithes in *Abram.* . ." The corrected Harvard and Newberry
copies read ". . . *Abraham,* & all the faithful with themselves included
in him, cannot both give & take tithes in the same respect. . ." Also
on p. 36, line 15, "verse" is changed to "Verse"; and on p. 35, bottom
line, "thir" is changed to "their." Parker, II, 1069–70, n. 93, prints a
finding list of other copies. Collation: 12mo; A-G^{12}, H^6; 90 leaves (but
A12 is missing from all copies examined); pp. [24] 1–153 [3]. Contents: [Ar-Av], blank; [A2], title page (verso blank); A3-[A11v],
"To the Parlament"; [A12], presumably blank; B-[H5], the work;
[H5v-H6v], blank.

A TREATISE OF Civil power

IN Ecclesiastical causes:

SHEWING

That it is not lawfull for any power on earth to compell in matters of

Religion.

The author J. M.

London, Printed by *Tho. Newcomb*,
Anno 1 6 5 9.

TO THE PARLAMENT OF THE COMMONWEALTH OF ENGLAND WITH THE DOMINIONS THEROF.

I HAVE *prepar'd, supream Councel, against the much expected time of your sitting,*[1] *this treatise; which, though to all Christian magistrates equally belonging, and therfore to have bin written in the* [A2] *common language of Christendom,*[2] *natural dutie and affection hath confin'd, and dedicated first to my own nation: and in a season wherin the timely reading therof, to the easier accomplishment of your great work, may save you much labor and interruption: of two parts usually propos'd, civil and ecclesiastical, recommending civil only to your proper care, ecclesi-*[A2v]*astical to them only from whom it takes both that name and nature. Yet not for this cause only do I require or trust to finde acceptance, but in a two-fold respect besides: first as bringing cleer evidence of scripture and protestant maxims to the Parlament of* England, *who in all thir late acts, upon occasion, have professd to assert only the true protestant Christian re-*[A3]*ligion,*[3] *as it is containd in the holy scriptures:*[4] *next, in regard that your power being but for a time,*[5] *and having in your selves a Christian libertie of your own, which at one time or other may be oppressd, therof truly sensible, it will concern you while you are in power, so to*

[1] Richard's Parliament began meeting on January 27, 1659, and Milton's pamphlet was published two or three weeks later. See Introduction above, p. 46.

[2] Latin. After the Latin exercises which he wrote in college, Milton always wrote in English for an English audience and (except perhaps for his *Logic*) in Latin for a Continental one.

[3] 1659: *Christianre-*.

[4] The Humble Petition and Advice, which became the new written constitution of the Protectorate when Cromwell formally accepted it from his second Parliament on May 25, 1657, provided that "the true Protestant Christian religion, as it is contained in the Holy Scriptures of the Old and New Testament, and no other, be held forth and asserted for the public profession of these nations." Gardiner, *Constitutional Documents*, p. 454.

[5] Although the Humble Petition and Advice did not limit the duration of parliamentary sessions, as (*e.g.*) the Agreement of the People of January 1649 had sought to do, the assumption of those who established the Protectorate was that they would be reasonably brief: see *A True State of the Case of the Commonwealth* (1654), pp. 22–25. Milton cannot have foreseen, however, that Richard Cromwell would be forced by his generals to dissolve this Parliament on April 22.

regard other mens consciences, as you would your own should be re-
garded in the power of others; and to consider [A3v] *that any law*
against conscience is alike in force against any conscience, and so may
one way or other justly redound upon your selves. One advantage I
make no doubt of, that I shall write to many eminent persons of your
number, alreadie perfet and resolvd in this important article of
Christianitie. Some of whom I remember to have heard often for several
years, at a [A4] *councel next in autoritie to your own,*[6] *so well joining*
religion with civil prudence, and [6a] *yet so well distinguishing the*
different power of either, and this not only voting, but frequently
reasoning why it should be so, that if any there present had bin before
of an opinion contrary, he might doubtless have departed thence a
convert in that point, and have confessd, that [A4v] *then both com-*
monwealth and religion will at length, if ever, flourish in Christendom,
when either they who govern discern between civil and religious, or
they only who so discern shall be admitted to govern. Till then nothing
but troubles, persecutions, commotions can be expected; the inward
decay of true religion among our selves, and the utter overthrow [A5]
at last by a common enemy. Of civil libertie I have written heretofore
by the appointment, and not without the approbation of civil power: [7]
of Christian liberty I write now; which others long since having don
with all freedom under heathen emperors, I should do wrong to suspect,
that I now shall with less under Christian governors, and such especially
as profess openly [A5v] *thir defence of Christian libertie; although I*
write this not otherwise appointed or induc'd then by an inward per-
swasion of the Christian dutie which I may usefully discharge herin to
the common Lord and Master of us all, and the certain hope of his
approbation, first and chiefest to be sought: In the hand of whose
providence I remain, praying all success [A6] *and good event on your*
publick councels to the defence of true religion and our civil rights.

John Milton. [A6v]

[6] *I.e.,* at the Council of State under the Commonwealth between 1649 and
1651.

[6a] 1659: *aud.*

[7] The two Latin *Defences* and probably *Eikonoklastes,* which Milton says the
Council of State ordered him to write: "there appeared a book attributed to
the king, and plainly written with great malice against Parliament. Bidden to
reply to this, I opposed to the *Eikon* the *Eikonoklastes,*" *Second Defence, Com-*
plete Prose, IV, 628.

A TREATISE OF CIVIL POWER
IN ECCLESIASTICAL CAUSES.

Two things there be which have bin ever found working much mischief to the church of God, and the advancement of truth; force on the one side restraining, and hire on the other side corrupting the teachers thereof. Few ages have bin since the ascension of our Saviour, wherin the one of these two, or both together have not prevaild. It can be at no time therfore unseasonable to speak of these things; since by them the church is either in continual de-[1]triment and oppression, or in continual danger. The former shall be at this time my argument; the latter as I shall finde God disposing me, and opportunity inviting.[8] What I argue, shall be drawn from the scripture only; and therin from true fundamental principles of the gospel; to all knowing Christians undeniable. And if the governors of this commonwealth since the rooting out of prelats have made least use of force in religion, and most have favord Christian liberty of any in this Iland before them since the first preaching of the gospel, for which we are not to forget our thanks to God, and their due praise, they may, I doubt not, in this treatise finde that which not only will confirm them to defend still the Christian liberty which [2] we enjoy, but will incite them also to enlarge it, if in aught they yet straiten it.[9] To them who perhaps herafter, less experienc'd in religion, may come to govern or give us laws, this or other such, if they please, may be a timely instruction: however to the truth it will be at all times no unneedfull testimonie; at least some discharge of that general dutie which no Christian but according to what he hath receivd, knows is requir'd of him if he have aught more conducing to the advancement of religion then what is usually endeavourd, freely to impart it.

[8] This is *Hirelings,* published the following August but addressed to another Parliament, the Restored Rump.

[9] For the Cromwellian religious settlement of 1654, and the Protectorate's subsequent efforts to hold a middle course between Presbyterians who desired a single, exclusive, state-supported church and sectaries who denied the civil magistrate any authority over religion, see Introduction above, pp. 27–45.

It will require no great labor of exposition to unfold what is here meant by matters of religion; being as soon apprehended as defin'd, such things as belong [3] chiefly to the knowledge and service of God: and are either above the reach and light of nature without revelation from above, and therfore liable to be variously understood by humane reason, or such things as are enjoind or forbidden by divine precept, which els by the light of reason would seem indifferent to be don or not don; and so likewise must needs appeer to everie man as the precept is understood. Whence I here mean by conscience or religion, that full perswasion whereby we are assur'd that our beleef and practise, as far as we are able to apprehend and probably make appeer, is according to the will of God & his Holy Spirit within us, which we ought to follow much rather then any law of man, as not only his word every where bids [4] us, but the very dictate of reason tells us. *Act.* 4. 19. *whether it be right in the sight of God, to hearken to you more then to God, judge ye.* That for beleef or practise in religion according to this conscientious perswasion no man ought be punishd or molested by any outward force on earth whatsoever,[10] I distrust not, through Gods implor'd assistance, to make plane by these following arguments.

First it cannot be deni'd, being the main foundation of our protestant religion, that we of these ages, having no other divine rule or autoritie from without us warrantable to one another [11] as a common ground but the holy scripture, and no other within us but the illumination of the Holy Spirit so interpreting that scripture as warrantable only to our selves and [5] to such whose consciences we can so perswade, can have no other ground in matters of religion but only from the scriptures. And these being not possible to be understood without this divine illumination, which no man can know at all times to be in himself, much less to be at any time for certain in any other, it follows cleerly, that no man or body of men in

---

[10] This is Milton's thesis, which the rest of the tract will argue. His emphasis upon the sole authority of scripture as interpreted by the "Holy Spirit within us" dominates his mature thinking. Such emphasis upon the guidance of the Spirit opposes him to all traditions supporting external authority (*i.e.,* the authority of the historical church as exemplified by the Church of Rome and the Church of England) and leads to concurrence with such diverse groups as the Quakers, the Baptists, and the radical Arminians (see William B. Hunter, Jr., "John Milton: Autobiographer," *Milton Quarterly,* VIII [1974], 101–04). Reliance upon such inner motivation could produce extremes of individuality and eccentricity, as contemporary sects were abundantly demonstrating.

[11] 1659: oneanother.

these times can be the infallible judges or determiners in matters of
religion to any other mens consciences but thir own. And therfore
those Beroeans are commended, *Act.* 17. 11, who after the preach-
ing even of S. *Paul, searchd the scriptures daily, whether those things
were so.* Nor did they more then what God himself in many places
commands us by the same apostle, to search, to try, to judge [6] of
these things our selves: And gives us reason also, *Gal.* 6. 4, 5. *let
every man prove his own work, and then shall he have rejoicing in
himself alone, and not in another: for every man shall bear his own
burden.* If then we count it so ignorant and irreligious in the papist
to think himself dischargd in Gods account, beleeving only as the
church beleevs, how much greater condemnation will it be to the
protestant his condemner, to think himself justified, beleeving only
as the state beleevs? With good cause therfore it is the general con-
sent of all sound protestant writers, that neither traditions, councels
nor canons of any visible [12] church, much less edicts of any magis-
trate or civil session, but the scripture only can be the final judge or
rule in mat-[7]ters of religion, and that only in the conscience of
every Christian to himself. Which protestation made by the first
publick reformers of our religion against the imperial edicts of
Charls the fifth, imposing church-traditions without scripture, gave
first beginning to the name of *Protestant;* [13] and with that name
hath ever bin receivd this doctrine, which preferrs the scripture be-
fore the church, and acknowledges none but the Scripture sole inter-
preter of it self to the conscience. For if the church be not sufficient
to be implicitly beleevd, as we hold it is not, what can there els be
nam'd of more autoritie then the church but the conscience; [14] then
which God only is greater, 1 *Joh.* 3.20? But if any man shall pre-
tend, that the scripture judges to his conscience for [8] other men,
he makes himself greater not only then the church, but also then
the scripture, then the consciences of other men; a presumption too

---

[12] 1659: visibie.

[13] The second diet of Spires (or Speyer) in 1529 supported the anti-Lutheran
conclusions of the Diet of Worms. Several German princes and cities formally
objected on various grounds, including the fact that this action would "denye
gods worde . . . , which were the moste heynous offense that coulde be com-
mitted. . . . And as for mens tradicions, they are grounded on a weake
foundation." Thus, the statement concludes, "this is in dede the first original of
the name of Protestauntes." John Sleidan, *Commentaries,* trans. John Daus
(London, 1560), pp. lxxxi verso–lxxxii verso.

[14] Instead of "conscience" the Authorized Version translates "heart." See
Preface above, p. 235.

high for any mortal; since every true Christian able to give a reason of his faith, hath the word of God before him, the promisd Holy Spirit, and the minde of Christ within him, 1 *Cor.* 2. 16; a much better and safer guide of conscience, which as far as concerns himself he may far more certainly know then any outward rule impos'd upon him by others whom he inwardly neither knows nor can know; at least knows nothing of them more sure then this one thing, that they cannot be his judges in religion. 1 *Cor.* 2. 15. *the spiritual man judgeth all things, but he himself is judgd of no man.* Chiefly for this cause do all true [9] protestants account the pope antichrist, for that he assumes to himself this infallibilitie over both the conscience and the scripture; *siting in the temple of God,* as it were opposite to God, *and exalting himself above all that is called god, or is worshipd,* 2 Thess. 2. 4. That is to say not only above all judges and magistrates, who though they be calld gods, are far beneath infallible, but also above God himself, by giving law both to the scripture, to the conscience, and to the spirit it self of God within us. Whenas we finde, *James* 4. 12, *there is one lawgiver, who is able to save and to destroy: who art thou that judgest another?* That Christ is the only lawgiver of his church and that it is here meant in religious matters, no well grounded Christian will deny. Thus also [10] *S. Paul,* Rom. 14. 4. *who art thou that judgest the servant of another? to his own Lord he standeth or falleth: but he shall stand; for God is able to make him stand.* As therfore of one beyond expression bold and presumptuous, both these apostles demand, *who art thou* that presum'st to impose other law or judgment in religion then the only lawgiver and judge Christ, who only can save and can destroy, gives to the conscience? And the forecited place to the *Thessalonians* by compar'd effects resolvs us, that be he or they who or wherever they be or can be, they are of far less autoritie then the church, whom in these things as protestants they receive not, and yet no less antichrist in this main point of antichristianism, no less a pope or popedom than he at *Rome,* if [11] not much more; by setting up supream interpreters of scripture either those doctors whom they follow, or, which is far worse, themselves as a civil papacie assuming unaccountable supremacie to themselves not in civil only but ecclesiastical causes. Seeing then that in matters of religion, as hath been prov'd, none can judge or determin here on earth, no not church-governors themselves against the consciences of other beleevers, my inference is, or rather not mine but

our Saviours own, that in those matters they neither can command
nor use constraint; lest they run rashly on a pernicious consequence,
forewarnd in that parable *Mat.* 13. from the 26 [15] to the 31 verse:
least while ye gather up the tares, ye root up also the wheat with
them. Let [12] *both grow together until the harvest: and in the*
time of harvest I will say to the reapers, Gather ye together first the
tares &c. whereby he declares that this work neither his own min-
isters nor any els can discerningly anough or judgingly perform with-
out his own immediat direction, in his own fit season; and that they
ought till then not to attempt it. Which is further confirmd 2 *Cor.*
1. 24. *not that we have dominion over your faith, but are helpers of*
your joy. If apostles had no dominion or constraining power over
faith or conscience, much less have ordinary ministers. 1 *Pet.* 5. 2, 3.
feed the flock of God not by constraint &c. *neither as being lords*
over Gods heritage. But some will object, that this overthrows all
church-discipline, all censure of errors, if no man can determin. [13]
My answer is, that what they hear is plane scripture; which forbids
not church-sentence or determining, but as it ends in violence upon
the conscience unconvinc'd. Let who so will interpret or determin,
so it be according to true church-discipline; which is exercis'd on
them only who have willingly joind themselves in that covnant of
union, and proceeds only to a separation from the rest,[16] proceeds
never to any corporal inforcement or forfeture of monie; which in
spiritual [17] things are the two arms of Antichrist, not of the true
church; the one being an inquisition, the other no better then a
temporal indulgence of sin for monie, whether by the church exacted
or by the magistrate; both the one and the other a temporal satis-
faction for what Christ hath [14] satisfied eternally; a popish com-
muting of penaltie, corporal for spiritual; a satisfaction to man
especially to the magistrate, for what and to whom we owe none:
these and more are the injustices of force and fining in religion,
besides what I most insist on, the violation of Gods express com-
mandment in the gospel, as hath bin shewn. Thus then if church-
governors cannot use force in religion, though but for this reason,

[15] Should be 29.
[16] For Milton the corporate church is a voluntary association of like-minded
believers; a member may be excommunicated ("a separation from the rest")
but not otherwise punished. See *Christian Doctrine*, I, xxxii, in *Complete Prose*,
VI, 607–14. At the end of that chapter Milton briefly summarizes his views
upon the separation of church and state.
[17] 1659: spiri ual.

because they cannot infallibly determin to the conscience without convincement, much less have civil magistrates autoritie to use force where they can much less judge; unless they mean only to be the civil executioners of them who have no civil power to give them such commission, no nor yet ecclesiastical to any force or [15] violence in religion.[18] To summe up all in brief, if we must beleeve as the magistrate appoints, why not rather as the church? if not as either without convincement, how can force be lawfull? But some are ready to cry out, what shall then be don to blasphemie? Them I would first exhort not thus to terrifie and pose the people with a Greek word: but to teach them better what it is; being a most usual and common word in that language to signifie any slander, any malitious or evil speaking, whether against God or man or any thing to good belonging: [19] blasphemie or evil speaking against God malitiously, is far from conscience in religion; according to that of *Marc 9. 39. there is none who doth a powerfull work in my name, and can likely* [20] *speak evil of* [16] *me.* If this suffice not, I referre them to that prudent and well deliberated act *August 9.* 1650; where the Parlament defines blasphemie against God, as far as it is a crime belonging to civil judicature,[21] *pleniùs ac meliùs Chrysippo & Crantore;* [22] in plane English more warily, more judiciously, more orthodoxally then twice thir number of divines have don in many a

[18] This was the goal of the Presbyterians and of some Independents. See Introduction above, pp. 34–45.

[19] Although Milton often uses the word in its ordinary pejorative sense, he employs a definition similar to this in the *Christian Doctrine (Complete Prose,* VI, 699): "all Greek writers, sacred as well as prophane, use the word *blasphemy* in a general sense to mean any kind of evil-speaking, directed at any person." He goes on to object to the limitation of the definition to "evil-speaking against God."

[20] The Authorized Version, which Milton is closely paraphrasing, reads *lightly.* See Preface above, p. 236.

[21] The *Act Against several Atheistical, Blasphemous and Execrable Opinions* of this date was aimed mainly against the Ranters, with whose excesses Milton can have felt no sympathy. For uttering certain of their more shocking opinions, which it specified, it imposed six months' imprisonment for a first offense and banishment for a second. Though rigorous, it was much less so than *An Ordinance for the punishing of Blasphemies and Heresies* which the unpurged Long Parliament had passed on May 2, 1648. This had prescribed the death penalty for a wider range of opinions, many of which were heretical rather than blasphemous, and some of which Milton himself was to hold. See Firth and Rait, *Acts and Ordinances,* I, 1133–36, and II, 409–12.

[22] In Epistle I, ii, 4, Horace asserts that the Homeric poems are "fuller and better" guides than the philosophers Chrysippus or Crantor.

prolix volume: although in all likelihood they whose whole studie and profession these things are should be most intelligent and authentic therin, as they are for the most part, yet neither they nor these unnerring always or infallible. But we shall not carrie it thus; another Greek apparition stands in our way, *heresie* and *heretic;* in like manner also rail'd at to the people as in a tongue un-[17]known. They should first interpret to them, that heresie, by what it signifies in that language, is no word of evil note; [23] meaning only the choise or following of any opinion good or bad in religion or any other learning: and thus not only in heathen authors, but in the New testament it self without censure or blame. *Acts* 15. 5. *certain of the heresie of the Pharises which beleevd.* and 26. 5. *after the exactest heresie* [24] *of our religion I livd a Pharise.* In which sense Presbyterian or Independent may without reproach be calld a heresie. Where it is mentiond with blame, it seems to differ little from schism 1 *Cor.* 11. 18, 19. *I hear that there be schisms among you* &c. *for there must also heresies be among you* &c; though some who write of heresie after their own heads, would make [18] it far worse then schism; whenas on the contrarie, schism signifies division, and in the worst sense; heresie, choise only of one opinion before another, which may bee without discord. In apostolic times therfore ere the scripture was written, heresie was a doctrin maintaind against the doctrin by them deliverd: [25] which in these times can be no otherwise defin'd then a doctrin maintaind against the light, which we now only have, of the scripture. Seeing therfore that no

---

[23] Milton similarly tolerates heresy in the "Epistle" to the *Christian Doctrine:* "since the compilation of the New Testament, nothing can correctly be called heresy unless it contradicts that," *Complete Prose,* VI, 123. Again in *Of True Religion* (1673), p. 6, he wrote, "Heresie is in the Will and choice profestly against Scripture; error is against the Will, in misunderstanding the Scripture after all sincere endeavours to understand it rightly." Barbara Lewalski contrasts this position with that of the "orthodox" Puritan William Ames, who "defines heresy as error that is 'contrary to that doctrine which belongs to the summe and substance of faith and manners' and that is held with stubbornness, that is, the heretic 'opposeth himselfe to the plaine Scripture, and will not through the naughtinesse of his mind perceive the sense of it,'" *Conscience with the Power and Cases Thereof* (London, 1643), IV, 9–10; cited in *The Prose of John Milton,* ed. J. Max Patrick (New York, 1967), p. 472, n. 10. See also the parliamentary statements referred to above in note 21.

[24] Translated *sect* in both verses in the Authorized Version. See Preface above, p. 235.

[25] *E.g.,* in Romans 16:17 and II John 1:10.

man, no synod, no session of men, though calld the church, can judge definitively the sense of scripture to another mans conscience,[26] which is well known to be a general maxim of the Protestant religion, it follows planely, that he who holds in religion that beleef or those [19] opinions which to his conscience and utmost understanding appeer with most evidence or probabilitie in the scripture, though to others he seem erroneous, can no more be justly censur'd for a heretic then his censurers; who do but the same thing themselves while they censure him for so doing. For ask them, or any Protestant, which hath most autoritie, the church or the scripture? they will answer, doubtless, that the scripture: and what hath most autoritie, that no doubt but they will confess is to be followd. He then who to his best apprehension follows the scripture, though against any point of doctrine by the whole church receivd, is not the heretic; but he who follows the church against his conscience and perswasion grounded on the scripture.[27] To make this [20] yet more undeniable, I shall only borrow a plane similie, the same which our own writers, when they would demonstrate planest that we rightly preferre the scripture before the church, use frequently against the Papist in this manner. As the Samaritans beleevd Christ, first for the womans word, but next and much rather for his own,[28] so we the scripture; first on the churches word, but afterwards and much more for its own, as the word of God; yea the church it self we beleeve then for the scripture. The inference of it self follows: if by the Protestant doctrine we beleeve the scripture not for the churches saying, but for its own as the word of God, then ought we to beleeve what in our conscience we apprehend the scripture to say, though the visible [21] church with all her doctors gainsay; and being taught to beleeve them only for the scripture, they who so do

[26] On the other hand, in their *Westminster Confession of Faith,* Chapter 31, 3, the Assembly of Divines had asserted that "It belongeth to synods and councils . . . to determine controversies of faith, and cases of conscience." Schaff, III, 669, and Preface above, p. 231.

[27] A more famous statement of this judgment had appeared in *Areopagitica:* "A man may be a heretick in the truth; and if he beleeve things only because his Pastor sayes so, or the Assembly so determine, without knowing other reason, though his belief be true, yet the very truth he holds, becomes his heresie." *Complete Prose,* II, 543; see also Sirluck's introductory statement, II, 167.

[28] In John 4:39–42 (a commonplace; see also *Christian Doctrine* in *Complete Prose,* VI, 590).

are not heretics, but the best protestants: and by their opinions, whatever they be, can hurt no protestant, whose rule is not to receive them but from the scripture: which to interpret convincingly to his own conscience none is able but himself guided by the Holy Spirit; and not so guided, none then he to himself can be a worse deceiver. To protestants therfore whose common rule and touchstone is the scripture, nothing can with more conscience, more equitie, nothing more protestantly can be permitted then a free and lawful debate at all times by writing, conference or disputation of what opinion soever, disputable by scri-[22]pture: concluding, that no man in religion is properly a heretic at this day, but he who maintains traditions or opinions not probable by scripture; who, for aught I know, is the papist only; he the only heretic, who counts all heretics but himself. Such as these, indeed, were capitally punishd by the law of *Moses,* as the only true heretics, idolaters, plane and open deserters of God and his known law: [29] but in the gospel such are punishd by excommunion only. *Tit.* 3. 10. *an heretic, after the first and second admonition, reject.* But they who think not this heavie anough and understand not that dreadfull aw and spiritual efficacie which the apostle hath expressd so highly to be in church-discipline, 2 *Cor.* 10. of which anon, and think weakly that the church of God [23] cannot long subsist but in a bodilie fear, for want of other prooff will needs wrest that place of S. *Paul Rom.* 13.[30]

[29] *E.g.,* Leviticus 20:1–5.

[30] The biblical citations which Milton explicates in the next few sentences are all taken from Romans 13:1–6. He had earlier considered this same text when he denied the interpretation given it by Salmasius (*First Defense, Complete Prose,* IV, 382–86); still earlier he had had to discuss it in *Tenure (Complete Prose,* III, 209–10). The fundamental importance attached to St. Paul's words may, however, best be understood in the fact that they are cited as the primary proof texts beginning Chapter 23 of the *Westminster Confession,* "Of the Civil Magistrate," which in paragraph 3 asserts that "The civil magistrate . . . hath authority, and it is his duty to take order, that unity and peace be preserved in the Church, that the truth of God be kept pure and entire, that all blasphemies and heresies be suppressed, all corruptions and abuses in worship and discipline prevented or reformed; and all the ordinances of God duly settled, administered, and observed. For the better effecting whereof, he hath power to call synods, to be present at them, and to provide that whatsoever is transacted in them be according to the mind of God." The Savoy Declaration modified this to have the magistrate "to take care that men of corrupt minds and conversations do not licentiously publish and divulge blasphemy and errors, in their own nature subverting the faith and inevitably destroying the souls of them that receive them," but in strictly religious matters "there is no warrant

to set up civil inquisition, and give power to the magistrate both of civil judgment and punishment in causes ecclesiastical. But let us see with what strength of argument. *Let every soul be subject to the higher powers.* First, how prove they that the apostle means other powers then such as they to whom he writes were then under; who medld not at all in ecclesiastical causes, unless as tyrants and persecuters; and from them, I hope, they will not derive either the right of magistrates to judge in spiritual things, or the dutie of such our obedience. How prove they next, that he intitles them here to spiritual causes, from whom he witheld, as much as in him lay, [24] the judging of civil; 1 *Cor.* 6. 1, &c.[31] If he himself appeald to *Cesar,* it was to judge his innocence, not his religion.[32] *For rulers are not a terror to good works, but to the evil.* then are they not a terror to conscience, which is the rule or judge of good works grounded on the scripture. But heresie, they say, is reck'nd among evil works *Gal.* 5. 20: [33] as if all evil works were to be punishd by the magistrate; wherof this place, thir own citation, reck'ns up besides heresie a sufficient number to confute them; *uncleanness, wantonness, enmitie, strife, emulations, animosities, contentions, envyings;* all which are far more *manifest* to be judgd by him then heresie, as they define it; and yet I suppose they will not subject these evil works nor many more such like to his cognisance [25] and punishment. *Wilt thou then not be affraid of the power? do that which is good and thou shalt have praise of the same.* This shews that religious matters are not here meant; wherin from the power here spoken of they could have no praise. *For he is the minister of God to thee for good.* true; but in that office and to that end and by those means which in this place must be cleerly found, if from this place they intend to argue. And how for thy good by forcing, oppressing and insnaring thy conscience? Many are the

---

for the magistrate under the gospel to abridge them of their liberty." Schaff, III, 653 and 720. See Preface above, p. 231.

[31] "Dare any of you . . . go to law before the unjust [pagans], and not before the saints [Christians]?"

[32] Charged in court with "grievous complaints" by the Jews, Paul appealed his case "unto Caesar"—that is, to the Roman courts. Acts 25:11.

[33] Heresy is listed in this verse among the many "works of the flesh" which are "manifest." Milton goes on to give most of the sins from verses 19–21, which the Authorized Version names as "adultery, fornication, uncleanness, lasciviousness, idolatry, witchcraft, hatred, variance, emulations, wrath, strife, seditions, heresies, envyings, murders, drunkenness, revilings, and such like." For Milton's alterations see Preface above, p. 236.

ministers of God, and thir offices no less different then many; none more different then state and church-government. Who seeks to govern both must needs be worse then any lord prelat or church-pluralist: for he in his own fa-[26]cultie and profession, the other not in his own and for the most part not throughly understood makes himself supream lord or pope of the church as far as his civil jurisdiction stretches, and all the ministers of God therin, his ministers, or his curates rather in the function onely, not in the government: while he himself assumes to rule by civil power things to be rul'd only by spiritual: when as this very chapter v. 6 appointing him his peculiar office, which requires utmost attendance, forbids him this worse then church-plurality from that full and waightie charge, wherin alone he is *the minister of God, attending continually on this very thing*. To little purpose will they here instance *Moses*, who did all by immediate divine direction, [27] no nor yet *Asa*, *Jehosaphat*, or *Josia*,[34] who both might when they pleasd receive answer from God, and had a commonwealth by him deliverd them, incorporated with a national church exercis'd more in bodily then in spiritual worship, so as that the church might be calld a commonwealth and the whole commonwealth a church: nothing of which can be said of Christianitie, deliverd without the help of magistrates, yea in the midst of thir opposition; how little then with any reference to them or mention of them, save onely of our obedience to thir civil laws, as they countnance good and deterr evil: which is the proper work of the magistrate, following in the same verse, and shews distinctly wherin he is the minister of God, *a revenger* [28] *to execute wrath on him that doth evil*.[35] But we must first know

[34] These were good men who exercised the law of Moses in Old Testament history: II Chronicles 14–16; 20:31–37; 34–35. They are also cited in the proof texts of the *Westminster Confession*, Chapters 20 and 23. Moses is instanced in the same way from Deuteronomy 13:5, 6, and 12. Milton goes on to respond that at this period of Old Testament history no real distinction was made between church and state.

[35] The magistrate, according to Romans 13:4, is "the minister of God to thee for good [and] a revenger to execute wrath upon him that doeth evil." Chapter 20 of the *Westminster Confession*, "Of Christian Liberty, and Liberty of Conscience," concludes that those "who, upon pretence of Christian liberty, shall oppose any lawful power, or the lawful exercise of it, whether it be civil or ecclesiastical, resist the ordinance of God." They then "may lawfully be called to account, and proceeded against by the censures of the Church, and by the power of the Civil Magistrate." Romans 13:1–8 is a proof text for the first statement, and Romans 13:3–4 the first proof text for the final clause. Schaff, III, 645. This paragraph is omitted from the Savoy Declaration. See Preface above, p. 231.

who it is that doth evil: the heretic they say among the first. Let it be known then certainly who is a heretic: and that he who holds opinions in religion professdly from tradition or his own inventions and not from Scripture [36] but rather against it, is the only heretic; and yet though such, not alwaies punishable by the magistrate, unless he do evil against a civil Law, properly so calld, hath been already prov'd without need of repetition. *But if thou do that which is evil, be affraid.*[37] To do by scripture and the gospel according to conscience is not to do evil; if we therof ought not to be affraid, he ought not by his judging to give cause; [38] causes therfore of Religion are not here [29] meant. *For he beareth not the sword in vain.* Yes altogether in vain, if it smite he knows not what; if that for heresie which not the church it self, much less he, can determine absolutely to be so; if truth for error, being himself so often fallible, he bears the sword not in vain only, but unjustly and to evil. *Be subject not only for wrath, but for conscience sake:* how for conscience sake against conscience? By all these reasons it appeers planely that the apostle in this place gives no judgment or coercive power to magistrates, neither to those then nor these now in matters of religion; and exhorts us no otherwise then he exhorted those *Romans.* It hath now twice befaln me to assert, through Gods assistance, this most wrested and vexd place [30] of scripture; heretofore against *Salmasius* [39] and regal tyranie over the state; now against *Erastus* [40] and state-tyranie over the church. If from such uncertain or rather such improbable grounds as these they endue magistracie with spiritual judgment, they may as well invest him in the same spiritual kinde with power of utmost punishment, excommunication; and then turn spiritual into corporal, as no worse authors did then *Chrysostom, Jerom* and *Austin,* whom *Erasmus* and others in thir notes on the New Testament have cited to interpret

---

[36] 1659: Scripture.

[37] This and the next two quotations are also from Romans 13:4–5.

[38] 1659: cause . causes.

[39] See above, note 30.

[40] Thomas Erastus (1524–83), a German-Swiss theologian, had asserted in his posthumous *Explicatio Gravissimae Quaestionis* (London, 1589) that civil rather than ecclesiastical authority should punish offenses against the latter; hence arises "Erastianism," the doctrine that the state has power to intervene in religious matters. A translation of Erastus's book was published later in 1659 with the title, *The Nullity of Church Censures* (Thomason E 1783.[2.]). The *Westminster Confession,* the Humble Petition and Advice, and Cromwell's state church were all Erastian.

that *cutting off* which S. *Paul* wishd to them who had brought back the Galatians to circumcision, no less then the amercement of thir whole virilitie; [41] and *Grotius* addes that this concising [42] punishment of circumcisers became a penal law [31] therupon among the *Visigothes:* [43] a dangerous example of beginning in the spirit to end so in the flesh: wheras that cutting off much likelier seems meant a cutting off from the church, not unusually so termd in scripture, and a zealous imprecation, not a command. But I have mentiond this passage to shew how absurd they often prove who have not learnd to distinguish rightly between civil power and ecclesiastical. How many persecutions then, imprisonments, banishments, penalties and stripes; how much bloodshed have the forcers of conscience to answer for, and protestants rather than papists! For the papist, judging by his principles, punishes them who beleeve not as the church beleevs though against the scripture: but the protestant, teaching every one to beleeve [32] the scripture though against the church, counts heretical and persecutes, against his own principles, them who in any particular so beleeve as he in general teaches them; them who most honor and beleeve divine scripture, but not against it any humane interpretation though universal; them who interpret scripture only to themselves, which by his own position none but

---

[41] See Galatians 5:12: "I would that they were even cut off which trouble you." Annotating this verse, Erasmus cited two interpretations for such "cutting off": gelding and excommunication. As Lewalski notes (*Prose*, ed. Patrick, p. 473, n. 18), Erasmus finds support for the former sense in "Ambrose, Theophylactus, and Chrysostom . . . but indicates his own belief that the latter meaning is more in keeping with the dignity of the Apostle." He then "cites Augustine [Austin] for still a third meaning which Milton seems to have remembered wrongly, to the effect that the apostle here begs the false teachers to . . . cease disturbing the church by their preaching of circumcision." *Annotationes ad Novum Testamentum* (*Opera*, VI [London, 1705], p. 823). One of the "others" who interprets the verse as meaning circumcision is the Presbyterian John Downame, *Annotations upon All Books of the Old and New Testament* (2 vols., London, 1651, 2nd ed.), II, *ad* Gal. 5:12.

[42] "Mutilating," a rare word derived from *concision* (for circumcision) in Phil. 3:2.

[43] In his *Annotationes in Epistolam ad Galatas*, Hugo Grotius cites Chrysostom as interpreting the verse, "Ne circumcidantur solum, sed, si id malunt, etiam abscindantur. . . . Nec aliter Hieronymus, *Si putant sibi hoc prodesse, non solum circumcidantur, sed etiam abscindantur: si enim exspoliatio membri proficit, multo magis abolitio*. Videtur ad hunc locum respicere Wisigottica XII, III, 4. *Illi vero qui carnis circumcisiones in Iudaeis vel Christianis exercere praesumserint, quisquis haec aut intulit alteri aut fieri ab altero permiserit sibi, veretri ex toto amputatione plectetur*," *Operum Theologicorum* (London, 1679), II, ii, 877.

they to themselves can interpret; them who use the scripture no
otherwise by his own doctrine to thir edification, then he himself
uses it to thir punishing: and so whom his doctrine acknowledges
a true beleever, his discipline persecutes as a heretic. The papist
exacts our beleef as to the church due above scripture; and by the
church, which is the whole people of God, understands the [33]
pope, the general councels prelatical only and the surnam'd fathers:
but the forcing protestant though he deny such beleef to any
church whatsoever, yet takes it to himself and his teachers, of
far less autoritie then to be calld the church and above scripture
beleevd: which renders his practise both contrarie to his beleef, and
far worse then that beleef which he condemns in the papist. By all
which well considerd, the more he professes to be a true protestant,
the more he hath to answer for his persecuting then a papist. No
protestant therfore of what sect soever following scripture only,
which is the common sect wherin they all agree, and the granted
rule of everie mans conscience to himself, ought, by the common
doctrine of protestants, to be forc'd or molested for religi-[34]on.
But as for poperie and idolatrie, why they also may not hence plead
to be tolerated, I have much less to say. Their religion the more
considerd, the less can be acknowledgd a religion; but a Roman
principalitie rather, endevouring to keep up her old universal do-
minion under a new name and meer shaddow of a catholic religion;
being indeed more rightly nam'd a catholic heresie against the scrip-
ture; supported mainly by a civil, and, except in *Rome,* by a forein
power: justly therfore to be suspected, not tolerated by the magis-
trate of another countrey. Besides, of an implicit faith, which they
profess, the conscience also becoms implicit; and so by voluntarie
servitude to mans law, forfets her Christian libertie. Who then can
plead for such a consci-[35]ence, as being implicitly enthrald to
man instead of God, almost becoms no conscience, as the will not
free, becoms no will. Nevertheless if they ought not to be tolerated,
it is for just reason of state more then of religion; which they who
force, though professing to be protestants, deserve as little to be
tolerated themselves, being no less guiltie of poperie in the most
popish point. Lastly, for idolatrie, who knows it not to be evidently
against all scripture both of the Old and New Testament, and ther-
fore a true heresie, or rather an impietie; wherin a right conscience
can have naught to do; and the works therof so manifest, that a

magistrate can hardly err in prohibiting and quite removing at least the publick and scandalous use therof. [36]

From the riddance of these objections I proceed yet to another reason why it is unlawfull for the civil magistrate to use force in matters of religion; which is, because to judge in those things, though we should grant him able, which is prov'd he is not, yet as a civil magistrate he hath no right. Christ hath a government of his own, sufficient of it self to all his ends and purposes in governing his church; but much different from that of the civil magistrate; and the difference in this verie thing principally consists, that it governs not by outward force, and that for two reasons. First because it deals only with the inward man and his actions,[44] which are all spiritual and to outward force not lyable: secondly to shew us the divine excellence of his spiritual [37] kingdom, able without worldly force to subdue all the powers and kingdoms of this world, which are upheld by outward force only. That the inward man is nothing els but the inward part of man, his understanding and his will, and that his actions thence proceeding, yet not simply thence but from the work of divine grace upon them, are the whole matter of religion under the gospel, will appeer planely by considering what that religion is; whence we shall perceive yet more planely that it cannot be forc'd. What euangelic religion is, is told in two words, faith and charitie; or beleef and practise.[45] That both these flow either the one from the understanding, the other from the will, or both jointly from both, once indeed naturally free, but now only [38] as they are regenerat and wrought on by divine grace,[46] is in part evident to common sense and principles unquestiond, the rest by scripture: concerning our beleef, *Mat.* 16. 17. *flesh and blood hath not reveald it unto thee, but my father which is in heaven:* concerning our practise, as it is religious and not meerly civil, *Gal.*

[44] St. Paul develops the idea of the "inward man" in Romans 7:22 and II Corinthians 4:16.

[45] These are the traditional divisions underlying Milton's arrangement of the *Christian Doctrine* into two books.

[46] This traditional belief, that man's understanding and free will both were enfeebled at Adam's fall and could be regained only by God's extension of grace to the depraved individual, is part of the plan of God in *Paradise Lost;* see III, 188 ff. According to the *Christian Doctrine,* "The change in man which follows his vocation is that whereby the mind and will of the natural man are partially renewed and are divinely moved towards knowledge of God, and undergo a change for the better." *Complete Prose,* VI, 457.

5. 22, 23 [47] and other places declare it to be the fruit of the spirit only. Nay our whole practical dutie in religion is contained in charitie, or the love of God and our neighbour, no way to be forc'd, yet the fulfilling of the whole law; [48] that is to say, our whole practise in religion. If then both our beleef and practise, which comprehend our whole religion, flow from faculties of the inward man, free and unconstrainable of themselves by [39] nature, and our practise not only from faculties endu'd with freedom, but from love and charitie besides, incapable of force, and all these things by transgression lost, but renewd and regenerated in us by the power and gift of God alone, how can such religion as this admit of force from man, or force be any way appli'd to such religion, especially under the free offer of grace in the gospel, but it must forthwith frustrate and make of no effect both the religion and the gospel? And that to compell outward profession, which they will say perhaps ought to be compelld though inward religion cannot, is to compell hypocrisie not to advance religion, shall yet, though of it self cleer anough, be ere the conclusion further manifest. The other reason why Christ [40] rejects outward force in the goverment of his church, is, as I said before, to shew us the divine excellence of his spiritual kingdom, able without worldly force to subdue all the powers and kingdoms of this world, which are upheld by outward force only: by which to uphold religion otherwise then to defend the religious from outward violence, is no service to Christ or his kingdom, but rather a disparagement, and degrades it from a divine and spiritual kingdom to a kingdom of this world: [49] which he denies it to be, because it needs not force to confirm it: *Joh.* 18. 36. *if my kingdom were of this world, then would my servants fight, that I should not be deliverd to the Jewes.* This proves the kingdom of Christ not governd by outward force; as [41] being none of this world, whose kingdoms are maintaind all by force onely: and yet disproves not that a Christian commonwealth may defend it self against outward force

[47] "The fruit of the spirit is love, joy, peace . . . ; against such there is no law."

[48] Asked by the Pharisees, "Which is the great commandment in the law?," Jesus answered, "Thou shalt love the Lord thy God . . . and thy neighbor as thyself. On these two commandments hang all the law and the prophets." Matthew 22:36–40, quoting Deut. 6:5 and Lev. 19:18.

[49] This is a central idea in *Paradise Regained*, especially Satan's offer to Jesus of all the kingdoms of the world (IV, 163).

in the cause of religion as well as in any other; [50] though Christ himself, coming purposely to dye for us, would not be so defended. 1 *Cor.* 1. 27. *God hath chosen the weak things of the world to confound the things which are mighty.* Then surely he hath not chosen the force of this world to subdue conscience and conscientious men, who in this world are counted weakest; but rather conscience, as being weakest, to subdue and regulate force, his adversarie, not his aide or instrument in governing the church. 2 *Cor.* 10. 3, 4, 5, 6. *for though we walk in the flesh,* [42] *we do not warre after the flesh: for the weapons of our warfare are not carnal; but mightie through God to the pulling down of strong holds; casting down imaginations and everie high thing that exalts it self against the knowledge of God; and bringing into captivitie everie thought to the obedience of Christ: and having in a readiness to aveng all disobedience.* It is evident by the first and second verses of this chapter, that the apostle here speaks of that spiritual power by which Christ governs his church, how allsufficient it is, how powerful to reach the conscience and the inward man with whom it chiefly deals and whom no power els can deal with. In comparison of which as it is here thus magnificently describ'd, how uneffectual and weak is outward force with all her boi-[43]strous tooles, to the shame of those Christians and especially those churchmen, who to the exercising of church discipline never cease calling on the civil magistrate to interpose his fleshlie force; an argument that all true ministerial and spiritual power is dead within them: who think the gospel, which both began and spread over the whole world for above three hundred years under heathen and persecuting emperors, cannot stand or continue, supported by the same divine presence and protection to the worlds end, much easier under the defensive favor onely of a Christian magistrate, unless it be enacted and settled, as they call it,[51] by the state, a statute or a state-religion: and understand not

---

[50] Chapter 23 of the *Westminster Confession* (followed by the Savoy Declaration) permits considerably more leeway: Christians "may lawfully, now under the New Testament, wage war upon just and necessary occasions." Schaff, III, 652.

[51] Milton's ironic allusions in this sentence to "settled, as they call it," to "settle . . . religion," to "thir settling petition," and to "thir setled confession" all suggest the Humble Petition and Advice, which prays in its first sentence that God will use Cromwell and the Army "in the settling and securing our liberties" (Gardiner, *Constitutional Documents,* p. 448).

that the church it self cannot, much less the state, [44] settle or impose one tittle of religion upon our obedience implicit, but can only recommend or propound it to our free and conscientious examination: unless they mean to set the state higher then the church in religion, and with a grosse contradiction give to the state in thir settling petition [52] that command of our implicit beleef, which they deny in thir setled confession [53] both to the state and to the church. Let them cease then to importune and interrupt the magistrate from attending to his own charge in civil and moral things, the settling of things just, things honest, the defence of things religious settled by the churches within themselves; and the repressing of thir contraries determinable by the common light of nature; which [45] is not to constrain or to repress religion, probable by scripture, but the violaters and persecuters therof: of all which things he hath anough and more then anough to do, left yet undon; for which the land groans and justice goes to wrack the while: let him also forbear force where he hath no right to judge; for the conscience is not his province: least a worse *woe* arrive him, for worse offending, then was denounc'd by our Saviour *Matt.* 23. 23. against the Pharises: ye have forc'd the conscience, which was not to be forc'd; but judgment and mercy ye have not executed: this ye should have don, and the other let alone. And since it is the councel and set purpose of God in the gospel by spiritual means which are counted weak, to overcom all [46] power which resists him; [54] let them not go about to do that by worldly strength which he hath decreed to do by those means which the world counts weakness, least they be again ob-

[52] The Humble Petition directed that "a Confession of Faith . . . according to the rule and warrant of the Scriptures, be asserted" and that "none may be suffered or permitted to revile [it]." More than a year later, the Savoy Conference met.

[53] The Savoy Declaration is almost identical with the *Westminster Confession,* Chapter 20, which asserts that "God alone is Lord of the conscience, and has left it free from the doctrines and commandments of men"—a statement immediately modified, however, to permit an Erastian interpretation: "free from the doctrines and commandments of men which are in any thing contrary to his Word, or beside it in matters of faith or worship." On the other hand, it continues, "the requiring of an implicit faith, and an absolute and blind obedience, is to destroy liberty of conscience and reason." As has been stated above, note 35, the chapter concludes with assertion of the power of the civil magistrate in religious matters, which the Declaration omits. Schaff, III, 644 and 719–20.

[54] "God hath chosen the weak things of the world to confound the things which are mighty," I Corinthians 1:27.

noxious to that saying which in another place is also written of the
Pharises, *Luke* 7. 30. *that they frustrated the councel of God*. The
main plea is, and urgd with much vehemence to thir imitation, that
the kings of *Juda,* as I touchd before, and especially *Josia* both
judgd and us'd force in religion. 2 *Chr.* 34. 33. *he made all that
were present in Israel to serve the Lord thir God:* [55] an argument,
if it be well weighed, worse then that us'd by the false prophet
Shemaia to the high priest, that in imitation of *Jehojada* he ought
to put *Jeremie* in the stocks, *Jer.* 29. 24, 26, &c. for which he re-
ceivd [47] his due denouncement from God.[56] But to this besides
I return a threefold answer: first, that the state of religion under
the gospel is far differing from what it was under the law: [57] then
was the state of rigor, childhood, bondage and works, to all which
force was not unbefitting; now is the state of grace, manhood, free-
dom and faith; to all which belongs willingness and reason, not
force: the law was then written on tables of stone, and to be per-
formd according to the letter, willingly or unwillingly; the gospel,
our new covnant, upon the heart of every beleever, to be interpreted
only by the sense of charitie and inward perswasion: the law had
no distinct government or governors of church and commonwealth,
but the Priests and Levites judg'd in [48] all causes not ecclesi-
astical only but civil, *Deut.* 17. 8, &c. which under the gospel is
forbidden to all church-ministers, as a thing which Christ thir
master in his ministerie disclam'd *Luke* 12. 14; as a thing beneathe
them 1 *Cor.* 6. 4; [58] and by many of our statutes, as to them who

[55] A proof text for the final clause of Chapter 20 of the *Westminster Con-
fession* cited above in note 35.

[56] The false prophet Shemaiah had directed the priests at Jerusalem, as
exercisers of the authority of the earlier priest and leader Jehoiada (II Chron-
icles 22:11–24:16), that they should jail and put into the stocks "every man
that is mad, and maketh himself a prophet"—including Jeremiah. After Jeremiah
heard about this, the Lord told him to notify everyone that because Shemaiah
had prophesied without divine authorization "he caused you to trust in a lie"
and will be punished by not having "a man to dwell among this people; neither
shall he behold the good that I will do for my people," Jeremiah 29:24–32.

[57] The contrast between the externally delivered Old Testament Law and the
internally experienced New Testament Gospel was a fundamental Christian
principle. Milton elaborates some details in the clauses which follow, and it
frequently appears elsewhere in his writing; see, *e.g.*, *Hirelings*, below, p. 281.

[58] In the passage which Milton cites from Deuteronomy the priests make
civil judgments; in that from Luke Jesus refuses to decide the rights in a
patrimony case; in that from I Corinthians judges are to be those "who are
least esteemed in the church."

have a peculiar and far differing government of thir own. If not, why different the governors? why not church-ministers in state-affairs, as well as state-ministers in church-affairs? If church and state shall be made one flesh again as under the law, let it be withall considerd, that God who then joind them hath now severd them; [59] that which, he so ordaining, was then a lawfull conjunction, to such on either side as join again what he hath severd, would be nothing now but thir [49] own presumptuous fornication. Secondly, the kings of *Juda* and those magistrates under the law might have recours, as I said before, to divine inspiration; [60] which our magistrates under the gospel have not, more then to the same spirit, which those whom they force have oft times in greater measure then themselves: and so, instead of forcing the Christian, they force the Holy Ghost; and, against that wise forewarning of *Gamaliel*,[61] fight against God. Thirdly, those kings and magistrates us'd force in such things only as were undoubtedly known and forbidden in the law of *Moses*, idolatrie and direct apostacie from that national and strict enjoind worship of God; wherof the corporal punishment was by himself expressly set down: but magi-[50]strates under the gospel, our free, elective and rational worship, are most commonly busiest to force those things which in the gospel are either left free, nay somtimes abolishd when by them compelld, or els controverted equally by writers on both sides, and somtimes with odds on that side which is against them. By which means they either punish that which they ought to favor and protect, or that with corporal punishment and of thir own inventing, which not they but the church hath receivd command to chastise with a spiritual rod only. Yet some are so eager in thir zeal of forcing, that they refuse not to descend at length to the utmost shift of that parabolical prooff *Luke* 14. 16, &c. *compell them to come in.* therfore magistrates may compell in

[59] This extended comparison with the union in marriage may have greater force for someone like Milton who believed in divorce. It is impossible, he argues, to reunite what God has severed; to attempt to do so produces not the marriage union but fornication.

[60] *I.e.,* from the prophets, as King Josiah did in the passage referred to, II Chronicles 34–35. Christians, on the other hand, consult the Spirit of God—or conscience—within themselves.

[61] Acts 5:38–39. Gamaliel advised his fellow Jews not to proceed against Peter, for if what Peter was doing was the work of men nothing could come of it; if it were of God nothing could stop it, and they might "be found even to fight against God."

religion.[62] [51] As if a parable were to be straind through every word or phrase, and not expounded by the general scope therof: which is no other here then the earnest expression of Gods displeasure on those recusant Jewes, and his purpose to preferre the gentiles on any terms before them; expressd here by the word *compell*. But how compells he? doubtless no otherwise then he draws, without which no man can come to him, *Joh.* 6. 44: and that is by the inward perswasive motions of his spirit and by his ministers; not by the outward compulsions of a magistrate or his officers. The true people of Christ, as is foretold *Psal.* 110. 3, *are a willing people in the day of his power*. then much more now when he rules all things by outward weakness, that both his inward [52] power and their sinceritie may the more appeer. *God loveth a chearfull giver:* [63] then certainly is not pleasd with an unchearfull worshiper; as the verie words declare of his euangelical invitations. *Esa.* 55. 1. *ho, everie one that thirsteth, come. Joh.* 7. 37. *if any man thirst. Rev.* 3. 18. *I counsel thee.* and 22. 17. *whosoever will, let him take the water of life freely*. And in that grand commission of preaching to invite all nations *Marc* 16. 16, as the reward of them who come, so the penaltie of them who come not is only spiritual. But they bring now some reason with thir force, which must not pass unanswerd; that the church of *Thyatira* was blam'd *Rev.* 2. 20 for suffering the false *prophetess to teach and to seduce*.[64] I answer, that seducement is to be hinderd by [53] fit and proper means ordaind in church-discipline; by instant and powerfull demonstration to the contrarie; by opposing truth to error, no unequal match; truth the strong to error the weak though slie and shifting.[65] Force is no honest confutation; but uneffectual, and for the most part unsuccessfull, oft

---

[62] The "Parable of the Great Supper," Luke 14:16–23, which says that when a man invited a large number of people to a meal each made excuses not to come. In their place he then invited the poor and the sick. When the number of guests was still not enough he sent "into the highways and hedges" with the direction, "compel them to come in, that my house may be filled." As Milton observes, this is scarcely authority to compel religious conformity, but see Downame's interpretation of the passages in just this sense (*Annotations, ad* Luke 14:16 ff.).

[63] II Corinthians 9:7.

[04] The proof text is appended to the *Westminster Confession*, Chapter 20.4.

[65] The echo of the panegyric upon Truth in *Areopagitica* is clear: "Let her and Falshood grapple; who ever knew Truth put to the wors, in a free and open encounter." *Complete Prose*, II, 561.

times fatal to them who use it: sound doctrine diligently and duely taught, is of herself both sufficient, and of herself (if some secret judgment of God hinder not) alwaies prevalent against seducers. This the *Thyatirians* had neglected, suffering, against Church-discipline, that woman to teach and seduce among them: civil force they had not then in thir power; being the Christian part only of that citie, and then especi-[54]ally under one of those ten great persecutions, wherof this the second was raisd by *Domitian:* [66] force therfore in these matters could not be requir'd of them, who were then under force themselves.

I have shewn that the civil power hath neither right nor can do right by forcing religious things: I will now shew the wrong it doth; by violating the fundamental privilege of the gospel, the new-birthright of everie true beleever, Christian libertie. 2 *Cor.* 3. 17. *where the spirit of the Lord is, there is libertie. Gal.* 4. 26. *Jerusalem which is above, is free; which is the mother of us all.* and 31. *we are not children of the bondwoman but of the free.* It will be sufficient in this place to say no more of Christian libertie, then that it sets [55] us free not only from the bondage of those ceremonies, but also from the forcible imposition of those circumstances, place and time in the worship of God: [67] which though by him commanded in the old law, yet in respect of that veritie and freedom which is euangelical, S. *Paul* comprehends both kindes alike, that is to say, both ceremonie and circumstance, under one and the same con-temtuous name of *weak and beggarly rudiments, Gal.* 4. 3. 9, 10. *Col.* 2. 8. with 16: conformable to what our Saviour himself taught *John* 4. 21, 23. *neither in this mountain nor yet at Jerusalem. In spirit and in truth: for the father seeketh such to worship him.*[68] that is to say, not only sincere of heart, for such he sought ever, but also, as the words here chiefly import, not compelld to [56] place, and by the same reason, not to any set time; as his apostle by the

[66] Roman emperor, 81–96. The tradition that John was banished to Patmos (where he wrote Revelation) during this reign goes back to the *Ecclesiastical History* of Eusebius Pamphilus, III, 18. See *A Select Library of Nicene and Post-Nicene Fathers*, Second Series, I, 148.

[67] Old Testament Law, which prescribed these details, has been abrogated by the New Testament, the usual Christian understanding of the relationship be-tween the Testaments.

[68] In all of these passages St. Paul asserts a new dispensation for Christians. *Rudiments* is *elements* in Galatians 4:9, Authorized Version. See Preface above, p. 235.

same spirit hath taught us *Rom.* 14. 6,[69] &c. *one man esteemeth one day above another, another* &c. *Gal.* 4. 10. *Ye observe dayes, and moonths* &c. *Coloss.* 2. 16. These and other such places of scripture the best and learnedest reformed writers have thought evident anough to instruct us in our freedom not only from ceremonies but from those circumstances also, though impos'd with a confident perswasion of moralitie in them, which they hold impossible to be in place or time. By what warrant then our opinions and practises herin are of late turnd quite against all other Protestants, and that which is to them orthodoxal, to us become scandalous and punishable by statute, I wish were once [57] again better considerd; if we mean not to proclame a schism in this point from the best and most reformed churches abroad. They who would seem more knowing, confess that these things are indifferent, but for that very cause by the magistrate may be commanded. As if God of his special grace in the gospel had to this end freed us from his own commandments in these things, that our freedom should subject us to a more greevous yoke, the commandments of men. As well may the magistrate call that common or unclean which God hath cleansd, forbidden to S. *Peter Acts* 10. 15; as well may he loos'n that which God hath strait'nd, or strait'n that which God hath loos'nd,[70] as he may injoin those things in religion which God hath [58] left free, and lay on that yoke which God hath taken off. For he hath not only given us this gift as a special privilege and excellence of the free gospel above the servile law, but strictly also hath commanded us to keep it and enjoy it. *Gal.* 5. 13. *you are calld to libertie.* 1 *Cor.* 7. 23. *be not made the servants of men. Gal.* 5. 14.[71] *stand fast therfore in*

[69] Milton begins his quotation with Romans 14:5. His point is that no time *per se* is holy (as the Sabbath is for the Jew). The same view appears elsewhere, as in *Christian Doctrine*, II, 7 (*Complete Prose*, VI, 708–15), and in *Hirelings*, below, p. 295. In the *Westminster Confession* (which the Savoy Declaration follows) on the other hand, Chapter 21 supports public worship, which is "not carelessly or wilfully to be neglected or forsaken," and the appointment of "one day in seven for a Sabbath." Schaff, III, 648. The public law which Milton is questioning, An Act for the better observation of the Lord's Day, was passed on June 26, 1657 (Firth and Rait, *Acts and Ordinances*, II, 1162–70). It required attendance at "some Church or Chappel . . . or other convenient Meeting-place of Christians, not differing in matters of Faith from the publique Profession of the Nation," p. 1167. See Introduction above, p. 51.

[70] Expanded from God's ironic question of Job (38:31): "Canst thou bind the sweet influences of Pleiades, or loose the bands of Orion?"

[71] This should be Galatians 5:1, but later it is correctly identified.

*the libertie wherwith Christ hath made us free; and be not intangl'd
again with the yoke of bondage.* Neither is this a meer command,
but for the most part in these forecited places accompanied with the
verie waightiest and inmost reasons of Christian religion: [72] *Rom.
14. 9, 10. for to this end Christ both dy'd and rose and reviv'd, that
he might be Lord both of the dead and living. But why dost thou
judge thy brother?* [59] &c. how presum'st thou to be his lord, to
be whose only Lord, at least in these things, Christ both dy'd and
rose and livd again? *We shall all stand before the judgment seat of
Christ.* why then dost thou not only judge, but persecute in these
things for which we are to be accountable to the tribunal of Christ
only, our Lord and lawgiver? 1 *Cor. 7. 23. ye are bought with a
price; be not made the servants of men.* some trivial price belike,
and for some frivolous pretences paid in their opinion, if bought
and by him redeemd who is God from what was once the service of
God, we shall be enthrald again and forc'd by men to what now is
but the service of men. *Gal. 4. 31,* with 5. 1. *we are not children of
the bondwoman* &c. *stand fast therfore* &c. *Col. 2. 8.* [60] *beware
least any man spoil you,* &c. *after the rudiments of the world, and
not after Christ.* Solid reasons wherof are continu'd through the
whole chapter. *v. 10. ye are complete in him, which is the head of
all principalitie and power.* not completed therfore or made the more
religious by those ordinances of civil power, from which Christ thir
head hath dischargd us; *blotting out the handwriting of ordinances,
that was against us, which was contrarie to us; and took it out of
the way, nailing it to his cross, v.* 14: blotting out ordinances written
by God himself, much more those so boldly written over again by
men. ordinances which were against us, that is, against our frailtie,
much more those which are against our conscience. *Let no man ther-
for judge you in* [61] *respect of* &c. *v.* 16.[73] *Gal. 4. 3,* &c. *even so
we, when we were children, were in bondage under the rudiments of
the world: but when the fullness of time was come, God sent forth*

---

[72] Beginning here Milton imagines a series of biblical quotations (in italics)
being put forward by an Erastian as supportive of his position. The answering
interpretations, usually ironic, follow immediately (in roman). Milton has al-
ready employed most of the adverse material in his own argument. The presence
of this dialogue explains the unusual punctuation (periods not followed by
capitals) in the text. See a somewhat similar dialogue between Milton and a de-
fender of forced tithing in *Hirelings* below, pp. 298–99, and Preface above, p. 234.

[73] "in respect of meat, or in drink, or in respect of a holy day." Modern
practice would insert ellipses [. . .] for *etc.* in the passage that follows.

his son &c. to redeem them that were under the law, that we might
receive the adoption of sons &c. Wherfore thou art no more a ser-
vant, but a son &c. But now &c. how turn ye again to the weak and
beggarly rudiments, wherunto ye desire again to be in bondage?
ye observe dayes &c. Hence it planely appeers, that if we be not free
we are not sons, but still servants unadopted; and if we turn again
to those weak and beggarly rudiments, we are not free; yea though
willingly and with a misguided conscience we desire to be in bond-
age to them; how much more then if unwillingly and against our
con-[62]science? Ill was our condition chang'd from legal to euan-
gelical, and small advantage gotten by the gospel, if for the spirit
of adoption to freedom, promisd us, we receive again the spirit of
bondage to fear; if our fear which was then servile towards God
only, must be now servile in religion towards men: strange also and
preposterous fear, if when and wherin it hath attaind by the re-
demption of our Saviour to be filial only towards God, it must be
now servile towards the magistrate. Who by subjecting us to his
punishment in these things, brings back into religion that law of
terror and satisfaction, belonging now only to civil crimes; and
thereby in effect abolishes the gospel by establishing again the law
to a far worse yoke of servi-[63]tude upon us then before. It will
therfore not misbecome the meanest Christian to put in minde Chris-
tian magistrates, and so much the more freely by how much the
more they desire to be thought Christian (for they will be thereby,
as they ought to be in these things, the more our brethren and the
less our lords) that they meddle not rashly with Christian libertie,
the birthright and outward testimonie of our adoption: least while
they little think it, nay think they do God service, they themselves
like the sons of that bondwoman [74] be found persecuting them who
are freeborne of the spirit; and by a sacrilege of not the least aggra-
vation bereaving them of that sacred libertie which our Saviour with
his own blood purchas'd for them. [64]

A fourth reason why the magistrate ought not to use force in reli-
gion, I bring from the consideration of all those ends which he can
likely pretend to the interposing of his force therin: and those

[74] Genesis 21:9 depicts Ishmael, son of the bondwoman Hagar, mocking Isaac,
son of her mistress Sarah. Paul, addressing backsliding converts (Galatians 4:29)
applies this incident in an allegory, in which the "sons of the bondwoman," ad-
hering to the covenant of Sinai, are in effect mocking the adherents of the newer
covenant, "But as he that was born after the flesh persecuted him that was born
after the spirit, even so is it now."

hardly can be other then first the glorie of God; [75] next either the spiritual good of them whom he forces, or the temporal punishment of their scandal to others. As for the promoting of Gods glory, none, I think, will say that his glorie ought to be promoted in religious things by unwarrantable means, much less by means contrarie to what he hath commanded. That outward force is such, and that Gods glory in the whole administration of the gospel according to his own will and councel ought to be fulfilld by weakness, at least so refuted, not [65] by force; or if by force, inward and spiritual, not outward and corporeal, is already prov'd at large. That outward force cannot tend to the good of him who is forc'd in religion, is unquestionable. For in religion whatever we do under the gospel, we ought to be therof perswaded without scruple; and are justified by the faith we have, not by the work we do. *Rom.* 14.5. *Let every man be fully perswaded in his own mind.* The other reason which follows necessarily, is obvious *Gal.* 2. 16, and in many other places of St. *Paul,* as the groundwork and foundation of the whole gospel, that we are *justified by the faith of Christ, and not by the works of the law.* if not by the works of Gods law, how then by the injunctions of mans law? Surely force cannot [66] work perswasion, which is faith; cannot therfore justifie nor pacifie the conscience; and that which justifies not in the gospel, condemns; is not only not good, but sinfull to do. *Rom.* 14. 23. *Whatsoever is not of faith, is sin.* It concerns the magistrate then to take heed how he forces in religion conscientious men: least by compelling them to do that wherof they cannot be perswaded, that wherin they cannot finde themselves justified, but by thir own consciences condemnd, instead of aiming at thir spiritual good, he force them to do evil; and while he thinks himself *Asa, Josia, Nehemia,* he be found *Jeroboam,* who causd Israel to sin; [76] and thereby draw upon his own head all those sins and shipwracks of implicit faith and conformitie, which he [67] hath forc'd, and all the wounds given to those *little ones,* whom to offend he will finde worse one day then that violent drowning men-

[75] The first question in the Presbyterian *Shorter Catechism* defines man's chief end as "to glorify God and enjoy him forever." Schaff, III, 676.

[76] See above, note 34, for Asa and Josiah. Nehemiah led a Jewish restoration movement at Jerusalem a century after the Babylonian captivity. His example is cited in support of the final clause of the *Westminster Confession,* Chapter 20, which authorizes the power of the civil magistrate in religious matters. Jeroboam, on the other hand, instituted idol worship (I Kings 12:25–33) and after failing to heed warnings of prophets was punished by the death of his son (I Kings 14:17).

tioned *Matt*. 18. 6.[77] Lastly as a preface to force, it is the usual pretence, That although tender consciences shall be tolerated, yet scandals thereby given shall not be unpunishd, prophane and licentious men shall not be encourag'd to neglect the performance of religious and holy duties by color of any law giving libertie to tender consciences.[78] By which contrivance the way lies ready open to them heerafter who may be so minded, to take away by little and little, that liberty which Christ and his gospel, not any magistrate, hath right to give: though this kinde of his giving be but to give with one hand and take away with the o-[68]ther, which is a deluding not a giving. As for scandals, if any man be offended at the conscientious liberty of another, it is a taken scandal not a given. To heal one conscience we must not wound another: and men must be exhorted to beware of scandals in Christian libertie, not forc'd by the magistrate; least while he goes about to take away the scandal, which is uncertain whether given or taken, he take away our liberty, which is the certain and the sacred gift of God, neither to be touchd by him, nor to be parted with by us. None more cautious of giving scandal then St. *Paul*. Yet while he made himself *servant to all,* that he *might gain the more,* he made himself so of his own accord, was not made so by outward force, testifying at the same time [69] that he *was free from all men,* 1 *Cor*. 9. 19: and therafter exhorts us also *Gal*. 5. 13. *ye were calld to libertie* &c. *but by love serve one another:* then not by force. As for that fear least prophane and licentious men should be encourag'd to omit the performance of religious and holy duties, how can that care belong to the civil magistrate, especially to his force? For if prophane and licentious persons must not neglect the performance of religious and holy duties, it implies, that such duties they can perform; which no Protestant will affirm. They who mean the outward performance, may so explane it; and it will then appeer yet more planely, that such performance of religious and holy duties especialy by prophane and licentious persons, is a

---

[77] "But whoso shall offend one of these little ones which believe in me, it were better for him that a millstone were hanged about his neck, and that he were drowned in the depth of the sea."

[78] Lewalski suggests (*Prose*, ed. Patrick, p. 474, n. 29) that this is directed against the Savoy Declaration. But it seems even more pointedly opposed to the *Westminster Confession,* which after defending liberty of conscience in Chapter 20 states that "they who, upon pretence of Christian liberty, shall oppose any lawful power . . . , whether it be civil or ecclesiastical, resist the ordinance of God" and should be punished. Schaff, III, 645. The paragraph is omitted from the Savoy Declaration. See Preface, p. 231.

dishonoring rather then a [70] worshiping of God; and not only by
him not requir'd but detested: *Prov. 21. 27. the sacrifice of the
wicked is an abomination: how much more when he bringeth it
with a wicked minde?* To compell therfore the prophane to things
holy in his prophaneness, is all one under the gospel, as to have com-
pelld the unclean to sacrifise in his uncleanness under the law. And
I adde withall, that to compell the licentious in his licentiousness,
and the conscientious against his conscience, coms all to one; tends
not to the honor of God, but to the multiplying and the aggravating
of sin to them both. We read not that Christ ever exercis'd force but
once; and that was to drive prophane ones out of his temple,[79] not
to force them in: and if thir beeing there was an of-[71]fence, we
finde by many other scriptures that thir praying there was an abomi-
nation: and yet to the Jewish law that nation, as a servant, was
oblig'd; but to the gospel each person is left voluntarie, calld only,
as a son, by the preaching of the word; not to be driven in by edicts
and force of arms. For if by the apostle, *Rom.* 12. 1, we are *be-
seechd* as *brethren by the mercies of God* to *present* our *bodies a
living sacrifice, holy, acceptable to God, which is* our *reasonable ser-
vice* or worship,[80] then is no man to be forc'd by the compulsive
laws of men to present his body a dead sacrifice, and so under the
gospel most unholy and unacceptable, because it is his unreasonable
service, that is to say, not only unwilling but unconscionable. But if
prophane and licenti-[72]ous persons may not omit the performance
of holy duties, why may they not partake of holy things? why are
they prohibited the Lords supper;[81] since both the one and the other
action may be outward; and outward performance of dutie may at-
tain at least an outward participation of benefit? The church deny-
ing them that communion of grace and thanksgiving, as it justly
doth,[82] why doth the magistrate compell them to the union of per-
forming that which they neither truly can, being themselves unholy,
and to do seemingly is both hatefull to God, and perhaps no less
dangerous to perform holie duties irreligiously then to receive holy

[79] John 2:14–16 describes how Christ drove the money-lenders from the
temple.
[80] The words printed in roman in this quotation adapt it to Milton's context.
[81] I Corinthians 11:27–28 denies communion to the unworthy.
[82] *E.g., Westminster Confession,* Chapter 29.8, followed by the Savoy Declara-
tion. Parliament had confirmed on August 29, 1648, the power of churches to
suspend members from the sacrament for a long series of "scandalous offenses."
See Firth and Rait, *Acts and Ordinances,* I, 1206.

signes or sacraments unworthily. All prophane and licentious men, so known, can be considerd but either so without the church [73] as never yet within it, or departed thence of thir own accord, or excommunicate: if never yet within the church, whom the apostle, and so consequently the church have naught to do to judge, as he professes 1 *Cor*. 5. 12,[83] then [84] by what autoritie doth the magistrate judge, or, which is worse, compell in relation to the church? if departed of his own accord, like that lost sheep *Luke* 15. 4, &c. the true church either with her own or any borrowd force worries him not in again, but rather in all charitable manner sends after him; and if she finde him, layes him gently on her shoulders; bears him, yea bears his burdens; his errors, his infirmities any way tolerable, *so fulfilling the law of Christ, Gal.* 6. 2: if excommunicate, whom the church hath bid go out, in whose [74] name doth the magistrate compell to go in? The church indeed hinders none from hearing in her publick congregation, for the doors are open to all: nor excommunicates to destruction, but, as much as in her lies, to a final saving. Her meaning therfore must needs bee, that as her driving out brings on no outward penaltie, so no outward force or penaltie of an improper and only a destructive power should drive in again her infectious sheep; therfore sent out because infectious, and not driven in but with the danger not only of the whole and sound, but also of his own utter perishing. Since force neither instructs in religion nor begets repentance or amendment of life, but, on the contrarie, hardness of heart, formalitie, hypocrisie, and, as I said before, everie way [75] increase of sin; more and more alienates the minde from a violent religion expelling out and compelling in, and reduces it to a condition like that which the *Britains* complain of in our storie, driven to and fro between the *Picts* and the sea.[85] If after excommunion he be found intractable, incurable, and will not hear the church, he becoms as one never yet within her pale, *a heathen or a publican, Mat.* 18. 17; not further to be judgd, no

[83] "For what have I to do to judge them also that are without [the church]? do not ye judge them that are within?"

[84] 1659: them.

[85] In his *History of Britain*, III, Milton writes that despite the conversion of many of them to Christianity the Scots and Picts continued to make raids upon the Britons. The latter protested to Aetius, Consul of Rome at the time: "*The barbarians drive us to the Sea, the Sea drives us back to the barbarians; thus bandied up and down between two deaths we perish, either by the Sword or by the Sea.*" *Complete Prose*, V, 138. See Bede, *Ecclesiastical History* (Loeb edition), I, xiii.

not by the magistrate, unless for civil causes; but left to the final
sentence of that judge, whose coming shall be in flames of fire; [86]
that *Maran athà*,[87] 1 *Cor.* 16. 22; then which to him so left nothing
can be more dreadful and ofttimes to him particularly nothing
more speedie, that is to say, the Lord cometh: In the mean while
de-[76]liverd up to Satan, 1 *Cor.* 5. 5. 1 *Tim.* 1. 20. that is, from
the fould of Christ and kingdom of grace to the world again which
is the kingdom of Satan; and as he was receivd *from darkness to
light, and from the power of Satan to God Acts* 26. 18, so now de-
liverd up again from light to darkness, and from God to the power
of Satan; yet so as is in both places manifested, to the intent of
saving him, brought sooner to contrition by spiritual then by any
corporal severitie. But grant it belonging any way to the magistrate,
that prophane and licentious persons omit not the performance of
holy duties, which in them were odious to God even under the law,
much more now under the gospel, yet ought his care both as a magis-
trate and a Christian, to be much more [77] that conscience be not
inwardly violated, then that licence in these things be made out-
wardly conformable: since his part is undoubtedly as a Christian,
which puts him upon this office much more then as a magistrate, in
all respects to have more care of the conscientious then of the pro-
phane; and not for their sakes to take away (while they pretend [88]
to give) or to diminish the rightfull libertie of religious consciences.

On these four scriptural reasons as on a firm square this truth,
the right of Christian and euangelic liberty, will stand immoveable
against all those pretended consequences of license and confusion,
which for the most part men most licentious and confus'd them-
selves, or such as whose severitie [78] would be wiser then divine
wisdom, are ever aptest to object against the waies of God: as if
God without them when he gave us this libertie, knew not of the
worst which these men in thir arrogance pretend will follow: yet
knowing all their worst, he gave us this liberty as by him judgd
best. As to those magistrates who think it their work to settle reli-
gion, and those ministers or others, who so oft call upon them to do

[86] Revelation 1:14.

[87] "A Syriack word, signifying our Lord cometh. . . . It is a word used in
the greatest excommunication among the Christians, implying that they sum-
moned the excommunicated before the dreadfull Tribunall at the last coming
of the Sonne of God." Downame, *Annotations, ad* I Corinthians 16:22.

[88] 1659: ptetend.

so, I trust, that having well considerd what hath bin here argu'd, neither they will continue in that intention, nor these in that expectation from them: when they shall finde that the settlement of religion belongs only to each particular church by perswasive and spiritual means within it self, and that the defence only of the church [79] belongs to the magistrate. Had he once learnt not further to concern himself with church affairs, half his labor might be spar'd, and the commonwealth better tended. To which end, that which I premis'd in the beginning, and in due place treated of more at large, I desire now concluding, that they would consider seriously what religion is: and they will find it to be in summe, both our beleef and our practise depending upon God only. That there can be no place then left for the magistrate or his force in the settlement of religion, by appointing either what we shall beleeve in divine things or practise in religious (neither of which things are in the power of man either to perform himself or to enable others) I perswade me in the Christian ingenuitie of all religi-[80] ous men, the more they examin seriously, the more they will finde cleerly to be true: and finde how false and deceivable that common saying is, which is so much reli'd upon, that the Christian Magistrate is *custos utriusque tabulæ,* keeper of both tables; unless is meant by keeper the defender only: neither can that maxim be maintaind by any prooff or argument which hath not in this discours first or last bin refuted. For the two tables, or ten commandements, teach our dutie to God and our neighbour from the love of both; give magistrates no autoritie to force either: they seek that from the judicial law; though on false grounds, especially in the first table, as I have shewn; and both in first and second execute that autoritie for the most part [81] not according to Gods judicial laws but thir own. As for civil crimes and of the outward man, which all are not, no not of those against the second table, as that of coveting; in them what power they have, they had from the beginning, long before *Moses* or the two tables were in being. And whether they be not now as little in being to be kept by any Christian as they are two legal tables, remanes yet as undecided, as it is sure they never were yet deliverd to the keeping of any Christian magistrate. But of these things perhaps more some other time; [89] what may serve the present hath bin above discourst

[89] Milton also concerns himself with the subject in the *Christian Doctrine,* I, xxvii (*Complete Prose,* VI, 525–31). In his view there, "all the old covenant,

sufficiently out of the scriptures: and to those produc'd might be added testimonies, examples, experiences of all succeeding ages to [82] these times asserting this doctrine: but having herin the scripture so copious and so plane, we have all that can be properly calld true strength and nerve; the rest would be but pomp and incumbrance. Pomp and ostentation of reading is admir'd among the vulgar: but doubtless in matters of religion he is learnedest who is planest.[90] The brevitie I use, not exceeding a small manual, will not therfore, I suppose, be thought the less considerable, unless with them perhaps who think that great books only can determin great matters. I rather chose the common rule, not to make much ado where less may serve. Which in controversies and those especially of religion, would make them less tedious, and by consequence read ofter, by many more, and with more benefit.

The end. [83]

---

in other words the entire Mosaic law, is abolished." For the Presbyterians, on the other hand, God gave Adam "a law, as a covenant of works," which after the Fall "continued to be a perfect rule of righteousness; and, as such, was delivered by God upon mount Sinai in ten commandments." This is the law "commonly called moral," and it "doth for ever bind all, as well justified persons as others, to the obedience thereof." *Westminster Confession*, Chapter 19; Schaff, III, 640–41. The same statement appears in the Savoy Declaration.

[90] The same claims against a learned ministry appear in *Hirelings*. See below, p. 302.

Confiderations

TOUCHING

The likelieſt means to remove

HIRELINGS

out of the church.

Wherein is alſo diſcourc'd

Of { *Tithes,*
Church-fees,
Church-revennes ;

And whether any maintenance
of miniſters can be ſettl'd
by law.

The author *J. M.*

LONDON:
Printed by *T. N.* for *L. Chap-*
man at the Crown in Popes-
head Alley. 1659.

TO THE PARLAMENT OF THE COMMONWEALTH OF ENGLAND WITH THE DOMINIONS THEROF.

O WING to your protection, supream Senat, this libertie of [A3] writing which I have us'd these 18 years [1] on all occasions to assert the just rights and freedoms both of church and state, and so far approv'd, as to have bin trusted with the represent-ment and defence of your actions to all Christendom against an [A3v] adversarie of no mean repute, to whom should I address what I still publish on the same argument, but to you whose magnanimous councels first opend and unbound the age from a double bondage under prelatical and regal tyrannie; [A4] above our own hopes heartning us to look up at last like men and Christians from the slavish dejection, wherin from father to son we were bred up and taught; and thereby deserving of these nations, if they be not barbarously in-[A4v]grateful, to be acknowledgd, next under God, the authors and best patrons of religious and civil libertie, that ever these Ilands brought forth. The care and tuition of whose peace and safety, after a short but scandalous night [A5] of interruption,[2] is now again by a new dawning of Gods miraculous providence among us, revolvd upon [3] your shoulders. And

---

[1] Milton begins with an outline of his writing for various public causes, from *Of Reformation* (1641) to his support of the Commonwealth against "an adversarie of no mean repute"—Salmasius—in the first Latin *Defensio*. Conspicuously missing is mention of the divorce pamphlets and *Areopagitica*, which Milton could hardly pretend represented the view of any contemporary Parliament.

[2] Best understood as the six years between Oliver Cromwell's dissolution of the Rump in 1653 and the Army's restoration of it late in the spring of 1659, although this period does not seem very "short." See Introduction above, pp. 85–87, and Austin Woolrych, "Milton and Cromwell: 'A Short but Scandalous Night of Interruption?'," in *Achievements of the Left Hand,* esp. pp. 200–09. Milton is obliquely referring to a Parliamentary Act of May 11, 1659, which declared that "the Style and Title to be used in all legal proceedings and process shall and ought to be, *The Keepers of the Liberty of England by Authority of Parliament*," resuming a title which had been replaced on December 16, 1653, by the "Name and style of Lord Protector." Firth and Rait, *Acts and Ordinances,* II, 1271 and 813.

[3] Restored to.

to whom more appertain these considerations which I propound, then to your selves and the debate [A5v] before you, though I trust of no difficultie, yet at present of great expectation, not whether ye will gratifie, were it no more then so, but whether ye will hearken to the just petition of many thousands best affected both to religi-[A6]on and to this your returne,[4] or whether ye will satisfie, which you never can, the covetous pretences and demands of insatiable hirelings, whose disaffection ye well know both to your selves and your resolutions. That I, though among many [A6v] others in this common concernment, interpose to your deliberations what my thoughts also are, your own judgment and the success therof hath given me the confidence: which requests but this, that if I have prosperously, God so favoring [A7] me, defended the publick cause of this commonwealth to foreiners, ye would not think the reason and abilitie, wheron ye trusted once, and repent not, your whole reputation to the world, either grown less by more maturitie and longer [A7v] studie, or less available in *English* then in another tongue: but that if it suffic'd som years past to convince and satisfie the uningag'd of other nations in the justice of your doings, though then held paradoxal, it may as well suffice [A8] now against weaker opposition in matters, except here in *England* with a spiritualtie of men devoted to thir temporal gain, of no controversie els among Protestants.[5] Neither do I doubt, seeing daily the acceptance which they [A8v] finde who in thir petitions venture to bring advice also and new modells of a commonwealth,[6] but that you will interpret it much more the dutie of a Christian to offer what his conscience perswades him may be of moment to the [A9] freedom and better constituting of the church: since it is a deed of highest charitie to help undeceive the people, and a work worthiest your autoritie, in all things els authors, assertors and now recoverers of our libertie, to deliver us, [A9v] the only people of all Protestants left still undeliverd, from the oppressions of a Simonious decimating clergie; who shame not against the judgment and practice of all other churches reformd, to maintain, though very weakly, thir [A10] Popish and oft refuted positions, not in a point of conscience, wherin they might be blameles, but in a point of covetousnes and unjust claim to other mens goods; a contention foul and odious in any man, but most of all in mini-[A10v]sters of the gospel, in whom contention, though for thir own right, scarce is allowable. Till

[4] For the petitions addressed to Parliament in the early summer of 1659, see Introduction above, pp. 74–75.

[5] As Milton argues in the body of the pamphlet (below, p. 289), England was the only Protestant country with forced tithing.

[6] For the "new modells" of government being proposed for England in the summer of 1659, see Introduction above, pp. 101 ff.

which greevances be remov'd and religion set free from the monopolie of hirelings, I dare affirme, that no modell whatsoever of a common-[A11]wealth will prove succesful or undisturbd; and so perswaded, implore divine assistance on your pious councels and proceedings to unanimitie in this and all other truth.

John Milton. [A11v]

CONSIDERATIONS TOUCHING THE LIKELIEST MEANS TO REMOVE HIRELINGS OUT OF THE CHURCH.

THE former treatise,[7] which leads in this, begann with two things ever found working much mischief to the church of God, and the advancement of truth; force on the one side restraining, and hire on the other side corrupting the teachers therof. The latter of these is by much the more [1] dangerous: for under force, though no thank to the forcers, true religion oft-times best thrives and flourishes: but the corruption of teachers, most commonly the effect of hire, is the very bane of truth in them who are so corrupted. Of force not to be us'd in matters of religion, I have already spoken; and so stated matters of conscience and religion in faith and divine worship, and so severd them from blasphemie and heresie, the one being such properly as is despiteful, the other such as stands not to the rule of Scripture, and so both of them not matters in religion, but rather against it, that [2] to them who will yet use force, this only choise can be left, whether they will force them to beleeve, to whom it is not given from above, being not forc'd thereto by any principle of the gospel, which is now the only dispensation of God to all men, or whether being Protestants, they will punish in those things wherin the Protestant religion denies them to be judges, either in themselves infallible or to the consciences of other men, or whether, lastly, they think fit to punish error, supposing they can be infallible that it is so, being not wilful, but conscientious, and, according to the best light of him who [3] errs, grounded on scripture: which kinde of error all men religious, or but only reasonable, have thought worthier of pardon; and the growth therof to be prevented by spiritual means and church-discipline, not by civil laws and outward force; since it is God only who gives as well to beleeve aright, as to beleeve at all; and by those means which he ordaind sufficiently in his church to the full

[7] *A Treatise of Civil Power,* published the previous February.

execution of his divine purpose in the gospel. It remanes now to speak of hire; the other evil so mischeevous in religion: wherof I promisd then to speak further, when I should finde God dis-[4]posing me, and opportunity inviting. Opportunity I finde now inviting; and apprehend therin the concurrence of God disposing; since the maintenance of church-ministers, a thing not properly belonging to the magistrate, and yet with such importunity call'd for, and expected from him, is at present under publick debate.[8] Wherin least any thing may happen to be determind and establishd prejudicial to the right and freedom of church, or advantageous to such as may be found hirelings therin, it will be now most seasonable, and in these matters wherin every Christian hath his free suffrage, [5] no way misbecoming Christian meeknes to offer freely, without disparagement to the wisest, such advice as God shall incline him and inable him to propound. Since heretofore in commonwealths of most fame for government, civil laws were not establishd till they had been first for certain dayes publishd to the view of all men, that who so pleasd might speak freely his opinion therof, and give in his exceptions, ere the law could pass to a full establishment. And where ought this equity to have more place, then in the libertie which is unseparable from Christian religion? This, I [6] am not ignorant, will be a work unpleasing to some: but what truth is not hateful to some or other, as this, in likelihood, will be to none but hirelings. And if there be among them who hold it thir duty to speak impartial truth, as the work of thir ministry, though not performd without monie, let them not envie others who think the same no less their duty by the general office of Christianity, to speak truth, as in all reason may be thought, more impartially and unsuspectedly without monie.

Hire of it self is neither a thing unlawful, nor a word [7] of any evil note, signifying no more then a due recompence or reward; as when our Saviour saith, *the laborer is worthy of his hire*.[9] That which makes it so dangerous in the church, and properly makes the

[8] For the debates on tithing in Parliament which ended on June 27, 1659, see Introduction above, pp. 74 ff.

[9] Matthew 10:10, Luke 10:7, or I Timothy 5:18, a major support for those favoring tithes. It is the first evidence offered by William Prynne in his *A Gospel Plea* (1653), pp. 3 ff., one of the main books to which Milton was responding. On June 27, 1659 (according to the inscription on Thomason's copy), Prynne published a six-page restatement of his views, *Ten Considerable Quæries Concerning Tithes*.

hireling, a word always of evil signification, is either the excess thereof, or the undue manner of giving and taking it. What harme the excess therof brought to the church, perhaps was not found by experience till the days of *Constantine:* [10] who out of his zeal thinking he could be never too liberally a nursing father of the church, might be not unfitly said to have either overlaid it or [8] choakd it in the nursing. Which was foretold, as is recorded in ecclesiastical traditions, by a voice heard from heaven on the very day that those great donations and church-revenues were given, crying aloud, *This day is poison pourd into the church.*[11] Which the event soon after verifi'd; as appeers by another no less ancient observation, *That religion brought forth wealth, and the daughter devourd the mother.*[12] But long ere wealth came into the church, so soone as any gain appeerd in religion, hirelings were apparent; drawn in long before by the very s[c]ent thereof. *Judas* therefor, the first [9] hireling,[13] for want of present hire answerable to his coveting, from the small number or the meanness of such as then were the religious, sold the religion it self with the founder therof, his master. *Simon Magus* the next, in hope only that preaching and the gifts of the holy ghost would prove gainful, offerd beforehand a sum of monie to obtain

[10] An old tradition—to which the historian Eusebius, for example, testifies in his *Life of Constantine* (*Vita Constantini,* in J. P. Migne, *Patrologiae Latinae,* VIII, 9–29)—was the benevolence showered upon the Church by the Emperor Constantine after his conversion. Later a forgery, *Constitutum Constantini,* circulated; it endowed Pope Silvester (Constantine's contemporary) and his successors with supremacy in religion and temporal dominion over Rome. By 1440 Laurentius Valla was quite properly questioning its authenticity, but at least for polemical purposes Milton accepted the tradition of the Donation. Much the same argument as here appears in *Of Reformation;* see *Complete Prose,* I, 554 ff. The historian and supporter of tithes, Sir Henry Spelman, also believed in the Donation; see his *Larger Worke of Tithes,* printed posthumously in a collection of pamphlets, *Tithes too hot to be Toucht* (London, 1646), p. 24. For a detailed discussion of Constantine's influence see Christopher B. Coleman, *Constantine the Great and Christianity,* Columbia University Studies in History, Law, and Economics, No. 146 (New York, 1914).

[11] Milton had used this quotation before, in *An Apology* (*Complete Prose,* I, 946–47), where he traces it to John Gower's *Confessio Amantis* (II, 3475–96). It appears again in the *Second Defence* (*Complete Prose,* IV, 651), and Moses Wall picked it up from Milton to quote it back in a letter to him of May 26, 1659, printed below, pp. 510–13. For a full study of the use of the phrase see M. C. Jochums, "As Ancient as Constantius," *SEL,* IV (1964), 101–07.

[12] Again a quotation which Milton had used earlier (in *Eikonoklastes, Complete Prose,* III, 518, where the editor, Merritt Y. Hughes, traces it to St. John Chrysostom, Homily 85 on Matthew).

[13] The testimony is in all the synoptic gospels; see *e.g.,* Matthew 26:14–15.

them.[14] Not long after, as the apostle foretold, hirelings like wolves came in by herds, *Acts* 20. 29. *For, I know this, that after my departing shall greevous wolves enter in among you, not sparing the flock*. Tit. 1. 11. *Teaching things which they ought not, for* [10] *filthy lucres sake*. 2 Pet. 2. 3. *And through covetousnes shall they with feigned words make merchandise of you*. Yet they taught not fals doctrin only, but seeming piety: 1 *Tim.* 6. 5. *supposing that gain is Godlines*. Neither came they in of themselves only, but invited oft-times by a corrupt audience: 2 *Tim.* 4. 3. *For the time will come, when they will not endure sound doctrin, but after thir own lusts they will heap to themselves teachers, having itching ears:* and they on the other side, as fast heaping to themselves disciples, *Acts* 20. 30, doubtles had as itching palmes. 2 *Pet.* 2. 15. *Following the way of* Balaam, [11] *the son of* Bosor, *who lovd the wages of unrighteousnes*. Jude 11. *They ran greedily after the error of* Balaam *for reward*.[15] Thus we see that not only the excess of hire in wealthiest times, but also the undue and vitious taking or giving it, though but small or mean, as in the primitive times, gave to hirelings occasion, though not intended, yet sufficient, to creep at first into the church.[16] Which argues also the difficulty, or rather the impossibility, to remove them quite; unless every minister were, as St. *Paul*, contented to teach *gratis:* [17] but few such are to be found. As therefor we cannot justly take away all [12] hire in the church, because we cannot otherwise quite remove all hirelings, so are we not for the impossibility of removing them all, to use therefor no endevor that fewest may come in: but rather, in regard the evil, do what we can, will alwayes be incumbent and unavoidable, to use our utmost diligence, how it may be least dangerous. Which will be likeliest effected, if we consider, first, what recompence God hath ordaind should be given to ministers of the church; (for that a recompence ought to be given them, and may by them justly be received, our Saviour himself from the very [13] light of reason and of equity hath declar'd:

[14] The story of Simon, in Acts 8:9–24, is the origin of the word *simony*.

[15] As Acts 20:30 says, men shall "arise, speaking perverse things, to draw away disciples after them." The quotations from II Peter 2 and Jude exhibit the effect of false teachers upon their followers; Balaam, cited from Numbers 31:16 and Revelation 2:14, is an example of such a person.

[16] The idea is developed from such texts as Micah 3:11 and John 10:12–13, and, of course, appears also in *Lycidas*, l. 115.

[17] According to Acts 18:3, Paul supported himself as a tent-maker.

Luke 10. 7. *The laborer is worthy of his hire*) next by whom; and lastly, in what manner.

What recompence ought be given to church-ministers, God hath answerably ordaind according to that difference which he hath manifestly put between those his two great dispensations, the law and the gospel. Under the law he gave them tithes; under the gospel, having left all things in his church to charity and Christian freedom, he hath given them only what is justly given them.[18] That, as well under the gospel as under the law, say our English divines, [14] and they only of all Protestants, is tithes; and they say true, if any man be so minded to give them of his own the tenth or twentith: but that the law therefor of tithes is in force under the gospel, all other Protestant divines, though equally concernd, yet constantly deny. For although hire to the laborer be of moral and perpetual right, yet that special kinde of hire, the tenth, can be of no right or necessity, but to that special labor for which God ordaind it. That special labor was the Levitical and ceremonial service of the tabernacle, *Numb*. 18. 21, 31.[19] which is now abolishd: the right therefor [15] of that special hire must needs be withall abolishd, as being also ceremonial. That tithes were ceremonial, is plane; not being given to the Levites till they had bin first offerd a heave-offering to the Lord, *Vers*. 24, 28. He then who by that law brings tithes into the gospel, of necessity brings in withall a sacrifice, and an altar; [20] without which tithes by that law were unsanctifi'd and polluted, *Vers*. 32. and therefor never thought on in the first Christian times, till ceremonies, altars, and oblations, by an ancienter corrup-

[18] Like everyone else in his day, Milton distinguished the Old Testament ("the law") from the New ("the gospel"). Supporters of tithing found much of their authority in the former which, to be valid for Christians, had to reveal its full significance in the latter. Milton is arguing that the New Testament teaching about voluntary support for the ministry differs from the obligatory support required by Old Testament law. See also his discussion of the authority of the Old Testament in *Civil Power* above, p. 259.

[19] In Numbers 18:21–31 the Lord promises the sons of Levi Israel's tithes for the religious services they perform. Tithes are their sole inheritance: the Levites can own no property. Milton's argument is that these duties were abolished for Christians when Christ abolished the law.

[20] Old Testament sacrifices were made at the altar by the priests, who were supported by tithes. Milton's point is that if, as his opponents argued, the modern priest is a Levitical equivalent, then he too celebrates a sacrifice at an altar, with the implication that the Puritan communion table becomes a Roman Catholic altar and the service a mass.

tion were brought back long before. And yet the *Jewes* ever since thir temple [16] was destroid, though they have Rabbies and teachers of thir law, yet pay no tithes, as having no Levites to whom, no temple where to pay them, no altar wheron to hallow them; which argues that the *Jewes* themselves never thought tithes moral, but ceremonial only.[21] That Christians therefor should take them up, when *Jewes* have laid them down, must needs be very absurd and preposterous. Next, it is as cleer in the same chapter, that the priests and Levites had not tithes for their labor only in the tabernacle, but in regard they were to have no other part nor inheritance in [17] the land, *Vers.* 20, 24. and by that means for a tenth lost a twelfth.[22] But our levites undergoing no such law of deprivement, can have no right to any such compensation: nay, if by this law they will have tithes, can have no inheritance of land, but forfeit what they have. Besides this, tithes were of two sorts, those of every year, and those of every third year: of the former, every one that brought his tithes, was to eat his share. *Deut.* 14. 23. *Thou shalt eat before the Lord thy God, in the place which he shall chuse to place his name there, the tithe of thy corn, of thy wine, and of thine oyle, &c.* Nay, though [18] he could not bring his tithe in kinde, by reason of his distant dwelling from the tabernacle or temple, but was thereby forc'd to turn it into monie, he was to bestow that monie on whatsoever pleasd him; oxen, sheep, wine, or strong drink; and to eat and drink therof there before the Lord both he and his household, *Ver.* 24, 25, 26. As for the tithes of every third year, they were not given only to the Levite, but to the stranger, the fatherles, and the widdow, *Vers.* 28, 29. & *Chap.* 26. 12, 13. So that ours, if they will have tithes, must admitt of these sharers with them. Nay, these tithes were not paid in [19] at all to the Levite, but the Levite himself was to come with those his fellow guests and eat his share of them only at his house who provided them; and this not in regard of his ministerial office, but because he had no part nor inheritance in the land. Lastly, the priests and Levites, a tribe, were of a far different constitution from

[21] If ceremonial, they would disappear when the ceremony did (that is, when the Romans razed the Temple in 70 A.D.); if moral, they would be a universal and continuing obligation. Spelman argues the latter interpretation, *Larger Worke*, p. 141: "the end whereunto Tithe was ordained is plainly *Morall.*"

[22] In order that it might receive its tithe, or tenth, from the other eleven tribes, the tribe of Levi surrendered its hereditary twelfth part of the Promised Land, its share by virtue of its descent from one of the twelve sons of Jacob.

this of our ministers under the gospel: [23] in them were orders and degrees both by family, dignity and office, mainly distinguishd; the high priest, his brethren and his sons, to whom the Levites themselves paid tithes, and of the best, were eminently superior, *Num.* [20] 18. 28, 29. No Protestant, I suppose, will liken one of our ministers to a high priest, but rather to a common Levite. Unless then, to keep their tithes, they mean to bring back again bishops, archbishops and the whole gang of prelatry, to whom will they themselves pay tythes, as by that law it was a sin to them, if they did not, *v.* 32. Certainly this must needs put them to a deep demurr, while the desire of holding fast thir tithes without sin, may tempt them to bring back again bishops as the likenes of that hierarchy that should receive tithes from them, and the desire to pay none, may advise [21] them to keep out of the church all orders above them. But if we have to do at present, as I suppose we have, with true reformed Protestants, not with Papists or prelates, it will not be deni'd that in the gospel there be but two ministerial degrees, presbyters and deacons: which if they contend to have any succession, reference or conformity with those two degrees under the law, priests & Levites, it must needs be such whereby our presbyters or ministers may be answerable to priests, and our deacons to Levites: by which rule of proportion it will follow, that we must pay our tithes to the deacons [22] only, and they only to the ministers. But if it be truer yet that the priesthood of *Aaron* typifi'd a better reality,[24] 1 *Pet.* 2. 5. signifying the Christian true and *holy priesthood, to offer up spiritual sacrifice;* it follows hence, that we are now justly exempt from paying tithes, to any who claim from *Aaron,* since that priesthood is in us now real, which in him was but a shaddow. Seeing then by all this which hath bin shewn that the law

[23] There is no ministerial hierarchy in the Reformed churches, which, as Milton goes on to remark, recognize from such passages as I Timothy 3:8 and 5:17 only the offices of presbyters and deacons.

[24] Details appearing in the Old Testament were called *types* of the New (on such authority as I Corinthians 10:10 and Hebrews 8:5), meaning that the full import of such details became clear only as they could be interpreted in New Testament terms. The earlier priesthood of Aaron thus anticipated "a better reality" in Christians, who become a "holy priesthood." Sometimes, as at the end of this sentence, the "type" is called a "copy" or "shadow," again from Hebrews 8:5. The elaborate discussion of Melchizedek, which follows, is another example of such typology. See William G. Madsen, *From Shadowy Types to Truth* (New Haven, 1968), and Jean Daniélou, *From Shadows to Reality: Studies in the Typology of the Fathers,* trans. W. Hibberd (London, 1960).

of tithes is partly ceremonial, as the work was for which they were given, partly judicial, not of common, but of particular right to the tribe of *Levi*, nor [23] to them alone, but to the owner also and his houshold, at the time of thir offering, and every three year to the stranger, the fatherles, and the widdow, thir appointed sharers, and that they were a tribe of priests and deacons improperly compar'd to the constitution of our ministery, and the tithes given by that people to those deacons only, it follows that our ministers at this day, being neither priests nor Levites, nor fitly answering to either of them, can have no just title or pretence to tithes, by any consequence drawn from the law of *Moses*. But they think they have yet a better plea in the [24] example of *Melchisedec,* who took tithes of *Abram* ere the law was given: [25] whence they would inferr tithes to be of moral right. But they ought to know, or to remember, that not examples, but express commands oblige our obedience to God or man: next, that whatsoever was don in religion before the law written, is not presently to be counted moral, when as so many things were then don both ceremonial and Judaically judicial, that we need not doubt to conclude all times before Christ, more or less under the ceremonial law. To what end servd els those altars and sacrifices, that di-[25]stinction of clean and unclean entring into the ark, circumcision and the raising up of seed to the elder brother, *Gen.* 38. 8? [26] If these things be not moral, though before the law, how

[25] Having answered the argument for tithing derived from Old Testament law, Milton turns to a more complicated one from Melchizedek, who, according to Genesis 14:18–20, was the King of Salem, a "priest," who offered Abram "bread and wine" (*cf.* the Christian sacrament) and blessed him. Abram, who had been at war, gave him in turn "tithes of all." This happened, of course, long before God revealed the law to Moses on Mount Sinai.

Hebrews, Chapter 7, elaborately interprets these few verses as typifying the revelation to mankind of the Son of God. Because Abram gave Melchizedek tithes and was blessed, he is viewed as recognizing a special priesthood "after the order of Melchizedek," superior to the Jewish priesthood which later developed. The difference was reinforced for Christians by Psalm 110:4, which said, "Thou [Christ, as Christians interpreted] art a priest for ever, after the order of Melchizedek." Because Abram gave him tithes long before the Law so directed, tithers like Prynne (*A Gospel Plea,* pp. 57 ff.) and Spelman (*Larger Worke,* pp. 104 ff.) argued that tithing to support the Christian priesthood was a universal moral duty, not limited to Jews as the laws of Moses were. At the very beginning (pp. 1–4) of his *History of Tithes* (London, 1618), John Selden considered this interpretation as he, like Milton, questioned the practice of forced tithing.

[26] This Old Testament passage describes the so-called levirate marriage, "by which the brother or next of kin to a deceased man was bound under certain

are tithes, though in the example of *Abram* and *Melchisedec?* But
this instance is so far from being the just ground of a law, that after
all circumstances duly waighd both from *Gen.* 14. and *Heb.* 7, it will
not be allowd them so much as an example. *Melchisedec,* besides his
priestly benediction, brought with him bread and wine sufficient to
refresh *Abram* and his whole armie; incited to do so, first, by the
secret providence of [26] God, intending him for a type of Christ
and his priesthood; next by his due thankfulnes and honor to *Abram,*
who had freed his borders of *Salem* from a potent enemie: *Abram*
on the other side honors him with the tenth of all, that is to say,
(for he took not sure his whole estate with him to that warr) of
the spoiles, *Heb.* 7. 4. Incited he also by the same secret providence,
to signifie as grandfather of *Levi,* that the Levitical priesthood was
excelld by the priesthood of Christ.[27] For the giving of a tenth de-
clar'd it seems in those countreys and times, him the greater who
receivd it. That [27] which next incited him, was partly his grati-
tude to requite the present, partly his reverence to the person and
his benediction: to his person, as a king and priest; greater therefor
then *Abram;* who was a priest also, but not a king. And who un-
hir'd will be so hardy as to say, that *Abram* at any other time ever
paid him tithes, either before or after; or had then, but for this
accidental meeting and obligement; or that els *Melchisedec* had de-
manded or exacted them, or took them otherwise, then as the vol-
untarie gift of *Abram?* But our ministers, though neither priests
nor kings more then [28] any other Christian, greater in thir own
esteem then *Abraham* and all his seed, for the verbal labor of a
seventh dayes preachment, not bringing, like *Melchisedec,* bread or
wine at thir own cost, would not take only at the willing hand of
liberality or gratitude, but require and exact as due the tenth, not
of spoiles, but of our whole estates and labors; nor once, but yearly.
We then it seems by the example of *Abram* must pay tithes to these

---

circumstances to marry the widow" (*OED*). Milton's purpose is to discount
any universal authority of pre-Mosaic practices.

[27] Hebrews 7:9–10 observes that "Levi also, who receiveth tithes, paid tithes
in Abraham. For he was yet in the loins of his father, when Melchizedek met
him." In other words, even before its actual origin in Levi through his ancestor
Abram, the Old Testament priesthood was inferior to the New Testament order
represented by Melchizedek because Melchizedek blessed Abram. Milton loosely
uses "grandfather" here as meaning "forefather" (for Abram actually was Levi's
great-grandfather); in the same way he had used "grandsire" in *Eikonoklastes:*
"Our Gransire Papists in this realm," *Complete Prose,* III, 534.

melchisedecs: but what if the person of *Abram* can either no way represent us, or will oblige the ministers to pay tithes no less then other men? *A-*[29]*bram* had not only a priest in his loines, but was himself a priest; and gave tithes to *Melchisedec* either as grandfather of *Levi,* or as father of the faithful. If as grandfather (though he understood it not) of *Levi,* he oblig'd not us but *Levi* only, the inferior priest, by that homage (as the apostle to the *Hebrewes* cleerly anough explanes) to acknowledge the greater. And they who by *Melchisedec* claim from *Abram* as *Levi*'s grandfather, have none to seek thir tithes of but the Levites, where they can finde them. If *Abram* as father of the faithful paid tithes to *Melchisedec,* then certainly the [30] ministers also, if they be of that number, paid in him equally with the rest. Which may induce us to beleeve, that as both *Abram* and *Melchisedec,* so tithes also in that action typical and ceremonial, signifi'd nothing els but that subjection, which all the faithful, both ministers and people owe to Christ, our high priest and king. In any literal sense from this example they never will be able to extort that the people in those dayes paid tithes to priests; but this only, that one priest once in his life, of spoiles only, and in requital partly of a liberal present, partly of a benediction, gave voluntary tithes, [31] not to a greater priest then himself as far as *Abram* could then understand, but rather to a priest and king joind in one person. They will reply, perhaps, that if one priest paid tithes to another, it must needs be understood that the people did no less to the priest. But I shall easily remove that necessitie by remembring them that in those dayes was no priest, but the father, or the first born of each familie; and by consequence no people to pay him tithes, but his own children and servants, who had not wherewithall to pay him, but of his own. Yet grant that the people then paid [32] tithes, there will not yet be the like reason to enjoin us: they being then under ceremonies, a meer laitie, we now under Christ, a royal priesthood, 1 *Pet.* 2. 9, as we are coheirs, kings and priests with him, a priest for ever after the order or manner of *Melchisedec.* As therefor *Abram* paid tithes to *Melchisedec* because *Levi* was in him, so we ought to pay none because the true *Melchisedec* is in us, and we in him who can pay to none greater, and hath freed us by our union with himself, from all compulsive tributes and taxes in his church. Neither doth the collateral place, *Heb.* 7, make other use of this [33] story, then to prove Christ, personated by

Melchisedec, a greater priest then *Aaron: Vers. 4. Now consider how great this man was, &c.* and proves not in the least manner that tithes be of any right to ministers, but the contrary: first the Levites had *a commandment to take tithes of the people according to the law, that is of thir brethren, though they com out of the loines of Abraham, Vers.* 5. The commandment then was, it seems, to take tithes of the *Jewes* only, and according to the law. That law changing of necessity with the priesthood, no other sort of ministers, as they must needs be another [34] sort, under another priesthood, can receive that tribute of tithes which fell with that law, unless renu'd by another express command and according to another law: no such law is extant. Next, *Melchisedec* not as a minister, but as Christ himself in person blessd *Abraham,* who *had the promises, Vers.* 6; and in him blessd all both ministers and people, both of the law and gospel: that blessing declar'd him greater and better then whom he blessd, *Vers.* 7; receiving tithes from them all not as a maintenance, which *Melchisedec* needed not, but as a signe of homage and subjection to their king and [35] priest: wheras ministers bear not the person of Christ in his priesthood or kingship, bless not as he blesses, are not by their blessing greater then *Abraham,* & all the faithful with themselves included in him, cannot both give & take tithes in the same respect, cannot claim to themselves that signe of our allegiance due only to our eternal king and priest, cannot therefor derive tithes from *Melchisedec.* Lastly, the eighth Verse hath thus: *Here men that die receive tithes: There he received them, of whom it is witnesd that he liveth.* Which words intimate that as he offerd himself once for us, so he received once of us [36] in *Abraham,* and in that place the typical acknowledgment of our redemption: which had it bin a perpetual annuitie to Christ, by him claimd as his due, *Levi* must have paid it yearly, as well as then, *Vers.* 9. and our ministers ought still to som *Melchisedec* or other, as well now as they did in *Abraham.* But that Christ never claimd any such tenth as his annual due, much less resign'd it to the ministers, his so officious receivers without express commission or assignement, will be yet cleerer as we proceed. Thus much may at length assure us, that this example of *Abram* & *Melchisedec,* though I see of late [37] they build most upon it, can so little be the ground of any law to us, that it will not so much avail them as to the autoritie of an example. Of like impertinence is that example of *Jacob, Gen.* 28.

22,[28] who of his free choise, not enjoind by any law, vowd the tenth of all that God should give him: which, for aught appeers to the contrarie, he vowd as a thing no less indifferent before his vow, then the foregoing part thereof; That the stone which he had set there for a pillar, should be God's house. And to whom vowd he this tenth, but to God; not to any priest; for we read of none to him greater then [38] himself? and to God, no doubt, but he paid what he vowd; both in the building of that *Bethel* with other altars els where, the expence of his continual sacrifices, which none but he had right to offer. However therefor he paid his tenth, it could in no likelihood, unless by such an occasion as befell his grandfather, be to any priest. But, say they, *All the tithe of the land, whether of the seed of the land, or of the fruit of the tree, is the Lords, holy unto the Lord, Levit.* 27. 30. And this before it was given to the Levites; therefor since they ceasd. No question; *For the whole earth is the Lords, and* [39] *the fulnes therof, Psal.* 24. 1; and the light of nature shews us no less: but that the tenth is his more then the rest, how know I, but as he so declares it? He declares it so here of the land of *Canaan* only, as by all circumstance appeers; and passes by deed of gift this tenth to the Levite; yet so as offerd to him first a heave-offring, and consecrated on his altar, *Numb.* 18. all which I had as little known, but by that evidence. The Levites are ceasd, the gift returns to the giver. How then can we know that he hath given it to any other, or how can these men presume to take it unofferd first to God, unconse-[40]crated, without an other cleer and express donation, wherof they shew no evidence or writing? Besides, he hath now alienated that holy land: who can warrantably affirme, that he hath since hallowd the tenth of this land; which none but God hath power to do or can warrant? Thir last prooff they cite out of the gospel, which makes as little for them; *Matth.* 23. 23; [29] where our Saviour denouncing woe to the Scribes and Pharises, who paid tithe so exactly, and omitted waightier matters, tels them, that these they ought to have don, that

---

[28] After God had revealed his promise about Canaan in a dream, Jacob set up a stone to mark the place (Bethel), and swore that "of all that thou [God] shalt give me I will surely give the tenth unto thee." In his *History of Tithes*, pp. 4 ff., Selden had concluded that this statement does not establish tithing, for Jacob was a priest rather than a layman; but Spelman, *Larger Worke*, p. 109, holds that it does as "a law of nature and reason."

[29] Prynne, *A Gospel Plea*, pp. 129 ff., argues from this text (but it is not his "last prooff . . . out of the gospel").

is, to have paid tithes. For our Saviour spake then to [41] those
who observd the law of *Moses,* which was yet not fully abrogated,
till the destruction of the temple. And by the way here we may ob-
serve out of thir own prooff, that the Scribes and Pharises, though
then chief teachers of the people, such at least as were not Levites,
did not take tithes, but paid them: So much less covetous were the
Scribes and Pharises in those worst times then ours at this day. This
is so apparent to the reformed divines of other countreys, that when
any one of ours hath attempted in Latine to maintain this argument
of tithes, though a man would think they might suffer [42] him with-
out opposition in a point equally tending to the advantage of all
ministers, yet they forbear not to oppose him, as in a doctrin not fit
to pass unoppos'd under the gospel. Which shews the modestie, the
contentednes of those forein pastors with the maintenance given
them, thir sinceritie also in the truth, though less gainful, and the
avarice of ours: who through the love of their old Papistical tithes,
consider not the weak arguments, or rather conjectures and surmises
which they bring to defend them. On the other side, although it be
sufficient to have prov'd in general the abolish-[43]ing of tithes, as
part of the Judaical or ceremonial law, which is abolishd all, as well
that before as that after *Moses,* yet I shall further prove them abro-
gated by an express ordinance of the gospel, founded not on any
type, or that municipal [30] law of *Moses,* but on moral, and general
equitie, given us instead: 1 *Cor.* 9. 13, 14. *Know ye not, that they
who minister about holy things, live of the things of the temple; and
they which wait at the altar, are partakers with the altar? so also
the Lord hath ordaind, that they who preach the gospel, should live
of the gospel.* He saith not, Should live on things which were of
the temple or [44] of the altar, of which were tithes, for that had
given them a cleer title: but abrogating that former law of *Moses,*
which determind what and how much, by a later ordinance of
Christ, which leaves the what and how much indefinit and free, so
it be sufficient to live on, he saith, *The Lord hath so ordaind, that
they who preach the gospel, should live of the gospel;* which hath
neither temple, altar nor sacrifice: *Heb.* 7. 13. *For he of whom these
things are spoken, pertaineth to another tribe, of which no man gave
attendance at the altar:* his ministers therefor cannot thence have
tithes. And where the Lord [45] hath so ordaind, we may finde

[30] Of a particular state as distinguished from international law (*OED*); *i.e.,*
limited to Israel.

easily in more then one evangelist: *Luke* 10. 7, 8. *In the same house remane, eating and drinking such things as they give: For the laborer is worthy of his hire, &c. And into whatsoever citie you enter, and they receive you, eat such things as are set before you.* To which ordinance of Christ it may seem likeliest, that the apostle referrs us both here and 1 *Tim.* 5. 18, where he cites this as the saying of our Saviour, *That the laborer is worthy of his hire:* and both by this place of *Luke,* and that of *Matth.* 10. 9, 10, 11, it evidently appeers that our Saviour ordaind no [46] certain maintenance for his apostles or ministers publickly or privatly in house or citie receivd, but that, what ever it were, which might suffice to live on: and this not commanded or proportiond by *Abram* or by *Moses,* whom he might easily have here cited, as his manner was, but declar'd only by a rule of common equitie which proportions the hire as well to the abilitie of him who gives as to the labor of him who receives, and recommends him only as worthy, not invests him with a legal right. And mark wheron he grounds this his ordinance; not on a perpetual right of tithes from *Melchi-*[47]*sedec,* as hirelings pretend, which he never claimd either for himself, or for his ministers, but on the plane and common equitie of rewarding the laborer; worthy somtimes of single, somtimes of double honor, not proportionable by tithes. And the apostle in this forecited chapter to the *Corinthians, Vers.* 11, affirms it to be no great recompence, if carnal things be reapd for spiritual sown; but to mention tithes, neglects here the fittest occasion that could be offerd him, and leaves the rest free and undetermind. Certainly if Christ or his apostles had approv'd of tithes, they would have [48] either by writing or tradition recommended them to the church: and that soone would have appeerd in the practise of those primitive and the next ages. But for the first three hundred years and more, in all the ecclesiastical storie, I finde no such doctrin or example: [31] though error by that time had brought back again priests, altars and oblations; and in many other points of religion had miserably Judaiz'd the church. So that the defenders of tithes, after a long pomp and tedious preparation out of Heathen authors, telling us that tithes were paid to *Hercules* and

---

[31] The first three hundred years of the Church (to the time of Constantine and the Council of Nicaea) were admired by Protestants for their religious purity. Prynne, *A Gospel Plea,* pp. 146 ff., and Spelman, *Larger Worke,* Chapter IV, try to counter this argument, which had been advanced by Selden (*History of Tithes,* Chapter IV), by showing that the early clergy received free-will offerings, as Milton also observes.

Apollo, which perhaps was imi-[49]tated from the *Jewes,*[32] and as it were bespeaking our expectation, that they will abound much more with autorities out of Christian storie, have nothing of general approbation to beginn with from the first three or four ages, but that which abundantly serves to the confutation of thir tithes; while they confess that churchmen in those ages livd meerly upon freewill offerings. Neither can they say, that tithes were not then paid for want of a civil magistrate to ordain them, for Christians had then also lands, and might give out of them what they pleasd; and yet of tithes then given [50] we finde no mention. And the first Christian emperors, who did all things as bishops advis'd them, suppli'd what was wanting to the clergy not out of tithes, which were never motiond, but out of thir own imperial revenues; as is manifest in *Eusebius, Theodorit* and *Sozomen,* from *Constantine* to *Arcadius.*[33] Hence those ancientest reformed churches of the *Waldenses,*[34] if

[32] In his *History of Tithes,* Chapter III, Selden makes this point at length; and Prynne, *A Gospel Plea* (p. 73) quotes Hugo Grotius's *De jure belli ac pacis* (1625) for pagan examples which were supposedly equivalent to Christian tithing. The point is that such universality implies a universal moral law. Spelman devotes pp. 114–28 of *Larger Worke* to a similar argument. Hellenic civilization was often thought to be descended from an antecedent Jewish one. As applied to one aspect, for instance, see Don Cameron Allen, "Some Theories of the Growth and Origin of Language in Milton's Age," *PQ,* XXVIII (1949), 5–16.

[33] These three ancient historians are major authorities for the development of Christianity to the death of the Emperor Arcadius in 408.

[34] For all of his adult life Milton admired the Waldensians, a religious group in the Italian Alps and Bohemia who were considered either to be the first Protestants or to have actually preserved as a living tradition the purity of the primitive church from the earliest times. Their "Massacre" at Easter, 1655, by the forces of the Duke of Savoy provoked passionate responses from Protestant Europe and especially from the English. See the *State Papers, Complete Prose,* IV, 685–709, and Milton's sonnet "On the late Massacher in Piemont." It should, however, be remarked that Milton is surprisingly silent on the massacre in this tract.

Quite apart from his interest in such contemporary events is Milton's conviction of the group's religious purity. He had cited their skill in languages in the *Commonplace Book* (*Complete Prose,* I, 379), their resistance to tyranny in *Tenure* (*Complete Prose,* III, 227), their avoidance of episcopacy in *Eikonoklastes* (*Complete Prose,* III, 513 f.). From the several references to them in *Hirelings,* it is evident that Milton was quite familiar with all of the major books about them. Here he is paraphrasing "an ancient tractate inserted in the *Bohemian* historie," his announced source cited also in the passage in *Eikonoklastes.* In editing that work Merritt Y. Hughes identified this "historie" as *The History of the Bohemian Persecution,* supposedly by Václav Hájek (London, 1650); see notes 14 and 15 in *Complete Prose,* III, 513 f. Examination of this book offers, however, no evidence that Milton had ever read it. Instead, he

they rather continu'd not pure since the apostles, deni'd that tithes were to be given, or that they were ever given in the primitive church; as appeers by an ancient tractate inserted in the *Bohemian* historie. Thus far hath the church bin al-[51]waies, whether in her prime, or in her ancientest reformation, from the approving of tithes: nor without reason; for they might easily perceive that tithes were fitted to the *Jewes* only, a national church of many incomplete synagogues; uniting the accomplishment of divine worship in one temple; and the Levites there had thir tithes paid where they did thir bodilie work; to which a particular tribe was set apart by divine appointment, not by the peoples election: but the Christian church is universal; not ti'd to nation, dioces or parish, but consisting of many particular churches complete [52] in themselves; gatherd, not by compulsion or the accident of dwelling nigh together, but by free consent chusing both thir particular church and thir church-officers. Wheras if tithes be set up, all these Christian privileges will be disturbd and soone lost, and with them Christian libertie. The first autoritie which our adversaries bring, after those fabulous apostolic canons, which they dare not insist upon,[35] is a provincial councel held at *Cullen*,[36] where they voted tithes to be *Gods rent,* in the year three hundred fifty six; at the same time per-

---

seems to be referring to *De Waldensibus, Eorumque Doctrina et Moribus, Liber a Pontificio Doctore (Reinerium quidam putant) ante ccc. annos scriptus,* one of a group of documents collected in *Rerum Bohemicarum Antiqui Scriptores.* This collection in turn is part of John Dubrau's *Historia Bohemica ab Origine Gentis,* which is Milton's *"Bohemian* historie." In the Hanau, 1602, edition "Reinerius's" statement appears on pp. 222–32 of the collection of documents. It was for Milton an "ancient tractate" in that it is dated "ante ccc. annos scriptus." He is here referring to p. 223: "decimae non sint dandae: quia in primitiva Ecclesia non dabantur"—a statement detailing Waldensian practices. See further William B. Hunter, Jr., "Milton and the Waldensians," *SEL,* XI (1971), 153–64.

[35] These "canons" conclude the *Apostolic Constitutions,* an apocryphal work supposedly transmitted from the original apostles to the Church by Clement of Rome. Selden had questioned their authenticity in his *History of Tithes,* p. 42: "no man that willingly and most grossly deceives not himself, can beleeve that this *Constitution* [is] of anytime neer the age of the Apostles, but many hundred yeers after." But Spelman, *Larger Worke,* pp. 88 f., considered them to be authoritative, being "very ancient and neer the time of the Apostles." Book VII, 29, supports tithing: "all the first fruits . . . shalt thou give to the priests," *The Ante-Nicene Fathers,* ed. Alexander Roberts and James Donaldson, 10 vols. (Buffalo and New York, 1885–97), VII, 471.

[36] This is the Council of Agrippinense, or Cologne (Cullen), which according to Spelman, *Larger Worke,* p. 89, decreed tithes to be "Gods rent."

haps when the three kings [53] reignd there, and of like autoritie.[37]
For to what purpose do they bring these trivial testimonies, by
which they might as well prove altars, candles at noone,[38] and the
greatest part of those superstitions, fetchd from Paganism or Jewism,
which the Papist, inveigl'd by this fond argument of antiquitie, re-
tains to this day? to what purpose those decrees of I know not what
bishops, to a Parlament and people who have thrown out both
bishops and altars, and promisd all reformation by the word of God?
And that altars brought tithes hither, as one corruption begott an-
other, is evident by one of [54] those questions which the monk
Austin propounded to the Pope, *Concerning those things, which by
offerings of the faithful came to the altar;* as *Beda* writes, *l.* 1. *c.*
27.[39] If then by these testimonies we must have tithes continu'd, we
must again have altars. Of fathers, by custom so calld, they quote
Ambrose, Augustin, and som other ceremonial doctors of the same
leaven: [40] whose assertion without pertinent scripture, no reformed
church can admitt; and what they vouch, is founded on the law of
Moses, with which, every where pitifully mistaken, they again in-
corporate the gospel; [55] as did the rest also of those titular fa-
thers, perhaps an age or two before them, by many rights and
ceremonies, both Jewish and Heathenish introduc'd; whereby think-
ing to gain all, they lost all: and instead of winning Jewes and
Pagans to be Christians, by too much condescending they turnd
Christians into Jewes and Pagans. To heap [41] such unconvincing

---

[37] A disparaging reference to the historical truth of the medieval romance by
John of Hildesheim, *The Three Kings of Cologne.* See *EETS,* Original Series, 85.

[38] Parliament had forbidden both the burning of votive candles and wor-
shipping at altars in an Ordinance of August 26, 1643 (Firth and Rait, *Acts and
Ordinances,* I, 265).

[39] Bede, *Ecclesiastical History* (Loeb edition, I, 117).

[40] Tithers often relied upon patristic authority. In *A Gospel Plea,* p. 143,
Prynne cites a number of fathers, beginning with Ambrose, Jerome, and
Augustine.

[41] *"Prynn"* is added in the margin of the reprint in the *Complete Collection
of the Historical, Political, and Miscellaneous Works* (1698), II, 796. He is the
"Quaerist" in the next sentence who in both *A Gospel Plea* (p. 144) and *Ten
Considerable Quæries* (p. 3) had cited the Roman Catholic writers Alphanus
Tyndarus and Pierre Rebuffus in support of tithing. Their tracts, both entitled
De Decimis, had been published respectively in Venice in 1584 and in Lyons in
1566. As Milton indicates, both of Prynne's works are, as usual with him,
heavily annotated in their margins. Milton, on the other hand, almost always
inserts his documentation into the text. A canceled line of his "New Forcers
of Conscience" makes the same slighting judgment: "Clip ye as close as mar-
ginal P——s ears."

citations as these in religion, wherof the scripture only is our rule, argues not much learning nor judgment, but the lost labor of much unprofitable reading. And yet a late hot Quærist for tithes, whom ye may know by his wits lying ever [56] beside him in the margent, to be ever beside his wits in the text, a fierce reformer once, now ranckl'd with a contrary heat, would send us back, very reformedly indeed, to learn reformation from *Tyndarus* and *Rebuffus,* two canonical Promooters. They [42] produce next the ancient constitutions of this land, *Saxon* laws, edicts of kings, and thir counsels, from *Athelstan,* in the year nine hundred twenty eight, that tithes by statute were paid: and might produce from *Ina,* above two hundred years before,[43] that *Romescot,* or *Peters* penny, was by as good statute law paid to the Pope, from [57] seven hundred twenty five, and almost as long continu'd. And who knows not that this law of tithes was enacted by those kings and barons upon the opinion they had of thir divine right, as the very words import of *Edward* the Confessor, in the close of that law: *For so blessed* Austin *preachd and taught;* meaning the monk, who first brought the *Romish* religion into *England* from *Gregory* the Pope.[44] And by the way I add, that by these laws, imitating the law of *Moses,* the third part of tithes only was the priests due; the other two were appointed for the poor, and to adorne or repare churches; as [58] the canons of *Ecbert* and *Elfric* witnes: *Concil. Brit.*[45] If then these laws were

[42] As Milton now moves to arguments in support of tithing taken from British history, his opponent is primarily Spelman, whose *Concilia, Decreta, Leges, Constitutiones, in Re Ecclesiarum Orbis Britannici* (London, 1639) was a major compilation of constitutional and legal facts from which a tithing structure from British history could be drawn. Most tithers, including Spelman himself, invoke such evidence. As the author of the yet-unpublished *History of Britain (Complete Prose,* V, i), Milton was probably better equipped than any living contemporary to respond (John Selden had died in 1654). Athelstan's laws concerning tithes appear on pp. 398 and 402 of *Concilia,* and are cited in his *Larger Worke,* p. 129 (but dated 924), and by Prynne in *A Gospel Plea,* p. 145.

[43] Equaling Spelman as a historian here, Milton had observed in his *History of Britain (Complete Prose,* V, i, 228) that Ina's laws are "the first of *Saxon* that remain extant to this day." They authorize the payment of "Romescot, or Peters penny," a tax levied by the Church upon land before the Reformation. Spelman described the law in *Concilia,* p. 230, where it is dated 725. Milton is observing ironically that Peter's pence—which all Protestants agree are abolished—have as good authority as tithes.

[44] In the section of *Concilia* concerned with the ecclesiastical laws of King Edward, Spelman reports, p. 621: "Haec enim beatus Augustinus praedicavit & docuit, & haec concessa sunt a Rege, & Baronibus, & populo."

[45] Now Milton expressly cites the *Concilia:* the Canons of Egbert (c. 750),

founded upon the opinion of divine autoritie, and that autoritie be
found mistaken and erroneous, as hath bin fully manifested, it fol-
lows, that these laws fall of themselves with thir fals foundation.
But with what face or conscience can they alleage *Moses,* or these
laws for tithes, as they now enjoy or exact them; wherof *Moses* or-
dains the owner, as we heard before, the stranger, the fatherles and
the widdow partakers with the Levite; [46] and these fathers which
they cite, and these though Romish rather then English laws,
al-[59]lotted both to priest and bishop the third part only. But
these our Protestant, these our new reformed English presbyterian
divines, against thir own cited authors, and to the shame of thir pre-
tended reformation, would engross to themselves all tithes by statute;
and supported more by thir wilful obstinacie and desire of filthie
lucre then by these both insufficient and impertinent autorities,
would perswade a Christian magistracie and parlament, whom we
trust God hath restor'd for a happier reformation, to impose upon
us a Judaical ceremonial law, and yet from that law to be more ir-
regular and [60] unwarrantable, more complying with a covetous
clergie, then any of those Popish kings and parlaments alleagd. An-
other shift they have to plead, that tithes may be moral as well as
the sabbath, a tenth of fruits as well as a seaventh of dayes.[47] I an-
swer, that the prelats who urge this argument, have least reason to
use it; denying morality in the sabbath, and therin better agreeing
with reformed churches abroad then the rest of our divines. As there-
for the seaventh day is not moral, but a convenient recourse of wor-
ship in fit season,[48] whether seaventh or other num-[61]ber, so
neither is the tenth of our goods, but only a convenient subsistence
morally due to ministers. The last and lowest sort of thir arguments,

#5 (p. 259), repeated in the Canons of Aelfric, #24 (p. 578): "Sancti etiam
patres statuerunt, ut Ecclesiae Dei decimas suas quique conferant, tradanturque
eae Sacerdoti, qui easdem in tres distribuat portiones: unam, ad Ecclesiae repa-
rationem: alteram, pauperibus erogandam, tertiam vero Ministris Dei qui Ec-
clesiam ibi curant."

[46] From Deuteronomy 14:29, paraphrased above, p. 282.

[47] Spelman, for instance, argues that although Christians have no command-
ment to keep the Sabbath, "Yet durst never any man say, that the Sabbath
was therefore to be abolished, but . . . the morall use of the commandement,
which is, that the seventh part of our time must be dedicate to the generall
service of God, remaineth forever. . . . So likewise in tithing," *Larger Worke,*
pp. 148–49. See also Prynne, *A Gospel Plea,* pp. 87–88.

[48] The *Christian Doctrine* even more positively questions keeping the Sab-
bath; see *Complete Prose,* VI, 351–55 and 704–15, and Introduction above,
p. 51, especially Hill's *Society and Puritanism* cited there in n. 22.

that men purchas'd not thir tithe with thir land and such like petti-
foggerie, I omitt; as refuted sufficiently by others: I omitt also thir
violent and irreligious exactions, related no less credibly: thir seising
of pots and pans from the poor, who have as good right to tithes
as they; from som, the very beds; thir sueing and imprisoning; [49]
worse then when the canon law was in force; worse then when those
wicked sons of *Eli* were priests,[50] [62] whose manner was thus to
seise thir pretended priestly due by force, 1 *Sam*. 2. 12, &c. *Whereby
men abhorrd the offering of the Lord;* and it may be feard that
many will as much abhorr the gospel, if such violence as this be suf-
ferd in her ministers, and in that which they also pretend to be the
offering of the Lord. For those sons of *belial* within som limits made
seisure of what they knew was thir own by an undoubted law; but
these, from whom there is no sanctuarie, seise out of mens grounds,
out of mens houses thir other goods of double, somtimes of treble
value, for that, which did [63] not covetousnes and rapine blinde
them, they know to be not thir own by the gospel which they preach.
Of som more tolerable then these, thus severely God hath spoken:
Esa. 46. 10,[51] &c. *They are greedy dogs*; *they all look to thir own
way, every one for his gain, from his quarter*. With what anger then
will he judge them who stand not looking, but under colour of a
divine right, fetch by force that which is not thir own, taking his
name not in vain, but in violence? Nor content as *Gehazi* [52] was to
make a cunning, but a constrain advantage of what thir master bids
them to give freely, [64] how can they but returne smitten, worse
then that sharking minister, with a spiritual leprosie? And yet they
cry out sacrilege, that men will not be gulld and baffl'd the tenth of
thir estates by giving credit to frivolous pretences of divine right.
Where did God ever cleerly declare to all nations, or in all lands

[49] According to Prynne in *A Gospel Plea*, p. 29, "in cases of necessity, when
the wants of the Apostles, Ministers and Saints of God require it, Christians
are not bound to pay them the Tithes of their Lands and other setled Dues, but
even to sell their very Lands, Houses, Estates, and lay them down at the
Apostles and Ministers feet."

[50] "Now the sons of Eli were sons of Belial," I Samuel 2:12. The passage
continues to detail how these false priests demanded their due; if anyone de-
murred, he was told, "Thou shalt give it to me now: and if not, I will take it
by force." See another use of this material in *Paradise Lost*, I, 490 ff.

[51] The text should be Isaiah 56:11. See Preface above, p. 235.

[52] In II Kings 5 the prophet Elisha healed Naaman but refused payment for
his service. Later, when Elisha's servant Gehazi sought the payment for himself,
the prophet caused Gehazi to become leprous.

(and none but fooles part with thir estates, without cleerest evidence, on bare supposals and presumptions of them who are the gainers thereby) that he requir'd the tenth as due to him or his son perpetually and in all places? Where did he demand it, that we might certainly know, as in [65] all claimes of temporal right is just and reasonable? or if demanded, where did he assigne it, or by what evident conveyance to ministers? unless they can demonstrate this by more then conjectures, thir title can be no better to tithes then the title of *Gehazi* was to those things which by abusing his masters name he rookd from *Naaman*. Much less where did he command that tithes should be fetchd by force, where left not under the gospel whatever his right was, to the freewill-offrings of men? Which is the greater sacrilege, to bely divine autoritie, to make the name of Christ accessory to [66] violence, and, robbing him of the very honor which he aimd at in bestowing freely the gospel, to committ Simonie and rapin, both secular and ecclesiastical, or on the other side, not to give up the tenth of civil right and proprietie to the tricks and impostures of clergie men, contriv'd with all the art and argument that thir bellies can invent or suggest; yet so ridiculous and presuming on the peoples dulnes or superstition, as to think they prove the divine right of thir maintenance by *Abram* paying tithes to *Melchisedec,* when as *Milchisedec* in that passage rather gave maintenance to *Abram;* in whom [67] all both priests and ministers, as well as lay-men paid tithes, not receivd them. And because I affirmd above, beginning this first part of my discourse, that God hath given to ministers of the gospel that maintenance only which is justly given them, let us see a little what hath bin thought of that other maintenance besides tithes, which of all Protestants, our English divines either only or most apparently both require and take. Those are, fees for christnings, marriages, and burials: which, though whoso will may give freely, yet being not of right, but of free gift, if they be exacted or [68] establishd, they become unjust to them who are otherwise maintaind; and of such evil note, that even the councel of *Trent, l. 2. p.* 240, makes them lyable to the laws against Simonie, who take or demand fees for the administring of any sacrament: *Che la sinodo volendo levare gli abusi introdotti, &c.*[53] And in the next page, with like severity condemns the giving

[53] Quoted from Paulo Sarpi, *Historia del Concilio Tridentino* (London, 1619): ". . . for the Council, wishing to correct the abuses which have been

or taking for a benefice, and the celebrating of marriages, christ-
nings, and burials, for fees exacted or demanded: nor counts it less
Simonie to sell the ground or place of burial. And in a state assembly
at *Orleans*, 1561, it was [69] decreed, *Che non si potesse essiger
cosa alcuna, &c, p.* 429. *That nothing should be exacted for the ad-
ministring of sacraments, burials, or any other spiritual function.*[54]
Thus much that councel, of all others the most Popish, and this as-
sembly of Papists, though, by thir own principles, in bondage to the
clergie, were induc'd, either by thir own reason and shame, or by
the light of reformation then shining in upon them, or rather by the
known canons of many councels and synods long before, to con-
demne of Simonie spiritual fees demanded. For if the minister be
maintaind for his whole ministry, why [70] should he be twice paid
for any part therof? why should he, like a servant, seek vailes [55]
over and above his wages? As for christnings, either they themselves
call men to baptism, or men of themselves com: if ministers invite,
how ill had it becomd *John* the Baptist to demand fees for his bap-
tising, or Christ for his christnings? Far less becoms it these now,
with a greedines lower then that of tradesmen calling passengers [56]
to thir shop, and yet paid beforehand, to ask again, for doing that
which those thir founders did freely. If men of themselves com to
be baptiz'd, they are either brought by [71] such as already pay the
minister, or com to be one of his disciples and maintainers: of whom
to ask a fee as it were for entrance, is a piece of paultry craft or
caution, befitting none but beggarly artists.[56a] Burials and marriages
are so little to be any part of thir gain, that they who consider well,
may finde them to be no part of thir function.[57] At burials thir at-
tendance they alleage on the corps; all the guests do as much un-
hir'd: But thir praiers at the grave; superstitiously requir'd: yet if

---

brought in," etc. It goes on to direct that the sacraments shall be given without
any charge whatsoever; violators will be accused of simony. Sarpi's *Historia*
presents the view of the Council of Trent generally accepted by Protestants.
Some of the arguments in *Areopagitica* are based upon it. See the notes by
E. Sirluck in *Complete Prose*, II, 500 ff., as well as many citations in the
Commonplace Book, Complete Prose, I, Index, *s.v.* Sarpi. There is a full-length
study by John Lievsay, *Paolo Sarpi, Venetian Phoenix* (Lawrence, Kans., 1973).

[54] 1659: *funstion*. Milton translates from Sarpi's Italian.

[55] Gratuities.

[56] Passers-by.

[56a] Mechanics or artisans.

[57] The sentences that follow are to be read as a dialogue. See Preface above,
p. 235.

requir'd, thir last performance to the deceasd of thir own flock. But
the funeral sermon: at thir choise: or if [72] not, an occasion of-
ferd them to preach out of season, which is one part of thir office.
But somthing must be spoken in praise: if due, thir duty; if undue,
thir corruption: a peculiar Simonie of our divines in *England* only.
But the ground is broken, and especially thir unrighteous posses-
sion, the chancel. To sell that will not only raise up in judgment the
Councel of *Trent* against them, but will lose them the best champion
of tithes, thir zealous antiquary, Sir *Hen: Spelman*; who in a book
written to that purpose, by many cited canons, and som even of
times corruptest in the church, proves that fees [73] exacted or de-
manded for sacraments, marriages, burials, and especially for inter-
ring, are wicked, accursed, Simoniacal and abominable.[58] Yet thus
is the church, for all this noise of reformation, left still unreformd,
by the censure of thir own synods, thir own favorers, a den of
theeves and robbers. As for marriages that ministers should meddle
with them, as not sanctifi'd or legitimat without their celebration,
I finde no ground in scripture either of precept or example. Likeliest
it is (which our *Selden* hath well observd, *l. 2, c. 28, ux. Eb.*[59]) that
in imitation of heathen priests who were wont at nu-[74]ptials to
use many rites and ceremonies, and especially, judging it would be
profitable, and the increase of thir autoritie, not to be spectators
only in busines of such concernment to the life of man, they insinu-
ated that marriage was not holy without their benediction, and for
the better colour, made it a sacrament; being of it self a civil ordi-
nance, a houshold contract, a thing indifferent and free to the whole
race of mankinde, not as religious, but as men: best, indeed, under-
taken to religious ends, and, as the apostle saith, 1 *Cor.* 7, *in the
Lord.* Yet not therefor invalid or unholy without [75] a minister
and his pretended necessary hallowing, more then any other act,
enterprise or contract of civil life, which ought all to be don also in
the Lord and to his glorie. All which, no less then marriage, were

---

[58] According to Spelman, *Concilia*, p. 259, "Ut nullus Presbyter sacrum
officium, sive baptismatis sacramentum, aut aliquid donorum spiritualium pro
aliquo precio vendere praesumat," a law dated c. 750. But Milton is referring
here more specifically to Spelman's *De Sepultura* (London, 1641; Thomason
E.158.[19]), its thesis being "the reproofe of a customc grown up amongst *us
Christians* [of] *Selling of graves and the duty of buriall,*" p. 2. Spelman then
cites various church canons on the subject, pp. 4 ff. The same attack on burial
fees had appeared in *Of Reformation, Complete Prose,* I, 591 and 608.

[59] This section of John Selden's *Uxor Hebraica* (London, 1646) is also
quoted in the *Commonplace Book* (*Complete Prose,* I, 402 and n.).

by the cunning of priests heretofore, as material to thir profit, trans-
acted at the altar. Our divines denie it to be a sacrament; yet re-
taind the celebration, till prudently a late parlament recoverd the
civil liberty of marriage from thir incroachment; and transferrd the
ratifying and registring therof from the canonical shop to the proper
cognisance of civil magistrates.[60] Seeing then, that God hath [76]
given to ministers under the gospel, that only which is justly given
them, that is to say, a due and moderat livelihood, the hire of thir
labor, and that the heave-offering of tithes is abolishd with the altar,
yea though not abolishd, yet lawles, as they enjoy them, thir Mel-
chisedecian right also trivial and groundles, and both tithes and fees,
if exacted or establishd, unjust and scandalous, we may hope, with
them remov'd, to remove hirelings in some good measure, whom
these tempting baits, by law especially to be recoverd, allure into
the church. [77]

The next thing to be considerd in the maintenance of ministers,
is by whom it should be given. Wherin though the light of reason
might sufficiently informe us, it will be best to consult the scripture:
Gal. 6. 6. *let him that is taught in the word, communicate, to him
that teacheth, in all good things:* that is to say, in all manner of
gratitude, to his abilitie. 1 *Cor.* 9. 11. *if we have sown unto you
spiritual things, is it a great matter if we reap your carnal things?*
to whom therefor hath not bin sown, from him wherefor should be
reapd? 1 *Tim.* 5. 17. *let the elders that rule well, be counted worthie
of double honor;* [78] *especially they who labor in the word and
doctrin.* By these places we see, that recompence was given either
by every one in particular who had bin instructed, or by them all
in common, brought into the church-treasurie, and distributed to
the ministers according to thir several labors: and that was judgd
either by som extraordinarie person, as *Timothie,* who by the apostle
was then left evangelist at *Ephesus,* 2 *Tim.* 4. 5,[61] or by som to
whom the church deputed that care. This is so agreeable to reason
and so cleer, that any one may perceive what iniquitie and violence
hath prevaild since in [79] the church, whereby it hath bin so or-
derd, that they also shall be compelld to recompense the parochial

---

[60] The Marriage Act, passed by the Nominated Parliament on August 24,
1653, had made these changes. As Masson observed (*Life,* V, 281), Milton's
second marriage to Katherine Woodcock in 1656 was performed by a justice
of the peace. For the Act see Firth and Rait, *Acts and Ordinances,* II, 715–18.

[61] Paul directs Timothy to "watch . . . in all things, endure afflictions, do
the work of an evangelist, make full proof of thy ministry."

minister, who neither chose him for thir teacher, nor have receivd
instruction from him, as being either insufficient, or not resident, or
inferior to whom they follow; wherin to barr them thir choise, is to
violate Christian liberty. Our law-books testifie, that before the
councel of *Lateran*, in the year 1179, and the fifth of our *Henry* 2,
or rather before a decretal epistle of Pope *Innocent* the third, about
1200, and the first of king *John, any man might have given his tithes
to what spiritual person he* [80] *would:* [62] and, as the L. *Coke* notes
on that place, *instit. part* 2, that *this decretal bound not the subjects
of this realm; but, as it seemd just and reasonable.*[63] The Pope took
his reason rightly from the above cited place, 1 *Cor.* 9. 11: but falsly
suppos'd every one to be instructed by his parish-priest. Whether
this were then first so decreed or rather long before, as may seem
by the laws of *Edgar* and *Canute*,[64] that tithes were to be paid, not
to whom he would that paid them, but to the cathedral church or the
parish-priest, it imports not; since the reason which they themselves
bring, built on fals sup-[81]position, becomes alike infirme and ab-
surd, that he should reap from me, who sows not to me; bee the
cause either his defect, or my free choise. But here it will be readily
objected, What if they who are to be instructed be not able to main-
tain a minister, as in many villages? I answer, that the scripture
shews in many places what ought to be don herin. First I offer it
to the reason of any man, whether he think the knowledge of Chris-
tian religion harder then any other art or science to attain. I sup-
pose he will grant that it is far easier; both of it self, and in regard
of Gods assisting spirit, not particularly [65] [82] promisd us to the

[62] As Selden observes, *History of Tithes*, pp. 137–38, "of the General Coun-
cels . . . , the first that names Tithes, is the Eleventh, that was held under
Alexander the third, in M.C.LXXX." But, he continues, it directed only how
they were to be consecrated. Selden cites "that Assertion amongst our com-
mon Lawiers, *that, before the Councell of* Lateran, *every man might have given
his Tithes to what Church he would.* . . . But . . . wee find that Canon of
Lateran, under *Alexander* the third, to be differently interpreted by *Innocent*
the Third, within twentie or thirtie yeers after the making of it."

[63] Edward Coke, *The Second Part of the Institutes of the Lawes of England*
(London, 1642), p. 641: "This Epistle Decretall bound not the Subjects of this
Realme, but the same being just and reasonable they allowed the same."

[64] According to the *Leges Ecclesiasticae Edgarii Regis* (A.D. 967), Cap. 3, in
Spelman's *Concilia*, pp. 444–45, "Atque si quis decimas . . . dare noluerit,
praepositus regius, illius loci Episcopus, & Sacerdos conveniunto, atque eo vel
invito decimam Ecclesiae cui debeatur partem, nona ei reliqua facta, reddunto:
quod ad residuas octo partes attinet, quatuor dominus, quatuor Episcopus
habeto. . . ." The laws of Canute, dated 1032, repeat this (p. 544).

[65] 1659: pariularly.

attainment of any other knowledge, but of this only: since it was preachd as well to the shepherds of *Bethleem* by angels, as to the eastern Wisemen by that starr: and our Saviour declares himself anointed to preach the gospel to the poore, *Luke* 4. 18. then surely to thir capacitie. They who after him first taught it, were otherwise unlearned men: they who before *Hus* and *Luther* first reformd it, were for the meanenes of thir condition calld, *the poore men of Lions:* [66] and in *Flanders* at this day, *les gueus,* which is to say, beggars. Therefor are the scriptures translated into eve-[83]ry vulgar tongue, as being held in main matters of belief and salvation, plane and easie to the poorest: and such no less then thir teachers have the spirit to guide them in all truth, *Joh.* 14. 26, *&* 16. 13. Hence we may conclude, if men be not all thir life time under a teacher to learn Logic, natural Philosophie, Ethics or Mathematics, which are more difficult, that certainly it is not necessarie to the attainment of Christian knowledge that men should sit all thir life long at the feet of a pulpited divine; [67] while he, a lollard [68] indeed over his elbow-cushion, in almost the seaventh part of 40. or 50. [84] years teaches them scarce half the principles of religion; and his sheep oft-times sit the while to as little purpose of benifiting as the sheep in thir pues at *Smithfield;* [69] and for the most part by som Simonie or other, bought and sold like them: or, if this comparison be too low, like those woemen, 1 *Tim.* 3. 7. *ever learning and never attaining*; [70] yet not so much through thir own fault, as through the unskilful and immethodical teaching of thir pastor, teaching here and there at random out of this or that text as his ease or fansie, and

---

[66] The Waldensians, who antedated such early Reformation leaders as John Hus and Martin Luther. They were frequently called "the poor men of Lyons [France]," where they may have originated as the followers of Peter Waldo (whence their name). See above, n. 34.

[67] An important argument for tithing was the cost of the necessary education for ministers. Prynne, for instance, stated that they should be schooled for "sixteen or twenty years . . . , double the years, study, industry, that most other Artists (except Lawyers and Physicians) spend," *A Gospel Plea,* p. 31. For Milton, on the other hand, the guidance of the Holy Spirit (the subject of the two texts just quoted from John) in the reading of the Bible is sufficient education. He does not favor a learned ministry but an inspired one. See Barbara Lewalski, "Milton on Learning and the Learned-Ministry Controversy," pp. 267–81, and *Civil Power* above, p. 242, n. 10.

[68] A follower of the reformer Wycliffe, with an intended pun on "lolling."

[69] London meat market (*OED*).

[70] Milton refers rather to II Timothy 3:7: "Ever learning, and never able to come to the knowledge of the truth." See Preface above, p. 235.

oft-times as his stealth guides him. Seeing then that Christian religi-[85]on may be so easily attaind, and by meanest capacities, it cannot be much difficult to finde waies, both how the poore, yea all men may be soone taught what is to be known of Christianitie, and they who teach them, recompenc'd. First, if ministers of thir own accord, who pretend that they are calld and sent to preach the gospel, those especially who have no particular flock, would imitate our Saviour and his disciples who went preaching through the villages, not only through the cities, *Matth.* 9. 35, *Mark* 6. 6, *Luke* 13. 22, *Acts* 8. 25. and there preachd to the poore as well as to the rich, [86] looking for no recompence but in heaven: *John* 4. 35, 36. *Looke on the fields; for they are white alreadie to harvest: and he that reapeth, receiveth wages, and gathereth fruit unto life eternal.* This was their wages. But they will soone reply, we our selves have not wherewithall; who shall bear the charges of our journey? To whom it may as soone be answerd, that in likelihood they are not poorer then they who did thus; and if they have not the same faith which those disciples had to trust in God and the promise of Christ for thir maintenance as they did, and yet intrude into the ministerie [87] without any livelihood of thir own, they cast themselves into a miserable hazzard or temptation, and oft-times into a more miserable necessitie, either to starve, or to please thir paymasters rather then God: and give men just cause to suspect, that they came neither calld nor sent from above to preach the word, but from below, by the instinct of thir own hunger, to feed upon the church. Yet grant it needful to allow them both the charges of thir jorney and the hire of thir labor, it will belong next to the charitie of richer congregations, where most commonly they abound with teachers, to send som [88] of thir number to the villages round, as the apostles from *Jerusalem* sent *Peter* and *John* to the citie and villages of *Samaria, Acts* 8. 14, 25; or as the church at *Jerusalem* sent *Barnabas* to *Antioch, chap.* 11. 22; and other churches joining sent *Luke* to travail with *Paul,* 2 *Cor.* 8. 19: though whether they had thir charges born by the church or no, it be not recorded. If it be objected that this itinerarie preaching will not serve to plant the gospel in those places, unless they who are sent, abide there som competent time, I answer, that if they stay there a year or two, which was the longest time [89] usually staid by the apostles in one place, it may suffice to teach them, who will attend and learn, all the points of religion necessary to salvation; then sorting them into several congregations of a moderat number, out of the ablest and zealousest among them to create elders, who, exercising and requiring from themselves what they have learnd (for no learning is retaind without constant exercise and methodical repetition) may teach and govern the rest: and so exhorted to continue faithful and stedfast, they may securely be committed to the providence of God and the guidance of his holy [90] spirit, till God may offer som opportunitie to visit them again and to confirme them: which when they have don, they have don as much as the apostles were wont to do in propagating the gospel, *Acts* 14. 23. *And when they had ordaind them elders in every church, and had praied with fasting, they commended them to the Lord, on whom they beleevd.* And in the same chapter, *Vers.* 21, 22, *When they had preachd the gospel to that citie, and had taught many, they returned again to* Lystra *and to* Iconium *and* Antioch, *confirming the soules of the disciples,* and *exhorting them to continue in the faith.* And [91] *Chap.* 15. 36. *Let us go again and visit our brethren.* And *Vers.* 41. *He went thorow* Syria *and* Cilicia, *confirming the churches.* To these I might add other helps, which we enjoy now, to make more easie the attainment of Christian religion by the meanest: the entire scripture translated into English with plenty of notes; and som where or other, I trust, may be found som wholsom bodie of divinitie, as they call it, without schoole terms and metaphysical notions,[71] which have obscur'd rather then explan'd our religion, and made it seem difficult without cause. Thus taught once for all, and [92] thus now and then visited and confirmd, in the most destitute and poorest places of the land, under the government of thir own elders performing all ministerial offices among them, they may be trusted to meet and edifie one another whether in church or chappel, or, to save them the trudging of many miles thether, neerer home, though in a house or barn. For notwithstanding the gaudy superstition of som devoted still ignorantly to temples, we may be well assur'd that he who disdaind not to be laid in a manger, disdains not to be preachd in a barn; and that by such meetings as these, being, indeed, [93] most apostolical and primitive, they will in a short time advance more in Christian

---

[71] Milton's own *Christian Doctrine* attempts to fit this definition in its avoidance of theological and philosophical terminology, but it is addressed to an audience of intellectual sophistication. See Hunter, "The Theological Context of Milton's *Christian Doctrine*," *Achievements of the Left Hand*, pp. 269–87.

knowledge and reformation of life, then by the many years preaching of such an incumbent, I may say, such an incubus oft times, as will be meanly hir'd to abide long in those places. They have this left perhaps to object further, that to send thus and to maintaine, though but for a year or two, ministers and teachers in several places, would prove chargeable to the churches, though in towns and cities round about. To whom again I answer, that it was not thought so by them who first thus propagated the [94] gospel, though but few in number to us, and much less able to sustain the expence. Yet this expence would be much less, then to hire incumbents or rather incumbrances, for life-time; and a great means (which is the subject of this discourse) to diminish hirelings. But be the expence less or more, if it be found burdensom to the churches, they have in this land an easie remedie in thir recourse to the civil magistrate; who hath in his hands the disposal of no small revenues; left, perhaps, anciently to superstitious, but meant undoubtedly to good and best uses; and therefor, once made publick, appliable [95] by the present magistrate to such uses as the church or solid reason from whomsoever shall convince him to think best. And those uses may be, no doubt, much rather then as glebes and augmentations [72] are now bestowd, to grant such requests as these of the churches; or to erect in greater number all over the land schooles and competent libraries to those schooles, where languages and arts may be taught free together, without the needles, unprofitable and inconvenient removing to another place. So all the land would be soone better civiliz'd, and they who are taught freely at the publick [96] cost, might have thir education given them on this condition, that therewith content, they should not gadd for preferment out of thir own countrey, but continue there thankful for what they receivd freely, bestowing it as freely on thir countrey, without soaring above the meannes wherin they were born. But how they shall live when they are thus bred and dismissd, will be still the sluggish objection. To which is answerd, that those publick foundations may be so instituted, as the youth therin may be at once brought up to a competence of learn-

[72] Glebes were lands forming part of a parish clergyman's benefice; augmentations were cash additions to the annual value of his living, if it was considered inadequate. Augmentations were dispensed in the sixteen-fifties mainly by the Trustees for the Maintenance of Ministers, who doubtless incurred Milton's particular distrust as agents of the secular state. See Shaw, *English Church*, II, 216–33.

ing and to an honest trade; and the [97] hours of teaching so or-
derd, as thir studie may be no hindrance to thir labor or other calling.
This was the breeding of S. *Paul,* though born of no mean parents,
a free citizen of the Roman empire: so little did his trade debase
him, that it rather enabld him to use that magnanimitie of preach-
ing the gospel through *Asia* and *Europe* at his own charges: thus
those preachers among the poor *Waldenses,* the ancient stock of our
reformation, without these helps which I speak of, bred up them-
selves in trades, and especially in physic and surgery as well as in
the studie of scripture (which is the only true [98] theologie) that
they might be no burden to the church; and by the example of
Christ, might cure both soul and bodie; through industry joining
that to their ministerie, which he joind to his by gift of the spirit.
Thus relates *Peter Gilles* in his historie of the *Waldenses* in *Pie-
mont.*[73] But our ministers think scorn to use a trade, and count it
the reproach of this age, that tradesmen preach the gospel. It were
to be wishd they were all tradesmen; they would not then so many
of them, for want of another trade, make a trade of thir preaching:
and yet they clamor that tradesmen preach; and yet they [99]
preach, while they themselves are the worst tradesmen of all. As
for church-endowments and possessions, I meet with none consider-
able before *Constantine,* but the houses and gardens where they met,
and thir places of burial: and I perswade me, that from them the
ancient *Waldenses,* whom deservedly I cite so often, held, *that to
endow churches is an evil thing*; and, that the church then fell off
and turnd whore sitting on that beast in the *Revelation,* when under
Pope *Sylvester* she receivd those temporal donations. So the fore-
cited tractate of thir doctrin testifies.[74] This also thir own traditions
of that [100] heavenly voice witnesd,[75] and som of the ancient fa-
thers then living, foresaw and deplor'd. And indeed, how could these

[73] The standard history of the Waldensians, *Histoire Ecclesiastique des Eglises
Reformées, Recueillies en Quelques Valées de Piedmont . . . commençant dès
l'an 1160* (Geneva, 1644), pp. 15–16. Milton had earlier entered a statement
from these same pages in his *Commonplace Book (Complete Prose,* I, 379).

[74] Reinerius, in Dubrau, p. 223: "malum sit dotare & fundare Ecclesias &
claustra." And a few sentences earlier, "Romana Ecclesia sit illa meretrix in
Apocalypsi." This was the regular Protestant interpretation of the Whore of
Babylon in Revelation 17:4 ff.

[75] As observed above, n. 11, when referring to the voice from heaven which
spoke at the Donation of Constantine, Milton traced the allusion to Gower's
Confessio Amantis. Here he correctly observes that the tradition also figures in
Reinerius, who reports the Waldensian tradition that the Church "defecerit a
Sylvestro, cum venenum temporalium in Ecclesiam infusum sit," p. 223.

endowments thrive better with the church, being unjustly taken by those emperors, without suffrage of the people, out of the tributes and publick lands of each citie, whereby the people became liable to be oppressd with other taxes. Being therefor given for the most part by kings and other publick persons, and so likeliest out of the publick, and if without the peoples consent, unjustly, however to publick ends of much concernment to the good or evil of a common-[101]wealth, and in that regard made publick though given by privat persons, or which is worse, given, as the clergie then perswaded men, for thir soul's health, a pious gift, but as the truth was, ofttimes a bribe to God or to Christ for absolution, as they were then taught, from murders, adulteries, and other hainous crimes, what shall be found heretofore given by kings or princes out of the publick, may justly by the magistrate be recalld and reappropriated to the civil revenue: what by privat or publick persons out of thir own, the price of blood or lust, or to som such purgatorious and superstitious [102] uses, not only may but ought to be taken off from Christ, as a foul dishonor laid upon him, or not impiously given, nor in particular to any one, but in general to the churches good, may be converted to that use, which shall be judgd tending more directly to that general end. Thus did the princes and cities of *Germany* in the first reformation; and defended thir so doing by many reasons, which are set down at large in *Sleidan, l.* 6, *an.* 1526, and *l.* 11, *an.* 1537, and *l.* 13, *an.* 1540.[76] But that the magistrate either out of that church revenue which remanes yet in his hand, or e-[103]stablishing any other maintenance instead of tithe, should take into his own power the stipendiarie maintenance of church-ministers or compell it by law, can stand neither with the peoples right nor with Christian liberty, but would suspend the church wholly upon the state, and turn her ministers into state-pensioners. And for the magistrate in person of a nursing father to make the church his meer ward, as alwaies in minoritie, the church, to whom he ought as a magistrate, *Esa.* 49. 23, *To bow down with his face toward the earth, and lick up the dust of her feet,* her to subject to his political drifts [104] or conceivd opinions by mastring her revenue, and so by his examinant committies to circumscribe her free election of

---

[76] Milton often referred to the standard history of the Reformation, John Sleidan's *De statu religionis et reipublicae.* In the translation by John Daus (London, 1569), the passages mentioned here begin on fols. lxvii, cxliii, and clxx verso.

ministers, is neither just nor pious; no honor don to [77] the church, but a plane dishonor: and upon her,[78] whose only head is in heaven, yea upon him, who is her only head, sets another in effect, and, which is most monstrous, a human on a heavenly, a carnal on a spiritual, a political head on an ecclesiastical bodie; which at length by such heterogeneal, such incestuous conjunction, transformes her oft-times into a beast of many heads and many horns.[79] For if the [105] church be of all societies the holiest on earth, and so to be reverenc'd by the magistrate, not to trust her with her own belief and integritie, and therefor not with the keeping, at least with the disposing of what revenue shall be found justly and lawfully her own, is to count the church not a holy congregation, but a pack of giddy or dishonest persons, to be rul'd by civil power in sacred affairs. But to proceed further in the truth yet more freely, seeing the Christian church is not national, but consisting of many particular congregations, subject to many changes, as well [106] through civil accidents as through schism and various opinions, not to be decided by any outward judge, being matters of conscience, whereby these pretended church-revenues, as they have bin ever, so are like to continue endles matter of dissention both between the church and magistrate, and the churches among themselves, there will be found no better remedie to these evils, otherwise incurable, then by the incorruptest councel of those *Waldenses,* our first reformers, to remove them as a pest, an apple of discord in the church, (for what els can be the effect of riches and the snare of monie in re-[107]ligion?) and to convert them to those more profitable uses above expressd or other such as shall be judgd most necessarie; considering that the church of Christ was founded in poverty rather then in revenues, stood purest and prosperd best without them, receivd them unlawfully from them who both erroneously and unjustly, somtimes impiously, gave them, and so justly was ensnar'd and corrupted by them. And least it be thought that these revenues withdrawne and better imploid, the magistrate ought in stead to settle by statute som maintenance of ministers, let this be considerd first, that [108] it concerns every mans conscience to what religion he contributes; and that the civil magistrate is intrusted with civil rights only, not

[77] 1659: to to.

[78] The Church, whose head or spouse is Christ.

[79] The beast upon which the Whore of Babylon rode, Revelation 13:1 and 17:3.

with conscience, which can have no deputy or representer of it self, but one of the same minde: next, that what each man gives to the minister, he gives either as to God, or as to his teacher; if as to God, no civil power can justly consecrate to religious uses any part either of civil revenue, which is the peoples, and must save them from other taxes, or of any mans proprietie, but God by [80] special command, as he did by *Moses,* or the owner himself [109] by voluntarie intention and the perswasion of his giving it to God; forc'd consecrations out of another mans estate are no better then forc'd vowes; hateful to God, who *loves a chearful giver,*[81] but much more hateful, wrung out of mens purses to maintaine a disapprov'd ministerie against thir conscience; however, unholy, infamous and dishonorable to his ministers and the free gospel, maintaind [82] in such unworthy manner as by violence and extortion: If he give it as to his teacher, what justice or equitie compells him to pay for learning that religion which leaves freely to his choise whether [110] he will learn it or no, whether of this teacher or another, and especially to pay for what he never learnd, or approves not; whereby, besides the wound of his conscience, he becoms the less able to recompence his true teacher? Thus far hath bin enquir'd by whom church-ministers ought to be maintaind; and hath bin prov'd most natural, most equal and agreeable with scripture, to be by them who receive thir teaching; and by whom, if they be unable. Which waies well observd, can discourage none but hirelings, and will much lessen thir number in the church. [111]

It remanes lastly to consider in what manner God hath ordaind that recompence be given to ministers of the gospel: and by all scripture it will appeer that he hath given it them not by civil law and free-hold,[83] as they claim, but by the benevolence and free gratitude of such as receive them: *Luke* 10. 7, 8. *Eating and drinking such things as they give you. If they receive you, eate such things as are set before you. Matth.* 10. 7, 8. *As ye go, preach, saying, The kingdome of God is at hand, &c. Freely ye have receivd, freely give.* If God have ordaind ministers to preach freely, whether they [112] receive recompence or not, then certainly he hath forbidd both them to compell it, and others to compell it for them. But freely given, he

[80] property, unless God permits it by.

[81] From II Corinthians 9:7.

[82] The *Complete Collection* of 1698 (II, 773) punctuates: "however unholy, infamous and dishonorable to his ministers, and the free gospel maintaind . . ."

[83] Legal tenure.

accounts it as given to himself: *Phillip*. 4. 16, 17, 18. *Ye sent once
and again to my necessitie. Not because I desire a gift; but I desire
fruit that may abound to your account. Having receivd of* Epaphro-
ditus *the things which were sent from you, an odour of sweet smell,
a sacrifice acceptable, well pleasing to God.* Which cannot be from
force or unwillingness. The same is said of almes, *Heb.* 13. 16. *To
do good and to communicate, forgett not: for with such sacrifices
God is well pleasd.* Whence [113] the primitive church thought it
no shame to receive all thir maintenance as the almes of thir audi-
tors. Which they who defend tithes, as if it made for thir cause,
when as it utterly confutes them, omitt not to set down at large;
proving to our hands out of *Origen, Tertullian, Cyprian,* and others,
that the clergie livd at first upon the meer benevolence of thir hear-
ers: [84] who gave what they gave, not to the clergie, but to the
church; out of which the clergie had thir portions given them in
baskets; and were thence calld *sportularii, basket-clerks:* [85] that thir
portion was a very mean allow-[114]ance, only for a bare liveli-
hood; according to those precepts of our Saviour, *Matth.* 10. 7, *&c;*
the rest was distributed to the poore. They cite also out of *Prosper,*
the disciple of St. *Austin,* that such of the clergie as had means of
thir own, might not without sin partake of church-maintenance; not
receiving thereby food which they abound with, but feeding on the
sins of other men: that the holy ghost saith of such clergie men, they
eat the sins of my people: and that a councel at *Antioch,* in the year
340, sufferd not either priest or bishop to live on church-maintenance
without necessitie.[86] Thus [115] far tithers themselves have con-
tributed to thir own confutation, by confessing that the church livd
primitively on almes. And I add, that about the year 359, *Constan-
tius* the emperor having summond a general councel of bishops to

[84] As Spelman observes, *Larger Worke,* p. 16, "Touching their maintenance,
the means thereof arise chiefly (as appeareth by *Tertullian, Origen, Cyprian,*
and others) out of the oblations of the people, benevolences, first fruits, tithes,
etc." In *A Gospel Plea,* p. 146, Prynne recognized that the primitive church
did not tithe, but then answers arguments based on this fact.

[85] Spelman goes on (pp. 18 ff.) to consider how in the early church gifts
were presented in baskets.

[86] St. Prosper of Aquitaine supported Augustine in the Pelagian controversy.
Again Milton is answering Spelman's *Larger Worke,* pp. 27 f., which quotes a
paragraph of Prosper, who "will not suffer that a Minister able to live of
himself should participate any thing of Church goods." The paragraphs preced-
ing and following both cite the Council of Antioch (340), Canon 25, on this
issue.

Ariminum in *Italie,* and provided for thir subsistence there, the *British* and *French* bishops judging it not decent to live on the publick, chose rather to be at thir own charges.[87] Three only out of *Britain* constraind through want, yet refusing offerd assistance from the rest, accepted the emperor's provision; judging it more convenient to subsist by publick then by [116] privat sustenance. Whence we may conclude, that *bishops* then in this Iland had thir livelihood only from benevolence: in wch regard this relater *Sulpitius Severus,* a good author of the same time, highly praises them. And the *Waldenses,* our first reformers, both from the scripture and these primitive examples, maintaind those among them who bore the office of ministers, by almes only. Take thir very words from the historie written of them in *French, Part. 3. l. 2. c. 2. La nourriture & ce de quoy nous sommes couverts &c. Our food & cloathing is sufficiently administerd & given to us by way of gratuitie and almes, by the good people* [117] *whom we teach.*[88] If then by almes and benevolence, not by legal force, not by tenure of freehold or copyhold: [89] for almes, though just, cannot be compelld; and benevolence forc'd, is malevolence rather, violent and inconsistent with the gospel; and declares him no true minister therof, but a rapacious hireling rather, who by force receiving it, eats the bread of violence and exaction, no holy or just livelihood, no not civilly counted honest; much less beseeming such a spiritual ministry. But, say they, our maintenance is our due, tithes the right of Christ, unseparable from the priest, no where repeald; if [118] then, not otherwise to be had, by law to be recoverd: for though *Paul* were pleasd to forgoe his due, and not to use his power, 1 *Cor.* 9. 12,[90] yet he had a power, *v.* 4,[91] and bound not others. I answer first, because

---

[87] Milton had cited the same incident in *Of Reformation* (*Complete Prose,* I, 543), tracing it there to Sulpicius Severus's *Historia Sacra.* See *A Select Library of Nicene and Post-Nicene Fathers,* Second Series, XI, 116. The information also appears in Spelman, *Concilia,* p. 24.

[88] The quotation is from Jean Paul Perrin, *Histoire des Vaudois* (Geneva, 1619), pp. 228–29, in Part 3; the work had been translated into English as *Luthers Fore-Runners* (London, 1624), but Milton quotes directly from the original.

[89] Copyhold was a form of land tenure warranted by the manorial court; the tenant held a copy of the entry in the court roll which recorded his tenement.

[90] "If others be partakers of this power over you, are not we rather? Nevertheless we have not used this power."

[91] "Have we not the power to eat and to drink?" Prynne had argued from

I see them still so loath to unlearn thir decimal arithmetic, and still grasp thir tithes as inseparable from a priest, that ministers of the gospel are not priests; and therefor separated from tithes by thir own exclusion; being neither calld priests in the new testament, nor of any order known in scripture: not of *Melchisedec,* proper to Christ only; not of *Aaron,* as they themselves will confess; and [119] the third priesthood,[92] only remaining, is common to all the faithful. But they are ministers of our high priest. True; but not of his priesthood, as the Levites were to *Aaron:* for he performs that whole office himself incommunicably. Yet tithes remane, say they, still unreleasd, the due of Christ; and to whom payable, but to his ministers? I say again, that no man can so understand them, unless Christ in som place or other so claim them. That example of *Abram* [93] argues nothing but his voluntarie act; honor once only don, but on what consideration, whether to a priest or to a king, whether [120] due the honor, arbitrarie that kinde of honor or not, will after all contending be left still in meer conjecture: which must not be permitted in the claim of such a needy and suttle spiritual corporation pretending by divine right to the tenth of all other mens estates; nor can it be allowd by wise men or the verdit of common law. And the tenth part, though once declar'd holy, is declar'd now to be no holier then the other nine, by that command to *Peter Act.* 10. 15. 28: whereby all distinction of holy and unholy is remov'd from all things.[94] Tithes therefor though claimd, and holy under the law, yet are now re-[121]leasd and quitted both by that command to *Peter,* and by this to all ministers, above-cited *Luke* 10; *eating and drinking such things as they give you:* made holy now by thir free gift only. And therefor S. *Paul,* 1 *Cor.* 9. 4, asserts his power, indeed; but of what? not of tithes, but, *to eat and drink such things as are given* in reference to this command: which he calls not holy things or things of the gospel, as if the gospel had any consecrated things in answer to things of the temple, *v.* 13, but he calls them *your carnal things, v.* 11. without changing thir property. And what

---

this text a proof that the church has the power to require tithes (*A Gospel Plea,* pp. 41–42).

[92] That is, the priesthood of all Christian believers (see I Peter 2:5 and 9).
[93] When he met Melchizedek.
[94] In a dream Peter is told that he may eat anything, including foods defined by Mosaic law as unclean: "what God hath cleansed, that call not thou common."

power had he? not the [122] power of force but of conscience only,
whereby he might lawfully and without scruple live on the gospel;
receiving what was given him, as the recompence of his labor. For
if Christ the master hath professd his kingdom to be not of this
world,[95] it suits not with that profession either in him or his min-
isters to claim temporal right from spiritual respects. He who refus'd
to be the divider of an inheritance between two brethren,[96] cannot
approve his ministers by pretended right from him to be dividers of
tenths and freeholds out of other mens possessions, making thereby
the gospel but a cloak of carnal [123] interest, and, to the contra-
diction of thir master, turning his heavenly kingdom into a kingdom
of this world, a kingdom of force and rapin. To whom it will be one
day thunderd more terribly then to *Gehazi,* for thus dishonoring a
far greater master and his gospel, *is this a time to receive monie
and to receive garments and olive-yards and vinyards and sheep and
oxen?* [97] The leprosie of *Naaman* linkd with that apostolic curse of
perishing imprecated on *Simon Magus,* may be feard will *cleave to*
such *and to* thir *seed for ever.* So that when all is don, and bellie
hath us'd in vain all her cunning shifts, I [124] doubt not but all
true ministers, considering the demonstration of what hath bin here
prov'd, will be wise, and think it much more tolerable to hear, that
no maintenance of ministers, whether tithes or any other, can be
settl'd by statute; but must be given by them who receive instruc-
tion; and freely given, as God hath ordaind. And indeed what can
be a more honorable maintenance to them, then such whether almes
or willing oblations as these, which [98] being accounted both alike as
given to God, the only acceptable sacrifices now remaining, must
needs represent him who receives them [125] much in the care of
God and neerly related to him, when not by worldly force and con-
straint, but with religious awe and reverence, what [99] is given to
God, is given to him, and what to him, accounted as given to God.
This would be well anough, say they; but how many will so give?

[95] John 18:36.

[96] Luke 12:13–14: "And one of the company said unto him, Master, speak
to my brother, that he divide the inheritance with me. And he said to him, Man,
who made me a judge or a divider over you?"

[97] II Kings 5:26.

[98] The *Complete Collection* of 1698 (II, 775) punctuates: "than such, whether
Alms or willing Oblations, as these; which . . ."

[99] The *Complete Collection* of 1698 (II, 775) punctuates "reverence;
what . . ."

I answer, as many, doubtles, as shall be well taught; as many as
God shall so move. Why are ye so distrustful both of your own doc-
trin and of Gods promises, fulfilld in the experience of those disci-
ples first sent: *Luke 22. 35. When I sent you without purse and
scrip and shooes, lackd ye anything? And they said, Nothing.* How
[126] then came ours, or who sent them thus destitute, thus poor
and empty both of purse and faith? Who stile themselves embas-
sadors of Jesus Christ, and seem to be his tithe-gatherers, though
an office of thir own setting up to his dishonor, his exacters, his
publicans rather, not trusting that he will maintain them in thir em-
bassy, unless they binde him to his promise by a statute law that
we shall maintain them. Lay down for shame that magnific title,
while ye seek maintenance from the people: it is not the manner of
embassadors to ask maintenance of them to whom they are sent. But
he who is [127] Lord of all things, hath so ordaind: trust him then;
he doubtles will command the people to make good his promises of
maintenance more honorably unaskd, unrak'd for.[100] This they
know, this they preach, yet beleeve not: but think it as impossible
without a statute law to live of the gospel, as if by those words
they were bid go eat thir bibles, as *Ezechiel* and *John* did thir
books;[101] and such doctrins as these are as bitter to thir bellies:
but will serve so much the better to discover hirelings, who can have
nothing, though but in appearance, just and solid to answer for them-
selves against [128] what hath bin here spoken, unless perhaps this
one remaning pretence, which we shall quickly see to be either fals
or uningenuous. They pretend that thir education either at schoole
or universitie hath bin very chargeable;[102] and therefor ought to be
repar'd in future by a plentiful maintenance: whenas it is well
known that the better half of them, and oft times poor and pittiful
boyes of no merit or promising hopes that might intitle them to the
publick provision but thir povertie and the unjust favor of friends,
have had the most of thir breeding both at schoole and universitie
by schollarships, [129] exhibitions[103] and fellowships at the pub-

[100] Unsought.

[101] Ezekiel 3:1 and Revelation 10:10.

[102] Expensive. As observed above, n. 67, Prynne had made this same point in
A Gospel Plea, p. 31. It is also argued in *A Resolution of a Doubt touching
the alienation of Tithes*, pp. 10 ff., the last tract included in the collection
Tithes too hot to be Toucht, in which Spelman's *Larger Worke* also appeared.

[103] Financial support.

lick cost; which might ingage them the rather to give freely, as they
have freely receivd. Or if they have missd of these helps at the lat-
ter place, they have after two or three years left the cours of thir
studies there, if they ever well began them, and undertaken, though
furnishd with little els but ignorance, boldnes and ambition, if with
no worse vices, a chaplainship in som gentlemans house, to the fre-
quent imbasing of his sons with illiterate and narrow principles. Or
if they have livd there upon thir own, who knows not that seaven
years charge of living [130] there, to them who fly not from the
government of thir parents to the license of a universitie, but com
seriously to studie, is no more then may be well defraid and reim-
bours'd by one years revenue of an ord'nary good benifice? If they
had then means of breeding [104] from thir parents, 'tis likely they
have more now; and if they have, it needs must be mechanique [105]
and uningenuous in them to bring a bill of charges for the learning
of those liberal arts and sciences, which they have learnd (if they
have indeed learnd them, as they seldom have) to thir own benefit
and accomplishment. But [131] they will say, we had betaken us
to som other trade or profession, had we not expected to finde a
better livelihood by the ministerie. This is that which I lookd for,
to discover them openly neither true lovers of learning, and so very
seldom guilty of it, nor true ministers of the gospel. So long agoe
out of date is that old *true saying*, 1 *Tim.* 3. 1. *if a man desire a
bishoprick, he desires a good work:* for now commonly he who de-
sires to be a minister, looks not at the work but at the wages; and
by that lure or loubel [106] may be toald from parish to parish all the
town over. But what can be planer Simonie, then thus [132] to be
at charges beforehand to no other end then to make thir ministry
doubly or trebly beneficial? to whom it might be said as justly as
to that *Simon, thy monie perish with thee, because thou hast thought
that the gift of God may be purchas'd with monie: thou hast neither
part nor lot in this matter.*[107] Next, it is a fond error, though too
much beleevd among us, to think that the universitie makes a min-
ister of the gospel; what it may conduce to other arts and sciences,
I dispute not now: but that which makes fit a minister, the scrip-

[104] Education.
[105] Like a tradesman presenting his account.
[106] According to *OED*, a bell used for hunting at night which frightened
birds into motionlessness, when they might be caught.
[107] Acts 8:20–21.

ture can best informe us to be only from above; whence also we are
bid to seek [133] them; *Matth. 9. 38. Pray ye therefor to the Lord
of the harvest, that he will send forth laborers into his harvest.* Acts
20. 28. *The flock, over which the holy ghost hath made you over-
seers.* Rom. 10. 15. *How shall they preach, unless they be sent?* by
whom sent? by the universitie, or the magistrate, or thir belly? no
surely: but sent from God only, and that God who is not thir belly.
And whether he be sent from God or from *Simon Magus,* the inward
sense of his calling and spiritual abilitie will sufficiently tell him;
and that strong obligation felt within him, which was felt by the
apostle, will often express [134] from him the same words: 1 *Cor.
9. 16. Necessity is laid upon me, yea, woe is me, if I preach not the
gospel.* Not a beggarly necessity, and the woe feard otherwise of
perpetual want, but such a necessitie as made him willing to preach
the gospel *gratis,* and to embrace povertie rather then as a woe to
fear it. 1 *Cor. 12. 28. God hath set som in the church, first apostles,
&c.* Eph. 4. 11, *&c. He gave som apostles, &c. For the perfeting of
the saints, for the work of the ministerie, for the edifying of the
body of Christ, till we all come to the unitie of the faith.* Whereby
we may know that as he made them at the first, [135] so he makes
them still, and to the worlds end. 2 *Cor. 3. 6. Who hath also made
us fit or able ministers of the new testament.* 1 Tim. 4. 14. *The gift
that is in thee, which was given thee by prophesie and the laying on
of the hands of the presbyterie.* These are all the means which we
read of requir'd in scripture to the making of a minister. All this is
granted you will say: but yet that it is also requisite he should be
traind in other learning; which can be no where better had then at
universities. I answer, that what learning either human or divine can
be necessary to a minister, may as easily and less chargeably [136]
be had in any private house. How deficient els and to how little pur-
pose are all those piles of sermons, notes, and comments on all parts
of the bible, bodies and marrows of divinitie,[108] besides all other
sciences, in our English tongue; many of the same books which in
Latine they read at the universitie? And the small necessitie of going
thether to learn divinitie, I prove first from the most part of them-
selves, who seldom continue there till they have well got through
Logic,[109] thir first rudiments; though, to say truth, Logic also may

[108] Such as William Ames's *Medulla, or Marrow of Divinity (1627),* which
Milton had himself used.
[109] Part of the first-year curriculum at universities.

much better be wanting in disputes of divinitie, then in [137] the suttle debates of lawyers and statesmen, who yet seldom or never deal with syllogisms. And those theological disputations there held by Professors and graduates are such as tend least of all to the edification or capacitie of the people, but rather perplex and leaven pure doctrin with scholastical trash then enable any minister to the better preaching of the gospel. Whence we may also compute, since they com to recknings, the charges of his needful library: which, though som shame not to value at 600 l,[110] may be competently furnishd for 60 l. If any man for his own curiositie or de-[138]light be in books further expensive, that is not to be recknd as necessarie to his ministerial either breeding or function. But Papists and other adversaries cannot be confuted without fathers and councels, immense volumes and of vast charges. I will shew them therefor a shorter and a better way of confutation: *Tit.* 1. 9. *Holding fast the faithful word, as he hath bin taught, that he may be able by sound doctrin, both to exhort and to convince gain-sayers:* who are confuted as soon as heard, bringing that which is either not in scripture or against it. To persue them further through the obscure [139] and intangld wood of antiquitie, fathers and councels fighting one against another, is needles, endles, not requisite in a minister, and refus'd by the first reformers of our religion. And yet we may be confident, if these things be thought needful, let the state but erect in publick good store of libraries, and there will not want men in the church, who of thir own inclinations will become able in this kinde against Papist or any other adversarie. I have thus at large examind the usual pretences of hirelings, colourd over most commonly with the cause of learning and universities: as if with [140] divines learning stood and fell; wherin for the most part thir pittance is so small: and, to speak freely, it were much better, there were not one divine in the universitie; no schoole-divinitie known, the idle sophistrie of monks, the canker of religion; and that they who intended to be ministers, were traind up in the church only, by the scripture and [111] in the original languages therof at schoole; without fetching the compas of other arts and sciences, more then what they can well

---

[110] The author of *A Resolution of a Doubt,* p. 11, had cited this amount. Prynne, *A Gospel Plea,* p. 32, makes the same argument for financial support of the ministry but gives no sum.

[111] The *Complete Collection* of 1698 (II, 777) punctuates: "Church only by the scripture, and . . ."

learn at secondary leasure and at home. Neither speak I this in contempt of learning or the ministry, but hating [141] the common cheats of both; hating that they who have preachd out [112] bishops, prelats and canonists, should, in what serves thir own ends, retain thir fals opinions, thir Pharisaical leaven, thir avarice and closely [113] thir ambition, thir pluralities, thir nonresidences, thir odious fees, and use thir legal and Popish arguments for tithes: that Independents should take that name, as they may justly from the true freedom of Christian doctrin and church-discipline subject to no superior judge but God only, and seek to be Dependents on the magistrate for thir maintenance; which two things, independence and [142] state-hire in religion, can never consist long or certainly together. For magistrates at one time or other, not like these at present our patrons of Christian libertie, will pay none but such whom by thir committies of examination, they finde conformable to their interest and opinions: and hirelings will soone frame themselves to that interest and those opinions which they see best pleasing to thir paymasters; and to seem right themselves, will force others as to the truth. But most of all they are to be revil'd and sham'd, who cry out with the distinct voice of notorious hirelings, that if ye settle not [143] our maintenance by law, farwell the gospel: then which nothing can be utterd more fals, more ignominious, and, I may say, more blasphemous against our Saviour; who hath promisd, without this condition, both his holy spirit and his own presence with his church to the worlds end: nothing more fals (unless with thir own mouths they condemne themselves for the unworthiest and most mercenary of all other ministers) by the experience of 300. years after Christ, and the churches at this day in *France, Austria, Polonia,* and other places witnessing the contrary under an advers magistrate not a favo-[144]rable: nothing more ignominious, levelling or rather undervaluing Christ beneath *Mahomet.* For if it must be thus, how can any Christian object it to a Turk, that his religion stands by force only; and not justly fear from him this reply, yours both by force and monie in the judgment of your own preachers. This is that which makes atheists in the land, whom they so much complain of: not the want of maintenance or preachers, as they alleage, but the many hirelings and cheaters that have the gospel in thir hands;

[112] Rid the country of, from the pulpit.
[113] Secretly (*OED*).

hands that still crave, and are never satisfi'd. Likely ministers, indeed, to proclaim the [145] faith or to exhort our trust in God, when they themselves will not trust him to provide for them in the message wheron, they say, he sent them; but threaten for want of temporal means to desert it; calling that want of means, which is nothing els but the want of thir own faith; and would force us to pay the hire of building our faith to their covetous incredulitie. Doubtles, if God only be he who gives ministers to his church till the worlds end; and through the whole gospel never sent us for ministers to the schooles of Philosophie, but rather bids us beware of such *vain deceit, Col. 2. 8.* (which [146] the primitive church, after two or three ages [114] not remembring, brought herself quickly to confusion) if all the faithful be now *a holy and a royal priesthood,* 1 *Pet. 2. 5. 9,* not excluded from the dispensation of things holiest, after free election of the church and imposition of hands, there will not want ministers, elected out of all sorts and orders of men, for the Gospel makes no difference from the magistrate himself to the meanest artificer, if God evidently favor him with spiritual gifts, as he can easily and oft hath don, while those batchelor divines and doctors of the tippet [115] have bin [147] passd by. Heretofore in the first evangelic times (and it were happy for Christendom if it were so again) ministers of the gospel were by nothing els distinguishd from other Christians but by thir spiritual knowledge and sanctitie of life, for which the church elected them to be her teachers and overseers, though not thereby to separate them from whatever calling she then found them following besides, as the example of S. *Paul* declares, and the first times of Christianitie. When once they affected to be calld a clergie, and became as it were a peculiar tribe of levites, a partie, a distinct order in the [148] commonwealth, bred up for divines in babling schooles and fed at the publick cost, good for nothing els but what was good for nothing, they soone grew idle: that idlenes with fulnes of bread begat pride and perpetual contention with thir feeders the despis'd laitie, through all ages ever since; to the perverting of religion, and the disturbance of all Christendom.

---

[114] Centuries.

[115] One of the ecclesiastical vestments retained by the Anglican clergy, and particularly associated in Milton's time with the Laudian bishops: a band of silk or other stuff worn round the neck, with two ends hanging in front from the shoulders.

And we may confidently conclude, it never will be otherwise while they are thus upheld undepending on the church, on which alone they anciently depended, and are by the magistrate publickly maintaind a numerous faction [149] of indigent persons, crept for the most part out of extream want and bad nurture, claiming by divine right and freehold the tenth of our estates, to monopolize the ministry as their peculiar,[116] which is free and open to all able Christians, elected by any church. Under this pretence exempt from all other imployment, and inriching themselves on the publick, they last of all prove common incendiaries, and exalt thir horns [117] against the magistrate himself that maintains them, as the priest of *Rome* did soone after against his benefactor the emperor,[118] and the presbyters of late in *Scotland*.[119] Of which [150] hireling crew together with all the mischiefs, dissentions, troubles, warrs meerly of their kindling, Christendom might soone rid herself and be happie, if Christians would but know thir own dignitie, thir libertie, thir adoption,[120] and let it not be wonderd if I say, thir spiritual priesthood, whereby they have all equally access to any ministerial function whenever calld by thir own abilities and the church, though they never came neer commencement or universitie. But while Protestants, to avoid the due labor of understanding thir own religion are content to lodge it in the breast or rather in the books [151] of a clergie man, and to take it thence by scraps and mammocks [121] as he dispences it in his sundays dole, they will be alwaies learning and never knowing, alwaies infants, alwaies either his vassals, as laypapists are to their priests, or at odds with him, as reformed principles give them som light to be not wholly conformable, whence infinit disturbances in the state, as they do, must needs follow. Thus much I had to say; and, I suppose, what may be anough to them who are not avariciously bent otherwise, touching the likeliest means to remove hirelings out of the church; then which no-[152]thing

[116] As exclusive to themselves.

[117] This phrase, used several times in I Samuel and Psalms, usually means to rise in power.

[118] Constantine.

[119] The most recent difficulties with Scotland had taken place in the summer of 1653, when the meeting of the Presbyterian General Assembly in Edinburgh had to be forcibly adjourned. But there were no serious troubles with the group towards the end of the decade, when *Hirelings* was published.

[120] By God into the priesthood of believers.

[121] Shreds.

can more conduce to truth, to peace and all happines both in church and state. If I be not heard nor beleevd, the event will bear me witnes to have spoken truth: and I in the mean while have borne my witnes not out of season to the church and to my countrey.

The end. [153]

A LETTER TO A FRIEND,
CONCERNING THE RUPTURES
OF THE COMMONWEALTH

October 20, 1659

PREFACE AND NOTES BY ROBERT W. AYERS

A *Letter to a Friend, Concerning the Ruptures of the Commonwealth* was so titled when first published in *A Complete Collection of the Historical, Political, and Miscellaneous Works of John Milton* (3 vols., Amsterdam [London], 1698), II, 779–81. It was printed there from a manuscript which John Toland had from a friend, who had it from Milton's nephew, and which Toland "imparted . . . to the Publishers of the new Edition."[1] A slightly different and apparently prior version appears on pp. 21–23 of the Columbia Manuscript.[2] Both texts are dated at the end, October 20, 1659.

Occasioned by Milton's discussion, with a friend, of Lambert's *coup d'état* of October 13, the letter first recalls events which have brought the nation to its present peril within the single year since Cromwell's death on September 3, 1658: (1) the Declaration of the Officers of the Army (May 6, 1659) in which—after having forced dissolution of Richard's Parliament on April 22—the officers confessed "their backsliding from the good old cause" and called for restoration of the Rump, the "old famous parlament, which they had without just autority dissolved" in 1653; (2) Lambert's "signall victory" over the royalist "Cheshire Rebells" under Booth in August; (3) the army's acknowledgment of the Rump as "the supreme authority of these nations" in the Derby Petition of mid-September and the Humble Representation and Petition of October

---

[1] Toland, *Life of Milton*, in *A Complete Collection*, 1698, I, 37.

[2] Phillipps 3993, Columbia University Library shelf number X823M64/S62; contents listed, French, IV, 277–80; see also Maurice Kelley, *Complete Prose*, I, 954–57. All printings of the *Letter* prior to the present one, including that in Columbia *Works* (text, ed. William Haller, VI, 101–06, notes, VI, 357) have reproduced the Toland text.

5; (4) the "intentions against the parlament" intimated by the officers' epistolary solicitation of additional signatures to the Humble Representation and Petition after its rejection by the Rump; (5) the subsequent and consequent "discommissioning [on October 12 of the] nine great officers in the Army" who had undertaken the solicitation; and finally, (6) the army's retaliatory subdual of the "supreme power that sett them up" in Lambert's action of October 13.

Turning in the latter portion of the *Letter* to the desperate question of "what remedies may be likelyest to save us from approaching ruine," Milton articulates the basic ideas which were to be developed through the *Proposalls of Certaine Expedients* to their fullest and most urgent expression in the two editions of the *Readie & Easie Way*. While castigating the army's *coup* as motivated by the "close ambition" of certain officers, he realistically acknowledges what could not be denied, that the army "only now have the power." But since the army is unable to discharge at once both military and civil offices, the nation is now in anarchy, and what is needed is a "counselling & governing power," a senate or general council of state. For this purpose, Milton proposes reconvening the Rump, or so many among the Rumpers as may be reliably dedicated to two essential principles: "Liberty of conscience to all professing Scripture the rule of their faith & worship, And the Abjuracion of a single person." Both officers and councilmen should be kept in their places for life. Other reforms are regarded as of secondary importance; unless these matters are first settled, Milton anticipates ruin or servitude under a single person, "the secret author & fomenter of all these disturbances."

TEXTUAL NOTE: *A LETTER TO A FRIEND*

The text which follows is that of the Columbia Manuscript, with all contractions except the ampersand expanded, but with spellings otherwise unaltered. Selected and possibly significant variants from the Toland text appear in the notes.

I wish to acknowledge the expert aid of Mrs. Laetitia Yaendle, Curator of Manuscripts at the Folger Shakespeare Library.

ROBERT W. AYERS

Georgetown University

A LETTER TO A FRIEND

Sɪʀ[1] upon the sad & serious discourse which we fell into last night[2] concerning these dangerous ruptures of the common wealth, scarce yet in her infancy, which cannot be without some in ward flaw in her bowells, I began to consider more intensly thereon then hitherto I have bin wont resigni[n]g my selfe to the wisedome & care of those who had[3] the government, & not finding that either God or the publick required more of me then my prayers for them that govern. And since you have not only stirred up my thoughts by acquai[n]ting me with the state of affaires more inwardly[4] then I knew before, but also have desired me to set downe my opinion thereof, trusting to your ingenuity, I shall give you freely my apprehension both of our present evills & what expedients (if God in mercy regard us) may remove them. I will begin with telling you how I was overjoyed, when I heard that the Army under the working of Gods holy spiritt, as I thought & still hope well, had bin so far wrought to Christian humility & self-denyall, as to confesse in publick their backsliding from the good old cause, & to shew the fruits of their repentance in the righteousnesse of their restoring the old famous parlament, which they had without just autority dissolved.[5] I call it the famous parlament, though not the blame-

---

[1] The addressee has not been identified. Masson (V, 618; see also Barker, *Milton and the Puritan Dilemma*, pp. 260, 393) suggests Vane or Sir Philip Meadows, but these are unlikely. Meadows was not close enough to the center of affairs or weighty enough politically to have played the part Milton suggests here. There is no independent evidence whatsoever of contact or communication between Vane and Milton during this period, and Vane was, indeed, in continuing close touch with Lambert. See discussion by Woolrych, introduction, above, p. 121, which advances another possibility—the dying John Bradshaw.

[2] Presumably the night of October 19, 1659, since the text is dated October 20.

[3] Prior to October 13, the Rump; at the time of writing, Lambert and the army.

[4] An indication that the friend was privy to events and the inner workings of the government.

[5] Under pressure from the army led by Fleetwood, Richard Cromwell was forced to order the dissolution of his Parliament, and the session ended on the morning of April 22, 1659. For two weeks or so, no one knew what form of government would be imposed upon the nation, but it gradually became evident to the officers that since the army and the Long Parliament had together been re-

lesse,[6] since none well affected but will confesse, they have deserved much more of these nations, then they have undeserved. And I perswade me that God was pleased with their restitution, signing it as he did, with such a signall victory, when so great a part of the nation were desperately conspir'd to call back again their Egyptian bondage. So much the more it now amazes mee that they whose lips were yet scarce clos'd from giveing thanks for that great deliverance should be now relapsing & so soon again backsliding into the same fault which they confessed so lately & so solemnly to god & the world & more lately punished in those Cheshire Rebells,[7] that they should ∧ dissolve that parlament which they themselves reestab-

now

---

sponsible for the execution of Charles and the establishment of a free state in 1649, now in 1659 the two must stand together, or together fall. Accordingly, on Friday, May 6, in "A Declaration of the Officers of the Army" (*Somers Tracts*, VI, 505), the officers, "led to look back, and examine the cause of the Lord's withdrawing his wonted presence from us," admitted that they themselves had contributed to the present vicissitudes "by wandering divers ways, from righteous and equal paths," so that "the Good Old Cause itself"—i.e., a pure and absolute republic such as had existed from 1649 until Cromwell dissolved it in April, 1653 —"became a reproach." Acknowledging that the Long Parliament—consisting of the members who continued there sitting until April 20, 1653—"were eminent assertors of that cause, and had a special presence of God with them," they invited those members to return "to the exercise and discharge of their trust." See Woolrych, introduction, above, pp. 66–76, for detailed discussion of these events.

[6] Toland: harmles.

[7] Although the fall of the Protectorate in the person of Richard and the recall of the Rump on May 6, 1659 had seemed to royalists dismal and desperate changes, their hopes soon began to feed on the evident and extreme factionalism in the Rump, the army, and the republicans; and supporters of Charles began to aspire to armed insurrection. By early June the Council of State knew a great deal concerning royalist plans, and had in fact undertaken precautionary measures such as the arrest of notable conspirators and reinforcement of the army in areas where it was known there would be uprisings. But no such measures were undertaken in Cheshire, where Sir George Booth, in earlier times a valiant supporter of the Parliamentary cause, led a fleetingly successful revolt and seized Chester in the early morning of August 2. Hearing of this rebellion, the Rump with some hesitation appointed Lambert commander in chief of a force assigned to counter Booth. After slight casualties, Lambert prevailed at Winnington Bridge on August 19, and on August 24 captured Booth himself, in women's clothes, at Newport Pagnell. See David Underdown, *Royalist Conspiracy in England 1649–1660* (New Haven: Yale University Press, 1960), pp. 254–85; J. R. Jones, "Booth's Rising of 1659," *Bulletin of the John Rylands Library*, XXXIX (1956–57), 413–43; Woolrych, introduction, above, pp. 107–09.

lished & acknowledged for the [8] supreme power in thir other dayes humble representacion: [9] & all this for no apparent cause of publick concernment to the Church or commonwealth, but only for the [10] discommissioning of [11] nine great officers in the Army; which had not bin done [21] as is reported, but upon notice of their intentions against the parlament.[12] I presume not to give my censure

[8] Toland: thir.

[9] The "Humble Representation and Petition of the Officers of the Army to the Parliament of the Commonwealth of England," October 5, 1659 (text in Baker, *Chronicle,* pp. 679–81). See below, n. 12.

[10] Toland omits.

[11] Toland omits.

[12] Following defeat of the Cheshire rebels, about mid-September, 1659, some fifty officers of Lambert's force at Derby met to consider how they might best exploit their victory; to this end, three of the group—apparently without consulting Lambert—set to drafting the Derby Petition, which has been described (Davies, *Restoration,* p. 147) as "the spark which started the conflagration that destroyed the Commonwealth." Addressed to "the supreme authority of these nations, the Parliament of the Commonwealth of England," in it the officers "aspersed the Parliament for not endeavouring to suppress the late rebellion with such vigour as they ought, for not punishing those who had been engaged in it, and for not rewarding the officers who had defeated the enemy. They pressed for a settlement of the government after their own mode, in a representative of the people, and a select senate. And for the better discovery of their arbitrary designs, they demanded that Lieutenant-General Fleetwood might be made Commander-in-Chief of the army . . . Col. Lambert appointed Major-General, Col. Desborow Lieutenant-General of the Horse, and Col. Monk Major-General of the Foot. To which they added, that no officer of the army should be dismissed from his command, unless by a court martial" (Ludlow, II, 118). Parliament's rash response was to order Fleetwood to admonish the officers for their irregular proceedings and to resolve that "to have any more general officers in the army than are already settled by the Parliament is needless, chargeable, and dangerous to the Commonwealth" (Ludlow, II, 118, n.). The results of Fleetwood's subsequent meeting with the officers were the direct opposite of those intended by the Rump, and the public silence which had prevailed since the officers' meeting of September 23 was broken on October 5, when Desborough headed a group of officers who presented yet another petition —the "Humble Representation and Petition of the Officers of the Army to the Parliament of the Commonwealth of England." This was actually a very unhumble document, which, after what Ludlow describes (II, 135, 136) as "specious promises of obedience," went on to make a number of demands, "most of which," he says, "were as absurd for the army to ask, as for the Parliament to grant."

The Rump was itself in an uncompromising mood, and its determination was stiffened when, during its consideration of this latest petition, it learned that Lambert, Desborough, and seven other officers were by letter soliciting additional signatures to the Derby Petition. By a large majority the Rump im-

upon [13] this action, not knowing, as I [14] doe not, the bottome of
it. I speak only what it appeares to us without doors, till better
cause be declared, & I am confident [15] to all other nacions most ille-
gall & scandalous, I fear me barbarous, or ^ rather scarce ~~not~~ to be
exampled among any Barbarians, that a paid army should for no
other cause, thus subdue the supreme power that sett them up. this
I say other nacions will judge to the sad dishonour of that army
lately so renowned for the civilest & best ordered in the world, & by
us here at home for the most conscientious. Certainly if the great
officers & soldiers of the Holland, French, or Venetian forces should
thus sitt in Councell & write from garison to garison against their
superiors, they might as easily reduce the King of France, or Duke
of Venice & put the United provinces into like confusion.[16] why do
they not being most of them held ignorant of trew religion? because
the light of Nature, the Lawes of Humane Society, the reverence of
their Magistrates, covenants, engagements, loyalty, allegiance keeps
them in awe. How greivous will it then be, how infamous to the true
religion which [we] [17] professe, how dishonourable to the Name of
God, that his fear & the power of his Knowledge in an Army pro-
fessing to be his, should not work that obedience, that fidelity to their
supreme Magistrates, that levied them, & payed them, which [18] the
light of Nature, the lawes of Humane society, covenant & contract,[19]
yea common shame works in other Armies, among [20] the worst of

---

mediately stripped of their commissions the nine officers who had signed the
objectionable letter, removed Fleetwood from his command, and put the army
under a commission of seven members, who ordered the regiments of Morley
and Moss to occupy the Parliamentary precincts and guard them against an an-
ticipated move by the army. Lambert recognized the challenge, accepted it,
and called together the dismissed officers. They decided to expel the Rump, and
on the morning of October 13 an army unit which had lain in a nearby church-
yard overnight surrounded the Parliamentary guard and turned back members
of the Rump attempting to reach the House. See further, introduction, above,
pp. 112–17.

[13] Toland: on.
[14] Toland: as yet I.
[15] Toland: sure.
[16] Toland: in like Disorder and Confusion.
[17] From Toland.
[18] Toland: when.
[19] Toland: Covenants, and Contracts.
[20] Toland: amongst.

Men.[21] Which will undoubtedly pull downe the heavy judgments [22] of God among us, who cannot but avenge these hypocrisies & violacions [23] of truth & holynesse, if they be indeed so, as they yett seeme. For neither do I speak this in reproach to the Army, but as Jealous of their honour, inciting them to manifest & publish with all speed some better cause of these their late acions, then hath hitherto

appeared,[24] & to finde out that Achan [25] among [26] them whose ~~secret~~ close

[21] Toland: them?

[22] Toland: Judgment.

[23] Toland: Hypocrisies, Violations.

[24] In *Mercurius Politicus,* October 27–November 3, 1659, p. 833, date October 27, it was reported that "[The General Council] agreed upon a Declaration, Entituled, *A Declaration of the General Council of the Officers of the Army,* and ordered it to be forthwith printed and published."

The text of the *Declaration,* "Concerning the Grounds and Reasons of the late Actings, and of their Intentions as to their future proceedings," asserts that it was in order "that a full and through [*sic*] Reformation of the Law may be effected, as also that a Faithful godly, and painful gospel-preaching Ministery [*sic*] may be encouraged and provided for, by some certain way that may be less troublesome to them, and less vexatious to the people, than that of Tithes." (So see *Hirelings,* above, pp. 294 ff.).

"And we do further Declare, That we have no aim or ends to set up a Military or Arbitrary Government over this Commonwealth; but have already provided that the Civil and Executive part of Government may be lodged in a Committee of safety, and they obliged in a short time, to prepare such a form of Government, as may best suit and comport with a free State and Commonwealth, without a Single Person, King-ship or House of Peers." Dated October 29, 1659, p. 834.

[25] Achan ("troubler"), son of Carmi, of the tribe of Judah (Joshua 7:1). Joshua (7:8–12) learns that the defeat at Ai was due to the transgression of Jahweh's covenant by Achan, who, after an inquiry, is singled out as the transgressor. Achan confesses that after the capture of Jericho he had hidden part of the spoil, the whole of which had been placed under the ban—i.e., devoted to Jahweh, and was therefore unlawful for men to touch. Both he and his family are stoned to death and burned.

The allusion had appeared prominently in Cromwell's "Declaration for a Solemn Fast" (Proclamation, March 14, 1656, BM Press Mark 669f20(25), ref. Gardiner, *Commonwealth and Protectorate,* IV, 264). Therein Cromwell desired that the people would apply themselves to the Lord, "to discover that Achan which had so long obstructed the settlement of these distracted nations."

Vane, replying to Cromwell's "Declaration" in *Healing Question* (March, 1656; reprinted *Somers Tracts,* VI, 304–13, esp. 310), strongly implied that Cromwell himself was Achan: "Nay, if in stead of favouring and promoting the peoples common good and welfare, self-interest and private gain should evidently appear to be the things we have aimed at all along; if those very tyrannical principles and antichristian reliques which God by us hath punished in

ambition in all likelyhood abuses their honest natures against their meaning to these disorders, the [27] readiest way to bring in again the Common enemie, & with him the destrucion of true religion & civill liberty. But because our evills are now growne more dangerous & extreme then to be remedied by complaints, it concernes us now to finde out what remedies may be likelyest to save us from approaching ruine. Being now in Anarchy without a counselling & governing power & the Army I suppose finding themselves insufficient to discharge at once both military & civill offices,[28] the 1st thing to be found out with all speed, without which no common wealth can subsist, must be a senate or generall Councell of State in whome must be the power 1st to preserve the publick peace, next the commerce with forraigne nacions, & lastly to raise moneys for the manageing [29] of these affaires. This must be either the parlament readmitted to sitt, or a councell of State,[30] allowed of by the Army since they only now have the power.

---

our predecessors, should again revive, spring up afresh, and shew themselves lodged also and retained in our bosomes, rendring us of the number of those that have forgot they were purged from their old sins, and declaring us to be such as to please a covetous mind, do withhold from destruction that which God hath designed to the curse of his vengeance. If all those great advantages of serving the Lords will and design in procuring and advancing his peoples true welfare and outward safety, which (as the fruit of his blessing upon our armies) have so miraculously fallen into our hands, shall at last be wrested and mis-improved to the enriching and greatning of our selves: If these things should ever be found amongst us, (which the Lord in mercy forbid) shall we need to look any further for the accursed thing? . . . And did the action of Achan import any more than these two things? First, he saved and kept from destruction the goodly Babylonish garment, which was devoted by God thereunto. Secondly, he brought not in the fruit and gain of the conquest into the Lords treasure, but covetously went about to convert it to his own proper use. To do this is to take of the accursed thing, which (Josh. 7) all Israel was said to do in the sin of Achan, and to have stolen and dissembled likewise, and to put it amongst their own stuffe. This caused the anger of the Lord to kindle against Israel, and made them unable to stand before their enemies, but their hearts melted as water. And thus far the Lord is concerned, if such an evil as this shall lie hid in the midst of us."

Milton's use of the allusion here seems to be a thrust at Lambert.

[26] Toland: amongst.

[27] Toland: thir.

[28] Toland: Affairs.

[29] Toland: Management.

[30] Milton's terminology changes between *Letter to a Friend* and *Readie & Easie Way*. Here "Councell of State" means roughly the same as Senate in

The termes to be stood on are Liberty of conscience to all professing Scripture the [31] rule of their faith & worship, And the Abjuracion of a single person. If the parlament be again thought on, to salve honour on both sides, the well affected partie of the citie, & the congregated churches may be induc'd to mediate by publick addresses & brotherly beseechings, which if there be that Saintship among us which is talked of, ought to be of highest & undeniable persuasion to a reconcilement. If the parlament be thought well dissolv'd, as not complyeing fully to grant liberty of conscience & the necessary consequence thereof, The Removall of a forc't maintenance [32] from Ministers, then must the Army forthwith chuse a councell of State, whereof as many to be of the parlament as are undoubtedly affected to these two condicions proposed. That which I conceive only able to ciment & unite for ever the Army either to the parlament recall'd, or this chosen councell, must be a mutuall league & oath private or publick not to desert one another till death: that is to say, that the Army be kept up & all these officers in their places during life,[33] & so likewise the parlament men or counsellors of State; which wilbe no

Readie & Easie Way: a sovereign assembly, preferably with life membership. In *Readie & Easie Way,* the Council of State is to be a (smaller) executive board, subordinate to the Senate in the way that the Rump's Council of State had been subordinate to Parliament. See *Readie & Easie Way,* below, pp. 368 and 433 for this and for similar statements concerning the responsibilities and functions of the sovereign assembly. See also Woolrych, introduction, above, p. 132, for discussion of the degree to which the Committee of Safety of October–December, 1659, conformed to Milton's alternative proposal here.

[31] Toland: Scripture to be the. This sentence begins a new paragraph without indentation.

[32] After dissolution of Richard's Parliament on April 22, 1659, and restoration of the Rump on May 7, in June powerful popular pressures produced a campaign of petitions against tithes. One asked whether it was any part of the Lord's work "To set the Magistrate in Christs throne to try and judge who are fit to be his Ministers, and to send out and restraine whom he thinks fit, and to force a maintenance for them, even from those that for conscience sake cannot hear them, nor own them" [*The Copie of a Paper Presented to the Parliament,* June 29, 1659, E988(24)]. On receiving it the House resolved that "the Payment of Tythes shall continue as now they are unless this Parliament shall find out some other more equal and comfortable Maintenance, both for the Ministry, and Satisfaction of the People" (*Commons Journals,* VII, 694). See more fully, Woolrych, introduction, above, pp. 74–76.

[33] Considering the conduct of the army in the spring, summer, and fall of 1659, and Milton's severe strictures against its leaders earlier in the letter, such a grant of life tenure of their commands would have been indeed a desperate and potentially dangerous expedient.

wayes [34] unjust considering their knowne merits on either side in councell or in feild; unless any be found false to either [35] of those two principles, or otherwise personally criminous in the judgment of both parties. If such Union [36] as this be not accepted on the Armies part, be confident there is a single person [37] working [38] underneath. That the Army be upheld, the necessity of our affairs & factions will constraine long enough perhaps to content the longest liver in the Army. And whether the civill government be an annuall democracy or a perpetuall Aristocracy,[39] is too nice [40] a consideracion for the extremities [22] wherein wee are & the hazard of our safety from a [41] common enemie, gapeing at present to devour us.

That it be not an Oligarchy or the faction of a few, may be easily prevented by the numbers of their owne chusing. who may be found infallibly constant to those conditions afore nam'd.[42] Full liberty of conscience, & the abjuracion of Monarchy propos'd: & the well ordered committies [43] of their faithfullest adherents in every county [44] may give this government the resemblance & effects of a perfect democracie. As for the reformacion of lawes & the places of judica-

[34] Toland: way.

[35] Toland: any.

[36] Toland: such a Union.

[37] As in the Achan passage (above, n. 25), presumably Lambert, but conceivably Richard Cromwell, whose interest might be supported by frustrated army leaders.

[38] Toland omits.

[39] By the following February and March Milton had come to feel that the question was no longer "too nice," but in fact central to the problems of the nation. He therefore argued in both editions of *Readie & Easie Way* that the Senate should be perpetual. See below, pp. 369, 433.

[40] Toland: not to me.

[41] Toland: our.

[42] Toland: those two Conditions forenam'd. This sentence seems conclusive that Milton had in mind a considerably larger national assembly than the twenty-three of the Committee of Safety of October–December. See discussion by Woolrych, above, pp. 132–33.

[43] Milton came to regret the terminology, and said in the second edition of *Readie & Easie Way* (below, p. 443) that "the people then will have thir several ordinarie assemblies (which will henceforth quite annihilate the odious power and name of Committies) in the chief towns of every countie." In both editions of the *Readie & Easie Way* he indicated that these assemblies would be made up of the "nobilitie and chief gentry." See below, pp. 383 and 458, and Woolrych, above, p. 122.

[44] See *Readie & Easie Way,* below, pp. 383, 458.

ture, whether to be here, as at present, or in every county as hath bin long aim'd,[45, 46] & many other [47] such proposalls, tending no doubt to publick good, they may be considered in due time, when we are passed these pernicious pangs in a hopefull way of health & firme constitution. But unlesse these things which I have above propos'd one way or other be 1st [48] settled, in my fear, which god avert, we instantly ruine; or at best become the servants of one or other single person, the secret author & fomenter of all [49] these disturbances. You have the summe of my present thoughts on [50] as much as I understand of these affaires, freely imparted at your request, & the persuasion which you wrought in mee that I might chance hereby to be some way serviceable to the commonwealth in a time when all ought to be endeavoring what good they can whether much or but little. With this you may doe what you please: [51] put out, put in, communicate, or suppresse; you offend not mee who only have obeyed your opinion, that in doing what I have done, I might happen to offer something which might be ∧ of some use in this great time of need However I have not bin wanting to the opportunity which you presented to [52] mee of shewing the readynesse which I have in the

---

[45] Toland: aim'd at.

[46] Popular courts in every county or hundred had been a prominent plank in the Leveller platform; and the demand had continued after the decline of the Leveller movement; so see Richard Overton, *An Appeale* [July 17, 1647; E398(28)], reprinted in *Leveller Manifestoes*, ed. Don M. Wolfe (New York, 1944), pp. 156–95, esp. p. 190; *A Letter . . . Concerning . . . An Agreement of the People* [January 20, 1649; reprinted July 23, 1649; 669f14(59)], reprinted *ibid.*, pp. 333–54, esp. p. 353. See further, Henry Robinson, *Certaine Considerations in Order to a More Speedy, Cheap, and Equall Distribution of Justice* [November 14, 1650; E616(22)]; James Freze, *A Moderate Inspection into the Corruption of the Pratique Part of the Common Law* [June 17, 1656; E882(4)]; *England's Safety in the Law's Supremacy* [June 23, 1659; E988 (13)]; William Cole, *A Rod for the Lawyers, Who are Hereby Declared to Be the Grand Robbers and Deceivers of the Nation* [July 12, 1659; E989(15)], p. 13. See also, Stuart E. Prall, *The Agitation for Law Reform During the Puritan Revolution: 1640–1660* (The Hague: Martinus Nijhoff, 1966), pp. 55, 128–29, 137, 138.

[47] Toland omits.

[48] Toland: once.

[49] Toland omits.

[50] Toland omits.

[51] An almost certain indication that the letter was intended as a private com-

midst of my unfitnesse to what ever may be required of mee as a publick dutie.

J. M.[53]

Octob. 20th.[54]
1659. [23]

---

munication. *Cf.* Woolrych, above, p. 120: "It sounds as though Milton were furnishing a man nearer the center of affairs with matter for a speech or writing of his own, but he may well have kept a copy with the idea of circulating it more widely or of working up its proposals at greater length."

[52] Toland: before.
[53] Toland omits.
[54] Toland: 20.

PROPOSALLS OF CERTAINE EXPEDIENTS FOR THE PREVENTING OF A CIVILL WAR NOW FEARD, & THE SETTLING OF A FIRME GOVERNMENT

October 20–December 26, 1659

PREFACE AND NOTES BY MAURICE KELLEY

Proposalls of Certaine Expedients appears in the Columbia Manuscript,[1] pp. 19–21, and seems to be the fourth of Milton's writings on the ecclesiastical and civil problems vexing the English government on the eve of the Restoration. Zera S. Fink[2] dates the *Proposalls* after *A Letter to a Friend*, October 20, 1659, but before Parliament resumed its sitting on December 26 of the same year. Scholars have described the essay as a draft of *The Readie & Easie Way*[3] or as an independent tract,[4] with Mabbott and French[5] suggesting that Sir Roger L'Estrange's reference in *No Blinde Guides,* 1660, to a *"Proposalls of the benefits of a Free-State"* by Milton may indicate a printed edition, now lost, in late 1659 or early 1660.

---

[1] Described and discussed in *Complete Prose* I, 954–57, and French, *Life Records,* IV, 277–80.

[2] "The Date of Milton's Proposalls for a Firme Government," *MLN,* LV (1940), 407–10. Barbara Lewalski ("Milton: Political Beliefs and Polemical Methods, 1659–60," *PMLA,* LXXIV [1959], 194) tacitly accepts Fink's dating. For October 27–December 24, see Woolrych, above, pp. 139–42. If either date is correct, then the Columbia Manuscript scribe did not enter the *Proposalls* in its proper chronological order, for it (pp. 19–21) precedes rather than follows *A Letter to a Friend* (pp. 21–23).

[3] *Book Auction Records,* XVIII (1920–21), 534.

[4] Columbia Milton, XVIII, 501. Fink (*MLN,* LV [1940], 409) does not attempt to resolve the matter.

[5] "Milton's 'Proposalls of Certaine Expedients,' 1659," *N&Q,* CLXXIII (1937), 66.

Although perhaps referred to as early as 1836,[6] the *Proposalls* did not receive modern editing until the Columbia Milton (XVIII, 3–7), where except for three errors in spelling and the silent expansion of abbreviations, the text is commendably correct. Our text is a new transcript of the manuscript, with all abbreviations except the ampersand expanded. The punctuation, though lacking by modern and perhaps seventeenth-century standards, is that appearing in the manuscript.

I wish to acknowledge the expert aid of Mrs. Laetitia Yaendle, Curator of Manuscripts at the Folger Shakespeare Library.

MAURICE KELLEY

Princeton University

[6] *Gentleman's Magazine,* n.s. VI, 462.

Proposalls of certaine expedients for the preventing of a civill war now feard, & the settling of a firme government by J.M.

FIRST to lay before them in power the scorne we are to forreigne nacions by these our continuall changes; & the danger we are in, not only from the common enemy at home, but from two potent kingdomes abroad Spaine & France by most certaine intelligence, designing with joynt forces a speedy invasion of this Iland. Whose united power we should have much adoe to resist, though all united & settled among our selves; but in this distracted anarchy without confederates & such condicion as none will treat with us, wee cannot hope to withstand.

2.dly that the present committee of safety do go on with all vigour & watchfulnesse to provide for the publick safety both at home & from abroad, & hasten as much as may be the settling of som firme & durable government.

3.dly in regard that no government is like to continue unlesse founded upon the publick autority & consent of the people which is the parlament the only probable way in all appearance can be, & the only prevention of this civill war now at point to ensue, that the parlament be again treated with to sitt on these following condicions. [19] That they begin 1.st with an Act of oblivion for what is past between them & the Army.

2.dly that the main condicions of their agreement be full liberty of conscience to all who professe their faith & worship by the scriptures only, & against single government by any one person in cheif & house of Lords.

3.dly that a former Act of their owne be reinforced, whereby they sitt indissolubly, & that they & all henceforth to be chosen into the parlament do retaine their places during life, unlesse by particular faults they deserve removall.for although Magistracies be annuall in most commonwealths yet the place of Senator hath bin always during life both in Rome, Venice, & elsewhere: the Senate being the basis & foundacion of government; which cannot be moveable without great danger to the whole building, & especially in this common wealth & in our condicion not without just fear of novelties & commocions upon every chang of parliament.

4.^ly that the par[la]ment having thus resolved, do confirm the continuance of this Army, & all the cheif officers thereof in their places also during life, together with successive advancement, as superior places shalbe vacant; which must needs content them who are not unreasonable, & remove ambition the comon cause of disturbance. & they may the more willingly from the highest to the lowest souldier of them take an oath of obedience to the supreme autority, unlesse that fall off from the two maine principles above named, Liberty of conscience, & the other against a single person & house of Lords.

5. because the name of parlament is a Norman or French word,[1] a monument of our Ancient Servitude, commonly held to consist necessarily of 3. Estates, King, Lords, & commons; [2] & the two latter to be called by the King to parlie with him about the great affairs of his

realme, it might be very agreeable with our freedome to ∧ the *chang* name of parliament (especially now having outlived its honour by soe many dissolucions) into the name of a Grand or Supreme Counsell: whose power may be in a manner the same with that of parlaments, to make lawes, peace, war, league, & treatie with forreigne nacions to raise taxes,[3] coyne mony & the like which have bin formerly called regalities.

6. that the Elecions of them who shall here after sit in this supreme councell may be of such as are certainly known to have besides their ability, the two qualificacions above named, & to the persisting in them shall take their oath, whither they be nominated by the grand Councell, & elected by the well affected [4] people, or nominated by

[1] *Cf. History of Britain, Complete Prose,* V, 377: "Then began the English to lay aside thir own antient Customes, and in many things to imitate French manners, the great Peers to speak French in thir Houses, in French to write thir Bills and Letters, as a great peece of Gentility, asham'd of thir own: a presage of thir subjection shortly to that people, whose fashions and language they affected so slavishly."

[2] *Cf. Articles of Peace, Complete Prose,* III, 314–15; "As for Parlaments by three Estates, wee know that a Parlament signifies no more then the Supream and generall Councell of a Nation, consisting of whomsoever chos'n and assembld for the public good; which was ever practis'd, and in all sorts of Government, before the word *Parlament,* or the formality, or the possibility of those three Estates, or such a thing as a Titular Marquess had either name or being in the World."

[3] "taxes" seems first begun as "tal" or "tas."

[4] Well disposed toward existing authority. Perhaps a Civil War development: the first *NED* citation is 1643; and for 1659–60 usages, see Lewalski, *PMLA,* LXXIV (1959), 193, n. 16; 194, n. 25.

those of the people & elected by the grand Councell. The people also, especially such as look to be entrusted with offices or places of advantage & elections in the Common wealth, should be enjoyned by oath to the same two principles.

7. that the number of those who are to be of the grand counsell be so many as shalbe judged sufficient to carry on the great affaires committed to them, & in regard they are to sitt during life, & perhaps not without Salary, & lastly for the more honour & Majesty of so great a councell it may perhaps be thought requisite, if there should be any among them, they who are generally knowne & judged insufficient or otherwise a disparagement that such be dismissed & worthier chosen in their roome, but this is not urged, lest it be misinterpreted.

8. that the supreme councell chuse out of their owne number & to them, if it be thought fit, some others also of eminent ability, to be a councell of State, with the same power which it had under the parlament, & to the same intents.

9. that both councells do deale as little as may be with the execution of lawes, but leave that to the severall [20] appointed Magistrates; & both maintenance of Minist[ers] & all matters Ecclesiasticall to the church in her severall congregacions: by which meanes they shall rid their hands of much trouble & businesse not appertai[n]ing to them, furder then to defend religion from outward violence, which wilbe an undoubted cause of great peace and quietnesse among us, & of great ease & health to themselves, by many dayes of leasure & intermission from the toile of their constant sitting.

10. & lastly, that the administration of Civill Justice may be in the City or cheif towne of every county without appeal, Judges & all such officers by themselves chosen, whereby they shall have no cause to clamour against the supreame Councell, nor can hope for more equall Justice in any other place. As for those of severall Countyes who have causes & suites, there may be still a common Judicature, as ther is here, in the Capitall citty.

Other particulars might be mencioned, as the reforming of som nationall lawes, the liberty to erect [5] schooles where all arts & sciences may be taught in every citty & great towne, which may then be honoured with the name of citty whereby the land would become much more civilized; the just division of wast Commons, whereby the nation would become much more industrious, rich & populous:

[5] "erect" perhaps corrected from "erects."

but those are of a second consideracion; these now presented are the maine, & the most of them absolutely necessary; without which wee are like to fall into evills & discords incurable, the speedy end whereof wilbe utter ruine, which God of his mercy prevent!

THE READIE & EASIE WAY TO ESTABLISH A FREE COMMONWEALTH

February 23–29, 1660

PREFACE AND NOTES BY ROBERT W. AYERS

I

W HEN MILTON emerged from political retirement with *A Letter to a Friend* (October, 1659) and *Proposalls of Certaine Expedients* (November, 1659), he had been so disillusioned with the succession of Parliaments since 1649 that in order to prevent the return of the king or some other single person, and to escape the vortex of turmoil and anarchy into which the nation was descending, he urged that the Rump, which Lambert had turned out on October 13, be restored, and that it, or a Council of State made up from it, should sit indissolubly. But a tide of popular sentiment was gathering at this very time in support of "full and free" successive Parliaments or re-admission of the secluded members (those turned out of the House in Pride's Purge) ; either event, it was generally assumed, would result in return of the king.[1]

Notwithstanding the force of this movement and in the very face of it, after reconvening on December 26 the Rump voted on January 3 to hold elections to fill the seats of those members who had died and on January 5 of those who had been secluded.[2] Monck, who from October on had supported the return of the Rump as at least the remnant of a legal governing authority while he simultaneously exerted every effort for a return to successive parliaments, determined to be on the scene to see that the Rump did not perpetuate itself. He therefore began a slow march down from Scotland almost as soon as the Rump assembled, and arrived in London on Friday, February 3, just a day before the House, in another action signaling its refusal to return to the full House as constituted before Pride's Purge, resolved to bring its strength up to 400, with seats apportioned as "they were agreed in the year 1653." It was well known that many representations had been made to the

[1] See above, Woolrych, introduction, pp. 156–71.
[2] *Ibid.,* p. 162.

General in the English counties all along the route of his march; he referred to these when he addressed the House on Monday, February 6:

> As I marched from *Scotland* hither, I observed the People in most Counties in great and earnest Expectations of Settlement; and they made several Applications to me, with numerous Subscriptions. The chiefest Heads of their Desires were, For a free and full Parliament, and that you would determine your sitting . . . and for Admittance of the Members secluded before 1648, without any previous Oath or Engagement.[3]

Almost daily thereafter, Monck pressed the Parliament to prepare for new elections. On the 9th, reporting to the House his partial compliance with orders to act against the rebellious City of London, he besought the members to "hasten your Qualifications, that the Writs may be sent out."[4] On the same day, "Lovers of the Good Old Cause," "constant Adherers to this Parliament," noting the "general Boldness . . . to plead a Necessity of returning to the Government of Kings and Lords, a taking in of the King's Son; or, which is all one, for a Return of the justly-secluded Members, or a Free Parliament, without due Qualifications,"[5] submitted to the House a "Representation and Address," in which they asked that no one be allowed to sit or vote in Parliament or the Council of State who would not abjure Charles, or any other single person, and that anyone who should move to introduce any single person would be declared guilty of high treason.[6]

Himself one who had refused to take the Oath of Abjuration, Monck took the Rump's orders against the City and its sympathetic reception of the "Representation and Address" to be nearly conclusive evidence that, unless forced, the House would never move to remedy "The grand Cause of the present Heats and Dissatisfactions in the Nation . . . [that] they are not fully represented in Parliament."[7] He therefore stepped up his pressure in a letter of Saturday the 11th, in which he demanded that the House issue writs by "Friday next," February 17,[8] for an election to fill up their number according to qualifications which would exclude only those who had actually been in arms against Parlia-

[3] *Old Parliamentary History*, XXII, 88–89.
[4] *Ibid.*, p. 93; *cf.* p. 121, where it is said that "[The members of the Rump] were deaf to all salutary Counsel, and resolved to finish the Work with the new Instruments which they had chosen. To this End they proceeded on the Bill for filling up the House; which, by wise Men, was thought a most dangerous Expedient in that Conjuncture, unless *Monke* should prove more honest than they could believe him to be."
[5] *Ibid.*, p. 95.
[6] *Ibid.*, pp. 96–97.
[7] *Ibid.*, p. 101.
[8] *Ibid.*, p. 102; see above, Woolrych, introduction, p. 171.

ment, and those who in the late wars had declared their disaffection to the Parliament. He reminded the House that "the Time hastens wherein you have declared your intended Dissolution; which the People and ourselves desire you would be punctual in," and observed that "Hereby the Suspicion of your Perpetuation will be taken away, and the People will have Assurance that they shall have a Succession of Parliaments of their own Election; which is the undoubted Right of the *English* Nation." "You have promised and declared no less," he said. Then he implied the threat of force: "Both the People and your Armies do live in the Hope and Expectation of it." This open declaration for a free Parliament was in effect something close to a declaration for the king, and that night there was riotous rejoicing in the City, with ringing of bells, burning of bonfires, and roasting of rumps.

The Rump pretended to shrug off Monck's threat, but after a week of work, on the 17th, as he had demanded, it duly defined and published the form of writs for elections; [9] and on the next day, Saturday the 18th, passed an act decreeing qualifications for candidates so restrictive that compliance would result in filling up the House with supporters of the Rump.[10] But even as the Rump thus swiftly worked to entrench its power and position, frequent meetings—including one on the 18th—at Monck's quarters with some secluded members and certain of the House intimated urgent, perhaps immediate, danger to the proposed elections; so the Rump ordered the Clerk of the Commonwealth in Chancery to issue writs with speed, and it was announced that some would in fact be issued on Monday, the 20th.[11]

When he examined the narrow qualifications decreed on the 18th, Monck must have concluded that an election according to them would prolong the inequities of representation in Parliament which he regarded as the primary cause of tumult in the nation, and would probably result in perpetuation of the Rump itself. Monck moved swiftly to avert that danger; possibly at his suggestion, when ordered on the 20th to sign the warrants for issuance of the writs, the Speaker refused, arguing that he might thereby expose himself to suit* by the secluded members.[12] Whether the consequent delay was fortuitous or by the Speaker's or Monck's design, it served Monck's purpose. Early the next morning, the 21st, seventy-three of the secluded members went

---

[9] The form of the writs was published in *Mercurius Politicus,* February 16–23, 1660, pp. 1114–15, February 17; also in *Publick Intelligencer,* p. 1124.

[10] See *Old Parliamentary History,* XXII, 131–32, and above, introduction, p. 174.

[11] *Mercurius Politicus, loc. cit.,* p. 1117.

[12] Above, introduction, p. 174.

to Monck's quarters in Whitehall, where his secretary read to them a "Speech and Declaration," in which the General averred his devotion to a settlement of the government upon commonwealth foundations, directed them to "take care" for issuing writs for a new Parliament to meet April 20, and—repeatedly and emphatically—directed them to "make way for Succession of Parliaments." [13] Thereafter they were escorted to the House, where, Monck having withdrawn the guard which for so long had prevented their entrance, their first act was to vote nullification, voiding and obliterating all earlier votes relating to elections—including, of course, that of the 18th.[14] Later that day, Monck sent a letter to all regiments and garrisons announcing re-admission of the secluded members "in order to a legal Dissolution of this Parliament," and assuring the army that this Parliament would sit no longer than necessary for "putting the Government into successive Parliaments." [15] That night, as on the 11th, there were again bonfires and bells in the City.

Such were the events that immediately preceded and precipitated the composition and publication of the first edition of *The Readie & Easie Way to Establish a Free Commonwealth,* and the work must be read in the closest relation to them.

II

The introductory paragraph of *The Readie & Easie Way* distinguishes between that paragraph and the "treatise," or body of the work, which follows: evidently the treatise was (a) written first, and (b) completed *before* "the members [were] readmitted from exclusion, to sit again in Parlament"—i.e., before the morning of February 21. At the same time, within the treatise itself clear and unambiguous reference to the "just and necessarie qualifications decreed in Parlament" shows that it was completed *after* the House's action on the morning of February 18.

Indeed, it appears likely that composition of the treatise was *begun* after that action. Only after the decree of qualifications on the 18th but before the return of the secluded members on the morning of the 21st could perpetuation of the Rump as a ready and easy way to establish a free commonwealth simultaneously have seemed to Milton an immediate possibility—and to Monck an imminent danger. And only

---

[13] Text in *Old Parliamentary History*, XXII, 140–43, and in *Mercurius Politicus, loc. cit.*, pp. 1121–22.

[14] *Common Journals*, VII, 846; *cf. Old Parliamentary History*, XXII, 134.

[15] Text in *Old Parliamentary History*, XXII, 170–72, and *Mercurius Politicus, loc. cit.*, pp. 1119–20.

within that short period of some two-and-a-half days could Milton
have written the very important passage which appears almost in the
middle of the first edition:

> And now is the opportunitie, now the very season wherein we may obtain
> a free Commonwealth, and establish it forever in the land, without diffi-
> culty or much delay. The Parlament have voted to fill up their number:
> and if the people, laying aside prejudice and impatience, will seriously
> and calmly now consider thir own good, thir own libertie and the only
> means therof, as shall be heer laid before them, and will elect thir
> Knights and Burgesses able men, and according to the just and neces-
> sarie qualifications decreed in Parlament, men not addicted to a single
> person or house of lords, the work is don.[16]

It is clear that Milton looked upon the decree of qualifications on
the 18th as a long-sought but instant opportunity, given right action,
to perpetuate the existing Parliament, and several features of the
pamphlet bespeak the haste with which he moved to seize it: its length
(a mere 18 quarto pages, some 6000 words); its style (terse, earnest
and urgent, summary, elliptical, relatively undocumented, and assertive
rather than argumentative); and rather numerous errors or infelicities
(imprecision, vagueness, redundancy, and factual error),[17] such as
would surely have been corrected during any prolonged process of
composition, and such as were indeed corrected in the separately and
late-printed errata [18] or removed in the second edition.

But what Milton seized upon as a last chance, Monck looked upon as
a last straw; and while Monck's move on the 21st ended work on his
"treatise," in Milton's mind not all was necessarily lost. In its general
form, the central proposal of the treatise was for a parliamentary
"Grand Councel . . . firmly constituted to perpetuitie"—still, Milton
must have thought, a possibility for that portion of the Long Parlia-
ment constituted by the House after readmission of the secluded mem-
bers. Following that event (and referring to it), therefore—but before
the morning of the 22nd, when the newly enlarged House resolved that
a new Parliament should be summoned to meet April 25, ordered the
issuance of new writs, and appointed a committee to prepare qualifica-
tions for a new election [19] (actions which rendered his advocacy of the
perpetuation of the Long Parliament in any form passé and completely

---

[16] Below, pp. 366–68.

[17] See below, preface to 2nd ed., p. 400, nn. 25, 27, and annotations to text.

[18] Advertisement and errata for the first edition were published in *Mercurius
Politicus*, March 1–8, 1660, p. 1151; reprinted, French, *Life Records*, IV, 303.
See below, n. 22.

[19] *Commons Journals*, VII, 848.

irrelevant)—Milton added the prefatory paragraph and transmitted the manuscript to the printer.

Printing, too, was hurried. The press appears not to have been stopped for the correction of any of the numerous auctorial or printer's errors,[20] so that the copies I have examined show no variants whatsoever. There was not even time for the compilation of an errata sheet; the pamphlet was put together without one, and the defect was explicitly attributed to the printer's haste when the errata were printed in *Mercurius Politicus* on March 8.[21] Finally, in the second edition Milton himself testifies that not only printing but distribution of the first edition was precipitous, as he asserts that "in the former edition through haste, many faults escap'd,[22] and many books were suddenly dispersd, ere the note to mend them could be sent." [23]

In summary, then, the evidence indicates that (1) the treatise was certainly completed and was probably begun between the morning of February 18 and the morning of February 21; [24] (2) the introductory paragraph was written on February 21, or perhaps early on February 22; [25] and (3) the complete pamphlet was probably published early in the final week of February, 1660.[26]

[20] See below, n. 22.

[21] See above, n. 18.

[22] The errata appear to have been compiled from manuscript, not from printed sheets, for they correct several almost certainly auctorial or amanuensal errors, while they leave uncorrected numerous errors characteristic of printers.

Corrected (see citation, above, n. 18): "Page 9. line 32. for the *Areopagus,* read of *Areopagus.* p. 10. l. 3. for full Senate, true Senate, l. 4. for sits, is the whole Aristocracy, l. 7. Provincial States, States of every City, p. 17. l. 29. for cite, citie, l. 30, for left, felt." Uncorrected: p. 7, l. 1, Protestanus *for* Protestants; p. 7. l. 14, goverment *for* government; p. 9. l. 24, Commonweath *for* Commonwealth; p. 11. l. 33, intricases *for* intricasies; p. 12. l. 1, friviously *for* frivolously; p. 12. l. 34, do *for* to; p. 13. l. 2, made made *repetition;* p. 13. l. 32, assing'd *for* assign'd; p. 14. l. 18, kinship *for* kingship.

[23] Below, p. 409.

[24] *Cf.* Masson (V, 640), who says that Milton "had begun it just after Monk's arrival in London . . . and it seems to have been ready for the press about or not long after the middle of February." *Cf.* also Clark (p. xiv): "The body of the work was certainly written during the interval Feb. 4 to Feb. 21, and probably in the ten days between Feb. 4 and Feb. 15."

[25] *Cf.* Clark (p. xii): "The preface was therefore written in the interval Feb. 21 (probably Feb. 22)–Feb. 29."

[26] The Thomason copy is dated "March. 3. 1659," but Thomason did not always receive copies promptly, or perhaps he did not always immediately date them. Wood, I, 883, accurately describes the publication as "in two sheets and an half in qu.," and says that it was "Published in *Feb.*" White Kennet, *A Register and Chronicle* (London, 1728), p. 73, lists the work among *"Some*

III

The moment which seemed to Milton to be the Rump's greatest opportunity—February 18–20, 1660—was in fact the moment of its greatest peril. After the decree of restrictive qualifications on the 18th, the Rump raced to issue writs for elections that would secure and perpetuate its power—even as Monck's meetings with the secluded members ominously intimated that the surging tide of public sentiment for monarchy might instantly overwhelm the Rump and the Commonwealth.

There was no time to lose, no time now to debate peripheral particulars or constitutional circumstances. There was time only to strive to save the nation from the impending disaster of monarchy. In Milton's mind, this could not be done with successive Parliaments; it was a succession of Parliaments since 1649 which had brought the nation by way of changes, novelties, and uncertainties to its present crisis. Nor could it be accomplished by a Parliament representative of the whole people; the revolution had been brought about originally, and had been sustained to the present moment, by only a minority of the best-affected and best-principled,[27] and it was a majority who were now running headlong again with full stream wilfully and obstinately into the old bondage of the once abjured and detested thraldom of kingship. In the nation's present extremity, what was wanted was a ready and easy way to establish the free commonwealth so long expected but unattained. The way Milton now proposed he had in fact already twice earlier set down—often using the same phrases—in the unpublished *Letter to a Friend* and *Proposalls of Certaine Expedients*: perpetuate the Parliament already in power—while augmenting its membership with "men not addicted to a single person or house of lords." A second absolute condition of the earlier documents—liberty of conscience for all professing Scripture to be the rule of their faith and worship—he no longer insisted upon; the Rump itself had acted in June, 1659, to continue the "forc'd maintenance" of ministers by tithes.[28] And Monck being now in unquestioned command—and opposed to the Rump— Milton no longer proposed that the chief officers hold their commands

---

Books and Papers published within this Month of February, 1659." See French, *Life Records*, IV, 300–01. French notes that on the title page of one of two Bodleian copies the "60" in the printed date is stricken, and "59:ffeb" written in what seems to be a contemporary hand.

[27] This argument is stressed by an addition to the second edition, below, pp. 411–16.

[28] See above, *Letter to a Friend*, p. 330, n. 32.

for life. Indeed, all other recommendations—for strengthening of local or county provincial governments, reform of legal institutions and procedures, establishment of local schools or academies, etc.—are secondary and subordinate to the single central proposal for perpetuation of the Rump.

His support of this single central proposal in particular and the exigencies of the political situation in general required that Milton extol the advantages of a free commonwealth while enumerating and enlarging upon the disadvantages and thraldom of kingship. And these paired conceptions control not only the diction and the imagery but the organization and the proportions of the draft, although extensive use of the sometimes rambling loose sentence, often with vague or uncertain conjunctions or relatives, frequent omission of transitions, and seemingly inconsistent paragraphing—all perhaps marks of the haste in which the work was composed and published—often obscure the order and coherence of the underlying argument.

In the exordium and narration, after terse praise of Parliament and the people for justly and magnanimously abolishing kingship and turning regal bondage into a free commonwealth,[29] Milton argues that a return now to the thraldom of kingship would be attended by such manifold evils—which he enumerates—that a people who would do so must be "madd or strangely infatuated," and one must wonder how "any man . . . can presume . . . to be a king and lord over his brethren." [30]

Milton moves into the confirmation, the heart of his argument, with the contention that since the ground and basis for a just and free government is a General Council of ablest men, and the present Parliament, the Rump, is made up of such ("the remainder of those faithfull worthies, who at first freed us from tyrannie"), a free commonwealth and its benefits might at this moment be easily attained by filling up their body and perpetuating them in office. If this is done, there is no reason why peace, justice, and all prosperity should not ensue forever, while, if there should be a king, which the inconsiderate multitude are so mad upon, we will have all of the many woes—and Milton enlarges upon them—flowing from the unbounded power of a king exercised for his selfish benefit against a defenseless people.[31]

Having shown with what ease a free commonwealth and its benefits might be obtained, and having displayed the difficulties and troubles which would attend a return to kingship, Milton continues in the

[29] Below, pp. 353–57.
[30] Below, pp. 357–66.
[31] Below, pp. 366–80.

confirmation to "shew more particularly wherein our freedom and flourishing condition will be more ample and secure to us under a free Commonwealth then under kin[g]ship." As for liberty, the main end of government, Milton avers: spiritual liberty—liberty of conscience—is promoted by a commonwealth which is most confident of its own fair proceedings, but it is obstructed, feared and hated by kingship and its bishops; and civil liberty—"the civil rights and advanc'ments of every person according to his merit"—may be soonest and best obtained, not from monarchs, who wish their people base and servile, but from a commonwealth, "if every county . . . were made a little commonwealth . . . where the nobilitie and chief gentry . . . may bear part in the government, make their own judicial lawes, and execute them by their own elected judicatures . . . in all things of civil government between man and man." [32]

In peroration, Milton says that few and easy things seasonably done will save the nation, while on the other hand, if the people must set to sale all concernments divine and human to keep up trading, they will be brought to those calamities which always and unavoidably attend on luxury. He would have spoken thus if only to trees and stones, Milton declares, but hopes that he will have spoken to some sensible and ingenuous men, who will give a stay to these ruinous proceedings and to this general defection of the misguided and abused multitude.[33]

IV

The first edition of *The Readie & Easie Way* was reprinted in *The [English Prose] Works of Mr. John Milton* (London, 1697), pp. 361–71. In *The Ready and Easy Way to Establish a Free Commonwealth,* ed. Evert M. Clark (New Haven: Yale Studies in English, 1915), the "first edition . . . [was] reproduced as the basis of the . . . text, and into this [were] inserted all the variants and additions found in the revised edition" (p. iv).

TEXTUAL NOTE: *THE READIE & EASIE WAY TO ESTABLISH A FREE COMMONWEALTH* (FEBRUARY 23–29, 1660)

The present text is that of the Princeton University Library copy, Ex 3857 . 376. Collation: 4°: A-B⁴, C² [$2 (-A1, title page; C2) signed]; 10 leaves; pp. [ii] 1–18. Contents: [A1], title page (verso blank); A2-[C2v], the work. This copy has been collated with other copies as follows: Christ's College Library, Cambridge; Cornell Uni-

[32] Below, pp. 379–83.
[33] Below, pp. 380–88.

versity Library; Harvard University Library; Henry E. Huntington Library; University of Illinois Library; Newberry Library; University of Texas Library; Alexander Turnbull Library; Yale University Library.[1]

ROBERT W. AYERS

Georgetown University

[1] Parker, *Milton,* p. 1072, lists a few additional copies.

THE
R E A D I E & E A S I E
VV A Y
TO
E S T A B L I S H
A
Free Commonwealth,
AND
The E X C E L L E N C E therof
Compar'd with
The inconveniences and dangers of
readmitting kingſhip in this nation.

The author J. Milton

LONDON,
Printed by T. N. and are to be ſold by Livewell Chapman
at the Crown in Popes-Head Alley. 1660.

NOTES ON THE TITLE PAGE

a The type ornament is found on p. 1, *A Treatise of Civil Power* . . . *Printed by Tho. Newcomb,* Anno 1659 (Wing, *STC,* M2185). Although Newcomb was for years the printer of *Mercurius Politicus* under the supervision of Milton and Marchamont Needham (Masson, IV, 325, 433; V, 52), and printer of several of Milton's tracts (Masson, IV, 581; V, 404–05, 572, 581; French, IV, 273), as well as several editions of *Eikon Basilike* [F. F. Madan, *A New Bibliography of the Eikon Basilike of King Charles the First* (London, 1950), pp. 16–22, 40], he "ratted in time," as Masson says (VI, 167). On May 5, 1660, he was appointed one of two official printers to the Restoration House of Commons (Masson, VI, 167). See further, *DNB,* and Henry R. Plomer, *A Dictionary of the Booksellers and Printers . . . in England, Scotland and Ireland from 1641 to 1667* (London, 1907), pp. 136–37.

b Chapman was also the bookseller for *Considerations Touching the Likeliest Means* (August, 1649; see above, pp. 229 ff., and French, IV, 273). He had published so much of the anti-Cromwellian literature that Woolrych ["The Good Old Cause and the Fall of the Protectorate," p. 151, n. 98] says that "his share of responsibility for the [fall of the Protectorate] may well have been considerable." He was also active in the antiroyalist cause during the period immediately prior to Charles II's return, and on March 28, 1660, the Council of State ordered his surrender or arrest for causing "several seditious and treasonable books to be printed and published." See *Tudor and Stuart Proclamations: 1485–1714,* calendared by Robert Steele (2 vols., London, 1910), I, 382; Masson, V, 670; Plomer, p. 44. Warrants for his apprehension were issued on March 27, April 3, and April 28 (*CSPD,* 1659–60, 572, 575). *Mercurius Politicus,* March 29–April 5, 1660, p. 1211, for March 31, reported that "This week, the Council of State put forth a Proclamation against *Livewel Chapman* Stationer of *London,* for his printing and dispersing divers Books against the present Government; requiring him to appear before the council on Monday next, 2. of *April*." On April 8 Col. John Desborough and R. Hughes wrote to him in London, informing him of plans for armed action to preserve the Commonwealth (*CSPD,* 1659–60, 409–11).

THE READIE & EASIE WAY
TO ESTABLISH A FREE
COMMONWEALTH, &C.

LTHOUGH since the writing of this treatise, the face of things
hath had some change, writs for new elections have bin
recall'd, and the members at first chosen, readmitted from
exclusion, to sit again in Parlament,[1] yet not a little rejoicing to hear

[1] In the No-Address Resolutions of January 1–15, 1648, the Long Parliament
(November 3, 1640–March 16, 1660) voted to break off negotiations for a
constitutional settlement with Charles I. Since a majority of the House con-
tinued to wish and work for a treaty between king and Parliament in order to
avoid a settlement imposed by the army, the increasingly powerful army leaders
decided to "purge" the House by preventing the admittance of those who fa-
vored such negotiated settlement. This was done on December 6, 1648, in
"Pride's Purge." From that time until it was dissolved by Cromwell on April
20, 1653, this purged minority "Rump" of the Long Parliament ruled the coun-
try as a commonwealth. Richard Cromwell's abdication as Protector in May,
1659, was followed by restoration of the Rump (May 7–October 13, 1659),
now representing a revived alliance between army leaders and anti-Protectorate
republicans. But renewed antagonisms between civil and military elements un-
dermined the restored Rump, so that it was dissolved a second time, by Lam-
bert's *coup d'état*, on October 13, 1659. Although it was again convened on
December 26, 1659, the Rump's ineffectiveness—a consequence generally of its
radically unrepresentative character—contributed to the general confusion and
an apparent drift towards anarchy. This was the situation when General George
Monck, whose position was somewhat apart from most army leaders, started
south from Scotland to support the Rump in its struggle against other powerful
elements of the army. Once in London, however, Monck had first-hand ex-
perience with the perversity of the Rump, and, with the support of the City—
and pursuant to a resolution of the House (February 4) that it should be filled
up to the number of 400 for England and Wales (Masson, V, 532)—he de-
manded that the Rump within a week issue writs to fill up its members. On
February 18 a bill to this effect was passed and ordered printed and published.
Meanwhile, Monck seems to have concluded that no reasonable hope whatso-
ever could be reposed in the Rump, and began consulting with members of the
House who had been excluded in Pride's Purge. They agreed in writing to a
number of conditions for their readmission to the House—including those of
issuing writs for a new Parliament to meet April 20, and of dissolving the
House—i.e., the Long Parliament—as soon as possible. As a consequence, on
February 21 Monck withdrew the guard at Westminster so that the excluded
members might enter and take their seats. With these members sitting, on the

declar'd, the resolutions of all those who are now in power, jointly
tending to the establishment of a free Commonwealth,[2] and to remove

---

morning of that day a resolution was passed voiding all earlier votes of the
House relating to future elections—including that of the 18th (*Commons Jour-
nals*, VII, 846), which would have filled up the House only on terms stipulated
by the Rump. On the next day, February 22, the House directed the issuing of
writs for election of a new Parliament returnable April 25, and a committee was
appointed to recommend qualifications.

Milton's opening sentence indicates that the body of the treatise—beginning
with paragraph two—was written before the morning of February 21, and that
the introductory paragraph was written subsequent to that time. But his ap-
parent ignorance of the House's actions of February 22—when it resolved that
a new Parliament should be summoned to appear April 25, ordered the issu-
ance of writs, and appointed a committee to prepare qualifications—clearly in-
dicates that the introductory paragraph was written and the whole pamphlet
given to the printer before those events, i.e., it was written in the afternoon
or evening of February 21 or the early morning of February 22.

See *Commons Journals* various dates, except for Pride's Purge, notices of
which were stricken, and Masson, *passim*. The *Parliamentary or Constitutional
History of England* (24 vols., 1751–66), XVIII, 447–61—commonly known as
Old Parliamentary History—includes a highly circumstantial account by John
Rushworth of the planning of Pride's Purge. See also, for the events of 1659–60,
Woolrych, introduction, above, *passim*.

[2] "Those . . . now in power": Monck, the army officers, and the House.
Shortly after his return from Scotland Monck said to Ludlow that "we must
live and die together for a Commonwealth," and that if the House should
undertake to bring in the king, he would "interrupt them therein" (Ludlow,
Memoirs, II, 227). On February 14 the House passed a resolution that mem-
bers of the Council of State should engage to "be true and faithful to the
Commonwealth of *England*, and the Government thereof, in the way of a Com-
monwealth and Free State, without a King, Single Person, or House of Lords"
(*Commons Journals*, VII, 843). At a meeting on February 17, Monck had his sec-
retary read his views to some secluded members: "The writing imported . . .
that the interest of the city of London would be best preserved by the gov-
ernment of a commonwealth" (Clarendon, *History of the Rebellion*, ed.
W. Dunn Macray [6 vols., Oxford, 1888], VI, 175 [xvi, 133–34]). On Febru-
ary 21, the very day on which Milton wrote this introductory paragraph, there
were several "resolutions of all those . . . in power, jointly tending to the es-
tablishment of a free Commonwealth." On that morning, before the admission of
the secluded members, the army officers, being consulted, indicated that they
were willing enough to have the secluded members sit, "on Condition they would
promise to declare for a Commonwealth Government," and "The secluded mem-
bers declared, as to Government, they intended no Alteration in it" [Sir Richard
Baker, *A Chronicle of the Kings of England*, add. by Edward Phillips (Lon-
don, 1670), p. 710]. In a "Speech and Declaration" to Parliament later that
same day, Monck assured the House that he desired "the Settlement of these
nations upon Commonwealth foundations" (*Old Parliamentary History*, XXII,
140–43; see also Pepys, *Diary*, of date). In the afternoon and evening, when
the House had concluded its sitting for the day, Monck conferred with all of

if it be possible, this unsound humour of returning to old bondage, instilld of late by some cunning deceivers,[3] and nourished from bad principles and fals apprehensions among too many of the people, I thought best not to suppress what I had written,[4] hoping it may perhaps (the Parlament now sitting more full and frequent) [5] be now much more useful then before: yet submitting what hath reference to the state of things as they then stood, to present constitutions; and so the same end be persu'd, not insisting on this or that means to obtain it. The treatise was thus written as follows.

The Parlament of *England* assisted by a great number of the people who appeard and stuck to them faithfullest in the defence of religion and thir civil liberties, judging kingship by long experience a government burdensom, expensive, useless and dangerous, justly and magnanimously abolishd it; [6] turning regal-bondage into a

---

the officers about London on a letter to be sent to all commanders, regiments, and garrisons throughout the three kingdoms in order to solicit their concurrence in the admission of the secluded members. The document was drawn up by a committee with special instructions "That nothing was intended for Alteration of Government," and that "it should continue as a free State and Commonwealth" (Baker, *Chronicle*, p. 710).

[3] Milton recalls this passage in *Brief Notes*, below, p. 469, par. 1, where he characterizes Matthew Griffith, author of *Fear of God and the King* (1660), as one of them.

[4] Presumably beginning par. 2.

[5] That is, more crowded or full; see *NED*, s. v. frequent, a. 1. Early lists differ from one another, and are often indeed internally inconsistent; the numbers are therefore uncertain, although certainly few. Although ordinary attendance before readmission of the secluded members might vary from 20 to 80, there were seldom as many as 60. About 90 were present on February 21, 114 on February 23, thereafter usually an average of 100 to 120, with never more than 150. See Davies, *Restoration*, p. 259, n. 16; p. 293; D. Brunton and D. H. Pennington, *Members of the Long Parliament* (London, 1954), pp. 38–47, esp. 41; and introduction, above, p. 174.

[6] On January 4, 1649, Commons resolved "That the People are, under God, the Original of all just Power," that "the Commons . . . representing, the People, have the supreme Power in this Nation," and that "whatsoever is enacted, or declared for Law, by the Commons . . . hath the Force of Law . . . although the Consent and Concurrence of King, or House of Peers, be not had thereunto" (*Commons Journals*, VI, 111). Charles was executed on January 30, and that afternoon an act was passed prohibiting the proclamation of any successor to him (*Commons Journals*, VI, 125). On February 6, 1649, it was resolved that "the House of Peers . . . is useless and dangerous, and ought to be abolished" (*Commons Journals*, VI, 132). On the following day it was further resolved that "the Office of a King in this Nation, and to have the Power thereof

free Commonwealth, to the admiration and terror of our neighbours, and the stirring up of *France* it self, especially in *Paris* and *Bourdeaux,* to our imitation.[7] Nor were our actions less both at home and abroad then might become the hopes of a glorious rising Commonwealth; nor were [1] the expressions both of the Army and of the People, whether in thir publick declarations or several writings, other then such as testifi'd a spirit in this nation no less noble and well fitted to the liberty of a Comonwealth, then in the ancient Greeks or Romans. After our liberty thus succesfully fought for, gaind and many years possessd, except in those unhappie interruptions,[8] which God hath remov'd, and wonderfully now the third time brought together our old Patriots, the first Assertours of our religious and civil rights, now that nothing remains but in all reason the certain hopes of a speedy and immediate settlement to this nation for ever in a firm and free Commonwealth, to fall back, or rather to creep back so poorly as it seems the multitude would, to thir once abjur'd

---

in any Single Person, is unnecessary, burdensome, and dangerous to the Liberty, Safety, and publick Interest of the People of this Nation; and therefore ought to be abolished" (*Commons Journals,* VI, 133). The two acts—abolishing the office of the king and the House of Lords, respectively—were passed on the following March 17 and 19. So see *Commons Journals,* VI, 133, 166, 168. Texts in Firth and Rait, *Acts and Ordinances,* II, 18–20, 24. See also Godfrey Davies, *Early Stuarts* (2nd ed., Oxford, 1959), p. 160. While Milton's words here clearly recall those of the resolution of January 4 and the act of March 17, 1649, the revised edition uses the precise words of those documents.

[7] Paris was the center of the "Fronde of the Parlement" in 1648–49. Bordeaux witnessed a much more radical movement in the organization known as the Ormée, which was at its height in 1652–53, and to which the Council of State of the English Commonwealth sent Colonel Sexby as its agent. For the latest and fullest discussion of the extent to which England's example and encouragement affected these revolutionary movements in France, see Philip A. Knachel, *England and the Fronde* (Ithaca: Cornell University Press for the Folger Shakespeare Library, 1967), which has an excellent bibliography.

[8] "Our old Patriots, the first Assertours of our religious and civil rights," are the members of the Rump, those remaining in Parliament after Pride's Purge, December 6, 1648 (see above, p. 353, n. 1), who condemned and executed the king. Dissolved by Cromwell, April 20, 1653, it was restored May 7, 1659, following the deposition of Richard Cromwell. Again dissolved by Lambert's *coup d'état,* October 13, 1659, it was for "the third time brought together," December 26, 1659. Among the "unhappy interruptions," therefore, was the whole of the Protectorate. See Woolrych's discussion of Milton's reference to a "short but scandalous night of interruption" in *The Likeliest Means,* introduction, above, pp. 85–87.

and detested thraldom of kingship, not only argues a strange degenerate corruption suddenly spread among us, fitted and prepar'd for new slaverie, but will render us a scorn and derision to all our neighbours. And what will they say of us, but scoffingly as of that foolish builder mentiond by our Saviour, who began to build a Tower, and was not able to finish it: [9] where is this goodly tower of a Common-wealth which the *English* boasted they would build, to overshaddow kings and be another *Rome* in the west? The foundation indeed they laid gallantly, but fell into a worse confusion, not of tongues, but of factions, then those at the tower of *Babel;* [10] and have left no memorial of thir work behind them remaining, but in the common laughter of *Europ.* Which must needs redound the more to our shame, if we but look on our neighbours the United Provinces,[11] to us inferiour in all outward advantages: who notwithstanding, in the midst of greater difficulties, couragiously, wisely, constantly went through with the same work, and are settl'd in all the happie injoiments of a potent and flourishing Republick to this day. [2]

Besides this, if we return to kingship, and soon repent, as undoubtedly we shall, when we begin to finde the old incroachments coming on by little and little upon our consciences, which must necessarily proceed from king and bishop united inseparably in one interest,[12] we may be forc'd perhaps to fight over again all that we

[9] Luke 14:28–30: "For which of you, intending to build a tower, sitteth not down first, and counteth the cost, whether he have sufficient to finish it? Lest haply, after he hath laid the foundation, and is not able to finish it, all that behold it begin to mock him, saying, This man began to build, and was not able to finish."

[10] For the story of Babel, see Genesis 11: 1–9.

[11] The seven provinces represented in the States-General of the Dutch Republic were Holland, Zealand, Gelderland, Utrecht, Overyssel, Friesland, and Groningen. An eighth, Drente, enjoyed rights of self-government similar to those of the seven, but sent no representatives to the States-General. Their century-long struggle for independence from Spain, from 1568 to 1648 (punctuated only by the Twelve Years' Truce of 1609–21), had been an object of intense concern and admiration to Protestant Englishmen, many of whom had learned the arts of war in the Dutch campaigns. This cordiality had been strained, especially after 1621, by rivalries in trade and colonization, and more recently by the Anglo-Dutch War of 1652–54. Milton's admiration had survived these trials, but this was by no means so with all Englishmen; *cf.* Woolrych, introduction, above, p. 201, and below, nn. 68, 77, 79, 112.

[12] An alliance of church and state was of course immemorial in England. The interests of the two were practically identified by James I at the Hampton

have fought, and spend over again all that we have spent, but are never like to attain thus far as we are now advanc'd, to the recoverie of our freedom, never likely to have it in possession, as we now have it, never to be voutsaf'd heerafter the like mercies and signal assistances from heaven in our cause, if by our ingratefull backsliding we make these fruitless to our selves, all his gratious condescensions and answers to our once importuning praiers against the tyrannie which we then groand under to become now of no effect, by returning of our own foolish accord, nay running headlong again with full stream wilfully and obstinately into the same bondage: making vain and viler then dirt the blood of so many thousand faithfull and valiant Englishmen, who left us in this libertie, bought with thir lives; losing by a strange aftergame of folly, all the battels we have wonne, all the treasure we have spent, not that corruptible treasure only,[13] but that far more precious of all our late miraculous

---

Court Conference, on Monday, January 16, 1604, when he declared that "I approve the calling and use of bishops in the church; and it is my aphorism, 'No bishop, no king'" [Thomas Fuller, *The Church History of Britain* (3rd ed., 3 vols., London, 1868), III, 201]. Jeremy Taylor [*The Whole Works*, ed. Reginald Heber and Charles Eden (10 vols., London, 1862), V, 11] later expressed the view that it "were natural and consonant to the first justice that kings should defend the rights of the church, and the church advance the honour of kings." *Eikon Basilike* [1649; ed. Philip A. Knachel (Ithaca, 1966), p. 101] expressed the Stuart conception in the statement that "I find it impossible for a prince to preserve the state in quiet unless he hath such an influence upon churchmen and they such a dependence on him as may best restrain the seditious exorbitancies of ministers' tongues."

Milton frequently condemned this union of interests. In *Commonplace Book* (*Complete Prose*, I, 476) he noted "That the combining of ecclesiastical and political government (when, that is to say, the magistrate acts as minister of the Church and the minister of the Church acts as magistrate) is equally destructive to both religion and the State." In *Eikonoklastes* (1649; *Complete Prose*, III, 511) he said of Charles I that "when both Interests of Tyrannie and Episcopacie were incorporat into each other, the King . . . fatally driv'n on, set himself to the extirpating of those men whose Doctrin, and desire of Church Discipline he so fear'd would bee the undoing of his Monarchie."

Much new light is cast on the changing relationships between kings and bishops by William M. Lamont in *Godly Rule: Politics and Religion, 1603–1660* (London: Macmillan, 1969).

[13] *Cf.* I Peter 1:18–19: "Ye know that ye were not redeemed with corruptible things, as silver and gold . . . but with the precious blood of Christ."

In *The Century of Revolution, 1603–1714* (Edinburgh: 1961), p. 160, Christopher Hill says that "It has been calculated that during the Interregnum over £80 million was raised in England—an average of over £4 million a year." This should be compared with Charles I's annual average of ordinary revenues from

deliverances; and most pittifully depriving our selves the instant fruition of that free government which we have so dearly purchasd, a free Commonwealth, not only held by wisest men in all ages the noblest, the manliest, the equallest, the justest government, the most agreeable to all due libertie and proportiond equalitie, both humane, civil and Christian, most cherishing to vertue and true religion, but also (I may say it with greatest probabilitie) planely commended or rather enjoind by our Saviour himself, to all Christians, not without remarkable disallowance and the brand of *Gentilism* upon kingship.[14] God in much displeasure gave a king to the *Israelites*, and imputed it a sin to them that they sought one: [15] [3] but Christ apparently forbids his disciples to admitt of any such heathenish government: *the kings of the gentiles, saith he, exercise lordship over them; and they that exercise autoritie upon them, are call'd benefactors. But ye shall not be so: but he that is greatest among you, let him be as the younger; and he that is chief, as he that serveth.*[16] The occasion of these his words, was the ambitious desire of *Zebede's* two sons to be exalted above their brethren in his kingdom, which they thought was to be ere long upon earth. That he speaks of

---

1631 to 1635 of £618,376, from 1636 to 1641 of £899,482 [G. E. Aylmer, *The King's Servants: The Civil Service of Charles I: 1625–1642* (London: Routledge & Kegan Paul, 1961), p. 64], and the £1,200,000 which the Convention decided in 1660 to be sufficient for the ordinary needs of government.

[14] In response to the request that James and John, sons of Zebedee, be allowed to occupy places of favor in his kingdom (Matthew 20:25–27), "Jesus called them unto him, and said, Ye know that the princes of the Gentiles exercise dominion over them, and they that are great exercise authority upon them. But it shall not be so among you: but whosoever will be great among you, let him be your minister; and whosoever will be chief among you, let him be your servant." See also Mark 10:42–44, Luke 22:25–26, and *Tenure,* in *Complete Prose,* III, 216–17.

[15] I Samuel 8. The aged Samuel appointed his sons Joel and Abiah judges over Israel, but they turned to bribes and injustice, so that the elders pled with Samuel for a king. The Lord instructed Samuel to show them the kind of king who should rule over them—an oppressive and unjust one—and the lamentations they should consequently sound in regret at insisting upon a king. "And the Lord said unto Samuel, Hearken unto the voice of the people in all that they say unto thee: for they have not rejected thee, but they have rejected me, that I should not reign over them" (7). Both royalists and republicans used this text; *cf. Complete Prose,* III, 202, n. 55; 206, n. 68; 207, n. 69; and 580, n. 31. Reference to it is therefore frequent elsewhere in Milton's works, particularly in *A Defence (Complete Prose,* IV, 347, 349, 354, 364, 378).

[16] Luke 22:25–26, but the Authorized Version reads "doth serve" for "serveth." See above, n. 14.

civil government, is manifest by the former part of the comparison, which inferrs the other part to be alwaies in the same kinde.[17] And what government comes neerer to this precept of Christ, then a free Commonwealth; wherin they who are greatest, are perpetual servants and drudges to the publick at thir own cost and charges,[18] neglect thir own affairs; yet are not elevated above thir brethren, live soberly in thir families, walk the streets as other men, may be spoken to freely, familiarly, friendly, without adoration. Whereas a king must be ador'd like a Demigod,[19] with a dissolute and haughtie court about him, of vast expence and luxurie,[20] masks and revels, to the debaushing of our prime gentry both male and female; nor at his own cost, but on the publick revenue; and all this to do nothing but bestow the eating and drinking of excessive dainties, to set a pompous face upon the superficial actings of State, to pageant himself up and down in progress among the perpetual bowings and

[17] *I.e.*, rulers among the gentiles (therefore worldly or civil) compared to civil rulers among the Christians.

[18] Members of Parliament had an ancient legal right, fixed by statute in 1323, to wages from their constituencies: four shillings a day for every knight of the shire, two shillings for every citizen or burgess. In the sixteenth century, especially under Elizabeth, agreements for part wages and reduced traveling expenses were made almost invariably by resident members, while non-resident members went further and entered into agreements to serve altogether without pay. Such agreements were really bribes to the constituencies, for if wages and expenses were reduced or removed, local taxes to cover these charges were reduced or removed. There were only isolated instances of local payment of wages during the Commonwealth, the practice having generally disappeared long before. Andrew Marvell received wages until his death in 1678, and was evidently among the last members of the House to receive wages regularly and freely paid by his constituents. See Edward Porritt, *The Unreformed House of Commons* (2 vols., 1903), I, 51, 155, 157; Sir William Holdsworth, *History of English Law* (16 vols., 2nd ed., repr., London, 1966), IV, 93–94; J. E. Neale, *The Elizabethan House of Commons* (New Haven, 1950), p. 156; Andrew Marvell, *Complete Works*, ed. Alexander B. Grosart (4 vols., 1875), II, xxxv, xxxvi, 518.

[19] *Cf. Commonplace Book* in *Complete Prose*, I, 431; *Observations* in III, 307; *A Defence* in IV, 369; and n. 34, below.

[20] See *Eikonoklastes*, in *Complete Prose*, III, 358, 448, 569, and *A Defence*, in IV, 520–21, for charges of expense and luxury against Charles I. Aylmer, *The King's Servants*, p. 27, says that under Charles I the royal household accounted for over forty percent of all peacetime royal expenditure, and (p. 31) "Its glaring wastefulness, due to bad methods of catering and accounting, to redundancy and sinecurism, and to downright fraud, made it an obvious, though not for that reason necessarily an easy, target for financial and administrative reformers."

cringings of an abject people, on either side deifying and adoring
him who for the most part deserves none of this by any good done
to the people (for what can he more then another man?) but even
in the expression of a late court-Poet, sits only like a great cypher
set to no purpose before a long row of other significant figures.[21]
Nay it is well and happy for the people if thir king be but a cypher,
being oft times a mischief, a pest, a scourge of the nation, and which
is worse, [4] not to be remov'd, not to be contrould, much less
accus'd or brought to punishment, without the danger of a common
ruin, without the shaking and almost subversion of the whole land.
Wheras in a free Commonwealth, any governour or chief coun-
selour offending, may be remov'd and punishd, without the least
commotion.[22] Certainly then that people must needs be madd or
strangely infatuated, that build the chief hope of thir common hap-
piness or safetie on a single person; [23] who if he happen to be good,
can do no more then another man, if to be bad, hath in his hands to
do more evil without check, then millions of other men. The happi-

---

[21] In *Notes and Queries*, n. s., I (1954), 473, Elsie Duncan-Jones suggests
Charles I's poet-laureate, Sir William Davenant, *Gondibert* (1651), II.ii.14:
"Nature too oft by birthright does preferr / Less perfect Monarchs to an
anxious Throne; / Yet more than her, Courts by weak Counc'lers err, / In
adding Cyphers where she made but one." But the figure was common: *cf.*
George Chapman, *Bussy D'Ambois* (1607), I.i.34–36; Shakespeare, *Winter's
Tale* (1623), I.ii.6–9. It had in fact appeared in at least one political tract of
1659, *A Seasonable Word, Or, Certain Reasons Against a Single Person* (May
5), quoted in Woolrych, introduction, above, p. 67.

[22] *Cf. Tenure* in *Complete Prose*, III, 236–37: "They that shall boast, as we
doe, to be a free Nation, and not have in themselves the power to remove, or to
abolish any governour supreme, or subordinat, with the goverment it self upon
urgent causes, may please thir fancy with a ridiculous and painted freedom,
fit to coz'n babies; but are indeed under tyranny and servitude; as wanting that
power, which is the root and sourse of all liberty, to dispose and *oeconomize* in
the Land which God hath giv'n them, as Maisters of Family in thir own house
and free inheritance." See also *A Defence*, in *Complete Prose*, IV, 468, where
Milton asserts that in either monarchical or popular government the magistrate
may be deposed or punished "Because . . . the people did not surrender all
their power to the magistrate." But in *Readie & Easie Way* Milton is con-
spicuously silent as to how, or by whom, members of the perpetual Grand
Council may be removed.

[23] The phrase is common in republican literature after 1649, and refers to a
king or a protector under any name whatsoever. See House of Commons reso-
lution, February 7, 1649, p. 355, n. 6, above, and the act abolishing kingship,
March 17, 1649, in Firth and Rait, *Acts and Ordinances*, II, 19. See further,
the Engagement resolution of the House, February 14, 1660, p. 354, n. 2, above.

ness of a nation must needs be firmest and certainest in a full and free Councel of their own electing,[24] where no single person, but reason only swayes. And what madness is it, for them who might manage nobly their own affairs themselves, sluggishly and weakly to devolve all on a single person; and more like boyes under age then men, to committ all to his patronage and disposal, who neither can perform what he undertakes, and yet for undertaking it, though royally paid, will not be thir servant, but thir lord? [25] how unmanly must it needs be, to count such a one the breath of our nostrils, to hang all our felicitie on him, all our safety, our well-being, for which if we were aught els but sluggards or babies, we need depend on none but God and our own counsels,[26] our own active vertue and industrie. *Go to the Ant, thou sluggard,* saith *Solomon, consider her waies, and be wise; which having no prince, ruler, or lord, provides her meat in the summer, and gathers her food in the harvest.*[27] Which evidently shews us, that they who think the nation undon without a king, though they swell and look haughtie, have not so much true spirit and understanding in them as a Pismire. It may

---

[24] *Cf. Letter to a Friend,* above, pp. 329–30: "The 1ˢᵗ thing . . . without which no common wealth can subsist, must be a senate or generall Councell of State. . . . This must be either the parlament readmitted to sitt, or a councell of State, allowed of by the Army since they only now have the power. . . . If the parlament be thought well dissolv'd . . . then must the Army forthwith chuse a councell of State, whereof as many to be of the parlament as are undoubtedly affected to [the] condicions proposed." In *The Present Means,* below, p. 394, Milton refers to the "Parlament, or (as it will from henceforth be better called) the Grand or General Council of the Nation." *Cf.* also *Proposalls of Certaine Expedients,* above, p. 337: "It might be very agreeable with our freedome to chang the name of parliament (especially now having outlived its honour by soe many dissolucions) into the name of a Grand or Supreme Counsell."

[25] *Cf. A Defence,* in *Complete Prose,* IV, 379: "A Christian king is the minister of the people, as indeed all good magistrates are. Amongst Christians, then, there will either be no king at all, or else one who is the servant of all; for clearly one cannot wish to dominate and remain a Christian." *Cf.* above, p. 359, n. 14.

[26] See *Eikonoklastes,* in *Complete Prose,* III, 542: "The happiness of a Nation consists in true Religion, Piety, Justice, Prudence, Temperance, Fortitude, and the contempt of Avarice and Ambition. They in whomsoever these vertues dwell eminently, need not Kings to make them happy, but are the architects of thir own happiness; and whether to themselves or others are not less then Kings."

[27] Proverbs 6:6–8. For "prince, ruler, or lord," Authorized Version reads "guide, overseer, or ruler." *Cf. Tenure,* in *Complete Prose,* III, 238.

be well wonderd that any nation, styling themselves free, can suffer
any man to pretend right over them as thir lord; [28] whenas by
acknowledging that right, they conclude [5] themselves his servants
and his vassals, and so renounce thir own freedom. Which how a
people can do, that hath fought so gloriously for libertie, how they
can change thir noble words and actions heretofore so becoming the
majestie of a free people, into the base necessitie of court-flatteries
and prostrations, is not only strange and admirable,[29] but lamentable
to think on; that a nation should be so valorous and courageous
to winne thir libertie in the field, and when they have wonn it, should
be so unwise in thir counsels, as not to know how to value it, what
to do with it, or with themselves; but after ten or twelve years pros-
perous war and contestation with tyrannie,[30] basely and besottedly to
run thir necks again into the yoke which they have broken, and
prostrate all the fruits of thir victorie for nothing at the feet of
the vanquishd, besides our loss of glorie, will be an ignominie, if it
befall us, that never yet befell any nation possessd of thir libertie:
worthie indeed themselves, whosoever they be, to be for ever slaves;
but that part of the nation which consents not with them, as I per-
swade me of a great number, far worthier then by their means to
be brought into the same bondage, and reservd, I trust, by Divine
providence to a better end; since God hath yet his remnant,[31] and

[28] *Cf. Paradise Lost,* XII, 70–72: "Man over men / He made not Lord; such
title to himself / Reserving, human left from human free." See also *Common-
place Book,* in *Complete Prose,* I, 433, and *A Defence,* in *Complete Prose,* IV,
393 and n. 81. As it appears here, the implication is not strictly consonant with
Milton's view clearly expressed elsewhere earlier, as in *Tenure,* in *Complete
Prose,* III, 199, 200, 206, where he concedes that a king may rule by right
through delegation of powers by the people. Milton himself evidently recog-
nized the inconsistency and the inaccuracy in expression of his convictions, and
so inserted "hereditary" in the second edition.

[29] "To be wondered at." *NED,* 1 (1660), uses this line in illustration.

[30] Since the phrase is indefinite, its referent is uncertain, but perhaps either
1639–1651 (first Bishops' War to the Worcester campaign: rather more than
twelve years) or 1642–1651 (outbreak of the first English Civil War to the
Worcester campaign: rather less than ten years). In any case, a reference to
the period of actual "war and contestation with tyrannie."

[31] The idea of the remnant is frequent in the Old Testament, and that of the
"saving remnant" is particularly notable in Isaiah. As Milton wrote this first
edition of the *Readie & Easie Way,* the dwindling republican remnant included
the Rump. The fact that it no longer existed by the time of the writing of the
second edition in March may explain suppression of the sentence there.

hath not yet quenchd the spirit of libertie among us. Considering these things, so plane, so rational, I cannot but yet further admire [32] on the other side, how any man who hath the true principles of justice and religion in him,[33] can presume or take upon him to be a king and lord over his brethren, whom he cannot but know, whether as men or Christians, to be for the most part every way equal or superiour to himself: [34] how he can display with such vanitie and ostentation his regal splendour so supereminently above other mortal men; or, being a Christian, can assume such extraordinarie honour and worship to himself, while the kingdom of Christ, our common King and Lord, is hid to this world,[35] and such *Gentilish* imitation [36] forbid in express words by him-[6]self to all his disciples? All Protestants [37] hold, that Christ in his Church hath left no vicegerent of his kingly power,[38] but himself without deputy, is the only head thereof, governing it from heaven: how then can any Christian man derive his kingship from Christ, but with worse usurpation then the Pope his headship over the Church, since Christ not only hath not left the least shadow of a command for any such vicegerence from him in the State, as the Pope pretends for his in the Church, but hath expressly declar'd that such regal dominion is from the gentiles,[39] not from him, and hath strictly charg'd us, not to imitate them therein?

I doubt not but all ingenuous and knowing men will easily agree with me, that a free Commonwealth without single person or house

[32] See above, p. 363, n. 29.

[33] See above, p. 362, n. 26.

[34] See further, *Eikonoklastes,* in *Complete Prose,* III, 463: "And he . . . might have rememberd that the Parlament sit in that body, not *as his Subjects* but as his Superiors, call'd, not by him but by the Law." See also *A Defence,* in *Complete Prose,* IV, 466: "Certainly by the law of nature all good kings always consider the Senate or people as their equal and their superior. Since however a tyrant is by nature the lowest of all men, whoever has more power than he must be considered his equal and superior."

[35] Jesus, being asked by Pilate, "Art thou the King of the Jews?" answered (John 18:36), "My kingdom is not of this world." See *Complete Prose,* I, 420, n. 2; 576, n. 19. On millenarian connotations, see Michael Fixler, *Milton and the Kingdoms of God,* pp. 200–07.

[36] See above, p. 359, nn. 14 and 16.

[37] Quarto: Protestanus.

[38] *Cf. Of Civil Power,* above, p. 244, and *Christian Doctrine* in *Complete Prose,* VI, 435.

[39] See above, p. 359, and n. 16.

of lords,[40] is by far the best government,[41] if it can be had; but we have all this while, say they, bin expecting it, and cannot yet attain it. I answer, that the cause thereof may be ascrib'd with most reason to the frequent disturbances, interruptions and dissolutions which the Parlament hath had [42] partly from the impatient or disaffected people,[43] partly from some ambitious leaders in the armie; much contrarie, I believe, to the minde and approbation of the Armie it self and thir other Commanders,[44] when they were once undeceivd, or in thir own power. Neither ought the small number of those remaining in Parlament, be made a by-word of reproach [45] to them, as it

[40] The language recalls not only resolutions of January and February, 1649, and acts of March, 1649, abolishing kingship and the House of Lords (see above, nn. 6 and 23, and Gardiner, *Constitutional Documents*, p. 388), but much more recent acts, declarations, and oaths, such as the Engagement of Parliament on February 14, 1660 (see above, nn. 2 and 23). The phrase had become a republican shibboleth.

[41] Quarto: goverment.

[42] See above, nn. 1 and 8. *Cf.* "A Declaration of the Parliament," January 23, 1660: "The Parliament . . . would have accomplished their Intentions in these Things, and settled the Commonwealth upon the Basis and Foundation [of a Commonwealth and Free-State], if they had not been so often interrupted, and thereby prevented hitherto from doing that which always was, and is, the utmost Desire and Intention of their Hearts." *Old Parliamentary History*, XXII, 59.

[43] Perhaps the London mob's invasion of the Parliament in August, 1647. See Samuel R. Gardiner, *History of the Great Civil War, 1642–1649* (4 vols., New York: AMS Press, 1965), III, 336–38.

[44] The army had never been a homogeneous body. The junior officers and the rank and file were much influenced by the egalitarian doctrines of the Levellers, so that there was a "divided interest" between them and the ambitious leaders. This was evident as the grandees forced Richard Cromwell to dissolve his Parliament, but were forced by their subordinates to recall the Rump. When Lambert again turned out the Rump on October 13, 1659, only Fleetwood among the seven army commissioners (who had been appointed by the Rump the day before in order to supersede Fleetwood's authority as commander in chief; the others were Ludlow, Haslerig, Morley, Walton, Monck, and Overton) openly supported his move. Monck, in Scotland, outspokenly favored the Rump. See Masson, V, 493 ff., and Davies, *Early Stuarts*, pp. 87, 145, 356–57.

[45] Because it was a fragment of the Long Parliament (see above, n. 1), called the "Rump," a term said (*NED*, 3.b.) to have been applied to Parliament in a pamphlet, "The Bloody Rump," prior to the trial of Charles I, otherwise "from Mr. Clem. Walker in his *History of Independency* [II (1649), 32: "this fagge end, this Rump of a Parliament with corrupt Maggots in it"] printed in 1648 and was given to those . . . members that strenuously oppos'd the King." D. Brunton and D. H. Pennington, *Members of the Long Parliament*, p. 41, say that "A Perfect List of Rumpers" (March, 1660) contained 121

is of late by the rable, whenas rather they should be therefor honourd, as the remainder of those faithfull worthies, who at first freed us from tyrannie, and have continu'd ever since through all changes constant to thir trust; which they have declar'd, as they may most justly and truly, that no other way they can discharge, no other way secure and confirme the peoples libertie, but by setling them in a free Commonwealth.[46] And doubtless, no Parlament will be ever able under royaltie to free the people from slavery: and when they go about it, [7] will finde it a laborious task; and when they have don all, they can, be forc'd to leave the contest endless between prerogative and petition of right,[47] till only dooms-day end it: And

---

names. But far fewer customarily attended; see above, p. 355, n. 5. See also Masson, V, 518–19; Clark, 104; and Walker (as above), II, 40.

[46] On May 19, 1649, the House declared England to be "a Commonwealth and Free State . . . without any King or House of Lords." See above, p. 355, n. 6. On May 7, 1659, the Restored Rump resolved "to apply themselves to the faithful Discharge of the Trust reposed in them; and to endeavour the Settlement of this Commonwealth upon such a Foundation, as may assert, establish, and secure the Property and the Liberties of the People . . . and that without a single Person, Kingship, or House of Peers." See Gardiner, *Constitutional Documents*, p. 388, and "Declaration of the Officers of the Army" and "Declaration of Parliament," in *Commons Journals*, May 7, 1659 (VII, 645).

[47] Although the two terms appear to be used here as synecdoches in a general opposition of royal power to subject rights and freedoms, the conceptions underlying the terms are so great and important that their opposition provides the philosophical cause of the Civil War.

Strictly speaking, royal prerogative is the legal exercise of royal authority. Its province has varied in extent at different times in English history; it always included the power of summoning and dissolving parliaments, of coining money, of creating peers, and of pardoning criminals; and before 1377 it had included powers of legislation and taxation. In the Tudor period it was extended to the Church, and to such courts as the Star Chamber and the Court of High Commission—i.e., courts not limited by statute, dependent upon and controlled by the Crown.

Upon the accession of James I to the English throne, this Tudor doctrine of "royal prerogative" was for a time—in theory—extended to become the Stuart doctrine of "absolute prerogative." In 1616, James himself addressed judges, saying, "As for the absolute Prerogatiue of the Crowne, that is no Subiect for the tongue of a Lawyer, nor is lawfull to be disputed. It is Athiesme and blasphemie to dispute what God can doe: good Christians content themselues with his will reuealed in his word, so, it is presumption and high contempt in a Subject, to dispute what a King can doe, or say that a King cannot doe this, or that; but rest in that which is the Kings reuealed will in his Law" [*Political Works*, ed. Charles H. McIlwain (Cambridge, Mass., 1918), p. 333]. In his later Parliaments, James surrendered this theoretical position.

By the time Charles' Parliament of 1628 met, men were alarmed: they had

now is the opportunitie, now the very season wherein we may obtain a free Commonwealth, and establish it forever in the land, without difficulty or much delay.[48] The Parlament have voted to fill up their number: [49] and if the people, laying aside prejudice and impatience, will seriously and calmly now consider thir own good, thir own libertie and the only means therof, as shall be heer laid

---

seen the supporters of the king identify the doctrine of the public good with the absolute prerogative to justify royal actions, no matter how much they encroached upon the rights of the subject or how grievous they were to him. Soldiers had been billeted, martial law proclaimed, forced loans taken, men imprisoned for refusing to pay—and under claim of absolute prerogative imprisoned for no cause shown at all. The opposition was able to show that by long-established law and custom the individual Englishman had his own rights in property not subject to royal prerogative. To this, in the parliamentary view, attached also his personal rights—i.e., they argued that if the king had no absolute power over their land or goods, then he had no such power over their persons. This linking of property and personal rights was the foundation of the parliamentary case. In the Petition of Right, accepted by Charles, June 7, 1628, they set forth as absolute certain rights of the subject, without any reference to the king's prerogative or intrinsic sovereign power: "that no man . . . be compelled to make or yield any gift, loan, benevolence, tax, or such like charge, without common consent by Act of Parliament and that no freeman . . . be imprisoned or detained [without cause shown under the laws]; and that [the king should] remove the said soldiers and mariners [from enforced billeting upon private citizens]; and that . . . commissions for proceeding by martial law ["against soldiers and mariners, or other dissolute persons joining with them"], may be revoked and annulled." Text in Gardiner, *Constitutional Documents,* pp. 66–70. See further, Margaret A. Judson, *The Crisis of the Constitution* (New Brunswick, 1949), pp. 44–67; Frances H. Relf, *The Petition of Right* (Minneapolis, 1917). *Cf.* below, nn. 82, 96.

The issue involved was expressed on the eve of the Civil War in the "Protestation of the Lords and Commons" of May 26, 1642, as "this erroneous maxim being infused into princes that their kingdoms are their own, and that they may do with them what they will, as if their kingdoms were for them, and not they for their kingdoms." See Francis D. Wormuth, *The Royal Prerogative: 1603–1649* (Ithaca, 1939), esp. pp. 69–107; Judson, *Crisis,* pp. 23–34; and J. P. Kenyon, *The Stuart Constitution: 1603–1688: Documents and Commentary* (Cambridge, 1966), pp. 7–11, 12–13. *Cf. Eikonoklastes, Complete Prose,* III, 459: "He met at first with doctrines of unaccountable Prerogative; in them he rested, because they pleas'd him; they therfore pleas'd him, because they gave him all." *Cf.* also *Tenure, ibid.,* p. 214, n. 86.

[48] The Rump, presumably made up of adherents to the Good Old Cause of a free commonwealth, was still sitting as Milton wrote, and Monck, repeatedly pledged to establishment of a commonwealth, was on hand with an army to support it. See above, p. 353, n. 1.

[49] By a series of votes beginning on January 3. See Woolrych, introduction, above, pp. 162 ff.

before them, and will elect thir Knights [50] and Burgesses [51] able men, and according to the just and necessarie qualifications decreed in Parlament,[52] men not addicted to a single person or house of lords, the work is don; at least the foundation is firmly laid of a free Commonwealth, and good part also erected of the main structure. For the ground and basis of every just and free government (since men have smarted so oft for committing all to one person) is a general Councel of ablest men, chosen by the people to consult of publick affairs from time to time for the common good. This Grand Councel must have the forces by sea and land in thir power, must raise and mannage the Publick revenue, make lawes, as need requires, treat of commerce, peace, or war with forein nations; and for the carrying on som particular affairs of State with more secrecie and expedition, must elect, as they have already out of thir own number and others, a Councel of State.[53] And although it may seem strange

[50] Representatives from counties and shires (*NED*, 4.c.).

[51] Representatives from towns, boroughs, and universities (*NED*, 1.6.spec.).

[52] In various resolutions and acts of January and February, 1660, the Rump disqualified royalists, sons of royalists, those who had engaged in plots or conspiracies on behalf of the king or his family, Catholics and other abettors of the Irish Rebellion, any who had "advised, promoted, or abetted any Single Person to the Supreme Magistracy"—not to speak of "profaners of the Lord's Day, Swearers or Cursers, Drunkards, or common haunters of Taverns or alehouses." See *Commons Journals*, January 3, 5, February 8, 11, 13, 14, 18; *Old Parliamentary History*, XXII, 131; and *Publick Intelligencer*, p. 1124, where the form of the writs is published.

A burlesque, "The Qualifications of Persons declared capable, by the Rump-Parliament, to elect, or be elected, members to supply their house" [1660; printed in *Harleian Miscellany*, ed. William Oldys and Thomas Park (10 vols., London, 1803–13), VII, 124–31], adds any who "hath called the present parliament Rump, Arse, Bum, Tail, or Breech." The Rump was, by now, obviously in bad odor.

[53] On Wednesday, February 7, 1649, the day on which kingship was declared abolished (see above, p. 355, n. 6), the House ordered "that there be a Council of State erected, to act and proceed according to such instructions as shall be given to them by this House" (Masson, IV, 11), and it met for the first time on February 17. Upon its restoration in May, 1659, the Rump reverted to the same constitution of the Council of State that it had instituted in February, 1649—i.e., twenty-one M.P.'s and ten non-members, all elected by the House. After its second restoration on December 26, 1659, the Rump elected a new Council of State, making a clean sweep of all who had acted with the Committee of Safety in any way. In addition to Monck, hitherto a supporter of the Commonwealth, this new Council included six regicides, as well as others who had long labored for the Good Old Cause. For the membership

at first hearing, by reason that mens mindes are prepossessd with the conceit of successive Parlaments, I affirm that the Grand or General Councel being well chosen, should sit perpetual: for so their business is, and they will become thereby skilfullest, best acquainted with the people, and the people with them. The ship of the Commonwealth [54] is alwaies undersail; they sit at the stern; and if [8] they stear well, what need is ther to change them; [55] it being rather dangerous? Adde to this, that the Grand Councel is both foundation and main pillar of the whole State; and to move pillars and foundations, unless they be faultie, cannot be safe for the building. I see not therefore how we can be advantag'd by successive Parlaments; [56] but that they are much likelier continually to unsettle rather then to settle a free government, to breed commotions, changes, novelties and uncertainties; and serve only to satisfie the ambition of such men, as think themselves injur'd, and cannot stay till they be orderly chosen to have thir part in the government. If the ambition of such be at all to be regarded, the best expedient will be, and with least danger, that everie two or three years a hundred or some such

---

of this Council see *Commons Journals,* December 31, 1659, and January 2, 1660, and Masson, V, 519–20.

Pursuant to a resolution of February 13, 1649, to appoint a special Secretary for Foreign Tongues, on March 5 Milton became an official of the body and began to attend its meetings (French, *Life Records,* II, 236, and references). He served this and succeeding Councils of State, apparently until the very eve of the Restoration (French, *Life Records,* IV, 280–81, and Masson, V, 624–25, 672–75).

[54] The metaphor is a commonplace in writings on politics since Plato, *Republic,* VI, 488–89, tr. Paul Shorey (2 vols., Cambridge, Mass.: Loeb Classical Library, 1946), II, 19–27. [*govern* ‹OF *governer* ‹L *gubernare* to steer ‹Gk κυβερνάω]. Milton himself uses the figure several times: *Of Reformation* (*Complete Prose,* I, 601), *Eikonoklastes* (*ibid.,* III, 408, 501), and second edition of *Readie & Easie Way* (see below, p. 458).

[55] This proposed life membership is what most distinguishes Milton's from all other contemporary models of a commonwealth; it is adumbrated in *Letter to a Friend,* above, p. 331.

[56] "Successive Parlaments" had been asked for and promised so often as to become a catch phrase. See below, p. 373, n. 72. *Cf.* Jean Bodin, *The Six Bookes of a Commonweale,* ed. Kenneth Douglas McRae (Cambridge, 1962), p. 233: "The Genowaise [Genoese] use every yeare to change their great Counsell of fower hundred, and Senat of three score, with other their Magistrats. . . . Whereas the great Counsell of Geneva, the Senat, and privie counsell are once chosen for ever . . . whereby it commeth to passe, that the Commonweal of Geneva is more firme, and less subject unto alteration or seditious innovation than is that of Genua [Genoa]."

number may go out by lot or suffrage of the rest, and the like number
be chosen in thir places; (which hath bin already thought on heer,[57]
and done in other Commonwealths:) but in my opinion better noth-
ing mov'd, unless by death or just accusation: and I shall make
mention of another way [58] to satisfie such as are reasonable, ere I end
this discourse. And least this be thought my single opinion, I shall
adde sufficient testimonie. Kingship it self is therefore counted the
more safe and durable, because the king and for the most part, his
Councel, is not changd during life: but a Commonwealth [59] is held
immortal; and therein firmest, safest and most above fortune; for
that the death of a king, causeth oft-times many dangerous altera-
tions; but the death now and then of a Senatour is not felt; the main
body of them still continuing unchang'd in greatest and noblest
Commonwealths, and as it were eternal. Therefore among the Jews,
the supream Councel of seaventie, call'd the *Sanhedrim,*[60] founded
by *Moses,* in *Athens* that of [61] *Areopagus,*[62] in *Lacedæmon* that

[57] Chiefly by James Harrington, *Oceana* [1656; ed. John Toland (London,
1787), pp. 33–228, esp. 54, 55, 57]. Harrington and others presented the idea in
a "Humble Petition of Divers well affected Persons" (*ibid.*, pp. 541–46), July
6, 1659; see esp. section 3. See also Zera S. Fink, *The Classical Republicans*
(2nd ed., Evanston, 1962), pp. 31–32, 65–66, 113, 115, 131. But whereas
Harrington categorically proposed the outright and automatic annual retirement
and replacement of a third of the membership, Milton's acceptance of the idea
here is reluctant and tentative, and the rotation he suggests would be much less
frequent, would involve smaller numbers, and would perhaps be contingent
("by lot"). In the second edition of *Readie & Easie Way,* pp. 434–35, below,
Milton accepts—still reluctantly—something much closer to Harrington's
scheme. See Woolrych, introduction, above, pp. 210–11.

[58] See below, p. 383, n. 109, "every county . . . a little commonwealth."

[59] Quarto: Commonweath.

[60] Sanhedrim: variant for *Sanhedrin,* the name in ancient Judea for assemblies
or synods convoked at various times, nominally of 70 members, following the
example of Moses (Numbers 11:16–17). These bodies exercised primarily moral
authority, in a theocratic context, as interpreters of the Law (Torah), both the
Written Law of the Hebrew Scriptures and traditional Oral Law. The term, of
Greek origin (*synedrion,* council), was most commonly used during the three
centuries following the Maccabee establishment of a Jewish commonwealth
about 160 B.C. Seventeenth-century Europe supposed it to have been a supreme
council, legislative and judicial, with a history continuous from the time of Moses.

[61] Quarto: the. Corrected in errata. See above, pp. 344, 345, nn. 18, 22.

[62] The oldest court or council at Athens, which held its sessions on a hill
northwest of the Acropolis, the Areopagus [<L<Gk Ἀρειοπᾶγος <Ἄρειος of
Ares +Πάγος hill]. It originated in the king's advisory body of chief men, and
was composed of ex-archons, who were chosen for life. It was entrusted with
the safeguarding of the state's most sacred traditions. See Aristotle, *The*

of the Ancients,[63] in *Rome* the Senat,[64] consisted of members
chosen for term of life; and by that means remaind still the same to
generati-[9]ons. In *Venice* they change indeed ofter then everie year
som particular councels of State, as that of six, or such others; but
the true [65] Senate, which upholds and sustains the government, is
the whole Aristocracy immovable.[66, 67] So in the United Provinces,
the States General, which are indeed but a Councel of State delegated
by the whole union, are not usually the same persons for above three
or six years; but the States of every City,[68] in whom the true sov-

---

Athenian Constitution, and Milton, Areopagitica, in Complete Prose, II, 486, n. 1.

[63] Lacedæmon: the southeastern district of the Peloponnesus, bounded on the north by Argolis and Arcadia, on the east by Messenia, and on the south and east by the Aegean Sea; its capital was Sparta. Plutarch, "Lycurgus," in *Plutarch's Lives*, tr. Bernadotte Perrin (10 vols., London: Loeb Classical Library, 1914), I, 219–25, describes the council of Ancients as thirty men over sixty years of age, elected for life, and the supreme authority in the government. For the Spartan constitution, see Xenophon, *Constitution of the Lacedaemonians*, in *Scripta Minora*, tr. E. C. Marchant (Cambridge, Mass.: Loeb Classical Library, 1946), pp. 135–90.

[64] [<OF senat <L senatus, literally, council of old men <senex, senis, old], in ancient Rome, the state council, whose extensive powers were curtailed under the empire. At first chosen by the kings, later by the consuls, and after the plebiscitum of Ovinius, by the censors; membership was *de facto* permanent.

[65] Quarto: full. Corrected in errata. See above, pp. 344, 345, nn. 18, 22.

[66] Quarto: sits immovable. Corrected in errata. See above, pp. 344, 345, nn. 18, 22.

[67] The Venetian executive consisted of a Doge, elected for life, and six councillors (one from each of the six tribes into which the city was divided), chosen for terms of eight months. The Senate consisted of sixty members elected annually by the Great Council, and sixty others chosen by the first sixty. The Great Council, made up of all patrician males over twenty-five years of age, was perpetual. There was also a Council of Ten, elected annually by the Great Council, which customarily sat with the Doge and the Council of Six. For discussion and references, see Fink, *The Classical Republicans*, pp. 28–32; for parallels between Milton's proposals and Venetian institutions, see Fink, "Venice and Political Thought in the Seventeenth Century," *MP*, XXVIII (1940), 155–72.

[68] Quarto: Provincial States. Corrected in errata. See above, pp. 344, 345, nn. 18, 22. After publication, Milton was evidently informed that he had been wrong in supposing that delegates to the provincial States served for life. By means of the errata, therefore, he shifts the sovereignty from the provincial States to the "States"—more properly, the town council or *vroedschap*—of each constituent city. It is true that the town councils had by this time become permanent bodies, "without succession," and composed of a narrow class of hereditary regents. In the States of Holland, which completely dominated the Republic from 1650 to 1672, eighteen towns had one vote each, and the nobility only one

rantie is plac'd, are a standing Senate, without succession, and accounted chiefly in that regard the main prop of thir libertie. And why they should be so in everie well ordered Commonwealth, they who write of policie,[69] give these reasons; "That to make the whole Senate successive, not only impairs the dignitie and lustre of the Senate, but weakens the whole Commonwealth, and brings it into manifest danger; while by this means the secrets of State are frequently divulgd, and matters of greatest consequence committed to inexpert and novice counselors, utterly to seek in the full and intimate knowledg of affairs past." I know not therefor what should be peculiar in *England* to make successive Parlaments thought safest, or convenient heer more then in all other nations, unless it be the fick'lness which is attributed to us as we are Ilanders.[70] But good education and acquisite wisdom ought to correct the

---

vote collectively. The town delegates to the States were drawn exclusively from the regent class, and it was reasonable to conclude, as Sir William Temple did, too, that sovereignty in this period lay ultimately in the towns rather than in the provincial States. But it is significant that Milton is here commending the closest and most uncontrolled oligarchy in Europe—one moreover that was undergoing a rapid progress of "aristocratization," even to the point in some cases of purchasing titles from the king of France. As for liberty, it has been said that "in order to emphasize the unlimited sovereignty of the States of Holland, . . . some of their supporters went so far as to propound absolutist political theories; in practice their power was restrained neither by an 'eminent head' of princely birth nor by their 'subjects'": D. J. Hoorda, "The Ruling Classes in Holland in the Seventeenth Century," *Britain and the Netherlands*, ed. J. S. Bromley and E. H. Kossman (Groningen: Wolters, 1964), II, p. 126. To Hoorda's article as a whole I am greatly indebted for this note.

[69] Clark argues (pp. lxii–lxiii) that the ensuing quotation, ending with "affairs past," is translated from Jean Bodin, *De Republica* (Frankfurt, 1641), iii.1: "mea tamen sententia commodius est, senatores perpetuos esse, . . . quin tanta varietate mutabiles efficiunt, . . . *non modo senatus splendorem obscurant, ac Reip. dignitatem labefactant, verumetiam Remp. in apertum discrimen coniiciunt, dum arcana promulgantur ac novis Senatoribus rerum praeteritarum ignaris summa Reip. gubernacula committuntur.*"

[70] A version of the theory of climatic influence upon the mental and physical characteristics of a people as a result of its effect upon the humors of the body. In its general form, it is traceable to Aristotle, *Politics*, VII, vii, and was regarded by Bodin as so important that he devoted a complete chapter (*Commonweale*, V.i) to it. The idea was accepted and repeatedly expressed by Milton; see Zera S. Fink, "Milton and the Theory of Climatic Influence," *MLQ*, II (1941), 67–80, and *The Classical Republicans*, pp. 91–94 and nn. 19–21, pp. 191–92; also T. B. Stroup, "Implications of the Theory of Climatic Influence in Milton," *MLQ*, IV (1943), 185–89. In its specific form, the idea that islanders and shore folk have "uncertain and unfaithful ways" occurs as

fluxible fault,[71] if any such be, of our watrie situation. I suppose therefor that the people well weighing these things, would have no cause to fear or murmur, though the Parlament, abolishing that name, as originally signifying but the *parlie* of our Commons with thir *Norman* king when he pleasd to call them,[72] should perpetuate themselves, if thir ends be faithfull and for a free Commonwealth, under the name of a Grand or General Councel: nay till this be done, I am in doubt whether our State will be ever certainlie and throughly setl'd: and say again therefor, that if the **Parlament** do this, these nations [73] will have so little cause to [10] fear or suspect them, that they will have cause rather to gratulate and thank them: nay more, if they understand thir own good rightly, will sollicit and entreat them not to throw off the great burden from thir shoulders which none are abler to bear, and to sit perpetual; never likely till then to see an end of thir troubles and continual changes, or at least never the true settlement and assurance of their libertie. And the government being now in so many faithful and experienc'd hands, next under God, so able, especially filling up their number, as they intend,[74] and abundantly sufficient so happily to govern us,

---

early as Plato, *Laws*, IV, 704–05. Bodin (*Commonweale*, p. 564), following Plato, asserts that "inhabitants upon the Sea coast . . . are more subtill, politike, and cunning, than those that lie farre from the sea and traffique." On May 30, 1659, Francesco Giavarina, Venetian Resident in England, wrote to the Doge and Senate that "In a country like this, so subject to change from the instability of the climate, which renders men themselves volatile and inconstant, it is impossible to say what form the government will take since the fall of the Protector, whether as a free state or republic and if it is likely to endure for long" (*CSP Ven.*, 1659–61, p. 23).

[71] Like Milton, both Plato and Bodin (*Commonweale*, p. 565, D) consider education a corrective for the "fluxible fault" of islanders.

[72] The thought is glancingly considered in *A Defence* (*Complete Prose*, IV, 484, but it is quite explicit in *Proposalls*, above, p. 337: "because the name of parlament is a Norman or French word, a monument of our Ancient Servitude, commonly held to consist necessarily of 3. Estates, King, Lords, & commons; & the two latter to be called by the King to parlie with him about the great affairs of his realme, it might be very agreeable with our freedome to chang the name of parliament (especially now having outlived its honour by soe many dissolucions) into the name of a Grand or Supreme Counsell: whose power may be in a manner the same with that of parlaments, to make lawes, peace, war, league, & treatie with forreigne nacions to raise taxes, coyne mony & the like which have bin formerly called regalities."

[73] England, Scotland, and Ireland.

[74] Like other passages above, such as p. 367: "Parlament have voted to fill up," this was certainly written after January 3 and 5, when the House voted to

why should the nation so little know thir own interest as to seek change, and deliver themselves up to meer titles and vanities, to persons untri'd, unknown, necessitous, implacable, and every way to be suspected: to whose power when we are once made subject, not all these our Patriots nor all the wisdom or force of the well affected joind with them can deliver us again from most certain miserie and thraldom. To return then to this most easie, most present and only cure of our distempers, the Grand Councel being thus firmly constituted to perpetuitie, and still, upon the death or default of any member, suppli'd and kept in full number, ther can be no cause alleag'd why peace, justice, plentiful trade and all prosperitie should not therupon ensue throughout the whole land; with as much assurance as can be of human things, that they shall so continue (if God favour us, and our wilfull sins provoke him not) even to the coming of our true and rightfull and only to be expected King, only worthy as he is our only Saviour, the Messiah, the Christ, the only heir of his eternal father, the only by him anointed and ordaind, since the worke of our redemtion finishd, universal Lord of all mankind.[75] The way propounded is plain, easie and open before us; without intricasies,[75a] without the mixture of inconveniencies, or any considerable objection to be [11] made, as by some frivolously,[76] that it is not practicable: and this facilitie we shall have above our next neighbouring Commonwealth,[77] (if we can keep us from the fond conceit of somthing like a duke of *Venice*, put lately into many

---

fill its vacant seats, and probably after February 18, when a bill was passed to issue writs for the elections, but certainly before the readmission of the secluded members on February 21, on which day they voided all earlier votes relating to future elections, and before February 22, when the enlarged House directed the issuance of writs for the election of a new Parliament, returnable April 25.

[75] The passage should not be regarded as either utopian or Fifth Monarchist. Although Milton's polemical purpose made it essential to stress the durability of the benefits which would follow upon establishment of a perpetual Grand Council, their continuance would be subject to only "as much assurance as can be of human things," and the prediction pertains only to the period prior to the Second Coming of Christ. *Cf.* Fixler, *Milton and the Kingdoms of God*, p. 205; on millenarianism, see Barker, *Milton and the Puritan Dilemma*, ch. xii and pp. 287–88; on utopianism, Howard F. Schultz, *Milton and Forbidden Knowledge* (New York: Modern Language Association, 1955), p. 147; and Wolfe, *Milton in the Puritan Revolution*, ch. xi and p. 287.

[75a] Quarto: intricases. Corrected in errata. See p. 345, above.

[76] Quarto: friviously.

[77] The Netherlands.

mens heads, by som one or other [78] suttly driving on under that prettie notion his own ambitious ends to a crown) that our liberty shall not be hamperd or hoverd over by any ingag'ment to such a potent family as the house of *Nassaw*,[79] of whom to stand in perpetual doubt and suspicion, but we shall live the cleerest and absolutest free nation in the world. On the contrarie, if ther be a king, which the inconsiderate multitude are now so madd upon,[80] marke how far short we are like to com of all those happinesses, which in a free State we shall immediately be possessd of. First, the Grand Councel, which, as I said before, is both the basis and main pillar in everie government, and should sit perpetually, (unless thir leisure give them now and then some intermissions or vacations easilie manageable by the Councel of State left sitting) shall be call'd, by the kings good will and utmost endeavour, as seldome as may be; [81] and then for his own ends: for it will soon return to that, let no man hope otherwise, whatever law or provision be made to the contrarie. For it is only the kings right, he will say, to call a Parlament; and this he will do most commonly about his own affairs rather then the kingdom's, as will appear planely so soon as they are call'd. For what will thir business then be and the chief expence of thir time, but an endless tugging between right of subject and royal prerogative,[82] especially

[78] Possibly Richard Cromwell, whom some proposed to re-install as Protector, but probably Monck, who was suspected in February and March of aspiring to higher places. Woolrych, introduction, above, p. 182, cites contemporary authorities.

[79] A renowned and powerful family of Germany, from which have sprung the stadtholders and sovereigns of Holland, as well as William III, King of England. The House of Orange had been pro-Stuart through the 1640's, but following the death (1650) of William II, Count of Nassau, Prince of Orange, the States Party (i.e., republicans) under John de Witt was fully in command all through the 1650's and 1660's, and had actually abolished the office of stadtholder. Naturally, English royalists tended to be Orangist in sympathy, while English republicans looked to De Witt's party to maintain the terms of the Anglo-Dutch peace of 1654, whereby William III was to be excluded from the Stadtholderate (Milton identified William with single-person government). The standard work in English is Pieter Geyl, *The Netherlands in the Seventeenth Century* (2 vols., New York, 1961), but for an excellent brief account see E. H. Kossman in *New Cambridge Modern History* (Cambridge University Press, 1961), V, 278 ff.

[80] Milton here acknowledges the dominant royalist sentiment.

[81] Milton frequently noted the reluctance of English kings to call parliaments. See *Eikonoklastes*, in *Complete Prose*, III, 383, and *A Defence, ibid.*, IV, 521.

[82] See above, pp. 366–67, n. 47, "prerogative and petition of right."

about the negative voice,[83] militia,[84] or subsidies,[85] demanded and oft-times extorted without reasonable cause appearing to the Commons, who are the only true representatives of the people; [86] but will be then mingl'd with a court-faction; besides which, within thir own walls, the sincere part of them who stand faithful to the people, will again have to [87] deal with two troublesome [12] counter-working adversaries from without, meer creatures of the king, temporal and spiritual lords,[88] made [89] up into one house, and nothing concernd with the peoples libertie. If these prevail not in what they please, though never so much against the peoples interest, the Parlament shall be soon dissolvd,[90] or sit and do nothing; not sufferd to

[83] A corollary of the royal prerogative (see above, p. 366, n. 47), a veto over Parliament's determinations. See *Eikonoklastes,* in *Complete Prose,* III, 409 and n. 9, 412, 415, 501, and Gardiner, *Great Civil War,* IV, 7, 326. The royal veto over Parliamentary bills was restored in 1660, and, although not abolished since, Queen Anne was the last monarch to employ it.

[84] Military forces, land or sea. Naturally, power of the militia, or arming of the subject, hitherto regarded as among the king's prerogatives (Gardiner, *Constitutional Documents,* p. 248), was challenged and demanded by the Parliamentary forces; see, *e.g.,* "The Militia Ordinance," March 5, 1642 (*ibid.,* pp. 245–47), "The King's Proclamation Condemning the Militia Ordinance," May 27, 1642 (*ibid.,* 248–49), "The Declaration of the Houses in Defence of the Militia Ordinance," June 6, 1642 (*ibid.,* pp. 254–58), and item 9 of "The Nineteen Propositions Sent by the Two Houses of Parliament to the King at York," June 1, 1642 (*ibid.,* pp. 249–54). See also, Gardiner, *Great Civil War,* III, 127. The matter is a main concern of chapter ten of *Eikonoklastes,* in *Complete Prose,* III, 445–56. Royal control over the armed forces was specifically restored and Parliament's right to dispose of them specifically denied in the Militia Act of 1661. See David Ogg, *England in the Reign of Charles II* (2 vols., 2d ed., Oxford, 1955), I, 198.

[85] Technically, a pecuniary aid granted by Parliament to the sovereign to meet special needs, but used by Milton here as a generic term for all parliamentary grants.

[86] See House resolution of January 4, 1649, above, p. 355, n. 6. *Cf. Eikonoklastes,* in *Complete Prose,* III, 410 and 524.

[87] Quarto: do.

[88] On abolition of the House of Lords, see Commons resolution of February 6, and act of March 19, 1649, above, p. 355, n. 6. In *A Defence* (*Complete Prose,* IV, 509), Milton had described the lords temporal and spiritual as "appointed by the king and were his companions, his domestics, as it were, his shadows."

[89] Quarto: made made.

[90] Charles dissolved his first (June 18–August 12, 1625), his second (February 6–June 11, 1626), his third (March 17, 1628–March 10, 1629, with prorogation from June 26 until January 20, 1629) Parliaments, and the so-called Short Parliament (April 13–May 5, 1640). He did not, of course, dissolve the Long Parliament (Masson, I, 368–70; II, 126–33, 216, *et passim*). Even the royalist Edward Hyde, Earl of Clarendon, said at the beginning of his *History of the*

remedie the least greevance, or enact aught advantageous to the people. Next, the Councel of State shall not be chosen by the Parlament, but by the king, still his own creatures, courtiers and favorites; who will be sure in all thir counsels to set thir maister's grandure and absolute power, in what they are able, far above the peoples libertie. I denie not but that ther may be such a king,[91] who may regard the common good before his own, may have no vitious favorite, may hearken only to the wisest and incorruptest of his Parlament; but this rarely happ'ns in a monarchie not elective; [92] and it behoves not a wise nation to committ the summ of thir well-being, the whole state of thir safetie to fortune. And admitt, that monarchy

Rebellion (ed. W. Dunn Macray, I, 5) that "Parliaments were summoned, and again dissolved. . . . And here I cannot but let myself loose to say, that no man can shew me a source from whence these waters of bitterness we now taste have more probably flowed, than from this unseasonable, unskilful, and precipitate dissolution of Parliaments."

The first Parliament elected after Charles II's return (in 1661) was not dissolved until 1679, and it was the Country party which in the mid-1670s attacked the government for keeping it in being. Nevertheless, the three Exclusion Parliaments of 1678–81 were all frustrated by early dissolutions.

[91] As the statement implies, Milton did not oppose monarchy as such, but only absolute and hereditary monarchy (see *A Defence,* in *Complete Prose,* IV, 472). A people, he says there, have the right to choose and change their form of government as they will (*ibid.,* 344), and "The form of state [is] to be fitted to the peoples disposition [, for] some live best under monarchy [.] others otherwise [,] so that the conversions of commonwealths happen not always through ambition or malice" (*Commonplace Book, ibid.,* I, 420). But no other form of government so easily slips into tyranny as monarchy (*ibid.,* IV, 427), and it is "fittest to curb degenerate, corrupt, idle, proud, luxurious people" (*Brief Notes,* pp. 481–82, below; *cf. Commonplace Book, loc. cit.*).

But since *A Defence* and even *A Second Defence,* Milton's opinion (as part of his whole reaction against the Protectorate) had hardened, so that by 1660 he regarded even the best regulated monarchy as inferior to a commonwealth.

Woolrych discusses the evolution of Milton's attitudes towards the Protectorate at length *et passim,* in introduction, above.

[92] In *Commonplace Book* (*Complete Prose,* I, 475) Milton quotes Machiavelli, *Discorsi* [in *Tutte le Opere,* 1550, p. 5], I.ii: "After it became customary for the ruler to rule by right of succession, and not by election, the heirs soon began to degenerate from the standards of their ancestors, and leaving off virtuous deeds they thought that rulers had to do nothing but surpass others in luxury and in lust and in every other form of pleasure." *Cf.* Bodin, *Commonweale,* p. 414: "Neither ought it unto any man to seeme straunge, if there have bene but few princes for their vertues famous: for . . . they to whome their kingdomes come by succession, commonly have their education polluted with so many vices, as that . . . it is almost a myracle if one of them shall be able to get out of such a gulfe of all maner of vices."

of it self may be convenient to som nations, yet to us who have thrown it out, received back again, it cannot but prove pernicious. For the kings to com, never forgetting thir former ejection, will be sure to fortifie and arme themselves sufficiently for the future against all such attempts heerafter from the people: who shall be then so narrowly watch'd and kept so low,[93] as that besides the loss of all thir blood, and treasure spent to no purpose, though they would never so fain and at the same rate, they never shall be able to regain what they now have purchasd and may enjoy, or to free themselves from any yoke impos'd upon them. Besides this, a new royal-revenue must be found; which being wholly dissipated or bought by private persons, or assign'd [94] for service don, and especially to the Armie,[95] cannot be recovered without a general confusion to men's estates,[96] or a heavy imposition on all men's purses. [13] Not to speak of revenges and offences that will be rememberd and returnd,[97]

[93] *Cf.* Milton's quotation from Guicciardini, *Historia* (Florence, 1636), pp. 126–27, in *Commonplace Book, Complete Prose,* I, 471: "Kings in the past, fearing an attack by the people, have kept them disarmed and estranged from military practice."

[94] Quarto: assing'd.

[95] "An Act for sale of the Honors, Manors, Lands heretofore belonging to the late King, Queen and Prince" (16 July, 1649; Firth and Rait, *Acts and Ordinances,* II, 168–91) resulted in the conveyance of many royal properties to the Army grandees. But the army leaders and their parties had been prime beneficiaries of the confiscations in other ways. They profiteered from their subordinates, and became landed proprietors at their expense, by buying at discount prices from the soldiers the debentures issued for arrears of pay when ready money was not available. See Davies, *Restoration,* pp. 168, 358; "A Word to the Army," in "A Rod for the Lawyers" (1659), in *Harleian Miscellany,* VII, pp. 34–35; and references, below, n. 96.

[96] Crown, church, and delinquents' lands were sold into new hands during the Interregnum, and the problem of disentangling profit, use, and ownership rights at the time of the Restoration has been described by Joan Thirsk, "The Restoration Land Settlement," *Journal of Modern History,* XXVI (1954), 316, as "one of the most vexatious of Restoration problems." See also Thirsk, "The Sales of Royalist Land during the Interregnum," *Economic History Review,* 2nd ser., V (1952–53), 188–205, and H. J. Habbakuk, "Landowners and the Civil War," *ibid.,* XVIII (1965), 130–51.

[97] On April 4/14, 1660, Charles II promised "a free and general pardon . . . to all our subjects . . . excepting only such persons as shall hereafter be excepted by Parliament," and pledged that "no crime whatsoever, committed against us or our royal father . . . shall ever rise in judgment, or be brought in question, against any of them, to the least endamagement of them, either in their lives, liberties or estates" (Gardiner, *Constitutional Documents,* pp. 465–66). For the manner in which the Convention embodied the king's promise in the

not only by the chief person, but by all his adherents; accounts and reparations that will be requir'd, suites and inditements, who knows against whom, or how many, though perhaps neuters, if not to utmost infliction, yet to imprisonment, fines, banishment; or if not these, yet disfavour, discountnance, disregard and contempt on all but the known royalist, or whom he favours, will be plentious; whatever conditions be contriv'd or trusted on.

Having thus far shewn with what ease we may now obtain a free Commonwealth, and by it with as much ease all the freedom, peace, justice, plentie that we can desire, on the otherside, the difficulties, troubles, uncertainties nay rather impossibilities to enjoy these things constantly under a monarch, I will now proceed to shew more particularly wherein our freedom and flourishing condition will be more ample and secure to us under a free Commonwealth then under kingship.[98]

The whole freedom of man consists either in spiritual or civil libertie.[99] As for spiritual, who can be at rest, who can enjoy any thing in this world with contentment, who hath not libertie to serve God and to save his own soul, according to the best light which God hath planted in him to that purpose, by the reading of his reveal'd will and the guidance of his holy spirit? That this is best pleasing to God, and that the whole Protestant Church allows no supream judge or rule in matters of religion, but the scriptures, and these to be interpreted by the scriptures themselves,[100] which

---

Act of Indemnity and Oblivion (August 29, 1660), see Woolrych, introduction, above, pp. 221–22.

[98] Quarto: kinship.

[99] In the *Second Defence* (*Complete Prose*, IV, 624), Milton had distinguished three varieties of liberty—ecclesiastical, domestic or personal, and civil. Later, in *Civil Power*, above, pp. 239–40, and *The Likeliest Means*, above, p. 274, domestic or personal liberty is subsumed under civil liberty.

[100] The doctrine that the Protestant "allows no supream judge or rule in matters of religion, but the scriptures, and these to be interpreted by the scriptures themselves" according to the individual guidance by the Holy Spirit, was many times asserted "since the Reformation." See, *e.g.*, John Calvin, *Institutes of the Christian Religion*, ed. John T. McNeill (2 vols., Philadelphia, 1960), I, Bk. I, chs. vi–vii (pp. 69–81); "Of the Authoritie of the Scriptures," art. XIX, in *The Scotch Confession of Faith* in Schaff, III, 464; "Of the Sufficing of the Holy Scriptures for Salvation," sect. VI of *The Thirty Nine Articles of the Church of England* (1571), *ibid.*, 489; section VI of *The Westminster Confession of Faith* (1647), *ibid.*, 603–04. Milton himself repeatedly expresses this position, notably in *Treatise of Civil Power in Ecclesiastical Causes* (1659),

necessarily inferrs liberty of conscience, hath bin heertofore prov'd
at large in other treatises, and might yet further by the publick
declarations, confessions, and admonitions of whole Churches and
States, obvious in all historie, since the Reformation. He who
cannot be content with this libertie to himself, but seeks violently
to impose what he will have [14] to be the only religion, upon
other men's consciences, let him know, bears a minde not only un-
christian and irreligious, but inhuman also and barbarous. And in
my judgement civil States would do much better, and remove the
cause of much hindrance and disturbance in publick affairs, much
ambition, much hypocrisie and contention among the people, if they
would not meddle at all with Ecclesiastical matters, which are both
of a quite different nature from their cognisance, and have thir
proper laws fully and compleatly with such coercive power as be-
longs to them, ordaind by Christ himself and his apostles. If ther
were no medling with Church matters in State counsels, ther
would not be such faction in chusing members of Parlament, while
every one strives to chuse him whom he takes to be of his religion;
and everie faction hath the plea of Gods cause. Ambitious leaders of
armies would then have no hypocritical pretences so ready at hand
to contest with Parlaments,[101] yea to dissolve them and make way to
thir own tyrannical designs: in summ, I verily suppose ther would be
then no more pretending [102] to a fifth monarchie of the saints: [103] but

---

above, p. 242, and it is the whole basis of the introductory address to *Christian
Doctrine* (*Complete Prose*, VI, 117–24). That Milton is thinking especially of
his own *Treatise of Civil Power* becomes evident in the revised edition, where
he says that "I have heretofore prov'd [this point] at large in another treatise,"
below, p. 456.

[101] For a notable example of the way in which ambitious army leaders had
used religious pretexts for the breaking of Parliaments, see "Declaration by the
Lord General and the Council on the Dissolution of the Long Parliament"
(April 22, 1653; Gardiner, *Constitutional Documents*, pp. 400–04), issued
after the first expulsion of the Rump on April 20, 1653. There the Rump is
charged at length, and with some eloquence, with "bitterness and opposition
to the people of God, and His spirit acting in them; which grew so prevalent,
that those persons of honour and integrity amongst them, who had eminently
appeared for God and the public good, both before and throughout this war,
were rendered of no further use in Parliament, than by meeting with a corrupt
party to give them countenance to carry on their ends" (401).

[102] Aspiring, undertaking, venturing. See *NED* 9.

[103] A radical sect whose members aimed at bringing in the "Fifth Mon-
archy" (Daniel 2:44) to succeed the four monarchies of Assyria, Persia,

much peace and tranquillitie would follow; as the United Nether-
lands have found by experience: who while they persecuted the
Arminians,[104] were in much disquiet among themselves, and in dan-

---

Greece, and Rome. During this monarchy, Christ was to reign with his saints
for a thousand years (Revelation 20:4). In league with the army, they ap-
proved of the execution of Charles as one whose reign delayed the ad-
vent of the monarchy of Christ, and their importance gradually increased
until Cromwell dissolved the Barebones Parliament (July 4–December 12,
1653), in which they were especially prominent, because he believed their
reforming zeal was pushing the Commonwealth toward disorder and chaos. Op-
posing Cromwell from that time on, their theocratic hopes revived upon his
death, and their activity waxed through the summer and fall of 1659, when they
contributed their full quota to the flood of advice to Parliament on the form
the government should take after Lambert's *coup d'état* of October 13. After
an unsuccessful uprising on January 6, 1661, its leaders were beheaded, and the
sect died out. See Louise F. Brown, *The Political Activities of the Baptists and
Fifth Monarchy Men in England During the Interregnum* (Washington, 1912);
John Rogers, *Some Account of the Life and Opinions of a Fifth Monarchy
Man* (London, 1687); P. G. Rogers, *The Fifth Monarchy Men* (London: Ox-
ford University Press, 1966); B. S. Capp, *The Fifth Monarchy Men* (Totowa,
N.J., 1972). See also, introduction, above, pp. 125–28.

    On Milton's explicit repudiation of Fifth Monarchists here, see Fixler, *Milton
and the Kingdoms of God,* pp. 206–07. *Cf.* also Barker, *Milton and the Puritan
Dilemma,* pp. 278–81.

[104] Jacobus Arminius (1560–1609) studied theology at Leyden and at Ge-
neva, under Beza, he came to doubt the Calvinistic doctrine of predestination.
In 1603 he was appointed to the chair of theology at Leyden, where the learned
Franciscus Gomarus, leader of the strict Calvinist school, had already served
for eight years. Prolonged and heated disputes by them and devoted disciples
on doctrines of predestination and free will led to appeals to the States Gen-
eral and the Estates of Holland to convene a synod to settle the disputed
questions. As the quarrel grew more embittered, Johannes Uyttenbogaert as-
sumed leadership of the Arminians, and, after consultation with John of Olden-
barnevelt, Advocate of Holland, convened Arminian preachers and laymen at
Gouda (June, 1610). There they drafted for presentation to the Estates a peti-
tion in five articles, known as the Remonstrance of Gouda, defining the points
in which they differed from orthodox Calvinistic doctrines. They insisted that
divine sovereignty was compatible with real free will in man, that Jesus Christ
died for all men—not for the elect only—and that both antelapsarian and
postlapsarian views of predestination were unbiblical. The nation divided into
a Calvinist camp, headed by Maurice of the House of Orange (who was reported
to have declared that he did not know whether predestination was blue or
green) with the majority in the Estates General, and an Arminian camp,
headed by Oldenbarnevelt with the majority in the States of Holland. Much
strife followed as the central government struggled to subdue the provinces.
The Synod of Dort (1618), to which delegates from other nations were
invited, ended in a complete Calvinist victory, and Oldenbarnevelt was con-
demned and executed. Persecution of the Arminians ceased only with the
death of Maurice in 1625. See the standard authority in English, Pieter

ger to have broke asunder into a civil war; since they have left off persecuting, they have livd in much more concord and prosperitie. And I have heard from *Polanders* themselves,[105] that they never enjoid more peace, then when religion was most at libertie among them; that then first began thir troubles, when that king [106] by instigation of the Jesuites began to force the *Cossaks* in matters of religion. This libertie of conscience, which above all other things ought to be to all men dearest and most precious, no government more inclinable not only to favour but to protect, then a free Commonwealth; as being most magnanimous, most fearless and confident of its own fair proceedings. Wheras kingship, though looking big, yet indeed most pusillanimous, full of fears, full of jealousies, startl'd at everie umbrage, as it hath bin observd of old to have ever suspected most and mistrusted them who were in most esteem for vertue and generositie of [15] minde, so it is now known to have most in doubt and suspicion them who are most reputed to be religious. Q. *Elizabeth,* though her self accounted so good a Protestant, so moderate, so confident of her subjects love, would never give way so much as to Presbyterian reformation in this land, though once and again besought, as *Cambden* [107] relates, but imprisond and

---

Geyl, *The Netherlands in the Seventeenth Century*, I, 38–83; Douglas Nobbs, *Theocracy and Toleration: A Study of the Disputes in Dutch Calvinism from 1600 to 1650* (Cambridge University Press, 1938); A. W. Harrison, *Arminianism* (London, 1937). For documents, see Schaff, I, 508; III, 545–97.

[105] Among them perhaps Samuel Hartlib (*ca.* 1600–*ca.* 1670), of Polish and English parentage but Prussian birth, whose father, a Protestant, was forced to flee from Poland to Prussia in order to escape Jesuit persecution. Milton dedicated *Of Education* (1644; *Complete Prose*, II, 362–415) to Hartlib, and evidently wrote it at his request. See G. H. Turnbull, *Hartlib, Dury and Comenius* (London, 1947), and Henry Dircks, *A Biographical Memoir of Samuel Hartlib* (London, 1865). Also *Complete Prose*, I, 151–66; II, 357–60, 362, n. 2; and Masson, III, 193–233.

[106] Sigismund III (1566–1632), whose long and turbulent reign (1587–1632) was marked by the grandiose plans and dreams of the zealous crusader for God, the Catholic faith, and the Vasa dynasty. A close friend of the Jesuits, he attempted to enforce Catholic worship, and to suppress the non-Catholic churches to which the Cossacks belonged. See *The Cambridge History of Poland,* ed. W. F. Reddaway, *et al.* (2 vols., Cambridge, 1950), II, 451–74.

[107] William Camden, *Annales . . . regnante Elizabetha ad annum . . . 1589* (I, 1615; II, 1627), I, 23. Camden, noted antiquary and historian, was educated at Christ's Hospital, St. Paul's School, and Magdalen College and Christ Church, Oxford, and was made Headmaster of Westminster School in 1593. After tours of

persecuted the verie proposers therof, alleaging it as her minde and maxim unalterable, that such reformation would diminish regal authoritie. What libertie of conscience can we then expect from others far worse principld from the cradle, traind up and governd by Popish and *Spanish* counsels,[108] and on such depending hitherto for subsistence? For they hear the Gospel speaking much of libertie, a word which monarchie and her bishops both fear and hate; but a free Commonwealth both favours and promotes; and not the word only, but the thing it self.

The other part of our freedom consists in the civil rights and advanc'ments of every person according to his merit: the enjoiment of those never more certain, and the access to these never more open, then in a free Commonwealth. And both in my opinion may be best and soonest obtain, if every county in the land were made a little commonwealth,[109] and thir chief town a city, if it be not so call'd alreadie; where the nobilitie and chief gentry may build, houses or palaces, befitting their qualitie, may bear part in the government, make their own judicial lawes, and execute them by their own elected judicatures, without appeal, in all things of civil government between man and man. So they shall have justice in thir own hands, and none to blame but themselves, if it be not well administerd. In these imployments they may exercise and fit themselves till their lot fall to be chosen into the Grand Councel, according as their worth and merit shall be taken notice of by the people. As for controversies that shall happen between men of several counties, they may repair, as they do now, to the capital citie. They should have heer also

---

antiquarian investigation all around England, he published his *Britannia* (1586), which went through many editions. The *Annales,* published some years later, was largely a panegyric of Elizabeth. Milton cites the *Annales* repeatedly in the *Commonplace Book,* and in *Of Reformation (Complete Prose,* I, 539), says that "[Elizabeth's] private *Councellors* . . . perswaded her (as *Camden* writes) that the altering of *Ecclesiasticall Policie* would move sedition." For Elizabeth's treatment of Presbyterians and other radical reformers, see Patrick Collinson, *The Elizabethan Puritan Movement* (Berkeley: University of California Press, 1967), *passim.*

[108] An allusion to Charles II, with Henrietta Maria, his French Catholic mother, and his years of residence in the Spanish Netherlands. Other Catholics in the exiled court are presumably included in the reference.

[109] The federal principle here enunciated is a vital part of Milton's scheme, but the reference to "the nobilitie and chief gentry" indicates that the dominant powers in the counties would be local oligarchies.

schools and academies [110] at thir own choice, wherin their children may be bred up in thir own sight to all learning and noble education, not in grammar only, but in all liberal arts and exercises. [16] This would soon spread much more knowledge and civilitie, yea religion, through all parts of the land: this would soon make the whole nation more industrious, more ingenuous at home, more potent, more honourable abroad. To this a free Commonwealth will easily assent; (nay the Parlament hath had alreadie som such thing in designe) for of all governments a Commonwealth aims most to make the people flourishing, vertuous, noble and high spirited. Monarchs will never permitt: whose aim is to make the people, wealthy indeed perhaps and wel-fleec't for thir own shearing, and for the supply of regal prodigalitie; but otherwise softest, basest, vitiousest, servilest, easiest to be kept under; and not only in fleece, but in minde also sheepishest; and will have all the benches of judicature annexd to the throne,[111] as a gift of royal grace that we have justice don us; whenas nothing can be more essential to the freedom of a people, then to have the administration of justice and all publick ornaments in thir own election and within thir own bounds, without long travel-

[110] These schools and academies in which the "nobilitie and chief gentry" would bring up their children "to all learning and noble education, not in grammar only, but in all liberal arts and exercises," should be distinguished from those proposed in *The Likeliest Means* (p. 305, above), where "languages and arts may be taught free together" to "tradesmen," who are to become ministers of religion. *Cf.* Wolfe, *Milton in the Puritan Revolution,* pp. 356–58; Barker, *Milton and the Puritan Dilemma,* pp. 276, 281; Woolrych, introduction, above, pp. 90–91 and 183–84.

Cf. "A Declaration of the Parliament," January 23, 1660: "The Parliament do declare, That they will uphold the public Universities and Schools of this Land, and not only continue to them the Privileges and Advantages they now enjoy, but shall be ready to give them such further Countenance as may encourage them in their Studies, and promote Godliness, Learning, and good Manners amongst them." *Old Parliamentary History,* XXII, 62.

[111] Milton presumably anticipates here that the appointment of all judges will revert to the crown. The dismissal of judges who would not toe the "high prerogative" line had been a keen grievance before the Civil War, especially the Stuart practice of appointing judges *durante beneplacito* instead of *quam diu bene se gesserint:* so see the *Grand Remonstrance* (Gardiner, *Constitutional Documents,* p. 213) and Nineteen Propositions (p. 253). Charles did in fact revive the practice of appointing judges *durante beneplacito,* and this again became a major issue in the troubles of 1678–1688, especially in the Rye House Plot trials and Bloody Assize. After the Revolution of 1688, judges were always appointed *quam diu bene se gesserint,* but this was not embodied in a statute until the Act of Settlement (1701).

ing or depending on remote places to obtain thir right or any civil accomplishment; so it be not supream, but subordinate to the general power and union of the whole Republick. In which happie firmness as in the particular above mentioned, we shall also far exceed the United Provinces, by having, not many sovranties in one Commonwealth, but many Commonwealths under one sovrantie.[112]

I have no more to say at present: few words will save us, well considerd; few and easie things, now seasonably don. But if the people be so affected, as to prostitute religion and libertie to the vain and groundless apprehension, that nothing but kingship can

[112] Kossman in *New Cambridge Modern History*, V, 276–77: "The political structure of the Dutch Republic was cumbersome and complicated: it did in fact not constitute one republic but a federation of seven sovereign provinces, each with its special characteristics. The federal government was weak. The most important of the federal institutions was the States General to which each of the provinces sent a delegation bound to vote as instructed by its principals. Unanimity was required for the States General to take a decision committing all their members. . . . They acted as the representative of the Union, conducted foreign affairs, controlled defence and federal taxation. . . . They nominated, finally, the captain-general and the admiral-general of the Union, offices usually held by the Prince of Orange. However, the States General were clearly not a sovereign body. Sovereignty resided in the States of the various provinces, the composition of which varied greatly. The States of Holland consisted of nineteen delegations each having one vote: the nobility and eighteen towns. In the States just as in the States General important decisions were normally taken unanimously: the principle of Dutch government was that none of its members could be coerced to comply with the majority. In practice a decision was reached only after long negotiations and thanks to the persuasiveness of the leading statesmen.

"The centrifugal forces in the government were sometimes checked by two important officials: the Grand Pensionary and the stadholder. The Grand Pensionary was the legal adviser of the States of Holland who acted as the president of the States and of their committees, led the provincial deputation to the States General, often carried on the correspondence of the Republic with the Dutch ambassadors abroad and received their dispatches. . . . The function of stadholder was more ambiguous. The incumbent of the stadholdership of Holland was always the Prince of Orange. He was appointed by the sovereign States and was therefore in theory a provincial official just as the Grand Pensionary. But since he was always stadholder of more than one province at the same time (Holland, Zeeland, Utrecht, Overijssel, and Guelderland normally nominated the Prince of Orange, Groningen and Drente, not represented in the States General, often did so, whereas Friesland always appointed a member of the Nassau branch of the family) and acted also as captain-general and admiral-general of the Union, he quite naturally participated in the making of federal policy. The enormous prestige, moreover, of his noble birth and the popularity of his great House gave him an influence and power not defined by any constitutional laws but none the less real and important."

restore trade, not remembring the frequent plagues and pestilences [113] that then wasted this citie,[114] such as through God's mercie, we never have felt [115] since, and that trade flourishes no where more, then in the free Commonwealths of *Italie, Germanie* and the Low Countreys,[116] before thir eyes at this day, yet if trade be grown so craving and importunate through the profuse living of tradsmen that nothing can support it, but the luxurious expences of a nation upon trifles or superfluities, so as if the people generally should betake themselves to frugalitie, it might prove a dangerous matter, least tradesmen should mutinie [17] for want of trading, and that therefor we must forgoe and set to sale religion, libertie, honour, safetie, all concernments divine or human to keep up trading,[117] if lastly, after all this

---

[113] The last major outbreak of the bubonic plague in London had occurred in 1625. An outbreak of 1665 is the basis for Defoe's *Journal of the Plague Year*. See Charles Creighton, *A History of Epidemics in Britain* (2nd ed., 2 vols., London, 1965), I, *passim*—an eccentric and interesting work. But the allusion is conceivably metaphorical and related to the idea of the Egyptian captivity, which becomes explicit within the next few lines.

[114] Quarto: cite. Corrected in errata. See above, pp. 344, 345, nn. 18, 22.

[115] Quarto: left. Corrected in errata. See above, p. 344, 345, nn. 18, 22.

[116] The statement is similar to that in "A Declaration of the Parliament," January 23, 1660: "[The people of England have their] Navigation and Trade encouraged and promoted, which in all Monarchies is stinted and restrained." *Old Parliamentary History*, XXII, 59.

[117] After 1649 there was at first a great increase in confidence and business, but with a shortage of money, falling prices, perhaps overproduction of certain commodities, and political instability, a depression began in 1659. Early in the year it was reported that there had never been greater complaints in the City for want of trade: the war with Spain had brought grave financial strain and interruption especially to the cloth and shipping trades; trade with Ireland had almost ceased because of the depredations of privateers in the Irish Channel; house rents had fallen by an average of ten percent; and bad harvests in 1658 and 1659 had resulted in markedly higher food prices. Towards the close of the year the depression tended to crisis as thousands, without employment, were hard pressed simultaneously by hunger and high taxation; and in December business was frequently suspended in London because of riots. Petitions presented on behalf of the contending political parties during this winter allude again and again to the general depression of trade and the pressure of taxes. Discounting some exaggeration because of political motives, there can be little doubt that the crisis was a serious one. Trade in general was pictured as very depressed, "to the utter ruin of many and fear of the like to others." See Whitelocke, *Memorials*, 1732 ed., p. 689; William Cunningham, *The Growth of English Industry and Commerce* (2 vols., 1910; repr. New York, 1968), II, 927; William R. Scott, *The Constitution and Finance of English, Scottish and Irish Joint-Stock Companies to 1720* (3 vols., Cambridge, 1912), I, 359–62; Maurice Ashley, *Financial and Commercial Policy under the Cromwellian Protectorate* (London: Frank Cass & Co., 1962),

light among us, the same reason shall pass for current to put our necks again under kingship, as was made use of by the *Jews* to return back to *Egypt* [118] and to the worship of thir idol queen,[119] because they falsly imagind that they then livd in more plenty and prosperitie, our condition is not sound but rotten, both in religion and all civil prudence; and will bring us soon, the way we are marching, to those calamities which attend alwaies and unavoidably on luxurie, that is to say all national judgments under forein or domestic slaverie: so far we shall be from mending our condition by monarchizing our government; what ever new conceit now possesses us. However wth all hazard I have ventur'd what I thought my dutie, to speak in season, & to forewarn my country in time: wherin I doubt not but there be many wise men in all places and degrees, but am sorrie the effects of wisdom are so little seen among us. Many circumstances and particulars I could have added in those things whereof I have spoken; but a few main matters now put speedily into execution, will suffice to recover us, and set all right: and ther will want at no time who are good at circumstances, but men who set thir mindes on main matters and sufficiently urge them, in these most difficult times I finde not many. What I have spoken, is the language of the good old cause: [120] if it seem strange to any, it will

esp. pp. 174–78; Charles Wilson, *England's Apprenticeship, 1603–1760* (London: Longmans, 1965).

Cf. "A Declaration of the Parliament," January 23, 1660: "The Parliament being very sensible of the great Decay of the Trade of these Nations, will apply themselves to such Councils and Means as shall be found most proper both for the speedy restoring and increasing thereof, judging that there is no one Thing in the Affairs of State more important to the Welfare, Strength, and Glory of a Commonwealth, especially of this, being an Island, than the Encouragement of Trade and Navigation." *Old Parliamentary History,* XXII, 62.

[118] Clark, ed., suggests Exodus 16:3: "And the children of Israel said . . . Would to God we had died by the hand of the Lord in the land of Egypt, when we sat by the fleshpots, and when we did eat bread to the full; for ye have brought us forth into this wilderness, to kill this whole assembly with hunger."

[119] Clark suggests Hathor, cow-goddess of Dendorah and Aphroditopolis, hence upper Egypt, goddess of fertility and plenty. Does the molten (golden) calf of Exodus 32:4 ("These be thy gods, O Israel, which brought thee up out of the land of Egypt") recall the worship of Hathor?

[120] An intentionally vague blanket phrase whose use was to unite as many as possible against the drift back to monarchy. See introduction, above, pp. 19–26; Woolrych, "The Good Old Cause and the Fall of the Protectorate," *Cambridge Historical Journal,* XIII (1957), 133–61; and Christopher Hill and Edmund Dell, eds., *The Good Old Cause: The English Revolution of 1640–60: Its Causes, Course and Consequences: Extracts from Contemporary Sources* (London, 1949).

not seem more strange, I hope, then convincing to backsliders.[121] Thus much I should perhaps have said, though I were sure I should have spoken only to trees and stones, and had none to cry to, but vvith the Prophet, *O earth, earth, earth:* [122] to tell the verie soil it self what God hath determined of *Coniah* and his seed for ever. But I trust, I shall have spoken perswasion to abundance of sensible and ingenuous men: to som perhaps, whom God may raise of these stones, to become children of libertie,[123] and may enable and unite in thir noble resolutions to give a stay to these our ruinous proceedings and to this general defection of the misguided and abus'd multitude.

The End. [18]

[121] See especially Hosea and Jeremiah.

[122] Jeremiah, 22:24–29. Coniah (Jehoiachin, Jeconiah), king of Judah and worthless son of the profligate and evil King Jehoiakim, surrendered to the Chaldeans under Nebuchadnezzar and was confined in Babylon for thirty-seven years. "Saith the Lord . . . I will cast thee out, and thy mother that bare thee, into another country, where ye were not born; and there shall ye die. But to the land whereunto they desire to return, thither shall they not return. Is this man Coniah a despised broken idol? is he a vessel wherein is no pleasure? Wherefore are they cast out, he and his seed, and are cast into a land which they know not? O earth, earth, earth, hear the word of the Lord. Thus saith the Lord, Write ye this man childless, a man that shall not prosper in his days: for no man of his seed shall prosper, sitting upon the throne of David, and ruling any more in Judah." It seems clear that Milton here conceives Charles I as Jehoiakim, Charles II as Jeconiah his son, Charles II's European exile as the Babylonian exile, etc.

[123] *Cf.* the voice of another crying in the wilderness, John the Baptist, preaching repentance and imminent judgment to the Pharisees and Sadducees in Judea (Matt. 3:7–9, Luke 3:8): "Think not to say within yourselves, we have Abraham to our father: for I say unto you, that God is able of these stones to raise up children unto Abraham."

THE PRESENT MEANS, AND BRIEF DELINEATION OF A FREE COMMONWEALTH

February 23–March 4, 1660

PREFACE AND NOTES BY ROBERT W. AYERS

T*he Present Means, and Brief Delineation of a Free Common-wealth* seems, from internal evidence, to be the dictated jottings for a letter—public or private—to General Monck,[1] and appears to have been first published "from the Manuscript," in *A Complete Collection of the Historical, Political and Miscellaneous Works of John Milton* (3 vols., Amsterdam [London], 1698), II, 799–800.[2]

Not only is there no evidence that it was ever sent, received, or printed in Milton's lifetime; there is no evidence that it was ever in fact finished. As printed in 1698 it is undated, unsigned, and lacking address or addressee; and there are roughnesses in the text which Milton would surely have removed from a draft for dispatch or publication.[3]

It is impossible to fix the precise date of composition of *The Present Means*. In the first sentence, mention of "ensuing Elections" establishes that it was subsequent to the House's action of February 22,[4] and an allusion to the first edition of *The Readie & Easie Way* shows that it was later than "that Book." [5] What is surely a reference to the stringent electoral qualifications decreed on February 18, and assumes

---

[1] There are three allusions to "your Excellency" and a reference to "your publish'd Letters to the Army, and your Declaration recited to the Members of Parliament" [669f23(54); E1016(2)], as well as to "[your] having a faithful Veteran Army . . . to assist you." See *Way* I, above, p. 354, n. 2.

[2] Printed also in Columbia, VI, 107–09; see note by William Haller, pp. 357–58. See above, p. 322.

[3] The opening sentence lacks a main verb, and so is not the kind of prose Milton usually wrote for publication, even with his left hand; the exceedingly long third sentence is confused in structure; and, as noted below, the antecedent of the important "they" in the first sentence of the second paragraph is uncertain.

[4] See below, p. 392, n. 1.

[5] See below, p. 394, n. 16.

their applicability to the "ensuing Elections," [6] indicates composition before the qualifications of February 18 were superseded by very much less stringent ones on March 14.[7]

But several considerations suggest a date early within this indicated period from February 23 to March 14. One is Milton's clear stress upon speed [8] as necessary to save what he regarded as a rapidly worsening situation, even while he assumes that there is still time for operation of his time-consuming plan [9]—convocation of chief gentry in London, issuance of writs, and two-stage elections—before April 25, when it was already determined that the new Parliament should meet. Even his apparently forthright trust in the sincerity of Monck's declaration to the Parliament and his letters to the army [10] hints that it was in all probability before March 5, when a Presbyterian House under the domination and perhaps the control of Monck reinstituted the Solemn League and Covenant, with its Article III—binding the Parliament "to preserve and defend the King's Majesty's person and authority, in the preservation and defense of the true religion, and liberties of the kingdom," [11] and before March 13, when it revoked the Engagement to "be true and faithful to the Commonwealth of *England,* as the same is now established, without a King, or House of Lords." [12] Altogether, assumption of a date of composition within a few days of March 1, 1660—and rather earlier than later—seems reasonable.[13]

The purpose of the draft was not, as has been said, to summarize the essential argument of the first edition of *The Readie & Easie Way;* it was rather to propose a means by which the elections decided upon on February 22 might be so managed that "the ensuing Election be

---

[6] *Cf.* below, p. 392, n. 2.

[7] See *Way* II, below, p. 432, n. 112, and above, Woolrych, introduction, p. 190.

[8] So in the title: "without Delay." In the text: "all endeavours speedily to be us'd," "speediest prevention," "speediest way will be . . . forthwith," "you will not longer delay . . . but put into thir hands forthwith . . . if they will first return immediately."

[9] Above, introduction, pp. 190–91: "Under the conditions of travel in an English March three centuries ago, it would probably have taken two weeks to send to the leading gentry of the remoter English counties and assemble them in London and at least another week for them to return home and bring their local 'standing Councils' into being—longer, indeed, if the process were to be remotely democratic. Yet it is only after this has been done that the Parliamentary elections are to proceed."

[10] See below, p. 393, and n. 5.

[11] See below, p. 409, n. 22.

[12] *Ibid.*

[13] This is in essential agreement with Masson, V, 655–56. For other views, see Wolfe, *Milton in the Puritan Revolution,* pp. 294, 461, and Lewalski, *PMLA,* LXXIV, 195.

of such as are already firm, or inclinable to constitute a free Common-
wealth . . . without single Person, or House of Lords." Milton's pro-
posal is for Monck to convoke a number of the chief gentry from every
county who should return to their own towns or territories and manage
elections by the "rightly qualifi'd" to local or regional "standing coun-
cils," which would then elect representatives to the national Grand
Council. If the gentlemen so convoked should refuse Monck's offer
of liberty and happy condition, there are others who will thankfully
accept them, and "your Excellency . . . [has] a faithful Veteran Army,
so ready, and glad to assist you in the prosecution therof." These, as
well as other details indicated in the footnotes, depart from the first
edition and look forward to the second edition of *The Readie & Easie
Way*.

THE PRESENT MEANS, AND BRIEF DELINEATION OF A FREE COMMONWEALTH, EASY TO BE PUT IN PRACTICE, AND WITHOUT DELAY. IN A LETTER TO GENERAL *MONK*.

Published from the Manuscript.

Fᴵʀsᴛ, all endeavours speedily to be us'd, that the ensuing Election [1] be of such as are already firm, or inclinable to constitute a free Commonwealth (according to the former qualifications [2] decreed in Parlament, and not yet repeal'd, as I hear) [3]

[1] On February 22 it had been resolved "That a New Parliament be summoned to appear, upon the 25th Day of *April* 1660." See *Way* II, below, p. 396, n. 5, and Introduction, above, p. 190.

[2] *Cf. Way* I, above, pp. 367–68: "If the people . . . will elect thir Knights and Burgesses . . . according to the just and necessarie qualifications decreed in Parlament, men not addicted to a single person or house of lords, the work is don." *Cf.* also *Way* II, below, p. 431: "If the people . . . will elect thir Knights and Burgesses . . . according to the just and necessarie qualifications (which for aught I hear, remain yet in force unrepeald, as they were formerly decreed in Parlament) men not addicted to a single person or house of lords, the work is don."

This statement concerning the qualifications is curious and puzzling. Qualifications for an election to fill up the Rump had indeed been fixed by a series of votes ending on February 18. While not being *specifically* repealed, they were *positively* and comprehensively repealed by a vote of the House on February 21, after the readmission of the secluded members, which vacated "all Votes of this House, touching new Elections of Members to sit and serve in this Parliament" (*Commons Journals*, VII, 846). On the following day, after the vote for a new Parliament to meet April 25, a new committee was appointed to consider qualifications for electing or being elected to that Parliament, and to "bring in an Act for repealing the Act appointing the Form of a Writ for Members to sit and serve in Parliament" (*ibid.*, p. 848).

Although the reference to "this next Parlament" makes it certain that Milton wrote the present passage after February 22, for some reason he seems to be unaware of the action of February 21.

[3] Was Milton already away from London? Or was he being left rather severely alone?

without single Person, or House of Lords. If these be not such, but the contrary, who foresees not, that our Liberties will be utterly lost in this next Parlament, without some powerful course taken, of speediest prevention? [4] The speediest way will be to call up forthwith the chief Gentlemen out of every County; to lay before them (as your Excellency hath already, both in your publish'd Letters to the Army, and your Declaration [5] recited to the Members of Parlament) the Danger and Confusion of readmitting Kingship in this Land; especially against the Rules of all Prudence and Example, in a Family once ejected,[6] and therby not to be trusted with the power of Revenge: [7] that you will not longer delay them with vain expectation, but will put into thir hands forthwith the possession of a free Commonwealth; if they will first return immediately and elect them, by such at least of the People as are rightly qualifi'd,[8] a standing Council [9] in every City, and great Town, which may then be dignified with the name of City, continually to consult the good and flourishing state of that Place, with a competent Territory adjoin'd; to assume the judicial Laws, either these that are, or such as they themselves shall new make severally, in each Commonalty, and all Judicatures, all Magistracies, to the Administration of all Justice between man and man, and all the Ornaments of publick Civility, Academies, and such like, in thir own hands. Matters appertaining to men of several Counties, or Territories, may be determin'd, as they are here at *London,* or in some more convenient Place, under equal Judges.[10]

Next, That in every such Capital Place, they will choose them [11]

[4] The purpose of the pamphlet is not simply to summarize the *Readie & Easie Way,* and its emphasis is not so much on the Grand Council as on insuring that the coming Parliament would consist of men well affected to a Commonwealth, and so be fit for the role that Milton was to cast it for in the second edition of *Readie & Easie Way.* The means is to be the managing of the forthcoming elections.

[5] See *Way* I, above, p. 354 and n. 2.

[6] *Cf. Way* II, below, p. 449.

[7] *Cf. Way* I, above, p. 378, and *Way* II, below, p. 449.

[8] *Cf. Way* II, below, p. 443.

[9] The "ordinarie assemblies . . . in the chief towns of every countie," *Way* II, below, p. 443. This is Milton's first indication of the way in which these local assemblies should be elected.

[10] In *Way* II, below, pp. 443–44, Milton considerably expanded the role that these bodies were to play. *Cf. Way* I, above, p. 383.

[11] Who are "they"? The grammatical indication is not the total electorate,

394 THE PRESENT MEANS

the usual number of ablest Knights and Burgesses, engag'd for a Commonwealth, to make up the Parlament, or (as it will from henceforth be better called) the Grand or General Council [12] of the Nation: whose Office must be, with due Caution, to dispose of Forces, both by Sea and Land, under the conduct of your Excellency, for the preservation of Peace, both at home and abroad; must raise and manage the publick Revenue, but with provided inspection of thir Accompts; [13] must administer all forein Affairs, make all General Laws, Peace, or War, but not without Assent of the standing Council in each City, or such other general Assembly [14] as may be call'd on such occasion, from the [799] whole Territory, where they may without much trouble, deliberate on all things fully, and send up thir Suffrages within a set time, by Deputies [15] appointed. Though this grand Council be perpetual (as in that Book [16] I prov'd would be best and most conformable to best examples) yet they will then, thus limited, have so little matter in thir Hands, or Power to endanger our Liberty; and the People so much in thirs, to prevent them, having all Judicial Laws in thir own choice, and free Votes in all those which concern generally the whole Commonwealth, that we shall have little cause to fear [17] the perpetuity of our general Senat; which will be then nothing else but a firm foundation and custody of our Public Liberty, Peace, and Union, through the whole Commonwealth, and the transactors of our Affairs with forein Nations.

---

but the members of the local standing councils. Milton's suggestion is that Monck should invite hand-picked members of the gentry "out of every County" to London, to be charged to return to their localities and elect standing councils, which should in turn elect the members of the Grand Council. Elections managed by this means Milton conceived to be the only way to stay the royalist deluge that was overwhelming the nation.

[12] Cf. Way I, above, p. 368, and Way II, below, p. 432.

[13] The idea appears again in Way II, below, p. 433, where Milton speaks of "inspectors deputed for satisfaction of the people, how [the public revenue] is imploid."

[14] Cf. Way II, below, p. 459: "more general assemblies . . . on such occasion," and n. 221; cf. introduction, above, pp. 210, 213.

[15] Cf. Way II, below, p. 459: "[They may] declare and publish thir assent or dissent by deputies within a time limited sent to the Grand Councel."

[16] The first edition of Readie & Easie Way.

[17] Cf. Way II, below, p. 444: "The people well weighing and performing these things, I suppose would have no cause to fear, though the Parlament . . . should, with certain limitations of thir power, sit perpetual."

If this yet be not thought enough, the known Expedient may at length be us'd, of a partial Rotation.[18]

Lastly, if these Gentlemen convocated, refuse these fair and noble Offers of immediate Liberty, and happy Condition, no doubt there be enough in every County who will thankfully accept them, your Excellency once more declaring publickly this to be your Mind, and having a faithful Veteran Army, so ready, and glad to assist you in the prosecution therof.[19] For the full and absolute Administration of Law in every County,[20] which is the difficultest of these Proposals, hath bin of most long desired; and the not granting it, held a general Grievance. The rest when they shall see the beginnings and proceedings of these Constitutions propos'd, and the orderly, the decent, the civil, the safe, the noble Effects therof, will be soon convinc'd, and by degrees come in of thir own accord, to be partakers of so happy a Government. [800]

[18] The phrase appears also in *Way* II, below, p. 435. Note the modification of Milton's ideas on rotation from *Way* I, above, pp. 369–70.

[19] *I.e.*, in the institution of these local standing councils by Monck's fiat.

[20] Demands for the decentralization of justice, by means of courts in every county or hundred, had been frequently voiced by the Levellers, and had continued after the decline of the Leveller movement. See Charles R. Niehaus, *The Issue of Law Reform in the Puritan Revolution* (unpublished dissertation, Harvard, 1957), and Stuart E. Prall, *The Agitation for Law Reform During the Puritan Revolution* (The Hague: Nijhoff, 1966), *passim*. Recent reiterations of these demands had appeared in James Freze, *A Moderate Inspection into . . . the Common Law* [June 17, 1656; E882(4)]; *England's Safety in the Law's Supremacy* [June 23, 1659; E988(13)]; and William Cole, *A Rod for the Lawyers* [July 12, 1659; E989(15)].

THE READIE AND EASIE WAY
TO ESTABLISH A FREE
COMMONWEALTH

April 1–10, 1660

PREFACE AND NOTES BY ROBERT W. AYERS

I

IMMEDIATELY upon taking their seats in the House on the morning of February 21 the secluded members, royalist and Presbyterian, voted to void all earlier votes touching new elections of members to sit in the current Parliament. Thus they wiped out the vote of qualifications of the 18th—and wrecked the whole scheme to fill up the Rump.[1]

Next, they set to work on the program Monck's secretary had laid before them earlier that morning, of "settling the Conduct [command] of the Armies" and "providing sufficient Maintenance for them," appointing a Council of State which would issue writs for the calling of a new Parliament, a legal dissolution of the present Parliament "to make Way for Succession of Parliaments," and—in religion—a "moderate, not rigid, Presbyterian Government."[2]

On the first day they settled the command of the army by making Monck Commander in Chief,[3] as he, for his part, began a purge of officers which continued "till he had not left a Zealot or a Preacher amongst them."[4] On the following day they resolved that a new Parliament should be summoned to appear on the 25th of April,[5] and on the 23rd they created a new Council of State, excluding republicans, but including Monck himself along with a majority of "new royaliz'd presbyterians." Within a week, on the 28th, they began consideration of a Militia Bill for a force "in which . . . neither Independent, Ana-

---

[1] See preface to *Way* I (February, 1660), above, p. 342, n. 10, and note, p. 353. For general background, February 22–April 25, see introduction, above, pp. 192–97.

[2] *Old Parliamentary History*, XXII, 142–43; *cf.* introduction above, p. 174.

[3] *Old Parliamentary History*, XXII, 134.

[4] *Ibid.*, p. 173.

[5] See below, p. 431, n. 112, and *Commons Journals*, VII, 848.

baptist, Fifth-Monarchy-Man or Quaker, [would have] any Sort of Command," [6] and which would be under new commissioners, to include Sir George Booth, leader of the royalist uprising in Cheshire of the previous August. On this day, too, the House began to settle religious matters, when a bill was brought in for approbation of ministers before their admittance to any public benefice.[7]

Within another week, on March 5, the Presbyterian majority revived the Westminster Confession of Faith as the standard of doctrine in a national church and reinstituted the Solemn League and Covenant, which bound the signatories to "preserve and defend the King's Majesty's person and authority, in the preservation and defense of the true religion and liberties of the Kingdom." [8] And on the 13th they annulled the Engagement "to be true and faithful to the Commonwealth of England, as the same is now established, without a King, or House of Lords." [9]

All of these events—occurring within about three weeks of the readmission of the secluded members—signaled the cresting force of the tide running towards monarchy. Still, there were cross currents; there were many besides Milton to whom the restoration of Charles was abhorrent. The republican intrigue of February for the restoration of Richard Cromwell as Protector was followed by a March movement to offer supreme power to Monck—who would have none of it.[10] And although some officers in the army who survived Monck's purge had signed their acceptance of the secluded members, they interpreted their submission to the authority of the enlarged House to extend only so far as it was grounded upon a "Free State"—a phrase Monck had used in his letter of the 21st to the regiments and garrisons. By now they did not trust the good intentions of the House respecting such a government; nor, indeed, did they trust Monck, who had refused the offer of crown lands and even the crown itself.[11] So they drafted a petition, the sense of which was that the government should be a commonwealth, without a king or single person, that the present Parliament should be required to pass the petition into an act as a fundamental constitution not to be altered by future Parliaments, and that the army should on no other terms maintain the Parliament's authority. When they presented their petition to him, Monck sternly re-

[6] *Old Parliamentary History,* XXII, 173.
[7] *Ibid.,* p. 147.
[8] See below, p. 409, n. 22, and *Old Parliamentary History,* XXII, 150.
[9] See *ibid.*
[10] *Old Parliamentary History,* XXII, 174.
[11] *Ibid.*

minded them that they were under the command of Parliament and that it was contrary to the discipline of an army to meddle with civil government; but there was understandably renewed agitation among them when the Engagement was annulled on the 13th.[12]

There was, finally, trouble from Parliament itself; as the day set for its dissolution drew near, a number of the Presbyterian majority, fearing that Charles would reintroduce episcopacy, and despite the terms of their readmission by Monck, sought to prolong their own hold on power and to alter the form of the government themselves rather than to leave this work to the incoming Parliament. Prynne said openly "that, if the King must come in, it was safest for them that he should come in by their Votes, who had made War against his Father." [13] But Prynne was muzzled, and under pressure from Monck on the 16th the House enacted writs for the election of a new Parliament to be according to "The Keepers of the Liberties of England by Authority of Parliament," [14] and on the same day dissolved its sitting.[15]

The nation did not tarry in this stage of its journey, but hastened to new elections as fast as the writs came down. On the 19th the writs were proclaimed for Middlesex,[16] and elections appear to have been appointed and held daily from no later than the 24th,[17] until by the first two weeks in April they were in full swing, with many reported as already having taken place.[18]

II

Although it is clear from the prefatory paragraph of the second edition of *The Readie & Easie Way* that the body of this edition, like that of the first, was composed before the prefatory paragraph, an updated and slightly modified version of the same passage which enables rather precise dating of the first edition makes it certain that composition of the body of the revised work postdates the March 16 dissolu-

[12] *Ibid.*, p. 176.

[13] *Ibid.*

[14] See below, p. 430, n. 110.

[15] See *ibid.*

[16] *Mercurius Politicus*, March 15–22, 1660, p. 1190.

[17] The latest date, it would appear, for the election at Canterbury. See *Mercurius Politicus*, March 22–29, 1660, p. 1195: "On Monday the 26. instant, will be the Election of Knights for *Yorkshire*. On Tuesday the 27, the Members of Parliament for the City of *London* are to be Elected; and on Wednesday the 28. those of the City of *Westminster*.

"Out of Kent it is certified, That at Canterburry [*sic*] they have already made their Election, and chosen *Sir Anthony Ager,* and *Heneage Finch,* Esquire."

[18] See *Mercurius Politicus*, March 29–April 5, 1660, pp. 1113, 1122; April 5–12, 1660, pp. 1238, 1244–45, 1252–53, 1254.

tion of the Long Parliament and the almost immediate dispatch of writs
for the new election:

> Now is the opportunitie, now the very season wherein we may obtain a
> free Commonwealth and establish it for ever in the land, without dif-
> ficulty or much delay. Writs are sent out for elections, and which is
> worth observing in the name, not of any king, but of the keepers of our
> libertie, to summon a free Parlament. . . . and if the people, laying
> aside prejudice and impatience, will seriously and calmly now consider
> thir own good both religious and civil, thir own libertie and the only
> means thereof, as shall be heer laid before them, and will elect thir
> Knights and Burgesses able men, and according to the just and necessarie
> qualifications (which for aught I hear, remain yet in force unrepeald,
> as they were formerly decreed in Parlament) men not addicted to a
> single person or house of lords, the work is don.[19]

The Rump with its select membership having passed out of existence
and the scheme Milton contemplated in *The Present Means* for man-
aging the elections never having been realized, the cause of a common-
wealth now depended entirely on the character and quality of the
representatives to be freely elected to the forthcoming Parliament. Thus
both this passage, contemplating the possibility that "the people . . .
will elect thir Knights and Burgesses able men," and the prefatory
paragraph, expressing hope that the work "may now be of much more
use and concernment to be freely publishd, in the midst of our Elec-
tions to a free Parlament, or their Sitting to consider freely of the Gov-
ernment," [20] suggest Milton's expectation that his revised counsel would
be available to the public early in this crucial period of deliberation;
indeed, it must if it were to have any effect. When he completed the
revision is not certain, but after March 27 (when the Council of State
issued the first of several warrants for the arrest of Livewell Chapman,
bookseller for the first edition of *The Readie & Easie Way*), or the next
day (when it issued a proclamation ordering Chapman's surrender and
arrest for causing "several seditious and treasonable books to be printed
and publishd," and he was ordered to appear before it on Monday,
April 2), Milton would surely not have taken it for granted that his
work would in fact be "freely publishd." [21]

Appearance of the volume with neither printer's nor bookseller's
name surely reflects their reluctance to be identified, and that, as well
as the extreme rarity of extant copies,[22] suggests fugitive printing, pos-
sibly because of the actions against Chapman. I therefore hypothesize

[19] Below, pp. 430–32.
[20] Below, p. 408.
[21] See above, p. 352, n. b.
[22] See textual note below, p. 404.

composition before March 28 and publication no later than the first week or so of April, when the elections appear to have been at their very height—in any case, before the certain mid-April composition and publication of *Brief Notes upon a Late Sermon*.[23]

III

The errata for the first edition, tardily published in *Mercurius Politicus*, March 8, 1660, had mended a few of the many faults in that hastily composed and speedily printed edition, but it had left most of them uncorrected. There remained, in addition to numerous typographical errors,[24] frequent redundancies and superfluities to be removed,[25] occasional inaccuracies to be clarified or corrected,[26] and imprudent remarks to be canceled.[27] But there were much more important reasons for revision and enlargement. The first edition, composed when the Rump was still sitting, had argued its central proposal for a representative perpetual senate in terms of special pleading for the perpetuation of a radically unrepresentative Rump which much of the nation had come to despise, and—to make matters worse—it had been published when that body no longer existed. Its confusion of the general with the particular had thus made it politically offensive, and the time of printing had made it anachronistic and irrelevant. And although by mid-March the greater part of the nation seemed past reason and recovery to be devoted to kingship, still, as we have seen, there were those who did not yield. To confirm them, therefore, Milton felt compelled to articulate again his central proposal for a "Grand

[23] Masson, V, 678, n. 1, concludes only that "Milton did publish his second and enlarged edition some time in April 1660"; and he accounts for the rarity of original copies of the second edition by supposing that "either the impression was seized before many copies had got about, or the Restoration itself came so rapidly after the publication as to make it all but abortive." Clark (p. xvi) says that "we may be reasonably certain that to . . . April 9–22, belongs the composition of the second edition. We do not know the exact date of its publication; but there is evidence that the book appeared after April 20." Elsewhere (p. xvii) he says that "The conclusion, then, is that the second edition was written certainly between March 16 and April 25, and very likely during the interval April 9–22; and that it was published upon the eve of the Restoration, almost certainly after April 20, and probably in the last six days before the setting up of kingship on the 1st of May."

[24] See above, *Way* I, p. 345, n. 22.

[25] See *e.g.*, below, p. 407, n. 4; p. 421, n. 73; p. 423, nn. 82, 83; p. 430, n. 107; p. 432, n. 113; p. 434, n. 123; p. 437, n. 136; p. 446, n. 169.

[26] See, *e.g.*, below, p. 420, n. 67; p. 433, n. 119; p. 435, n. 128; p. 436, n. 131; p. 436, n. 134.

[27] See below, p. 409, n. 18.

Councel . . . firmly constituted to perpetuitie" [28]—now without any prejudicial association with the Rump, and with greater precision, comprehensiveness, and clarity. This must be done in order to show its application to present constitutions, "least it be said hereafter, that we gave up our libertie for want of a readie way or distinct form propos'd of a free Commonwealth." [29]

This purpose, itself defined within a drastically altered political situation, accounts for deletion of all of the first edition's numerous references to the Rump, as it does for omission of a long passage on "medling with Church matters in State counsels," [30] a discussion rendered pointless if not, indeed, inflammatory by reinstitution of the Westminster Confession and the Solemn League and Covenant. And the looming certainty that Charles would be restored made unapt the first edition's concluding reference to him as a Coniah [31] who was never to return to his homeland; that too was therefore eliminated.

Following a sizable new passage which discusses the conditions, motivations, and legal grounds which underlay the original rebellion,[32] there appear enlargements and additions enough to nearly double the length of the work, especially, as Milton himself indicates, in "that part which argues for a perpetual Senat." [33] This comes about not only because he augments his original arguments justifying perpetuation,[34] but because he considers at much greater length and with far greater particularity safeguards against the abuse of authority by a perpetual Senate: [35] carefully stipulated conditions and purposes for which certain limited powers would be delegated to the national Senate,[36] with all other governmental authority to be reserved to the several regional governments; [37] membership in the Senate to be limited to "principal men" (more to be trusted, Milton says, than lesser ones), and, if necessary, to be rotated; membership, and participation in elections to membership, to be restricted to the well-affected; and, finally, the enlistment of an army or militia of the well-affected, who would certainly resist any abuse of legislative authority.[38]

[28] Below, p. 444.
[29] Below, p. 446.
[30] Above, *Way* I, pp. 379–82.
[31] *Ibid.*, p. 388.
[32] Below, pp. 409–20.
[33] Below, pp. 437–44.
[34] Below, pp. 433, 434–36, 445–46.
[35] Below, pp. 437–44.
[36] Below, pp. 432–33.
[37] Below, pp. 437–44, 459–60.
[38] For a summary of safeguards, see below, p. 461.

Elsewhere, the rhetorical need to sway forgetful or heedless voters and parliamentarians causes Milton to dilate upon the absurdity of seeking what must needs be an incapable and corrupt king to manage the nation's affairs; [39] it gives point to new passages which recall Charles' perfidy in the past [40] and prophesy, with his restoration, the return of a corrupt court [41] and a Catholic queen,[42] the confusion of men's estates, the imposition of a Cavalier army to work the king's will upon a groveling and prostrate nation—and the utter and irrecoverable extirpation of civil and religious liberty.[43]

Milton makes these and many other additions without substantial modification of the sequence and structure of the original argument, but not without a marked, even striking, alteration in tone. The approach of the dread event causes the earnestness of the first edition to sharpen to alarm and its hopefulness to sink into resignation [44] edged by ironic scorn for "a people and thir leaders especially . . . who [having] fought so gloriously for liberty . . . can change thir noble words and actions, heretofore so becoming the majesty of a free people, into the base necessitie of court flatteries and prostrations." [45]

As he moves into the darkness and splendor of his final sentences, Milton cries out to the earth [46] in the words of Jeremiah, and we are made aware that—as a messenger of God's will revealed in His Word and His works, a missionary of repentance recalling a Chosen People to God's righteousness—he has spoken with the prophet's voice from the first. Like earlier prophets inspired with a vision of the coming of the Kingdom of God, Milton intervenes in the political affairs of his nation, attempting to shape its history in accordance with what he conceives to be the will of God. In so doing, he expounds the articles of a national covenant with God of which Israel is the paradigm and archetype. This involves a moral contrast between the iniquitous thraldom of kingship and the virtuous liberty of a commonwealth,[47] like that between Egypt and Canaan; and it involves the distinctive historiographic view which, overleaping the present, extends past promises to His peculiar people unto a millennium that stands now, even at

[39] Below, pp. 447–49.
[40] Below, p. 451.
[41] Below, pp. 425–26.
[42] Below, p. 425.
[43] Below, pp. 449–50.
[44] See below, pp. 428–29, n. 105.
[45] Below, p. 428.
[46] Below, p. 462.
[47] Below, p. 409.

the door, requiring one last great act in order to realize itself: "The Grand Councel being thus firmly constituted to perpetuitie," Milton proclaims, "ther can be no cause alleag'd why peace, justice, plentifull trade and all prosperitie should not thereupon ensue throughout the whole land . . . even to the coming of our true and rightfull and only to be expected King, only worthie as he is our only Saviour, the Messiah, the Christ." [48]

The present strange and lamentable craving of the English people for monarchy is like that of the Children of Israel who yearned for a return to Egyptian servitude,[49] or like that of the "Gentilizing" Israelites [50] who, because of the alleged misgovernment of Samuel's sons, clamored for a king. And while envisioning the possibility that a saving remnant may survive the calamities to come—"som," that is, "whom God may raise of these stones to become children of reviving libertie," [51] Milton warns the nation against its evident desire to choose a captain back for Egypt,[52] and, lifting up his voice like unto a Son of Thunder, prophesies avenging judgment upon the iniquities of a Chosen People [53] no longer mindful of God's manifold wonders and mercies.[54]

By means of this archetype Milton unites English history with the history of the Reformation,[55] and the history of the Reformation in turn with the whole history of redemption; [56] so his denunciations of his people and his prophecies concerning them come to stand as a preview of the larger ordering of human history which God is enacting.

IV

The Readie and Easie Way to Establish a Free Commonwealth has been reprinted in all major collections of Milton's prose since 1698 [57] and in numerous selections. With exceptions observed in the prefatory note to the February edition, above, p. 348, all appear to have presented the text of this revised edition.

[48] Below, pp. 444–45.
[49] Below, p. 462; *cf.*, p. 450.
[50] Below, p. 449.
[51] Below, p. 463.
[52] Below, p. 463.
[53] Below, pp. 450, 462.
[54] Below, pp. 421, 423–24, 450.
[55] Below, pp. 413, 422.
[56] Below, p. 445.
[57] See editions listed in *Complete Prose*, I, 514–15.

TEXTUAL NOTE: *THE READIE AND EASIE WAY TO
ESTABLISH A FREE COMMONWEALTH*
(APRIL 1–10, 1660)

Our text presents that of the Harvard University Library copy (14496.17.2*). Collation: 12°: A-D¹², E⁶ [$5 (-A1, title page; E5) signed; E4 mis-signed B4]; 54 leaves; pp. [ii] 3–108. Contents: [A1], title page (verso blank); A2-[E6v], the work. This has been collated with the two other known extant copies: Bibliothèque Nationale (8° Nc. 1132), and The Royal Library at Copenhagen (Sfr. I. 529). There are no variants.

The readie and easie way

to establish a

free Commonwealth;

and the excellence therof com
par'd with the inconveniencies
and dangers of readmit-
ting Kingship in
this Nation.

The second edition revis'd and
augmented.

The author J. M.

LONDON,
Printed for the Author, 1660.

NOTES ON THE TITLE PAGE

Latin motto:

ᵃ Masson (V, 678) translates: "We have advised Sulla himself, advise we now the People." Adapted from Juvenal, I, 15–16: "et nos / consilium dedimus Sullae." Lucius Cornelius Sulla (138–78 B.C.) was a ruler the quasi-regal character of whose dictatorship, unlimited in power and duration, set the model of the undisguised monarchies of Caesar and the second Triumvirate. Milton is presumably referring to Monck as Sulla, and the advice may be that given in the first edition of the *Readie & Easie Way*, or that in the *Present Means and Brief Delineation of a Free Commonwealth* (pp. 392–95, above), believed to be a letter to Monck. In any case, the implication is clear that Milton no longer trusted Monck's professions of republicanism. See introduction, above, pp. 189–92, and below, p. 440.

ᵇ The printer was evidently unwilling to be identified, and is unknown. I have been unable to identify the ornamental capital on p. 3.

THE READIE AND EASIE WAY
TO ESTABLISH A FREE
COMMONWEALTH

ALTHOUGH since the writing of this treatise, the face of things hath had som change, writs for new elections have bin recall'd, and the members at first chosen, readmitted from exclusion,[1] yet not a little rejoicing to hear declar'd the resolution [2] of those [3] who are in power,[4] tending [5] to the establishment of a free Commonwealth, and to remove, if it be possible, this [3] noxious [6] humor of returning to bondage,[7] instilld of late by som deceivers,[8]

[1] The words, "to sit again in Parlament," are deleted in the revised version. They were unnecessary in the first edition; they were irrelevant in the second edition, for by the time of writing their sitting (*i.e.*, the Long Parliament's) was over.

[2] The plural of the first edition has statutory and public connotations; the singular of the revised form is general and collective, and perhaps moral or psychological in orientation. In the strict sense, "those who are in power" should have meant the Council of State elected on February 23 (Masson, V, 543–44), although there is no reason to suppose Milton was being so precise. In any case, the Council as well as the army was headed by Monck, who had been ready with resolutions for a commonwealth at the drop of a hat.

[3] The omission of "all" in the revised edition results in a more generalized and less specific reference. It may reflect recognition of Monck's pre-eminent power—or Milton may very well have learned of exceptions to the original statement before the writing of the second.

[4] The revised edition omits "now." In the first edition it was redundant. Not only would it have been redundant in the second edition, but its presence might have led the reader to think too precisely of the Council of State, entrusted with supreme authority in the interval between the two Parliaments. The Council had published no "resolution," and its composition and temper were very far from "tending to the establishment of a free Commonwealth."

[5] "Jointly tending" of the first edition connotes cooperation or collaboration, perhaps of Parliament and army. The omission of "jointly" divests the revised passage of such connotations.

[6] The change from "unsound" to "noxious" produces a far more precise and emphatic characterization of the "humour of returning to old bondage" as Milton viewed it.

[7] The phrase "old bondage" in the first edition suggests a rather comfortable distance and separation between the abhorred past and the free present, while the removal of the adjective in the revised version seems to heighten implications of the immediacy and imminence of the anticipated return to bondage.

[8] The omission of "cunning" results in a revised version emphatic, vivid,

and nourishd from bad principles and fals apprehensions among too many of the people, I thought best not to suppress what I had written, hoping that [9] it may now [10] be of much more use and concernment to be freely publishd,[11] in the midst of our Elections to a free Parlament, or [12] their sitting to consider freely of the Government; whom it behoves to have all things represented to them that may direct thir judgment therin; and I never read of any State, scarce of any tyrant grown so incurable, as to refuse counsel from [4] any in a time of public deliberation; much less to be offended. If thir absolute determination be to enthrall us, before so long a Lent of Servitude, they may permitt us a little Shroving-time [13] first, wherin to

---

explicit, and more general. *Cf.* Milton's statement in *Brief Notes,* below, p. 469: "I affirmd in the Preface of a late discourse, Entitl'd, *The ready way to establish a free Commonwealth, and the dangers of readmitting Kingship in this Nation,* that *the humor of returning to our old bondage, was instilld of late by some deceivers.*"

[9] Addition of the subordinating conjunction produces a revised version somewhat more formal.

[10] The remainder of this paragraph is importantly revised and expanded from the first edition. The revelation that "in the former edition through haste, many faults escap'd, and many books were suddenly dispersd, ere the note to mend them could be sent," supports earlier indications (see above, p. 354, n. 1) that the first edition should be dated very soon after February 21. The nation being "now . . . in the midst of our Elections to a free Parlament," the revised edition must be subsequent to March 16 (when the Long Parliament, including the secluded members, passed the act regulating the forthcoming elections, and finally enacted its own dissolution) and prior to April 25 (when the "free [Convention] Parlament" assembled). The assumption, implicit in the first edition, that reasonable composition of reasonable differences is possible, "so the same end"—establishment of a free commonwealth—"be persu'd, not insisting on this or that means," yields to ironical recognition that not all, indeed, do pursue that same end.

[11] On March 28 the Council of State ordered the arrest of Livewell Chapman, publisher of the first edition of *Readie & Easie Way.* See above, p. 352, n. b.

[12] Not here a particle coordinating phrases between which there is an alternative (*NED,* B.1. or B.4.), for the phrases are not of parallel construction, and their referents are not alternatives: first the election will be held; later, the parliament will sit. "Or" must therefore be the variant form of "ere," preposition meaning "before" in time (see *NED,* II.B.1.; *cf.* II.B.16., which cites "Ode on Christ's Nativity," 86).

[13] *I.e.,* Shrovetide, the few days before Ash Wednesday, particularly Shrove Tuesday (March 6, 1660), formerly a period set aside for going to confession, and also for lively recreation prior to Lent. Here it ironically anticipates not only a penitential "Lent of Servitude" under Charles II, but an Easter day of freedom as God may later "raise [men] of these stones to become children of reviving libertie" (below, p. 463, n. 237).

speak freely, and take our leaves of Libertie. And because in the former edition through haste,[14] many faults escap'd,[15] and many books were suddenly dispersd, ere the note to mend them could be sent, I took the opportunitie from this occasion to revise and somwhat to enlarge the whole discourse, especially that part which argues for a perpetual Senat. The treatise thus revis'd and enlarg'd, is as follows. [5]

The Parliament of *England,* assisted by a great number of the people who appeerd and stuck to them faithfullest in defence [16] of religion and thir civil liberties, judging kingship by long experience a government unnecessarie, burdensom and dangerous,[17] justly and magnanimously abolishd it; turning regal bondage into a free Commonwealth, to the admiration and terrour of our emulous neighbours.[18] They took themselves [19] not bound by the light of nature or religion,[20] to any former covnant,[21] from which the King himself by many forfeitures of a latter date or discoverie, and our [6] own longer consideration theron had more & more unbound us, both to himself and his posteritie; as hath bin ever the justice and the prudence of all wise nations that have ejected tyrannie. They covnanted *to preserve the Kings person and autoritie in the preservation of the true religion and our liberties;* [22] not in his endeavoring to

---

[14] The hasty printing and sudden dispersion of copies strongly suggests a date close to February 22 for the first edition.

[15] Errata for the first edition were printed in *Mercurius Politicus,* March 1–8, 1660, reprinted in French, *Life Records,* IV, 303. They are included without notation in the collation of the first and second editions in Columbia, VI, 359–67. See also above, *Way* I, preface, p. 345, n. 22.

[16] Deletion of the definite article before "defence" seems to make the phrase more colloquial.

[17] Although the first edition recalls the language of the Act of March 17, 1649, as well as the House resolution of the preceding February 7 (see above, *Way* I, p. 355, n. 6, the second edition in this passage precisely reproduces it.

[18] The addition of "emulous" and deletion of "and the stirring up of *France* it self, especially in *Paris* and *Bordeaux,* to our imitation," results in a great gain of economy (one word for sixteen) and concentration. On reflection, Milton may also have realized that most Englishmen would regard the Fronde as a thoroughly discreditable episode, of which it would be impolitic to remind them.

[19] Milton adds a long passage which dwells upon the conditions and motivations that brought about the rebellion in the first place. This makes more persuasive his portrayal of the evils to come if the king should return.

[20] See below, p. 412, n. 35.

[21] *I.e.,* the Solemn League and Covenant with the Scots, entered into by the House of Commons, September 25, 1643. See following note.

[22] In the Solemn League and Covenant with the Scots (September 25, 1643;

bring in upon our consciences a Popish religion, upon our liberties thraldom,[23] upon our lives destruction, by his occasioning, if not complotting, as was after discoverd, the *Irish* massacre,[24] his fomenting and arming the rebellion, his covert leaguing with the rebels against us, his refusing more [7] then seaven times, propositions [25]

Gardiner, *Constitutional Documents*, p. 268), the parties undertook "the reformation of religion in the kingdoms of England and Ireland, in doctrine, worship, discipline and government, according to the Word of God, and the example of the best reformed Churches." In Article II they pledged "without respect of persons, [to] endeavour the extirpation of Popery [and] prelacy (that is, Church government by Archbishops, Bishops . . . and all other ecclesiastical offices depending on that hierarchy)." Article III bound them "mutually to preserve the rights and privileges of the Parliaments, and the liberties of the kingdoms, and to preserve and defend the King's Majesty's person and authority, in the preservation and defence of the true religion and liberties of the kingdoms" (*ibid.*, p. 269). Milton's argument here is that Charles himself assaulted the true religion and liberties of the kingdoms, and so had forfeited any rights to defense of his own "person and authority." See *Eikonoklastes,* in *Complete Prose,* III, 592–97, and Hughes' introduction, *ibid.,* 80–88; see also Rushworth, V, 478, and Gardiner, *Great Civil War,* I, 229–36. As a test of allegiance to the Commonwealth, the Solemn League and Covenant was superseded by the "Engagement" test of Parliament (October 11, 1649; see Masson, IV, 124), later extended to all male subjects over eighteen (January 2, 1650; Gardiner, *Constitutional Documents*, p. 391), to "be true and faithful to the Commonwealth of *England,* as the same is now established, without a King, or House of Lords" (*Commons Journals,* VI, 306). But after the return of the secluded members to the House on February 21, 1660 (see above, *Way* I, p. 353, n. 1), on March 5 Commons ordered that the Solemn League and Covenant be published, forthwith be read in every church, and thereafter be read once a year. It was also to be set up in the House itself (*Commons Journals,* VII, 862). For text see Gardiner, *Constitutional Documents,* pp. 267–71.

[23] See above, *Way* I, p. 366, n, 47: "Prerogative and petition of right."

[24] On October 23, 1641, while Charles was in Scotland, several Irish counties erupted in insurrection, during the course of which some thousands of English Protestants were massacred. Sir Phelim O'Neill, who assumed leadership of the movement during the first few months, claimed to be acting by the authority of Charles, and displayed a commission under the great seal of Scotland, dated October 1 at Edinburgh, purporting to be from Charles [text in *The Mysterie of Iniquity* (1643), pp. 35–36] and empowering the Irish to "arrest and seize the Goods, Estates, and Persons of all the English Protestants within the said Kingdom to Our Use." Milton discusses this incident at length in *Eikonoklastes,* ch. XII, *Complete Prose,* III, 470–85, *q. v.* A good brief account and bibliography appear in J. C. Beckett, *The Making of Modern Ireland, 1603–1923* (New York: Knopf, 1966), pp. 82 ff., 471–72. See also Masson, II, 308–14, and Wolfe, introduction, *Complete Prose,* I, 168–70.

[25] It is impossible to determine precisely what Milton had in mind here. Perhaps (1) The Nineteen Propositions sent by The Two Houses of Parliament to the King at York (June 1, 1642; Gardiner, *Constitutional Documents,* p. 249); (2) The Propositions Presented to the King at the Treaty of Oxford

most just and necessarie to the true religion and our liberties, tenderd him by the Parlament both of *England* and *Scotland*. They made not thir covnant concerning him with no difference between a king and a god, or promisd him as *Job* did to the Almightie, *to trust in him, though he slay us:* [26] they understood that the solemn ingagement, wherin we all forswore kingship, was no more a breach of the covnant,[27] then the covnant was of the protestation before,[28] but a faithful and prudent going on both in the words, well weighd, and in the true sense of the covnant, *without respect* [8] *of persons,*[29] when we could not serve two contrary maisters,[30] God and the king, or the king and that more supreme law, sworn in the first place to maintain, our safetie and our libertie.[31] They knew the people of *England* to be a free people, themselves the representers of that freedom; [32] & although many were excluded,[33] & as many fled (so they

---

(February 1, 1643; pp. 262–67); (3) The Propositions of the Houses Presented to the King at Oxford, and Subsequently Discussed at the Trealy of Uxbridge (November 24, 1644; pp. 275–86); (4) "Proposals" of the Scots to Charles (February and March, 1646; Gardiner, *Great Civil War*, III, 71–73); (5) The Propositions of the Houses Sent to the King at Newcastle (July 13, 1646; Gardiner, *Constitutional Documents*, pp. 290–306); (6) The Four Bills, with the Propositions Accompanying Them (December 14, 1647; pp. 335–47); (7) "The Three Propositions" embodied in the Treaty of Newport (September 18, 1648; *Great Civil War*, IV, 159, 214).

[26] Job 13:15: "Though he slay me, yet will I trust in him."

[27] Duodecimo: covant.

[28] For the "Engagement" (October 11, 1649), see above, p. 410, n. 22. On December 25, 1649, it was proposed "That it be referred to a Committee, to consider of a Declaration to be published, to satisfy the People, That the Engagement is not against the former Protestation and Covenant" (*Commons Journals*, VI, 337). In "The Protestation" of May 3, 1641, Parliament had inveighed against "a Popish army levied in Ireland, and two armies brought into the bowels of this kingdom, to the hazard of His Majesty's royal person." Signers promised, among other things, "to maintain and defend . . . the true reformed Protestant religion," and to "maintain and defend His Majesty's royal person and estate, as also the power and privilege of Parliaments, [and] the lawful rights and liberties of the subjects" [Gardiner, *Constitutional Documents*, pp. 155–56, and *Documents Illustrative of English Church History*, ed. Henry Gee and William J. Hardy (New York, 1896), pp. 545–47].

[29] See above, p. 410, n. 22.

[30] *Cf.* Matthew 6:24: "No man can serve two masters: for either he will hate the one, and love the other; or else he will hold to the one, and despise the other." See also Luke 16:13.

[31] The phrases are from the Solemn League and Covenant. See above, p. 410, n. 22.

[32] See Commons resolution of January 4, 1649, above, *Way* I, p. 355, n. 6.

[33] Milton's chronology creates ambiguity here. He has just mentioned the

pretended) from tumults to *Oxford*,[34] yet they were left a sufficient number to act in Parlament; therefor not bound by any statute of preceding Parlaments, but by the law of nature [35] only, which is the

---

Engagement of 1649, yet his next words refer to the royalist members' secession to Oxford in 1643–44 as if subsequent to these exclusions. Monopolists and "army plotters" had been expelled in 1640–41 and many active royalists from 1642 onward, but the "many excluded" must surely also embrace the victims of Pride's Purge in December 1648. His theme is the Parliament as it was constituted in 1649; whatever its incompleteness, he argues, it was competent to abolish the monarchy. The number secluded by force in Pride's Purge cannot be established precisely, though in effect at least 231 men ceased to be members: compare David Underdown, *Pride's Purge* (Oxford, 1971), pp. 210–13 with Blair Worden, *The Rump Parliament* (Cambridge, 1974), pp. 391–92. Between 205 and 211 M.P.s sat in the Rump at some time, not counting ten who were elected after the Purge: see Worden, pp. 389–91.

[34] After members of the Parliament at Westminster had covenanted on June 6 to support the forces raised in defence of Parliament against those raised by the king, on June 20, 1643, Charles declared the Parliament to be no longer free. Thereafter, on August 7, a mob of 5000 partisans of the Parliament clamored in Palace Yard for rejection of peace propositions, and the few peers remaining at Westminster abandoned their seats. Then, after Parliament's conclusion of the Solemn League and Covenant in September, and in anticipation of the incursion of the Scots against his forces, Charles summoned an anti-Parliament, to consist of all members expelled or willing to withdraw from the Parliament at Westminster, and to meet at Oxford, January 22, 1644. The group that assembled on that day included the great majority of the Peers and about a third of the Commons. But the Oxford Parliament accomplished little, and was prorogued by Charles on April 16, 1644. See Gardiner, *Great Civil War*, I, *passim*.

[35] *NED*, s. v. Natural, a., I.1: "Of law or justice: Based upon the innate moral feeling of mankind; instinctively felt to be right and fair, although not prescribed by any enactment or formal compact."

The phrase "natural law" is ambiguous, the same writers frequently using it in different senses; but the central idea is that of an ultimate principle of fitness with regard to the nature of man as a rational and social being, which is, or should be, the justification of every form of positive (enacted) law. If not the source, the fountainhead is probably the passage in the *Nicomachean Ethics* (V.vii) in which justice as a necessary element in the state is divided into natural (*naturale:* rules universally recognized among civilized men) and conventional (*legale:* rules dealing with matters indifferent or indeterminate until a definite stipulation is laid down by some specific authority). Although strictly speaking *ius naturale* should signify rules of conduct deducible by reason from the general conditions of human society and *ius gentium* so much of those rules as is actually received among all civilized peoples, the terms were generally regarded as synonymous. Later, the process was carried further by the author or authors of the *Decretum* of Gratian, who identified the Law of Nature with the Law of God (the golden rule, comprised in the Law and the Gospel), and so argued that it is immutable, by antiquity and dignity supreme over all kinds of law, and prevailing over both custom and express ordinance.

For Milton's earlier use of the conception, see Sirluck, introduction, *Complete*

only law of laws truly and properly to all mankinde fundamental; the beginning and [9] the end of all Government; to which no Parlament or people that will throughly reforme, but may and must have recourse; as they had and must yet have in church reformation (if they throughly intend it) to evangelic rules; [36] not to ecclesiastical canons,[37] though never so ancient, so ratifi'd and establishd in the land by Statutes, which for the most part are meer positive laws,[38] neither natural nor moral, & so by any Parlament for just and serious considerations, without scruple to be at any time repeal'd. If others of thir number, in these things were under force,[39] they were

---

Prose, II, 1–52, 132–36, *passim*, and Hughes, introduction, *ibid.*, III, 65–80. Otherwise, from a vast bibliography, see esp. F. Pollock, "The History of the Law of Nature," in *Essays in the Law* (London, 1922), pp. 31–79; O. Gierke, *Natural Law and the Theory of Society, 1500–1800* (2 vols., London, 1934); C. G. Haines, *The Revival of Natural Law Concepts* (Cambridge, 1930).

[36] See *Treatise of Civil Power* (1659), above, p. 255: "What euangelic religion is, is told in two words, faith and charitie; or beleef and practise. That both these flow either the one from the understanding, the other from the will, or both jointly from both . . . is in part evident to common sense and principles unquestiond, the rest by scripture." See also, *ibid., passim*, especially p. 242: "Our beleef and practise, as far as we are able to apprehend and probably make appeer, is according to the will of God & his Holy Spirit within us, which we ought to follow much rather then any law of man, as not only his word every where bids us, but the very dictate of reason tells us." *Cf.* above, p. 412, n. 35, on identification of the law of nature with the law of God and the golden rule. Milton's general point seems to be to draw a parallel between the law of nature (which is anterior and superior to Parliamentary statutes) on the one hand, and the precepts and precedents of the New Testament (which are anterior and superior to the canons of the church) on the other.

[37] *Cf. Treatise of Civil Power* (1659), above, p. 243: "With good cause therfore it is the general consent of all sound protestant writers, that neither traditions, councels nor canons of any visible church, much less edicts of any magistrate or civil session, but the scripture only can be the final judge or rule in matters of religion, and that only in the conscience of every Christian to himself. Which protestation made by the first publick reformers of our religion against the imperial edicts of *Charls* the fifth, imposing church-traditions without scripture, gave first beginning to the name of *Protestant;* and with that name hath ever bin receivd this doctrine, which preferrs the scripture before the church, and acknowledges none but the Scripture sole interpreter of it self to the conscience."

[38] "Formally laid down or imposed; arbitrarily or artificially instituted; proceeding from enactment or custom; conventional; opp. to *natural*" (*NED*, s.v. Positive, a. I.1.). See especially quotation from *Rolls of Parliament*, V, 122.2 (1467–8): "All the Lawes of the world . . . resteth in three; . . . the Lawe of God, Lawe of nature and posityve Lawe."

[39] On December 11, 1648, was published "A Solemne Protestation of the imprisoned and secluded Members of the Commons House: Against the Horrid

not, but under free conscience; if others were [10] excluded by a power which they could not resist, they were not therefore to leave the helm of government [40] in no hands, to discontinue thir care of the public peace and safetie, to desert the people in anarchie and confusion; no more then when so many of thir members left them,[41] as made up in outward formalitie a more legal Parlament of three estates [42] against them. The best affected also and best principl'd of the people, stood not numbring or computing on which side were most voices in Parlament, but on which side appeerd to them most reason, most safetie, when the house divided upon [11] main matters: what was well motiond and advis'd, they examind not whether fear or perswasion carried it in the vote; neither did they measure votes and counsels by the intentions of them that voted; knowing that intentions [43] either are but guessd at, or not soon anough known; and although good, can neither make the deed such, nor prevent the consequence from being bad: suppose bad intentions in things otherwise welldon; what was welldon, was by them who so thought, not the less obey'd or followd in the state; since in the church, who had not rather follow *Iscariot* [44] or *Simon* the magi-

---

force and violence of the Officers and Souldiers of the Army, on Wednesday and Thursday last, the 6. and 7. of *Decemb.* 1648." From that time until the time of Milton's writing of *Readie & Easie Way* the opponents of the Commonwealth argued that everything done by Parliament after Pride's Purge was done under the pressure of the army. See Clement Walker, *History of Independency,* II (1649), 30, 35.

[40] See above, *Way* I, p. 369, n. 54.

[41] *I.e.,* for the Oxford Parliament. See above, p. 412, n. 34.

[42] In *Proposalls,* p. 337, above, Milton says that "the name of parlament is a Norman or French word . . . commonly held to consist necessarily of 3. Estates, King, Lords, & commons; & the two latter to be called by the King to parlie with him about the great affairs of his realme." See also, *NED,* Estates, 6, 7. Since the king sat with lords and commons in the Oxford Parliament, and only lords and commons sat at Westminster, the Oxford gathering was "in outward formalitie a more legal Parliament of three estates."

[43] "These may seem dangerous doctrines in a treatise whose central proposal is a perpetual Grand Council whose decisions in many great matters of state are to be as unquestionable by the people as its members are to be irremovable, except presumably by itself. . . . Milton, however, is concerned here to denounce the terms that the majority in the Long Parliament had been bent on concluding with Charles I in the later months of 1648—terms that were often referred to in March and April, 1660, as a possible basis for the restoration of Charles II." Woolrych, in introduction, above, p. 209.

[44] See John 12:3–6: "Then took Mary a pound of ointment of spikenard, very costly, and anointed the feet of Jesus, and wiped his feet with her hair:

cian,[45] [12] though to covetous ends, preaching, then *Saul*, though
in the uprightness of his heart persecuting the gospell? [45a] Safer they
therefor judgd what they thought the better counsels, though carried
on by some perhaps to bad ends, then the wors, by others, though
endevord with best intentions: and yet they were not to learn [46] that
a greater number might be corrupt within the walls of a Parlament
as well as of a citie [47]; wherof [48] in matters of neerest concernment all
men will be judges; nor easily permitt, that the odds of voices in thir
greatest councel, shall more endanger them by corrupt or credulous
votes, then [13] the odds of enemies by open assaults; judging that
most voices ought not alwaies to prevail where main matters are in
question; if others hence will pretend to disturb all counsels, what
is that to them who pretend not, but are in real danger; not they
only so judging, but a great though not the greatest, number of thir
chosen Patriots, who might be more in waight, then the others in
number; there being in number little vertue,[49] but by weight and

---

and the house was filled with the odor of the ointment. Then saith one of his
disciples, Judas Iscariot, Simon's son, which should betray him, Why was not
this ointment sold for three hundred pence, and given to the poor? This he
said, not that he cared for the poor; but because he was a thief, and had the
bag, and bare what was put therein."

[45] Simon Magus ["which . . . used sorcery . . . giving out that himself
was some great one," Acts 8:9], the shallowness of whose beliefs was revealed
as he offered to buy from the Apostles Peter and John the power of conferring
the Holy Ghost. He has given his name to the word—simony—for "buying or
selling ecclesiastical preferments, benefices, or emoluments." *NED*, 1.

[45a] Saul—later Paul—living "the most straitest sect of our religion . . . a
Pharisee," and being "jealous toward God" before his conversion on the road
to Damascus, "verily thought with myself, that I ought to do many things con-
trary to the name of Jesus of Nazareth. Which thing I did also in Jerusalem:
and many of the saints did I shut up in prison, having received authority from
the chief priests; and when they were put to death, I gave my voice against
them. And I punished them oft in every synagogue, and compelled them to
blaspheme; and being exceedingly mad against them, I persecuted them even
unto strange cities" (Acts 26:4, 9–11; cf. 8:3, 22:3–5).

[46] *I.e.*, they already knew.

[47] *I.e.*, a Presbyterian majority in Parliament as well as in the City of
London, with a view to saving the life of Charles and preserving the institu-
tion of kingship, wished to continue negotiations with the king in the latter
months of 1648. See Masson, III, 602–03.

[48] *I.e.*, "concerning [the soundness or corruptness of] which"—a typical
syntactical shortcut.

[49] The argument is not sophistical for Milton, who seems always to have be-
lieved in the superiority of the "fit audience . . . though few" (*Paradise Lost*,
VII, 31; *cf. First Prolusion*, in *Complete Prose*, I, 220, and *Eikonoklastes*, in

measure wisdom working all things: and the dangers on either side they seriously thus waighd: from the treatie,[50] short fruits of long labours and seaven [14] years warr; [51] securitie for twenty years,[52]

---

ibid., III, 339–40, 348). It is in fact fundamental; later (p. 455, below), in a remarkable passage, he will argue that, liberty being one main end of government, "They who seek nothing but thir own just libertie, have alwaies right to winn it and to keep it, when ever they have power, be the voices never so numerous that oppose it."

[50] *I.e.*, "treating of matters with a view to settlement, discussion of terms, conference, negotiation" (*NED*, 2). The reference is to discussions at Newport on the Isle of Wight, beginning September 8, 1648, as the Parliament essayed a final attempt at agreement with Charles. Parliament's demands, based on the Propositions of Newcastle (Gardiner, *Constitutional Documents*, pp. 290–306), included, among other things, control of the militia for twenty years, abolition of episcopacy and establishment of Presbyterianism, and confiscation of all lands belonging to bishops. Although he finally consented to Parliamentary control of the militia for twenty years (Rushworth, *Historical Collections*, VII, 1291), Charles would agree to the practice of Presbyterianism for only three years, and—although willing to allow their use under ninety-nine-year leases—would not consent to alienation of the bishops' lands. A letter presented to Parliament on Monday, October 2, 1648 (Rushworth, VII, 1281), set out his initial—and in most respects final—position: "In brief, concerning Religion his Majesty will consent, *That the calling and sitting of the Assembly of Divines at* Westminster *be confirmed for three years by Act of Parliament, and confirms for three years the Directory, and the form of Church-Government, to be used for the Churches of* England *and* Ireland, *and Dominion of* Wales. . . . *Concerning the Bishops Lands and Revenue, his Majesty will consent to an* [*Act*] *or Acts of Parliament, whereby Legal Estates for Lives, or for Years, not exceeding 99, shall be made for those Lands towards the satisfaction of the Purchasers, and to others to whom they are engaged, whereby they may receive satisfaction;* . . . *provided that the Propriety and Inheritance of those Lands may still remain to the Church.* . . . *Touching the Militia, his Majesty will consent to an Act of Parliament, to be in the Parliaments hands for ten years.* . . . *And lastly, proposeth* . . . *that an Act of Oblivion and Indempnity may pass, to extend to all Persons, for all matters relating to the late unhappy Differences, which being agreed to by his two Houses of Parliament, his Majesty will be ready to make these his Concessions binding, by giving them the force of Laws by his Royal Assent.*" The Commons immediately voted this message unsatisfactory.

For these negotiations, see particularly Rushworth, VII, 1281–1338, as above, and Sir Edward Walker, *Historical Discourses upon Several Occasions* (1705). Walker was Secretary of War to Charles I, and the latter part of his volume has as subtitle, "Perfect Copies of all the Votes, Letters, Proposals, and Answers . . . in the Treaty Held at Newport." These run to 98 folio pages. Also see Clarendon, IV, 426–52 [§ xi, 153–87]; *Cobbett's Parliamentary History*, III, cols. 1013–1133; Masson, III, 605–10; Gardiner, *Great Civil War*, III, 197; IV, 217–18, 222.

[51] The seven years may be supposed to run from 1642 (beginning of the First Civil War; Gardiner, *Great Civil War*, I, 1 ff.) through 1648 (the Second

if we can hold it; reformation in the church for three years [53]: then put to shift again with our vanquishd maister. His justice, his honour, his conscience declar'd quite contrarie to ours; which would have furnishd him with many such evasions, as in a book entitl'd *an inquisition for blood*,[54] soon after were not conceald: bishops not totally remov'd,[55] but left as it were in ambush, a reserve, with

---

Civil War, determined by the Battle of Preston, the surrender of Colchester, Cromwell's intervention in Scotland and siege of Pontefract; *ibid.*, IV, pp. 143–202).

[52] On Wednesday, October 11, 1648, the Parliament's commissioners treating with Charles on the Isle of Wight reported "that his Majesty had consented for the settling of the Militia by Sea and Land in the Parliament's hands for 20 years, as desired in the Propositions" (Rushworth, VII, 1291). But see above, p. 416, n. 50.

[53] See above, p. 416, n. 50.

[54] The preamble to the first propositions made to Charles in the Treaty of Newport (September–October, 1648) began, "Whereas both Houses of Parliament have been necessitated to take up Arms in their just and lawful Defence," etc. On Tuesday, September 19, Charles consented to the propositions, but without this preamble, acceptance of which would of course prejudicially acknowledge the justness of Parliamentary opposition to him. But on the morning of September 25 he agreed to the preamble as well as the particular propositions, "provided that nothing be binding, unless the whole be agreed upon, betwixt His Majesty and Parliament by this Treaty" (Rushworth, VII, 1275). "As Charles had himself no expectation that an understanding would ever be reached," Gardiner (*Great Civil War*, IV, 214) says, "he was thus enabled to promise whatever he found convenient, without regarding himself as in any way bound by his words." *An Inquisition After Blood* (July, 1649) acknowledged (p. 1) that "There be many, and they not only Presbyterians and Independents, but *Cavaliers* also, who think that the King had taken the guilt of all this blood upon himselfe, in regard of that Concession he passed in the preamble of the late Treaty at the *Isle of Wight*." But, the author argued, "touching the expressions and words of this Grant, they were not his owne, nor did he give order for dictating or penning thereof; the King was not the *Author* of them, but an *Assenter* only unto them" (p. 2); "Besides, He pass'd them as he doth all Lawes and Acts of Parlement . . . in his *politic* capacity, therefore they cannot prejudice his *person* any way" (p. 3); he passed them "When the razor was as it were at his throat" (p. 3); "Moreover, His Majesty pass'd this Concession with these two provisos and reservations, First, that it should be of no vertu or validity at all, till the whole Treaty were intirely consummated. Secondly, that he might when he pleas'd inlarge and cleer the truth with the reservedness of his meaning herein, by Public Declaration" (p. 3); "Add hereunto, that this *Grant* was but a meer preambular Proposition, 'twas not of the essence of the Treaty it self: And as the Philosophers and Schoolemen tell us, there is *no valid proof can be drawn out of Proemes, Introductions* or *Corallaries* in any science, but out of the positive assertions and body of the Text" (pp. 3–4).

[55] The Parliament's commissioners at Newport reported on Wednesday, Oc-

ordination in thir sole power; thir lands alreadie sold,[56] not to be alienated, but rented, and the sale of them call'd *sacrilege;* [57] delinquents [58] few of many brought to condigne punish[15]ment; acces-

---

tober 11, 1648, that Charles "is not satisfied in his Conscience, or can be content to the utter abolishing of Episcopacy; the substance whereof he conceives to consist in the Power of Ordination and Jurisdiction, as they were exercised by the Apostles themselves and others, by authority derived from them, superior to Prisbyters and Deacons in the primitive times" (Rushworth, VII, 1291; *cf.* 1301, 1302, 1303). See *Commons Journals,* VI, 62 (October 27, 1648): "*Resolved* . . . That the King's Answer . . . is not satisfactory. . . . 1. That the King doth not utterly abolish the Function and Power of Bishops . . . but only suspendeth the Exercise of their Function as to Ordination, for the Term of three Year's, and no more. . . . 2. That, during the Term of Three Years, the King may make Bishops in the old Manner; and, at the End of Three Years, the Exercise of their Function, as to the Point of Ordination in the Old Manner, is revived in such of the old Bishops as shall be then living; and in such other new Bishops as the King hath or shall make. . . . 3. Thirdly, That the Form of Church Government, presented to the King by the Houses, is, by his Answer, limited only to the Term of Three Years; and that, at the End thereof, Provision is only made for Ordination in a Way different from what the Houses have proposed; and no certain Way settled for any other Thing concerning Ecclesiastical Discipline and Government, which will be as necessary to be provided as that of Ordination. And this, the Houses do judge, at the End of the Three Years, will expose the Kingdom to new Distractions."

[56] See above, *Way* I, p. 378, n. 95: "Assign'd . . . to the Armie," and n. 96 and references therein.

[57] Through the Parliament's Commissioners, on Thursday, November 23, 1648, Charles submitted his "ultimate Answer concerning Bishops and Bishops Lands": "As to these particulars, his Majesty doth again clearly profess, that he cannot with a good Conscience consent to the total Abolition of the Function and Power of Bishops, nor to the intire and absolute Alienation of their Lands, as is desired, because he is yet perswaded in his Judgment that the former is of Apostolical Institution, and that to take away the latter is Sacrilege" (Rushworth, VII, 1334).

[58] On September 5, 1642 (*Commons Journals,* II, 753), Parliament decreed that "those great Charges and Damages wherewith all the Commonwealth hath been burthened . . . sithence his Majesty's Departure from the Parliament, may be born by the Delinquents, and other malignant and disaffected Persons; and that all his Majesty's good and well-affected Subjects; who by the Loan of Monies, or otherwise, at their Charge, have assisted the Commonwealth . . . may be repaid all Sums of Money by them lent for those Purposes . . . out of the Estates of the said Delinquents, and of the malignant and disaffected Party in this Kingdom." An "Ordinance for sequestring notorious Delinquents Estates" (March 27, 1643; text in Firth and Rait, *Acts and Ordinances,* I, 106), in effect defined a Delinquent as any "person and persons . . . as have raised or shall raise Arms against the Parliament . . . or have voluntarily contributed, or shall voluntarily contribute . . . any . . . Ayd or Assistance, for,

sories punishd; [59] the chief author,[60] above pardon, though after utmost resistance, vanquish'd; not to give, but to receive laws; yet besought,[61] treated with, and to be thankd for his gratious concessions,[62] to be honourd, worshipd, glorifi'd. If this we swore to do,[63] with what righteousness in the sight of God, with what assurance that we bring not by such an oath the whole sea of blood-guiltiness [64]

---

or towards the maintenance of any forces raised against the Parliament." Severe penalties of forfeiture were proposed for the various categories of delinquents in the Parliament's Propositions of Newcastle of July, 1646 (Gardiner, *Constitutional Documents*, pp. 302–03), but, these negotiations proving unsuccessful, the sequestrations earlier ordered were extended in a resolution of December 8, 1646 (*Commons Journals*, V, 6), so "That if any Person or Persons whatsoever shall, from henceforth, raise Arms, or maintain Arms, against both or either of the Houses of Parliament, or their Forces, that every such Person and Persons shall die without Mercy: And that his and their whole Estates shall be confiscated." In the negotiations at Newport, September, 1648, the Parliament would not agree to Charles' demand for an act of oblivion which would remove both his own and his supporters' delinquency, and the hazard it brought upon their lives and property.

[59] It has been suggested that the reference here is chiefly to Laud and Strafford. This seems doubtful, since the contrast is with "the chief author," clearly meaning the author of the Civil Wars, to which Laud and Strafford were not immediate accessories, since they were imprisoned in 1640. It seems more likely that Milton had in mind such men as Sir Charles Lucas (1613–48) and Sir George Lisle (d. 1648), brave and able commanders of royal forces, both of whom Fairfax had shot on August 28, 1648, after Colchester surrendered. See *DNB*, XI, 1219–20; XII, 229–30, and Gardiner, *Great Civil War*, IV, 203–06.

[60] In *Tenure* and *Eikonoklastes* Milton repeatedly refers to Charles as the author of England's troubles, and in *Observations upon the Articles of Peace* (May 16, 1649; *Complete Prose*, III, 328), he says of the Presbyterians in Parliament who wished before Pride's Purge to bring Charles back upon the basis of his concessions, such as they were, in the Newport negotiations, that "They had no privilege to sit there and vote home the author, the impenitent author of all our miseries . . . for a few fraudulent if not destructive concessions."

[61] See "The Commissioners Reply" (November 20, 1648; Rushworth, VII, 1335–36) to Charles' letter of November 18, 1648, concerning bishops and bishops' lands, in which they "humbly leave to [his] Majesty's Consideration," "humbly offer," "humbly say," "humbly beseech," etc.

[62] *Ibid.*

[63] *I.e.*, by swearing to the Solemn League and Covenant. See above pp. 409–10, n. 22.

[64] See *Eikonoklastes, Complete Prose*, III, 533: "As his own lipps acquitted the Parliament, not long before his death, of all the blood spilt in this Warr, so now his prayer unwittingly drawes it upon himself. . . . So that now whether purposely, or unaware he hath confess'd both to God and Man the blood-guiltiness of all this Warr to lie upon his own head."

upon our own heads? If on the other side we preferr a free government, though for the present not obtain, yet all those suggested fears and difficulties, as the event will prove, easily [16] overcome, we remain finally secure from the exasperated regal power, and out of snares; shall retain the best part of our libertie, which is our religion, and the civil part will be from these who deferr us,[65] much more easily recoverd, being neither so suttle nor so awefull as a King reinthron'd. Nor were thir [66] actions less both at home and abroad then might become the hopes of a glorious rising Commonwealth: nor were the expressions both of armie and people,[67] whether in thir publick declarations or several writings other then such as testifi'd a spirit in this nation no less noble and well fitted to the liberty of a Com[17]monwealth, then in the ancient *Greeks* or *Romans*. Nor was the heroic cause unsuccesfully defended to all Christendom against the tongue of a famous and thought invincible adversarie; [68]

[65] Strictly speaking, the government was in the hands of the Council of State appointed on February 23, but both it and the army were dominated by Monck.

[66] By changing the original "our" to "thir" Milton causes the statement to refer to the glorious actions of those "chosen Patriots" (above, p. 415) who brought about establishment of the Commonwealth in the first place—those whose actions have been considered at length in the preceding addition.

[67] The effect of a change from "both of the Army and the People" to "both of armie and people" is to clarify an implication that in the glorious days in which the Commonwealth was first established, army and people were one.

[68] In November, 1649, following the execution of Charles in January, Claude de Saumaise [L. Salmasius] (1588–1653), French classical scholar of prodigious reputation, published a long attack upon the regicides and the Commonwealth, the *Defensio Regia pro Carolo I ad Serenissimum Magnae Britanniae regem Carolum II. Filium natu majorem, Heredem & Successorem legitimum* [The Royal Defense of Charles I, to the Most Serene King of Great Britain, Charles II, His Son, His Heir, and by birth his legitimate Successor]. Basically a call for the kings of Europe to unite against the new English republic and enthrone Charles the son, then a refugee at The Hague, it appeared in many editions, but it added little to Salmasius' reputation, and is remembered principally for the fact that it evoked in December, 1651, Milton's powerful "written monument" in rejoinder—the *Pro Populo Anglicano Defensio Contra Claudii . . . Salmasii Defensionem Regiam* [A Defence of the English People, against the Royal Defence of Claudius Salmasius]. This, too, went through many editions, including two authorized revised editions, the last of which appeared in 1658. In a passage added to the conclusion of this edition, Milton said, "Such as it is, this memorial, I see, will not easily perish. It may be that civil freedom has

nor the constancie and fortitude that so nobly vindicated our liberty, our victory at once against two the most prevailing usurpers over mankinde, superstition and tyrannie unpraisd or uncelebrated in a written monument, likely to outlive detraction, as it hath hitherto convinc'd [69] or silenc'd not a few of our detractors, especially in parts abroad.[70] After our liberty and religion [71] thus prosperously fought for, gaind [18] and many years possessd, except in those unhappie interruptions, which God hath remov'd,[72] now that nothing remains, but in all reason the certain hopes of a speedie and immediat settlement [73] for ever in a firm and free Commonwealth,[74]

---

been more freely defended, but never in a greater or more outstanding instance. If then, we believe that a deed so lofty and noble was not successfully undertaken and completed without divine inspiration, there is good reason for us to suppose that the same assistance and guidance led to its being recorded and defended by my words of praise" (*Complete Prose,* IV, 536; *cf. Second Defence, ibid.,* 549).

[69] Duodecimo: covinc'd

[70] "Nor was the heroic cause . . . in parts abroad" is an autobiographical addition. As in the dedicatory address to *The Likeliest Means,* above, p. 274, Milton alludes to his performance against Salmasius in *A Defence* (1651) (*Complete Prose,* IV), as if he gained strength for his desperate resistance to collapse of the Good Old Cause by recalling the nation's and his own days of glory and triumph.

[71] In changing "liberty" to "liberty and religion" Milton makes the revised edition support the concern earlier expressed (*Way* I, above, p. 356) with both civil and religious matters; and in replacing "successfully" by the more tentative "prosperously" causes the revised version to reflect the hazard in which he felt English liberty and religion now stood, in the shadow of the Restoration.

[72] Milton deletes a reference to the third convening of the Rump, since it had been overwhelmed by admission of the secluded members on February 21, and the Parliament had been dissolved on March 16.

[73] The phrase "to this nation" following "settlement" in the first edition was superfluous.

[74] The addition, "for this . . . voutsaf't from heaven," augments the earlier addition (see above, p. 420, n. 68) concerning the repute of the nation after the elimination of Charles and publication of Milton's own *Defence of the English People.* But more importantly, to those who still have ears to hear, Milton is recalling the vision of England as an—even *the*—Elect Nation, which had inspired so many sermons and tracts, including Milton's own, in the 1640's. For this theme and the ideology of the English Revolution in general, see William Haller, *Foxe's Book of Martyrs and the Elect Nation* (London: Jonathan Cape, 1963), esp. pp. 238–42, and William Lamont, *Godly Rule.*

for this extolld and magnifi'd nation, regardless both of honour
wonn or deliverances voutsaf't from heaven, to fall back or rather
to creep back so poorly as it seems the multitude would to thir once
abjur'd and detested thraldom of Kingship,[75] to be our selves the
slanderers of our own just and religious deeds, though don by som
to covetous and ambitious ends,[76] [19] yet not therefor to be staind
with their infamie, or they to asperse the integritie of others, and
yet these now by revolting from the conscience of deeds welldon
both in church and state, to throw away and forsake, or rather to
betray a just and noble cause for the mixture of bad men who have
ill manag'd and abus'd it (which had our fathers don heretofore,
and on the same pretence deserted true religion, what had long ere
this become of our gospel and all protestant reformation so much
intermixt with the avarice and ambition of som reformers?) and by
thus relapsing, to verifie all the [20] bitter predictions of our tri-
umphing enemies, who will now think they wisely discernd and justly
censur'd both us and all our actions as rash, rebellious, hypocritical
and impious, not only argues a strange degenerate contagion [77] sud-
denly spread among us fitted and prepar'd for new slaverie, but will
render us a scorn and derision to all our neighbours. And what will
they at best [78] say of us and of the whole *English* name,[79] but scoff-
ingly as of that foolish builder, mentiond by our Saviour, who

[75] The addition, "to be our selves . . . hypocritical and impious," gives new
emphasis to the idea of religious liberty, and adduces an historical argument
for consistency: if our forefathers had argued and acted as the royalists now
argue and act, the "just and noble cause" of the protestant reformation itself
would have been abandoned and lost because of the base motivations and
actions of a few corrupt reformers. Again, Milton notes the irony of a situa-
tion in which we should "be our selves the slanderers of our own just and re-
ligious deeds, though don by som to covetous and ambitious ends."

[76] The reference here seems to be primarily to the army officers who erected
the Protectorate, and who were more recently responsible for the *coup d'état* of
October 13, 1659, and the fiasco of the Committee of Safety. The "just and
noble cause" was superior to "the mixture of bad men who have ill manag'd
and abus'd it."

[77] The change of "corruption" to "contagion" emphasizes the *infectious*
character of the corruption which Milton will later (below, p. 463) characterize
as an "epidemic madness."

[78] The addition, "at best," is hyperbolical. The effect is to introduce or
heighten an ironical and taunting tone by emphasizing what will be alleged as
the vast gulf between the promises and the performance of the English reform-
ers if the king should return.

[79] "and of the whole *English* name" added. See previous note.

began to build a tower, and was not able to finish it. Where is this goodly tower of a Commonwealth, which the English boasted [21] they would build to overshaddow kings, and be another *Rome* in the west? The foundation indeed they laid gallantly; but fell into a wors confusion, not of tongues, but of factions, then those at the tower of *Babel;* and have left no memorial of thir work behinde them remaining, but in the common laughter of *Europ*. Which must needs redound the more to our shame, if we but look on our neighbours the United Provinces, to us inferior in all outward advantages; who notwithstanding, in the midst of greater difficulties, courageously, wisely, constantly went through with the same work, [22] and are setl'd in all the happie enjoiments of a potent and flourishing Republic to this day.

Besides this, if we returne to Kingship, and soon repent, as undoubtedly we shall, when we begin to finde the old encroachments coming on by little and little upon our consciences, which must necessarily proceed from king and bishop united inseparably in one interest, we may be forc'd perhaps to fight over again all that we have fought, and spend over again all that we have spent, but are never like to attain thus far as we are now advanc'd to the recoverie of our freedom, never [80] to have [23] it in possession as we now have it, never to be voutsaf't heerafter the like mercies and signal assistances from heaven [81] in our cause, if by our ingratefull backsliding we make these fruitless; flying now to regal concessions from his divine condescensions and gratious answers [82] to our once importuning praiers against the tyrannie which we then groand under [83]: making vain and viler then dirt the blood of so many thousand

[80] Deletion of the qualifying "likely" makes the revised version stronger and more categorical in its prophecy of the gravely adverse consequences to flow from the return of kingship.

[81] *The Censure of the Rota* (March 26; Thomason, March 30) seems to attribute the phrase to Cromwell: "You are not ashamed to rob Oliver Cromwell himself, and make use of his canting, with signal assistances from heaven, and answering condescensions." In *Harleian Miscellany*, VII, 119.

[82] The prepositional phrase "to our selves" in the first edition was unnecessary, and is so deleted. The revision from "gratious condescensions and answers" to "divine condescensions and gratious answers" is one of a number of small touches that stress the impiety, even the apostasy, involved in betraying the cause of the Elect Nation that God had blessed. In addition, the irony is heightened.

[83] Deleted following "under," a redundant passage ("to become . . . bondage").

faithfull and valiant *English* men, who left us in this libertie, bought with thir lives; losing by a strange after game of folly, all the battels we have wonn,[84] together with all *Scotland* as to our conquest, [24] hereby lost, which never any of our kings could conquer, all the treasure we have spent, not that corruptible treasure only, but that far more precious of all our late miraculous deliverances; treading back again with lost labour all our happie steps in the progress of reformation; [85] and most pittifully depriving our selves the instant fruition of that free government which we have so dearly purchasd, a free Commonwealth, not only held by wisest men in all ages the noblest, the manliest, the equallest, the justest government, the most agreeable to all due libertie and proportiond equalitie, both human, civil, and [25] Christian, most cherishing to vertue and true religion, but also (I may say it with greatest probabilitie) planely commended, or rather enjoind by our Saviour himself, to all Christians, not without remarkable disallowance, and the brand of *gentilism* upon kingship. God in much displeasure gave a king to the *Israelites*, and imputed it a sin to them that they sought one: but *Christ* apparently forbids his disciples to admitt of any such heathenish government: *the kings of the gentiles,* saith he, *exercise lordship over them;* and they that *exercise authoritie upon them, are call'd benefactors: but ye shall not be so; but he that* [26] *is greatest among you, let him be as the younger; and he that is chief, as he that serveth.* The occasion of these his words was the ambitious desire of *Zebede's* two sons, to be exalted above thir brethren in his kingdom, which they thought was to be ere long upon earth. That he speaks of civil government, is manifest by the former part of the comparison,

---

[84] Milton adds a reference to the conquest of Scotland, and anticipates its loss, should Charles return. Although Cromwell had carried through the conquest in 1650–51, negotiations over the formal union of the two Commonwealths were so protracted that the Rump had not completed them when it was dissolved in April, 1653; see C. H. Firth, ed., *Scotland and the Commonwealth* (Edinburgh: Scottish Historical Society, 1895), esp. pp. xxiii–xxviii, and C. Sanford Terry, *The Cromwellian Union* (Edinburgh: Scottish Historical Society, 1902), *passim.* The union was thereafter promulgated by an Ordinance of Cromwell and the Council of State (April 12, 1654) and confirmed by an Act of Parliament passed on June 26, 1657 (Firth and Rait, *Acts and Ordinances,* II, 871–75, 1131). As Milton correctly foresaw, these measures, like all others enacted without the king's assent, became void at the Restoration, and permanent union with Scotland was not achieved until 1707.

[85] The metaphor in the addition, "treading . . . reformation," vividly and pathetically expresses the loss to religion and reformation.

which inferrs the other part to be alwaies in the same kinde. And what government coms neerer to this precept of Christ, then a free Commonwealth; wherin they who are greatest, are perpetual servants and drudges to the public at thir own cost and [27] charges, neglect thir own affairs; yet are not elevated above thir brethren; live soberly in thir families, walk the streets as other men, may be spoken to freely, familiarly, friendly, without adoration. Wheras a king must be ador'd like a Demigod, with a dissolute and haughtie court about him, of vast expence and luxurie, masks and revels, to the debaushing of our prime gentry both male and female; [86] not in thir passetimes only, but in earnest, by the loos imploiments of court service, which will be then thought honorable. There will be a queen also of no less charge; in most likelihood outlandish [87] [28] and a Papist; [88] besides a queen mother [89] such alreadie; together with both thir courts and numerous train: then a royal issue,[90] and ere long severally thir sumptuous courts; to the multiplying of a servile crew, not of servants only, but of nobility and gentry, bred up then to the hopes not of public, but of court offices; to be stewards, chamberlains, ushers, grooms, even of the close-stool; [91] and the lower

[86] While the first edition stressed the financial cost of royal "masks and revels," the new passage, "not . . . but to bestow," stresses the likely moral and social effects of a haughty, dissolute, and Catholic court: a servile, debased, and sycophantic people, and the loss of reformation. Again, the ironical tone is heightened.

[87] Ambiguously, "foreign" or "bizarre, uncouth" (*NED*, 1, 2).

[88] Milton may have anticipated the likelihood of a Catholic match because of Charles' alliance with Spain following his expulsion from refuge in France, as a consequence of the French alliance established by Cromwell. In any case, on May 21, 1662, Charles married Catherine of Braganza, a princess of the royal house of Portugal, although Portugal was at that time still fighting for independence from Spain; and the match was strongly encouraged by France, with whom Charles renewed close ties after the Restoration.

[89] Henrietta Maria, wife of Charles I and Queen Mother to Charles II, was the youngest sister of the late king of France, Louis XIII, and, like her queen successor, both "outlandish and a Papist."

[90] As Clark (p. 89) says, "Charles died without legitimate offspring, but not without a numerous bastard progeny."

[91] Close-stool: "A chamber utensil enclosed in a stool or box" (NED, s. v., which quotes this passage). See "Ordinances made by King Charles II for the Government of His Household," in *A Collection of Ordinances and Regulations for the Government of the Royal Household . . . from King Edward III to King William and Queen Mary* (London, 1790), p. 364, where Charles declares that "For our Bedchamber and Back-staires Wee recommend the care and government thereof to the Groome of the Stole." Earlier, Henry VI had listed

thir mindes debas'd with court opinions, contrarie to all vertue and reformation, the haughtier will be thir pride and profuseness: we may well remember this not long since at home; or need but [29] look at present into the *French* court,[92] where enticements and preferments daily draw away and pervert the Protestant Nobilitie. As to the burden of expence, to our cost we shall soon know it; for any good to us, deserving to be termd no better then the vast and lavish price of our subjection and their debausherie; which we are now so greedily cheapning,[93] and would so fain be paying most inconsideratly to a single person; who for any thing wherin the public really needs him, will have little els to do, but to bestow the eating and drinking of excessive dainties, to set a pompous [30] face upon the superficial actings of State, to pageant himself up and down in progress among the perpetual bowings and cringings of an abject people, on either side deifying and adoring him [94] for nothing don that can deserve it. For what can hee more then another man? who even in the expression of a late court-poet, sits only like a great cypher set to no purpose before a long row of other significant figures. Nay it is well and happy for the people if thir King be but a cypher, being oft times a mischief, a pest, a scourge of the nation, and which is wors, not to be remov'd, not [31] to be controul'd, much less accus'd or brought to punishment, without the danger of a common ruin, without the shaking and almost subversion of the whole land. Wheras in a free Commonwealth, any governor or chief counselor offending,

---

William Grymesby as "Yoman of the Stoole" (*ibid*, p. *18); and Henry VIII had ordained that "It is the King's pleasure, that Mr. Norres shall be in the roome of Sir William Compton, not onely giveing his attendance as groome of the King's stoole, but also in his bed-chamber, and other privy places, as shall stand with his pleasure; and the King's expresse commandment is, that none other . . . presume to enter or follow his Grace into the said bed chamber, or any other secret place, unlesse he shall be called and admitted thereunto by his said grace," *ibid.*, p. 156.

[92] Although the splendor and voluptuousness of the court of Louis XIV are legend, he did not assume the full exercise of his royal authority until March, 1661, following the death of Mazarin. From 1643 until that time it was Mazarin and Anne of Austria, Queen Mother, who presided over the French court and set its tone.

[93] Ambiguously, "bargaining over," "lowering the price of," and "bringing into contempt" (*NED*, 1, 3, 3.b.).

[94] The revision, "for nothing . . . even," categorically excludes the possibility —allowed by the first version—that a king can at all deserve the "bowings and cringings of an abject people."

may be remov'd and punishd without the least commotion. Certainly then that people must needs be madd or strangely infatuated, that build the chief hope of thir common happiness or safetie on a single person: who if he happen to be good, can do no more then another man, if to be bad, hath in his hands to do more evil without check, then millions of other [32] men. The happiness of a nation must needs be firmest and certainest in a full and free Councel of thir own electing, where no single person, but reason only swaies. And what madness is it, for them who might manage nobly thir own affairs themselves, sluggishly and we[a]kly to devolve all on a single person; and more like boyes under age then men, to committ all to his patronage and disposal, who neither can performe what he undertakes, and yet for undertaking it, though royally paid, will not be thir servant, but thir lord? how unmanly must it needs be, to count such [33] a one the breath of our nostrils, to hang all our felicity on him, all our safetie, our well-being, for which if we were aught els but sluggards or babies, we need depend on none but God and our own counsels, our own active vertue and industrie; *Go to the Ant, thou sluggard,* saith *Solomon; consider her waies, and be wise; which having no prince, ruler, or lord, provides her meat in the summer, and gathers her food in the harvest.* which evidently [95] shews us, that they who think the nation undon without a king, though they look grave or haughtie,[96] have not so much true spirit and understanding in them [34] as a pismire: [97] neither are these diligent creatures hence concluded to live in lawless anarchie, or that commended, but are set the examples to imprudent and ungovernd men, of a frugal and self-governing democratie or Commonwealth; safer and more thriving in the joint providence and counsel of many industrious equals, then under the single domination of one imperious Lord. It may be well wonderd that any Nation styling themselves free, can suffer any man to pretend hereditarie right [98] over them as thir lord; when as

[95] Duodecimo: evidently.

[96] The revision concentrates on the signs of pride of understanding—solemnity and hauteur in appearance and demeanor.

[97] The addition, "neither . . . Lord," interprets the Biblical text, Proverbs 6:6–8, as supporting from nature Milton's argument for a commonwealth.

[98] The insertion of "hereditarie" renders the revised version consistent with Milton's long-held belief that a king may rule by right through delegation of powers by the people (see above, *Way* I, p. 363, n. 28). At the same time, if introduced into the text early in the process of revision, perhaps early or mid-March (the title-page motto notwithstanding, as a possible last touch before

by acknowledging that right, they conclude themselves his [35] servants and his vassals, and so renounce thir own freedom. Which how a people and thir leaders especially [99] can do, who [100] have fought so gloriously for liberty, how they can change thir noble words and actions, heretofore so becoming the majesty of a free people, into the base necessitie of court flatteries and prostrations, is not only strange and admirable, but lamentable to think on. That a nation should be so valorous and courageous to winn thir liberty in the field, and when they have wonn it, should be so heartless and [101] unwise in thir counsels, as not to know how to use it, value it, what to do with it [36] or with themselves; but after ten or twelve years prosperous warr and contestation with tyrannie, basely and besottedly to run their necks again into the yoke which they have broken, and prostrate all the fruits of thir victorie for naught [102] at the feet of the vanquishd, besides our loss of glorie,[103] and such an example as kings or tyrants never yet had the like to boast of, will be an ignomine if it befall us, that never yet befell any nation possessd of thir libertie; worthie indeed themselves, whatsoever [104] they be, to be for ever slaves: but that part of the nation which consents not with them, as I perswade me [37] of a great number, far worthier then by their means to be brought into the same bondage.[105]

---

publication), it is not inconsistent with Milton's contemplation of the assumption of the crown by Monck as a lesser evil than the restoration of Charles II (see below, *Brief Notes*, p. 482, and above, Woolrych, introduction, p. 203).

[99] The revision shifts primary responsibility for the base and foolish turn to royalism from the people to "thir leaders especially," the ruling Council of State, perhaps more particularly to Monck, who, after having "fought so gloriously for liberty," was moving away from his seemingly "noble words and actions" of mid-February to accommodation with the royalists. Milton may, indeed, have been thinking also of the forthcoming Convention.

[100] The change of the relative pronoun from "that" to "who" confirms and supports the shift of emphasis resulting from the preceding revision. See *NED*, s.v. "that," rel. pron., 2, 3a, b.

[101] The addition results in a rhetorically strong opposition between valor and courage (heart) and heartlessness.

[102] The revised form, replacing "nothing" by "naught," seems somewhat poetical and stylistically superior.

[103] By the addition, Milton both stresses the uniqueness of the impending event and inserts a vivid set of rhetorical parallels: unique example of voluntary return to servitude; unique example for the boast of kings and tyrants; unique reason for a people's shame.

[104] Milton replaces "whosoever." See *NED*, s.v. "whatsoever," 2.b.

[105] With deletion of both a reference to a saving "remnant" and the state-

Considering these things so plane, so rational, I cannot but yet furder admire on the other side, how any man who hath the true principles of justice and religion in him, can presume or take upon him to be a king and lord over his brethren, whom he cannot but know whether as men or Christians, to be for the most part every way equal or superior to himself: how he can display with such vanitie and ostentation his regal splendor so supereminently above other mortal men; or being a Christian, can as[38]sume such extraordinarie honour and worship to himself, while the kingdom of Christ our common King and Lord, is hid to this world, and such *gentilish* imitation forbid in express words by himself to all his disciples. All Protestants hold that Christ in his church hath left no vicegerent of his power, but himself without deputie, is the only head therof, governing it from heaven: how then can any Christian-man derive his kingship from Christ, but with wors usurpation then the Pope his headship over the church, since Christ not only hath not left the least shaddow of a command for any such vice[39]gerence from him in the State, as the Pope pretends for his in the Church, but hath expressly declar'd, that such regal dominion is from the gentiles, not from him, and hath strictly charg'd us, not to imitate them therin.

I doubt not but all ingenuous and knowing men will easily agree with me, that a free Commonwealth without single person or house of lords, is by far the best government, if it can be had; but we have all this while say they bin expecting it, and cannot yet attain it.[106]

---

ment that "God . . . hath not yet quenched the spirit of libertie among us," the revised version here reflects a radically reduced confidence in the survival of liberty.

[106] Here, "Tis true. . . . Yet," Milton adds an acknowledgment that delay, despite the opportunity of settling the nation in the form of a commonwealth, was an error which left the nation unprepared for present stresses. He expresses the same opinion in the "Character of the Long Parliament" (Columbia, XVIII, 248–55; *Complete Prose*, V, 442–50). But shortly before Milton wrote the present passage, much the same position was being taken by James Harrington, in *The Wayes and Meanes whereby an Equal & Lasting Commonwealth May be suddenly introduced and Perfectly founded with the Free Consent and Actual Confirmation of the Whole People of England* (February 6, 1660), p. 4: "Well, but now saith the Protectorian Family, O that we had set up the equal Commonwealth; so say broken Parliaments and Statesmen, so say the sadly mistaken Sectaries; so say the casheered Officers; so sayes he that would have no nay, but Oligarchy was a good word, and so will more say after these, except they learn to say after another, *Aut reges non exigendi fuerunt, aut plebi re, non*

Tis true indeed, when monarchie was dissolvd, the form of a Commonwealth should have forthwith bin fram'd; and the [40] practice therof immediatly begun; that the people might have soon bin satisfi'd and delighted with the decent order, ease and benefit therof: we had bin then by this time firmly rooted past fear of commotions or mutations, & now flourishing: this care of timely setling a new government instead of ye old, too much neglected, hath bin our mischief. Yet the cause therof may be ascrib'd with most reason to the frequent disturbances, interruptions and dissolutions which the Parlament hath had partly from the impatient or disaffected people, partly from som ambitious leaders in the Armie; much contrarie, I beleeve, to the mind and [41] approbation of the Armie it self and thir other Commanders,[107] once undeceivd, or in thir own power.[108] Now is the opportunitie, now the very season wherein we may obtain a free Commonwealth and establish it for ever in the land, without difficulty or much delay.[109] Writs are sent out for elections, and which is worth observing in the name, not of any king, but of the keepers of our libertie,[110] to summon a free Parlament: which then only will

---

verbo danda libertas, either the Kings ought not to have been driven out, or the People to have their liberty not in word, but in deed."

[107] After "Commanders," Milton has removed the unnecessary adverbial phrase "when they were."

[108] Milton deletes from the second edition a defense of the Rump which, had he not been in extreme haste to publish, he would surely have deleted from the first edition as soon as the Rumpers were swamped by the restored secluded members, February 21.

[109] Milton deletes the statement that "The Parlament have voted to fill up their number"; that vote—actually a series of votes beginning on January 3 and culminating on February 18—had been nullified on the morning of February 21 (see above, *Way* I, p. 353, n. 1). Like the immediately preceding deletion, this one would surely have been made in the first edition, if Milton had had time and opportunity. He adds reference to the writs for new elections and emphasizes the authority under which they have been issued, the "keepers of our libertie." This passage was certainly written subsequent to March 16, since the vote enacting the form of the writs came about on that day and the form of the writs was published the next day, March 17 (Thomason). See following note.

[110] Parliament and members of Parliament were first styled "Keepers of the liberty of England" in "An Act declaring what offences shall be adjudged Treason" (July 17, 1649; text in Gardiner, *Constitutional Documents,* pp. 388–91) soon after the act establishing the Commonwealth (May 19, 1649). After Cromwell's dissolution of Parliament on April 22, 1653, the "Instrument of Government," which settled legislative authority in him, declared (Art. III): "That all writs, processes, commissions, patents, grants, and other things, which now run in the name and style of the keepers of the liberty of England by authority of

indeed be free, and deserve the true honor of that supreme title, if
they preserve us a free people. Which never Parlament was more
free to do; being now call'd, not as here[42]tofore, by the summons
of a king, but by the voice of libertie: and if the people, laying aside
prejudice and impatience, will seriously and calmly now consider
thir own good [111] both religious and civil, thir own libertie and the
only means thereof, as shall be heer laid before them, and will elect
thir Knights and Burgesses able men, and according to the just and
necessarie qualifications [112] (which for aught I hear, remain yet in

Parliament, shall run in the name and style of the Lord Protector" (Gardiner,
Constitutional Documents, p. 406). On February 22, 1660, the second day of the
Parliament of the Secluded Members, a committee was "appointed to bring in an
Act for repealing the Act appointing the Form of a Writ for Members to sit and
serve in Parliament" (*Commons Journals*, VII, 848). The complexities and am-
biguities of the political situation in March, 1660, precipitated agitated debate
on the question in whose name the writs for the coming Parliament should be
issued. There was no longer a Protector; the Long Parliament was finally
coming to an end; and the return of Charles was at this time only putative. On
the last day of the Parliament, March 16, "An Act for Dissolving the Parlia-
ment begun the third of November 1640. And for the Calling and Holding of a
Parliament at Westminster the 25th April 1660" enacted "that the Form of
the Writ . . . to the said Parliament, be as followeth . . . The Keepers of the
Liberties of England by Authority of Parliament," etc. (Firth and Rait, *Acts
and Ordinances*, II, 1469–70).

[111] In the second edition Milton again specifies the two kinds of liberty, re-
ligious and civil. The phrases were common in current political debate.

[112] See above, *Way* I, pp. 353–54, nn. 1, 2; p. 368, n. 52. The added words,
"which . . . formerly," are very important. Following a resolution of the Rump
on February 4 that it should be filled up to the number of 400 for England and
Wales, on February 14 the House had resolved that members should engage to
"be true and faithful to the Commonwealth of *England,* and the Government
thereof, in the way of a Commonwealth and Free State, without a King, Single
Person, or House of Lords" (*Commons Journals*, VII, 843); on the 17th the
form of the writs was determined (*Mercurius Politicus*, February 16–23, 1660,
pp. 1114–15), and on the 18th a bill was passed fixing the qualifications of elec-
tors (voters) to fill up the Rump. No text of this bill having survived, our
understanding of even the amendments recorded in *Commons Journals* is limited;
however, many were disqualified: all who had advocated a single person or su-
preme magistrate, those who were guilty of blasphemy, married to Papists,
denied the scriptures to be the Word of God, were drunkards, were the sons of
sequestrated fathers, etc. But immediately after their readmission to the House
on February 21, the secluded members resolved "that all Votes of this House,
touching new Elections of Members to sit and serve in this Parliament, be, and
are hereby, vacated" (*Commons Journals*, VII, 846); this effectively wiped out
the vote of the 18th, itself the culmination of a series of votes beginning in early
January. On the following day, February 22, it was resolved "that a New Parlia-
ment be summoned to appear, upon the 25th Day of *April* 1660," and a new

force unrepeald, as they were formerly decreed in Parlament) men not addicted to a single person or house of lords, the work is don; at least the foundation [113] firmly laid of a free Common[43]wealth, and good part also erected of the main structure. For the ground and basis of every just and free government (since men have smarted so oft for commiting all to one person) is a general councel of ablest men, chosen by the people to consult of public affairs from time to time for the common good. In this Grand Councel must the sovrantie, not transferrd, but delegated only,[114] and as it were deposited, reside; [115] with this caution they must have the forces by sea and

---

committee was appointed to consider qualifications, and to "bring in an Act for repealing the Act appointing the Form of a Writ for Members to sit and serve in Parliament" (*ibid.*, VII, 848). This was directed at the action of the 17th. Moreover, on March 5 the Solemn League and Covenant—Article III of which bound the parties "mutually to preserve the rights and privileges of the Parliaments . . . and to preserve and defend the King's Majesty's person and authority"—had been revived; and on March 13 it was resolved "That the Engagement, appointed to be taken by Members of Parliament, and others [to "be true and faithful to the Commonwealth of England, as the same is now established, without a King, or House of Lords"] be discharged, and taken off the File" (VII, 872; see also VI, 306). Thus the action of February 14 was nullified. On the same day it was ordered "That it be referred to a Committee, to consider, What hath been done in this House concerning the Lords House" (*ibid.*, 872). The Act of March 16 dissolving the Long Parliament (Firth and Rait, *Acts and Ordinances*, II, 1469; *Commons Journals*, VII, 880) also called for a new Parliament to assemble on April 25, and included the form for the writs. As distinguished from the Act of February 18, this one imposed no qualifications whatsoever on electors. However, all who had abetted the Irish rebellion or were Roman Catholics and all who had taken part in the wars against Parliament, together with their sons, were declared incapable of being elected, "unless he or they have since manifested their good affection to this Parliament." *Mercurius Politicus*, pp. 1180–81, publishes the form of the writs for the new Parliament and "Principal Points of Qualifications." See, in addition, Godfrey Davies, "The General Election of 1660," *HLQ*, XV (1952), 211–35.

[113] Again, this revision omits the unnecessary verb.

[114] Delegated, that is, by the "People, [who] have the Supreme Power in this Nation" (*Commons Journals*, January 4, 1649, VI, 111; see *Way* I, p. 355, n. 6. See also *Tenure*, in *Complete Prose*, III, 202: "The power of Kings and Magistrates is nothing else, but what is only derivative, transferr'd and committed to them in trust from the People, to the Common good of them all, in whom the power yet remaines fundamentally, and cannot be tak'n from them, without a violation of thir natural birthright."

[115] Woolrych, above, introduction, pp. 199–200, suggests that pointed criticisms in L'Estrange's *Be Merry and Wise* and in *The Censure of the Rota* (March 26) may have thrown Milton on the defensive as regards his central proposal, with the consequence that he revised and enlarged this passage to stipulate the conditions and purposes under which power would be delegated to the pro-

land committed to them for preservation of the common peace and libertie; must raise and manage the public revenue, at least with som in[44]spectors deputed for satisfaction of the people,[116] how it is imploid; must make or propose, as more expressly shall be said anon, civil laws; treat of commerce, peace, or warr with forein nations, and for the carrying on som particular affairs with more secrecie and expedition, must elect, as they have alreadie out of thir own number and others, a Councel of State.[117]

And although it may seem strange at first hearing, by reason that mens mindes are prepossessed [117a] with the notion [118] of successive Parlaments, I affirme that the Grand or General Councel being well chosen, should be perpetual: [119] for so [45] thir business is [120] or may be, and oft times urgent; the opportunitie of affairs gaind or lost in a moment. The day of counsel cannot be set as the day of a festival; but must be readie alwaies to prevent or answer all occasions. By this continuance they will become everie way skilfullest, best provided of intelligence from abroad, best acquainted with the people at home, and the people with them. The ship of the Common-

---

posed Grand Council. But the first edition, although written in haste, shows that Milton was mindful of objections to his proposal, and *The Present Means,* almost certainly written before these pamphlets of Milton's detractors, shows him moving to meet some of the objections. Moreover, the second edition of the *Readie & Easie Way* must have been composed before these pamphlets were published. See above, preface, pp. 398–400, for argument that the revision probably was completed before March 28.

[116] It is unnecessary to attribute the idea to Plato, *Laws* [VI, 761: "No judge or official should hold office without being subject to an audit, excepting only those who, like kings, form a court of final appeal," tr. R. G. Bury (2 vols., London: Loeb Classical Library, 1926), I, 427]. The Rumpers and the army grandees had often been charged with corruption.

[117] Paragraphing at this point gives emphasis to the conception of the perpetual parliament that it did not have in the first edition.

[117a] Duodecimo: prepossed.

[118] Context suggests that Milton wished to move away from the objective and logical connotations of "concept" (*NED,* s.v. "conceit," I.c.) to the pejorative implications of subjective and private fancy in "notion."

[119] The second edition is more precise, for although as a continuing body the Grand Council would "be perpetual," it would not always be in session ("sit perpetual").

[120] Evidently sensing a need to offer more specific reasons for perpetuation of his Grand Council, Milton augments the original passage, considering the need to exploit momentary opportunity in affairs of state, the continuing character of the problems with which the Council will grapple, and the intimacy of knowledge which continuing exposure to those problems will confer.

wealth is alwaies under sail; they sit at the stern; and if they stear well, what need is ther to change them; it being rather dangerous? Add to this, that the Grand Councel is both [46] foundation and main pillar of the whole State; and to move pillars and foundations, not faultie,[121] cannot be safe for the building. I see not therefor, how we can be advantag'd by successive and transitorie [122] Parlaments; but that they are much likelier continually to unsettle rather then to settle a free government; to breed commotions, changes, novelties and uncertainties; [123] to bring neglect upon present affairs and op- portunities, while all mindes are suspense with expectation of a new assemblie, and the assemblie for a good space taken up with the new setling of it self. After which, if they finde no great work to do, [47] they will make it, by altering or repealing former acts, or making and multiplying new; that they may seem to see what thir predeces- sors saw not, and not to have assembld for nothing: till all law be lost in the multitude of clashing statutes. But if the ambition of such as think themselves injur'd that they also partake not of the government, and are impatient till they be chosen, cannot brook the perpetuitie of others chosen before them, or if it be feard that long continuance of power may corrupt sincerest men, the known expe- dient is, and by som lately propounded, that annually (or if the space be lon[48]ger, so much perhaps the better) the third part of Senators may go out according to the precedence of thir election, and the like number be chosen in thir places, to prevent the setling of too absolute a power,[124] if it should be perpetual: and this they

---

[121] The second edition is both more economical and more precise in articula- tion of Milton's thought. Proposing erection of a "foundation and main pillar of the whole State" which he conceives to be "not faultie," he has no reason to consider what might be done with a "faultie" foundation.

[122] By the added phrase, "and transitorie," Milton heightens the idea of im- permanency which he associates with successive parliaments.

[123] By dwelling at greater length on the arguments for perpetuity in the Senate, the second edition makes clear the concessive character of Milton's agreement to rotation. It also makes explicit the assumption that the "setled militia" is to be made up of the "well-affected," and that this would prevent the usurpation or abuse of power by a perpetual Senate. *Cf.* Bodin, *Common- weale*, p. 277.

[124] *The Censure of the Rota* [March 26, 1660; in *Harleian Miscellany*, VII, 123 ff., reprinted in facsimile in William R. Parker, *Milton's Contemporary Reputation* (Columbus, 1940)], evidently written in response to the first edi- tion, since it refers to Milton's design to perpetuate the present members, com- ments on "Rotation, which [Milton] implicitly reject[s]": "You have really

call *partial rotation*.[125] But I could wish that this wheel [126] or partial wheel in State, if it be possible, might be avoided; as having too much affinitie with the wheel of fortune. For it appeers not how this can be don, without danger and mischance of putting out a great number of the best and ablest: in whose stead new elections may bring in [49] as many raw, unexperienc'd and otherwise affected, to the weakning and much altering for the wors of public transactions. Neither do I think a perpetual Senat, especially chosen and entrusted by the people, much in this land to be feard, where the well-affected either in a standing armie, or in a setled militia [127] have thir arms in thir own hands. Safest therefor to me it seems and of least hazard or interruption to affairs, that none of the Grand Councel be mov'd, unless by death or just conviction of som crime: [128] for what can be

---

proposed the most ready and easy way to establish downright slavery upon the nation that can possibly be contrived, which will clearly appear to any man that does but understand this plain truth, that wheresoever the power of proposing and debating, together with the power of ratifying and enacting laws, is intrusted in the hands of any one person, or any one council, as you would have it, that government is inevitably arbitrary and tyrannical, because they may make whatsoever they please lawful and unlawful. And that tyranny hath the advantage of all others that hath law and liberty among the instruments of servitude." See above, p. 432, n. 115.

[125] I have not found the phrase as such in Harrington's writings. "Partial" seems more appropriate to the proposals in the first edition, where only 100 or so are to retire every two or three years, "by lot or suffrage of the rest"— which might well enable an "old guard" to go on sitting until they died. Here Milton at least grudgingly concedes the possibility of the one-third who had sat longest retiring annually, although he would wish the interval to be longer. "Partial" seems to mean no more than that only part of the Senate should go out at any one time—but if all went out it would not be rotation. Woolrych suggests that "Milton felt so little at home in these waters that his usual verbal exactitude deserted him."

[126] Rotation < L. *rota,* wheel, hence Rota Club; *cf.* above, pp. 129–30. The wheel was the symbol of the goddess Fortuna, who was herself associated with temporal change, instability, and decay. See Boethius, *The Consolation of Philosophy;* H. R. Patch, *The Tradition of Boethius* (New York, 1935); and esp. Patch, *The Goddess Fortuna in Medieval Literature* (Cambridge, Mass.: 1927), pp. 147–77.

[127] The distinction is between the regular or standing professional army, and an auxiliary citizen force. In *A Letter to a Friend* (above, p. 330) and *Proposalls of Certaine Expedients* (above, p. 337) Milton is prepared to have the Grand Council concede life tenure to the military officers. After the downfall of the grandees, he characteristically soft-pedals the role of a standing army, knowing its desperate unpopularity, and offers a militia as an alternative.

[128] The justice and preferability of requiring conviction, rather than mere accusation, as ground for removal from the Senate is evident.

expected firm or stedfast from a floating foundation? however, I forejudge [50] not any probable expedient, any temperament that can be found in things of this nature so disputable on either side. Yet least this which I affirme, be thought my single opinion, I shall add sufficient testimonie. Kingship it self is therefor counted the more safe and durable,[129] because the king and, for the most part, his councel, is not chang'd during life: but a Commonwealth is held immortal; and therin firmest, safest and most above fortune: for [130] the death of a king, causeth ofttimes many dangerous alterations; but the death now and then of a Senator is not felt; the main bodie of them still continuing perma[51]nent [131] in greatest and noblest Commonwealths, and as it were eternal. Therefor among the *Jews,* the supreme councel of seaventie, call'd the *Sanhedrim,* founded by *Moses,* in *Athens,* that of *Areopagus,* in *Sparta,*[132] that of the Ancients, in *Rome,* the Senat, consisted of members chosen for term of life; and by that means remain as it were [133] still the same to generations. In *Venice* they change indeed ofter then every year som particular councels of State, as that of six, or such other; [134] but the true Senat, which upholds and sustains the government, is the whole aristocracie immovable. So in the United Provinces, the [52] States General, which are indeed but a councel of state deputed [135] by the whole union, are not usually the same persons for above three or six

[129] *Cf.* Bodin, *Commonweale,* p. 413, C.

[130] The awkward and redundant conjunction "that" is removed, and the sentence thereby improved.

[131] Again, the revision results in greater precision, for as a continuing body of gradually changing membership the perpetual Senate would remain permanent despite change.

[132] Although Sparta and Lacedaemon are used interchangeably by Homer for the dwelling place of Menelaus, Lacedaemon generally refers to the territory, Sparta to the capital city of the territory. See *The Oxford Classical Dictionary,* ed. M. Cary, *et al.* (Oxford, 1949), *s. v.* Sparta.

[133] The added phrase implicitly and precisely recognizes that representative bodies of these ancient cities, continuing with changing memberships, "remaind still the same" in a qualified and even figurative sense.

[134] The change from the plural of the first edition appears to be correction of an error.

[135] Although the words are generally synonymous, "deputed" of the second edition occurs more frequently in the passive construction than "delegated" of the first edition. See *NED,* s. vv.

years; but the States of every citie, in whom the sovrantie hath bin plac'd time out of minde,[135a] are a standing Senat, without succession, and accounted chiefly in that regard the main prop of thir liberty. And why they should be so in every well orderd Commonwealth, they who write of policie, give these reasons; "That to make the Senat [136] successive, not only impairs the dignitie and lustre of the Senat, but weakens the whole Commonwealth, and [53] brings it into manifest danger; while by this means the secrets of State are frequently divulgd, and matters of greatest consequence committed to inexpert and novice counselors, utterly to seek in the full and intimate knowledge of affairs past." I know not therefor what should be peculiar in *England* to make successive Parlaments thought safest, or convenient here more then in [137] other nations, unless it be the fickl'ness which is attributed to us as we are Ilanders: but good education and acquisit wisdom ought to correct the fluxible fault, if any such be, of our watry situation. It [54] will be objected,[138] that in those places where they had perpetual Senats, they had also popular remedies against thir growing too imperious: as in *Athens*, besides *Areopagus*, another Senat [139] of four or five hunderd; in *Sparta*,

---

[135a] See above, p. 371, n. 68.

[136] "Whole," deleted in the second edition, was superfluous. It does not appear in Bodin, *De Republica*, iii.1, which Clark (pp. lxii–lxiii) believes to be the original of the quoted passage. See above, *Way* I, p. 372, n. 69.

[137] Omitting "all" before "other," the revised edition is more precise and less categorical than the original edition.

[138] In this long addition, "will be . . . to fear," Milton considers "popular remedies" proposed against "too imperious [perpetual Senates]": rotation, the establishment of other legislative assemblies, Ephori, Tribunes, etc. But these, he argues, have in the past, and would again in the future, become contentious among themselves, unsettling in their continual alterations or movements, or ruinous with excessive power. It is preferable to dispense with these expedients, to choose one Senate of principal men—perhaps by multiple ballots of the "rightly qualifi'd," in which those first chosen would choose from among themselves "others of a better breeding . . . till . . . they only be left chosen who are the due number, and seem by most voices the worthiest." "To make the people fittest to chuse, and the chosen fittest to govern," we must "mend our corrupt and faulty education," and learn "to place every one his private welfare and happiness in the public peace, libertie and safetie."

[139] Under the first form of the Athenian constitution, the Areopagus, which administered the most important affairs of the state, was made up of Archons

the *Ephori;* [140] in *Rome,* the Tribunes [141] of the people. But the event tels us, that these remedies either little availd the people, or brought them to such a licentious and unbridl'd democratie, as in fine ruind themselves with thir own excessive power. So that the main reason urg'd why popular assemblies are to be trusted with the peoples libertie, rather then a Senat of principal men, because [55] great men will be still endeavoring to inlarge thir power, but the common sort will be contented to maintain thir own libertie, is by experience found false; none being more immoderat and ambitious

---

who were appointed for life. About 621 B.C., to allay discontent of the masses who objected to execution of the laws in the interests of the nobility, Draco enacted ordinances under which a Council was to be formed of 401 members chosen by lot from the citizenry. See Aristotle, *The Athenian Constitution,* tr. H. Rackham (London: Loeb Classical Library, 1938), IV, 1–4 [pp. 19–21]. Solon "made a Council of four hundred members, a hundred from each [of four tribes]" (VIII.4; p. 31); Cleisthenes (510 B.C.) divided the people into ten tribes instead of the existing four, and "made the Council to consist of five hundred members instead of four hundred, fifty from each tribe" (XXI.3; p. 65). Also see Plutarch, *Solon.*

[140] Ephori: Plutarch, *Lycurgus,* says that Lycurgus set up a senate, or Council of Elders, and about 130 years later his successors imposed the Ephors as a curb upon the Senate. Aristotle [*Politics,* tr. H. Rackham (London: Loeb Classical Library, 1932), II, vi, 14; p. 141] says that "the office was too powerful, and equal to a tyranny." The origin of the Ephorate is disputed; Aristotle (V, ix, 1) ascribes it to Theopompus, king of Sparta, *ca.* 770–720 B.C.

[141] The "tribuni plebis," officers of the plebs, first created 500–450 B.C., in order to protect the lives and property of the plebs from oppression by the patricians, by asserting a veto right over any act of the magistrates. First admitted only to listen to the debates of the Senate, at least from the third century B.C. they obtained the right of convening the Senate. In the second century membership in the tribunate became sufficient qualification for entry into the Senate, and from the fourth and third centuries B.C. the tribunate became particularly an instrument by which the Senate could control the magistrates through the veto. See A. H. J. Greenidge, *Roman Public Life* (London, 1901), p. 93, and H. F. Jolowicz, *Historical Introduction to the Study of Roman Law* (Cambridge, 1952), pp. 52–53.

to amplifie thir power, then such popularities; which was seen in the people of *Rome;* who at first contented to have thir Tribunes, at length contended with the Senat that one Consul,[142] then both; soon after, that the Censors [143] and Prætors [144] also should be created Plebeian, and the whole empire put into their hands; adoring lastly those, who most were advers to the Senat, till *Marius* [145] by fulfilling

[142] With the expulsion of Tarquinius Superbus (510 B.C.) Rome abolished the monarchy. An aristocratic republic was established, and two annually elected magistrates, later called consuls, were invested with *imperium*. Roman citizens were divided into classes—patricians and plebeians. The plebeians suffered injustices which they sought to redress by means of pressures brought by secessions, and by virtually creating a separate state within the state. During this struggle of the orders, the plebeians established their own officers (tribunes and *aediles*) and assembly (*concilium plebis*), and gradually forced the patricians to recognize these. In 367 B.C. the Licinian law opened the consulship to the plebeians, and representatives of the two orders shared the consulship until 172, when for the first time two plebeian consuls were elected. See Theodor Mommsen, *History of Rome,* tr. William P. Dickson, various editions, and Jolowicz, *Historical Introduction to the Study of Roman Law,* pp. 43–46.

[143] A Roman magistrate, probably instituted *ca.* 443 D.C. as a patrician civil magistracy, in order to make up and maintain the official list of citizens, or census. Although lacking in *imperium*, the censor possessed great authority, since he controlled public morals and supervised the leasing of public areas and buildings. The censorship became accessible to the plebeians at the latest in 351 B.C., and one of the *Leges Publiliae* declared that at least one censor must be a plebeian, although two collegiate plebeian censors were not elected until 131. See Jolowicz, *Historical Introduction to the Study of Roman Law,* pp. 36–37, 50–52.

[144] When the office of consul was opened to the plebeians about 367 B.C., the patricians were able to set up the praetors as judiciary officers, eligibility restricted to patricians, but from 337 the plebeians were also eligible. See Jolowicz, *Historical Introduction to the Study of Roman Law,* pp. 46–48, and Mommsen, *History of Rome,* I, 296, and III, 342–47.

[145] Gaius Marius (157–86 B.C.), served with credit in the Numantine War, became a tribune of the plebs, and married Julia, aunt of Julius Caesar. He came into prominence in the war against Jugurtha; in 107 he became consul, and by popular vote against the wishes of the Senate supplanted Metellus in command of the Roman army. The diplomacy of his quaestor, Sulla, enabled

thir inor[56]dinat desires, quite lost them all the power for which they had so long bin striving, and left them under the tyrannie of *Sylla:* [146] the ballance therefor must be exactly so set, as to preserve and keep up due autoritie on either side, as well in the Senat as in the people. And this annual rotation of a Senat to consist of three

---

him to capture Jugurtha himself and bring the war to an end, but his greatest achievement was his overthrow in 102–101 of the Teutones and Cimbri, Germanic tribes then invading Gaul and Italy. In 100 he entered into close relations with the extremist democrat demagogue, Saturninus, who, as tribune, executed various measures on Marius' behalf; but when the extremists insisted on pressing their land programs too far, Marius abandoned them. With the death of his former allies, Marius lost his popularity with the people and his influence with the Senate. After leaving Rome to travel in Asia in 89, after the Social War, he came into conflict with Sulla, who, like Marius, had taken a prominent part in that war, and who as a leader of the aristocratic party had been given by the Senate the command against Mithridates. Marius had wished this appointment for himself, and by a popular resolution the command was transferred to him. When Sulla, refusing defeat, marched on Rome, Marius fled to Africa. After Sulla's departure for the east in 88 B.C., Marius returned to Italy, joined the democratic leader Cinna, occupied Rome, and began to massacre his enemies. Thus the mutual jealousy of Marius and Sulla, combined with the bitterness of party feeling, led to the first great civil war at Rome. See F. W. Robinson, *Marius, Saturninus, and Glaucia* (Bonn, 1912); "Lycurgus," in *Plutarch's Lives,* I, 203–302, and "Sulla," *ibid.,* lV, 324–445.

[146] Lucius Cornelius Sulla, of an obscure patrician family, was undistinguished except for the part he played in the arrest of Jugurtha when quaestor to Marius in Africa, until he won a considerable military reputation in the Social War. This gained him command of the impending war against Mithridates, and he was drawn into party politics as an opponent to the *populares,* to prevent proposed transfer of his military command to Marius. When the proposal was passed, Sulla, with a disregard for the constitution that shocked patricians as well as plebs, inaugurated the period of military dictatorships by marching on Rome with his legions. After travel and fighting in the East, he returned to find Rome in the hands of the *populares,* assumed the name of "Fortune's Favorite," and after two years of ruthless civil war was triumphant. He now adopted in his turn Marius' policy of extermination of his enemies, adding the device of proscription, the posting of lists of victims who might be killed without trial and their property confiscated, while murderers and informers were rewarded. Although he undertook some desirable constitutional reforms his harsh treatment of municipalities which had opposed him and settlement of his victims in vanquished colonies prepared future discontents, and the quasi-regal character of his dictatorship, unlimited in power and duration, set the model for the undisguised monarchies of Caesar and the second Triumvirate. See *Appian's Roman History,* tr. Horace White (4 vols., London: Loeb Classical Library, 1913), II, *passim* ["The Civil Wars"]; and "Sulla" in *Plutarch's Lives,* IV, 324–445. Compare the epigraph on the title page of this edition, above, p. 405, and p. 406, n. a.

húnderd, as is lately propounded,[147] requires also another popular assembly upward of a thousand, with an answerable rotation. Which besides that it will be liable to all those inconveniencies found in the foresaid remedies, cannot but be troublesom and chargeable,[148] both in thir motion and thir session, to the whole land; unweildie with [57] thir own bulk, unable in so great a number to mature thir consultations as they ought, if any be allotted them, and that they meet not from so many parts remote to sit a whole year lieger [149] in one place, only now and then to hold up a forrest of fingers, or to convey each man his bean or ballot [150] into the box, without reason shewn or common deliberation; incontinent of secrets, if any be imparted to them, emulous and always jarring with the other Senat.[151] The much better way doubtless will be in this wavering condition of our affairs, to deferr the changing or circumscribing of our Senat, more then may be done with ease, [58] till the Commonwealth be throughly setl'd in peace and safetie, and they themselves give us the

[147] In *The Rota: Or, A Model of a Free-State* (January 9, 1660; E1013(7)), or Harrington's *The Wayes and Meanes* (February 6, 1660; E1015(4)).

[148] Inconvenient and expensive, both in their moving (to and from sittings) and their sitting (in session).

[149] To reside in the capacity of representative, ambassador, commissioner, or agent. See *NED*, s.v. "Ledger," II, 4, 5.

[150] With his alliterative clusters Milton neatly pillories the proposal for silent voting, which was all that Harrington would allow to his popular assembly of 1050 in *Oceana*, and—perhaps—also his reference to the parallel popular Athenian legislative body as the "Senate of the Bean" (*Oceana* [1656], p. 18; ed. Liljegren, p. 29). Harrington justified the silent voting with the argument that "The *election* or *suffrage* of the people, is *freest*, where it is made or given in such a manner, that it can neither oblige . . . nor disoblige another; or through fear of an enemy, or bashfulnesse towards a friend, impair a mans liberty. [¶] Wherefore saith *Cicero* . . . the Tablet (or Ballot of the people of *Rome*, who gave their votes by throwing tablets or little pieces of wood secretly into Urns marked for the negative or affirmative) was a welcome constitution, unto the people, as that which not impairing the assurance of their browes, encreased the freedom of their Judgment" (p. 23; ed. Liljegren, p. 33). See Sigonius, *De Rep. Athoniensium* (1564), p. 65 [II.3: "Suffragia Senatorum"]: "Suffragia vero fabas albas, nigrasq. fuisse, illas ad iubendum, has ad vetandum, Vlpianus notatum reliquit." See also Charles Blitzer, *Immortal Commonwealth*, pp. 224–25, on secrecy of the ballot in *Oceana*.

[151] Harrington proposed a parliament of two houses: one, known as the Senate, of about three hundred, to debate and propose laws; another, known as the Prerogative, of 1050, to ballot in silence for or against the proposals of the first. As a result of annual elections and three-year terms, one-third of each chamber would be replaced each year. See Woolrych, introduction, above, p. 102, and Blitzer, *Immortal Commonwealth*, pp. 234–48.

occasion. Militarie men hold it dangerous to change the form of battel in view of an enemie: neither did the people of *Rome* bandie with thir Senat while any of the *Tarquins* [152] livd, the enemies of thir libertie, nor sought by creating Tribunes to defend themselves against the fear of thir Patricians, till sixteen years after the expulsion of thir kings, and in full securitie of thir state, they had or thought they had just cause given them by the Senat. Another way will be, to wel-qualifie and refine elections: [153] [59] not committing all to the noise and shouting [154] of a rude multitude, but permitting

[152] According to tradition, Tarquinius Priscus was fifth king of Rome (616–579 B.C.) and left the kingdom to Servius Tullus (578–535 B.C.), who was murdered by his predecessor's son, Tarquinius Superbus (534–510 B.C.). According to legend, Lucrece, the wife of Tarquinius Collatinus, was raped by Sextus, son of Tarquinius Superbus, the first cousin of her husband. After pledging her father and her husband to revenge, she stabbed herself. This incident resulted in a popular uprising led by Junius Brutus against the Tarquins, and their expulsion from Rome (510 B.C.). See above, p. 438, n. 141.

[153] See Wolfe, *Milton in the Puritan Revolution,* p. 301, for graphic representation of Milton's election scheme. Milton's proposal should be compared with Harrington's elaborate scheme for a four-stage indirect election. See also introduction, above, p. 102, and Blitzer, *Immortal Commonwealth,* pp. 220–23.

[154] Until the seventeenth century each borough was free to evolve its own method of choosing representatives. County elections, on the other hand, were uniformly held at the county court, which met every fourth week on a fixed weekday, with the Sheriff, or, in his absence, his deputy presiding. "The initial proceedings at an election were those of a county court. The court was 'set,' then proclaimed, and a few cases called *pro forma*. After this, the election writ was read and the nomination of candidates followed. If procedure was decorous, the Justices and leading gentlemen, sitting on the bench with the Sheriff, usually proposed the candidates. If indecorous, the Sheriff took the nomination on himself, or the body of freeholders, like a noisy football crowd, bawled out the names. . . . [Occasionally] the nomination appears to merge, with no clear distinction, into the second stage of the proceedings, the election by voices, or, as it was sometimes called, 'the general election.' For this, everyone shouted his lustiest, calling the name of his man. 'Your friends must not be spare-voiced, but with their voices pronounce it roundly and fully,' wrote an anxious parent, coaching his son in election tactics in 1614; and, according to a witness of the result, 'the cry "A Phelips! A Phelips!" was so great and violent for three-quarters of an hour at least, that at the Cross and all about it, I heard no other noise nor sound but "A Phelips!" ' During the pandemonium, the Sheriff was supposed to discern who had the greatest number of voices."

This appears in J. E. Neale, *The Elizabethan House of Commons* (New Haven, 1950), pp. 86–87; much else that can be read with relish appears, *passim*. Davies describes some noisy elections at this very period—early April, 1660—in "The General Election of 1660," pp. 211–35; and for a particularly tumultuous and amusing one in 1679, see David Ogg, *England in the Reign of Charles II,* II, 476–77.

only those of them who are rightly qualifi'd, to nominat as many as
they will; and out of that number others of a better breeding, to
chuse a less number more judiciously, till after a third or fourth
sifting and refining of exactest choice, they only be left chosen who
are the due number, and seem by most voices the worthiest. To make
the people fittest to chuse, and the chosen fittest to govern, will be
to mend our corrupt and faulty education, to teach the people faith
not without vertue, temperance, modestie, sobrietie, parsi[60]monie,
justice; not to admire wealth or honour; to hate turbulence and
ambition; to place every one his privat welfare and happiness in the
public peace, libertie and safetie. They shall not then need to be
much mistrustfull of thir chosen Patriots in the Grand Councel;
who will be then rightly call'd the true keepers of our libertie, though
the most of thir business will be in forein affairs. But to prevent all
mistrust, the people then will have thir several ordinarie assemblies
(which will henceforth quite annihilate the odious power and name
of Committies) [155] in the chief towns of every countie, without the

[155] The county committees were local governing bodies with such powers
and responsibilities as were certain to make their name odious. So see D. H.
Pennington and I. A. Roots, ed., *The Committee at Stafford 1643–1645: The
Order Book of the Staffordshire County Committee* (Manchester University
Press, 1957), pp. xv–xvi: "In the seventeenth century the County was the
natural unit of local organisation and administration, in the military as in other
spheres. When civil war became a probability both sides looked to the existing
militia under the Lords Lieutenant and deputies in the counties to supply their
basic military strength. Moreover most of the small arms and equipment of
each county were to be found in the county magazines. . . . The county was
also the obvious unit for the assessment and collection of war revenue, more
especially as the subsidy (the normal parliamentary grant) was assessed and
collected by counties. When Charles I had sought free gifts, forced loans or
ship-money he had looked inevitably to the county as the essential link between
the localities and the central authority. . . . [T]he powers and functions of the
County Committees were extended by successive parliamentary ordinances and
by their own initiative. . . . No single legislative act initiated the system. . . .
Outstanding among [*ad hoc*] measures [establishing the system] were the Act
for raising £400,000 to which Charles gave his assent by commission in March
1642 [*Statutes of the Realm*, V, 145]; the Ordinance of 24 February 1643 for
the weekly assessment of England and Wales by counties [Firth and Rait,
Acts and Ordinances, I, 85]; the Ordinance of 27 March 1643 for the se-
questration of delinquents' estates [*ibid.*, 106]; and the Ordinance of 7 May
1643 for the one-fifth and one-twentieth [*ibid.*, 145]. Each of these enact-
ments appointed County Committees and delegated to them authority appro-
priate to each stage in the development of a system of regular war finance. . . .
Throughout the war and the Interregnum, Parliament continued to nominate

[61] trouble, charge, or time lost of summoning and assembling from far in so great a number, and so long residing from thir own houses, or removing of thir families, to do as much at home in thir several shires, entire or subdivided, toward the securing of thir libertie, as a numerous assembly of them all formd and conven'd on purpose with the wariest rotation. Wherof I shall speak more ere the end of this discourse: [156] for it may be referrd to time, so we be still going on by degrees to perfection. The people well weighing and performing these things, I suppose would have no cause to fear, though the *Parlament,* [62] abolishing that name, as originally signifying but the *parlie* of our Lords and [157] Commons with thir *Norman* king when he pleasd to call them, should, with certain limitations of thir power,[158] sit perpetual, if thir ends be faithfull and for a free Commonwealth, under the name of a Grand or General Councel. Till this be don, I am in doubt whether our State will be ever certainly and throughly setl'd; [159] never likely till then to see an end of our troubles [159a] and continual changes or at least never the true settlement and assurance of our libertie.[160] The Grand Councel being thus firmly constituted to perpetuitie, and still, upon [63] the death or default of any member, suppli'd and kept in full number, ther can be no cause alleag'd why peace, justice, plentifull trade and all prosperitie should not thereupon ensue throughout the whole land; with as much assurance as can be of human things, that they shall

---

new County Committees for specific purposes." See also the excellent pamphlet by Everitt, *The Local Community and the Great Rebellion.*

[156] See below, p. 461, n. 232.

[157] In explanation of the added phrase, "Lords and," see above, *Way* I, p. 373, n. 72.

[158] The added qualification, "with certain limitations of thir power," responds to objections such as are cited above, p. 434, n. 124.

[159] Parliament, in session when Milton wrote and published the first edition, had dissolved on March 16; after "setl'd" Milton therefore deletes as no longer relevant a passage ("and say . . . sit perpetual") which prophesies support from the three nations if Parliament should render itself perpetual.

[159a] With elimination of the reference to the three nations, "thir troubles" of the first edition becomes "our troubles."

[160] For "our libertie," see preceding note. Following "libertie," Milton deletes another outdated passage in praise of the Rump, "especially filling up their number as they intend," and warning of "certain misery and thraldom" if the nation should turn from these patriots. He would surely have removed this passage from the first edition itself had it not been "suddenly dispersd" upon the readmission of the secluded members on February 21.

so continue (if God favour us, and our wilfull sins provoke him not) even to the coming of our true and rightfull and only to be expected King, only worthie as he is our only Saviour, the Messiah, the Christ, the only heir of his eternal father, the only by him anointed and ordaind since the work of our redemption finishd, [64] Universal Lord of all mankinde. The way propounded is plane, easie and open before us; without intricacies, without the introducement [161] of new or obsolete forms, or terms, or exotic models; idea's that would effect nothing, but with a number of new injunctions to manacle the native liberty of mankinde; [162] turning all vertue into prescription, servitude, and necessitie, to the great impairing and frustrating of Christian libertie: I say again, this way lies free and smooth before us; is not tangl'd with inconveniencies; invents no new incumbrances; requires no perilous, no injurious alteration or circum[65]scription of mens lands and proprieties; secure, that in this Commonwealth, temporal and spiritual lords remov'd, no man or number of men can attain to such wealth or vast possession, as will need the hedge of an Agrarian law [163] (never

[161] The addition, "introducement . . . Commonwealth," warmly urges that "The way propounded is plane, easie and open before us"—and so, perhaps, to be distinguished from such complex and exotic proposals as those in Harrington's *Oceana* (1656). See above, introduction, p. 210, and below, n. 163.

[162] Milton expresses the idea throughout his works; *cf. Tenure*, in *Complete Prose*, III, 198–99: "No man who knows ought, can be so stupid to deny that all men naturally were borne free, being the image and resemblance of God himself, and were by privilege above all the creatures, born to command and not to obey: and that they liv'd so. Till from the root of *Adams* transgression, falling among themselves to doe wrong and violence, and foreseeing that such courses must needs tend to the destruction of them all, they agreed by common league to bind each other from mutual injury, and joyntly to defend themselves against any that gave disturbance or opposition to such agreement. Hence came Citties, Townes and Common-wealths."

[163] *Cf.* James Harrington, *Oceana*, ed. S. B. Liljegren, pp. 85–86. Apart from its constitutional provisions, the most important of the fundamental laws of Harrington's commonwealth, Oceana, was the Agrarian Law, "by the Ballance of dominion preserving equalitie in the Roote" (p. 85). This law, an integral part of the constitution, is designed to provide a stable and appropriate base for the government. Its essential aim is to provide that, in the future, landed estates in Oceana shall not exceed a given value—two thousand pounds annual income—while recognizing the inadvisability of enforcing such a limitation immediately, and so its terms relate to the inheritance of land in the case of estates so large that even equal distribution among the heirs of the owner would not bring the worth of the various parts below an annual value of two thousand pounds. See Blitzer, *Immortal Commonwealth*, pp. 226–34.

succesful, but the cause rather of sedition, save only where it began seasonably with first possession) to confine them from endangering our public libertie; to conclude, it can have no considerable objection made against it, that it is not practicable: least it be said hereafter, that we gave up our libertie for want of a readie way or distinct form propos'd of a free [66] Commonwealth. And this facilitie we shall have above our next neighbouring Commonwealth (if we can keep us from the fond conceit of somthing like a duke of *Venice,* put lately into many mens heads, by som one or other sutly driving on under that notion[164] his own ambitious ends to lurch [165] a crown) that our liberty shall not be hamperd or hoverd over by any ingagement to such a potent familie as the house of *Nassaw* of whom to stand in perpetual doubt and suspicion, but we shall live the cleerest and absolutest free nation in the world.[166]

On the contrarie, if ther be a king, which the incon[67]siderate multitude are now so madd upon, mark how far short we are like to com of all those happinesses, which in a free state we shall immediatly be possessd of. First, the Grand Councel, which, as I shewd [167] before,[168] should sit perpetually (unless thir leisure give them now and then som intermissions or vacations, easilie manageable by the Councel of State left sitting) shall be call'd, by the kings good will and utmost endeavor, as seldom as may be.[169] For it is only the king's right, he will say, to call a parlament; and this he will do most commonly about his own affairs rather then the kingdom's, as will [68] appeer planely so soon as they are call'd. For what will thir business then be and the chief expence of thir time, but an endless tugging between petition of right and royal prerogative,[170] especially about the negative voice, militia, or subsidies,

---

[164] Deletion of the pettily ironical "prettie" is consistent with the deepening seriousness and the elevated irony which often marks the second edition.

[165] Lurch: "To get hold of by stealth, pilfer, filch, steal" (*NED* 3).

[166] Paragraphing at this point emphasizes the turn in the argument, from numbering the advantages of a free commonwealth to numbering the disadvantages and detriments of a return to kingship.

[167] The change from the assertive "said" to the demonstrative "shewd" strengthens the statement.

[168] Deleted: "is both the basis and main pillar in everie government, and should." See above, p. 434, n. 121.

[169] Deleted: "and then . . . to the contrarie" (above, *Way* I, p. 375); redundant, considering the content of the sentence which immediately follows it.

[170] In the first edition, the text here recalls a general opposition of subject

demanded and oft times extorted without reasonable cause appeering to the Commons, who are the only true representatives of the people, and thir libertie,[171] but will be then mingl'd with a court-faction; besides which within thir own walls, the sincere part of them who stand faithfull to the people, will again have to deal with two troublesom counter-working [69] adversaries from without, meer creatures of the king, spiritual, and the greater part, as is likeliest, of temporal lords,[172] nothing concernd with the peoples libertie. If these prevail not in what they please, though never so much against the peoples interest, the Parlament shall be soon dissolvd, or sit and do nothing; not sufferd to remedie the least greevance, or enact aught advantageous to the people. Next, the Councel of State shall not be chosen by the Parlament, but by the king, still his own creatures, courtiers and favorites; who will be sure in all thir counsels to set thir maister's grandure and absolute [70] power, in what they are able, far above the peoples libertie. I denie not but that ther may

---

rights and royal powers; as revised it refers specifically to the Petition of Right (1628), in which subject rights were enumerated. See above, *Way* I, p. 366, n. 47.

[171] The added phrase, "and thir libertie," was important at a time when it appeared that a majority of the people yearned for the return of kingship, and in a document which argued that slavery would in such case certainly ensue. See Resolution of the House, January 4, 1649, above, *Way* I, p. 355, n. 6, "representers of that freedom," above, p. 411, n. 32, and "keepers of our libertie," above, p. 430, n. 110.

[172] With restoration of the Solemn League and Covenant on March 5, expungement of the Engagement "to be true and faithful to the Commonwealth of England, as the same is now established, without a King or House of Lords" on March 13 (see above, p. 411, n. 32), and, on the same day, an order "That it be referred to a Committee, to consider, What hath been done in this House concerning the Lords House" (*Commons Journals*, VII, 872), Milton now had every reason to suppose the Parliament would include not only a House of Commons but a reconstituted House of Lords. The revision ambiguously allows for the possibility that some few temporal lords might as a saving remnant (see above, p. 363, *Way* I, n. 31; p. 428, n. 105) be concerned for the liberties of the people.

The bishops were not restored in the Convention, but were promptly readmitted by the Cavalier Parliament in 1661, by an Act partly repealing that Act of 1642 which had excluded them. The temporal lords were restored in rapid stages. On April 27 Monck consented to the admission of the "young lords," sons of Royalists, about thirty in number. On May 14 several peers who had fought for the king were invited to resume their seats. These two groups, added to the Presbyterian or Parliamentary peers in attendance on April 25, brought the number of lords by June 1 to about eighty. See Ogg, *England in the Reign of Charles II*, I, 30, 198.

be such a king, who may regard the common good before his own, may have no vitious favorite, may hearken only to the wisest and incorruptest of his Parlament: but this rarely happens in a monarchie not elective; and it behoves not a wise nation to committ the summ of thir welbeing, the whole state of thir safetie to fortune. What [173] need they; and how absurd would it be, when as they themselves to whom his chief vertue will be but to hearken, may with much better management and dispatch, with much more [71] commendation of thir own worth and magnanimitie govern without a maister. Can the folly be paralleld, to adore and be the slaves of a single person for doing that which it is ten thousand to one whether he can or will do, and we without him might do more easily, more effectually, more laudably our selves? Shall we never grow old anough to be wise to make seasonable use of gravest autorities, experiences, examples? Is it such an unspeakable joy to serve, such felicitie to wear a yoke? to clink our shackles, lockt on by pretended law of subjection more intolerable and hopeless to be ever shaken off, then [72] those which are knockt on by illegal injurie and violence? *Aristotle,*[174] our chief instructer in the Universities, least this doctrine be thought *Sectarian,* as the royalist would have it thought, tels us in the third of his Politics,[175] that certain men at first, for the matchless excellence of thir vertue above others, or som great public benifit, were created kings by the people; in small cities and territories, and in the scarcitie of others to be found like them: but

---

[173] The argument of this long addition: it is unnecessary and absurd to seek a king to manage our affairs when we may find among ourselves men more able; furthermore, a single person, although good, is "the natural adversarie and oppressor of libertie," and, because of his exaltation, is easier to corrupt. The tone, reflecting Milton's impatience with popular acceptance of the absurdity, is ironical.

[174] In the conclusion to the *Third Prolusion* (*Complete Prose*, I, 247–48) Milton exhorts his audience "in all these studies [to] take as your instructor him who is already your delight—Aristotle, who has recorded all these things with learning and diligence for our instruction."

[175] See Aristotle, *Politics*, III.ix.7, tr. H. Rackham, p. 259: "And it was perhaps only owing to this that kingships existed in earlier times, because it was rare to find men who greatly excelled in virtue, especially as in those days they dwelt in small cities. Moreover they used to appoint their kings on the ground of public service, and to perform this is a task for the good men. But as it began to come about that many men arose who were alike in respect of virtue, they would no longer submit to royalty, but sought for some form of commonwealth, and set up a republican constitution."

when they abus'd thir power and governments grew larger, and the number of prudent men increasd, that then the people soon deposing thir tyrants, betook them, in [73] all civilest places, to the form of a free Commonwealth. And why should we thus disparage and prejudicate our own nation, as to fear a scarcitie of able and worthie men united in counsel to govern us, if we will but use diligence and impartiality to finde them out and chuse them, rather yoking our selves to a single person, the natural adversarie and oppressor of libertie, though good, yet far easier corruptible by the excess of his singular power and exaltation, or at best, not comparably sufficient to bear the weight of government, nor equally dispos'd to make us happie in the enjoyment of our libertie under him. [74]

But admitt, that monarchie of it self may be convenient to som nations; yet to us who have thrown it out, receivd back again, it cannot but prove pernicious. For kings [176] to com, never forgetting thir former ejection, will be sure to fortifie and arm themselves sufficiently for the future against all such attempts hereafter from the people: who shall be then so narrowly watchd and kept so low, that [177] though they would never so fain and at the same rate of thir blood and treasure, they never shall be able to regain what they now have purchasd and may enjoy, or to free themselves from any yoke impos'd [75] upon them: nor will they dare to go about it; utterly disheartn'd for the future, if these thir highest attempts prove un-succesfull; which will be the triumph of all tyrants heerafter over any people that shall resist oppression; and thir song will then be, to others, how sped the rebellious *English?* to our posteritie, how sped the rebells your fathers? This is not my conjecture, but drawn from God's known denouncement against the gentilizing [178] *Israelites;* who though they were governd in a Commonwealth [179] of God's own ordaining, he only thir king, they his peculiar people,[180] yet

[176] Deletion of the definite article results in stylistic improvement and a more generalized statement.

[177] The substance of the revision is the same as that of the original passage, but it is certainly simpler and more economical and coherent.

[178] Gentilizing: Wishing to have a king over them, in order that they might be "like all the [gentile] nations" (I Samuel 8:19), and so "to make gentile; to paganize" (*NED*, v. 2. 2). *Cf. Way* I, above, p. 359, n. 14.

[179] Duodecimo: Commouwealth.

[180] *Cf.* Deuteronomy 14: 2: "For thou art a holy people unto the Lord thy God, and the Lord hath chosen thee to be a peculiar people unto himself, above all the nations that are upon the earth."

affecting rather to [76] resemble heathen, but pretending the mis-government of *Samuel's* sons, no more a reason to dislike thir Commonwealth, then the violence of *Eli's* sons [181] was imputable to that priesthood or religion, clamourd for a king. They had thir longing; but with this testimonie of God's wrath; *ye shall cry out in that day because of your king whom ye shall have chosen, and the Lord will not hear you in that day.*[182] Us if he shall hear now, how much less will he hear when we cry heerafter, who once deliverd by him from a king, and not without wondrous acts of his providence, insensible and unworthie of those high mercies, [77] are returning precipitantly, if he withold us not, back to the captivitie from whence he freed us. Yet neither shall we obtain or buy at an easie rate this new guilded yoke which thus transports us: a new royal-revenue must be found,[183] a new episcopal; for those are individual: both which being wholy dissipated or bought by privat persons or assign'd for service don, and especially to the Armie, cannot be recoverd without a general detriment and [184] confusion to mens estates, or a heavie imposition on all mens purses; [185] benefit to none, but to the worst and ignoblest sort of men, whose hope is to be either the mini[78]sters of court riot and excess, or the gainers by it: But not to speak more of losses and extraordinarie levies on our estates, what will then be

[181] See I Samuel 2:12–17: "Now the sons of Eli were sons of Belial; they knew not the Lord. And the priest's custom with the people was, that, when any man offered sacrifice, the priest's servant came, while the flesh was in seething, with a fleshhook of three teeth in his hand; and he struck it into the pan, or kettle, or caldron, or pot; all that the fleshhook brought up the priest took for himself. So they did in Shiloh unto all the Israelites that came thither. Also before they burnt the fat, the priest's servant came, and said to the man that sacrificed, Give flesh to roast for the priest; for he will not have sodden flesh of thee, but raw. And if any man said unto him, Let them not fail to burn the fat presently, and then take as much as thy soul desireth; then he would answer him, Nay; but thou shalt give it me now: and if not, I will take it by force. Wherefore the sin of the young men was very great before the Lord: for men abhorred the offering of the Lord."

[182] I Samuel 8:18; see above, *Way* I, p. 359, n. 14.

[183] Milton adds a reference to bishops' revenues, indicating that the problem relating to them is inseparable from the problem relating to royal revenues. On the Restoration land-settlement as it involved royal and church lands, see above, *Way* I, p. 378, nn. 95, 96.

[184] The addition makes more explicit the idea of injury and damage.

[185] The effect, and the evident purpose, of the addition is to augment presentation and portrayal of both "extraordinarie levies on our estates" and the "revenges and offences" to be "rememberd and returnd"—all to malign and vicious ends.

the revenges and offences rememberd and returnd, not only by the
chief person, but by all his adherents; accounts and reparations that
will be requir'd, suites, inditements,[186] inquiries, discoveries, com-
plaints, informations, who knows against whom or how many, though
perhaps neuters, if not to utmost infliction, yet to imprisonment,
fines, banishment, or molestation; [187] if not these, yet disfavor,
discountnance, disregard and contempt on all but [79] the known
royalist or whom he favors, will be plenteous: [188] nor let the new
royaliz'd presbyterians perswade themselves that thir old doings,
though now recanted, will be forgotten; what ever conditions be
contriv'd or trusted on. Will they not beleeve this; nor remember the
pacification,[189] how it was kept to the *Scots;* how other solemn

---

[186] The additions—"inquiries, discoveries, complaints, informations"—effec-
tively particularize the vengeful and suspicious proceedings which Milton fore-
sees, "not only by the chief person, but by all his adherents."

[187] Milton extends the list of possible punishments.

[188] Milton warns the "new royaliz'd presbyterians," who, although opposed to
the Independents as they sought condemnation and execution of Charles I, and
now seeking the return of Charles II, had earlier been in the forefront of the
organization and prosecution of the Civil War, the attempt to force Charles I to
subscribe to the Solemn League and Covenant, and the effort to impose Presby-
terianism upon the nation. See introduction, *Complete Prose*, III, 1–9. Robert S.
Bosher, *The Making of the Restoration Settlement* (Westminster: Dacre
Press, 1951), p. 47, says that "The Cavaliers, in spite of the support Presby-
terians had given to the royal cause since 1648, in private still denounced them
as the originators of the rebellion." Marchamont Needham, in a clever im-
posture, *Newes from Brussels, in a Letter from a neer Attendant on His Maj-
esties Person* (March 10, 1660), imagined a fire-eating Cavalier speaking to
the same effect: "This Rebellion first bubbled up in Presbyterian Pulpits, yet
it's impollitick to say so much: we also know 'tis more for fear of the
Phanatiques than for love to us, they now are loyal: so also it is our necessity,
not choice, that makes us court them: Hug them you cannot hang, at least until
you can" (p. 4). And later, "We resolve, the Rogues that left the Rump, shall
feel the scourge that Loyal hearts lash Rebels with, as well as others; a Round-
head is a Roundhead; black and white Devils all alike to us.—Thinkest thou that
we can breath in peace, while we see a little finger left alive that hath been dipt
in Royal blood? or his adherents? No, a thought of mercy more hateful is than
Hell: but Cooks may be conquerors, and a plate perform equal execution with
a Pistol, and with less report. Be quiet then, let's use all art to make them take
the halter tamely" (pp. 7–8).

[189] Probably the Pacification of Berwick ("Birks"), June 18, 1639, which
ended the first Bishops' War against the Scots. By this treaty Charles promised
future regulation of all ecclesiastical and civil affairs in Scotland by free annual
Assemblies of the Kirk and free parliaments of the realm. The first free Gen-
eral Assembly met on August 6 of the same year, but before it dispersed
Charles announced that he would not engage to call annual Assemblies. The

promises many a time to us? Let them but now read the diabolical forerunning libells,[190] the faces, the gestures that now appeer foremost and briskest in all public places; as the harbingers of those that are in expectation to raign over us; let them but hear the insolencies, the mena[80]ces, the insultings of our newly animated common enemies crept lately out of thir holes, thir hell,[191] I might say, by the language of thir infernal pamphlets, the spue of every drunkard, every ribald; nameless, yet not for want of licence,[192] but for very shame of thir own vile persons, not daring to name themselves, while they traduce others by name;[193] and give us to foresee that they intend to second thir wicked words, if ever they have power, with more wicked deeds. Let our zealous backsliders forethink now with themselves, how thir necks yok'd with these tigers of

---

Parliament of the Realm assembled on August 31, but Charles took the position that, in the absence of the bishops, the Parliament was illegal. "Charles, in short, was to cozen the Scots by appearing to yield everything, whilst he was secretly preparing an excuse which would justify him in his own eyes in taking back all that he had yielded, whenever he was strong enough to do so." Gardiner, *History of England* (1894), IX, 40–50, esp. 49.

[190] See Woolrych, introduction, above, pp. 214–18.

[191] Perhaps a pun. After Pride's Purge, the mainly Presbyterian "imprisoned members," says Walker (*History of Independency*, II, 31), "were conveyed away to a Victualling House call[ed] HELL"; Clarendon (*History of the Rebellion*, IV, 466 [xi.207]) says that they were confined in "that place under the Exchequer which is commonly called Hell; where they might eat and drink at their own charge what they pleased." One suspects that the victualling house may have been, or have become, a royalist hangout. In any case, now, on the eve of the Restoration, the Presbyterians and other royalists were celebrating. Pepys (*Diary*, March 6, Shrove Tuesday) says that "Everybody now drinks the King's health without any fear, whereas before it was very private that a man dare do it."

[192] Possibly another pun, the word referring to "permission to print or publish" (*NED* n. 2) and also to "dissoluteness" (*NED* n. 2.c.). While royalist pamphlets were appearing more openly and more frequently, republican pamphleteers were coming under restraints. On March 28 the Council of State ordered the arrest of Livewell Chapman, publisher of the first edition of *Readie & Easie Way,* for causing "several seditious and treasonable books to be printed and published." See above, p. 352, nn. a and b; title page: bookseller, and references.

[193] Milton among them. See introduction, above, pp. 197–201; see also French, *Life Records,* IV, 304–09, and Parker, *Milton's Contemporary Reputation,* pp. 98–103, *et passim.*

Bacchus,[194] these new [81] fanatics of not the preaching but the sweating-tub,[195] inspir'd with nothing holier then the Venereal pox, can draw one way under monarchie to the establishing of church discipline with these new-disgorg'd atheismes: yet shall they not have the honor to yoke with these, but shall be yok'd under them; these shall plow [196] on their backs. And do they among them who are so forward to bring in the single person,[197] think to be by him trusted or long regarded? So trusted they shall be and so regarded, as by kings are wont reconcil'd enemies; neglected and soon after discarded, if not prosecuted for [82] old traytors; the first inciters, beginners, and more then to the third part actors [198] of all that fol-

---

[194] Bacchus, otherwise and more generally Dionysus, was the son of Zeus and Semele. As god of the vine, or rather of nature's fertility as exemplified in the vine, his worship was accompanied by wild orgiastic revels. Sacred to him were not only such plants as the vine, the ivy, the laurel, and the asphodel, but such animals as the tiger, the lynx, the panther, and the lion. In works of art the attributes most frequently depicted are the grapes, the cup, the thyrsus, the crown of vine or ivy, and the skin of the lynx or the panther. He rode in a chariot drawn by wild animals, usually leopards or tigers. See George Howe and G. A. Harrer, *A Handbook of Classical Mythology* (New York, 1947), pp. 83–86; *Larousse Encyclopedia of Mythology*, introd. Robert Graves (New York: Prometheus Press, 1959), pp. 180–81; W. H. D. Rouse, *Gods, Heroes and Men* (New York, 1957), p. 78; *cf. Paulys Real-Encyclopädie der Classischen Altertumswissenschaft*, ed. Georg Wissowa (Stuttgart, 1905), V, cols. 1038, 1041.

[195] A preaching tub was the pulpit, especially of a non-conformist, and so "fanatic," preacher (*NED* 4); a sweating-tub was formerly used in the treatment of venereal disease (*NED* 1.b.).

[196] "To gash, tear up, scratch" (*NED* v.3.), thus to lash or whip. *Cf.* Psalm 129, 2–3: "Many a time have they afflicted me from my youth: yet they have not prevailed against me. The plowers plowed upon my back: they made long their furrows."

[197] On March 2, 1660, Pepys noted that "Great is the talk of a single person, and that it would now be Charles [II], George [Monck], or Richard [Cromwell] again." On the following day Mr. Crewe told Pepys that he "feared there was new design hatching, as if Monck had a mind to get into the saddle." But by the time of the publication of the second edition of *Readie & Easie Way*—after mid-March—there was little or no doubt that Charles was the single person intended.

[198] Time and again at the beginning of the *Tenure* (1648; *Complete Prose*, III, 190–258) Milton attacks the Presbyterians as hypocritical turncoats; but this passage, with its metaphor of the Presbyterians as actors in a drama, is reminiscent specifically of a passage in *A Defence* (*Complete Prose*, IV, 512–14): "You next revert to those responsible for the punishment of the king: 'If the thing is taken by itself according to its own character and circumstances, we must ascribe the outcome of this fearful crime to the Independents, without going so far as to deprive the Presbyterians of their claims to the glory of its

lowd; it will be found also, that there must be then as necessarily as now (for the contrarie part will be still feard) a standing armie; [199] which for certain shall not be this, but of the fiercest Cavaliers, of no less expence, and perhaps again under *Rupert:* [200] but let this armie be sure they shall be soon disbanded, and likeliest without arrear or pay; [201] and being disbanded, not be sure but they may as soon be questiond for being in arms against thir king: the same let them fear, who have contributed monie; [83] which will amount to no small number that must then take thir turn to be made delinquents

origin and progress.' Hear that, you Presbyterians; has your apparent great reluctance to punish the king done anything now to preserve or promote your reputation for harmless loyalty? This accuser of yours, this royal advocate so full of talk, says that you 'went more than halfway'; you 'were observed up to the fourth act of this drama and longer out of breath and jumping to and fro.' . . . You Presbyterians, however, 'have well deserved branding as regicides; you paved the way for the murder of the king; you and no others struck his neck with that accursed axe.' . . . They can learn from this that, if the king should return, he would punish them not simply for the king's death but for all these old petitions, and for acts of the whole Parliament on the form of worship or on doing away with the bishops or on the Triennial Parliament or anything else passed with the full consent and approval of the people, as though these were treasonable acts and 'mad assertions of the Presbyterians.' "

[199] During Charles II's reign the standing army, including garrison troops, seldom exceeded 7000 men. They included a few fragments of guards recruited at the Restoration from regiments which had served the king in exile, and from the Coldstream Guards, drawn from Monck's regiments. See David Ogg, *England in the Reign of Charles II*, I, 253–54.

[200] Prince Rupert (1619–1682), son of Queen Elizabeth of Bohemia (daughter of James I of England) and Frederick V, Elector Palatine and King of Bohemia. In July, 1642, he was summoned to the assistance of Charles, his uncle, in England, and was made general of the horse. From this time until the close of the first Civil War in 1646 he was the dominant figure of the war. His strategy was bold as well as skillful. In November, 1644, in spite of defeat at Marston Moor, he was appointed general of the king's army. By 1645, accused of barbarity as well as ingratitude, he was allowed to leave England. For some time after this he commanded troops formed of English exiles in the French army, and later commanded a royalist fleet. At the Restoration he settled in England again, receiving from Charles II an annuity and becoming a member of the Privy Council. See C. H. Firth, in *DNB*.

[201] After the Restoration, Monck's main responsibility was to disband the army. For his proposals, see *Lords Journals*, August 30, 1660; for the Act giving effect to the proposals, *ibid.*, September 13. So far as the army in England was concerned, the process was completed by December. The different sums paid to different regiments are recorded in a general statement of "Declared Accounts" paid at disbanding, totaling £341,637-6-9, printed in *Athenaeum*, July 12, 1902, p. 52. See C. H. Firth and Godfrey Davies, *The Regimental History of Cromwell's Army* (2 vols., Oxford, 1940), I, xxxiii–xxxvi.

and compounders.[202] They who past reason and recoverie are devoted to kingship, perhaps will answer, that a greater part by far of the Nation will have it so; the rest therefor must yield. Not so much to convince these, which I little hope, as to confirm them who yield not, I reply; that this greatest part have both in reason and the trial of just battel, lost the right of their election what the government shall be: of them who have not lost that right, whether they for kingship be the greater number, [84] who can certainly determin? Suppose they be; yet of freedom they partake all alike, one main end of government: which if the greater part value not, but will degeneratly forgoe, is it just or reasonable, that most voices against the the [202a] main end of government should enslave the less number that would be free? More just it is doubtless, if it com to force, that a less number compell a greater to retain, which can be no wrong to them, thir libertie, then that a greater number for the pleasure of thir baseness, compell a less most injuriously to be thir fellow slaves. They who seek nothing but thir own just libertie, have [85] alwaies right to winn it [203] and to keep it, when ever they have power, be the voices never so numerous that oppose it. And how much we above others are concernd to defend it from kingship, and from them who in pursuance therof so perniciously would betray us and themselves to most certain miserie and thraldom, will be needless to repeat.

Having thus far shewn with what ease we may now obtain a free Commonwealth, and by it with as much ease all the freedom,

---

[202] Delinquents: see above, p. 418, n. 58. Compounders: On January 30, 1644, the Houses offered pardon to all delinquents who would submit before a certain date, and they were allowed to compound, that is, to redeem their estates from sequestration, by the payment of a certain sum to be assessed by the Parliament, such sums to be used in defraying public expenses. See Paul H. Hardacre, *The Royalists During the Puritan Revolution* (The Hague: Nijhoff, 1956), esp. chs. 2 and 4. Milton's fears that a Restoration would create a new class of delinquents and compounders proved groundless.

[202a] So in duodecimo.

[203] Cf. *A Defence, Complete Prose*, IV, 457: If a majority in Parliament prefer enslavement and putting the commonwealth up for sale, is it not right for a minority to prevent it if they can and preserve their freedom?" See also, Plato, *Laws*, III, 690, tr. R. G. Bury, I, 213: "The most important right is [that] which ordains that the man without understanding should follow, and the wise man lead and rule." See further, Cicero, *De Re Publica*, II.xxii, tr. Clinton W. Keyes (Cambridge, Mass.: Loeb Classical Library, 1951), p. 149: "The greatest number should not have the greatest power." Cf. *First Prolusion*, in *Complete Prose*, I, 220, and *Eikonoklastes, ibid.*, III, 339–40, 348.

peace, justice, plentie that we can desire, on the other side the difficulties, troubles, uncertainties, nay rather impossibilities to enjoy these [86] things constantly under a monarch, I will now proceed to shew more particularly wherin our freedom and flourishing condition will be more ample and secure to us under a free Commonwealth then under kingship.

The whole freedom of man consists either in spiritual or civil libertie. As for spiritual, who can be at rest, who can enjoy any thing in this world with contentment, who hath not libertie to serve God and to save his own soul, according to the best light which God hath planted in him to that purpose, by the reading of his reveal'd will and the guidance of his [87] holy spirit? That this is best pleasing to God, and that the whole Protestant Church allows no supream judge or rule in matters of religion, but the scriptures, and these to be interpreted by the scriptures themselves, which necessarily inferrs liberty of conscience, I have heretofore prov'd at large in another treatise,[204] and might yet furder by the public declarations, confessions and admonitions of whole churches and states, obvious in all historie since the Reformation.[205]

This liberty of conscience which above all other things ought to be to all men dearest and most precious, no government more inclinable [88] not to favor only but [206] to protect, then a free Commonwealth; as being most magnanimous, most fearless and confi-

---

[204] A general reference to other treatises becomes, in revision, a specific reference to his own *Treatise of Civil Power in Ecclesiastical Causes*, above, p. 242: "First it cannot be deni'd, being the main foundation of our protestant religion, that we of these ages, having no other divine rule or autoritie from without us warrantable to one another as a common ground but the holy scripture, and no other within us but the illumination of the Holy Spirit so interpreting that scripture as warrantable only to our selves and to such whose consciences we can so perswade, can have no other ground in matters of religion but only from the scriptures."

[205] After "Reformation," Milton deletes a long passage on the practical harms of forcing conscience in religion and "medling with Church matters in State counsels." Time and time again in other works, as well as in the first edition of *Readie & Easie Way*, Milton had inveighed against these actions, but their discussion in this place does not contribute to a showing "wherin our freedom and flourishing condition will be more ample and secure to us under a free Commonwealth then under kingship." It may be, too, that Milton felt that to argue these matters at this time compromised his plea for a Commonwealth. See introduction, above, p. 212.

[206] The effect of the shift, and its evident intent, is to emphasize the phrase which follows, "to protect."

dent of its own fair proceedings. Wheras kingship, though looking big, yet indeed most pusillanimous, full of fears, full of jealousies, startl'd at every ombrage, as it hath bin observd of old to have ever suspected most and mistrusted them who were in most esteem for vertue and generositie of minde, so it is now known to have most in doubt and suspicion them who are most reputed to be religious. Queen *Elizabeth* though her self accounted so good a Protestant, so moderate, so [89] confident of her Subjects love would never give way so much as to Presbyterian reformation [207] in this land, though once and again besought, as *Camden* relates, but imprisond and persecuted the very proposers therof; alleaging it as her minde & maxim unalterable, that such reformation would diminish regal autoritie. What liberty of conscience can we then expect of [208] others, far wors principl'd from the cradle, traind up and governd by *Popish* and *Spanish* counsels, and on such depending hitherto for subsistence? [209] Especially what can this last Parlament expect, who having reviv'd lately and [90] publishd the covnant,[210] have reingag'd themselves, never to readmitt Episcopacie: which no son of *Charls* returning, but will most certainly bring back with him, if he regard the last and strictest charge of his father, *to persevere in not the doctrin only, but government of the church of* England; *not to neglect the speedie and effectual suppressing of errors and schisms;* [211]

---

[207] Duodecimo: re-reformation.

[208] The substitution of "of" for "from" is evidently stylistic, avoiding the use of "from" in a sense different from that in the following phrase.

[209] The resurrection of the Solemn League and Covenant by Parliament on March 5, 1660 (see above, p. 409, n. 22) leads Milton to insert the question: how can a returning Charles II honor its exclusion of episcopacy and obey his dying father's injunction to preserve both the doctrine and the government of the Church of England?

[210] The Solemn League and Covenant; see above, p. 409, n. 22. An Act to Preserve the Person and Government of the King (1661) declared that the Solemn League and Covenant was an unlawful oath. The Corporation Act of the same year required a declaration to this effect from all members of city or borough corporations, and by the Act of Uniformity (1662) a similar declaration was required of all clergymen and schoolmasters. See William C. Costin and J. Steven Watson, *The Law and Working of the Constitution* (2 vols., London: Black, 1952), I, 7, 16, 24.

[211] Chapter xiv of *Eikon Basilike*, at that time generally believed to have been written by Charles I, discourses adversely at length "Upon the Covenant" (pp. 75–83). In chapter xxvii, "To the Prince of Wales," he is charged "to persevere [in the Church of England] as coming nearest to God's word for doctrine and

among which he accounted Presbyterie one of the chief: or if not-
withstanding that charge of his father, he submitt to the covnant,
how will he keep faith to us with disobedience to him; or regard that
faith given, which must [91] be founded on the breach of that last
and solemnest paternal charge, and the reluctance, I may say the
antipathie which is in all kings against Presbyterian and Indepen-
dent discipline? for they hear the gospel speaking much of libertie;
a word which monarchie and her bishops both fear and hate, but a
free Commonwealth both favors and promotes; and not the word
only, but the thing it self.[212] But let our governors beware in time,
least thir hard measure to libertie of conscience be found the rock
wheron they shipwrack themselves as others have now don before
them in the cours wherin God was di[92]recting thir stearage [213] to
a free Commonwealth, and the abandoning of all those whom they
call *sectaries*,[214] for the detected falshood and ambition of som, be a
wilfull rejection of thir own chief strength and interest in the free-
dom of all Protestant religion, under what abusive name soever
calumniated.

The other part of our freedom consists in the civil rights and ad-
vancements of every person according to his merit: the enjoyment
of those never more certain, and the access to these never more open,
then in a free Commonwealth. Both which [215] in my opinion may be
best and soonest obtain, if [93] every countie in the land were
made [216] a kinde of subordinate Commonaltie or Commonwealth,
and one chief town or more, according as the shire is in circuit,[217]
made cities, if they be not so call'd alreadie; where the nobilitie and

---

to the primitive examples for government" (p. 160), and is exhorted not "to ne-
glect a speedy reforming and effectual suppressing [of] errors and schisms."

[212] Milton adds a warning to Monck and the Presbyterians: Beware lest in
your zeal to promote Presbyterianism and suppress the "sectaries" you violate
that very liberty of conscience for which you earlier strove, against a king who
was brought to the block for violating it.

[213] See above, *Way* I, p. 369, n. 54.

[214] *Cf. Eikonoklastes, Complete Prose*, III, 348: "I never knew that time in
England, when men of truest Religion were not counted Sectaries."

[215] By use of the relative pronoun Milton tightens the connection between
this sentence and its logical antecedents.

[216] The revision is precise in stipulating subordination of county jurisdiction
to national jurisdiction.

[217] *I.e.*, depending upon the size of the shire.

chief gentry [218] from a proportionable compas of territorie annexd to each citie, may build, houses or palaces, befitting thir qualitie, may bear part in the government, make thir own judicial laws, or use these that are,[219] and execute them by thir own elected judicatures and judges [220] without appeal, in all things of civil government between man and man. so they shall have justice in thir own [94] hands, law executed fully and finally in thir own counties and precincts, long wishd, and spoken of, but never yet obtaind; they shall have none then to blame but themselves, if it be not well administerd; and fewer laws to expect or fear from the supreme autoritie; or to those that shall be made, of any great concernment to public libertie, they may without much trouble in these commonalties or in more general assemblies [221] call'd to thir cities from the whole territorie on such occasion, declare and publish thir assent or dissent by deputies within a time limited sent to the Grand Councel: yet so as this thir [95] judgment declar'd shal submitt to the greater number of other counties or commonalties, and not avail them to any exemption of themselves, or refusal of agreement with the rest, as it may in any of the United Provinces,[222] being sovran within it self, oft times to the great disadvantage of that union. In these imploiments they may [223] much better then they do now, exercise and fit themselves, till thir lot fall to be chosen into the Grand Councel, according as thir worth and merit shall be taken notice of by the

[218] The revision precisely indicates that the "nobilitie and chief gentry," as local or regional residents, shall be local or regional representatives.

[219] The revision, implicitly acknowledging the possible utility of laws already obtaining, seems intended to express a continuity Milton conceives to relate the present constitution to that which he proposes.

[220] The addition is in the interest of explicitness and precision.

[221] This provision for more general assemblies to assent to laws confirms the assumption that the standing councils in the counties are to be very oligarchic. Cf. introduction, above, pp. 210, 213.

[222] Decisions of the States General theoretically required the unanimity of all seven provinces. In fact, this was obviated in 1650–72 by the overriding influence of the States of Holland and their Grand Pensionary, and at other times —especially of war—by that of the stadtholder. But differences between the provinces could occasionally threaten deadlock, as over the terms of the Anglo-Dutch peace of 1654. See E. H. Kossman, "The Dutch Republic," in *New Cambridge Modern History* (Cambridge, 1961), V, 277 ff., 284–85.

[223] The addition, "much better then they do now," comparative in form, is also comparative in intent: under the proposed constitution men would be schooled in their local institutions for service in the national institutions to a greater extent than is now possible.

people. As for controversies that shall happen between men of several counties, they may repair, [96] as they do now, to the capital citie,[224] or any other more commodious, indifferent place and equal judges. And this I finde to have bin practisd in the old *Athenian* Commonwealth, reputed the first and ancientest place of civilitie in all *Greece;* that they had in thir several cities, a peculiar; in *Athens,* a common government; [225] and thir right, as it befell them, to the administration of both. They should have heer also schools and academies at thir own choice, wherin thir children may be bred up in thir own sight to all learning and noble education not in grammar only, but in all liberal arts [226] and exerci[97]ses. This would soon spread much more knowledge and civilitie, yea religion through all parts of the land,[227] by communicating the natural heat of government and culture more distributively to all extreme parts, which now lie numm and neglected, would soon make the whole nation more industrious, more ingenuous at home, more potent, more honorable abroad. To this a free Commonwealth will easily assent; (nay the Parlament hath had alreadie som such thing in designe) for of all governments a Commonwealth aims most to make the people flourishing, vertuous, noble and high spi[98]rited. Monarchs will never permitt: whose aim is to make the people, wealthie indeed perhaps and well fleec't, for thir own shearing and [228] the supplie of regal prodigalitie; but otherwise softest, basest, vitiousest, servilest, easiest to be kept under; and not only in fleece, but in minde also sheepishest; and will have all the benches of judicature annexd to the throne, as a gift of royal grace that we have justice don us; whenas nothing can be more essential to the freedom of a people,

---

[224] Milton introduces a classical precedent for a federal structure.

[225] See Aristotle, *Athenian Constitution,* xxi.3–xxii, tr. H. Rackham, pp. 65–66: "Next [Cleisthenes] made the Council to consist of five hundred members . . . fifty from each Tribe. . . . He also portioned out the land among the demes into thirty parts . . . and assigned them among the Tribes by lot, three to each, in order that each Tribe might have a share in all the districts. And he made all the inhabitants in each of the demes fellow-demesmen of one another."

[226] Duodecimo: ars.

[227] In the interest of vividness, Milton introduces the organic metaphor into the revised edition.

[228] By removal of the preposition "for," Milton causes the syntax to express the intimacy of the relationship between the "shearing [of the people] and the supplie of regal prodigalitie."

then to have the administration of justice and all public ornaments in thir own election and within thir own bounds, with[99]out long travelling or depending on remote places to obtain thir right or any civil accomplishment; so it be not supreme, but subordinate to the general power and union of the whole Republic. In which happy firmness as in the particular above mentiond, we shall also far exceed the United Provinces,[229] by having, not as they (to the retarding and distracting oft times of thir counsels on [229a] urgentest occasions) many Sovranties united [230] in one Commonwealth, but many Commonwealths under one united and entrusted Sovrantie.[231] And when we have our forces by sea and land, either of a faithful Armie [100] or a setl'd Militia, in our own hands to the firm establishing of a free Commonwealth, publick accounts under our own inspection, general laws and taxes with thir causes in our own domestic suffrages, judicial laws, offices and ornaments at home in our own ordering and administration, all distinction of lords and commoners, that may any way divide or sever the publick interest, remov'd, what can a perpetual senat have then wherin to grow corrupt, wherin to encroach upon us or usurp; or if they do, wherin to be formidable? Yet if all this avail not to remove the fear or envie of a perpetual [101] sitting, it may be easilie provided, to change a third part of them yearly or every two or three years, as was above mentiond; [232] or that it be at those times in the peoples choice, whether they will change them, or renew thir power, as they shall finde cause.

I have no more to say at present: few words will save us, well considerd; few and easie things, now seasonably don. But if the people be so affected, as to prostitute religion and libertie to the vain and groundless apprehension, that nothing but kingship can restore trade, not remembring the frequent plagues and pesti[102]lences that then wasted this citie, such as through God's mercie we never have felt since, and that trade flourishes no where more then in the

---

[229] In revision, Milton heightens and clarifies the difference between the government of the United Provinces and that which he proposes for England, to the clear disadvantage of the former. *Cf.* above, *Way* I, p. 385, n. 112.

[229a] Duodecimo: or.

[230] In the revision, Milton heightens the concept of unification by adding "united" to both terms of the opposition; with reference to England, he again expresses the idea of delegation or subordination by inserting "entrusted."

[231] Milton adds a summary recapitulation of his arguments for a perpetual Grand Council, stressing the safeguards against its autocracy.

[232] See above, p. 444, n. 156.

free Commonwealths of *Italie, Germanie,* and the Low-Countries before thir eyes at this day, yet if trade be grown so craving and importunate through the profuse living of tradesmen, that nothing can support it, but the luxurious expences of a nation upon trifles or superfluities, so as if the people generally should betake themselves to frugalitie, it might prove a dangerous matter, least tradesmen should mutinie for want of trading, and that therefor we must forgoe & set [103] to sale religion, libertie, honor, safetie, all concernments Divine or human to keep up trading, if lastly, after all this light among us, the same reason shall pass for current to put our necks again under kingship, as was made use of by the *Jews* to returne back to *Egypt* and to the worship of thir idol queen, because they falsly imagind that they then livd in more plentie and prosperitie, our condition is not sound but rotten, both in religion and all civil prudence; and will bring us soon, the way we are marching, to those calamities which attend alwaies and unavoidably on luxurie,[233] all national judgments [104] under forein or domestic slaverie: so far we shall be from mending our condition by monarchizing our government, whatever new conceit now possesses us. However with all hazard I have ventur'd what I thought my duty to speak in season, and to forewarne my countrey in time: wherin I doubt not but ther be many wise men in all places and degrees, but am sorrie the effects of wisdom are so little seen among us. Many circumstances and particulars I could have added in those things wherof I have spoken; but a few main matters now put speedily in [234] execution, will suffice to recover us, and set all right: and ther [105] will want at no time who are good at circumstances; but men who set thir mindes on main matters and sufficiently urge them, in these most difficult times I finde not many. What I have spoken, is the language of that which is not call'd amiss [235] *the good Old Cause:* if it seem strange to any, it will not seem more strange, I hope, then convincing to backsliders. Thus much I should perhaps have said though I were sure I should have spoken only to trees and stones; and had none to cry to, but with the Prophet, *O earth, earth, earth!* to tell the very soil it

---

[233] The shift to appositive construction is more economical.

[234] Milton corrects the preposition.

[235] Paradoxically, the language of the insertion here connotes both objectivity and proud acceptance of the phrase, and Milton's readiness to be openly identified with that which was now hooted at by so many.

self,[236] what her perverse inhabitants are deaf [106] to. Nay though what I have spoke, should happ'n (which Thou suffer not, who didst create mankinde free; nor Thou next, who didst redeem us from being servants of men!) to be the last words of our expiring libertie. But I trust I shall have spoken perswasion to abundance of sensible and ingenuous men: to som perhaps whom God may raise of these stones [237] to become children of reviving [238] libertie; and may reclaim,[239] though they seem now chusing them a captain back for *Egypt*, to bethink themselves a little and consider whether they are rushing; to exhort this torrent also of the people, not to be [107] so impetuos, but to keep thir due channell; and at length recovering and uniting thir better resolutions, now that they see alreadie how open and unbounded the insolence and rage is of our common enemies, to stay these ruinous proceedings; justly and timely fearing to what a precipice of destruction the deluge of this epidemic madness would hurrie us through the general defection of a misguided [240] and abus'd multitude.

The end. [108]

[236] By the time the revised edition appeared, the restoration of Charles, if not a foregone conclusion, was overwhelmingly probable, and a parallel with the exiled king of Judah who was not to return to his homeland was no longer likely to be valid. Eliminating the reference to Coniah and his seed, and so being less specifically directed at Charles, the revision properly sustains the earlier concern with a deaf and perverse people.

[237] Hughes (p. 898) cites Ezekiel's vision (Ezek. 37) of the dry bones which gradually revive as he preaches to them, but see above, *Way* I, p. 388, n. 123.

[238] The word explicitly adds to the revision the idea of resurrection or rebirth implicit in the concept of the "Lent of Servitude" (p. 408) upon which Milton sees the nation entering.

[239] The allusion to the Egyptian captivity sustains and heightens the theme of the sinfulness of the servitude which the people seem to be choosing; the rest of the addition vividly presents the actions of a heedless and unreasoning people in terms of the metaphor of a flooded, rushing, and ravaging stream.

[240] Perhaps because his argument requires the premise that there is indeed a saving remnant which even now wishes a commonwealth (see above, *Way* I, p. 363, n. 31), Milton substitutes the indefinite article for the definite, and so moves away somewhat from his original sweeping and categorical characterization of the whole people as "the misguided and abus'd multitude."

BRIEF NOTES UPON
A LATE SERMON

April 10–15, 1660

PREFACE AND NOTES BY ROBERT W. AYERS

FOLLOWING readmission of the secluded members in February, discharge of the Engagement, reinstitution of the Solemn League and Covenant, and particularly dissolution of the Parliament in March, royalist voices were heard more openly and more often in both press and pulpit. It was against this background of increasingly overt royalist activity that on March 25 Matthew Griffith—sometime Chaplain to Charles I and several times imprisoned for covert ministry to royalist congregations when he used the Book of Common Prayer— preached in Mercers' Chapel a presumptuous and unsettling sermon on the text of Proverbs 24:21: "My son, fear God and the King, and meddle not with them that be seditious, or desirous of change." Attacking all who had opposed Charles I and all who had governed since his death,[1] he characterized Charles II as the Lord's Anointed, who, given the sword of the militia at his coronation, would not bear that sword in vain, but would, like Samson, avenge his father and himself at last upon Presbyterians, Independents, and sectaries alike.[2]

While his vengeful tone immediately embarrassed those royalists who were proclaiming that they wished only to bind up the nation's wounds, Griffith shortly compounded his error. On March 31 he registered,[3] and immediately thereafter published, the offending sermon under the title of *Fear of God and the King*, along with *The Samaritan Revived*, a review of the rebellion from the time of Charles I. The combined volume he rashly dedicated to Monck, and openly appealed to the General to carry on "what you have already so happily begun in the name and cause of God, and his Anointed, till you have finish'd this great, and good work [of restoration of Charles II], and brought it to perfection."[4]

The embarrassment was now to the Council of State and to the cryptoroyalist Monck, who remained publicly committed to a com-

---

[1] See *Fear of God*, esp. pp. 49–51.
[2] *Ibid.*, pp. 8–9.
[3] *Stationers' Registers*, II, 255.
[4] *Fear of God*, p. A4.

monwealth without a single person or house of lords. The result was that on April 5 Griffith was sent to Newgate "for writing and publishing a seditious and libellous book entitled 'The Samaritan Revived.' "[5]

After Griffith's imprisonment on the 5th, possibly after it was noticed in *The Parliamentary Intelligencer* on the 9th,[6] but in any case well before the 20th,[7] Milton wrote and published *Brief Notes Upon a late Sermon, Titl'd, The Fear of God and the King; Preachd, and since Publishd, By Matthew Griffith, D.D. And Chaplain to the late King. Wherin many Notorious Wrestings of Scripture, and other Falsities are observd by J. M.*

The title gives a fair idea of the greater part of the contents of this short pamphlet. Milton exults over Griffith's imprisonment and reminds Monck of his reiterated public pledges to maintain the Commonwealth, but for the most part he casts back detailed and even trivial rejoinders to Griffith's use of Scripture. Only in the latter third of the publication (p. 8 ff.) does Milton come to those independent arguments now of most interest: Since it makes and unmakes positive law, Parliament is above that law; a king, however, reigns according to such law and at the election or appointment of Parliament. The Parliament abrogated both king and kingship by a law which was valid, although passed by a House which was less than full; furthermore, the people and Parliament overcame the king in a war which he himself acknowledged to be just; as a consequence he ceased to be king by "the deciding verdit of warr," which is just by the law of nations. But a free people retain the right to choose their form of government, and if we are so degenerate and despairing of our own virtue, industry, and abilities as to insist on having back a king, then let us at least choose one of our own number, "one who hath best aided the people, and best merited against tyrannie, the space of a raign or two we may chance to live happily anough, or tolerably." Milton's despairing suggestion is to elect Monck to the throne.

TEXTUAL NOTE: *BRIEF NOTES UPON A LATE SERMON*

Our text reproduces that of the Huntington Library copy, DX M2097. Collation: 4°: A-B⁴ [3 (-A1, title page; A3) signed]; 8 leaves;

---

[5] *CSPD*, 1658–59, 572.

[6] No. 15 (2–9 April, 1660), p. 229.

[7] In *No Blind Guides*, dated April 20 on the title page, Roger L'Estrange attacked Milton's performance in *Brief Notes. Brief Notes* was therefore certainly published in mid-April, probably April 10–15. The title page of the Alexander Turnbull Library copy bears the inscribed date, "23 Aprill 1660," apparently in a contemporary hand.

pp. [2] 1–13 [1] Contents: [A1], title page (verso blank); A2–[B4], the work; [B4v], blank.[1]

[1] In addition to the Huntington Library copy, copies I have examined in Xerox form which show correct page numbering: Alexander Turnbull Library, Bodleian Library, Dartmouth College Library, Harvard University Library, Niedersächsische Landesbibliothek (Hannover, Germany), Kongelige Bibliothek (Copenhagen), Worcester College Library, Oxford. Copies I have examined in Xerox form which show misnumbering of 1 as 5, and 5 as 1: British Museum, University of Illinois Library (4 copies), Pierpont Morgan Library, Newberry Library, Rutgers University Library, John Rylands Library, Yale University Library. Parker, *Milton,* p. 1073, gives a convenient finding list of copies.

BRIEF

NOTES

Upon a late

SERMON,

TITL'D,

The Fear of God and the King;

Preachd, and fince Publifhd, By
MATTHEW GRIFFITH, D.D.
And Chaplain to the late KING.

Wherin many Notorious Wreftings of Scripture,
and other Falfities are obfervd by *J.M.*

LONDON,
Printed in the Year 1660.

NOTES ON THE TITLE PAGE

[1] Preached March 25, 1660, at the Mercers' Chapel; registered for publication March 31 (*Stationers' Registers*, II, 255), and presumably issued soon thereafter, since Roger L'Estrange attacked *Brief Notes* in his *No Blinde Guides*, dated on the title page, April 20, 1660.

[2] (1599?–1665). B.A., Oxford, 1618; M.A., Christ's College, Cambridge, 1621. For preaching and publishing in 1642 a sermon entitled "A Pathetical Persuasion to Pray for Publick Peace," he was sequestered from his livings and imprisoned, but, regaining his liberty, took refuge with the king, was made D.D. at Oxford on June 16, 1643, and became one of the royal chaplains. Returning to London about 1647, he continued use of the liturgy by stealth to small gatherings of cavaliers, and for that reason was imprisoned four times. The likelihood of the early Restoration greatly excited him, and on Sunday, March 25, 1660, he preached the exceedingly royalist sermon to which Milton here replies. It was dedicated to Monck, and its vindictive spirit offended not only republicans, but even prudent royalists, who were disclaiming any intention of revenge. The Council of State sent him to Newgate on April 5 "for writing and publishing a seditious and libellous book entitled 'The Samaritan Revived' " (*CSPD*, 1658–1659, 572). On Charles' return, Griffith was restored to his rectory of St. Mary Magdalen, and subsequently obtained the rectory of Bladon, Oxfordshire, and the mastership of the Temple. He died at Bladon, October 14, 1665, after rupturing a blood vessel while preaching, and was buried in the chancel of the church (*DNB*). For Griffith's reference to the offending sermon and publication, see *Fear of God*, p. [A2v], and below, n. 8.

[3] The ornament on the title page, Sir Francis Walsingham's crest, a tiger's head with the motto "Auspicante Deo," is no. 296 in Ronald B. McKerrow, *Printers' & Publishers' Devices in England and Scotland, 1485–1640* (London: Bibliographical Society, 1949). I have been unable to trace its ownership into the Restoration period.

BRIEF NOTES UPON A LATE
SERMON, TITLED, THE FEAR
OF GOD AND THE KING, &C.

I AFFIRMD in the Preface of a late discourse, Entitl'd, *The ready way to establish a free Commonwealth, and the dangers of re-admitting Kingship in this Nation,* that *the humor of returning to our old bondage, was instilld of late by some deceivers;* [4] and to make good, that what I then affirmd, was not without just ground, one of those deceivers I present here to the people: and if I prove him not such, refuse not to be so accounted in his stead.

He begins in his Epistle to the General; [5] and moves cunningly for a licence to be admitted Physitian both to Church and State; [6] then sets out his practice in Physical terms, *an wholsom Electuary* [7] *to be taken every morning next our hearts:* [8] tells of the opposition which he met with from the Colledge of State-Physitians,[9] then laies before you his drugs and ingredients; *Strong purgatives in the Pul-*

---

[4] *Readie & Easie Way,* 1st ed., above, p. 355.

[5] *I.e.,* Matthew Griffith's dedicatory epistle, *Fear of God,* pp. A2–[A5], "To His Excellency, George Monck, Captain General of all the land forces of *England, Scotland* and *Ireland;* and one of the *Generals* of all the Naval-forces."

[6] *Fear of God,* p. A2: "My Lord, *If you will be pleased to allow me to be a* Physitian *in the same sense that all Morall* Divines *do acknowledge the Body-Politick (consisting both of* Church *and* State*) to be a* Patient, *then I will now give your* Highness *a just account, both how far, and how faithfully I have practised upon it, by vertue of my* Profession."

[7] "A medicinal conserve or paste, consisting of a powder or other ingredient mixed with honey, preserve, or syrup of some kind," here used figuratively, of course. See *NED,* 1. b., which cites Milton's use in *Church-Government* (1641); see also *Complete Prose,* I, 803.

[8] *Fear of God,* p. [A2v]: "*I thought it my duty, to prescribe an wholsomn* [*sic*] Electuary, (*out of the* 122. Psalm, *at the* 6. *verse, in a* Sermon *which* I *was called to Preach in the Cathedrall Church of Saint* Pauls, *Anno,* 1642. *and I soon after publish't by command, under this Title;* A Patheticall Perswasion to pray for the publique Peace) *to be duly and devoutly taken every morning next our hearts.*" See Psalm 122:6: "Pray for the peace of Jerusalem: they shall prosper that love thee."

[9] *Fear of God,* pp. [A2v]–A3: "*My self, and most of the Ancient* Orthodox Clergy *were sequestred and silenc'd.*"

*pit, contemperd of the myrrhe of mortification, the aloes of con-
fession and contrition, the rubarb of restitution and satisfaction;* [10]
a pretty fantastic dos of Divinity from a Pulpit-Mountibanck,[11] not
unlike the Fox, that turning Ped[1]ler, opend his pack of ware
before the Kid; [12] though he now would seem *to personate the good
Samaritan*,[13] undertaking *to describe the rise and progress of our
national malady, and to prescribe the onely remedy:* [14] which how he
performs, we shall quickly see.

First, he would suborn Saint *Luke* as his spokesman to the Gen-
eral, presuming, it seems, *to have had as perfect understanding of
things from the very first*,[15] as the Evangelist had of his Gospel; that
the General who hath so eminently born his part in the whole action,
might know the certainty of those things better from him a partial
Sequesterd enemy: [16] for so he presently appears, though covertly
and like the tempter; commencing his address with an impudent
calumnie and affront to his Excellence, that he would be pleasd *to
carry on what he had so happily begun in the name and cause* not of

[10] *Fear of God*, p. A3: *"I saw that it was high time . . . to prescribe strong
purgative medicines in the* Pulpit, *(contempered of the Myrrhe of* Mortifica-
tion; *the Aloes of* Confession, *and* Contrition; *The Rubarb of* Restitution *and*
Satisfaction."

[11] Mountebank, literally "mount-on-bench": "An itinerant quack who from
an elevated platform appealed to his audience by means of stories, tricks, jug-
gling, and the like," or, figuratively, "an impudent pretender to skill or knowl-
edge, a charlatan; one who resorts to degrading means to obtain notoriety."
NED, 1, 2. *Cf. Fear of God*, p. 104.

[12] The fable is related at length in the May Eclogue of Spenser's *Shepheardes
Calendar*. Wilhelm Riedner, *Spensers Belesenheit* (Leipzig, 1908), p. 43, identi-
fies the fable as Phaedrus, VII.8 [*Cf. Bobrius and Phaedrus*, ed. Ben E. Perry
(Cambridge, Mass.: Loeb Classical Library, 1965), p. 529)], but the parallels
he finds are not convincing.

[13] See Luke 10:30–37, and *Fear of God*, p. A3.

[14] *Fear of God*, pp. A3–[A3v]: *"In this imperfect and impolish'd piece . . .
my chief scope is to personate the good* Samaritan; *that as he cur'd the
wounded* Traveller, *by searching his wounds with* wine, *and suppleing them
with* Oyl: *so I have here, both described the* Rise, *and* Progress *of our nationall
malady, and also prescrib'd the onely Remedy."*

[15] *Fear of God*, p. [A3v]: *"And for both my present undertaking, and dedi-
cation, St.* Luke *(Chap.* I.3.) *makes an Apologie:* It seem'd good unto me,
having had perfect understanding of things from the very first, to write unto
thee in order (most excellent *Theophilus*) that thou might'st know the certainty
of those things wherein thou hast been instructed."

[16] Sequesterd: deprived of a benefice, *NED*, 1.b.; see above, p. 468, n. b.

God onely, which we doubt not, but *of his anointed*,[17] meaning the
late Kings son: which is to charge him most audaciously and falsly
with the renouncing of his own public promises and declarations
both to the Parlament and the Army,[18] and we trust his actions ere
long will deterr such insinuating slanderers from thus approaching
him for the future. But the General may well excuse him; for the
Comforter himself scapes not his presumption, avouchd as falsly,
to have *impowrd* to those designs *him and him only*,[19] who hath
solemnly declar'd the contrary. What *Phanatique* against whom
he so often inveighs, could more presumptuously affirm whom the
Comforter hath inpowrd, then this Antifanatic, as he would be
thought? [2]

The Text.

Prov. 24. 21. *My son, fear God and the King, and meddle not with
them that be seditious, or desirous of change,* &c.[20]

Letting pass matters not in controversie, I come to the main drift
of your Sermon, *the King;* which word here is either to signifie any
supreme Magistrate, or else your latter object of fear is not universal,
belongs not at all to many parts of Christendom, that have no King;
and in particular, not to us. That we have no King since the putting

[17] *Fear of God,* p. A4: *"Give me leave not onely to crave your Lordships
patronage to this poor* Vade mecum; *but also your gracious concurrence, &
couragious carrying on of what you have already so happily begun in the name
and cause of God, and his Anointed."*

[18] See above, *Way* I, p. 354, n. 2.

[19] *Fear of God,* p. A4: *"My Lord, as it must needs grieve you to see these
three distressed kingdoms lye, like a Body without a Head: so it may also chear
you to consider that the Comforter hath impowr'd you, (and in this nick of
time, you onely) to make these dead and dry bones, live."*

[20] Milton quotes Proverbs 24:21 precisely from *Fear of God,* p. 1. I have
found no translation which reads exactly this way, although the Geneva Bible
—which Griffith seems to quote (*Fear of God,* pp. 15 and 39), and which he
unaccountably describes in both places as the "last Translation"—reads, "Med-
dle not with them that are seditious." A marginal gloss reads, "Meaning, either
of the wicked and seditious, as verse 19 and 21, or, of them that feare not God
nor obey their King." See 1st ed., Geneva ("Breeches") Bible, Geneva, 1560
(STC B2093), or *The Bible,* printed by Robert Baker, London, 1615 (STC
B2239). *Cf.* Authorized Version, "My son, fear thou the Lord and the king; and
meddle not with them that are given to change."

down of Kingship in this Commonwealth,[21] is manifest by this last Parlament, who to the time of thir dissolving [22] not onely made no address at all to any King, but summond this next to come by the Writ formerly appointed of a free Commonwealth,[23] without restitution or the least mention of any Kingly right or power; which could not be, if there were at present any King of *England*. The main part therefore of your Sermon, if it mean a King in the usual sense, is either impertinent and absurd, exhorting your auditory to fear that which is not, or if King here be, as it is, understood for any supreme Magistrate, by your own exhortation they are in the first place not to *meddle* with you, as being your self most of all the *seditious* meant here, and the *desirous of change*, in stirring them up to *fear* a *King*, whom the present Government takes no notice of.

You begin [24] with a vain vision, *God and the King at the first blush* (which will not be your last blush) *seeming to stand in* your *text like those two Cherubims on the* [3] *mercy-seat, looking on each other*.[25] By this similitude, your conceited Sanctuary, worse then the Altar of *Ahaz*, patternd from *Damascus*,[26] degrades God to a Cherub,

---

[21] See above, *Way* I, p. 355, n. 6.

[22] March 16, 1660.

[23] See above, *Way* II, p. 430, n. 110.

[24] *I.e.*, after the dedicatory epistle to Monck, Griffith begins the body of his argument, *Fear of God*, p. 1.

[25] *Fear of God*, p. 1: "Prov. 24.21. *My son, fear God and the King, and meddle not with them that be seditious, or desirous of change*, &c. God, and the King, at the first blush, seem to stand in the Text, like those two *Cherubims* on the *Mercy-seat* (*Exod.* 37.9.) *looking on each other:* yet with this difference, That God is an heavenly King, and eternal, I *Tim.* 1. 17. but the King is an earthly, and dying God, *Psal.* 82. 6.—And yet in a qualified sence, they are both *Gods,* and both *Kings,* and therefore both to be feared, as you are exhorted in the Text." See Exodus, 37:8–9: "One cherub on the end on this side, and another cherub on the other end on that side: out of the mercy seat made he the cherubim on the two ends thereof. And the cherubim spread out their wings on high, and covered their wings over the mercy seat, with their faces one to another; even to the mercy seatward were the faces of the cherubim." *Cf. Paradise Lost*, XII, 253–54.

[26] II Kings, 16:10–11: Ahaz, son and successor of Jotham, king of Judah, came to the throne about 734 B.C. King Pekah of Israel and King Rezin of Damascus made an alliance against the Assyrians and tried to compel him to join the coalition. His refusal so exasperated them that they planned his deposition and the appointment of a creature of their own to the throne. Ahaz did not take the field, but shut himself up in Jerusalem, strengthened its fortifications, and sent a message to Tiglath-Pileser, king of Assyria, submitting himself unreservedly to him. Tiglath-Pileser was already on the march, and at once

and raises your King to be his collateral in place, notwithstanding the other differences you put: which well agrees with the Court-letters, lately publishd from this Lord to tother Lord, that cry him up for no less then Angelical and Celestial.[27]

Your first observation, *pag.* 8. is, *That God and the King are coupl'd in the text, and what the Holy Ghost hath thus firmely combin'd, we may not, we must not dare to put asunder;* and your self is the first man who puts them asunder by the first proof of your doctrine immediately following, *Iudg.* 7. 20. which *couples the sword of the Lord and Gideon,*[28] a man who not only was no King, but refus'd to be a King or Monarch, when it was offered him, in the very next chapter, *vers.* 22, 23. *I will not rule over you, neither shall my son rule over you; the Lord shall rule over you.*[29] Here we see that this worthy heroic deliverer of his Country thought it best governd, if the Lord governd it in that form of a free Commonwealth, which

---

laid siege to Damascus, thus freeing Jerusalem from its enemies. Two years later, Tiglath-Pileser entered Damascus, "And king Ahaz went to Damascus to meet Tiglath-Pileser king of Assyria, and saw an altar that was at Damascus: and king Ahaz sent to Urijah the priest the fashion of the altar, and the pattern of it, according to all the workmanship thereof. And Urijah the priest built an altar according to all that king Ahaz had sent from Damascus: so Urijah the priest made it against king Ahaz came from Damascus." The story apparently refers to the introduction of Assyrian deities into Jerusalem.

[27] See "A Letter out of *Flanders,* from a Person of Honor, who lately transported himself purposely to kisse the hands of His Sacred Majesty *King Charles* the second, to a Noble-man in England: Wherein divers Observations of his Majesties Personal Deportments, both Private and Publick are declared" [E1019(11); Thomason date March 31; signed G.S.]: "(By the description we have of Angels) I could not value him lesse then a heavenly Messenger of Gods mercies, and to be his Ark of Blessings to that Territory wheresoever he shall make his residence" [p. 3]; "The Celestial lines I measured in his sable Countenance resembled that divine Canticle of Lovely Beauty, Black and Comely" [p. 4]; "Couch all excentrick spirits to that most heavenly happiness of submission to their Lawful Soveraigne King *Charles* the Second, there being no readier way to do the Will of our Father which is in heaven, when by imitating his Holy Angels, which alwayes in their obedience do his will, a chief part whereof is to guard his Anointed on Earth" [pp. 4–5].

[28] Judges 7:20: "And [Gideon's] three companies [about the camp of the Midianites] blew the trumpets, and brake the pitchers, and held the lamps in their left hands, and the trumpets in their right hands to blow withal: and they cried, The sword of the Lord, and of Gideon."

[29] Judges 8:22–23: "Then the men of Israel said unto Gideon, Rule thou over us, both thou, and thy son, and thy son's son also: for thou hast delivered us from the hand of Midian. And Gideon said unto them, I will not rule over you, neither shall my son rule over you: the Lord shall rule over you."

they then enjoiq without a single person. And this is your first Scripture, abus'd and most impertinently cited, nay against your self, to prove that *Kings at thir Coronation have a sword given them*,[30] which you interpret *the Militia, the power of life and death put into thir hands*, against the declar'd judgement of our Parlaments, nay of all our Laws, which reserve to themselves only the power of life and death, and render you in thir just resent[4]ment of this boldness, another Doctor *Manwaring*.[31]

Your next proof is as false and frivolous, *The King*, say you, *is Gods sword-bearer;* true, but not the King only, for *Gideon* by whom you seek to prove this,[32] neither was, nor would be a King; and as you your self confess, *pag.* 40. *there be divers forms of government*.[33] *He bears not the sword in vain*, Rom. 13. 4.[34] this also is as

---

[30] *Fear of God*, p. 8: "Kings at their *Coronation*, have a sword given them; the *Militia;* the power of life and death is put into their hands; for the King is Gods Sword-bearer, and he *bears not the sword in vain*, saith the Apostle, Rom. 13. 4."

[31] Roger Manwaring (1590–1653), bishop of St. David's, graduated Oxford, B.A., 1608; M.A., 1611. About 1626 he was appointed chaplain in ordinary to Charles I. In 1627 he preached absolutist sermons supporting Charles' actions in levying taxes and loans without consent of Parliament. In the Parliament of 1628, the Commons impeached him for seeking to persuade the king that he wielded a power unbounded by the laws; Pym even charged Manwaring with "endeavouring to destroy the king and kingdom by his divinity." The Lords sentenced him to a fine of £1000 and imprisoned him; they also disabled him from holding any ecclesiastical dignity or office. Nevertheless, the king almost immediately pardoned him and gave him successive preferments, culminating in the bishopric of St. David's in 1635. Much later he was imprisoned by the Long Parliament on new charges (among which was that of "exhibiting a sociability and joviality ill befitting his office"), lost all of his preferments, and lapsed into poverty and obscurity (*DNB*). See *Fear of God*, p. 75, for Griffith's mention of Manwaring as a zealot, a "[citizen] of desperate Opinions, and despicable fortunes."

[32] *Fear of God*, p. 8: "What the holy Ghost hath thus firmly combin'd, we may not, we must not dare to put asunder; for in the seventh Chapter of *Judges*, at the 20. verse, *The Sword of the Lord and Gideon*, is spoken of as but one two-handed Sword; the Lord gives it, and *Gideon* girds it to himself; *Gideon* gives the blow, and the Lord gives the blessing."

[33] *Fear of God*, pp. 39–40: "Saint *Paul* (in the 13. Chapter to the *Romans*, 2.) hath this *Apostolicall Canon*, Let every soul be subject to the higher Powers; where speaking in the plurall number, of *powers*, he implyes, that there be *more* then *one;* divers *forms* of *govrnment, and all* of them are *powers*."

[34] Romans 13:1–4: "Let every soul be subject unto the higher powers. For there is no power but of God: the powers that be are ordained of God. Whosoever therefore resisteth the power, resisteth the ordinance of God: and they that resist shall receive to themselves damnation. For rulers are not a terror to

true of any lawful rulers, especially supreme, so that *rulers, vers.* 3. and therefor this present government, without whose authority you excite the people to a King,[35] bear the sword as well as Kings, and as little in vain. *They fight against God, who resist his Ordinance, and go about to wrest the sword out of the hands of his Anointed.*[36] This is likewise granted: but who is *his Anointed?* not every King, but they only who were anointed or made Kings by his special command; as *Saul, David,* and his race, which ended in the Messiah, (from whom no Kings at this day can derive thir title) *Iehu, Cyrus,*[37] and if any other were by name appointed by him to some particular service: as for the rest of Kings, all other supreme Magistrates are as much the Lords anointed as they; and our obedience commanded equally to them all; *For there is no power but of God, Rom.* 13.1.[38] and we are exhorted in the Gospell to obey Kings, as other Magistrates, not that they are call'd any where the Lord's anointed, but as they are *the ordinance of man,* I *Pet.* 2.13.[39] You therefor and other such false Doctors, preaching Kings to your auditory, as the Lord's only anointed, to withdraw people from the present Government, by your own text are [5] self-condemnd, and not to be followd, not to be *medl'd with,* but to be noted, as most of all others the *seditious and desirous of change.*

Your third proof is no less against your self. *Psal.* 105.15. *touch not mine anointed.*[40] For this is not spoken in behalf of Kings, but

---

good works, but to the evil. Wilt thou then not be afraid of the power? do that which is good, and thou shalt have praise of the same: for he is the minister of God to thee for good. But if thou do that which is evil, be afraid; for he beareth not the sword in vain: for he is the minister of God, a revenger to execute wrath upon him that doeth evil." See *Fear of God,* p. 8.

[35] Evidenced by his imprisonment in Newgate for it, April 5. See above, p. 468, n. b.

[36] *Fear of God,* p. 8.

[37] For the anointing of Saul, see I Samuel 10:1; for David, I Samuel 16:12–13; for Jehu, II Kings 9:1–6 and I Kings 19:16; for Cyrus, Isaiah 44:28 and esp. 45:1.

[38] See above, n. 34.

[39] I Peter 2:13–14: "Submit yourselves to every ordinance of man for the Lord's sake: whether it be to the king, as supreme; or unto governors, as unto them that are sent by him for the punishment of evildoers, and for the praise of them that do well."

[40] Psalm 105:13–15: "When [Israel] went from one nation to another, from one kingdom to another people; he suffered no man to do them wrong: yea, he reproved kings for their sakes; saying, Touch not mine anointed, and do my prophets no harm."

spoken to reprove Kings, that they should not touch his anointed
Saints and Servants, the seed of *Abraham,* as the verse next before
might have taught you: *he reproved Kings for their sakes; saying,
touch not mine anointed, and do my Prophets no harm;* according
to that *2 Cor.* 1.21. *He who hath anointed us, is God.*[41] But how
well you confirme one wrested Scripture with another: 1 *Sam.* 8.7.
They have not rejected thee, but me: [42] grosly misapplying these
words, which were not spoken to any who had *resisted or rejected* a
King, but to them who much against the will of God had sought
a King, and rejected a Commonwealth, wherin they might have livd
happily under the Raign of God only, thir King. Let the words
interpret themselves: *v. 6.7. But the thing displeased Samuel, when
they said, give us a King to judge us: and Samuel prayed unto the
Lord. And the Lord said unto Samuel, hearken unto the voice of the
people in all that they say unto thee; for they have not rejected thee,
but they have rejected me, that I should not reign over them.* Hence
you conclude, *so indissoluble is the Conjunction of God and the
King.*[43] O notorious abuse of Scripture! whenas you should have
concluded, So unwilling was God to give them a King, So wide was
the disjunction of God from a King. Is this the doctrin you boast of
to be *so clear in it self, and like a Mathematical principle, that* [6]
needs no farther demonstration.[44] Bad Logic, bad Mathematics (for
principles can have no demonstration at all) but wors Divinitie. O
people of an implicit faith no better then *Romish,* if these be thy

[41] II Corinthians 1:21: "Now he which stablisheth us with you in Christ, and
hath anointed us, is God."

[42] I Samuel 8:4-9: "Then all the elders of Israel . . . came to Samuel . . .
and said unto him . . . now make us a king to judge us like all the nations.
But the thing displeased Samuel, when they said, Give us a king to judge us.
And Samuel prayed unto the Lord. And the Lord said unto Samuel, Hearken
unto the voice of the people in all that they say unto thee: for they have not
rejected thee, but they have rejected me, that I should not reign over them."

[43] *Fear of God,* pp. 8-9: "They fight against God, who resist his Ordinance,
and go about to wrest the sword out of the hands of his Annointed; whom
(in the 105. *Psal.* 5.) he hath fenced about with a *Nolite Tangere,* &c. *Touch
not mine annointed;* for they that touch him, in the sense there prohibited, offer
violence to God himself: as he tells *Samuel; they have not resisted or rejected
thee, but me:* so indissoluble is the conjunction of *God and the King."*

[44] *Fear of God,* pp. 12-13: "Then, *My Son, fear God, and the King;* and in
thy *fear,* observe both the *fast combination* and *conjunction;* and also the
right order and disposition of them. And so I have soon done with the *Doctrine,*
which being so clear in it self, and (like a *Mathematicall* Principle) shining by
its own light, needs no farther demonstration."

prime teachers; who to thir credulous audience dare thus jugle with Scripture, to alleage those places for the proof of thir doctrin, which are the plane refutation: and this is all the Scripture which he brings to confirm his point.

The rest of his preachment is meer groundless chat, save heer and there a few granes of corn scatterd to intice the silly fowl into his net, interlac't heer and there with som human reading; though slight, and not without Geographical and Historical mistakes: as page 29, *Suevia* the German dukedom,[45] for *Suecia* the Northern Kingdom: *Philip of Macedon,* who is generally understood of the great *Alexanders* father only, made contemporanie, page 31, with *T. Quintus the Roman commander,* instead of *T. Quintius* and the latter *Philip:* [46] and page 44, *Tully* cited *in his third oration against Verres,* to say of him, *that he was a wicked Consul,* who never was a Consul: [47] nor Trojan *sedition ever portraid* by that verse of *Virgil,* which you cite page 47, as *that* of *Troy:* [48] school-boyes could have

[45] *Suevia:* the territory of a confederation of Germanic tribes called by the Romans *Suevi* (*Suebi;* see Tacitus, *Germania,* 178 ff.), which inhabited large territories in central Europe east of the Rhine. *Suecia:* Sweden. See *Fear of God,* p. 29: "We cannot but take notice how *praedominant* in all Ages, this desire of change hath bin in all *parts* of *Christendom,* What *chopping* and *changing* hath there been in *Bohemia, Portugall, Polonia, Suevia,* &c."

[46] *Fear of God,* p. 31: "Just as *Philip* of *Macedon* told certain *Graecians* that had *revolted* from him to *T. Quintus,* the *Roman Commander; Commutastis vestram catenam politiore quidem, sed longiore:* that is, You have *exchang'd* your *chain* (meaning their *servile condition*) for one that at first sight *seems* a little better *polished,* but you will find it in time to be much more *heavy,* and *lasting.*" Philip [II, king] of Macedon (359–336 B.C.) was father of Alexander [III] the Great, king of Macedon (336–323 B.C.). Philip V (238–179 B.C.), king of Macedon, was conquered at Cynoscephalae in Thessaly (197) by Roman forces under Titus Quinctius Flaminius, whose name is also found as Quintius Flamininus.

[47] *Fear of God,* p. 44: "*Tully* (in his third *Oration* against *Verres*) gives him this *ill character, viz.* That he was, *Malus civis,* a bad Citizen; *Improbus Consul,* a worse *Consul;* because like *Sylla,* he look'd more at his own *private gain,* then on the *publique good;* and *seditiosus homo,* a seditious man, that is, one that loved to engender strife, and raise tumults by ill arts among the people, then which nothing is more *dangerous* and *destructive.*" See Cicero, *Verrine Orations,* II.i.14.§37 [tr. L. H. G. Greenwood (2 vols., Cambridge, Mass.: Loeb Classical Library, 1928), I, 160–61]: "Malus civis, improbus consul, seditiosus homo Cn. Carbo fuit" [Carbo was a bad consul, a traitor and a rebel]. Cicero imagines Verres as uttering the statement concerning Gaius Popinius Carbo, one of the leaders who seized Rome when Sulla left for the east in 87. Carbo was a consul; Gaius Verres, impeached by Cicero, was propraetor in Sicily, 73–71 B.C. Griffith's quotation implied that Cicero was speaking of Verres.

[48] *Fear of God,* p. 47: "Sedition many times *ends* in the *conflagration* of

tould you, that ther is nothing of *Troy* in that whole portraiture, as
you call it, of *sedition*. These gross mistakes may justly bring in
doubt your other loos citations; and that you take them up som-
where at the second or third hand rashly and without due consider-
ing.

Nor are you happier in the relating or the moralizing your fable.
The frogs (being once a free na=[7]tion saith the fable) *petitioned
Jupiter for a King: he tumbl'd among them a log. They found it
insensible: they petitioned then for a King that should be active: he*
sent them a Crane (a Stork saith the fable) *which straight fell to
pecking them up.*[49] This you apply to the reproof of them who de-
sire change: wheras indeed the true moral shews rather the folly of
those, who being free seek a King; which for the most part either as
a log lies heavie on his Subjects, without doing aught worthie of his
dignitie and the charge to maintain him, or as a Stork is ever pecking
them up and devouring them.

But by our fundamental Laws, the King is the highest power, page
40.[50] If we must hear mooting and law-lectures from the Pulpit,

---

whole *Towns* and *Cities,* as *Virgil* Elegantly *portrays* it in that of *Troy;
Jamque faces, & Saxa volant, furor arma ministrat,"* from Virgil, *Aeneid,* I.
148–50, in which a storm at sea is described "as, when oft-times in a great na-
tion tumult has risen, the base rabble rage angrily, and now brands and stones
fly, madness lending arms" ["ac veluti magno in populo cum saepe coorta est /
seditio, saevitque animis ignobile volgus, / iamque faces et saxa volant (furor
arma ministrat)"; from *Aeneid,* tr. H. Rushton Fairclough (2 vols., Loeb Clas-
sical Library, 1950), I, 250–51].

[49] *Fear of God,* p. 36: "Upon a time the *Frogs* petition'd *Jupiter* to grant
them a *King;* in condescention whereunto he tumbled among them a *Log:* and
after they had leap'd a while both on it, and about it, and found it to be *in-
sensible;* then they *petition'd* again for a *King* that should be *active* and *stirring;*
and thereupon he sent them a *Crane,* which straight fell to *pecking them up:*
The *Morall* whereof shews plainly, that nothing can long give satisfaction to
this natural desire of change; whether the *Governour,* and *government* be a *log,*
or a *Crane.*" See "Of the frogges and Iupyter," in *Caxton's Aesop,* ed. R. T.
Lenaghan (Cambridge, 1967), pp. 90–91, where it is moralized: "And he that
hath lyberte ought to kepe hit wel / For nothying is better than lyberte." *Cf.*
Bernard Mandeville, *Aesop Dress'd, or a Collection of Fables Writ in Familiar
Verse* (1704; Augustan Reprint Society, 1966), pp. 62–63. Also *The Fabulist
Metamorphosed Or the Fables Of Esop, Translated out of Latine into English
Verse, and Moralized,* by R. A, (London, 1634), p. 15.

[50] *Fear of God,* p. 40: "The *higher* the *power* is, the more is our *subjection*
obliged thereunto: But by our *Fundamentall Laws;* The King is the *highest
power,* and all others that bear any rule among, and over us, are *subordinate*
unto him."

what shame is it for a Dr. of Divinitie, not first to consider, that no law can be *fundamental,* but that which is grounded on the light of nature or right reason, commonly call'd *moral law:* [51] which no form of Government was ever counted; but arbitrarie, and at all times in the choice of every free people, or thir representers. This choice of Government is so essential to thir freedom, that longer then they have it, they are not free.[52] In this land not only the late King and his posteritie, but kingship it self hath bin abrogated by a law; [53] which involves with as good reason the posteritie of a King forfeited to the people, as that Law heretofore of Treason against the King, attainted the children with the father.[54] This Law against both King and Kingship they who most question, do no less question all enacted without the King and his Antiparlament at *Oxford,*[55] though call'd Mungrell by himself.[56] If no Law must be held good, [8] but what passes in full Parlament, then surely in exactness of legalitie, no member must be missing: for look how many are missing, so many Counties or Cities that sent them, want thir representers. But if being once chosen, they serve for the whole Nation, then any number which is sufficient, is full, and most of all in times of discord, neces-

[51] See above, *Way* II, p. 412, n. 35.

[52] Milton frequently expresses the idea. See esp. *A Defence,* in *Complete Prose,* IV, 392: "He who deprives a people of the power to choose whatever form of government they prefer surely deprives them of all that makes up civil liberty."

[53] See above, *Way* I, p. 355, n. 6.

[54] The conception of treason before the Civil War, based upon the Act of 1351, was that it mainly consisted of an overt act proving the traitorous imagination or compassing the king's death or levying war against the king (*Statutes of the Realm* [9 vols., 1810–1822], I, 319–20); the legal consequences of conviction were condemnation to death, forfeiture of estate real and personal, corruption of blood so that the condemned could neither inherit nor transmit by descent, and, generally, extinction of all civil rights and capacities. On July 17, 1649, "An Act Declaring what Offences Shall be Adjudged Treason" recast the law to meet the new circumstances of the Commonwealth (text in Gardiner, *Constitutional Documents,* pp. 388–91). See *Christian Doctrine, Complete Prose,* VI, 388, and the valuable article by Conrad Russell, "The Theory of Treason in the Trial of Strafford," *English Historical Review,* LXXX (1965), 30–50.

[55] See above, *Way* II, p. 412, n. 34.

[56] Having on March 10 adjourned the Oxford Parliament, Charles wrote to the queen on March 13, 1645, that he was now *"freed from the place of base and mutinous motions (that is to say, our Mungrell Parliament here) as of the chief causers."* See *The Kings Cabinet Opened: or, Certain Packets of Secret Letters and Papers* (1645), p. 13.

sitie and danger. The King himself was bound by the old Mode of
Parlaments, not to be absent, but in case of sickness, or som
extraordinary occasion, and then to leave his substitute; much less
might any member be allowd to absent himself.[57] If the King then
and many of the members with him, without leaving any in his stead,
forsook the Parlament upon a meer panic fear,[58] as was at that time
judg'd by most men, and to leavie Warr against them that sat,
should they who were left sitting, break up, or not dare enact aught
of neerest and presentest concernment to public safety, for the punc-
tilio wanting of a full number, which no Law book in such extraor-
dinary cases hath determind? Certainly if it were lawfull for them
to fly from thir charge upon pretence of privat safety, it was much
more lawfull for these to sit and act in thir trust what was necessary
for public. By a Law therefor of Parlament, and of a Parlament that
conquerd both *Ireland, Scotland,* & all thir enemies in *England,*
defended thir friends, were generally acknowledgd for a Parlament
both at home & abroad, kingship was abolishd: [59] this Law now of
late hath bin negatively repeald; [60] yet Kingship not positively re-

[57] The *Modus Tenendi Parliamentum* [14th cent.?]—which William Prynne
dismissed as a "modern consarsination by some unskillfull Botcher"—pur-
ported to describe the manner of holding parliaments under Edward the Con-
fessor, the last Saxon king, as an example to be followed; it was incorporated
in John Hooker, *Order and Usage of the Keeping of a Parlement in England*
(1575?), ed. and tr. William Hakewill (1641). See p. 27: "The King ought
dayly to be present in the Parlement, unlesse he be sick or diseased . . . and
then he ought to send for xii persons of the great estates . . . to see his per-
son & to certifie of his estate, & in their presence he ought to commit power
. . . that they ioyntly and severally shall begin and continew the Parlament in
the Kings name, making expresse mention in his commission of his disease."
Cf. *Modus Tenendi Parliamentum,* ed. and tr. Thomas Duffus Hardy (London,
1846), p. 34: "The King is bound by all means to be personally present in
Parliament, unless hindered by corporal infirmity [in which case] he ought to
commission the archbishop of the province, the steward, and chief justice
jointly and severally to begin and continue the Parliament in his name, express
mention being made in that commission of the cause of his then absence."
For discussion and valuable references, see V. H. Galbraith, "The *Modus
Tenendi Parliamentum,*" *Journal of the Warburg and Courtauld Institutes,* XVI
(1953), 81–99.

[58] See above, *Way* II, p. 412, n. 34.

[59] See above, *Way* I, p. 355, n. 6.

[60] The "Engagement" oath to "be true and faithful to the Commonwealth of
England, as the same is now established, without a King or a House of Lords,"
was instituted by Parliament as a test of allegiance to the Commonwealth, on
October 11, 1649 (*Commons Journals,* VI, 306; see Masson, IV, 124). But

stor'd; and I suppose never was establishd by any certain Law in this Land, nor possibly could be: for how could our forefathers binde [9] us to any certain form of Government, more then we can binde our posteritie? If a people be put to warre with thir King for his misgovernment, and overcome him, the power is then undoubtedly in thir own hands how they will be governd. The warr was granted *just* by the King himself at the beginning of his last treatie; [61] and still maintaind to be so by this last Parlament, as appears by the qualification prescrib'd to the members of this next ensuing, That none shall be elected, who have born arms against the Parlament since 1641.[62] If the warr were *just*, the conquest was also just by the Law of Nations.[63] And he who was the chief enemie, in all right ceasd to be the King, especially after captivitie, by the deciding verdit of warr; and royaltie with all her Laws and pretentions, yet remains in the victors power, together with the choice of our future Government. Free Commonwealths have bin ever counted fittest and properest for civil, vertuous and industrious Nations, abounding with prudent men worthie to govern: monarchie fittest to curb degenerate,

---

after the readmission of the secluded members on February 21, 1660 (see above, *Way* I, p. 353, n. 1), Parliament revived the Solemn League and Covenant on March 5, 1660, and on March 13 ordered that the Engagement to be true to the Commonwealth as now established be taken off the file. See also above, *Way* II, p. 409, n. 22.

[61] See above, *Way* II, p. 417, n. 54.

[62] "An Act for Dissolving the Parliament begun the third of November 1640. And for the Calling and Holding of a Parliament at Westminster the 25th April 1660," March 16, 1660 (Firth and Rait, *Acts and Ordinances*, II, 1469–72), enacted "that all and every person and persons who have advised or voluntarily aided, abetted, or assisted in any Warr against the Parliament, since the First Day of January One thousand six hundred fourty one, and his or their Sons, unlesse he or they have since manifested their good affection to this Parliament, shall be incapable to be Elected to serve as Members in the next Parliament." Monck, particularly, laid much stress upon this bar against those who had opposed Parliament since 1641, but an astute army officer made the point that such qualifications were useless, since a majority of the House—now dominated by Presbyterians who had themselves opposed the Commonwealth—who might themselves be disqualified would be the judges of the fitness of their fellows (Baker, *Chronicle*, p. 716). Cavaliers were chosen, despite the ordinance against their election. This disturbed the Council of State, which issued a proclamation to be read at the time and place of electing that recited the provisions of the ordinance against choosing Cavaliers or their sons (Steele, *Tudor and Stuart Proclamations*, no. 3176, March 28). See further, Godfrey Davies, "The General Election of 1660," pp. 211–35.

[63] See above, *Way* II, p. 412, n. 35.

corrupt, idle, proud, luxurious people.[64] If we desire to be of the former, nothing better for us, nothing nobler then a free Commonwealth: if we will needs condemn our selves to be of the latter, desparing of our own vertue, industrie and the number of our able men, we may then, conscious of our own unworthiness to be governd better, sadly betake us to our befitting thraldom: yet chusing out of our own number one who hath best aided the people, and best merited against tyrannie, the space of a raign or two we may chance to live happily anough, or tolerably.[65] But [10] that a victorious people should give up themselves again to the vanquishd, was never yet heard of; seems rather void of all reason and good policie, and will in all probabilitie subject the subduers to the subdu'd, will expose to revenge, to beggarie, to ruin and perpetual bondage the victors under the vanquishd: then which what can be more unworthie?

From misinterpreting our Law, you return to do again the same with Scripture; and would prove the supremacy of *English* Kings from I *Pet.* 2. 13. as if that were the Apostles work: [66] wherin if he

---

[64] Cf. *Commonplace Book* in *Complete Prose*, I, 420: "the form of state to be fitted to the peoples disposition some live best under monarchy others otherwise. . . . as amoung the Romans who after thire infancy were ripe for a more free goverment then monarchy, beeing in a manner all fit to be Ks. afterward growne unruly, and impotent with overmuch prosperity were either for thire profit, or thire punishment fit to be curb'd with a lordly and dreadfull monarchy." Cf. also Michael's speech to Adam, *Paradise Lost*, XII, 82–101: "yet know withal, / Since thy original lapse, true liberty / Is lost, which always with right reason dwells / Twinned, and from her hath no dividual being; / Reason in man obscured, or not obeyed, / Immediately inordinate desires / And upstart passions catch the government / From reason, and to servitude reduce / Man till then free. Therefore since he permits / Within himself unworthy powers to reign / Over free reason, God in judgment just / Subjects him from without to violent lords; / Who oft as undeservedly enthrall / His outward freedom: tyranny must be, / Though to the tyrant thereby no excuse. / Yet sometimes nations will decline so low / From virtue, which is reason, that no wrong, / But justice, and some fatal curse annexed, / Deprives them of their outward liberty, / Their inward lost."

[65] This is the most surprising and interesting passage in the tract. Milton acknowledges the force of the popular sweep toward monarchy, as he suggests, in Woolrych's words, "Better . . . King George [Monck] than King Charles" (introduction, p. 203, above).

[66] *Fear of God*, pp. 39–41: "*Sedition is defin'd to be an insolent declination of self-conceited subjects, from such lawfull power as God hath set over them.* Saint *Paul* (in the 13. Chapter to the *Romans*, 2.) hath this *Apostolicall Canon,* Let *every soul be subject to the higher Powers;* where speaking in the plurall

saith that *the king is supreme,* he speaks so of him but as an *ordinance of man,* and in respect of those *Governours that are sent by him,* not in respect of Parlaments, which by the Law of this Land are his bridle; in vain his bridle, if not also his rider: and therefor hath not only *coordination* with him, which you falsly call *seditious,* but hath superioritie above him, and that neither *against religion,* nor *right reason:* no nor against Common Law; for our Kings reignd only by Law: but the Parlament is above all positive Law, whether civil or common, makes or unmakes them both, & still the latter Parlament above the former, above all the former Lawgivers, then certainly above all precedent Laws, entaild the Crown on whom it pleasd; and, as a great Lawyer saith, *is so transcendent and absolute, that it cannot be confin'd either for causes or persons, within any bounds.*⁶⁷ But your cry is, no Parlament without a King. If this be so, we have never had lawfull Kings, who have all bin created Kings either by such Parlaments,⁶⁸ or by conquest: if by such Parlaments, they are in your allowance none: if by conquest, that conquest [11] we have now conquerd. So that as well by your own assertion as by

---

number, of *powers,* he implyes, / that there be *more* then *one; divers forms* of *government,* and *all* of them are *powers; . . .* and the *higher* the *power* is, the more is our *subjection* obliged thereunto: But by our *Fundamentall Laws;* The King is the *highest power,* and all others that bear any rule among, and over us, are *subordinate* unto him: and St. *Peter* (in the second Chapter of his first *Epistle Generall*) asserts *positively,* that the King is *Supreme;* and the *Philosopher* will allow in *unoquoque genere,* but *unum summum.* So that the *coordination* which some seditious persons have so *fiercely* maintain'd of late, is *point-blanck* against, not onely *Religion,* but *right reason.* And as for the *new coyn'd* distinctions of the *consistorian schismaticks,* whereby they have done their utmost to *enervate* the *Kings Supremacy;* and with the *Cardinall* in King *Henry* the 8. dayes, who *set up* his *Cap* above the *Crown;* these would *set up* their *Kirks* above the *King,* (*Popery* and *Presbyterie,* both in / *opinions* and *practice,* differ in many things onely in *terms*) by a *Jesuiticall* evasion of *coordination,* and *subordination;* of the *Kings politick* capacity, and his *personall;* of *major singulis,* and *minor universis,* &c." *Cf.* above, n. 39.

⁶⁷ Sir Edward Coke, *The Fourth Part of the Institutes of the Laws of England: Concerning the Jurisdiction of Courts* (London, 1644), p. 36 [Chapter I: "Of the High and Most Honourable Court of Parliament," section on "The Power and Jurisdiction of the Parliament"]: "Of the power and jurisdiction of the Parliament, for making of laws in proceeding by Bill, it is so transcendent and absolute, as it cannot be confined either for causes or persons within any bounds."

⁶⁸ *Cf. Eikonoklastes,* in *Complete Prose,* III, 467: "Certainly it was a Parlament that first created Kings, and not onely made Laws before a King was in being, but those Laws especially, wherby he holds his Crown."

ours, there can at present be no King. And how could that person be absolutely supreme, who reignd, not under Law only, but under oath of his good demeanour given to the people at his coronation, ere the people gave him his Crown? [69] and his principal oath was to maintain those Laws which the people should chuse? If then the Law it self, much more he who was but the keeper and minister of Law, was in thir choice; and both he subordinat to the performance of his duty sworn, and our sworn allegiance in order only to his performance.

You fall next on the *Consistorian Schismatics;* for so you call Presbyterians, page 40; [70] and judge them to have *enervated the Kings Supremacie by thir opinions and practice, differing in many things only in terms from Poperie;* though some of those principles which you there cite concerning Kingship, are to be read in *Aristotles*

[69] The coronation oath of Henry IV, "that is or ought to be taken by the Kings of this Realm at their Coronation," was printed in Parliament's "Third Remonstrance," in *An Exact Collection of all Remonstrances . . . betweene the KINGS most Excellent Majesty and his High Court of Parliament . . . December 1641 . . . March the 21, 1643* (1643), p. 268, from *Rotuli Parliamentorum, H. 4. N. 7.* See also p. 713, and Arthur Taylor, *The Glory of Regality: An Historical Treatise of the Anointing and Crowning of the Kings and Queens of England* (London, 1820), 329–41. In response to questions by the Archbishop of Canterbury, the king pledged, first, to defend the church, second, to do justice. Then the Archbishop asked, "Concedis justas leges & consuetudines esse tenendas & promittis per te eas esse protegendas & ad honorem Dei corroborandas quas vulgus elegerit, secundum vires tuas?" A crucial question between royalists and Independents was whether "elegerit" was future ("shall choose") or future perfect ("shall have chosen"). If future perfect, the king undertook to govern only by such laws as the people had *already* chosen, and, in effect, retained a negative voice over any future legislation. See *Eikon Basilike,* ed. Knachel, p. 26: "So far am I from thinking the majesty of the crown of England to be bound by any coronation oath, in a blind and brutish formality, to consent to whatever its subjects in Parliament shall require, as some men will needs infer, while, denying me any power of a negative voice as king, they are not ashamed to seek to deprive me of the liberty of using my reason with a good conscience. . . . I think my oath fully discharged in that point by my governing only by such laws as my people, with the House of Peers, have chosen, and myself have consented to." Milton obviously takes the verb in the future tense.

[70] *Fear of God,* pp. 40–41: "And as for the *new coyn'd* distinctions of the *consistorian schismaticks,* whereby they have done their utmost to *enervate* the *Kings Supremacy;* and with the *Cardinall* in King *Henry* the 8. dayes, who *set up* his *Cap* above the *Crown;* these would *set up* their *Kirks* above the *King,* (*Popery* and *Presbyterie,* both in / *opinions* and *practice,* differ in many things onely in *terms*) by a *Jesuiticall* evasion of *co-ordination,* and *subordination;* of the *Kings politick* capacity, and his *personall.*"

Politics, long ere Popery was thought on. The Presbyterians therefor it concerns to be well forewarnd of you betimes; and to them I leave you.

As for your examples of seditious men, page 54, &c. *Cora, Absalom, Zimri, Sheba,*[71] to these you might with much more reason have added your own name, who *blow the Trumpet of sedition* from your Pulpit against the present Government: [72] in reward wherof they have sent you by this time, as I hear, *to* your *own place,*[73] for preaching open sedition, while you would seem to preach against it.

As for your appendix annext of the *Samaritan reviv'd,*[74] finding it so foul a libell against all the well-affected of this land, since the very time of *Ship-mo*[12]*ney,*[75] against the whole Parlament, both

---

[71] *Fear of God,* pp. 54–56. Cora [Korah], Dathan and Abiram (Numbers 16, 17), at the head of 250 princes of the congregation, revolted against Moses and Aaron, in the interests of the people at large against the tribe of Levi. Refusing to obey Moses' summons to appear before him, they and their households were swallowed up in the earth.

Absalom (II Samuel 13–18:9), third and favorite son of David, becoming heir-apparent, began undermining the loyalty of the people to his father, and set up the standard of rebellion at Hebron. After seizing Jerusalem and proclaiming his supersession of his father by publicly appropriating the royal harem, he offered battle to David's forces in the wood of Ephraim. "And Absalom rode upon a mule, and the mule went under the thick boughs of a great oak, and his head caught hold of the oak, and he was taken up between the heaven and the earth; and the mule that was under him went away." While he hung there he was stabbed to death by Joab.

Zimri (1 Kings 16:9–20) seized the throne of Israel by the murder of his king Elah, but held it only seven days before Omri, another general of the army, asserted himself as claimant and conquered Zimri's forces. Zimri himself retreated to the palace, and died in the fire which he set there.

Sheba (II Samuel 20:1–20), a "man of Belial," "blew a trumpet" and led a rebellion of Israelites against David and the men of Judah. Pursued by the forces of Joab and Abishai, he shut himself up in Abel-beth-maacah, a town in the extreme north. The place would speedily have been taken by assault had not a woman whose judgment was highly esteemed by the inhabitants persuaded them to kill Sheba and throw his head over the wall to Joab.

[72] See *Fear of God,* p. 55: "So *Sheba, a man of Belial,* for *blowing* the *trumpet* of *Sedition,* saying, *We have no part in David, every man to his tents, O Israel* (in I *Samuel* 20:1.) was soon after *beheaded* by the *men of Abel.*"

[73] To Newgate Prison, April 5, 1660. See above, p. 468, n. b.

[74] The appendix (pp. 59[106]) to *Fear of God* is entitled: "The Samaritan *revived; and the course he then took to cure the wounded Traveller, by pouring in* Wine *and* Oyl; *Historically applyed for the sound and speedy healing of our present dangerous Distractions.*"

[75] "An ancient tax levied in time of war on the ports and maritime towns,

Lords and Commons, except those that fled to *Oxford*,[76] against the whole reformed Church, not only in *England* and *Scotland*, but all over *Europ* (in comparison wherof you and your Prelatical partie are more truly schismatics and sectarians,[77] nay more properly *fanatics* in your *fanes* and guilded temples, then those whom you revile by those names) and meeting with no more Scripture or solid reason in your *Samaritane wine and oyle*, then hath already bin found sophisticated and adulterate, I leave your malignant narrative, as needing no other confutation, then the just censure already pass'd upon you by the Councel of State. [13]

---

cities, and counties of England to provide ships for the king's service" (*NED*). Charles I levied it in 1634, when England was not at war. He extended it to the inland counties in 1635, and thereafter annually; his right, though strongly challenged, was upheld by seven judges against five in Hampden's Case (1637). The Long Parliament outlawed ship money by statute on August 7, 1641, and impeached the judges who had found for the king. The best brief account is in Kenyon, *Stuart Constitution,* pp. 88–89, 105.

[76] "Those that fled to Oxford" were royalist. See above, nn. 55, 57, 58, and *Way* II, p. 412, n. 34.

[77] *The Samaritan Revived,* p. 91, so for [81]: "The Presbyterians, Independents, Anabaptists, and all other Schismatiques and Sectaries, may well be called *LEGION*, for they are many." *Cf.* p. 73, and see above, n. 66.

MILTON'S PRIVATE

CORRESPONDENCE

1656–1659

PREFACES, TRANSLATIONS, AND NOTES BY
W. ARTHUR AND ALBERTA T. TURNER

LETTER 27, TO RICHARD JONES, MAY OR JUNE [?], 1656

RICHARD JONES was born about 1641, the son of Arthur Jones, Viscount Ranelagh, and his wife, the former Katherine Boyle, the "Lady Ranelagh" mentioned by the early biographers as one of Milton's friends. It seems likely that he studied with Milton when Milton was living in the Holborn house (1647–1649), and perhaps later; Edward Phillips, writing forty years later, mentions the connection when writing of Lady Ranelagh's visits to Milton in Petty France in the period 1652–1660. But whatever the period, Jones must have stayed with Milton long enough to acquire a competence in Latin, for Milton's letters to him are in that language. Jones visited Milton whenever he was in London, and wrote to him as late as 1659. For his part, Milton knew Jones well enough to advise him and repeatedly exhort him to virtue.

Some time in the spring of 1656 young Jones went to Oxford, where he soon became a pupil of Oldenburg. As the Oldenburg-Milton, Milton-Oldenburg, and Milton-Jones letters below show, that relationship continued for at least three or four years. Whatever Jones' status at the university, his progress did not satisfy Oldenburg, so on April 16, 1657, he wrote to Robert Boyle, the boy's uncle. He had resolved, he said, to remove to a place where "your nephew may not more lose his time than he doth now here" (Birch, VI, 140). The place decided upon was Saumur. Tutor and pupil visited London, then went to Paris, and on to their destination. In the spring of 1658 they went to Germany; and a year later they were back in Paris, where they remained a considerable time.

In each of his letters to Jones, Milton attempted to incite the young man to virtue. Tillyard says (p. xi), "Milton apparently had nothing particular to say to Jones; so he played the game by filling out with a little rhetorical moralising." But there is no reason to suppose that Milton was merely playing a game; as his former teacher, Milton had a right, and he apparently saw a need, to advise Jones.

Milton clearly saw something pointing to trouble in the future, and it eventually came. When Jones returned to Ireland in 1661, he was elected to the lower house of the Irish Parliament for County Roscommon, and in 1668 he was appointed Chancellor of the Exchequer in Ireland. Upon the death of his father on January 16, 1669/70, he became third Viscount Ranelagh, and was raised to the upper house. However, he did not choose to stay in Ireland; in 1670 he went to England, joined the cabal of the Duke of Buckingham, and was soon in high intrigue. He and a few part-ners became farmers of the revenue for Ireland. Soon there were com-plaints, examinations, and evasions. Jones' whole career thereafter was apparently one of gross malfeasance; but, with powerful friends at court, he was never without a good place.

His infamy was not limited to politics. Lord Conway wrote to Sir George Rawdon that he could find no suitable home in which to place Rawdon's daughter:

> Mr. Speaker's Lady [Sir Edward Seymour's wife, Letitia] is a most virtuous person, but her husband is worse for women than my Lord Ranelagh. If she were in either of these families, the world would judge I might better have ventured her in a bawdy house. (*Conway Letters*, pp. 439–40)

The letter was written in 1677, but it reflects a reputation not built in a day.

Richard Jones, holder of many positions of honor and trust since 1661, and first Earl of Ranelagh since 1674, died on January 5, 1711/12. He was buried in Westminster Abbey—an honor not accorded his moralising old tutor, the greatest poet of the age.

The following letter is the earliest surviving between Milton and Jones. Since it summarizes an earlier letter from Jones to Milton in which Jones communicated his first impressions of Oxford, and since Jones was to be with Milton on June 25, 1656, it must have been written in May or early June—after Jones' arrival at Oxford, but before his visit to Milton. The fact that Milton still had drafts of this and other letters to Jones for use in the 1674 edition suggests that he had a more than perfunctory interest in Jones.

Letter 22 in the 1674 edition, undated, but out of place after Letter 19 [misnumbered 12], dated September 21, 1656; also in Masson, V, 267–68; Columbia, XII, 88–91; and French, *Life Records*, IV, 86–88.

SOURCES

Thomas Birch, ed., *The Works of the Honourable Robert Boyle* (6 vols., Lon-don, 1772), VI; Joseph L. Chester, ed., *The Marriage, Baptismal, and Burial Records of the Collegiate Church or Abbey of St. Peter, Westminster,* (Publ. Harl. Soc., Vol. X, 1875), p. 273; Columbia, XII, 88–90; Darbishire, *Early Lives;* DNB; French, *Life Records,* IV; Masson, V; M. H. Nicolson, ed., *The Conway Letters* (New Haven, 1930), pp. 439–40; Tillyard, *Private Correspon-dence.*

TO THE NOBLE YOUTH RICHARD JONES

I RECEIVED your letter long after you sent it, after it had lain, I think, fifteen days put aside somewhere at your mother's. From it at long last I gladly discerned your attachment to me and feeling of goodwill. Certainly my goodwill towards you and my constant advice have never disappointed your excellent mother's good opinion of me or confidence in me, nor your own inclination. There is indeed, as you say, much natural beauty and wholesomeness in the place you have retired to; and there are books enough for a university. If only that pleasure contributed as much to the character of the inhabitants as it does to their delight, the place would lack nothing in felicity. The library there, too, is extremely well furnished,[1] but unless the minds of the students come from it better furnished with the best education, you might more correctly call it a storeroom of books than a library. And so, you sensibly perceive that these advantages require zeal and industry. Take strict care that I never need to deal with you in a different frame of mind; this you will most easily avoid if you will carefully obey the firm and friendly precepts of the distinguished Henry Oldenburg, who is with you. Farewell my dearest Richard, and permit me to encourage and excite you, like another Timothy,[2] to virtue and piety by the example of that most excellent woman your mother.

From Westminster
[May or June, 1656.] [3]

LETTER XXVII, OLDENBURG TO MILTON, MAY OR JUNE [?] 1656

This letter and four later ones from Oldenburg to Milton were discovered by A. R. Hall of Imperial College, London, in Oldenburg's notebook,

[1] This tribute to the library is perhaps the most direct evidence we have that Milton had worked there, although we should assume that he had from the fact that he was incorporated M.A. at Oxford in 1635, during the Horton or Hammersmith period, when he was seeking books from all sources. The attack on the intellectual climate at Oxford is not to be regarded as a result of the biased opinion of an old Cantabrigian; we remember that Milton did not approve of the program of study at either university.

[2] Timothy. In the Bible, Timothy is a model of a dutiful son.

[3] Date. The printed letter in 1674 ends with *"Westmonasterio."* But see headnote above concerning date.

preserved in the archives of the Royal Society, of which Oldenburg was the first secretary. Oldenburg's hand is often nearly illegible, and he used cryptic abbreviations, shifts of tense or voice, etc. Final drafts of the letters were presumably in better condition.

Oldenburg had known Milton for at least two years. For further information about him, see headnote to Letter 23 in volume IV, p. 865, of the present edition.

Royal Society MS I, ff. 9–9ᵛ; first published, with translation, in French, *Life Records*, IV, 92–96.

To the most learned Mr. John Milton, Henry Oldenburg sends greetings.

HAVING FINISHED some of my business, I wanted as soon as possible to fulfill the promise which I gave you at parting, and challenge you, if you will, to an exchange of letters. If I have any plans in this retreat, you will be glad to know, they are two. I should like to contemplate more closely nature and its Author, and at the same time devote a little effort to my friends, if I can. These are the pleasures which I confess I pursue; if I can catch the quarry, I shall think I have spent my leisure well. I see this world as a completely furnished picture-gallery, in whose recesses lie so many treasures of divine wisdom that they take entire possession of one who examines them really closely and bind him to them with passion. Nor does Oxford lack men who apply themselves actively to this study, yet do not on that account neglect the refinements of the liberal arts. Many, meanwhile, still tread the customary path, and never stop brawling over both divine and natural subjects. We have had a contentious and garrulous learning long enough; I plan to substitute among you a more peaceful and useful one. You [1] consider learning to be, not that which disturbs the mind, but that which firmly settles it; and I have known nothing more certainly a criterion of truth than placement beyond the risk of argument. I have no doubt that the more exposed anything is to contention the farther it is from the truth. Meanwhile, however the theologians and philosophers may know this, they nevertheless continue to gather fuel for their fire, seizing hastily all that is sacred and profane for the purpose. Every man is mindful of his own advan-

[1] This *you* is singular, addressing Milton individually. The *you* in the preceding sentence is plural. The confusion of course does not exist in the Latin.

tage, says the comedian,[2] and they contend over the superiority of their talent rather than over the truth. Hence those tears; this the foundation of those griefs.[3] Nothing brings religion into contempt more than this and builds a cross in the souls of those who fear God. God will eventually cause this evil to be torn out root and branch, and the minds of men to unite in the pursuit of truth and virtue. I believe that you have already read the reply which Maresius has made to the defender of the pre-Adamites, to whom a certain Martini, a fellow-countryman sent to Rome as agent of the Chinese mission, will shortly undertake a rejoinder.[4] For this man reports, in the preface to a book which he has published about the Tartar war, that he has brought back with him very old books of Chinese history and calendars leading with extraordinary accuracy from the very flood of Noah; and thence he promises to reconcile Chinese chronology with that which our sacred writings record, than which nothing could better protect the antiquity of the Mosaic and Adamite epoch. But enough! Pardon my prolixity, and believe me

Your most devoted

Henry Oldenburg

[May or June (?), 1656.] [5]

[2] A verbatim quotation from Plautus, *Mercator,* line 1011.

[3] Quoted from Terence, *Andria,* 99.

[4] The participants in the pre-Adamite controversy discussed by Oldenburg can best be treated in a single note. The defender (or assertor) of the pre-Adamites was Isaac de la Peyrère (1594–1676), a Calvinist, whose book *Praeadamitae* appeared in 1655. Basing his argument on four Biblical passages, he asserted that there were people on earth before Adam. His book was immediately condemned by the Parlement of Paris, and in February, 1656, he was arrested, and was soon converted to Catholicism (*Biographie Universelle*). Maresius was the Latin name of Samuel Desmarets (1599–1673). An interesting coincidence is that he had studied at Saumur and had been minister to the Synod of Charenton, both places later visited by Oldenburg. Maresius' reply to La Peyrère appeared in *S. Maresii Refutatio Fabulae Praedamiticae* (Groningen, 1656). See *The Correspondence of Henry Oldenburg* (Madison, 1965), ed. A. Rupert and Marie Boas Hall, I, 99–101. Martin Martini (1614–61) was a Jesuit missionary to China who had devoted much time to the study of Chinese language and history. In 1651 he was sent back to report to Rome on the condition and needs of the mission. His *De bello Tartarico in Sinis* appeared in Rome in 1654 and was translated into French in the same year. The promised *Sinicae historiae decas prima,* Munich, 1658, traced the chronology back through the pre-Christian era (*Biographie Universelle*). But, as we see by Milton's reply, he was not much interested in the matter.

[5] Not dated; but Milton's next letter to Oldenburg, dated June 25, is obviously in answer to this, and in the first sentence Milton indicates that he has just received the letter.

LETTER 28, TO HENRY OLDENBURG, JUNE 25, 1656

Letter 18 in the 1674 edition; in Columbia, XII, 76–79; and French, *Life Records*, IV, 102–04.

TO HENRY OLDENBURG, AGENT FOR BREMEN WITH ENGLISH GOVERNMENT

YOUR LETTER,[1] brought by young Ranelagh,[2] has found me quite busy, so that I am forced to be briefer than I could wish. You have indeed fulfilled your parting promises so well that no one, I believe, could have more scrupulously discharged a financial debt. I congratulate you on your place of retirement because it gives you pleasure, though it be my loss; I congratulate you also on that happiness of disposition which you can raise so easily from either urban ambition or ease to the contemplation of higher things. But what that retreat contributes except plenty of books, I do not know, and I should think the companions of your studies whom you have found there would be such because of the very nature of the place rather than because of its instruction— unless perhaps on account of missing you I am too unfair to the place because it detains you. Meanwhile you yourself rightly observe that there are too many there who by their empty quibbling con- taminate both the divine and the human, lest they seem to be doing absolutely nothing worthy of the many taxes by which they are supported at grievous public expense. But you know all that better for yourself. That ancient Chinese calendar, from the Flood on, which you say is promised by the Jesuit Martini,[3] is doubtless ea- gerly anticipated because of its novelty; but I do not see what authority or support it could add to the Mosaic books. Our friend Cyriack,[4] whom you wished me to greet, greets you in return. Farewell.

From Westminster, June 25, 1656.

[1] Letter XXVII, above.
[2] Richard Jones. See headnote to Letter 27.
[3] See n. 3 to Letter XXVII.
[4] Cyriack Skinner, Milton's friend, student, and amanuensis. Since Oldenburg's letter had not mentioned Cyriack, the greeting was presumably transmitted by Jones, who had brought the letter.

LETTER 29, TO RICHARD JONES, SEPTEMBER 21, 1656

Misnumbered 12 for 19 in the 1674 edition; in Columbia, XII, 78–83; and French, *Life Records*, IV, 113–15.

TO THE MOST NOBLE YOUTH RICHARD JONES

REPEATEDLY as I was preparing to answer your last letter,[1] unexpected business of my usual kind prevented me; later I heard that you were on excursion to some places in the vicinity; now your most excellent mother, leaving for Ireland (her departure must grieve us both extremely, for she has been like a near relative to me also)[2] carries you this letter herself.[3] You are quite right to be convinced of my fondness for you, and you should daily feel more convinced of it the more you show me of your sincere disposition and worthwhile accomplishments. That, by God's grace, you not only undertake, but, as if I had provoked you by a wager, you give bail and bind yourself to do it; you do not refuse to abide the decision or to pay the forfeit if you fail. I am really delighted by your confidence in yourself, which you cannot now disappoint without at the same time not only seeming to have abandoned your promises but also to have foregone your bail. Your saying that Oxford does not displease you does not lead me to believe that you have become any more proficient or wiser there; *that* you will have to show me by far different proofs. The victories of princes, which you praise, and similar matters in which force prevails I would not have you admire too much, now that you are listening to philosophers. For what is so remarkable if strong horns spring forth in the land of mutton-heads which can powerfully butt down cities and towns? Learn now, from early youth, to consider and recognize great examples, not on the basis of force and strength, but of justice and moderation.[4] Farewell, and give

[1] The letter has not been found.

[2] Lady Ranelagh was among Milton's frequent visitors in Petty France (Phillips; Darbishire, p. 74). At that time Milton had recently become totally blind, his wife was dead, and he had daughters to care for. It must have been at this time that Lady Ranelagh stood in the place of a female relative to Milton.

[3] The delivery of the letter may have been delayed. Lady Ranelagh's pass to Ireland was not granted until October 7 (*CSPD*, 1656–57, p. 583).

[4] This and the preceding two sentences reflect here, in a private letter, the same distrust of force and admiration of moral strength which run through

my fondest greetings to your companion the distinguished Henry Oldenburg.

From Westminster, September 21, 1656

LETTER 30, TO PETER HEIMBACH, NOVEMBER, 1656

There are three letters to Heimbach in the 1674 edition, and one from him preserved in manuscript—enough to show that the friendship continued for several years, and that Milton thought well enough of the young man to keep copies of these communications.

Of Heimbach we know little more than we can infer from the correspondence. He apparently went to England in 1656—perhaps, as Masson says, in the train of some embassy or agency. Masson discovered that he had published in London a Latin letter of eulogy to Cromwell, "extremely enthusiastic and somewhat juvenile." He was probably among the many foreigners who, according to Phillips, visited Milton in Petty France. He was apparently just coming of age, for in 1656 Milton addressed him as *adolescenti,* in 1657 as *viro.* But youthful effusiveness seems to have remained a part of his nature, and one can see Milton tactfully recoiling from it even in his last letter. By 1664 Heimbach had become state councillor to the Elector of Brandenburg for the Duchy of Cleves. It was from this position that he wrote the last letter on record to Milton, answered by the last extant letter by Milton.

Number 20 in the 1674 edition; also in Columbia, XII, 82–85; and French, *Life Records,* IV, 124–25.

SOURCES

French, *Life Records,* IV, 109 *et passim;* Masson, V, 280–81, 380; VI, 500.

TO THE MOST HONORED YOUTH PETER HEIMBACH

ABUNDANTLY, my Heimbach, have you fulfilled your promises and all else which your excellence proclaims, except my longing for your return, which you promised would be within two months at most. Now, unless my longing makes me miscount, you have been absent almost three. Concerning the atlas, you have amply done all that I asked, not that you should get me one, but only that you should find out the lowest price of the book. You say that they ask one hundred and thirty florins. I think it must be the Mau-

---

Milton's poetry and prose tracts. It is in his praise of public leaders in *A Second Defense,* in his sonnets to Cromwell, Fairfax, and Vane, in *Paradise Lost,* in *Paradise Regained,* and in *Samson Agonistes.*

ritanian Mount Atlas, not the book, that you say is to be bought at such a steep price. Such now is the extravagance of typographers in printing books that the furnishing of a library seems to have become no less costly than that of a villa. Since to me, blind, pictured maps could hardly be useful, surveying as I do the actual globe with unseeing eyes, I fear that the more I paid for the book, the more I should mourn my loss. I beg you to do me the further favor to find out, so that you can tell me when you return, how many volumes there are in the whole work and which of the two editions, Blaeu's or Jansen's, is the fuller and more accurate.[1] This I hope to hear from you personally on your speedy return, rather than by another letter. Meanwhile farewell, and come back to us as soon as you can.

From Westminster, November 8, 1656

LETTER XXVIII, OLDENBURG TO MILTON, DECEMBER 28, 1656

Draft in Royal Society MS. I, ff. 11–11ᵛ (see headnote to Letter XXVII); first published, with translation, in French, *Life Records*, IV, 129–31.

To the most accomplished Mr. Milton, greetings. December 28, 1656

I WRITE you so rarely, most cordial Milton, not because of laziness nor forgetfulness, but because I would not interfere with your work. For this reason I would not write now, unless I thought your duties would be somewhat intermittent at this festive season. I do not wonder that the strong and entrenched custom of keeping holiday at this time is difficult to root out. But I do wonder that the birthday of the Lord was settled on the twenty-fifth of December by the Roman church, which could easily look at the census list; [1] for hardly ever (at least in a temperate zone) in winter, outdoors, especially at night, do shepherds act as it is well known they did at

---

[1] We do not know what atlas Milton had originally inquired about. That of John Jansen, *Novus Atlas*, was completed in six volumes in 1658; that of John Blaeu, *Geographia Blaeviana*, in eleven volumes in 1662. But individual volumes were on sale earlier. Blaeu advertised a four-volume atlas in 1650. All cost more than 130 florins (Masson, V, 280–81).

[1] It was not so easy as Oldenburg supposed, and the name of Jesus was apparently not on the census list. The exact date of His birth is still unknown.

the birth of Christ. Wherefore Scaliger,[2] the most careful investigator of the chronology, thinks it more suitable to September, when shepherds do work outdoors. And he who consults Nicephorus [3] will find that the Eastern churches did not observe this custom before the time of the Emperor Justinian.[4] If the Christian people would celebrate the memory of the Redeemer's birth at a different time, they might be tolerated. But when they hold Bacchanalian orgies in the name of Christ's holy birthday, they are unendurable. It is known that in olden times the Romans celebrated the Saturnalia in this month. It is equally well known that at these they glutted themselves with much wine, and the slaves sported with masters. I should say that the Christians have denied the name of Saturn but retain the fact; substituted the name of Christ but ignore the fact. I write freely to you about what I have been thinking these days, because this place, barren of new ideas, scarcely suggests any others. May these ideas, arising out of leisure, be good counsels, however barren and dry. I hope that the excellent Lawrence [5] is well and does active service for the state. I send him best wishes. Farewell, and continue to love me.

From Oxford [6]

LETTER 31, TO EMERIC BIGOT, MARCH 24, 1657

A native of Rouen and much younger than Milton, Emeric Bigot was devoted to literature, and was an industrious collector of books. A catalogue of his library was published in 1706. See Masson, V, 284–85, and *La Grande Encyclopédie Dictionnaire de Biographie Française*.

Letter 21 in the 1674 edition; also in Columbia, XII, 84–89; and French, *Life Records*, IV, 134–37.

---

[2] Joseph Justus Scaliger (1540–1609), the "founder of the science of chronology," whose *De Emendatione Temporum* (1583) and *Thesaurus Temporum* (1609) were well known.

[3] Probably Nicephorus Gregoras (ca. 1295–ca. 1359), one of the authors of the *Byzantine History*. He was particularly interested in the exact locating of holy days.

[4] Justinian the Great, emperor of Constantinople, 527–565 A.D.

[5] Edward Lawrence, one of Milton's young friends (now twenty-three), the person addressed in Sonnet XX. He was elected member of the House of Commons on Nov. 11, 1656. He died in 1657 (Parker, *Milton*, pp. 498–99 and note; p. 1058).

[6] The date is at the head of the letter in Oldenburg's notebook.

TO THE MOST ILLUSTRIOUS EMERY BIGOT

THAT on your crossing over to England I seemed to you more worthy than others to seek out and call upon was extremely and naturally gratifying to me; and that you greet me by letter [1] after so long an interval is even more welcome. For though at first you might have been led to me by the opinion of others, you could hardly return now by letter unless drawn back by your own judgment, or at least good will. Thus I surely have reason to congratulate myself; for many have become eminent by their published writings whose living voice and daily intercourse have displayed nothing but the feeble and the ordinary. If I can succeed so that I seem in mind and manners as I seem in my best writings, I shall myself both have added weight to the writings and received greater fame, no matter how small, from them in return, since I shall seem less to have taken what is honest and laudable from the most distinguished authors than to have brought it forth, pure and unalloyed, from the depths of my mind and spirit. I am glad therefore that you are convinced of my peace of mind in this severe loss of sight and in my willingness and eagerness to receive foreign guests. Why should I not quietly bear a loss of light which I expect is not so much lost as recalled and drawn inward to sharpen rather than dull the eye of the mind? For that reason I am not angry at written words nor do I entirely cease studying them, severely though they have punished me; for lest I be so peevish, I am instructed by the example of King Telephus [2] of the Mysians, who was not unwilling to be later healed by the weapon which wounded him. As to that book which you have, *On The Manner of Holding Parliaments,*[3] I have had the designated places either emended or, if they were doubtful, confirmed from the distinguished Lord Bradshaw's [4] manuscript, and also from

[1] The letter has not been found.

[2] Telephus, wounded by Achilles, was told by an oracle that the wound could be healed only by the one who inflicted it, and went to the Greek camp. The Greeks had been told by an oracle that they could not find Troy without the aid of Telephus. Achilles healed the wound with some rust from his spear, and Telephus showed the Greeks the way to Troy.

[3] Parker (*Milton,* p. 1061) identifies this as the medieval *Modus tenendi parliamentum.* See above, p. 480, n. 57.

[4] John Bradshaw, judge at the trial of Charles I, member of the Council of State, and a friend of Milton.

the Cotton manuscript,[5] as you will see from your note, herewith returned. In answer to your desire to know whether the autograph of this book exists in the Tower of London, I sent someone to ask the herald who has custody of the deeds,[6] and with whom I am on familiar terms. He answered that no copy of this book exists among those records. You in turn offer me welcome service in caring for my library: I lack, of the Byzantine histories, Theophanes' *Chronography*, Greek and Latin in folio, Constantine Manasses' *Epitome of History*, Codinus' *Excerpts from the Antiquities of Constantinople*, Greek and Latin in folio, Anastasius Bibliothecarius' *History and Lives of the Roman Popes* in folio, to which I would add, from the same press, Michael Glycas, and Joannes Cinnamus, the continuers of Anna Comnena, if they have published.[7] I do not add "as cheaply as you can," not only because it is unnecessary to remind a very frugal man like yourself, but because they say the price of these books is fixed and known to everyone. Mr. Stoupe [8] has undertaken to provide the money for you in cash and also to arrange for the most convenient method of transportation. I sincerely wish you all you choose and long for. Farewell.

From Westminster, March 24, 1657 [9]

LETTER XXIX, OLDENBURG TO MILTON, JUNE 27/JULY 7, 1657

As explained in the headnote to Letter 27, Oldenburg became dissatisfied with Oxford, and shortly before the date of this letter took his student, Richard Jones, to France.

---

[5] Several copies of the book were among the manuscripts of Sir Robert Cotton, later presented to the British Museum.

[6] William Ryley, Norroy King-at-arms, another friend of Milton.

[7] Parker (*Milton*, p. 502) identifies the first three of these books as the *Chronographia* of St. Theophanes (a chronicle of events 284–813 A.D.), the *Excerpta de Antiquitatibus Constantinopolitanis* of Georgius Codinus, and the *Breviarium Historicum* of Constantine Manasses, a metrical chronicle from the Creation to 1081 A.D. All three books had been published in 1655. The *Annales* of Michael Glycas, a history of the world from the Creation to 1118 A.D. was not published until 1660. The history of Johannes Cinnamus (or Sinnamus) was not published until 1670. It was a continuation of the *Alexiad* of Anna Comnena (b. 1083), largely a history of her father, the emperor Alexius Comnenus.

[8] Jean Baptiste Stoupe, a ubiquitous agent of Thurloe and the Council of State.

[9] 1656 in text (Old Style).

Draft in Royal Society MS. I, ff. 22ᵛ–23ʳ (see headnote to Letter
XXVII); first published, with translation, in French, *Life Records*, IV,
155–57.

TO THE MOST EXCELLENT MR. JOHN MILTON,
HENRY OLDENBURG SENDS GREETINGS

AFTER we came by a most agreeable journey to Saumur, the
darling of the River Loire, I wanted to inform you at once
of our good fortune; your manifest concern for us makes us
confident that you cherish a desire for our safety and happiness and
would therefore welcome a letter bringing that news. I can in turn
assure you, without exaggeration or pretense, that I love you and am
eager for a letter which will assure me of your health and safety. I
stayed only a week [1] in Paris, and attended only one meeting at
Charenton,[2] at the end of which I received on the return boat con-
firmation of the rumor that More [3] has been elected to the pastorate
of that church. These people are of such a nature that whoever
knows how to titillate their ears and soothe their passions with ornate
language can easily win favor among them, even if his life should
be entirely the opposite of his teaching. So it happens that certain
politicians cultivate religion (as many others who profess a purer
religion do, from custom, not from the promptings of the soul), and
they are more easily captivated by accomplished speaking than by
manner of living. Would that only those peoples who are sold to the
Roman Pontiff cultivated this species of religion, that only those
priests who have taken oath to that bishop turned religion to prop-
erty and profit. Our cause would be best served if we broke with
that unclean communion. But, alas, too many of us, whether clergy
or laity, dazzling with ornament, trample with words on truth fought
for by deeds. Therefore, when I perceived that shepherds along with
sheep were rushing to embrace this More, and that the eloquence
of his mouth bedaubed and disguised the ugliness of his life, I de-
cided it was not yet wise to show anyone your last treatise [4] against

---

[1] Perhaps "about a week." Oldenburg has *octiduum*.

[2] One of the chief Protestant churches in France, near Paris. See below, p.
502, n. 3.

[3] Alexander More, Milton's old enemy, whom Milton supposed to be the
author of the *Regii Sanguinis Clamor*.

[4] Presumably the *Pro Se Defensio* (Parker, *Milton*, p. 506).

this man. If I did so, I should surely kindle certain hostility against myself, and should probably separate the fewest people possible from their senseless enthusiasm for More. Forgive my speaking freely, and let us know at any time what you are doing and what you would like us to do or attend to for you. Farewell to you and your excellent wife,[5] and, if you please, give my kindest respects to Mr. Lawrence.[6]

From Saumur, July 7, 1657 (New Style)

LETTER 32, TO HENRY DE BRASS, JULY 15, 1657

Although Milton addresses him as a person of some distinction and promise, we know nothing of De Brass other than what is revealed by Milton's letters to him.

Letter 23 in the 1674 edition; also in Columbia, XII, 90–95; and French, *Life Records*, IV, 159–62.

TO THE MOST DISTINGUISHED MR. HENRY DE BRASS

I SEE, Sir, that you, like very few of today's youth who wander through foreign lands, travel rightly and wisely, not for childish aims, but in the manner of ancient philosophers, to gather richer learning from every source. Yet whenever I regard what you write, you seem to have come abroad not so much to acquire foreign knowledge as to impart knowledge to others, to barter good merchandise rather than to buy it. And I wish that it were as easy for me to assist and promote those admirable studies of yours in every way as it is truly agreeable and pleasant that one of your distinguished talents should ask it of me. Yet as to your writing that you have decided to write to me and ask me to resolve those problems about which for many ages historians seem to have been in the dark, I have certainly never assumed nor would I dare assume anything of the sort. Concerning what you write of Sallust, I will say frankly, since you wish me to say freely what I think, that I prefer Sallust to any other Latin historian whatever, which was also the nearly unanimous opinion of the ancients. Your Tacitus has his merits, but certainly the greatest of these in my judgment is that he imitated Sallust

---

[5] Katherine Woodcock, whom Milton had married in November 1656—a fact Oldenburg did not know when he wrote his previous letter.

[6] Edward Lawrence, as in Letter XXVIII.

with all his might. As far as I can tell from what you write, my dis-
cussing these matters personally with you seems to have made you
feel almost the same way yourself about that most sagacious writer;
and you even ask me, since he said at the beginning of the *Bellum
Catilinae* that history is extremely difficult to write "because the
style must be equal to the deeds," [1] just how I think a historian could
acquire such a style. I think thus: he who would write worthily of
worthy deeds ought to write with no less largeness of spirit and
experience of the world than he who did them,[2] so that he can
comprehend and judge as an equal even the greatest, and, having
comprehended, can narrate them gravely and clearly in plain and
temperate language. For I do not insist on ornate language; I ask
for a historian, not an orator. Nor would I favor injecting frequent
maxims or judgments on historical exploits, lest by breaking the
chain of events, the historian invade the province of the political
writer; if, in explaining plans and narrating deeds, he follows to the
best of his ability not his own invention or conjecture but the truth,
he truly fulfills his function. I would also add of Sallust, what he
himself praised most highly in Cato, that he can accomplish much in
few words, which I believe no one can do without sharp judgment
and a certain restraint. There are many in whose writing you will
miss neither grace of style nor abundance of fact, but in my opinion
the chief among the Latins who can join brevity with abundance, that
is, who can say much in few words, is Sallust. I think these should
be the excellences of the historian who expects to do justice to great
deeds in words. But why should I say all this to you, who, with
your ability, could reach these conclusions yourself, and who have
entered a course on which if you proceed you will soon be able to
consult no one more learned than yourself? And though you need no
one's urging, still, lest I seem wholly unresponsive to your great need
for my authority, I strongly urge and advise you to persevere. Fare-
well, and congratulations on your own excellence and on your zeal
for gaining wisdom.

From Westminster, July 15, 1657.[3]

[1] Milton does not use quotation marks, but his *"quod facta dictis exaequanda
sunt"* are the exact words of Sallust, *Bellum Catilinae*, III, 2.

[2] Compare Milton's similar requirement of greatness of character in the poet,
for instance, in Elegy VI.

[3] Milton has "Idibus Quintil."

LETTER 33, TO HENRY OLDENBURG, AUGUST 1, 1657

This letter is a reply to Letter XXIX, from Oldenburg.
Letter 24 in the 1674 edition; also in Columbia, XII, 96–99; and French, *Life Records*, IV, 165–67.

TO HENRY OLDENBURG

I AM glad you have arrived at Saumur, the end, I believe, of your travel; for you are not mistaken in thinking the news especially welcome to me, who both esteem you for own merit and know the reason for undertaking the journey to be so meritorious and praiseworthy.[1] As for what you have heard, that so infamous a priest[2] has been called to instruct so illustrious a church, I had rather anyone else had heard it in Charon's boat than you in that of Charenton;[3] for it is greatly to be feared that whoever expects to arrive at heaven by means of such a foul pilot will be a whole world off course. Woe to that church (may God avert the omen) where such ministers please the ears, as the Church, if she would truly be called reformed, would more properly eject than elect. In not having given copies of my writings[4] to anyone who does not ask, you have done well and judiciously, not in my opinion alone, but also in that of Horace:

> Err not by zeal for us, nor on our books
> Draw hatred by too vehement a care.[5]

A certain learned friend of mine[6] spent last summer at Saumur. He wrote me that the book was in demand in that region. I sent him just one copy. He wrote back that some of the learned men with

[1] Oldenburg had taken his pupil Richard Jones to France, where he thought Jones would make more progress than he was making at Oxford. See headnote to Letter 27, above.

[2] See above, n. 3 to Letter XXIX.

[3] Charenton is a town near Paris, on the Seine. More had recently been appointed minister there. Charon's boat took the souls of the dead across the Styx, into hell. Milton seems to mean that anyone who heard the news on Charon's boat would soon forget it and never tell anyone. Or he may mean that anyone who heard it on Charon's boat would have heard that Morus was already in hell.

[4] Presumably the *Pro Se Defensio* (Parker, *Milton*, p. 506).

[5] These and the three lines quoted below are from Horace, *Epistolae*, I, 13, 4–8.

[6] Probably Andrew Marvell, who was in Saumur in 1656 with his pupil William Dutton (Parker, *Milton*, p. 1061).

whom he had shared it had been more than pleased. Had I not thought I should please them, I would certainly have spared you the trouble and me the expense. Indeed,

> If my heavy pack of paper galls,
> Dump it at once, rather than in the end,
> Dash down the load in anger. . . .

To our friend Lawrence [7] I have given your greeting, as you asked. Finally, there is nothing I had rather have you do nor rather have happen, than that you and your pupil should be well and should return to us as soon as possible with all your wishes fulfilled.

From Westminster, August 1, 1657,[8]

LETTER 34, TO RICHARD JONES, AUGUST 1, 1657

For Jones' relations with Milton and his studies under Oldenburg, see above, p. 487, headnote to Letter 27.

Letter 25 in the 1674 edition; also in Columbia, XII, 98–101; and French, *Life Records*, IV, 163–64.

TO THE NOBLE YOUTH RICHARD JONES

THAT you have finished so long a journey without mishap, and, spurning the temptations of Paris, have hastened so quickly to that place where you can enjoy learned leisure and the company of learned men, I both rejoice and praise your nature for. As long as you stay there you will be in safe harbor; elsewhere you would have to beware the Syrtes and Scopulos, and the songs of the Sirens.[1] And I had rather you did not thirst too much after the Saumur vintage, with which you think you will while away the time, unless you also intend to dilute that must of Liber with more than a fifth part of the more liberal drink of the Muses.[2] But you have, even if I were silent, a first-rate adviser;[3] if you

[7] Edward Lawrence, as in Letter XXIX.

[8] Milton has "Calend. Sextil."

[1] Milton has *"Syrtes & Scopulos, & Sirenum cantus."* The Syrtes were two deep gulfs on the northern coast of Africa, proverbially dangerous to mariners. The word *scopulos* means cliffs, but capitalized may refer to the mountains forming the northern edge of the Great Desert (Sahara) between the two Syrtes, faced by salt marshes and also dangerous to mariners. The Sirens are are well known. The combination gives Milton a good alliteration.

[2] The name *Liber* was often given to Bacchus by Roman poets. Milton manages a pun in *"mustum illud Liberi liberiore Musarum latice."*

[3] That is, Oldenburg.

listen to him, you will indeed have acted in your own best interest, and both given gladness to your excellent mother [4] and daily increased her love for you—this you should daily pray Almighty God that you may do. Farewell, and see that you return to us upright and as accomplished as you can.[5] To me that will be the most joyful thing of all.

From Westminster, August 1, 1657.[6]

LETTER XXX, OLDENBURG TO MILTON,
OCTOBER 4/14, 1657

The handwriting is bad, and the coherence of Oldenburg's draft is sometimes uncertain, but the copy which Milton received would presumably have been much better. Our translation is based on French's transcription, and our own reading of the photostat which Professor French kindly sent us.

Draft in Royal Society MS. I, ff. 30–30ᵛ (see headnote to Letter XXVII); first printed, with translation, in French, *Life Records*, IV, 178–81.

OLDENBURG TO THE MOST EXCELLENT MILTON,
GREETINGS

Now that the grape harvest here is finished, which several weeks of all but continuous rain have made scant enough and weak, I could not refrain from telling you that your letters, duly delivered to us, made us extraordinarily glad, especially because they assured us of your health and confirmed the permanence of your feeling toward us. You must confidently promise yourself the same feeling in return, and you must not expect to be estranged from me by any interval of time or place. We had in mind to wander through this province of Anjou, to see the country and relax the mind.[1] But the too foul weather prevented us, and perhaps

---

[4] Lady Ranelagh.

[5] Tillyard (*Private Correspondence*, p. 133) called this "the most priggish letter Milton wrote." But for Milton's worry about Jones' character see the headnote to Letter 27. And Milton was fond enough of Jones to keep copies of this and other letters to him. In any case, at this time Jones was moved to industry and virtue either by Milton's urging or Oldenburg's daily care or his own initiative, for on September 8 Oldenburg wrote to Jones' uncle, Robert Boyle, that the boy had been so diligent for two or three months that he deserved a vacation (Parker, *Milton*, p. 505).

[6] Milton has "Calend. Sextil."

[1] See n. 5 to Letter 34, above.

will prevent us till next spring, if God lets us live. Christina of Sweden has now come to France on a second visit, but is less well received by the people.[2] They think it burdensome to entertain three queens,[3] and that at times this untamed sex, especially when placed in high position, is too apt and notorious at intrigue. I have heard that More has openly solicited the pastorate of Charenton; shortly, if he has not already presented himself, he is to be presented to that church.[4] He believes, from a diligent and unwearied canvass of this province, that you give yourself the severe blow he received from you; and thought to replace in you whatever tooth you had broken in him, by addressing the people with the most dazzling rhetoric. Meanwhile, no searcher of souls favors deceit toward God, however the multitude may toward men; nor need we fear for the safety of those who listen to such men so long as they preach the truth. Whoever receives the seed of the divine word, receives the seed of eternal life, by whomever it is sown; nor does good seed, though spread by an impure hand, fail to produce an ample harvest. Meanwhile they warn that mortals who live otherwise than as they should deserve the worst; I do not wish to be corrupted and much depleted the authority by which he is damned who must be damned for wavering in his duty.

You should not think me so feeble that I would throw away your writings,[5] which speak things worthy of immortality; and do not fear your expense, which I shall refund you in good faith on my return. We shall hardly visit Italy, which a plague consumes widely with creeping skin disease.[6] May the Highest Power drive it far from your Britain, and if by chance (which I fear) it has taken hold of any shore of it, may He turn it away, I plead in all my prayers. Stay well, and remember us.

Saumur, October 14, 1657, Gregorian Style.[7]

[2] Christina had liked Milton's first *Defence* and had turned against Salmasius. Milton had praised her highly in the *Second Defence*. She had abdicated in June 1654 (Parker, *Milton*, pp. 440–41).

[3] The three queens were presumably the queen of France, the exiled queen of England, and Christina.

[4] Apparently, when Oldenburg wrote Letter XXIX More had only been invited or considered; now he was to be "presented."

[5] See n. 4 to Letter 33.

[6] Oldenburg has *serpigine contages,* a Middle Latin term denoting such diseases as ringworm, eczema, and herpes. The word *serpigo* survives in *Webster's New Collegiate Dictionary,* but the reader would hardly look for it there.

[7] Oldenburg has "Salmurio prid. id. Octob. 1657. Styl. Gregor."

LETTER 35, TO HENRY DE BRASS,
DECEMBER 16, 1657

The letter to which this replies is lost, but either de Brass had not understood Milton's distinction (in Letter 32) between the style of the historian and the style of the orator, or he was teasing Milton. The busy Milton's reply—with his characteristic apology for tardiness—is courteous but brief and pointed, reminding de Brass of the distinction and giving him enough references to keep him busy for a while.

Letter 26 in the 1674 edition; also in Columbia, XII, 100–03; and French, *Life Records,* IV, 186–87.

TO THE MOST DISTINGUISHED MR. HENRY DE BRASS

HINDERED recently by business, illustrious Sir, I reply later than I wished. For I wished to answer sooner because I perceived that your letter, learned as it is, left me room not so much for advising you (which you ask, I believe, for my honor, not your need) as only for congratulating you. I especially congratulate, both myself on my apparent success in explaining the meaning of Sallust, and you on your assiduous and profitable reading of that wisest of authors. Concerning him I would dare say to you what Quintilian said of Cicero [1] that a man who delights in Sallust may be sure that he is not unproficient in history. As for that precept of Aristotle's from the third book of the *Rhetoric* which you wish explained,[2] that aphorism should be used in both narration and confirmation, for it is moral. I do not see what especially needs explanation, except that narration and confirmation, which is usually called proof, should here be understood as the rhetorician, not the historian uses them; for the functions of rhetorician and historian are different, whether they narrate or prove, just as the arts themselves are different from each other. You will, moreover, have learned what is suitable for the historian more directly from the ancient authors Polybius, Dionysius of Halicarnassus, Diodorus, Cicero, Lucian, and many others, who have handed down scattered precepts on the matter. I do earnestly wish you all prosperity and safety in your studies and travels, and success worthy of the will and perse-

[1] Quintilian, *Institutio Oratoria,* X, i, 112–13.
[2] Aristotle, *Rhetoric,* III, xvii, 9–10.

verance which I perceive that you devote to all things excellent. Farewell.

From Westminster, December 16, 1657.

LETTER 36, TO PETER HEIMBACH, DECEMBER 18, 1657

Letter 27 in the 1674 edition; in Columbia, XII, 102–05; and French, *Life Records*, IV, 189–90.

TO THE MOST HIGHLY ACCOMPLISHED PETER HEIMBACH

I HAVE received your letter dated The Hague, December eighteenth,[1] which, since I see that it concerns your business affairs, I thought I should answer on the same day it reaches me. In it, after thanking me for I know not what favors (which I wish were not nullities, since I would do anything you might desire), you ask me to recommend you through Lord Lawrence[2] to our minister-elect to Holland.[3] I grieve deeply that it is not in my power, both because my influential friends are very few (since I stay nearly always at home—and willingly) and because I believe that he has already sailed and is nearly there, and that he has with him the man whom he wants for secretary,[4] which is the position you seek. But the post is just leaving. Farewell.

From Westminster, December 18, 1657.

LETTER 37 [?], TO CHRISTOPHER MILTON, JANUARY 1657/8

Among the Rosenbach documents relating to Milton there is a brief note, with the left side torn off, which may be from Milton to his brother.

[1] Heimbach's letter would have been dated New Style, or December 8 Old Style. It must have pleased Milton to give his letter the same date as the letter he was answering. He broke all records by answering Heimbach's letter the day he received it.

[2] Henry Lawrence senior, member of the Council of State and the Protector's Councils from 1653 to 1659. He was the father of Milton's young friend, Edward Lawrence.

[3] The minister-elect was George Downing. The Council of State ordered his ship on December 18. On December 17 his letter of credentials to the United Provinces, translated by Milton, was prepared and dated (French, *Life Records*, IV, 188, and Parker, *Milton*, p. 1062).

[4] We do not know the name of the secretary.

First printed in Columbia, XVIII, 263, with a note at p. 521, it is also in French, *Life Records,* IV, 199, with slightly different readings. French says (p. 200), "Everything about this piece is highly uncertain: the author, the recipient, the date, and the meaning." He concludes, "This item is included with great diffidence on the chance that it may be Miltonic." Parker (*Milton,* p. 1049) dismisses it.

LETTER 38, TO JEAN LABADIE, APRIL 21,1659

Jean Labadie was a reforming French divine. A Jesuit who turned Protestant and founded the sect known as the Labadists, he was usually the subject of controversy, and sometimes scandal (Masson, V, 591–95). Since he sought Milton's aid through a common acquaintance, it would seem that they had not known one another personally, and that Milton had known little of him before. In any case, he did not accept the invitation Milton here transmits to him, and we hear of no further communication between them.

Letter 28 in the 1674 edition; in Columbia, XII, 104–09; and French, *Life Records,* IV, 259–63.

TO JEAN LABADIE, MINISTER OF ORANGE

IF I ANSWER you somewhat late, distinguished and Reverend Sir, our Durie,[1] I believe, will not refuse to let me transfer the blame to him. For since he supplied me with that note, which you wished read to me, concerning what you had done and suffered on behalf of the Gospel, I have not postponed preparing this letter to you, that I may give it to the first carrier, because I am concerned how you may interpret my long silence. Meanwhile I am most grateful to your Du Moulin of Nîmes,[2] who by his discourse and commendation of me, has put me in the good graces of so many worthy men in that region. And though I am not unaware that, whether because I did not refuse to engage so prominent an adversary at the request of the state, or because of the notoriety of the subject, or even because of my manner of writing, I have become known far

[1] It is not clear whether this is John Dury, or Durie, famous minister who spent many years working for unity of the Protestant churches of Europe and might well have known Labadie, or a G. Dury (possibly Giles) who was an elder of the French Church in London (see Parker, *Milton,* pp. 1069, 1285).

[2] Pierre Du Moulin the elder (1568–1659), famous French Protestant minister, father of the Anglican Du Moulin who was the real author of the *Clamor,* which Milton attributed to More. Milton apparently did not know that Du Moulin had died on March 10 (Parker, *Milton,* p. 1068). Du Moulin's praises of Milton seem to have been for his writings against Salmasius.

and wide, I still think I have only so much fame as I have a good name among good men. And I see plainly that this judgment is shared by you, who, kindled by zeal and love for Christian truth, have accomplished so much hard work and withstood so many enemies, and do it so courageously every day that, far from seeking fame from the wicked, you do not fear to call down on yourself their certain hatred and maledictions. O happy man, whom, alone from so many thousands of sage and learned men, snatched from the very gates and jaws of Hell, God has called to so distinguished and undaunted a proclamation of his Gospel. And I have now reason to think that it was by the singular providence of God that I did not answer you sooner; for when I understood from your letter that you, attacked and besieged on all sides by enemies, were looking about, quite rightly, to see where you might retreat if the worst came to the worst, and that you preferred England, I rejoiced for more reasons than one that you had made this decision, both from the hope of having you here, and because you think so highly of my country. I grieved that I could not then see a possible or suitable prospect here, especially as you do not know English. Now, however, it happens that a certain aged French minister departed this life a few days ago.[3] Those of most influence in his church, understanding that you are not safe where you are, earnestly wish (I report it not from uncertain rumors but directly from themselves) that you be chosen in that minister's place; in fact they invite you; they have resolved to provide the cost of your journey; and they offer you a living equal to that of any French minister here, so that you shall lack nothing that can lead to a willing assumption of a pastoral office among them.

---

[3] Parker discovered that the French minister was Jean d'Espagne, minister of the Somerset House Chapel, who died on April 25, 1659 (Parker, *Milton*, p. 525). Milton's Latin is *"Nunc vero peroportune accidit ut Minister quidam Gallicus aetate confectus, ante paucos dies è vita migraverit."* Masson (whose translation is used in the Columbia edition, V, 593) translates "Now, however, it has happened most opportunely that a certain French minister here, of great age, died a few days ago" (Columbia, XII, 107). French has "Now, however, it has happened most opportunely that a certain French minister here, worn out by age, departed this life a few days ago" (*Life Records*, IV, 262). Parker, who sometimes preferred his own translations of crucial passages, apparently accepted or agreed with Masson and French and said that the letter was misdated (*Milton*, p. 1069).

Wherefore, if you take my advice, Reverend Sir, fly hither as soon as possible, to those who are most eager to have you, where there is a harvest to be reaped, which though perhaps not so abundant in things of this world, still is such as I believe those like you most earnestly wish, a numerous harvest of souls. And be assured that you will be most welcome to all good men, and the sooner the better. Farewell.

From Westminster, April 21, 1659.

LETTER XXXI, MOSES WALL TO MILTON, MAY 26, 1659

Little is known of Moses Wall except what is implicit in this letter. One Moses Wall graduated B.A. from Oxford in 1612, and in 1613 became rector of Mickleham, Surrey; another Moses Wall entered Cambridge in 1627 and graduated B.A. in 1632 and M.A. 1635 (Parker, *Milton,* p. 1069). While Milton's letter is lost, Wall's implies that he and Milton had known each other personally before the Commonwealth period, but that they had not seen each other for a long time. The second Wall mentioned above might have known Milton at Cambridge. In any case, the author of this letter was a devout and learned man, deeply concerned about the church—and possessed of a remarkable memory. He had read Milton's latest book carefully, and was familiar with his earlier prose.

First printed in Richard Baron's revision (1753) of Birch's edition of the prose; reprinted in Columbia, XII, 333–36; and French, *Life Records,* IV, 267–68. The original is lost; a copy is in BM Add. MS. 4292, ff. 264^v–265^v, made by the Rev. Josiah Owen of Rochdale, who also copied Marvell's letter to Milton of June 2, 1654, which immediately precedes the present letter in the manuscript (see *Complete Prose,* IV, 861–62).

MOSES WALL TO MILTON

Sr

I RECEIVED Yo^{rs} the Day after you wrote and do humbly thank you that you are pleased to honor me, with your Letters. I confess I have (even in my Privacy in the Country) oft had thoughts of you, and that with much Respect, for your Friendliness to Truth in yor early Years and in bad Times.[1] But I was uncerten whether yor Relation to the Court, (though I think a Cõmonwealth was more friendly to you than a Court) had not clouded yor former Light, but

---

[1] Wall seems to be referring to the anti-episcopal tracts, but perhaps also to the *Tenure of Kings and Magistrates* and the Defences.

yor last Book ^{2} resolved that Doubt. You complaine of the Non-progresency of the nation, and of its retrograde Motion of late, in Liberty and Spiritual Truths. it is much to be bewailed; but yet let us pity humane Frailty when those who had made deep Protestations of their Zeal for our Liberty both spiritual and civill, and made the fairest offers to be asserters thereof, and whom we thereupon trusted; when those being instated in power, shall betray this good Thing committed to them, and lead us back to egypt, and by that Force which we gave them, to win us Liberty, hold us fast in Chains; what can poor people do You know who they were that watched o^r Savio^{rs} Sepulchre to keep him from rising. Besides whilst People are not free but straitened in Accommodations for Life, their Spirits will be dejected and servile; and conducing to that end there should be an improving of o^r native Comodities, as our manufactures, o^r Fisherie, o^r Fens Forests and Commons, & o^r Trade at Sea &c wch wold give the body of the nation a comfortable Subsistence, and the breaking that cursed yoak of Tythes wold much help y^{r}to. Also another Thing I cannot but mention, which is that the Norman Conquest and Tyranny is continued upon the nation without any Thought of removing it; ^{3} J mean the Tenure of Lands by Coppyhold, and holding for Life under a Lord (or rather Tyrant) of a Mannour; Whereby People care not to improve their Land by Cost upon it, not knowing how soon themselves or theirs may be outed it, nor what the House is in wch they live for the same Reason; and they are far more enslaved to the Lord: of the Mano^r, than the rest of the nation is to a King or supreme Magistrate! We have waited for Liberty, but it must be Gods work and not mans, Who thinks it sweet to maintaine his Pride and worldly Interest to the gratifying of the Flesh whatever becomes of the pretious Liberty of Mankind. but let us not despond but do our Duty; god will carry on that blessed work in despight of all opposites, and to their ruine if they persist y^{r}in.

^{2} The book would be the *Treatise of Civil Power in Ecclesiastical Causes*, as indicated by the date and the content. After Milton's final pleas for religious liberty in *A Second Defence* (1654) had gone unheeded, he had simply lapsed into silence on the subject. The court of course is Cromwell's. Now, with Cromwell dead, Milton had immediately spoken out again for the separation of the church from the state.

^{3} Here and in the following lines Wall seems to be referring to the surviving elements of the feudal system.

Sir, my humble Request is, That you wold proceed and give us
that other member of the Distribution mentioned in your Book; Sc.
that Hire doth greatly impede Truth and Liberty; [4] it is like if you
do you shall find Opposers; but remember that Saying Beatius est
pati quam frui [5] or in ye Apostles Words Μακαρίζομεν τὰ ὑπομένοντὰς
I have sometimes thought (concurring with yor Assertion of that
storied voice that shold speak from heaven) when Ecclesiasticks
were indowed with worldly preferments, Hodie venenum infunditur
in Ecclesiam,[6] for to use the speech of Gen. 4 ult. according to the
Sense wch it hath in the Hebrew—Then began men to corrupt the
worship of God.[7] I shall tell you a Supposal of mine wch is this, Mr
Dury [8] has bestowed about 30 years time in travell conference and
writing to reconcile Calvinists and Lutherans, and that with little
or no Success. But the Shortest way were, take away ecclesiastical
Dignities Preferments and Honor^rs on both Sides and all wold soon

[4] Milton had said in *Of Civil Power* that the two things working to the
greatest mischief in the church were force or control from without by the state,
and the corruption within, brought about by hire or state support. The former
was the subject of the treatise. Milton lost no time in writing *Considerations
Touching the Likeliest Means to Remove Hirelings*, which was out by August.

[5] See James 5:11.

[6] Milton first uses the story of the voice from heaven in *An Apology*, 1642.
He complains about tithes and luxury in the church and quotes a passage from
Gower's "Tale of Constantine and Sylvester" in the *Confessio Amantis*. Con-
stantine had supposedly left large possessions to Sylvester, and a voice cried
from heaven "this day venim is shad/In holy Church" (*Complete Prose*, I,
946–47). Again in *A Second Defence*, 1654, he complains of the luxury in which
the clergy and their wives and children live, and says that to give the pastors
new possessions (supposedly seized from the bishop) would be the same thing,
"ac siquis novum venenum, (quam olim pestem sub Constantino vox missa
coelitùs deflevit) in ecclesiam infudisset" (Columbia, VIII, 182); "as if to have
poured a new venom into the church [an evil which once under Constantine a
voice sent from heaven deplored]." See also *Complete Prose*, IV, 651. Wall's
"*Hodie*" suggests that he was recalling the *Apology*, but his use of Latin suggests
that he was recalling *A Second Defence*. Very likely he had read both, and, since
his quotation is *verbatim* from neither, was remembering Milton's early words,
which appear again in *Hirelings*, above, p. 279.

[7] The King James Version has "then began men to call upon the name of the
Lord" (Genesis 4:26). The Revised Standard Version and the New English
Bible are essentially the same. Wall's opinion is analogous to that of Rashi, the
most influential Rabbinical commentator, who interpreted Gen. 4:26 as "then
men began to bestow the name of God on the idol images which they made."

[8] Presumably John Dury, or Durie (1596–1680), who spent much of his life
working for a union of the Protestant churches of Europe. Masson and Parker
both give much attention to his activities. See bibliography of John Dury in
D. Bush, *English Literature in the Earlier 17th Century* (1962), p. 571.

be hushed; the Ecclesiasticks wold be quiet, and then the People wold come forth into Truth and Liberty. But I will not engage in this Quarrel yet I shall lay this Engagement upon myself to remaine

Your faithful Friend and Servant

M Wall

Causham [9] May 26, 1659.[10]

LETTER XXXII, OLDENBURG TO MILTON, DECEMBER 2/12, 1659

This is the last letter we have from one of Milton's most regular correspondents.

Draft in Royal Society MS. I, ff. 61–61^v; first printed, with translation, in French, *Life Records*, IV, 283–86.

TO THE MOST ILLUSTRIOUS MR. JOHN MILTON, GREETINGS

From Paris, December 12, 1659.[1]

IF I MAY interrupt your studies and business, I shall resume, if you please, that exchange of letters from which I have somehow held back so long. The trouble and effort of traveling, frequent intercourse with foreigners, an unsettled address, and much else, which there is no use listing here, kept me from proving my affection for you in more frequent letters. But now, since we have decided to make winter quarters here in Paris, we shall earnestly make up for the neglect. News of your health would greatly please us. Nor would it be unwelcome to learn whether you are preparing a history of the English revolution. If only it would subside and the cultivation of peace and justice succeed all war and injustice. Men squander men all too prodigally. The bottomless longing for wealth and power is the ancient cause of war and the waging of war. The French and Spanish have at last established peace between them, but it is to be feared that they may join forces to destroy those who

[9] Or Caversham.
[10] So dated in the copy. Professor A. H. Woolrych has suggested that in view of the rapid changes in the government earlier in May, Owen (see above, p. 510, headnote, par. 2), might have misread as May some abbreviation of March. This is certainly possible. But Richard Cromwell did not actually abdicate until May 25th, and Owen apparently had not heard of that.
[1] Oldenburg's date is New Style.

would protect liberty and the purer religion. Cardinal Mazarin is elevated by the courtiers to heaven, or at least to the Papacy, for giving these two nations peace, and is proclaimed arbiter of the fate of the entire globe. Someone recently praised him to the extent of saying there was nothing bloodstained about him except the tint of purple, and that all Europe justly wished him the supreme rank of the priesthood. The same person did not hesitate to add that this Cardinal was the hand and eye of the king of France, and that nature had made Mazarin to be a king, as he deserved. Many are convinced that a raging fury will henceforth attack the Protestants, both elsewhere and here in France. These, meanwhile, have finally, by much urging obtained a synod, which is being held at Loudon, near Saumur.[2] Many quarrels are to be broken up in that struggle, more composed, and the ambition of most ministers curbed. If all this is accomplished as resolved, the observation of Gregory Nazianzen will certainly have to be expanded, in which he aptly said in a letter to Procopius,[3] that he had never seen any good come of a synod and that the evils of the church had increased rather than decreased in assemblies of this sort, that is to say that the lust for controlling and domineering prevailed there. In that synod will be decided the suit of your adversary More, who has been invited and received into a pastorate in Paris. There are those, to be sure, who say that he has insinuated himself against the rules (and who have therefore kept the man at a distance) who may bring suit against him for surreptitious and illegal appointment. But men who are active and ready and who excel in the art of obliging those who have unlimited power, are accustomed to win even the most unjust case by number of votes. Rumor here, and not an idle one, says that the posthumous defense of Salmasius against you sweats under the press in Dijon.[4] As soon as it sees light, I will let you know. Meanwhile farewell and continue to love me. Given at Paris.

[2] The Synod of Loudon met from November 10, 1659, to January 10, 1660.

[3] Letter CXXX, to Procopius. Nazianzen (325–ca. 389) was one of the fathers of the Eastern church. He preferred the life of an ascetic but was often called upon to try to settle difficulties in the church. In 381, he was president of the Synod of Constantinople, which ended in disorder.

[4] The posthumous *Responsio* of Salmasius was published both in France and in England in September, 1660 (Parker, *Milton*, p. 1086). At the time Milton was in a precarious position because of the Restoration, and could not reply. It was reported that he considered the *Responsio* poorer than Salmasius' earlier books (French, *Life Records*, V, 461).

LETTER 39, TO HENRY OLDENBURG, DECEMBER 20, 1659

Letter 29 in the 1674 edition; in Columbia, XII, 108–11; and French, *Life Records*, IV, 287–89.

TO HENRY OLDENBURG

THAT Pardon which you ask for *your* silence you had better give to mine; it was, if I remember, my turn to write. It is certainly not a lessened regard for you (I assure you), but occupations or domestic cares which hindered me, or perhaps mere epistolary sluggishness, which makes me guilty of neglected courtesy. Since you wish to know, I am, with God's help, as well as usual. I am far from compiling a history of our political troubles, which you seem to urge; for they are worthier of silence than of publication. What we need is not one who can compile a history of our troubles but one who can happily end them. For I fear, as you do, lest to the lately united enemies of religion and liberty we shall, in the midst of civil dissensions or rather insanities, seem too vulnerable, though actually they will not have inflicted a greater wound on religion than we have long been doing by our crimes. But God, I hope, for his own glory, which is now made light of, will not allow the schemes and attacks of those enemies to succeed as they intend, whatever disturbance kings and cardinals mediate and contrive. Meanwhile for the Protestant Synod of Loudon, soon, you write, to convene, I wish what has never yet befallen any synod, a happy outcome, not like the Nazianzenian; but the outcome of this one will be happy enough if it has decreed nothing more than the expulsion of More. As for my posthumous adversary, as soon as he appears, I beg you, let me know at once.[1] Goodbye.

From Westminster, December 20, 1659

[1] For the Synod of Loudon and the posthumous adversary, see notes to Letter XXXII, above. Milton must have been disappointed when he learned the decision of the Synod on More: he was declared innocent and restored to his pastorate (Masson, V, 633–35).

LETTER 40, TO RICHARD JONES, DECEMBER 20, 1659

This letter responds to one from Jones which has not been found; but it appears that, as usual, Jones had written to Milton when his preceptor Oldenburg did so.

Letter 30 in the 1674 edition; in Columbia, XII, 110–13, and French, *Life Records*, IV, 289–90.

TO THE NOBLE YOUTH RICHARD JONES

FOR THE LONG BREAK in your correspondence with me you excuse yourself so modestly, although you could more justly accuse me of the same fault, that I scarcely know whether I should have preferred your performance to your apology. Let it never enter your mind that I measure your gratitude, if you owe me anything of the sort, by the regularity of your letters; I shall feel you most grateful to me when those services of mine which you commend have appeared not so much in frequent letters as in your laudable progress and praiseworthy achievement in the most valuable studies. You have certainly marked out the path of virtue in the field of the world which you have entered; but know that the path of virtue runs along with the path of vice and that you have to reach the point where they fork. And so you ought now to prepare yourself so that after leaving this double path, pleasant and flowry, you can climb by your own free will, even with effort and risk, that steep and dangerous slope which is virtue's alone. This, believe me, you who have obtained so trusty and skillful a guide, will be able to do much more easily than others. Farewell.

From Westminster, December 20, 1659

APHORISMS POLITICAL.

BY
James Harrington.

LONDON: *August* 31

Printed by *J. C.* for *Henry Fletcher*, at the signe of the three
Gilt Cups in St. *Pauls* Church-yard. *1659*

APPENDIX A

SELECTIONS FROM HARRINGTON'S
APHORISMS POLITICAL

James Harrington's *Aphorisms Political* fill a ten-page pamphlet which Thomason acquired on August 31, 1659.[1] That this was very close to the date of publication is confirmed by the reference on p. 7 to the defeat of Booth's rising on August 19. The royalist rising was probably the main occasion for writing it, since most of the text repeats in condensed form the arguments for Harrington's now familiar model of a commonwealth based on two elected assemblies, emphasizing that this is the only durable antidote to monarchy.

The aphorisms reprinted below are from pp. 2–5, and are all those that bear on religion. It seems likely that Harrington expanded them on reading *The Likeliest Means.* No. XXI, which takes up the words of Milton's title, would otherwise have followed logically upon no. XV; indeed XV–XX may have been all that Harrington's first draft devoted to questions of church and state. In no. XVIII he is already turning aside from them, and XIX and XX were probably aimed against those millenarians who still looked for some divinely inspired rule of the saints. It is a reasonable conjecture that Milton's treatise prompted him to insert, in aphorisms XXI–XXXVIII, a defense of a national religion and an endowed ministry, argued on the broadest philosophical grounds.

XV.

To hold that there can be any National Religion or Ministry without publick Indowment and Inspection of the Magistracy, or any Government without a National Religion or Ministry, is inconsistent with a Commonwealth.

XVI.

To hold that there may be Liberty, and not Liberty of Conscience, is inconsistent with a Commonwealth that hath the Liberty of her own Conscience, or that is not Popish.

[1] E995(8).

XVII.

Either Liberty of Conscience can have no security at all, or under Popular Government must have the greatest security.

XVIII.

To hold that a Government may be introduced by a little at once, is to wave prudence, and commit things unto chance.

XIX.

To hold that the Wisdom of God in the Formation of an House, or of a Government, goeth not universally upon natural principles, is inconsistent with Scripture.

XX.

To hold that the wisdom of man in the Formation of an House, or of Government, may go upon supernatural principles, is inconsistent with a Commonwealth, and cometh to a kind of breaking of Jests; as if one should say, God ordained the Temple, therefore it was not built by Masons; He ordained the Snuffers, therefore they were not made by a Smith.

XXI.

To hold that Hirelings, or an endowed Ministry, ought to be removed out of the Church, is inconsistent with a Commonwealth.

XXII.

Nature is of god.

XXIII.

Some part in every Religion is natural.

XXIV.

An universal Effect, demonstrateth an universal Cause.

XXV.

An universal Cause is not so much natural, as it is Nature it self.

XXVI.

Every man, either unto his terrour or consolation, hath some sense of Religion.

XXVII.

Man may rather be defined a Religious, then a Rational Creature; in regard that in other Creatures there is something of a Reason, but nothing of Religion.

XXVIII.

Government is of humane Prudence, and humane Prudence is adequate unto mans nature.

XXIX.

The prudence or Government that is regardless of Religion, is not adequate nor satisfactory unto mans nature.

XXX.

Where the Government is not adequate or satisfactory unto mans nature, it can never be quiet or perfect.

XXXI.

The major part of mankinde giveth it self up in the matter of Religion unto the publick leading.

XXXII.

That there may be a publick leading, there must be a National Religion.

XXXIII.

Where the minor part taketh away the National Religion, there the major part is deprived of the Liberty of Conscience by the minor.

XXXIV.

Where the major part is deprived of the Liberty of Conscience by the minor, there they will deprive the minor of that Liberty of Conscience which they might otherwise enjoy.

XXXV.

In *Israel* there was an endowed Clergie or Priesthood, and a National Religion under inspection of the Magistrate: whence the Christians in Apostolick times defraying their own Ministry, could have Liberty of Conscience; wheras if the Christians by going about take away Tythes, and abolish the National Religion, had endeavoured to violate the Conscience of the unconverted Jews, these far greater in number, must needs have taken away the Liberty of Conscience from the Christians.

XXXVI.

ld freely and undisturbedly convert *Dionysius* n *Athens* there was Liberty of Conscience: but ts had gone about to drive Hirelings, or an lergie out of that Church, who seeth not that ve driven *Paul* and his Converts out of

XXXVII.

of Conscience, there must be a Na-

XXXVIII.

Religion, there must be an endowed

siasm

ure only
. He de-
 y to the
reach and
e liable to
as are en-
t of reason
ewise must
2
nces as long
he stood with
enry Stubbe,
Overton, how-
apists, whereas
then others be
ggers also were
stles had no do-
e. In the case of
e strongly. "But
uglas Bush (Boston:
y, ed. Samuel L. Cald-
Providence, 1866–74),
, p. 113.

MILTON'S VIEWS ON CHURCH AND STATE IN 1659
By William J. Grace

I

In *A Treatise of Civil Power* Milton advocates a complete separa-
tion of church and state. Sonnet XVII (To Sir Henry Van
Younger), July, 1652, illustrates Milton's long-standing enthu
for this principle:

> . . . besides, to know
> Both spiritual power and civil, what each means,
> What severs each, thou hast learnt, which few have done.[1]

Milton intends to argue this thesis on the basis of script
where the true Protestant Christian religion is to be found
fines religion as pertaining to such matters "as belong chie
knowledge and service of God: and are either above the
light of nature without revelation from above, and therfor
be variously understood by humane reason, or such things
joind or forbidden by divine precept, which els by the lig
would seem indifferent to be don or not don; and so li
needs appeer to everie man as the precept is understood.'

Milton wanted complete toleration of religious differ
as such views were based on scripture. In a broad sense
Roger Williams, Henry Vane, Richard Overton, H
Leonard Busher, William Walwyn. Unlike Williams and
ever, Milton did not believe in toleration of the hated F
Williams wrote: "Why should their *Consciences* more
oppressed?"[3] Like Williams, the Quakers and the D
more tolerant of Catholicism than was Milton.

Milton's major historical premise is that the apo
minion or constraining power over faith or conscien
ordinary ministers, this principle holds even mo

[1] *The Complete Poetical Works of John Milton*, ed. D
Houghton Mifflin, 1965), p. 191.

[2] *Civil Power*, above, p. 242.

Roger Williams, *The Bloody Tenent Yet More Bloo*
Publications of the Narragansett Club (6 vols.,
. See also Wolfe, *Milton in the Puritan Revolutio*

XXXV.

In *Israel* there was an endowed Clergie or Priesthood, and a National Religion under inspection of the Magistrate: whence the Christians in Apostolick times defraying their own Ministry, could have Liberty of Conscience; wheras if the Christians by going about to take away Tythes, and abolish the National Religion, had endeavoured to violate the Conscience of the unconverted Jews, these being far greater in number, must needs have taken away the Liberty of Conscience from the Christians.

XXXVI.

Paul in *Athens* could freely and undisturbedly convert *Dionysius* and others; therefore in *Athens* there was Liberty of Conscience: but if *Paul* and his Converts had gone about to drive Hirelings, or an endowed Priesthood or Clergie out of that Church, who seeth not that the *Athenians* would have driven *Paul* and his Converts out of *Athens?*

XXXVII.

That there may be Liberty of Conscience, there must be a National Religion.

XXXVIII.

That there may be a National Religion, there must be an endowed Clergie.

APPENDIX B

MILTON'S VIEWS ON CHURCH AND STATE IN 1659
By William J. Grace

I

In *A Treatise of Civil Power* Milton advocates a complete separa-
tion of church and state. Sonnet XVII (To Sir Henry Vane the
Younger), July, 1652, illustrates Milton's long-standing enthusiasm
for this principle:

> . . . besides, to know
> Both spiritual power and civil, what each means,
> What severs each, thou hast learnt, which few have done.[1]

Milton intends to argue this thesis on the basis of scripture only
where the true Protestant Christian religion is to be found. He de-
fines religion as pertaining to such matters "as belong chiefly to the
knowledge and service of God: and are either above the reach and
light of nature without revelation from above, and therfore liable to
be variously understood by humane reason, or such things as are en-
joind or forbidden by divine precept, which els by the light of reason
would seem indifferent to be don or not don; and so likewise must
needs appeer to everie man as the precept is understood." [2]

Milton wanted complete toleration of religious differences as long
as such views were based on scripture. In a broad sense he stood with
Roger Williams, Henry Vane, Richard Overton, Henry Stubbe,
Leonard Busher, William Walwyn. Unlike Williams and Overton, how-
ever, Milton did not believe in toleration of the hated Papists, whereas
Williams wrote: "Why should their *Consciences* more then others be
oppressed?" [3] Like Williams, the Quakers and the Diggers also were
more tolerant of Catholicism than was Milton.

Milton's major historical premise is that the apostles had no do-
minion or constraining power over faith or conscience. In the case of
ordinary ministers, this principle holds even more strongly. "But

---

[1] *The Complete Poetical Works of John Milton*, ed. Douglas Bush (Boston:
Houghton Mifflin, 1965), p. 191.

[2] *Civil Power*, above, p. 242.

[3] Roger Williams, *The Bloody Tenent Yet More Bloody*, ed. Samuel L. Cald-
well, Publications of the Narragansett Club (6 vols., Providence, 1866–74),
IV, 312. See also Wolfe, *Milton in the Puritan Revolution*, p. 113.

some will object," Milton remarks, "that this overthrows all church-discipline, all censure of errors, if no man can determin." [4] Milton finds that scripture permits "church-sentence or determining" within a given religious group "exercis'd on them only who have willingly joind themselves in that covnant of union." [5] But there must be no violence to the unconvinced conscience, and punishment must not exceed separation from the religious body, and certainly not corporal punishment or fines. [6]

The next step follows logically. If a church itself cannot use force in religion, much less can civil magistrates do so in a field in which they are not competent much less expert. [7] Such magistrates place themselves in the ridiculous position of "civil executioners of them who have no civil power to give them such commission." [8] Milton takes the sting out of the word "heresy." It is not a word of evil note, and etymologically it simply means "the choise or following of any opinion good or bad in religion or any other learning." [9] The choice of one opinion before another may take place without discord.

In regard to the magistrate, Milton repeats some of his favorite arguments found in *The Tenure of Kings and Magistrates* and in *A*

---

[4] *Civil Power,* above, p. 245. In his *Essay in Defence of the Good Old Cause,* which appeared in September 1659 [Thomason E1841(1)], Henry Stubbe of Christ Church in general supported the extreme tolerationist views upheld by Milton in *Civil Power.* As a poor boy Stubbe had been sent by his seamstress mother to Westminster School, where his talents were recognized by the headmaster, who recommended him to Sir Henry Vane; Vane remained his constant friend thereafter. Admitted to Christ Church, Stubbe soon revealed brilliant gifts in languages and became a staunch supporter of Commonwealth principles. There is no evidence that he and Milton knew each other.

Stubbe cites the wide toleration granted the early Christians by Constantine and later emperors (*Essays in Defence of the Good Old Cause,* p. 52): "In the *Roman empire* there were many *Heresies* & Sects of Christians; As the Montanists, Sabbatians . . . the Arians . . . NO EMPEROUR HAVING EVER MOLESTED THEM." Nor were infidels required to renounce their errors. And what of the Essenes? Were they not "the *Quakers* of their Age . . . men of unspotted life, grave, reservedly superstitious"? Citing Jeremy Taylor's *Liberty of Prophesying,* Stubbe argues (p. 42) that "where there is wanting an infallible Expositor of the minde of God (which being to be accepted upon *Revelation,* is not to be discussed by Reason) there is not onely cause for a *Toleration,* (for why should any be forced from what he holds to be true, unto that which another can not evidence but it may be false?), but sufficient ground from former practices and usages to reestablish the like forbearance."

[5] See text of *Civil Power,* above, p. 245.

[6] *Ibid.*

[7] *Ibid.,* pp. 245–46.

[8] *Ibid.,* p. 246.

[9] *Ibid.,* p. 247.

Defence, including the rejection of opposing interpretations of the Pauline text, "Let every soul be subject to the higher powers." The magistrate is concerned merely with the outward man; the church with the inward and spiritual. "Christ hath a government of his own, sufficient of it self to all his ends and purposes in governing his church; but much different from that of the civil magistrate; and the difference in this verie thing principally consists, that it governs not by outward force, and that for two reasons. First because it deals only with the inward man and his actions, which are all spiritual and to outward force not lyable: secondly to shew us the divine excellence of his spiritual kingdom, able without worldly force to subdue all the powers and kingdoms of this world, which are upheld by outward force only." [10]

Milton reduces the organizational aspect of the church to a minimum, if he doesn't do away with it altogether. The church has an advisory capacity but no magisterium. "The church it self cannot, much less the state, settle or impose one tittle of religion upon our obedience implicit, but can only recommend or propound it to our free and conscientious examination." [11] "No man, no synod, no session of men, though calld the church, can judge definitively the sense of scripture to another mans conscience." [12] The whole matter of religion under the Gospel is man's use of his will and understanding and the work of divine grace upon them. Later in *The Likeliest Means to Remove Hirelings,* by insisting on the royal priesthood of the laity,[13] Milton inevitably moves from his complete insistence on the supremacy of the individual conscience to jeopardize any real need for a ministry at all.

It is both deeply ironic and endearing that the widely and profoundly read Milton, the creator of a rare religious epic, tries to come to grips with a mediocrity of religious spirit that must have appalled him. He has come to terms with his own intuitions about God, and he does not want any organizational threat, either from church or state authorities, to endanger them. His major idea, his rallying concept, is that of Christian liberty, which is Miltonic liberty as well.[14] Civil power in reference to religion violates "the fundamental privilege of the gospel, the new-birthright of everie true beleever, Christian libertie." [15] We are not children of the bondswoman; no more servants

[10] *Ibid.,* p. 255.
[11] *Ibid.,* p. 258.
[12] *Ibid.,* pp. 247–48.
[13] See *Likeliest Means,* above, p. 319.
[14] See *Civil Power,* above, pp. 263–64.
[15] *Ibid.,* p. 262.

but sons.[16] No external authority must threaten the new dignity of man under the Gospel.[17] Force in religion merely leads to formality and hypocrisy. "We read not that Christ ever exercis'd force but once; and that was to drive prophane ones out of his temple, not to force them in." [18] Milton (and God) are fully aware of the dangers of liberty, but all these dangers have been provided for. Any losses resulting from liberty are well worth the price. "This truth, the right of Christian and euangelic liberty, will stand immoveable against all those pretended consequences of license and confusion, which for the most part men most licentious and confus'd themselves, or such as whose severitie would be wiser then divine wisdom, are ever aptest to object against the waies of God: as if God without them when he gave us this libertie, knew not of the worst which these men in thir arrogance pretend will follow: yet knowing all their worst, he gave us this liberty as by him judgd best." [19]

II

Obviously nothing could be more obnoxious to a person with Milton's views about the supremacy of the individual conscience and about the meaning of Christian liberty than the ages-long system of ecclesiastical tithes. The Presbyterians had been distinguished by strong church organization, and, as early as 1646, Milton had become disenchanted with them. "New Presbyter is but old Priest writ large," he had acrimoniously observed in "On the New Forcers of Conscience under the Long Parliament." The Presbyterian William Prynne had zealously defended the tithes system in his *A Gospel Plea* (1653, 1660—the date of the second edition may be significant). The specifics of Milton's *The Likeliest Means to Remove Hirelings* are largely refutations of Prynne's arguments and examples. In the same year as the publication of Milton's tract (1659), Prynne published *Ten Considerable Quæries Concerning Tithes*. It seems obvious that this smouldering problem of tithes had come under reinforced attack from left-wing Puritanism in the last year of Cromwell's life. Prynne may have been fearful that the opponents of tithes might get the upper hand in the Rump Parliament, a Parliament he deeply deplored in his *Brief Narrative How Divers Members of the House of Commons Were Again Shut Out* (1660). Milton in *Likeliest Means* singles out the Presbyterians for vitriolic attack: "But these our Protestant,

[16] *Ibid.*
[17] *Ibid.*, pp. 262–63.
[18] *Ibid.*, p. 268.
[19] *Ibid.*, p. 270.

these our new reformed English presbyterian divines, against thir own cited authors, and to the shame of thir pretended reformation, would engross to themselves all tithes by statute; and supported more by thir wilful obstinacie and desire of filthie lucre then by these both insufficient and impertinent autorities, would perswade a Christian magistracie and parlament, whom we trust God hath restor'd for a happier reformation, to impose upon us a Judaical ceremonial law, and yet from that law to be more irregular and unwarrantable, more complying with a covetous clergie, then any of those Popish kings and parlaments alleagd." [20] Milton, who in *A Treatise of Civil Power* had maintained that "the spiritual man judgeth all things, but he himself is judgd of no man," [21] seized what has seemed to be a political opportunity: "Opportunity I finde now inviting; and apprehend therin the concurrence of God disposing; since the maintenance of church-ministers, a thing not properly belonging to the magistrate, and yet with such importunity call'd for, and expected from him, is at present under publick debate." [22] He strongly advises that any proposed civil law about tithes be not established until full opportunity for criticism has been provided.[23]

Milton stresses in *Likeliest Means,* as in his previous treatise, the difference between the two great dispensations, that of the law and that of the gospel. "Under the law he [Christ] gave them tithes; under the gospel, having left all things in his church to charity and Christian freedom, he hath given them only what is justly given them. That, as well under the gospel as under the law, say our English divines, and they only of all Protestants, is tithes; and they say true, if any man be so minded to give them of his own the tenth or twentith: but that the law therefor of tithes is in force under the gospel, all other Protestant divines, though equally concernd, yet constantly deny." [24]

Milton's attack on the system of tithes involves a great deal of scriptural exegesis, and at times he seems to follow Prynne's *A Gospel Plea* point for point, example for example, as he did with Salmasius in a controversy of greater magnitude. He attempts to show that many scriptural precedents for tithes are not, in fact, valid, as in the long account of the Levites and of the relation of Abraham to Melchisedek. But even if they were once valid, they are no longer binding. Even

[20] *Likeliest Means,* above, p. 295.
[21] *Civil Power,* above, p. 244.
[22] *Likeliest Means,* above, p. 278.
[23] *Ibid.*
[24] *Ibid.,* p. 281.

if the Hebrews paid tithes, they were "then under ceremonies, a meer laitie, we now under Christ, a royal priesthood . . . as we are coheirs, kings and priests with him, a priest for ever after the order or manner of Melchisedec." [25] Moreover, Milton argues, "that not examples, but express commands oblige our obedience." [26] Ministers cannot claim "to themselves that signe of our allegiance [the tithe as a symbol] due only to our eternal king and priest." [27]

Milton sees a great danger of turning ministers into state pensioners. The danger of a church financed by the state is that of setting "a human on a heavenly, a carnal on a spiritual, a political head on an ecclesiastical bodie," producing an "incestuous conjunction." [28] The church revenues now in fact in the hands of the magistrates could be used to erect in greater number schools and competent libraries.[29] Milton repeatedly cites the Waldenses [30] as shining contrasts to English Protestantism, for they understood "that the church of Christ was founded in poverty rather then in revenues, stood purest and prosperd best without them." [31] Ministers among the Waldenses were also trained in a trade or profession, "that they might be no burden to the church." [32]

Milton, while guarding ministers from any dangers of affluence, is surprisingly indifferent to their intellectual qualifications. They are basically pious men, who have no pressing need of theology: "it were much better, there were not one divine in the universitie; no schoole-divinitie known, the idle sophistrie of monks, the canker of religion." [33] He does not want pure doctrine mixed with scholastic trash.[34] He does not believe in expensive personal libraries for the clergy, but believes that the state should "erect in publick good store of libraries." [35] He does not want ecclesiastical examination committees because they will make examinees conformable to their interests.[36] Ultimately, if all the faithful be now "a holy and royal priesthood," [37] ministers of the gospel

[25] *Ibid.*, p. 286.
[26] *Ibid.*, p. 284.
[27] *Ibid.*, p. 287.
[28] *Ibid.*, p. 308.
[29] *Ibid.*, p. 305.
[30] See above, p. 291, n. 34.
[31] *Ibid.*, p. 308.
[32] *Ibid.*, p. 306.
[33] *Ibid.*, p. 317.
[34] *Ibid.*
[35] *Ibid.*
[36] *Ibid.*, p. 318.
[37] *Ibid.*, p. 319.

are distinguished "from other Christians but by thir spiritual knowledge and sanctitie of life." [38] Since obviously no juridical or other method could be determined to define such people, Milton does away not only with tithes but with any kind of formal ministry. He is wrathful at the idea of the clergy forming a separate class from the "despis'd laitie"; [39] they should never have been separated from any other occupation they had. He sees the "despis'd laitie" as their "feeders" through all ages.

Though Milton has not demanded high intellectual achievement as a mark of a Christian ministry, he at the same time resents an antiintellectual acceptance of religion. He presents the horrible image of an inert congregation taking understanding of religion "by scraps and mammocks" from the minister "as he dispences it in his sundays dole." [40] "They will be alwaies learning and never knowing, alwaies infants." [41]

William Prynne, in spite of his massive documentation, is a vigorous journalist, a scholar constantly lowering the boom. But Prynne, in contrast to Milton, adheres to a narrow theme, carefully argued within the limitations of scriptural literalism. He might win a few adherents from neutral opinion. Milton could only hope to persuade those who were prepared to do away with tithes, a formal ministry, and any pretense of an organizational church. He settles down to his task with real zest and enthusiasm; he reaffirms the ideal of a "pure" church, unspottedly spiritual. His vigorous anticlericalism is of the kind that always has some justification; but the unconvinced reader will always ask, is he realistic, is he truly aware of the real human situation? A church may be the home of saints, but can it altogether dispense with legal and socioeconomic ties, with perpetuation through institutional norms? Milton, drawing on the example of the Waldenses, believes that it can.

III

Arthur Barker, who has so searchingly analyzed the two tractates in his chapter, "Of Christian Liberty," in *Milton and the Puritan Dilemma, 1641–1660,* observes how extremely to the left was the position that Milton took. "In the pamphlets of 1659, Milton occupied a position which was well towards the Puritan left. His view of Christian

[38] *Ibid.*
[39] *Ibid.*
[40] *Ibid.*, p. 320.
[41] *Ibid.*

religion, of church association, and of the ministry, was scarcely distinguishable from that of the extreme sectaries." [42] But there were positions more extreme than those of Milton: "He could not pass, with Williams, Goodwin, and the Levellers, beyond Puritanism to a naturalism involving the strict segregation of the spiritual and the natural." [43] Milton differentiates between the liberty of all men and the rights of the elect: " 'the right of Christian and evangelic liberty' " was, by definition, " 'unseparable from Christian religion,' and the peculiar privilege of true believers: '2 Corinthians 3 : 17, where the Spirit of the Lord is, there is liberty.' " [44]

An alternative view to that of Woolrych (above, p. 42) is that the moderate Independent divines took the initiative to safeguard their position in the face of strict Presbyterians who could not dispense with the proper consistorial and classical forms, and of the Congregational ministers who also held aloof from voluntary associations. Their meetings at the Savoy, beginning in August, 1658, were efforts in reconciliation and diplomacy, manifesting a desire for *rapprochement* with the Presbyterians. This movement toward the center carried no appeal for Milton. His acrimonious remarks about the Presbyterians in *The Likeliest Means to Remove Hirelings* are not accidental, and the whole treatise is designed to pull the carpet from under all religious groups interested in securing status, economic support, or even some sort of recognition from the state. Not only has Milton rejected "the whole gang of prelatry," [45] but it would not be an exaggeration to say that he has also rejected the whole gang of ministers in favor of the very loose association of a lay church. Though as far back as *Lycidas*, "the pilot of the Galilean lake" could shake his *"Mitred* locks," Milton's anticlerical position is not exactly a late development. In Sonnet XVI, "To the Lord General Cromwell," he had warned in May, 1652, against the new foes who were now in 1659 once more showing their teeth for the maintenance of church ministers, "at present under public debate":

> . . . new foes arise
> Threat'ning to bind our souls with secular chains.
> Help us to save free conscience from the paw
> Of hireling wolves whose gospel is their maw.[46]

[42] Arthur Barker, *Milton and the Puritan Dilemma*, p. 257.
[43] *Ibid.*
[44] *Ibid.*
[45] *Likeliest Means*, above, p. 283.
[46] *Complete Poetical Works*, ed. Douglas Bush, pp. 190–91.

Milton's personal position remains curiously ironic. One of the world's great religious poets, a massive theologian in the *Christian Doctrine*, a deeply read classical scholar, he finds it practically impossible to discover a church bigger than he is himself. His deep concern for Christian liberty, for freedom of the conscience, was such that even the hint of founding his own church never crossed his mind. His function in these tractates is that of a penetrating critic; but even Milton's warmest admirers might admit that he is somewhat weak in making constructive, practical proposals, because of his lack of interest in juridical procedures and a lack of sympathy with the part that institutions, even when marked by deeply corrupt features, have played in society.

WILLIAM J. GRACE

Fordham University

INDEX

INDEX

INDEX TO AUTHORS AND WORKS

Most works are indexed under the authors' names. Cross references are made from the names of editors and translators to authors. When a work has more than one editor or translator, reference is made only from the one whose name is listed first in the series. Compilations and works of multiple, anonymous, or uncertain authorship are indexed under titles of the works. After the titles of such works will be found references to editors, translators, and probable authors.

For many works short titles have been used. Starred page references indicate that the longer titles or additional bibliographical information will be found on the cited pages. As a further bibliographical aid, known dates of publication are included in the index for pamphlets and other works published during or close to Milton's lifetime, and for certain important titles for which dating aids identification.